ROTHMANS RUGBY LEAGUE YEARBOOK 1989-90

**Raymond Fletcher
and David Howes**

ROTHMANS

Queen Anne Press

A *Queen Anne Press* **BOOK**

© **Rothmans Publications Ltd**

First published in Great Britain in 1989 by
Queen Anne Press, a division of
Macdonald & Co (Publishers) Ltd
66-73 Shoe Lane
London EC4P 4AB

A member of Maxwell Pergamon Publishing Corporation plc

Front Cover: World record recruit from Rugby Union, Jonathan Davies, in action for Widnes.

Back Cover: Great Britain prop forward Lee Crooks back on Test duty, against France in Avignon, after a two-year absence.

ACKNOWLEDGEMENTS
The compilers would like to acknowledge the assistance of the Rugby League Record Keepers' Club, club secretaries and individuals in providing material as a further source of reference for accuracy.

PHOTOGRAPHS
Modern day domestic photographs in this *Rothmans Rugby League Yearbook* are from the files of the *Rugby Leaguer,* the only weekly newspaper dedicated solely to the 13-a-side code. The compilers acknowledge the co-operation of Chief Photographer Gerald Webster and his staff.
The colour photographs on the front and back covers, plus a number of black-and-white contributions, are by freelance photographer Andrew Varley.
Photographic contributions have also been made by the *Halifax Courier.*

British Library Cataloguing in Publication Data
Rothmans Rugby League Yearbook — 1989-90
    1. Rugby football — Great Britain —
    Periodicals
    796.33.3.0941 GV945.9.G7

ISBN 0 356 17850 1

Photoset by New Rush Filmsetters, London

Reproduced, printed and bound in Great Britain by
Hazell Watson & Viney Ltd, Aylesbury, Bucks.
Member of the BPCC Group

Rothmans Rugby League Yearbook 1989-90

CONTENTS

FOREWORD

This is the ninth edition of the *Rothmans Rugby League Yearbook* and each year it has become more popular and increasingly authoritative; this year is no exception.

The season saw several milestones with the signing by Widnes of the Welsh Rugby Union stand off, Jonathan Davies, and Great Britain's victory over Australia for the first time in ten years. It was also a season of record sponsorship revenue and gate receipts.

We are delighted that David Howes and Raymond Fletcher are still prepared to devote themselves virtually night and day for several months to producing the leading reference book on Rugby League and know that their efforts will be appreciated by all those who regard this publication as their 'Bible'.

EDITORIAL PREFACE

As regular compilers of this best-selling annual, we are always conscious of the need to be topical. The 1989-90 *Rothmans Rugby League Yearbook* introduces a new feature with coaches for the past season being invited to select their own Select XIII. Typically, their participation in this fascinating poll was as enthusiastic as the numerous Rugby League aficionados who provide other invaluable assistance during the intense preparation of this tome. We thank the coaches for their co-operation.

The ever increasing amount of overseas material being featured in the Yearbook has put further pressure on the bid for the highest degree of accuracy and we again thank club officials, RLHQ staff, the RL Record Keepers' Club and a few individuals for their assistance, particularly George Bennison.

Behind every successful author is a supportive woman ... we have three, our wives and house editor Celia Kent. They have again supplied that ultimate, special encouragement.

One of the inspirations in the mammoth task of compiling this series of reference books is that the *Rothmans Rugby League Yearbook* mirrors the game's progress and rising stature. We are delighted that the following pages reflect a new era of development for the 13-a-side code.

● Facts and figures in this *Rothmans Yearbook* as at 1 June 1989.

RAYMOND FLETCHER, of the *Yorkshire Post*

DAVID HOWES, Rugby League Public Affairs Executive

COACHES SELECT XIII

For the first time, the coaches of the 14 clubs in the 1988-89 Stones Bitter Championship were invited to select their form team of the season as a new feature of the *Rothmans Rugby League Yearbook*.

The coaches were asked not to include members of their own club sides and to base their choices on opposition performances during the past campaign, while taking general form into account.

A total of 54 players were nominated, five in more than one position and 15 from overseas. The widest choice was for the second row positions with 16 individual selections, while 10 were put forward for the prop roles. There were only two contenders for the full back, scrum half and loose forward spots.

Both Widnes and Wigan supplied a total of 10 players in the selection process, while single nominations came from Hull K.R., Oldham, Salford and Wakefield Trinity.

In the Select XIII, only winger Martin Offiah and Great Britain and Wigan skipper Ellery Hanley polled 100 per cent support, Hanley being placed in the centre once. Andy Gregory, Phil McKenzie and Kevin Ward each polled 10 votes.

There was a three-man tie for the second row pairing with Australian Ron Gibbs and British Test men Mike Gregory and Andy Platt all receiving three commendations. At full back, new Test cap Alan Tait collected the odd vote in 13 to pip Great Britain rival Steve Hampson.

The Rothmans select side features only three overseas imports in Australians McKenzie and Gibbs, plus New Zealander Adrian Shelford. Of the remaining 10, nine represented Great Britain in the previous 12 months, while centre Andy Currier was a replacement during the 1988 Lions tour Down Under and travelling reserve for the Test at Avignon in February.

Featherstone Rovers coach Peter Fox declined the invitation to take part in the special poll.

Great Britain full back Alan Tait.

8

COACHES SELECT XIII

1. **Alan Tait** (Widnes)
2. **Des Drummond** (Warrington)
3. **Andy Currier** (Widnes)
4. **Joe Lydon** (Wigan)
5. **Martin Offiah** (Widnes)
6. **Shaun Edwards** (Wigan)
7. **Andy Gregory** (Wigan)
8. **Kevin Ward** (Castleford)
9. **Phil McKenzie** (Widnes)
10. **Adrian Shelford** (Wigan)
11. **Mike Gregory** (Warrington)
12. **Andy Platt** (Wigan)
    Ron Gibbs (Castleford)
13. **Ellery Hanley** (Wigan)

Great Britain wingman Des Drummond.

Great Britain tourist Andy Currier.

9

Great Britain centre Joe Lydon.

Great Britain winger Martin Offiah.

Great Britain stand off Shaun Edwards.

Great Britain scrum half Andy Gregory.

KEVIN ASHCROFT, Salford

1. Tait (Widnes)
2. Ettingshausen (Leeds)
3. Currier (Widnes)
4. Hanley (Wigan)
5. Offiah (Widnes)
6. Pearce (Hull)
7. Gregory (Wigan)
8. Ward (Castleford)
9. McKenzie (Widnes)
10. Roach (Warrington)
11. Davidson (Warrington)
12. Goodway (Wigan)
13. Miller (Hull K.R.)

ALAN HARDISTY, Halifax

1. Hampson (Wigan)
2. Drummond (Warrington)
3. Schofield (Leeds)
4. Loughlin (St. Helens)
5. Offiah (Widnes)
6. Steadman (Featherstone R.)
7. Gregory (Wigan)
8. Ward (Castleford)
9. McKenzie (Widnes)
10. Shelford (Wigan)
11. O'Neill (Widnes)
12. Gibbs (Castleford)
13. Hanley (Wigan)

TONY BARROW, Oldham

1. Hampson (Wigan)
2. Ford (Leeds)
3. Schofield (Leeds)
4. Lydon (Wigan)
5. Offiah (Widnes)
6. Woods (Warrington)
7. Gregory (Wigan)
8. Ward (Castleford)
9. McKenzie (Widnes)
10. Davidson (Warrington)
11. Miller (Hull K.R.)
12. Gregory (Warrington)
13. Hanley (Wigan)

BRIAN JOHNSON, Warrington

1. Tait (Widnes)
2. Quirk (St. Helens)
3. K. Iro (Wigan)
4. Currier (Widnes)
5. Offiah (Widnes)
6. Myler (Widnes)
7. D. Hulme (Widnes)
8. Ward (Castleford)
9. McKenzie (Widnes)
10. Shelford (Wigan)
11. Gibbs (Castleford)
12. Powell (Leeds)
13. Hanley (Wigan)

Great Britain prop forward Kevin Ward.

DOUG LAUGHTON, Widnes

1. Hampson (Wigan)
2. Drummond (Warrington)
3. Lydon (Wigan)
4. Loughlin (St. Helens)
5. Quirk (St. Helens)
6. Edwards (Wigan)
7. Gregory (Wigan)
8. Ward (Castleford)
9. Groves (St. Helens)
10. Shelford (Wigan)
11. Skerrett (Bradford N.)
12. Hobbs (Bradford N.)
13. Hanley (Wigan)

GRAHAM LOWE, Wigan

1. Tait (Widnes)
2. Drummond (Warrington)
3. Currier (Widnes)
4. Newlove (Featherstone R.)
5. Offiah (Widnes)
6. Ella (Wakefield T.)
7. D. Hulme (Widnes)
8. Ward (Castleford)
9. McKenzie (Widnes)
10. Skerrett (Bradford N.)
11. Vautin (St. Helens)
12. Gregory (Warrington)
13. Miller (Hull K.R.)

Australian import, hooker Phil McKenzie.

New Zealand Test prop forward Adrian Shelford.

ROGER MILLWARD, Hull K.R.

1. Hampson (Wigan)
2. Lydon (Wigan)
3. K. Iro (Wigan)
4. Loughlin (St. Helens)
5. Offiah (Widnes)
6. Lyons (Leeds)
7. Gregory (Wigan)
8. Ward (Castleford)
9. McKenzie (Widnes)
10. Sorensen (Widnes)
11. Platt (Wigan)
12. Koloto (Widnes)
13. Hanley (Wigan)

MALCOLM REILLY, Leeds

1. Tait (Widnes)
2. Drummond (Warrington)
3. Lydon (Wigan)
4. Loughlin (St Helens)
5. Offiah (Widnes)
6. Edwards (Wigan)
7. Gregory (Wigan)
8. Ward (Castleford)
9. Beardmore (Castleford)
10. Skerrett (Bradford N.)
11. Platt (Wigan)
12. Gregory (Warrington)
13. Hanley (Wigan)

ALEX MURPHY, St. Helens

1. Tait (Widnes)
2. Ettingshausen (Leeds)
3. K. Iro (Wigan)
4. Lydon (Wigan)
5. Offiah (Widnes)
6. Edwards (Wigan)
7. Gregory (Wigan)
8. Ward (Castleford)
9. McKenzie (Widnes)
10. Shelford (Wigan)
11. Eyres (Widnes)
12. Koloto (Widnes)
13. Hanley (Wigan)

BARRY SEABOURNE, Bradford N.

1. Tait (Widnes)
2. Drummond (Warrington)
3. Schofield (Leeds)
4. Lydon (Wigan)
5. Offiah (Widnes)
6. Woods (Warrington)
7. Gregory (Wigan)
8. Ward (Castleford)
9. Beardmore (Castleford)
10. Dannatt (Hull)
11. Ketteridge (Castleford)
12. Goodway (Wigan)
13. Hanley (Wigan)

Great Britain second row man Mike Gregory.   *Great Britain second row man Andy Platt.*

BRIAN SMITH, Hull

1. Hampson (Wigan)
2. T. Iro (Wigan)
3. K. Iro (Wigan)
4. McGowan (Bradford N.)
5. Offiah (Widnes)
6. O'Sullivan (Oldham)
7. D. Hulme (Widnes)
8. Harrison (Featherstone R.)
9. McKenzie (Widnes)
10. Shelford (Wigan)
11. Gibbs (Castleford)
12. Platt (Wigan)
13. Hanley (Wigan)

DAVID TOPLISS, Wakefield T.

1. Tait (Widnes)
2. Lydon (Wigan)
3. Currier (Widnes)
4. Newlove (Featherstone R.)
5. Offiah (Widnes)
6. Myler (Widnes)
7. Gregory (Wigan)
8. Crooks (Leeds)
9. McKenzie (Widnes)
10. England (Castleford)
11. Ketteridge (Castleford)
12. Fairbank (Bradford N.)
13. Hanley (Wigan)

DARRYL VAN DE VELDE, Castleford

1. Hampson (Wigan)
2. Quirk (St. Helens)
3. Currier (Widnes)
4. Williams (Salford)
5. Offiah (Widnes)
6. Steadman (Featherstone R.)
7. Gregory (Wigan)
8. Crooks (Leeds)
9. McKenzie (Widnes)
10. Sorensen (Widnes)
11. Fairbank (Bradford N.)
12. Dwyer (St. Helens)
13. Hanley (Wigan)

Australian import, second row man Ron Gibbs.

Great Britain skipper Ellery Hanley.

Hall opens
in honour
of 'greats'

MEMORIES

Attendance boom
smashes records

*World record
deal as Davies
joins Widnes*

Referee Lindop
given top job

*Record £900,000
Cup sponsorship*

Lowe puts
family
ahead of
Wigan

MEMORIES

1988-89 HEADLINES
Behind the facts and figures of the 1988-89 season were a number of stories which made extra impact:

JONATHAN DAVIES SIGNS
No single Rugby League event has ever made bigger headlines nationwide than Widnes's signing of Jonathan Davies, the Wales Rugby Union international captain and stand off, on 5 January. *The Times* report read like an obituary as they mourned the loss of one of Rugby Union's greatest players.

Estimates of the record deal went as high as £400,000 but Widnes later said the official figure was £150,000 for a four-year contract.

The Davies signing was one of six Rugby Union international moves which rocked the 15-a-side code. From Wales: David Bishop (Hull K.R.), Adrian Hadley (Salford), Paul Moriarty (Widnes) and Jonathan Griffiths (St. Helens). From England: John Bentley (Leeds).

CROWD BOOM CONTINUES
The Stones Bitter Championship had a second successive record campaign with the crowd average — up 25 per cent — the best for Division One since the reintroduction of two divisions in 1973. All but one of the 14 clubs reported a crowd increase on the previous season with Wigan reaching a record average of 14,543.

EXECUTIVE BOARD RULES
The Rugby League broke with tradition and took a momentous step forward in August when they appointed a six-man Board of Directors to govern the game. Bob Ashby (Featherstone Rovers) was elected chairman and was joined by David Oxley (Chief Executive), Maurice Lindsay (Wigan), Joe Seddon (St. Helens), Harry Jepson (Leeds) and Rodney Walker (Wakefield Trinity).

FOCUS ON REFEREES
With match officials coming under increasing pressure, Fred Lindop was appointed as the first Controller of Referees in November. The former top referee was to be responsible for the organisation of graded referees, overseeing appointments, assessments, examinations and fitness checks. He was to operate a new scheme in which the top ten referees would control all Division One matches within a promotion and relegation system for officials.

Mr Lindop's services to the game were recognised when he received the MBE in the Queen's New Year's Honours List.

DEWSBURY STAND FIRE
Struggling Dewsbury's only stand was destroyed by fire on 13 September, causing an estimated £100,000 worth of damage. Club and dressing rooms were lost along with all playing gear and club records. But with offers of help from several clubs and other sources Dewsbury battled on and no matches had to be postponed. The cause of the fire was arson.

NEW CLUB — NEW GROUNDS
A new club was formed at Chorley in May to replace Chorley Borough who moved to Manchester as Trafford Borough, having previously been Blackpool Borough and Springfield Borough.

York started the 1989-90 campaign with the prefix of Ryedale, having moved to the outlying district following the sale of their Clarence Street/Wigginton Road ground for development.

Hull Kingston Rovers made a similar move as they sold Craven Park and had a new ground built a short distance away. Mansfield Marksman were making plans to move grounds for the fourth time in their five-year history to the Harvey Haddon Stadium in Nottingham, and to be renamed Nottingham City.

RUNCORN DISPUTE

Runcorn Highfield first team players went on strike for more pay after the club forfeited home advantage to Wigan in the John Player Special Trophy first round because their own ground was too small. Runcorn fielded a team of reserves and trialists who suffered a club record 92-2 defeat. Coach Bill Ashurst came out of playing retirement but was sent off within 11 minutes of going on as substitute. The club fined the striking players £50 each, while Ashurst was fined £100 for bringing the game into disrepute. The Rugby League later handed the club a severe reprimand over the affair.

JUNE

Castleford and Wakefield Trinity vie for North Sydney's Kiwi forward Mark Graham .... St. Helens' bid for two-year deal with Australian packman Noel Cleal thwarted by Manly demand for £36,000 compensation .... Great Britain boosted by 28-12 success over Newcastle in first appearance in the Sydney area .... Kevin Tamati retires from New Zealand Test side after being appointed development officer for Warrington .... England B and Sheffield RU scrum half David Holmes signs for Halifax in £30,000 deal .... British tourist Shaun Edwards returns home with knee injury .... Wigan full back Steve Hampson cries off joining the tour party because of a slow-mending broken arm .... Featherstone Rovers sign veteran prop forward Jeff Grayshon .... Scarborough soccer club chairman Geoffrey Richmond considers the launch of a Rugby League side .... The British Lions crash to a shock 36-12 defeat by Northern Division at Tamworth .... Two days later the tourists are hammered 30-0 by Sydney Premiers, Manly .... Halifax back row man Paul Dixon shock choice as prop forward for the first Test in Sydney .... Great Britain go down fighting in the Centenary Test, 17-6, after leading Australia 6-0 at the interval .... Castleford end their

search for a new coach by recruiting Darryl Van de Velde from Brisbane club Redcliffe .... Wakefield Trinity win the race to sign Mark Graham .... Britain hit by wrist injury to Test man Andy Platt ... Centre Garry Schofield ruled out of the rest of the tour with a broken cheekbone as Britain beat Combined Brisbane 28-14 .... Five players involved in the Widnes-Warrington Premiership brawl fined a total of £800, Warrington's Mark Roberts and David Lyons £200 and banned for two matches each, teammate Barry Peters £200 and one match, with colleague Paul Cullen and Widnes forward Paul Hulme each fined £100 .... Hunslet appoint Nigel Stephenson as coach .... Tourist Paul Medley ordered home with a neck injury .... Widnes duo Andy Currier and Paul Hulme flown out as tour replacements for Garry Schofield and Paul Medley .... Martin Offiah bags four tries as Britain record 64-8 victory over Central Queensland at Rockhampton .... Castleford sign Gold Coast Australian forward Ron Gibbs .... St. Helens turned down by Australian Test star Wayne Pearce .... The British Lions beat Toowomba 28-12 .... Lions centre David Stephenson ruled out of the second Test with a shoulder injury .... Top Sydney side Manly eye Great Britain skipper Ellery Hanley .... A 65-yard special by Martin Offiah seals a 14-0 British victory over Wide Bay at Gympie .... Phil Ford given emergency role as British centre in the second Test in Brisbane .... The Lions crash 34-14 in the Brisbane encounter as Australia win the Ashes for the sixth successive time .... Eric Hughes resigns as coach of Rochdale Hornets to join the St. Helens coaching staff .... Workington Town name Maurice Bamford as their new coach .... Great Britain labelled 'headhunters' in second Test reviews .... Test packman Andy Platt, broken wrist, and Paul Dixon, broken thumb, sent home .... Wakefield Trinity join the chase for Australian centre Mal Meninga .... Bradford Northern recruit former Great Britain skipper

Harry Pinner from Leigh for £40,000 .... Jim Crellin joins Rochdale Hornets as coach.

JULY

Lee Crooks becomes the sixth British Lion to return home injured, his troublesome shoulder failing to respond to treatment .... Castleford skipper John Joyner and Widnes packman Richard Eyres called up as tour replacements .... Ellery Hanley signs a £2,000-a-match summer contract with Sydney club Balmain .... Kevin Ward is recruited by Sydney Premiers, Manly .... Top level talks staged to cut out high tackling in the third Test in Sydney .... Great Britain beat Western Division 28-26 at Orange .... Wakefield Trinity bid to sign Australians Garry Jack and Ben Elias .... Test hooker Kevin Beardmore suffers a shoulder injury as the British Lions fall 24-16 to a President's X111 at Canberra .... St. Helens sign Australian centre Mal Meninga for a second time .... Oldham list tourist Hugh Waddell at £90,000 .... York recruit Illawara duo Peter Spring and Chris Macklin-Shaw .... Eve of third Test withdrawals by Kevin Beardmore and Richard Eyres give Paul Hulme a Test debut in the emergency role of hooker .... Great Britain end 15-match losing run against Australia with 26-12 third Test success in Sydney .... Castleford sign Australian Test squad man Gary Belcher .... Warrington re-sign half back Paul Bishop from Australian club Cronulla .... The British Lions open their New Zealand visit with a 24-18 success over Wellington .... Kevin Beardmore returns for the World Cup-rated Test with New Zealand .... Mansfield Marksman appoint Billy Platt as coach .... Rochdale Hornets sign Swinton's Jeff Brown and Oldham's Chris Myler .... Great Britain miss out on a World Cup Final place in a 12-10 defeat by New Zealand in Christchurch .... Rest of the World coach Graham Lowe selects Great Britain's Henderson Gill, Andy Gregory, Kevin Ward, Mike Gregory and Ellery Hanley for the clash with Australia .... The British Lions party vote Paul Loughlin as the best tourist .... Oldham sign Parramatta skipper Paul Taylor .... Australia-based Kiwi forward Dane Sorensen turns down Carlisle .... Great Britain finish their 18-match tour with a 30-14 defeat by Auckland .... Salford move for loose forward John Westhead prompts Leigh to double the asking price to £100,000 .... St. Helens approach Welsh RU skipper Jonathan Davies .... Hull K.R. target Welsh RU duo David Bishop and Mark Ring .... Sacked Hunslet coach David Ward makes a comeback as skipper of Workington Town .... Former Leeds teammate Les Dyl also comes out of retirement to serve Bramley .... Prop forward Neil Clawson seeks a move from Oldham ... Swinton refuse to accept Oldham's bid for winger Tex Evans .... New Hull coach Brian Smith persuades young forwards Jon Sharp and Wayne Proctor to withdraw their transfer requests .... Oldham sign Rochdale Hornets hooker Andy Ruane .... Oldham fail to land Parramatta's Paul Mares .... St. Helens-bound Mal Meninga breaks his arm for the third time in the Australian Bicentennial 22-10 victory over the Rest of the World .... Bradford Northern offer new pay deal to winger Phil Ford before listing him at a world record £200,000 .... Leigh sign £25,000-rated St. Helens winger Barry Ledger .... Andy Gregory agrees to join Illawarra for the summer of 1989 .... Jonathan Davies turns down St. Helens .... David Bishop signs for Hull K.R. in estimated £100,000 deal .... Salford recruit New Zealand Test loose forward Mark Horo .... Swinton swap forward duo Mark Sheals and Mark Meadows for Chorley Borough packman Rory Howarth .... Wakefield Trinity fail in bid to sign Australian Test skipper Wally Lewis .... Hull K.R. offer Chris Burton at £80,000 and also list John Lydiat and Malcolm Beall.

AUGUST

Leeds sign Australian Test prop forward Sam Backo .... St. Helens join Hull K.R. in chase for newly-capped Australian Gavin Miller .... Wakefield Trinity snap up Sheffield Eagles forward John Glancy for £20,000 .... Rugby League Council introduce a six-man Board of Directors to replace the nine-member Management Committee .... Wakefield Trinity turned down by Australian Test skipper Wally Lewis and recruit Parramatta stand off Steve Ella .... Prop Neil Clawson makes peace with Oldham .... St. Helens capture Australian Test forward Paul Vautin .... Manly stand off Cliff Lyons joins Leeds for a second time .... York announce plans to change their name to Ryedale with their move from the city to the Ryedale district .... Hull recruit South Sydney scrum half Craig Coleman .... Barrow sign Australian prop Cavill Heugh .... Stomach injury stops Canberra stand off Ivan Henjak joining Oldham .... Hull K.R. win the race for Gavin Miller .... Bramley sign Graham Idle for the third time in 20 years .... Cronulla prop forward Michael Porter joins Hull K.R. .... Swinton winger Tex Evans moves to neighbours Salford .... Featherstone Rovers sign three-quarter Paul Newlove, son of former star John .... New Rugby League Board of Directors appointed with Chairman Bob Ashby and Chief Executive David Oxley joined by Harry Jepson, Maurice Lindsay, Joe Seddon and Rodney Walker .... Barrow's David Kendall moves to Carlisle for £15,000 .... Milton Huddart returns to Whitehaven from Leigh .... Oldham sign Canberra stand off Chris O'Sullivan and packman Ashley Gilbert .... Hull recruit South Sydney duo David Moon and David Boyle .... Scrum half Kevin Dick listed by Hull at £25,000 .... Manly half back Paul Shaw joins Salford .... Doug Laughton apointed coach of Lancashire for the Rodstock War of the Roses in succession to Alex Murphy .... Leigh sign forward Alan Platt from Hunslet .... New Zealander

Trevor Clark joins Featherstone Rovers .... Widnes lift the Okells Charity Shield, beating Wigan 20-14 on the Isle of Man .... Halifax player-coach Graham Eadie withdraws his resignation request after coaching role discussions .... Wigan face Australian club competition in quest for Ellery Hanley's signature on a new contract .... Hull K.R. sign former Australian Test player Chris Close .... Graham Eadie quits as coach of Halifax leaving newcomer Ross Strudwick in sole command .... Great Britain prop Hugh Waddell decides to stay at Oldham .... Nine players selected for the Whitbread Trophy Hall of Fame, all backs .... Wigan land a record sponsorship for a club with £250,000 three-year deal with Norweb .... Hunslet sign Batley's Neil Pickerill .... Whitehaven prop Tony Rose moves to Dewsbury .... After public protests, York decide to adopt the name York-Ryedale when leaving Wiggington Road .... Rugby League Tribunal fixes Alan Platt's move from Hunslet to Leigh at £40,000, £35,000 less than requested.

SEPTEMBER

Welsh RU winger Adrian Hadley turns professional with Salford .... Phil Ford turns down another Bradford Northern pay deal and threatens a move to Sydney .... Veteran Neil Hague moves from York to Hunslet .... Wakefield Trinity sign New Zealand Test prop Brent Todd .... Salford ordered by the Tribunal to pay £30,000 for Swinton's Tex Evans, £10,000 above their offer .... Former Welsh international Mick Murphy launches a takeover bid for Huddersfield .... Leeds hand over £20,000 for Castleford's Gary Lord .... Bradford Northern beat Hull K.R. and Wakefield Trinity for New Zealander Basil Ake .... Oldham protest dismissed by the League as Newcastle Knights sign centre Des Foy .... Wigan pay £140,000 for St. Helens Test forward Andy Platt .... Totting up system for sin bin offences scrapped .... St. Helens target New Zealand RU winger John

Kirwan .... Goalkicking Colin Whitfield listed by Halifax at £95,000 .... Jeff Edwards, £5,000-rated Oldham full back, transferred to Rochdale Hornets for £1,000 and four disused turnstiles .... New Zealand Test prop Peter Brown joins Salford .... Dewsbury stand destroyed by fire .... The League rule that only physiotherapists be allowed on the field to treat injuries during a game .... Halifax offer Steve Smith at £15,000 .... Swinton sign New Zealand duo David Ewe and Mike Kuiti .... Wigan Test star Shaun Edwards asks for a move .... Yorkshire maintain their Rodstock War of the Roses unbeaten record with a 24-14 success at Leeds .... Bradford Northern sign Leeds threequarter Erroll Johnson .... Leigh receive £50,000 from Oldham for centre John Henderson .... Prop forward Tim Street moves from Wigan to Leigh for £18,000 .... Chorley Borough recruit Salford pair Peter Glynn and Roy Wiltshire for £5,000 .... Wigan insist that Shaun Edwards honours his contract .... Ellery Hanley agrees a new three-year contract at Wigan .... Leeds deny an interest in Phil Ford as Bradford Northern offer him at a reduced £140,000 .... Hull K.R. list winger Steve Smith at £30,000 .... Wigan full back Steve Hampson to join teammate Andy Gregory for a summer stint with Sydney Premiership club Illawarra .... Australian Test coach Don Furner appointed as coach of the Rest of the World side to meet Great Britain .... Halifax offer of Colin Whitfield and £25,000 for Phil Ford turned down by Bradford Northern .... Halifax cross off Graham Eadie to make room on the quota system for Brisbane half back Peter Coyne.

OCTOBER

Whitehaven ordered by the Tribunal to hand over £10,000 for Milton Huddart, £25,000 less than being sought by Leigh .... Huddersfield receive Tribunal allocations of £6,500 for Tony Edwards from Rochdale

Hornets and £2,500 for Tony Kinsey from Swinton .... Graham Eadie elects to retire rather than join Wakefield Trinity .... The League's year-long ban on York director Albert Bond lifted after nine months .... New referees charter introduced by the League, featuring differential pay and appointments and the introduction of a Controller of Referees .... Wigan to sell part of ground for supermarket development in £2.5m deal .... Hull turn down Steve Norton's plea for a free transfer .... Leigh sign New Zealand centre Robert Moimoi .... Warrington move in for Llanelli scrum half Jonathan Griffiths .... Australian skipper Wally Lewis chosen to lead the Rest of the World in the Hall of Fame Challenge .... Local amateur club Elland fail in bid to sign Halifax's Graham Eadie .... Fulham sign Moroccan Hussein M'Barki for a second time .... St. Helens reject Leigh approach for forward Paul Forber .... Local council lend Rochdale Hornets £60,000 to stave off closure threats .... Leigh drop interest in South African winger Ray Mordt .... St. Helens recruit Welsh RU winger Mike Carrington in £65,000 deal .... Australia lift the World Cup, defeating New Zealand 25-12 in Auckland .... A broken arm in the World Cup Final rules Lewis out of Rest of the World duties .... Halifax launch official protest after Colin Whitfield is sin-binned for time-wasting during a first half penalty goal attempt .... Hull K.R. emerge as favourites to sign Wales RU international Mark Ring .... Castleford recruit Wakefield RU club duo Clive Yemm and Andy Clarke .... St. Helens' approach fails to tempt Oldham centre Des Foy to stay in Britain, opting to join Sydney Premiership outfit Newcastle Knights on a three-year contract .... Bev Risman dismissed as team manager of Fulham .... Steve Norton comes out of retirement at Hull to join former Boulevard teammate James Leuluai in move to Wakefield Trinity .... Oldham show interest in St. Helens winger Kevin McCormack ....

Bradford Northern chase Hull's Kevin Dick .... Colin Whitfield's sin bin offence for alleged time-wasting not recorded by the Disciplinary Committee .... Leeds beat Castleford 33-12 in an epic John Smiths Yorkshire Cup final .... Injury-hit Warrington go down 29-6 to visiting French tourists .... David Plange, Peter Williams and Kelvin Skerrett only three non-tourists in Great Britain's Hall of Fame Challenge 17-man squad .... France lose 24-18 to Halifax .... Leeds centre Erroll Johnson, valued at £60,000, moves to Bradford Northern priced at £30,000 by the Tribunal .... New Zealander Mark Graham appointed captain of the Rest of the World side .... France go down 18-13 to Cumbria at Whitehaven .... The League reject Halifax claim for a replay or share of the points in the Colin Whitfield sin-bin affair .... Hull K.R. drop interest in Mark Ring .... International Board delegates meeting in Auckland decide to scrap plans for a World Club Championship with a Tokyo final .... The League announce plans to go ahead with the European Club Championship fixture with Widnes and Le Pontet .... Sheffield Eagles list Derek Bridgeman at £15,000 .... Gary Hyde offered at £25,000 by Castleford .... Featherstone Rovers sign Glen Bell, brother of Wigan's Dean .... Whitehaven fined £500 for playing Kiwi Dave Watson without clearance .... Sheffield Eagles sign Australian packman Mark Geyer from Penrith .... Two-match ban and unsuccessful appeal put Salford full back Steve Gibson out of the Grunhalle Lager Lancashire Cup Final .... Wigan extend their record haul of the Lancashire Cup to 20 victories with a 22-17 defeat of Salford .... The Whitbread Trophy Hall of Fame is opened at the Bentley Arms, Oulton, near Leeds .... Great Britain beat the Rest of the World 30-28 at Headingley in the Hall of Fame Challenge encounter.

NOVEMBER

Doncaster pay club record £11,000 fee for Leeds international Kevin Rayne .... Hull K.R. chairman Colin Hutton calls for an end to the overseas quota system .... Warrington lift the British Coal Nines trophy, beating the Rest of the World 24-0 in the final .... Stones Bitter invest a record £750,000 in the League and Premiership campaigns in a new three-year deal .... Warrington protest about Ron Gibbs wearing gloves in the Nines tourney .... Oldham demand the appointment of full-time referees .... Roy Lester resigns as coach of Carlisle .... Swinton scrum half Tony Hewitt asks for a move and is listed at £15,000 .... Hull K.R. watch England RU three-quarter John Bentley .... Warrington and Wigan agree to meet in Milwaukee in June .... Chorley Borough centre Steve Donlan retires after second broken cheekbone .... Swinton offer Martin Lee at £19,000 .... Bradford Northern fined £1,000 for fielding a weakened side in the British Coal Nines .... Three-man board headed by former Welsh international Mick Murphy takes over at Huddersfield .... Halifax list want-away Great Britain tourist Ian Wilkinson at £30,000 .... League impose signing ban on Halifax for non-payment of transfer fee to Swinton for Les Holliday .... The League bans the wearing of gloves .... Oldham sack coaches Eric Fitzsimons and Iain MacCorquodale .... Wigan relieve Shaun Edwards of the captaincy and instal Great Britain skipper Ellery Hanley .... Warrington coach Tony Barrow resigns after 21-14 John Player Special Trophy victory over Oldham .... Huddersfield appoint Nigel Stephenson as coach .... Shaun Edwards in showdown at Wigan .... St. Helens' coach Alex Murphy invites disgraced Wimbledon soccer star Vinny Jones to play Rugby League .... Tony Barrow signs a three-and-a-half year contract as coach of Oldham .... Newly-retired man-in-the-middle Fred Lindop appointed the first-ever Controller of Referees .... Bradford Northern offer prop Brendan Hill at £90,000 and reduce the fee on Phil Ford to £140,000 .... John Fieldhouse makes his peace at St. Helens .... Strike-hit Runcorn Highfield go down 92-2 to Wigan in the John Player Special Trophy with out-of-retirement coach Bill Ashurst sent off .... Salford sign Keighley centre Ian Bragger for £20,000 .... Bill Ashurst suspended for four matches .... Leeds coach Malcolm Reilly signs a new 12-month contract to coach Great Britain part time .... Warrington bring Australian full back Brian Johnson back over to be coach .... England and Sale RU threequarter John Bentley signs for Leeds in estimated £80,000 deal .... Salford offer loose forward Mick McTigue at £30,000 .... Fulham appoint Australia-based former Great Britain hooker Mick Stephenson as coach .... Featherstone Rovers fail in a bid to land Hunslet second row man Sonny Nickle .... Oldham line up £40,000 package deal for Castleford duo David Roockley and Gary Hyde .... Featherstone Rovers utility back John Crossley returns to York for £4,000 .... Runcorn Highfield list four striking players, including captain Chris Middlehurst at £5,000 .... Wakefield Trinity's David Topliss appointed coach of Great Britain Under-21s .... The League advertises for a first-ever Marketing Executive .... York fail to sign Dewsbury second row man Stuart Morris .... Australian Brian Smith signs a new two-year contract as coach of Hull.

DECEMBER

St. Helens sign Jeff Clare from Wigan .... Oldham offer £65,000 for St. Helens Test forward John Fieldhouse .... St. Helens reject Leigh bid for scrum half Paul Doherty .... Oldham sign Widnes full back Duncan Platt for £35,000 .... Wigan centre Joe Lydon given a nine-month jail sentence suspended for two years for assaulting a boy spectator on the pitch after the Good Friday derby at St. Helens .... Hull K.R. interest in Great Britain utility back David Creasser warded off

by Leeds .... Mansfield Marksman appoint ex-Great Britain scrum half Steve Nash as coach .... New Controller of Referees, Fred Lindop, imposes a clampdown on high tackles .... Oldham sign Castleford's Gary Hyde for £15,000 .... Phil Ford returns to first team duty at Bradford Northern .... Salford sign Rochdale Hornets scrum half Mark Dobson .... Second row man Simon Bamber moves from Chorley Borough to Rochdale Hornets for £15,000 .... Bramley shell out a club record fee for Castleford prop Barry Johnson .... Fulham-bound Mike Stephenson makes 11th hour decision to stay in Australia .... Leeds recruit Dewsbury utility back Chris Vasey for £25,000 .... Ellery Hanley signs £85,000 contract to play summer rugby for Sydney Premiership side Western Suburbs .... Swinton offer full back Mark Villers at £12,000 and winger Terry Scott at £6,000 .... Coaches Barry Seabourne, of Bradford Northern, and Rochdale Hornets' Jim Crellin each fined £250 for verbal abuse of referees, heralding a new clampdown with suspension as the ultimate punishment .... Alex Murphy signs a new two-year contract as coach of St. Helens .... Dewsbury sack coach Terry Crooks .... New Zealand Test forwards Mark Graham and Brent Todd leave Wakefield Trinity to return home .... Hull hand over £25,000 for Barrow's Brian Blacker .... Castleford offer Welshman Brian Juliff at £6,000 .... Maurice Bamford resigns as coach of Workington Town, assistant Phil Kitchin taking over .... Halifax forward John Pendlebury fined £750 for missing a match and a training session .... Oldham's Australian recruit Paul Taylor forced to return home with a back injury .... Wigan accept a challenge from Queensland to meet in Brisbane in May .... Wembley fixes new capacity of 77,520 with 15,000 new seats replacing 30,000 standing places .... Maurice Bamford takes over as coach of Dewsbury .... Leigh ask £30,000 for former Under-21 hooker Gary Hughes .... Leeds sign Bradford Northern winger Phil Ford in a £95,000 deal including the part-exchange of utility back Mark Wilson .... Wigan put unsettled scrum half Andy Gregory on offer .... Hull K.R. sign Carlisle prop forward Colin Armstrong.

JANUARY

Hull K.R. pay £25,000 for Hunslet centre Jimmy Irvine .... Bill Ashurst resigns as coach of Runcorn Highfield .... Hull K.R., Bradford Northern and St. Helens join Halifax in the chase for Leeds second row man Paul Medley .... Australian John Cogger takes over as coach of Runcorn Highfield .... Price tag of £55,000 on Warrington's Billy McGinty puts off Oldham .... Wigan bid £120,000 for Halifax Test packman Paul Dixon .... St. Helens ask £75,000 for Tony Burke .... Hull K.R. move in for £25,000-rated St. Helens scrum half Paul Doherty .... Leeds and Halifax complete big exchange deal with £140,000-rated Paul Dixon moving to Headingley, £100,000-rated Paul Medley and half back John Lyons going to Thrum Hall .... Hull pay £25,000 for St. Helens scrum half Paul Doherty .... Welsh RU skipper Jonathan Davies signs for Widnes in a £150,000 record deal .... Wigan's Andy Gregory asks to come off the list .... Widnes call off their double European Club Championship fixture scheduled for March and agree a one-off meeting in France in May .... Oldham sign Widnes forward Keith Newton .... Warrington persuade Australian forward Les Boyd to return for another spell at Wilderspool .... Hull forward John Carroll moves to Dewsbury .... Welsh RU international centre John Devereux turns down a £100,000 package from Warrington .... Wigan lift the John Player Special Trophy for a record fourth time, beating Widnes 12-6 at Bolton .... After signing transfer forms with St. Helens in exchange for fellow prop Tony Burke, Bradford Northern's Brendan Hill moves to Halifax

.... York pay £2,500 for Halifax veteran forward Mick Scott .... Huddersfield stage triple signing session for David Heselwood (Featherstone Rovers), Gary Senior (Hunslet) and Bramley's Phil Johnson .... Hull K.R. hand over Chris Burton and £55,000 for Featherstone Rovers utility man Paul Lyman .... Leeds turn down Featherstone Rovers bid of £80,000 for Test three quarter Carl Gibson and an approach for forward Gary Price .... Oldham launch a £750,000 share issue .... Stand off Tony Myler recalled in the Great Britain squad to meet France at Wigan, then breaks an ankle .... David Ward returns as coach of Hunslet .... Jonathan Davies makes his debut for Widnes against Salford at Naughton Park as a 53rd minute substitute .... Hull K.R. sign Halifax scrum half Steve Robinson for £25,000 .... Bradford Northern introduces a fine system to curb indiscipline, rising to £200 for a dismissal .... York switch their home Silk Cut Challenge Cup tie with Leeds to York FC's Bootham Crescent ground .... Wigan's Andy Gregory and Leigh's Tim Street are the halfway stage leaders in the Greenalls First and Second Division Player of the Year polls .... A hip injury to Wigan full back Steve Hampson paves the way for ex-Scottish RU international Alan Tait, of Widnes, to make his Great Britain debut .... Hull K.R. ask £90,000 for winger Garry Clark .... Jonathan Davies makes his first full appearance in a Man of the Match performance for Widnes A-team, scoring three goals and creating three tries in a 32-20 Slalom Lager Alliance home success over Hull .... Great Britain Under-21s beat their French counterparts 30-0 at Leeds .... Widnes full back Alan Tait earns the Man of the Match award on his Great Britain debut in the 26-10 victory over France at Wigan .... The League decide to bring the Charity Shield from the Isle of Man to the mainland .... Great Britain coach Malcolm Reilly calls up forwards Lee Crooks and Keith England for the return French Test in Avignon ....

Controller of Referees Fred Lindop launches three new regional schools of excellence .... All available tickets for the 1989 Wembley Final sold out before the staging of the first round of the Silk Cut Challenge Cup .... Halifax loose forward John Pendlebury moves to Bradford Northern for £18,000 .... Hull hooker Lee Jackson called up for his Great Britain Under-21 debut as a replacement for injured captain Martin Dermott .... Warrington offer prop Tony Humphries at £35,000 .... St. Helens list hooker Mark Lee at £18,000 and cut the fee on Shaun Allen by £5,000 to £30,000 .... Leeds' Headingley complex to undergo £2.7m building facelift.

FEBRUARY

Mansfield Marksman seek their seventh coach in four years following the resignation of Steve Nash ... North Sydney forward Sean Willey rejoins York for a second spell of duty .... Rochdale Hornets sign Mansfield Marksman prop forward Les Chadwick .... Hull K.R. offer want-away prop forward Malcolm Beall at £40,000 .... Imperial Tobacco announce a new three-year sponsorship worth a record £825,000, the John Player Special Trophy being renamed the Regal Trophy .... Great Britain beat France 30-8 in Avignon .... Whitbread Trophy Bitter sponsorship of Great Britain not to be renewed .... Tribunal fixes £12,000 fee on Keith Newton's move from Widnes to Oldham .... Colin Whitfield makes his peace with Halifax .... Scotland B winger Derek Stark sought after by Halifax .... Wigan sign Orrell RU winger John Gilfillan .... Castleford forward Ron Gibbs reprimanded by the League's Disciplinary Committee after trial by video .... Wigan scrum half Andy Gregory goes on strike on the eve of second round Silk Cut Challenge Cup tie at Bradford after again being named substitute .... Halifax and Brendan Hill both reprimanded by the League for negotiating a transfer after Hill had signed for St. Helens .... Andy Gregory threatens to quit Wigan

.... Sydney club Eastern Suburbs sign Widnes winger Martin Offiah on a £50,000 summer contract .... Silk Cut announce a Rugby League record deal, sponsoring the Challenge Cup for a further three years for £900,000 .... Barrow chase St. Helens utility man Shaun Allen .... Andy Gregory returns to the fold at Wigan .... Wakefield Trinity's Australian import Steve Ella ruled out for the rest of the season with a dislocated shoulder .... Australian Ross Strudwick departs as coach of Halifax .... Alan Hardisty takes over as caretaker coach at Thrum Hall .... Wigan winger Mark Preston rejects a summer contract with Sydney club Cronulla .... British Coal take over sponsorship of Great Britain .... Oldham just manage to raise share flotation capital .... Sheffield Eagles loose forward Mark Fleming comes off the transfer list after a month's loan at Halifax .... Wakefield Trinity's record junior signing Gary Price put on offer at £95,000 .... The League bid to stage a World Club Challenge encounter in Britain in October .... Tony Fisher resigns as coach of Bramley .... Manchester City's Maine Road ground chosen as venue for a Wigan-Warrington Silk Cut Challenge Cup final, their first major match for 33 years .... Oldham turn down Bradford Northern offer of £65,000 for packman Paul Round .... Carlisle's £42,500-rated scrum half Dean Carroll joins Warrington on loan.

MARCH

Prop forward Barry Johnson appointed coach of Bramley .... Leeds agree two-year contract with Australian Test scrum half Peter Sterling .... Wigan linked with New Zealand RU winger John Kirwan .... Welsh Rugby League Players Association formed .... The League appoint Mike Turner as Sales Marketing Executive .... Oldham sign St. Helens utility man Shaun Allen on loan .... Police consider bringing charges against Salford hooker Ian Gormley after he jumps into the crowd at Halifax having been sent to the sin bin .... Gormley makes unreserved apology and is subject to a club suspension of four matches plus a £500 fine .... Manly approach Leeds for Test prop Hugh Waddell .... Western Suburbs recruit Bradford Northern prop forward Kelvin Skerrett for a summer stint .... Leeds scrum half Paul Delaney banned for three matches in trial by video for a tackle on Wakefield Trinity's Billy Conway .... The League launch a new sales division, Rugby League Enterprises .... MPs join in the protests as Welsh RU ban Jonathan Davies from commentating for the BBC at the Wales — England international in Cardiff .... St. Helens come to an agreement with Manly for the Wembley return of Paul Vautin and Michael O'Connor .... The autumn British Coal Tests with New Zeland to be staged at Old Trafford, Manchester; Elland Road, Leeds; and Wigan .... Australian RU winger David Campese rejects mammoth offer from St. Helens .... York sign Rochdale Hornets forward Dean Williams .... Hull offer prop forward Alan Tomlinson at £50,000 .... Leigh list hooker Carl Webb at £30,000 .... Hull put £27,500 price tag on scrum half Paul Doherty .... Great Britain Under-21 skipper Roy Southernwood listed by Castleford at his own request at £75,000 .... Hull recruit Balmain scrum half David Rowles for the rest of the season .... Balmain prop forward Steve Roach flies in from Sydney for the Silk Cut Challenge Cup semi-final with Wigan .... Chorley Borough offer 13 players in a bid to raise money pending the move to the Trafford area of Manchester .... Police decide not to press charges against Salford hooker Ian Gormley, now facing a League charge of bringing the game into disrepute .... Sheffield Eagles sign Hunslet second row man Sonny Nickles in a club record £20,000 deal .... Widnes return to Wales to recruit 21-cap RU international forward Paul Moriarty.

APRIL
Axed scrum half Bob Beardmore walks out

at Castleford .... Sydney club Balmain withdraw a summer contract for centre Garry Schofield after Leeds insist on 2 August return date .... St. Helens maintain interest in Australian RU star David Campese by inviting him to Wembley .... Wigan fail in bid to persuade New Zealand authorities to allow clearance-affected Test centre Kevin Iro to play in the title decider with Widnes .... Promoted Leigh and Barrow joined by Sheffield Eagles, going up in only their fifth season .... Relegated trio are Hull K.R., Halifax and Oldham .... Hull K.R. are defeated 16-13 by Widnes in the last-ever match at Craven Park .... Sheffield Eagles propose a three-division set-up for the 1989-90 campaign .... Four more players agree summer contracts Down Under, Joe Lydon to Eastern Suburbs, Shaun Edwards to Balmain, Hugh Waddell to Manly and Tracey Lazenby to Penrith .... Halifax target Canterbury Bankstown scrum half Steve Mortimer as new coach .... Salford hooker Ian Gormley banned for 10 matches and fined £1,000, six matches and £500 suspended for two years, for going into the stand during a game at Halifax .... Huddersfield handyman Keith Burhouse chosen as Traveleads Top Fan with a £4,000 holiday prize .... Widnes beat Wigan 32-18 to clinch the Stones Bitter Championship title and record £25,000 prize money .... St. Helens prop Tony Burke declares himself fit for Wembley after having 43 stitches in his ear during the last league match at Halifax .... The Board of Directors propose a transfer payment scheme of 50 per cent down and the rest over a maximum of one year .... Relegated Oldham list nine players in end-of-season clear out, including top-priced Ian Sanderson at £40,000 and former Test full back Mick Burke at £15,000 .... Wakefield Trinity ask £10,000 for former Batley forward Ian Douglas .... Chorley Borough plan a move to Altrincham, while current landlords Chorley AFC launch a bid for a new Rugby League club in the town .... Bradford

Northern subject to a takeover bid .... CIS Insurance announce sponsorship of the Charity Shield in a three-year, £50,000 deal .... Doncaster advertise for a new coach as John Sheridan confirms his retirement .... The League's request to have the fences taken down at Wembley is granted .... St. Helens protest to the League and Alex Murphy considers legal action following an outburst about Murphy from Wigan chairman Maurice Lindsay in the *Daily Mirror* .... Wigan offer New Zealand Test centre Kevin Iro a new three-year contract in face of Australian club competition .... Wigan lift the Silk Cut Challenge Cup with 27-0 victory over St. Helens, Ellery Hanley taking the Lance Todd Trophy.

MAY

International Board decide to stage a special month-long World Cup competition in Britain in 1995 to celebrate the Rugby Football League's centenary .... Castleford prop forward Kevin Ward opts for an abdominal operation instead of a summer contract with Sydney club Manly .... Leeds seal a two-year contract with Australian Test scrum half Peter Sterling .... Oldham list packman Terry Flanagan at £40,000 .... Forward Peter Regan offered at £10,000 by Salford .... Warrington reject Oldham's £30,000 bid for half back John Woods .... £185,000-rated stand off Graham Steadman agrees to join Castleford as Featherstone Rovers claim an illegal approach .... Graham Lowe quits as coach of Wigan to be with his two daughters in Brisbane .... St. Helens list 13 players, including four Wembley players, in a £406,000 clear out .... Great Britain and Wigan skipper Ellery Hanley named Greenalls Man of Steel for a record third time .... Widnes beat Hull 18-10 in the Stones Bitter Premiership final at Old Trafford, with Sheffield Eagles defeating Swinton 43-18 in the Second Division final .... Record crowd and receipts, 40,194 and £264,242, for the Stones Bitter Premiership doubleheader .... St. Helens sign Welsh RU scrum half Jonathan Griffiths .... Foster's launch a £50,000 sponsorship deal for the World Club Challenge encounter between Widnes and the 1989 Australian Grand Final winners to be staged at Old Trafford on 4 October .... Leeds centre Garry Schofield joins Sydney club Western Suburbs for a short summer stay .... Chorley AFC launch a new Rugby League club at Victory Park with Chorley Borough being given League permission to move to Altrincham as Trafford Borough .... Doncaster appoint former Castleford supremo Dave Sampson as coach .... The League announce a 12-match British Coal tour itinerary for New Zealand, including three British Coal Tests .... Gates for the Stones Bitter Championship rise by 25 per cent as 13 of the 14 clubs record an increase .... St. Helens target Australian Test stars Mal Meninga and Terry Lamb .... Le Pontet pull out three days before their European Club Championship encounter with Widnes because of disciplinary action by the French League, new French champions St. Esteve taking their place .... Rugby League introduce a kicking clinic for club players .... Bradford Northern sign Bramley RU full back David Cooper .... Widnes lift the European Club title by beating St. Esteve 60-6 at Arles .... Prop forward Tony Burke moves from St. Helens to Warrington for £50,000 .... Welsh RU packman Phil Davies decides to stay in the 15-a-side code after offers from St. Helens and Warrington .... Halifax appoint Australian and former Hull K.R. player John Dorahy as coach .... David Ward leaves coaching post at Hunslet to become assistant to Malcolm Reilly at Leeds.

Wakefield Trinity's Australian Test import, Steve Ella.

CLUBS

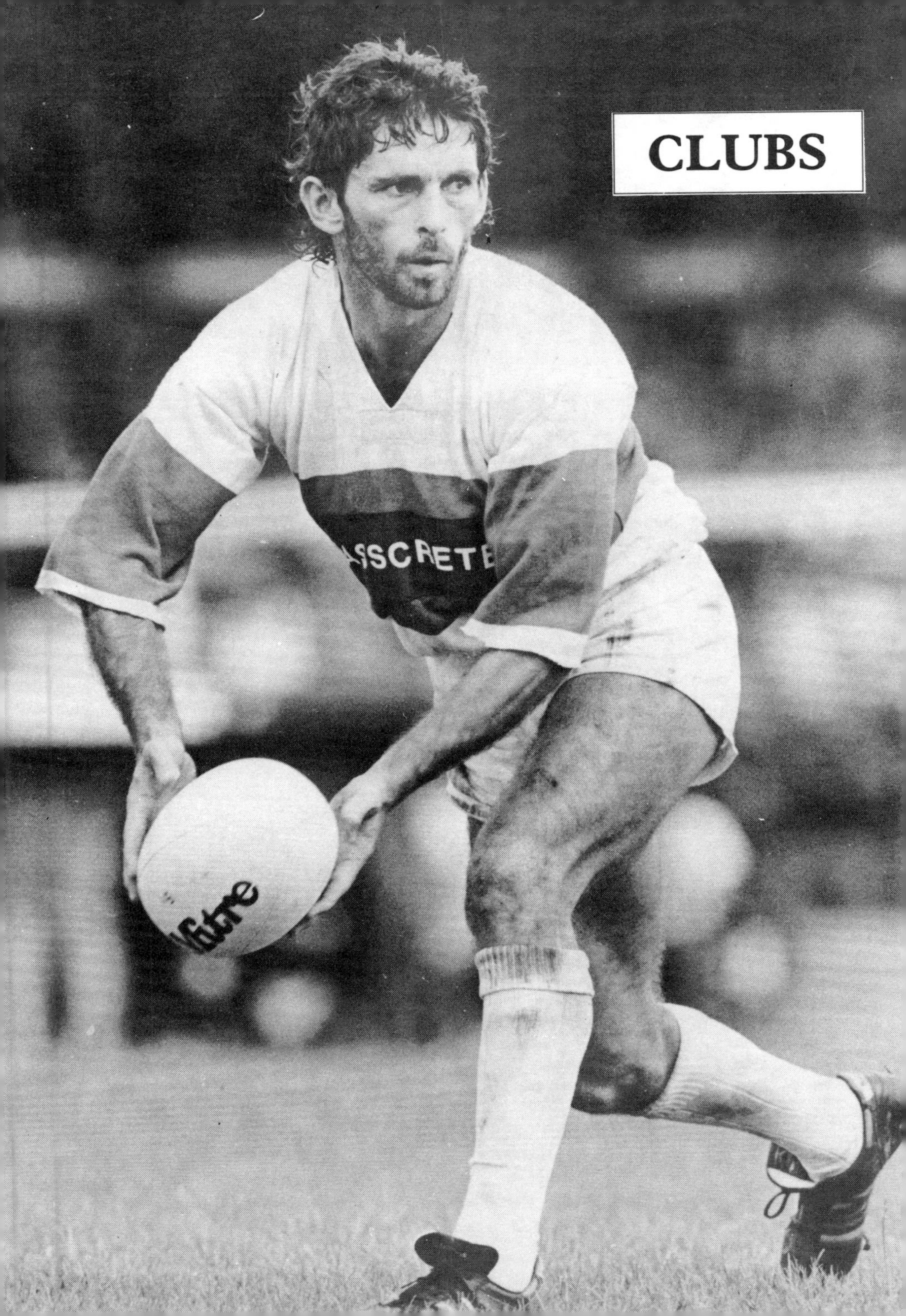

Salford's Australian full back Steve Gibson.

CLUBS

The following is a focus on the 34 professional Rugby League clubs, the section providing each club with a profile and an analysis of their 1988-89 campaign on a match by match basis with a summary for each first team player.

KEY

In the individual club profiles the following headings are featured:

First season refers to when the club gained senior league status. In some instances clubs have disbanded and re-formed, sometimes under different titles. For record purposes these changes are ignored except where there has been a break of more than one full season.

Honours. Until they were scrapped in 1970, the Yorkshire and Lancashire Leagues were among the honours in the professional game. Before 1903 they operated under the title of the Yorkshire and Lancashire Senior Competitions. Winners of these senior competitions are listed under Yorkshire and Lancashire League Champions. The pre-1903 Yorkshire Senior Competition should not be confused with the league operating for A-teams in Yorkshire which had the same title.

Coaches. Changes in the appointment of a club's coach since 1 June 1988 are shown in brackets.

Attendances. Crowds in brackets are at neutral venue.

Appearances. Players' totals are based on official teamsheets submitted to the League after each first team match. + indicates playing substitute appearance.

In the match by match review for each club the following abbreviations are used:

YC	— Yorkshire Cup	A	—	Away
LC	— Lancashire Cup	W	—	Won
SBC	— Stones Bitter Championship	L	—	Lost
SD	— Second Division	D	—	Drawn
JPS	— John Player Special Trophy	dg	—	Drop goal
CC	— Challenge Cup	Fr	—	France
PT	— Premiership Trophy	Aus	—	Australia
SDP	— Second Division Premiership	NZ	—	New Zealand
P	— Preliminary Round	PNG	—	Papua New Guinea
H	— Home	Pr	—	Probationer

BARROW

Ground: Craven Park
Colours: Royal blue
First Season: 1900-01
Nickname: Shipbuilders
Chairman: Bill Pears
Secretary: Wilf Livingstone
Coach: Rod Reddy (Nov 1987-)
Honours: **Challenge Cup** Winners, 1954-55
Beaten finalists, 1937-38, 1950-51, 1956-57, 1966-67
John Player Trophy Beaten finalists 1980-81
Lancashire Cup Winners, 1954-55, 1983-84
Beaten finalists, 1937-38
Division Two Champions, 1975-76, 1983-84
Records: Attendance: 21,651 v. Salford (League) 15 Apr, 1938
Season
Goals: 135 by J. Ball, 1956-57
Tries: 50 by J. Lewthwaite, 1956-57
Points: 305 by I. Ball, 1979-80
Match
Goals: 12 by F. French v. Maryport, 19 Feb, 1938; W. Horne v. Cardiff, 8 Sep, 1951; S. Tickle v. Kent Invicta, 8 Apr, 1984
Tries: 6 by V. Cumberbatch v. Batley, 21 Nov, 1936; J. Thornburrow v. Maryport, 19 Feb, 1938; F. Castle v. York, 29 Sep, 1951
Points: 28 by K. Jarrett v. Doncaster, 25 Aug, 1970; S. Tickle v. Kent Invicta, 8 Apr, 1984; D. Marwood at Runcorn H., 16 Apr, 1989
Highest score: 83-3 v. Maryport, 1937-38
Highest against: 71-15 v. St. Helens, 1958-59

1988-89 PLAYERS' SUMMARY

	App	Tries	Goals	Dr	Pts
Beckwith, Mark	8	4	—	—	16
Blacker, Brian	11 + 4	5	—	—	20
Brown, Ralph	1	—	—	—	—
Burns, Jeff	16 + 1	10	—	—	40
Burns, Paul	30 + 3	24	—	—	96
Clayton, Steve	31	2	—	—	8
Crarey, Paul	34	5	—	—	20
Du Toit, Nick	15	5	—	—	20
Dwyer, Tim	3 + 2	—	—	—	—
Hadley, Derek	0 + 3	—	—	—	—
Heugh, Cavill	24 + 1	9	—	—	36
Irvine, Paul	3	1	—	—	4
James, Mick	1	—	—	—	—
Kendall, Gary	26 + 1	5	—	—	20
Livesey, Dave	0 + 1	1	—	—	4
Maguire, Steve	31	4	1	2	20
Marshall, Ken	0 + 1	—	—	—	—
Marwood, Dean	33	5	114	1	249
Middleton, Glen	7 + 8	6	—	—	24
Morrison, Steve	6 + 2	—	—	—	—
Mossop, Andy	5	1	—	—	4
O'Neill, Ian	0 + 3	1	—	—	4
Pemberton, Keith	5 + 11	4	—	—	16
Shaw, Neil	23 + 8	4	—	—	16
Stott, Phil	30	18	—	—	72
Tees, Gary	9 + 5	2	—	—	8
Tickle, Steve	28 + 4	4	10	1	37
Totten, Greg	3	—	—	—	—
Trainor, Pat	0 + 6	1	—	—	4
Walker, Russ	29	9	—	—	36
Williams, Stewart	30 + 1	14	—	—	56

TOTALS:
| 31 players | | 144 | 125 | 4 | 830 |

Welshman Keith Jarrett, joint holder of the club record for most points in a match.

1988-89 MATCH ANALYSIS

Date	Competition	H/A	Opponent	Rlt	Score	Tries	Goals	Attendance	Referee
28.8.88	SD	A	Rochdale H.	L	26-36	Du Toit, Stott, Kendall, Walker, Heugh	Tickle (3)	—	—
4.9.88	SD	H	Mansfield M.	W	28-6	Maguire, Marwood, Stott, Walker, Clayton	Tickle (4)	1236	Volante
11.9.88	SD	A	Sheffield E.	D	11-11	Du Toit, Clayton	Marwood, Maguire (dg)	—	—
18.9.88	LC(1)	H	Wigan	L	10-24	Heugh	Marwood (2), Tickle	5528	Simpson
25.9.88	SD	H	Whitehaven	W	14-6	Mossop	Marwood (5)	1473	Allatt
2.10.88	SD	A	Chorley B.	W	18-16	P. Burns (2), Heugh	Marwood (3)	—	—
9.10.88	SD	H	Keighley	W	54-16	Stott (3), Walker (2), Heugh, Du Toit, P. Burns, Williams, Irving	Marwood (7)	1548	Dockray
18.10.88	SD	A	Hunslet	W	12-0	Blacker	Marwood (4)	—	—
23.10.88	SD	H	Rochdale H.	W	26-8	Du Toit, Stott, Marwood, Walker	Marwood (5)	1779	Berry
30.10.88	SD	A	Carlisle	W	28-6	Williams, Blacker, Heugh, Tickle, Stott	Marwood (4)	—	—
6.11.88	SD	H	Swinton	W	30-8	P. Burns (2), Marwood, Du Toit, Blacker, Stott	Marwood (3)	2007	Galtress
13.11.88	JPS(1)	A	Leigh	L	14-42	Maguire, Kendall	Marwood (3)	—	—
20.11.88	SD	A	York	W	18-12	Blacker, J. Burns	Marwood (5)	—	—
11.12.88	SD	A	Whitehaven	L	12-14	J. Burns, Stott	Marwood (2)	—	—
18.12.88	SD	H	Runcorn H.	W	36-6	P. Burns (2), Tickle, Stott (2), Blacker, J. Burns	Marwood (4)	1188	Tidball
26.12.88	SD	H	Carlisle	W	15-10	J. Burns, Williams	Marwood (3), Tickle (dg)	1446	Morris
1.1.89	SD	A	Workington T.	W	20-4	P. Burns (3), J. Burns	Marwood (2)	—	—
4.1.89	SD	H	Leigh	W	22-4	Williams (2), Stott, Tickle	Marwood (3)	2484	Whitelam
8.1.89	SD	H	Hunslet	W	40-0	Kendall (2), P. Burns (2), Pemberton, Stott, J. Burns	Marwood (6)	1712	Burke
22.1.89	SD	H	Chorley B.	W	44-12	Williams (2), Heugh (2), J. Burns, Shaw, Crarey, Kendall	Marwood (6)	1501	Berry
29.1.89	CC(1)	H	Huddersfield	W	38-16	P. Burns (2), Pemberton, Stott, Heugh, Middleton, Shaw	Marwood (5)	1859	Galtress
5.2.89	SD	A	Swinton	W	31-12	P. Burns, Maguire, Middleton, Livesey, Williams, Heugh	Tickle (2), Maguire (1, 1dg)	—	—
12.2.89	CC(2)	A	St. Helens	L	6-28	P. Burns	Marwood	—	—
19.2.89	SD	A	Bramley	W	26-21	J. Burns, P. Burns, Crarey, Scott	Marwood (5)	—	—
26.2.89	SD	A	Leigh	L	18-26	J. Burns, P. Burns, Crarey, Williams	Marwood	—	—
5.3.89	SD	H	York	L	12-26	Crarey	Marwood (4)	1694	Simpson
12.3.89	SD	A	Mansfield M.	W	36-12	Stott (2), Beckwith, Walker, P. Burns, Tickle, Pemberton	Marwood (4)	—	—
19.3.89	SD	H	Sheffield E.	L	20-24	Beckwith, O'Neill, Stott, J. Burns	Marwood (2)	1522	Cross
27.3.89	SD	H	Workington T.	W	32-0	Williams (2), Tees, Walker, Maguire, Shaw	Marwood (4)	1552	Smith
2.4.89	SD	A	Keighley	L	10-14	Walker, Williams	Marwood	—	—
9.4.89	SD	H	Bramley	W	27-16	P. Burns (2), Shaw, Middleton, Beckwith	Marwood (3, 1dg)	1175	Tidball
16.4.89	SD	A	Runcorn H.	W	60-0	Middleton (2), Marwood (2), Williams (2), P. Burns, Pemberton, Tees, Trainor	Marwood (10)	—	—
23.4.89	SDP (1)	H	Whitehaven	W	30-5	P. Burns (2), Beckwith, Walker, Middleton	Marwood (5)	1914	Tickle
7.5.89	SDP (SF)	H	Sheffield E.	L	6-9	Crarey	Marwood	1771	Tennant

BATLEY

Ground:	Mount Pleasant
Colours:	Cerise and fawn
First Season:	1895-96
Nickname:	Gallant Youths
Chairman:	Stephen Ball
Secretary:	Linda Hartley
Coach:	Paul Daley (July 1987-)

Honours: **Championship** Winners, 1923-24
Challenge Cup Winners, 1896-97, 1897-98, 1900-01
Yorkshire League Winners, 1898-99, 1923-24
Yorkshire Cup Winners, 1912-13
Beaten finalists, 1909-10, 1922-23, 1924-25, 1952-53

Records: Attendance: 23,989 v. Leeds (RL Cup) 14 Mar, 1925
Season
Goals: 120 by S. Thompson, 1958-59
Tries: 29 by J. Tindall, 1912-13
Points: 281 by J. Perry, 1950-51
Match
Goals: 9 by W. Davies v. Widnes, 27 Mar, 1909; S. Thompson v. Keighley, 20 Sep, 1958
Tries: 5 by J. Oakland v. Bramley, 19 Dec, 1908; T. Brannan v. Swinton, 17 Jan, 1920; J. Wale v. Bramley, 4 Dec, 1926 and v. Cottingham, 12 Feb, 1927
Points: 26 by J. Perry v. Liverpool C., 16 Sep, 1951
Highest score: 52-8 v. Widnes, 1908-09
Highest against: 78-9 v. Wakefield T., 1967-68

1988-89 PLAYERS' SUMMARY

	App	Tries	Goals	Dr	Pts
Arnold, Derek	18 + 8	1	—	—	4
Bownass, Mark	15 + 4	—	—	—	—
Carroll, Dean	3 + 1	1	—	1	5
Cook, Mark	10 + 3	2	—	—	8
Fortis, Mark	31	7	—	—	28
Gearey, Paul	29	22	—	—	88
Hemmingway, Neil	2 + 5	—	—	—	—
Hinchliffe, Mark	22 + 4	4	—	—	16
Illingworth, Neil	0 + 1	—	—	—	—
Jones, David	5	—	—	—	—
Kay, Andy	2	—	—	—	—
Kellett, Neil	8	1	—	—	4
Marshall, Paul	7	2	—	—	8
McGowan, John	24	9	—	—	36
McGrath, Damian	11	1	15	1	35
Parrish, Steve	2	—	—	—	—
Perry, David	1	—	—	—	—
Scott, Mark	19 + 6	4	—	—	16
Smith, Gary	9 + 16	4	—	—	16
Speight, Mark	31	1	—	—	4
Spendler, Mark	7 + 5	2	—	—	8
Stainburn, John	30 + 1	1	30	13	77
Storey, Paul	20 + 2	—	—	—	—
Thornton, Gary	4	—	—	—	—
Waites, Brian	16	7	—	—	28
Williams, Andy	31	10	—	1	41
Wilson, Simon	30 + 1	4	20	11	67
Wragg, Nicky	14 + 3	—	—	—	—
Trialist	2	—	—	—	—
TOTALS:					
29 players		83	65	27	489

Packman Paul Gearey, Batley's top try scorer.

1988-89 MATCH ANALYSIS

Date	Competition	H/A	Opponent	Rlt	Score	Tries	Goals	Attendance	Referee
26.8.88	SD	A	York	L	15-24	Geary, Scott	McGrath (3), Wilson (dg)	—	—
4.9.88	SD	A	Carlisle	D	17-17	Williams, Geary, Fortis	McGrath (2), Wilson (dg)	—	—
11.9.88	SD	A	Runcorn H.	L	28-31	Geary (2), Fortis (2), Scott	McGrath (4)	—	—
18.9.88	GC(1)	A	Halifax	L	14-36	Hinchliffe, Cook, Williams			
25.9.88	SD	A	Hunslet	L	14-31	Geary, Cook	McGrath (3)		
2.10.88	SD	A	Huddersfield	D	19-19	Williams (2), Wilson	Wilson (3, 1dg)	—	—
9.10.88	SD	A	Fulham	W	22-2	McGowan (2), Geary, Williams	Wilson (2, ldg), Stainburn (dg)	—	—
16.10.88	SD	A	Mansfield M.	W	8-6	Scott	Wilson (1, 2dg)	—	—
23.10.88	SD	A	Sheffield E.	W	17-10	Williams, Geary	Wilson (3), Stainburn (3dg)	—	—
30.10.88	SD	H	Rochdale H.	W	39-14	Geary (3), Spendler, Wilson, Williams, McGowan	Wilson (5), Stainburn (dg)	1000	Tidball
6.11.88	SD	H	Carlisle	L	6-13	Geary	Wilson	801	Whitelam
13.11.88	JPS(1)	A	Hull	L	10-26	Geary (2)	Wilson	—	—
20.11.88	SD	A	Whitehaven	D	2-2		Stainburn (dg), Williams (dg)	—	—
4.12.88	SD	H	Runcorn H.	W	34-0	Geary (3), Fortis, Williams, Smith	Stainburn (5)	606	Kendrew
11.12.88	SD	A	Rochdale H.	L	8-32	Geary, Spendler	Stainburn (5), Wilson (dg)	682	Smith
18.12.88	SD	H	Fulham	W	31-12	McGowan (2), Hinchliffe, Geary, Waites			
26.12.88	SD	A	Dewsbury	L	8-11	McGowan	Stainburn (2)	—	—
1.1.89	SD	H	Dewsbury	W	14-6	Carroll, Scott	Stainburn (2 ldg), Carroll (dg)	2061	Kendrew
8.1.89	SD	A	Bramley	L	8-22	Geary (2)	—	—	—
15.1.89	SD	H	Sheffield E.	L	4-42	McGowan	—	869	Spencer
29.1.89	CC(1)	A	Wakefield T.	L	4-34	Waites	—	—	—
5.2.89	SD	A	Workington T.	L	5-6	Fortis	Stainburn (dg)	—	—
12.2.89	SD	H	Hunslet	L	9-26	Arnold	McGrath (2, 1dg)	980	Allatt
19.2.89	SD	H	Doncaster	L	6-15	Waite	Stainburn (2dg)	1286	Spencer
26.2.89	SD	H	Mansfield M.	W	30-3	Williams (2), Geary, McGowan, Wilson	Stainburn (5)	504	Morris
5.3.89	SD	H	Bramley	W	15-12	Geary, Fortis, McGowan	Wilson, Stainburn (dg)	713	Tennant
12.3.89	SD	H	Huddersfield	W	13-0	Smith, Stainburn	Wilson (1, 1dg), Stainburn	897	Hawley (Pr)
19.3.89	SD	H	Workington T.	W	25-14	Smith (2), Hinchliffe, Marshall	Stainburn (4, 1dg)	617	Simpson
27.3.89	SD	A	Doncaster	W	22-11	Marshall, Waites, Wilson	Stainburn (5)	—	—
2.4.89	SD	H	York	L	19-20	Hinchliffe, Waites, McGrath	Wilson (1, 3dg), Stainburn	1059	Kendrew
16.4.89	SD	H	Whitehaven	W	23-15	Waites (2), Speight, Fortis, Kellett	Wilson, Stainburn (dg)	856	Houghton

33

BRADFORD NORTHERN

Ground.   Odsal Stadium
Colours: White, red, amber and black
First Season: 1895-96 as "Bradford". Disbanded
and became Bradford Northern in
1907-08. Disbanded during 1963-64
and re-formed for start of 1964-65
Nickname: Northern
Chairman: Chris Caisley
Secretary: Gary Tasker
Coach: Barry Seabourne (May 1985-)
Honours: **Challenge Cup** Winners, 1905-06,
1943-44, 1946-47, 1948-49
Beaten finalists, 1897-98, 1944-45,
1947-48, 1972-73
Championship Beaten finalists,
1947-48, 1951-52
Division One Champions, 1903-04,
1979-80, 1980-81
Division Two Champions, 1973-74
War-time Emergency League
Championship winners, 1939-40,
1940-41, 1944-45
Beaten finalists, 1941-42
Yorkshire League Winners,
1899-1900, 1900-01, 1939-40,
1940-41, 1947-48
Yorkshire Cup Winners, 1906-07,
1940-41, 1941-42, 1943-44,
1945-46, 1948-49, 1949-50,
1953-54, 1965-66, 1978-79,
1987-88
Beaten finalists, 1913-14, 1981-82,
1982-83
Premiership Winners, 1977-78
Beaten finalists, 1978-79, 1979-80
John Player Trophy Winners,
1974-75, 1979-80
Records: Attendance: 102,569 Warrington v.
Halifax (RL Cup Final replay)
5 May, 1954
Home: 69,429 v. Huddersfield
(RL Cup) 14 March, 1953
Season
Goals: 173 by E. Tees, 1971-72
Tries: 63 by J. McLean, 1951-52
Points: 364 by E. Tees, 1971-72

Match
Goals: 14 by J. Phillips v. Batley,
6 Sep, 1952
Tries: 7 by J. Dechan v. Bramley,
13 Oct, 1906
Points: 36 by J. Woods v. Swinton,
13 Oct, 1985
Highest score: 72-9 v. Doncaster,
1973-74; 72-12 v. Hunslet, 1984-85
Highest against: 75-18 v. Leeds,
1931-32

1988-89 PLAYERS' SUMMARY

	App	Tries	Goals	Dr	Pts
Ake, Basil	13 + 4	2	—	—	8
Barraclough, Glenn	1 + 1	—	—	—	—
Cornforth, Phil	1 + 1	3	—	—	12
Croft, David	0 + 2	—	—	—	—
Fairbank, Karl	34	20	—	—	80
Ford, Phil	2	1	—	—	4
Francis, Richard	13 + 2	3	—	—	12
Godfrey, Heath	4 + 1	1	—	—	4
Grayshon, Paul	1 + 1	—	—	—	—
Hamer, John	27 + 3	—	—	—	—
Harkin, Paul	29 + 1	4	5	5	31
Hill, Brendan	7 + 4	5	—	—	20
Hobbs, David	32	10	109	5	263
Johnson, Errol	15 + 1	4	—	—	16
McGowan, Steve	34	21	—	—	84
Mercer, Gary	19	4	1	—	18
Moxon, Darren	0 + 2	—	—	—	—
Mumby, Keith	33	1	—	—	4
Noble, Brian	34	4	—	—	16
Pendlebury, John	10	—	—	—	—
Pinner, Harry	20 + 4	1	—	—	4
Potts, Martin	1 + 1	—	—	—	—
Rhodes, Paul	4 + 2	—	—	—	—
Richards, Craig	0 + 1	—	—	—	—
Roebuck, Neil	2 + 6	—	—	—	—
Sidebottom, Gary	2	—	—	—	—
Simpson, Roger	29 + 1	9	—	—	36
Skerrett, Kelvin	31	8	—	—	32
Stewart, Russell	23	4	—	—	16
Wilkinson, Ian	11 + 1	5	—	—	20
Wilson, Mark	10 + 6	—	—	—	—

TOTALS:
| 31 players | | 110 | 115 | 10 | 680 |

1988-89 MATCH ANALYSIS

Date	Com-petition	H/A	Opponent	Rlt	Score	Tries	Goals	Atten-dance	Referee
28.8.88	SBC	A	St. Helens	L	16-23	Hill	Hobbs (6)	—	—
4.9.88	SBC	H	Salford	W	42-18	Hill (2), Simpson, Ake, Francis, Fairbank	Hobbs (9)	4403	Houghton
11.9.88	SBC	A	Halifax	L	14-26	Francis, Hobbs	Hobbs (3)	—	—
18.9.88	YC(1)	A	Leeds	L	21-24	McGowan, Francis, Harkin, Fairbank	Hobbs (2), Harkin (dg)	—	—
25.9.88	SBC	H	Wigan	L	17-20	Harkin (2)	Hobbs (4, ldg)	8769	Smith
2.10.88	SBC	A	Featherstone R.	W	48-20	Fairbank (3), Hobbs, Skerrett, Ake, Mumby, Noble	Hobbs (8)	—	—
9.10.88	SBC	H	Hull	W	32-20	McGowan (2), Johnson (2), Stewart, Noble	Hobbs (4)	3574	Tennant
16.10.88	SBC	A	Hull K.R.	L	22-24	Hill (2), McGowan	Harkin (5)	—	—
6.11.88	SBC	H	Leeds	L	10-18	Skerrett	Hobbs (3)	8663	Whitfield
13.11.88	JPS(1)	H	Dewsbury	W	34-18	Fairbank (3), Hobbs (2), Godfrey	Hobbs (5)	2555	Burke
20.11.88	SBC	A	Wakefield T.	W	23-14	Mercer (2), Stewart, Fairbank	Hobbs (3), Harkin (dg)	—	—
27.11.88	JPS(2)	A	Castleford	W	19-18	Johnson, Pinner, Fairbank	Hobbs (3, ldg)	—	—
4.12.88	JPS(3)	H	Leigh	W	6-0	Hobbs	Hobbs	3975	Allatt
11.12.88	SBC	A	Salford	L	18-33	Ford, Mercer, Hobbs	Hobbs (3)	—	—
17.12.88	JPS (SF)	Leeds	Wigan	L	5-16	—	Hobbs (2), Harkin (dg)	(6809)	Carter
1.1.89	SBC	A	Castleford	L	20-38	McGowan (2), Skerrett	Hobbs (4)	—	—
8.1.89	SBC	A	Hull	L	10-28	Stewart, McGowan	Hobbs	—	—
15.1.89	SBC	H	Warrington	W	15-4	Harkin, Fairbank	Hobbs (3), Harkin (dg)	3676	Steele
22.1.89	SBC	A	Oldham	W	30-14	McGowan (2), Hobbs, Fairbank, Johnson	Hobbs (5)	—	—
29.1.89	CC(1)	A	Fulham	W	28-10	McGowan (3), Wilkinson (2), Fairbank	Hobbs (2)	—	—
5.2.89	SBC	H	Halifax	W	30-18	Simpson, McGowan, Wilkinson, Stewart, Skerrett	Hobbs (5)	7229	Haigh
12.2.89	CC(2)	H	Wigan	L	4-17	—	Hobbs (2)	16,738	Whitfield
19.2.89	SBC	H	St. Helens	L	12-16	McGowan, Wilkinson, Simpson	—	4197	Holdsworth
22.2.89	SBC	H	Castleford	L	6-20	Wilkinson	Mercer	4404	Carter
5.3.89	SBC	A	Warrington	W	23-22	Skerrett (2), Fairbank	Hobbs (5, ldg)	—	—
12.3.89	SBC	A	Wigan	L	13-20	Mercer, Fairbank	Hobbs (2, ldg)	—	—
19.3.89	SBC	H	Widnes	D	16-16	McGowan, Hobbs, Skerrett	Hobbs (2)	5332	Kershaw
24.3.89	SBC	A	Leeds	L	7-10	Fairbank	Hobbs, Harkin (dg)	—	—
28.3.89	SBC	H	Wakefield T.	L	8-28	Fairbank	Hobbs (2)	4244	Kershaw
2.4.89	SBC	A	Widnes	W	22-12	McGowan, Simpson, Fairbank	Hobbs (5)	—	—
9.4.89	SBC	H	Featherstone R.	L	23-32	McGowan (2), Simpson, Noble	Hobbs (3, ldg)	4172	Whitfield
12.4.89	SBC	H	Oldham	W	30-10	Simpson (2), McGowan (2), Fairbank	Hobbs (5)	2927	Carter
16.4.89	SBC	H	Hull K.R.	W	38-14	Hobbs (2), Cornforth (2), Simpson, Noble, McGowan	Hobbs (5)	3012	Tennant
23.4.89	PT(1)	A	Widnes	L	18-30	Fairbank, Simpson, Skerrett, Cornforth	Hobbs	—	—

BRAMLEY

Ground: McLaren Field
Colours: Amber and black
First Season: 1896-97
Nickname: Villagers
Chairman: Jeff Wine
Secretary: Barry Rennison
Coach: Tony Fisher (Nov 1987-Feb 1989)
Barry Johnson (Feb 1989-)
Honours: **BBC2 Floodlit Trophy** Winners, 1973-74
Records: Attendance: 12,600 v. Leeds (League) 7 May, 1947
Season
Goals: 130 by J. Wilson, 1961-62
Tries: 34 by P. Lister, 1985-86
Points: 276 by G. Langfield, 1956-57
Match
Goals: 11 by B. Ward v. Doncaster, 1 Sep, 1974
Tries: 7 by J. Sedgewick v. Normanton, 16 Apr, 1906
Points: 28 by B. Ward v. Doncaster, 1 Sep, 1974
Highest score: 62-14 v. Dewsbury, 1988-89
Highest against: 92-7 v. Australia, 1921-22

1988-89 PLAYERS' SUMMARY

	App	Tries	Goals	Dr	Pts
Agar, Malcolm	5 + 2	—	7	1	15
Armitage, Des	2 + 2	—	—	—	—
Bibb, Trevor	4 + 3	—	—	—	—
Birch, Richard	2 + 2	—	—	—	—
Bond, Steve	7 + 3	1	—	—	4
Bowman, Chris	0 + 3	—	—	—	—
Brentley, Gary	33	3	—	—	12
Bridgeman, Derek	0 + 2	—	—	—	—
Carroll, Steve	25 + 1	8	77	1	187
Crawford, Adrian	11 + 2	1	—	—	4
Durham, Steve	28 + 2	1	11	—	26
Dyl, Les	23	4	—	—	16
Edmondson, Steve	16 + 4	3	—	—	12
Ellis, Andy	2	—	—	—	—
Fletcher, Paul	5 + 2	—	—	—	—
Gascoigne, Andy	22 + 1	3	—	—	12
Gerrard, Graham	9 + 3	5	—	—	20
Green, Karl	1	—	—	—	—
Hobbs, Gary	20	12	—	—	48
Holden, Barry	26 + 5	3	—	—	12
Hunter, Damian	3 + 3	1	—	—	4
Idle, Graham	0 + 2	—	—	—	—
Illingworth, Neil	17 + 2	3	6	—	24
Johnson, Barry	15 + 1	—	—	—	—
Langley, Paul	2 + 3	1	—	—	4
Lewis, Peter	25 + 1	26	—	—	104
Lister, Peter	32	28	4	4	124
McEvoy, Brett	2	2	—	—	8
Olpherts, Eric	7 + 1	3	—	—	12
Owen, Phil	2	—	—	—	—
Race, Wayne	32	10	—	—	40
Robinson, Andy	4	—	—	—	—
Sharp, Henry	1	—	—	—	—
Sharp, Ronnie	22 + 2	7	—	—	28
Smiles, Warren	2 + 3	—	—	—	—
Spedding, Paul	19 + 2	2	—	—	8
Thornton, Gary	3	—	—	—	—

TOTALS:

	App	Tries	Goals	Dr	Pts
37 players		127	105	6	724

Les Dyl, four tries in 23 matches.

Derek Bridgeman, two substitute appearances on loan from Sheffield Eagles.

1988-89 MATCH ANALYSIS

Date	Com-petition	H/A	Opponent	Rlt	Score	Tries	Goals	Atten-dance	Referee
28.8.88	SD	A	Sheffield E.	L	10-13	Lister (2)	Agar	—	—
31.8.88	YC(P)	H	Leeds	L	16-38	Sharp, Crawford, Carroll	Agar (2)	4258	Tennant
4.9.88	SD	H	Doncaster	L	16-32	Carroll, Race	Carroll (4)	1036	Carter
7.9.88	SD	H	Huddersfield	W	30-12	Hobbs (2), Edmondson, Carroll, Lister, Olpherts	Carroll (3)	710	Kershaw
11.9.88	SD	A	Mansfield M.	W	32-0	Lister (3), Olpherts, Sharp	Carroll (6)	—	—
25.9.88	SD	A	Fulham	W	30-20	Lewis (2), Gascoigne, Holden, Hobbs	Carroll (5)	—	—
2.10.88	SD	H	Swinton	W	34-22	Hobbs (3), Sharp (2), Lister	Carroll (5)	1122	Bowman
16.10.88	SD	H	Fulham	W	30-8	Carroll (2), Lister (2), Race	Carroll (5)	627	Holgate
23.10.88	SD	A	Chorley B.	W	25-7	Lister (2), Sharp, Gascoigne	Carroll (4), Lister (dg)	—	—
30.10.88	SD	H	Dewsbury	W	62-14	Hobbs (3), Lewis (3), Edmondson, Dyl, Carroll, Durham, Illingworth, Lister	Carroll (7)	1264	Whitelam
6.11.88	JPS(P)	H	Fulham	W	56-10	Lewis (2), McEvoy (2), Hobbs, Edmondson, Gascoigne, Gerrard, Lister, Brentley	Carroll (8)	850	Bowman
13.11.88	JPS(1)	H	Mansfield M.	W	32-6	Lewis (2), Dyl, Carroll, Spedding, Lister	Carroll (4)	1151	Kendrew
20.11.88	SD	A	Leigh	L	8-40	Illingworth	Durham (2)	—	—
27.11.88	JPS(1)	A	Warrington	L	10-42	Lister, Brentley	Durham	—	—
4.12.88	SD	H	Mansfield M.	W	36-2	Lewis (4), Dyl, Holden, Race	Durham (4)	573	Volante
11.12.88	SD	A	Doncaster	W	24-16	Race, Lister, Spedding, Lewis	Durham (4)	—	—
18.12.88	SD	A	York	W	20-11	Lister (2), Race, Gerrard	Illingworth (2)	—	—
27.12.88	SD	H	Hunslet	D	18-18	Race, Lister, Dyl	Illingworth (3)	2603	Kershaw
1.1.89	SD	A	Keighley	L	22-28	Lister, Gerrard, Race, Lewis	Lister (2), Illingworth	—	—
8.1.89	SD	H	Batley	W	22-8	Lister (3), Holden, Lewis	Lister	1001	Whitelam
15.1.89	CC(P)	A	Wakefield T.	L	10-18	Gerrard, Race	Lister	—	—
22.1.89	SD	A	Huddersfield	L	14-17	Illingworth, Sharp, Gerrard	Carroll	—	—
29.1.89	SD	A	Hunslet	L	18-27	Lister (2), Bond	Agar (3)	—	—
5.2.89	SD	H	Sheffield E.	W	13-9	Lister	Carroll (2), Agar (1, ldg), Lister (2 dg)	1071	Steele
19.2.89	SD	H	Barrow	L	21-26	Lewis (2), Lister, Race	Carroll (2), Lister (dg)	855	Simpson
26.2.89	SD	A	Dewsbury	L	14-33	Lewis, Olpherts	Carroll (3)	—	—
5.3.89	SD	A	Batley	L	12-15	Lewis (2), Hobbs	—	—	—
12.3.89	SD	H	Chorley B.	W	34-10	Lewis (2), Carroll, Brentley, Hobbs	Carroll (7)	497	Whitelam
19.3.89	SD	A	Swinton	L	0-16	—	—	—	—
27.3.89	SD	H	Keighley	L	14-29	Race, Langley	Carroll (3)	814	Burke
2.4.89	SD	H	Leigh	L	2-34	—	Carroll	1021	Haigh
9.4.89	SD	A	Barrow	L	16-27	Lewis, Hunter	Carroll (4)	—	—
16.4.89	SD	H	York	W	23-20	Lewis (2), Sharp, Lister	Carroll (3, 1dg)	856	Galtress

CARLISLE

Ground: Gillford Park
Colours: Blue, red and white
First Season: 1981-82. A Carlisle City team entered the League in 1928-29 but withdrew after 10 matches, winning one
Chairman: Alan Tucker
Secretary: Robert Carter
Coach: Roy Lester (June 1986-Nov 1988) Tommy Dawes (Dec 1988-)
Records: Attendance: 5,903 v. Workington T. (Div. 2) 6 Sep, 1981
Season
Goals: 113 by S. Ferres, 1981-82
Tries: 25 by M. Morgan, 1981-82; G. Peacham, 1984-85
Points: 242 by S. Ferres, 1981-82
Match
Goals: 9 by D. Carroll v. Mansfield M., 16 Mar, 1986; B. Vickers v. Mansfield M., 29 Jan, 1989
Tries: 4 by G. Peacham v. Workington T., 25 Jan, 1987 and K. Pape v. Rochdale H., 11 Feb, 1987
Points: 22 by B. Vickers v. Mansfield M., 29 Jan, 1989
Highest score: 58-1 v. Mansfield M., 1988-89
Highest against: 112-0 v. St. Helens, 1986-87

1988-89 PLAYERS' SUMMARY

	App	Tries	Goals	Dr	Pts
Armstrong, Colin	16 + 2	2	—	2	10
Bowness, Chris	1 + 3	—	—	—	—
Brierley, Steve	20 + 7	2	—	—	8
Carroll, Dean	3 + 3	1	—	—	4
Catton, Tony	11 + 3	2	—	1	9
Coles, Colin	18 + 1	8	5	—	42
Courty, Dave	1 + 1	—	—	—	—
Doyle, Mark	30	9	—	—	36
Ferguson, Gary	1	—	—	—	—
Graham, John	1 + 2	—	—	—	—
Kendall, Dave	21 + 3	3	—	—	12
Kirkby, Steve	24 + 1	6	—	1	25
Langton, Steve	16	6	—	—	24
Lithgow, Paul	2	—	—	—	—
Little, Alan	2 + 1	—	—	—	—
McAvoy, Brian	15 + 2	5	—	—	20
McMullen, Alan	3	—	—	—	—
Murdock, Gary	33	10	—	—	40
Murdock, Paul	0 + 4	—	—	—	—
Pape, Kevin	33	14	—	—	56
Peacham, Gary	2	—	—	—	—
Pitt, Darryl	19 + 1	7	—	—	28
Pollard, Damian	4 + 3	—	—	—	—
Rea, Steve	5 + 1	5	—	—	20
Richardson, Dave	3	2	—	—	8
Robinson, Paul	9 + 2	—	—	—	—
Schubert, Gary	31	2	—	—	8
Scott, Ian	0 + 2	—	—	—	—
Scott, Tony	33	4	—	—	16
Stafford, Peter	5 + 3	1	8	—	20
Thomason, Bryan	0 + 1	—	—	—	—
Thomason, Malcolm	32	8	—	—	32
Tunstall, Brian	1 + 2	—	—	—	—
Vickers, Barry	28	1	99	3	205
Wilkes, Mark	6 + 1	—	—	—	—
TOTALS:					
35 players		98	112	7	623

Steve Rea, five tries in six appearances.

Dave Kendall scoring his first-ever try for Carlisle, at home to Keighley.

1988-89 MATCH ANALYSIS

Date	Com-petition	H/A	Opponent	Rlt	Score	Tries	Goals	Atten-dance	Referee
28.8.88	SD	A	Swinton	L	20-28	Coles, Langton, Armstrong	Vickers (3, 2dg)	—	—
4.9.88	SD	H	Batley	D	17-17	Coles, Schubert	Vickers (4), Kirkby (dg)	675	Morris
11.9.88	SD	A	Workington T.	W	11-10	Langton	Vickers (3), Armstrong (dg)	—	—
18.9.88	LC(1)	H	Chorley B.	W	17-7	Langton, Doyle	Vickers (4), Armstrong (dg)	645	Tickle
25.9.88	SD	H	Huddersfield	W	40-1	Pape (2), Langton, Doyle, Thomason, Murdoch	Vickers (8)	701	Galtress
28.9.88	LC(2)	A	Warrington	L	18-34	Thomason, Brierley	Vickers (3), Stafford (2)	—	—
2.10.88	SD	H	Leigh	L	10-12	Langton	Stafford (3)	890	Holgate
9.10.88	SD	H	Doncaster	L	6-24	McAvoy	Stafford	812	Cross
16.10.88	SD	A	Keighley	L	12-26	Carroll, Murdoch	Stafford (2)	—	—
23.10.88	SD	H	Runcorn H.	W	30-10	Pape, Kirkby, McAvoy, Pitt	Vickers (7)	523	Burke
30.10.88	SD	H	Barrow	L	6-28	Langton	Vickers	785	Haigh
6.11.88	SD	A	Batley	W	13-6	McAvoy, Armstrong	Vickers (2, ldg)	—	—
13.11.88	JPS(1)	A	Wakefield T.	L	14-34	McAvoy, Pitt	Vickers (3)	—	—
20.11.88	SD	A	Chorley B.	L	4-18	—	Vickers (2)	—	—
4.12.88	SD	H	Dewsbury	W	26-15	Murdoch, Pitt, Pape, Doyle	Vickers (5)	395	Tickle
11.12.88	SD	A	Leigh	L	6-24	Pape	Vickers	—	—
18.12.88	SD	H	Swinton	L	6-28	Pitt	Vickers	563	Houghton
26.12.88	SD	A	Barrow	L	10-15	Thomason	Vickers (3)	—	—
1.1.89	SD	H	Whitehaven	W	9-8	Thomason	Vickers (2), Catton (dg)	902	Holgate
8.1.89	SD	H	Fulham	W	52-10	Pape (2), Richardson (2), McAvoy, Doyle, Thomason, Kirkby, Murdoch	Vickers (8)	512	Haigh
15.1.89	SD	A	Huddersfield	W	14-7	Thomason, Scott, Murdoch	Vickers	—	—
22.1.89	SD	H	Rochdale H.	W	44-12	Murdoch (2), Doyle, Catton, Stafford, Kirkby, Pape	Vickers (8)	635	Burke
29.1.89	CC(1)	H	Mansfield M.	W	58-1	Coles (3), Doyle (2), Scott, Pape, Pitt, Vickers, Thompson	Vickers (9)	663	Spencer
5.2.89	SD	H	Keighley	W	20-4	Kendall (2), Pitt	Vickers (4)	850	Berry
12.2.89	CC(2)	A	Leeds	L	4-24	Kirkby	—	—	—
26.2.89	SD	H	Chorley B.	L	8-17	Pape	Vickers (2)	650	Allatt
5.3.89	SD	A	Runcorn H.	W	48-4	Kirkby (2), Doyle (2), Schubert, Pitt, Kendall, Scott, Pape, Catton	Vickers (4)	—	—
12.3.89	SD	A	Dewsbury	L	4-14	—	Vickers (2)	—	—
27.3.89	SD	A	Whitehaven	L	14-30	Pape, Rea	Vickers (3)	—	—
2.4.89	SD	A	Fulham	W	26-22	Pape (2), Murdock, Brierley, Rea	Coles (3)	—	—
5.4.89	SD	A	Doncaster	L	6-15	Thomason	Vickers	—	—
9.4.89	SD	H	Workington T.	W	24-18	Coles (2), Rea, Murdock, Scott	Coles (2)	600	Tennant
16.4.89	SD	A	Rochdale H.	W	26-18	Rea (2), Murdock, Coles	Vickers (5)	—	—

CASTLEFORD

Ground: Wheldon Road
Colours: Yellow and black
First Season: 1926-27. There was also a
Castleford team from 1896-97 to
1905-06, inclusive
Nickname: Glassblowers
Chairman: David Poulter
Secretary: Denise Cackett
Coach: Darryl Van de Velde (July 1988-)
Honours: **Championship** Beaten finalists,
1938-39, 1968-69
Challenge Cup Winners, 1934-35,
1968-69, 1969-70, 1985-86
Yorkshire League Winners,
1932-33, 1938-39, 1964-65
Yorkshire Cup Winners, 1977-78,
1981-82, 1986-87
Beaten finalists, 1948-49, 1950-51,
1968-69, 1971-72, 1983-84,
1985-86, 1987-88, 1988-89
Eastern Division Championship
Beaten finalists, 1963-64
BBC2 Floodlit Trophy Winners,
1965-66, 1966-67, 1967-68, 1976-77
John Player Trophy Winners,
1976-77
Premiership Beaten finalists,
1983-84
Charity Shield Beaten finalists
1986-87
Records: Attendance: 25,449 v. Hunslet
(RL Cup) 3 Mar, 1935
Season
Goals: 158 by S. Lloyd, 1976-77
Tries: 36 by K. Howe, 1963-64
Points: 334 by R. Beardmore,
1983-84

Match
Goals: 17 by S. Lloyd v. Millom,
16 Sep, 1973
Tries: 5 by D. Foster v. Hunslet,
10 Nov, 1972; J. Joyner v. Millom,
16 Sep, 1973; S. Fenton v.
Dewsbury, 27 Jan, 1978; I. French
v. Hunslet, 9 Feb, 1986
Points: 43 by S. Lloyd v. Millom,
16 Sep, 1973
Highest score: 94-12 v.
Huddersfield, 1988-89
Highest against: 62-12 v. St.
Helens, 1985-86

1988-89 PLAYERS' SUMMARY

	App	Tries	Goals	Dr	Pts
Anderson, Grant	36	24	—	1	97
Battye, Neil	1 + 3	—	—	—	—
Beardmore, Kevin	34 + 1	9	—	—	36
Beardmore, Robert	22 + 1	3	9	—	30
Belcher, Gary	10 + 1	5	—	1	21
Blankley, Dean	3 + 1	—	—	—	—
Boothroyd, Giles	25 + 1	15	—	—	60
Chapman, Chris	24 + 1	10	—	—	40
Crabtree, Paul	6	—	—	—	—
England, Keith	36	3	—	—	12
Gibbs, Ron	23	4	—	—	16
Gibson, Mark	11 + 1	1	—	—	4
Hill, Kenny	5 + 8	1	—	—	4
Horo, Shane	17 + 1	11	—	—	44
Irwin, Shaun	10 + 2	2	—	—	8
Johnson, Barry	1 + 3	—	—	—	—
Joyner, John	35	7	—	—	28
Ketteridge, Martin	36	3	129	—	270
Marchant, Tony	35	13	—	—	52
McAllister, Terry	3 + 1	—	—	—	—
Mirfin, Phil	2 + 7	5	—	—	20
Plange, David	21	10	—	—	40
Roockley, David	18 + 6	6	5	1	35
Sampson, Dean	14 + 13	7	—	—	28
Southernwood, Graham	1	—	—	—	—
Southernwood, Roy	12 + 5	1	—	—	4
Thornton, Wayne	0 + 3	—	—	—	—
Ward, Kevin	27 + 2	2	—	—	8
TOTALS:					
28 players		142	143	3	857

1988-89 MATCH ANALYSIS

Date	Competition	H/A	Opponent	Rlt	Score	Tries	Goals	Attendance	Referee
28.8.88	SBC	A	Hull	W	18-8	Gibbs, Plange, K. Beardmore	Ketteridge (3)	—	—
4.9.88	SBC	H	Halifax	W	30-0	Marchant (2), Anderson, Ward, Roockley, Joyner	Ketteridge (2), Roockley	8455	Kershaw
11.9.88	SBC	A	St. Helens	D	14-14	Boothroyd, Anderson	Ketteridge (3)	—	—
18.9.88	YC(1)	H	Huddersfield	W	94-12	Chapman (3), Plange (3), K. Beardmore (3), Boothroyd (2), Belcher (2), Ketteridge (2), Joyner, Sampson	Ketteridge (13)	3144	Berry

MATCH ANALYSIS (continued)

Date	Competition	H/A	Opponent	Rlt	Score	Tries	Goals	Attendance	Referee
25.9.88	SBC	H	Oldham	W	22-19	K. Beardmore, Joyner, Chapman, Hill	R. Beardmore (3)	5496	Whitfield
28.9.88	YC(2)	H	York	W	40-14	Anderson (2), Chapman (2), Marchant, Plange, Boothroyd, Belcher	R. Beardmore (4)	3155	Cross
2.10.88	SBC	A	Wigan	W	20-12	K. Beardmore, Plange, Joyner, Anderson	Ketteridge (2)	—	—
5.10.88	YC(SF)	A	Halifax	W	12-8	Chapman, Marchant	Ketteridge (2)	—	—
9.10.88	SBC	H	Salford	W	38-12	Sampson, K. Beardmore, Anderson, R. Beardmore, England, Chapman	Ketteridge (7)	6208	Tickle
16.10.88	YC(F)	Elland Rd, Leeds	Leeds	L	12-33	Boothroyd, Joyner	Ketteridge (2)	(22,968)	Whitfield
23.10.88	SBC	H	Warrington	W	23-16	Anderson, Boothroyd, Plange	Ketteridge (5), Anderson (dg)	5318	Kershaw
30.10.88	JPS(P)	A	Workington T.	W	28-2	Roockley (2), Anderson (2), Plange	Ketteridge (4)	—	—
6.11.88	SBC	A	Featherstone R.	W	26-20	Anderson (2), Plange, Joyner, Belcher	Ketteridge (3)	—	—
12.11.88	JPS(1)	A	Leeds	W	21-12	Belcher, Boothroyd, K. Beardmore	Ketteridge (4), Belcher (dg)	—	—
20.11.88	SBC	H	St. Helens	W	46-12	Anderson (3), Horo (2), Boothroyd (2), Sampson, Plange	Ketteridge (5)	6608	Whitfield
27.11.88	JPS(2)	H	Bradford N.	L	18-19	Gibbs, Boothroyd	Ketteridge (5)	7688	Cross
18.12.88	SBC	A	Warrington	W	26-20	Anderson, Irwin, Marchant, Boothroyd, Horo	Ketteridge (2), R. Beardmore	—	—
26.12.88	SBC	H	Hull K.R.	W	38-20	Anderson (2), England, Horo, Boothroyd	Ketteridge (9)	6228	Berry
1.1.89	SBC	H	Bradford N.	W	38-20	Horo (2), R. Beardmore (2), Irwin	Ketteridge (9)	7420	Steele
8.1.89	SBC	A	Halifax	L	12-21	Sampson, Boothroyd	Ketteridge, R. Beardmore	—	—
22.1.89	SBC	H	Wakefield T.	W	38-14	Anderson (3), Gibbs (2), Marchant, Sampson	Ketteridge (5)	6411	Whitfield
28.1.89	CC(1)	A	Hull	W	7-4	Horo	Ketteridge, Roockley (dg)	—	—
11.2.89	CC(2)	H	Widnes	L	18-32	R. Southernwood, Horo	Ketteridge (5)	(10,765)	Cross
17.2.89	SBC	A	Salford	W	20-18	Joyner, Anderson, Roockley	Roockley (3), Ketteridge	—	—
22.2.89	SBC	A	Bradford N.	W	20-6	Marchant (2), Horo,	Ketteridge (4)	—	—
26.2.89	SBC	A	Wakefield T.	L	8-26	Marchant	Ketteridge (2)	—	—
5.3.89	SBC	H	Hull	L	16-23	Chapman, Horo, K.Beardmore	Ketteridge (2)	6263	Kershaw
19.3.89	SBC	A	Leeds	L	18-32	Boothroyd, Marchant, Gibson	Ketteridge (3)	—	—
24.3.89	SBC	H	Featherstone R.	D	14-14	Boothroyd, Anderson	Ketteridge (2), Roockley	6749	Carter
27.3.89	SBC	A	Hull K.R.	L	30-32	Roockley, Horo, Mirfin, Sampson	Ketteridge (7)	—	—
30.3.89	SBC	A	Widnes	L	4-36	Mirfin	—	—	—
2.4.89	SBC	H	Wigan	L	4-17	Roockley	—	7534	Tickle
9.4.89	SBC	A	Oldham	L	18-34	Mirfin, Anderson, Marchant	Ketteridge (3)	—	—
12.4.89	SBC	H	Widnes	L	22-24	Marchant, Ketteridge, Mirfin	Ketteridge (5)	6364	Kershaw
16.4.89	SBC	H	Leeds	W	38-10	Ward, Marchant, England, Sampson, Anderson, Mirfin	Ketteridge (7)	9864	Cross
23.4.89	PT(1)	A	Hull	L	6-32	Chapman	Ketteridge	—	—

CHORLEY BOROUGH

● **At the end of May 1989, the club changed its name to Trafford Borough and moved to Moss Lane, Altrincham, home of Altrincham F.C.**

Ground: Victory Park
First Season: 1954-55 as Blackpool Borough Changed to Springfield Borough in 1987-88 and became Chorley Borough at start of 1988-89.
Coach: Stan Gittins (Nov 1985-June 1988) Mike Peers (Aug 1987-)
Honours: **John Player Trophy** Beaten finalists, 1976-77
Records: Attendance: 7,614 v. Castleford (RL Cup) 14 Mar, 1964. There was an attendance of 21,000 in an RL Cup-tie against Leigh on Blackpool FC ground on 9 Mar, 1957
Season
Goals: 98 by M. Smith, 1987-88
Tries: 30 by T. Frodsham, 1985-86
Points: 201 by P. Fearis, 1957-58
Match
Goals: 11 by N. Turley v. Carlisle, 26 Apr, 1984;
Tries: 4 by T. Wilkshire v. Bradford N, 14 Jan, 1961; J. Stockley v. Doncaster, 1 Apr, 1984
T. Frodsham v. Bridgend, 14 Apr, 1985 and v. Mansfield M., 30 Nov, 1986
Points: 27 by N. Turley v. Carlisle, 26 Apr, 1984
Highest score: 56-2 v. Runcorn H., 1988-89
Highest against: 77-8 v. Wigan, 1963-64

CHORLEY

Formed by Chorley AFC and admitted for the 1989-90 season.
Ground: Victory Park
Colours: Black and white
First Season: 1989-90
Chairman: Syd Secker
Secretary: George Lunn
Coach: Stan Gittins

1988-89 PLAYERS' SUMMARY

	App	Tries	Goals	Dr	Pts
Abram, Darren	19 + 2	8	—	—	32
Bacon, David	11 + 5	4	—	—	16
Bamber, Simon	9 + 2	1	—	—	4
Bimson, Geoff	15	3	—	—	12
Briscoe, Carl	27 + 2	3	—	—	12
Brown, David	5 + 1	—	—	—	—
Brown, Mike	1	—	—	—	—
Broxton, Paul	2	1	—	—	4
Clayton, Richard	1	3	—	—	12
Donlan, Steve	8 + 1	—	—	—	—
Eccles, Bob	10	1	—	4	8
Eccles, Cliff	27 + 3	4	—	—	16
Garner, Steve	30 + 1	3	—	—	12
Glynn, Peter	24 + 1	3	—	1	13
Green, Jimmy	2	—	—	—	—
Griffiths, Steve	18	11	—	—	44
Grundy, Tracy	3 + 4	—	—	—	—
Hewitt, David	6	3	—	—	12
Hodson, Tony	16 + 5	2	—	—	8
Iddon, Tim	6 + 1	1	—	—	4
Jamieson, Ged	1 + 2	—	—	—	—
Jukes, David	1	—	—	—	—
Karalius, Graham	1 + 1	—	—	—	—
Litherland, Dennis	15 + 2	2	—	—	8
Mayo, John	10 + 3	—	—	—	—
Meadows, Mark	31 + 2	7	—	—	28
Middleshurst, Chris	7 + 1	1	2	—	8
O'Rourke, Gus	0 + 3	—	—	—	—
Phythian, David	1	—	—	—	—
Price, Billy	4 + 4	—	7	1	15
Reynolds, Paul	1	—	—	—	—
Shaw, Mark	5 + 1	—	—	—	—
Sheals, Mark	18	3	—	—	12
Smith, Graham	10	2	2	1	13
Smith, Mike	32	2	58	2	126
Stansfield, Phil	1	—	—	—	—
Stewart, Mike	29 + 1	5	—	—	20
Swindells, Andy	2 + 3	—	—	—	—
Thompson, Courtney	8 + 2	3	—	—	12
White, Tom	1	2	—	—	8
Whittle, Steve	0 + 1	—	—	—	—
Wilkinson, Chris	3	1	—	—	4
Wilson, Danny	3	1	—	—	4
Winnard, Ian	0 + 1	—	—	—	—
Wiltshire, Roy	5	1	—	—	4

TOTALS:
		Tries	Goals	Dr	Pts
45 players		81	69	9	471

Carl Briscoe, scorer of three tries in 29 games, supported by Steve Garner.

1988-89 MATCH ANALYSIS

Date	Com-petition	H/A	Opponent	Rlt	Score	Tries	Goals	Atten-dance	Referee
28.8.88	SD	A	Hunslet	W	18-6	Garner, Broxton, Bamber	M. Smith (2), R. Eccles (2dg)	—	—
4.9.88	SD	H	Workington T.	L	8-22	Hodson	M. Smith (2)	1030	Steele
7.9.88	SD	A	Keighley	L	12-26	Wilkinson, C. Eccles	M. Smith (2)	—	—
11.9.88	SD	A	Swinton	W	28-22	Meadows, Wiltshire, Sheals, Briscoe	M. Smith (6)	—	—
18.9.88	LC(1)	A	Carlisle	L	7-17	C. Eccles	M. Smith (1, 1dg)	—	—
25.9.88	SD	A	Workington T.	L	4-25	Abram	—	—	—
2.10.88	SD	H	Barrow	L	16-18	Glynn, Sheals, R. Eccles	M. Smith (2)	509	Carter
9.10.88	SD	H	Sheffield E.	L	4-14	Bacon	—	526	Kershaw
16.10.88	SD	A	Rochdale H.	L	25-28	Griffiths (3), Bacon	M. Smith (4), R. Eccles (dg)	—	—
23.10.88	SD	H	Bramley	L	7-25	Meadows	M. Smith, R. Eccles (dg)	493	Smith
30.10.88	SD	A	Whitehaven	L	14-36	Abram, Briscoe	M. Smith (3)	—	—
6.11.88	SD	H	Runcorn H.	W	22-13	White (2), Thompson, Abram	M. Smith (3)	291	Alba (Fr)
13.11.88	JPS(1)	A	Huddersfield	W	22-4	Hodson, Abram, M. Smith, Stewart	M. Smith (3)	—	—
20.11.88	SD	H	Carlisle	W	18-4	Meadows, Litherland, Abrams	M. Smith (3)	257	Dockray
27.11.88	JPS(2)	H	Hull K.R.	L	22-36	C. Eccles, G. Smith, Abram	M. Smith (5)	983	Morris
4.12.88	SD	H	Whitehaven	W	9-4	Thompson, Litherland	G. Smith (dg)	305	Tidball
11.12.88	SD	A	York	L	6-30	G. Smith	M. Smith	—	—
26.12.88	SD	H	Leigh	L	6-20	Garner	M. Smith	1506	Spencer
1.1.89	SD	A	Runcorn H.	W	56-2	Stewart (3), Bacon (2), Sheals, Abram, M. Smith, Griffiths, Meadows, Middlehurst	M. Smith (6)	—	—
8.1.89	SD	H	Keighley	W	22-6	Griffiths (2), Meadows (2)	M. Smith (3)	348	Cross
15.1.89	SD	A	Mansfield M.	D	16-16	Griffiths, Meadows, Garner	M. Smith (2)	—	—
22.1.89	SD	A	Barrow	L	12-44	Glynn, C. Eccles	Middlehurst (2)	—	—
29.1.89	CC(1)	H	Thatto Heath	W	8-4	Griffiths (2)	—	736	Whitelam
5.2.89	SD	H	Hunslet	L	10-13	Briscoe, Bimson	M. Smith	357	Galtress
12.2.89	CC(2)	A	Hull K.R.	L	4-28	Thompson	—	—	—
19.2.89	SD	H	Mansfield M.	W	28-18	Clayton (3), Griffiths (2) Hewitt	G. Smith (2)	188	Tickle
26.2.89	SD	A	Carlisle	W	17-8	Stewart, Bimson	M. Smith (4, 1dg)	—	—
5.3.89	SD	H	Swinton	L	7-31	Iddon	M. Smith, Glynn (dg)	679	Holgate
12.3.89	SD	A	Bramley	L	10-34	Glynn, Hewitt	M. Smith	—	—
19.3.89	SD	H	York	L	4-6	Abram	—	275	Spencer
24.3.89	SD	A	Leigh	L	6-14	Hewitt	M. Smith	—	—
27.3.89	SD	H	Rochdale H.	L	15-22	Wilson	Price (5, 1dg)	405	Berry
2.4.89	SD	A	Sheffield E.	L	8-26	Bimson	Price (2)	—	—

DEWSBURY

Ground: Crown Flatt
Colours: Red, amber and black
First Season: 1901-02
Chairman: Rodney Hardcastle
Secretary: Geoff Parrish
Coach: Terry Crook (Apr 1987-Dec 1988)
Maurice Bamford (Dec 1988-)
Honours: **Championship** Winners, 1972-73
Beaten finalists, 1946-47
Division Two Champions, 1904-05
Challenge Cup Winners, 1911-12, 1942-43
Beaten finalists, 1928-29
Yorkshire League Winners, 1946-47
Yorkshire Cup Winners, 1925-26, 1927-28, 1942-43
Beaten finalists, 1918-19, 1921-22, 1940-41, 1972-73
BBC2 Floodlit Trophy Beaten finalists, 1975-76
War League Championship Winners, 1941-42. (1942-43 won final but championship declared null and void because Dewsbury played an ineligible player.) Beaten finalists, 1943-44
Records: Attendance: 26,584 v. Halifax (Yorkshire Cup) 30 Oct, 1920
Season
Goals: 145 by N. Stephenson, 1972-73
Tries: 40 by D. Thomas, 1906-07
Points: 368 by N. Stephenson, 1972-73
Match
Goals: 10 by J. Ledgard v. Yorkshire Amateurs, 13 Sep, 1947; N. Stephenson v. Blackpool B, 28 Aug, 1972; C. Wilkinson v. Huddersfield, 27 Mar, 1989
Tries: 8 by D. Thomas v. Liverpool C, 13 Apr, 1907
Points: 29 by J. Lyman v. Hull, 22 Apr, 1919
Highest score: 72-0 v. Doncaster, 1984-85
Highest against: 82-0 v. Widnes, 1986-87

1988-89 PLAYERS' SUMMARY

	App	Tries	Goals	Dr	Pts
Bailey, Dennis	10	5	—	—	20
Bailey, Howard	9 + 1	2	4	—	16
Bates, Philip	0 + 1	—	—	—	—
Bowie, Ian	16	3	—	—	12
Burgess, Mark	5 + 2	—	—	—	—
Carroll, John	7 + 3	2	—	—	8
Cocks, Gary	31	10	—	—	40
Coen, Darren	26	4	1	—	16
Cornell, Paul	0 + 1	—	—	—	—
Fairhurst, Ian	2 + 1	—	—	—	—
Garforth, David	0 + 1	—	—	—	—
Garner, Peter	5 + 1	—	—	—	—
Graham, Nathan	0 + 1	—	1	—	2
Gregoire, Don	28	10	—	—	40
Haigh, Chris	9	2	—	—	8
Hinchliffe, Steve	9 + 3	4	—	—	16
Hooklyn, Terry	6 + 7	—	—	—	—
Howley, Pat	31	6	6	—	36
Hoyle, Robert	1 + 1	—	—	—	—
Hughes, Michael	10 + 1	1	—	—	4
Jennings, Paul	10 + 3	—	—	—	—
Johnson, Willie	11 + 1	2	—	2	10
Kelly, Neil	16	2	—	3	11
Marsden, Graham	10 + 3	1	—	—	4
McCabe, Martin	1 + 1	—	—	—	—
Moore, Gary	9	2	—	—	8
Moore, John	12 + 6	4	—	—	16
Morris, Stuart	13 + 5	4	—	—	16
Rose, Tony	18	—	—	—	—
Shaw, Alan	12 + 2	—	—	—	—
Shuttleworth, Paul	21	4	—	4	20
Simpson, Karl	0 + 2	—	—	—	—
Spooner, Chris	12 + 1	4	—	—	16
Squires, Chris	12 + 1	4	—	—	16
Toole, Timothy	7	1	—	—	4
Vasey, Chris	16	5	54	—	128
Westbury, Mark	3 + 2	—	—	—	—
Wilkinson, Chris	8	4	35	4	90
Womersley, Shaun	7	2	—	—	8
TOTALS: 39 players		88	100	13	565

1988-89 MATCH ANALYSIS

Date	Competition	H/A	Opponent	Rlt	Score	Tries	Goals	Attendance	Referee
28.8.88	SD	H	Runcorn H.	W	28-20	J. Moore, Gregoire, Squires, Hughes, Shuttleworth	Vasey (4)	541	Cross
4.9.88	SD	A	Whitehaven	L	2-24	—	Vasey	—	—
11.9.88	SD	H	Hunslet	W	16-5	Gregoire, Vasey	Vasey (4)	907	Whitelam
18.9.88	YC(1)	A	Wakefield T.	L	20-46	Vasey, Squires, Womersley	Vasey (3), Howley	—	—
25.9.88	SD	A	York	W	14-12	Squires	Vasey (5)	—	—
2.10.88	SD	A	Doncaster	L	19-48	Gregoire, Shuttleworth, Vasey	Vasey (3), Shuttleworth (dg)	—	—
9.10.88	SD	H	Rochdale H.	W	36-34	Morris (2), Shuttleworth, Coen, Cocks, Spooner	Vasey (6)	853	Bowman
16.10.88	SD	A	Huddersfield	W	26-12	Cocks, Spooner, Bowie, Shuttleworth	Vasey (5)	—	—
23.10.88	SD	H	York	L	6-45	Vasey	Vasey	732	Galtress
30.10.88	SD	A	Bramley	L	14-62	Marsden, Coen	Vasey (3)	—	—
6.11.88	SD	A	Hunslet	L	12-34	Toole, Gregoire	Vasey (2)	—	—
13.11.88	JPS(1)	A	Bradford N.	L	18-34	Gregoire (2), Cocks	Vasey (3)	—	—
20.11.88	SD	H	Workington T.	W	22-20	Cocks (2), Bowie (2)	Vasey (3)	439	Kershaw
27.11.88	SD	A	Mansfield M.	W	34-6	Cocks (2), Morris (2), Howley, Gregoire	Vasey (5)	—	—
4.12.88	SD	A	Carlisle	L	15-26	Kelly, Vasey	Vasey (3), Shuttleworth (dg)	—	—
11.12.88	SD	H	Mansfield M.	L	18-28	Spooner, Howley, Cocks	Vasey (3)	474	Holdsworth
18.12.88	SD	A	Sheffield E.	L	8-50	Cocks	Howley (2)	—	—
26.12.88	SD	H	Batley	W	11-8	J. Moore (2)	Howley, Shuttleworth (dg)	1699	Tidball
1.1.89	SD	A	Batley	L	6-14	Gregoire	Howley	1156	Tidball
8.1.89	SD	H	Doncaster	L	10-36	Howley, J. Moore	Howley	512	Bowman
22.1.89	SD	H	Fulham	L	16-18	Johnson, Spooner, Howley	Trialist (2)	2356	Dockray
29.1.89	CC(1)	H	Oldham	L	9-40	Womersley, Squires	Shuttleworth (dg)	458	Kershaw
5.2.89	SD	H	Whitehaven	L	10-12	G. Moore, Howley	Wilkinson	—	—
12.2.89	SD	A	Fulham	L	9-19	Johnson	Wilkinson (2, 1dg)	—	—
26.2.89	SD	H	Bramley	W	33-14	Wilkinson (2), D. Bailey, H. Bailey, Hinchcliffe	Wilkinson (6, 1dg)	659	Bowman
5.3.89	SD	A	Rochdale H.	L	30-32	Carroll (2), D. Bailey, Haigh, Gregoire	Wilkinson (5)	—	—
12.3.89	SD	H	Carlisle	W	14-4	Kelly, Wilkinson	Wilkinson (3)	506	Cross
19.3.89	SD	A	Runcorn H.	W	48-8	Hinchcliffe (3), D. Bailey (2), Cox, Coen, Howley	Wilkinson (8)	—	—
27.3.89	SD	H	Huddersfield	W	41-14	D. Bailey, Wilkinson, Gregoire, Haigh, H. Bailey	Wilkinson (10), Kelly (dg)	901	Tidball
2.4.89	SD	A	Workington T.	L	2-10	—	Wilkinson (2dg)	—	—
9.4.89	SD	H	Sheffield E.	W	18-11	Coen, G. Moore	H. Bailey, (2), Graham, Kelly (2dg), Johnson (2dg)	966	Smith

DONCASTER

Ground:	Tattersfield
Colours:	Blue and yellow
First Season:	1951-52
Nickname:	Dons
Chairman:	John Desmond
Secretary:	Granville Bowen
Coach:	John Sheridan (Jan 1988-Apr 1989) Dave Sampson (May 1989-)
Records:	Attendance: 5,274 v. Wigan (RL Cup) 29 Jan, 1989. There was an attendance of 10,000 for a Challenge Cup tie against Bradford N. at York Road Stadium on 16 Feb, 1952

Season

Goals: 118 by D. Noble, 1985-86
Tries: 20 by N. Turner, 1985-86; 1988-89
Points: 250 by D. Noble, 1986-87

Match

Goals: 9 by D. Towle v. York, 9 Sep, 1967
Tries: 4 by V. Grace v. Rochdale H, 4 Oct, 1952; B. Tasker v. Leeds, 26 Oct, 1963; J. Buckton v. Rochdale H., 30 Aug, 1981; T. Kemp v. Carlisle, 23 Nov, 1986
Points: 20 by K. Jones v. Whitehaven, 13 Mar, 1988; D. Noble v. Dewsbury, 2 Oct, 1988
Highest score: 50-6 v. Keighley, 1986-87
Highest against: 75-3 v. Leigh, 1975-76

1988-89 PLAYERS' SUMMARY

	App	Tries	Goals	Dr	Pts
Barrett, Dale	0 + 4	—	—	—	—
Carr, Alan	27 + 2	8	—	—	32
Chappell, Tony	2 + 6	3	—	—	12
Evans, John	31	10	—	—	40
Firth, Steve	0 + 2	—	—	—	—
Fletcher, Ian	4	1	—	—	4
Gibbon, Mark	30 + 1	3	—	—	12
Grace, Mick	7 + 5	2	—	—	8
Green, John	7	1	—	—	4
Hartley, Iain	26 + 1	3	—	—	12
Hudson, Shaun	4 + 1	—	—	—	—
Jones, Keith	16 + 2	3	—	—	12
Jones, Kevin	34	13	2	—	56
Moore, Gary	0 + 1	1	—	—	4
Noble, David	28 + 2	5	104	6	234
Parkhouse, Kevin	25 + 7	3	—	—	12
Payne, Phil	0 + 1	—	—	—	—
Pennant, Audley	27	3	—	—	12
Pennant, Milton	1	—	—	—	—
Pickerill, Neil	17	1	—	1	5
Potts, Martin	17	—	—	—	—
Rafferty, Roy	17	4	15	—	46
Rayne, Kevin	22	9	—	—	36
Roache, Mark	31 + 1	14	—	—	56
Roberts, Howard	1	—	—	—	—
Robinson, Kevin	8 + 7	1	—	—	4
Shillito, Alan	1 + 2	—	—	—	—
Sims, Mark	9 + 2	1	1	—	6
Smith, Stuart	0 + 2	—	—	—	—
Timson, Andy	12 + 6	2	—	—	8
Totten, Greg	1 + 1	—	—	—	—
Turner, Neil	30	20	—	—	80
Winkel, Brian	7 + 1	—	—	—	—
TOTALS:					
33 players		111	122	7	695

Doncaster's record signing, Great Britain second row man Kevin Rayne.

1988-89 MATCH ANALYSIS

Date	Competition	H/A	Opponent	Rlt	Score	Tries	Goals	Attendance	Referee
28.8.88	SD	H	Fulham	W	25-12	Turner, Pennant, Green, Roache, Gibbon	Noble (1, 1dg), Rafferty	1395	Berry
4.9.88	SD	A	Bramley	W	32-16	Evans (3), Kevin Jones, Carr	Noble (4, 2dg), Rafferty	—	—
11.9.88	SD	H	York	W	23-10	Roache, Carr, Parkhouse, Pennant	Noble (3, 1dg)	1902	Cross
18.9.88	YC(1)	A	Featherstone R.	L	8-38	Kevin Jones	Noble (2)	—	—
25.9.88	SD	A	Runcorn H.	W	18-10	Carr, Grace	Noble (5)	—	—
2.10.88	SD	H	Dewsbury	W	48-19	Turner (2), Carr, Moore, Roache, Gibbon, Noble, Kevin Jones	Noble (8)	2227	Tidball
9.10.88	SD	A	Carlisle	W	24-6	Roache (2), Grace, Turner	Noble (4)	—	—
16.10.88	SD	H	Workington T.	W	34-16	Carr (2), Roache, Kevin Jones, Turner, Evans	Noble (5)	2840	Morris
23.10.88	SD	A	Mansfield M.	W	32-10	Turner (3), Gibbon, Rafferty, Evans	Noble (4)	—	—
6.11.88	SD	A	Workington T.	L	14-22	Hartley, Rayne	Noble (2), Rafferty	—	—
13.11.88	JPS(1)	A	Swinton	W	16-13	Roache, Turner	Rafferty (4)	—	—
20.11.88	SD	H	Hunslet	W	18-2	Parkhouse, Rafferty, Chappell	Rafferty (3)	2416	Kendrew
27.11.88	JPS(2)	A	Leigh	L	8-40	Carr, Chappell	—	—	—
4.12.88	SD	A	York	L	10-20	Rafferty, Roache	Rafferty	—	—
11.12.88	SD	H	Bramley	L	16-24	Kevin Jones, Rafferty, Roache	Rafferty (2)	2125	Spencer
18.12.88	SD	H	Huddersfield	W	18-10	Turner, Robinson, Kevin Jones	Noble (3)	1743	Volante
26.12.88	SD	H	Sheffield E.	L	20-34	Roache, Keith Jones, Turner, Evans	Rafferty (2)	2536	Smith
8.1.89	SD	A	Dewsbury	W	36-10	Hartley, Roache, Turner, Noble, Rayne, Timson	Noble (6)	—	—
15.1.89	CC(P)	A (at Hull)	West Hull	W	48-2	Kevin Jones (2), Turner (2), Keith Jones, Rayne, Noble, Roache	Noble (6), Kevin Jones (2)	—	—
22.1.89	SD	A	Whitehaven	L	20-29	Rayne (2), Turner	Noble (4)	—	—
29.1.89	CC(1)	H	Wigan	L	6-38	Hartley	Noble	5274	Carter
5.2.89	SD	H	Runcorn H.	W	48-12	Turner (3), Roache (2), Rayne, Carr, Evans	Noble (8)	1606	Bowman
12.2.89	SD	H	Mansfield M.	W	18-12	Kevin Jones, Evans	Noble (5)	1817	Holgate
19.2.89	SD	A	Batley	W	15-6	Evans (2)	Noble (3, 1dg)	—	—
26.2.89	SD	H	Rochdale H.	L	18-28	Rayne (3)	Noble (3)	1711	Tickle
5.3.89	SD	A	Sheffield E.	W	26-25	Kevin Jones, Pennant, Parkhouse	Noble (7)	—	—
12.3.89	SD	H	Whitehaven	W	8-6	Keith Jones	Noble (2)	2087	Smith
19.3.89	SD	A	Hunslet	L	8-11	Pickerill	Noble, Sims	—	—
24.3.89	SD	A	Fulham	L	16-20	Kevin Jones (2), Noble	Noble (2)	—	—
27.3.89	SD	H	Batley	L	11-22	Noble	Noble (3), Pickerill (dg)	1982	Dockray
2.4.89	SD	A	Rochdale H.	L	18-44	Chappell, Turner	Noble (5)	—	—
5.4.89	SD	H	Carlisle	W	15-6	Timson, Kevin Jones	Noble (3, 1dg)	933	Whitelam
16.4.89	SD	A	Huddersfield	L	10-22	Fletcher, Sims	Noble	—	—
23.4.89	SDP(1)	A	Sheffield E.	L	10-28	Turner	Noble (3)	—	—

FEATHERSTONE ROVERS

Ground:	Post Office Road
Colours:	Blue and white
First Season:	1921-22
Nickname:	Colliers
Chairman:	Richard Evans
Secretary:	Terry Jones
Coach:	Peter Fox (May 1987-)

Honours: **Challenge Cup** Winners, 1966-67, 1972-73, 1982-83
Beaten finalists, 1951-52, 1973-74
Championship Beaten finalists, 1927-28
Division One Champions, 1976-77
Division Two Champions, 1979-80
Second Division Premiership Beaten finalists, 1987-88
Yorkshire Cup Winners, 1939-40, 1959-60
Beaten finalists, 1928-29, 1963-64, 1966-67, 1969-70, 1970-71, 1976-77, 1977-78
Captain Morgan Trophy Beaten finalists, 1973-74

Records: Attendance: 17,531 v. St. Helens (RL Cup) 21 Mar, 1959
Season
Goals: 163 by S. Quinn, 1979-80
Tries: 31 by C. Woolford, 1958-59
Points: 375 by S. Quinn, 1979-80
Match
Goals: 12 by D. Fox v. Stanningley, 8 Feb, 1964
Tries: 6 by M. Smith v. Doncaster, 13 Apr, 1968
Points: 29 by S. Quinn v. Doncaster, 4 Nov, 1979
Highest score: 66-14 v. Barrow, 1986-87
Highest against: 70-2 v. Halifax, 1940-41

1988-89 PLAYERS' SUMMARY

	App	Tries	Goals	Dr	Pts
Banks, Alan	35	8	—	—	32
Barker, Nigel	2 + 7	1	—	—	4
Bastian, John	23 + 5	3	—	—	12
Beach, Danny	10 + 5	1	—	—	4
Bell, Glenn	13 + 1	2	—	—	8
Bell, Keith	9 + 1	1	—	—	4
Bibb, Chris	34	13	—	—	52
Booth, Glen	3 + 9	2	—	—	8
Burton, Chris	14	1	—	—	4
Busby, Dave	0 + 1	—	—	—	—
Carey, Phil	3 + 2	—	—	—	—
Clark, Trevor	26 + 3	6	—	—	24
Crossley, John	1 + 7	1	—	—	4
Dakin, Alan	0 + 2	—	—	—	—
Fox, Deryck	35	9	19	9	83
Grayshon, Jeff	34	—	—	—	—
Harrison, Karl	32 + 2	5	—	—	20
Hughes, Paul	28 + 4	5	—	—	20
Lyman, Paul	17	7	—	—	28
Marsh, Richard	9	—	—	—	—
Newlove, Paul	30	18	9	—	90
Pearson, Martin	1 + 1	—	—	—	—
Quinn, Steve	9 + 2	—	23	—	46
Sharp, Tim	0 + 1	—	—	—	—
Siddall, Gary	1 + 9	—	—	—	—
Smales, Ian	28 + 1	9	4	—	44
Smith, Peter	31 + 1	—	—	—	—
Staniforth, Tony	1	—	—	—	—
Steadman, Graham	26	14	46	3	151
Sykes, David	0 + 2	—	—	—	—
TOTALS:					
30 players		106	101	12	638

Great Britain second row man Chris Burton, recruited from Hull K.R. in January 1989.

1988-89 MATCH ANALYSIS

Date	Competition	H/A	Opponent	Rlt	Score	Tries	Goals	Attendance	Referee
28.8.88	SBC	H	Leeds	L	18-32	Steadman, Lyman, Bibb	Quinn (3)	5822	Houghton
4.9.88	SBC	A	Hull K.R.	W	30-15	Steadman (2), Fox, Bibb, Crossley	Quinn (5)	—	—
11.9.88	SBC	H	Oldham	W	18-14	Steadman (2), Bibb	Quinn (3)	3731	Spencer
18.9.88	YC(1)	H	Doncaster	W	38-8	Lyman (3), K. Bell, Banks, Harrison, Steadman	Steadman (4), Quinn	2682	Kershaw
25.9.88	SBC	A	Widnes	L	2-58	—	Steadman	—	—
27.9.88	YC(2)	A	Hull	L	0-18	—	—	—	—
2.10.88	SBC	H	Bradford N.	L	20-48	Clark (2), Smales	Newlove (4)	3439	Simpson
9.10.88	SBC	A	Warrington	L	22-30	Newlove (2), Fox, Harrison	Newlove (3)	—	—
16.10.88	SBC	H	Halifax	W	21-17	Lyman (2), Steadman, Newlove	Newlove (2), Steadman (dg)	4724	Cross
30.10.88	JPS(P)	H	Hunslet	W	46-2	Newlove (2), Steadman (2), Bibb (2), Bastian, Lyman, Fox	Quinn (5)	1972	Cross
6.11.88	SBC	H	Castleford	L	20-26	Harrison, Banks, Bibb	Quinn (4)	6135	Volante
13.11.88	JPS(1)	A	Widnes	L	12-37	Newlove, Harrison	Quinn (2)	—	—
20.11.88	SBC	A	Hull	W	14-4	Smales, Steadman, Banks	Steadman	—	—
4.12.88	SBC	H	Salford	W	22-18	Smales, Steadman, Bibb	Steadman (5)	2637	Simpson
11.12.88	SBC	A	Leeds	L	18-36	Newlove (2), G. Bell	Steadman (3)	—	—
18.12.88	SBC	A	Salford	W	12-8	Newlove	Steadman (4)	—	—
26.12.88	SBC	H	Wakefield T.	L	14-15	Banks, Steadman	Steadman (3)	4632	Cross
1.1.89	SBC	A	Wakefield T.	L	12-19	Harrison, Bibb	Steadman (2)	—	—
15.1.89	SBC	H	St. Helens	W	13-12	Newlove, Clark	Steadman (2), Fox (dg)	3838	Carter
22.1.89	SBC	A	Halifax	W	24-4	Fox (2), Newlove, Steadman	Steadman (4)	—	—
29.1.89	CC(1)	A	Whitehaven	W	32-0	Newlove (2), Burton, Smales, G. Bell, Banks, Barker	Steadman (2)	—	—
12.2.89	CC(2)	A	Wakefield T.	W	10-4	Steadman	Steadman (2, 1dg), Fox (dg)	—	—
19.2.89	SBC	H	Widnes	L	10-22	Smales, Bibb	Fox	6132	Haigh
26.2.89	CC(3)	A	St. Helens	L	3-32	—	Steadman, Fox (dg)	—	—
1.3.89	SBC	H	Wigan	L	19-24	Clark (2), Fox	Smales (3), Fox (dg)	3960	Whitfield
5.2.89	SBC	A	Oldham	L	18-40	Hughes (2), Banks, Newlove	Smales	—	—
12.3.89	SBC	H	Hull K.R.	W	28-6	Hughes (2), Bibb, Newlove, Banks	Steadman (3), Fox	3673	Galtress
19.3.89	SBC	A	St. Helens	W	31-10	Bastian (2), Hughes, Smales, Banks	Fox (5, 1dg)	—	—
24.3.89	SBC	A	Castleford	D	14-14	Newlove, Fox	Steadman (3)	—	—
27.3.89	SBC	H	Hull	W	25-22	Smales, Bibb, Booth	Steadman (5), Fox (1, 1dg)	4584	Tickle
5.4.89	SBC	A	Wigan	L	10-14	Smales, Bibb	Fox	—	—
9.4.89	SBC	A	Bradford N.	W	32-23	Bibb, Beech, Smales, Newlove, Fox, Clark	Fox (4)	—	—
16.4.89	SBC	H	Warrington	W	15-14	Newlove	Fox (4, 3dg)	3623	Carter
23.4.89	PT(1)	A	Leeds	W	15-12	Fox, Booth	Fox (2), Steadman (1, 1dg)	—	—
7.5.89	PT(SF)	A	Hull	L	0-23	—	—	—	—

49

FULHAM

Ground:	Polytechnic of Central London Stadium, Chiswick
Colours:	Black, red and white
First Season:	1980-81
Chairman:	Mrs Barbara Close
Secretary:	Tim Lamb
Coach:	Bev Risman (May 1988-Feb 1989)
	Phil Sullivan (Feb 1989-Mar 1989)
	Bill Goodwin (Mar 1989-Apr 1989)
Honours:	**Division Two** Champions, 1982-83
Records:	Attendance: 15,013 v. Wakefield T. (RL Cup) 15 Feb, 1981 at Fulham FC

Season

Goals: 136 by S. Diamond, 1982-83

Tries: 27 by J. Crossley, 1982-83

Points: 308 by S. Diamond, 1982-83

Match

Goals: 11 by S. Guyett v. Huddersfield, 23 Oct, 1988

Tries: No player has scored more than 3

Points: 22 by A. Platt, v. Mansfield M., 10 May, 1986

Highest score: 61-22 v. Huddersfield, 1988-89

Highest against: 72-6 v. Whitehaven, 1986-87

1988-89 PLAYERS' SUMMARY

	App	Tries	Goals	Dr	Pts
Baker, David	4	—	—	—	—
Bibby, Neil	7 + 4	—	—	—	—
Boyce, Bob	20 + 3	2	—	—	8
Braniff, Gary	1 + 1	—	—	—	—
Bridge, Russ	24	3	—	—	12
Brown, Brian	6	1	—	5	9
Callow, Steve	3 + 1	—	—	—	—
Cheetham, Paul	2 + 2	1	—	—	4
Coutts, Jeff	30 + 1	9	11	3	61
Dutton, Joe	11 + 1	4	—	—	16
Fenn, Colin	7 + 2	—	2	—	4
Francis, Hugh	7 + 4	2	—	—	8
Garland, Earnie	6	2	—	—	8
Gillan, Dave	27 + 1	14	—	—	56
Grimoldby, Nick	8 + 1	—	—	—	—
Guyett, Steve	25 + 2	3	65	3	145
Helg, Albert	2 + 2	—	—	—	—
Hutchison, Mike	28 + 2	1	—	—	4
Jennings, Scott	16 + 1	1	2	—	8
Johansson, Lawrence	12 + 2	1	—	—	4
Keating, Noel	0 + 5	—	—	—	—
Lane, Gary	12	3	—	1	13
Leslie, Roy	5 + 5	—	—	—	—
Manning, Kevin	1	—	—	—	—
Mansfield, Glenn	26	9	—	—	36
M'Barki, Hussein	24	7	—	—	28
Mighty, Andrew	23 + 1	6	—	—	24
Murphy, Keiron	17 + 4	4	—	—	16
Pearce, Greg	2	1	—	—	4
Rees, Huw	13	3	—	—	12
Render, Andrew	2 + 4	—	1	—	2
Rotherham, David	1	—	—	—	—
Taylor, Craig	2	—	—	—	—
Trembath, Dennis	1 + 1	—	—	—	—
Walker, Paul	15	1	—	—	4
Wightman, Ian	5	—	—	—	—
Zillman, Andrew	7 + 1	2	—	—	8
Trialists (2)	1 + 1	1	—	—	4
TOTALS:					
39 players		81	81	12	498

Mike Hutchison, 30 apperances including two as substitute.

1988-89 MATCH ANALYSIS

Date	Com-petition	H/A	Opponent	Rlt	Score	Tries	Goals	Atten-dance	Referee
28.8.88	SD	A	Doncaster	L	12-25	Francis	Guyett (4)	—	—
4.9.88	SD	H	Sheffield E.	W	21-20	Coutts, Boyce, Mighty	Guyett (4), Brown (dg)	625	Tidball
11.9.88	SD	A	Huddersfield	W	28-16	Garland (2), Gillan, Brown	Guyett (5), Brown (2dg)	—	—
18.9.88	LC(1)	A	Rochdale H.	L	14-25	Guyett, Lane	Guyett (2), Brown (2dg)	—	—
25.9.88	SD	H	Bramley	L	20-30	Guyett, Gillan, Francis	Guyett (4)	620	Berry
9.10.88	SD	H	Batley	L	2-22	—	Guyett	488	Burke
16.10.88	SD	A	Bramley	L	8-30	Boyce	Guyett (2)	—	—
23.10.88	SD	H	Huddersfield	W	61-22	Gillan (3), M'Barki (2), Mighty (2), Coutts, Lane, Jennings	Guyett (10, 1dg)	643	Dockray
30.10.88	SD	A	Runcorn H.	L	12-20	Mansfield, Bridge	Guyett (1, 1dg), Lane (dg)	—	—
6.11.88	JPS(P)	A	Bramley	L	10-56	Mansfield, Lane	Fenn	—	—
20.11.88	SD	A	Mansfield M.	L	4-8	Coutts	—	—	—
27.11.88	SD	H	York	L	8-22	Dutton	Guyett (2)	535	Spencer
4.12.88	SD	A	Workington T.	W	17-16	Gillan (2), Mansfield	Jennings (2) Coutts (dg)	—	—
11.12.88	SD	H	Hunslet	L	10-16	Mansfield, Gillan	Guyett	537	Whitelam
18.12.88	SD	A	Batley	L	12-31	Gillan, Dutton	Guyett (2)	—	—
1.1.89	SD	H	Rochdale H.	L	10-20	Gillan, M'Barki	Guyett	622	Carter
8.1.88	SD	A	Carlisle	L	10-52	Bridge, Cheetham	Fenn	—	—
15.1.89	SD	H	Whitehaven	L	16-32	Mighty, Coutts, Dutton	Render, Coutts	566	Galtress
22.1.89	SD	A	Dewsbury	W	18-16	Coutts, Hutchison Gillan	Coutts (3)	—	—
29.1.89	CC(1)	H	Bradford N.	L	10-28	M'Barki, Mansfield	Coutts	1487	Smith
5.2.89	SD	H	Mansfield M.	W	26-12	Dutton, Mansfield, Walker, Coutts	Coutts (5)	515	Tidball
12.2.89	SD	H	Dewsbury	W	19-9	Murphy, M'Barki	Guyett (5, 1 dg)	515	Morris
19.2.89	SD	A	Whitehaven	L	0-60	—	—	—	—
26.2.89	SD	H	Runcorn H.	W	28-4	Mighty (2), Rees, Bridge, Mansfield, Murphy	Guyett, Coutts	491	Burke
5.3.89	SD	H	Workington T.	W	21-19	Rees, M'Barki, Murphy	Guyett (4), Coutts (dg)	617	Spencer
12.3.89	SD	A	York	L	10-30	Rees, Trialist	Guyett	—	—
24.3.89	SD	H	Doncaster	W	20-16	M'Barki, Gillan, Guyett, Mansfield	Guyett (2)	866	Holgate
26.3.89	SD	A	Sheffield E.	L	16-24	Johansson, Coutts	Guyett (4)	—	—
2.4.89	SD	H	Carlisle	L	22-26	Coutts, Mansfield, Gillan, Zillman	Guyett (3)	526	Morris
6.4.89	SD	A	Rochdale H.	L	12-26	Coutts, Zillman	Guyett (2)	—	—
9.4.89	SD	A	Hunslet	L	21-26	Pearce, Gillan, Murphy	Guyett (4), Coutts (dg)	—	—

HALIFAX

Ground:	Thrum Hall
Colours:	Blue and white
First Season:	1895-96
Nickname:	Thrum Hallers
Chairman:	Stan Ackroyd
General Manager:	Tony Beevers
Coach:	Graham Eadie (May 1988-Aug 1988)
	Ross Strudwick (Aug 1988-Feb 1989)
	Alan Hardisty (Feb 1989-Apr 1989)
Honours:	**Championship** Winners, 1906-07, 1964-65
	Beaten finalists, 1952-53, 1953-54, 1955-56, 1965-66
	Division One Champions, 1902-03, 1985-86
	War League Beaten finalists, 1942-43, 1944-45
	Challenge Cup Winners, 1902-03, 1903-04, 1930-31, 1938-39, 1986-87
	Beaten finalists, 1920-21, 1940-41, 1941-42, 1948-49, 1953-54, 1955-56, 1987-88
	Yorkshire League Winners, 1908-09, 1920-21, 1952-53, 1953-54, 1955-56, 1957-58
	Eastern Division Championship Winners, 1963-64
	Yorkshire Cup Winners, 1908-09, 1944-45, 1954-55, 1955-56, 1963-64
	Beaten finalists, 1905-06, 1907-08, 1941-42, 1979-80
	John Player Trophy Winners, 1971-72
	Premiership Trophy Beaten finalists, 1985-86
	Charity Shield Winners, 1986-87
	Beaten finalists, 1987-88
Records:	Attendance: 29,153 v. Wigan (RL Cup) 21 Mar, 1959
	Season
	Goals: 147 by T. Griffiths, 1955-56
	Tries: 48 by J. Freeman, 1956-57
	Points: 298 by C. Whitfield, 1986-87

Match

Goals: 14 by B. Burton v. Hunslet, 27 Aug, 1972
Tries: 8 by K. Williams v. Dewsbury, 9 Nov, 1957
Points: 31 by B. Burton v. Hunslet, 27 Aug, 1972
Highest score: 76-8 v. Hunslet, 1972-73
Highest against: 64-0 v. Wigan, 1922-23

1988-89 PLAYERS' SUMMARY

	App		Tries	Goals	Dr	Pts
Anderson, Tony	32		13	—	—	52
Atkinson, Colin	4		—	—	—	—
Beevers, Graham	9	+ 1	—	—	—	—
Bell, Peter	5	+ 4	1	—	—	4
Coyne, Peter	18		4	5	—	26
Dick, Kevin	1	+ 3	—	—	—	—
Dickinson, Roy	11	+ 1	—	—	—	—
Dixon, Paul	19		8	—	—	32
Eadie, Graham	5		—	7	—	14
Fairbank, Dick	32		5	—	—	20
George, Wilf	12	+ 2	4	—	—	16
Grogan, Bob	28	+ 1	5	—	—	20
Hancock, Andy	0	+ 1	—	—	—	—
Hill, Brendan	9	+ 2	1	—	—	4
Holliday, Les	15	+ 1	2	3	3	17
Holmes, David	14	+ 2	—	—	—	—
Hutchinson, Rob	13	+ 3	2	—	—	8
James, Neil	10	+ 1	3	—	—	12
Kemp, Martin	2	+ 4	—	—	—	—
Longstaff, Simon	9	+ 3	1	2	—	8
Lyons, John	14		1	5	—	14
McCallion, Seamus	29		6	—	1	25
Medley, Paul	6	+ 1	1	—	—	4
Milner, Richard	2		—	—	—	—
Parkinson, Andy	0	+ 3	—	—	—	—
Pendlebury, John	15		1	—	—	4
Ramshaw, Jason	15	+ 7	4	—	1	17
Riddlesden, Eddie	7		2	—	—	8
Robinson, Steve	5	+ 1	—	—	—	—
Scott, Mick	1		—	—	—	—
Simpson, Andy	0	+ 4	—	—	—	—
Smith, Steve	5	+ 3	1	6	—	16
Stains, Danny	17	+ 3	2	—	—	8
Taylor, Mike	22		6	—	—	24
Whitfield, Colin	22	+ 3	6	38	—	100
Wilkinson, Ian	5		—	—	—	—
Wilson, Scott	16	+ 4	4	—	—	16
Wood, Martin	0	+ 2	1	—	—	4

TOTALS:
38 players			84	66	5	473

1988-89 MATCH ANALYSIS

Date	Com-petition	H/A	Opponent	Rlt	Score	Tries	Goals	Atten-dance	Referee
28.8.88	SBC	H	Widnes	W	26-20	James (3), Dixon	Whitfield (5)	9001	Holdsworth
4.9.88	SBC	A	Castleford	L	0-30	—	—	—	—
11.9.88	SBC	H	Bradford N.	W	26-14	Dixon (2), Taylor (2), Fairbank	Eadie (3)	9547	Tickle
18.9.88	SYC(1)	H	Batley	W	36-14	George (2), McCallion (2), Anderson, Fairbank, Dixon	Eadie (4)	5370	Tidball
25.9.88	SBC	A	Hull K.R.	L	4-12	Taylor	—	—	—
28.9.88	YC(2)	H	Hull K.R.	W	24-2	Grogan, Anderson, Dixon, Wilson, Fairbank	Longstaff (2)	6296	Tennant
2.10.88	SBC	H	Warrington	L	4-16	—	Coyne (2)	8568	Haigh
5.10.88	YC(SF)	H	Castleford	L	8-12	Taylor	Whitfield (2)	8432	Berry
9.10.88	SBC	A	Widnes	L	4-5	Taylor	—	—	—
16.10.88	SBC	A	Featherstone R.	L	17-21	Dixon, Fairbank	Whitfield (4), McCallion (dg)	—	—
23.10.88	Tour	H	France	W	24-18	Taylor, Coyne, Wilson, Whitfield, Dixon	Whitfield (2)	4674	Holdsworth
6.11.88	SBC	H	Hull	L	6-14	—	Whitfield (3)	7340	Simpson
13.11.88	SBC	H	Salford	W	22-4	Coyne (2), Dixon, Anderson	Whitfield (3)	6661	Holdsworth
20.11.88	SBC	A	Oldham	W	14-12	Anderson, Hutchinson	Whitfield (3)	—	—
26.11.88	JPS(1)	A	Wigan	L	16-20	Anderson, Pendlebury	Whitfield (3), Coyne	—	—
4.12.88	SBC	H	Oldham	L	0-12	—	—	—	—
11.12.88	SBC	H	Wigan	L	16-20	McCallion, Grogan	Whitfield (4)	8822	Steele
18.12.88	SBC	A	St. Helens	L	16-50	McCallion, Stains, Whitfield	Whitfield (2)	—	—
26.12.88	SBC	A	Leeds	L	12-34	Grogan, Anderson	Coyne (2)	—	—
8.1.89	SBC	H	Castleford	W	21-12	Anderson (2), George	Lyons (4), Ramshaw (dg)	9231	Allatt
15.1.89	SBC	A	Wigan	L	12-26	Holliday, Grogan	Lyons, Whitfield	—	—
22.1.89	SBC	H	Featherstone R.	L	4-24	George	—	8012	Tickle
29.1.89	CC(1)	A	Warrington	L	8-25	Whitfield, Longstaff	—	—	—
5.2.89	SBC	A	Bradford N.	L	18-30	Anderson, Coyne, Holliday	Whitfield (3)	—	—
19.2.89	SBC	H	Hull K.R.	D	12-12	Anderson, Stains, Grogan	—	6676	Steele
26.2.89	SBC	A	Hull	L	4-24	Ramshaw	—	—	—
5.3.89	SBC	H	Salford	W	21-12	Whitfield, McCallion, Ramshaw	Whitfield (3), Holliday (3 dg)	6708	Holdsworth
19.3.89	SBC	A	Warrington	L	4-33	Wilson	—	—	—
24.3.89	SBC	A	Wakefield T.	L	10-27	Smith, Medley	Smith	—	—
27.3.89	SBC	H	Leeds	L	20-23	Anderson (2), Ramshaw, Lyons	Smith (2)	10,020	Carter
2.4.89	SBC	A	Salford	L	4-22	Wood	—	—	—
9.4.89	SBC	H	Wakefield T.	L	20-22	Riddlesden, Fairbank, Wilson, Whitfield	Smith (2)	6557	Steele
16.4.89	SBC	H	St. Helens	W	40-8	Whitfield, Bell, Riddlesden, Anderson, McCallion, Hill, Hutchinson, Ramshaw	Holliday (3), Smith	6774	Haigh

HUDDERSFIELD

Ground:	Fartown
Colours:	Claret and gold
First Season:	1895-96; added Barracudas to title from 1984-85 to 1987-88 inclusive
Nickname:	Fartowners
Chairman:	Mick Murphy
Secretary:	Neil Shuttleworth
Coaches:	Alan Jones and Neil Whittaker (Mar 1988-Nov 1988) Nigel Stephenson (Nov 1988-)
Honours:	**Championship** Winners, 1911-12, 1912-13, 1914-15, 1928-29, 1929-30, 1948-49, 1961-62 Beaten finalists, 1913-14, 1919-20, 1922-23, 1931-32, 1945-46, 1949-50 **Division Two** Champions, 1974-75 **Challenge Cup** Winners, 1912-13, 1914-15, 1919-20, 1932-33, 1944-45, 1952-53 Beaten finalists, 1934-35, 1961-62 **Yorkshire League** Winners, 1911-12, 1912-13, 1913-14, 1914-15, 1919-20, 1921-22, 1928-29, 1929-30, 1948-49, 1949-50, 1951-52 **Eastern Division** Beaten finalists, 1962-63 **Yorkshire Cup** Winners, 1909-10, 1911-12, 1913-14, 1914-15, 1918-19, 1919-20, 1926-27, 1931-32, 1938-39, 1950-51, 1952-53, 1957-58 Beaten finalists, 1910-11, 1923-24, 1925-26, 1930-31, 1937-38, 1942-43, 1949-50, 1960-61
Records:	Attendance: 35,136 Leeds v. Wakefield T. (RL Cup SF) 19 April 1947. Home: 32,912 v. Wigan (League) 4 Mar, 1950 **Season** Goals: 147 by B. Gronow, 1919-20 Tries: 80 by A. Rosenfeld, 1913-14 Points: 330 by B. Gronow, 1919-20

Match
Goals: 18 by M. Holland v. Swinton Park, 28 Feb, 1914
Tries: 10 by L. Cooper v. Keighley, 17 Nov, 1951
Points: 39 by M. Holland v. Swinton Park, 28 Feb, 1914
Highest score: 119-2 v. Swinton Park, 1913-14
Highest against: 94-12 v. Castleford, 1988-89

1988-89 PLAYERS' SUMMARY

	App	Tries	Goals	Dr	Pts
Bartle, Phil	11	1	—	—	4
Beckett, John	1	—	—	—	—
Boothroyd, Alan	5 + 1	—	—	—	—
Bostock, Mick	11	—	—	—	—
Brook, Tim	1 + 5	—	—	—	—
Brooke, Kevin	15	1	—	—	4
Cocker, Stuart	0 + 2	—	—	—	—
Cook, Billy	15 + 1	3	—	—	12
Cooper, Colin	3	1	—	—	4
Dickinson, Andy	19 + 7	3	—	—	12
Farrell, Anthony	24	8	2	—	36
Fitzpatrick, Dennis	0 + 1	—	—	—	—
Harris, Colin	6	—	—	—	—
Heselwood, Dave	3 + 2	—	—	—	—
Huck, Phil	22 + 2	3	—	—	12
Johnson, Jimmy	17 + 1	3	—	—	12
Johnson, Phil	0 + 1	—	—	—	—
Jowett, Bob	5	1	—	—	4
Kenworthy, Simon	24 + 6	2	48	4	108
Lee, Brian	8	1	—	—	4
Lee, Jimmy	2	—	—	—	—
Mackintosh, Andy	15	3	—	—	12
Massa, Mark	2 + 1	—	—	—	—
Meehan, Gary	25	2	—	4	12
Mitchell, Pat	1	—	—	—	—
Moore, John	1	—	—	—	—
Naidole, Tom	3 + 1	—	—	—	—
Nelson, Dave	27 + 2	7	—	—	28
Parker, Brad	1 + 2	—	—	—	—
Ramsden, Andrew	8	1	—	—	4
St. Hilaire, Darren	4	1	—	—	4
St. Hilaire, Lee	28	10	7	—	54
Sedgwick, Peter	2	—	—	—	—
Senior, Gary	7	1	—	—	4
Sewell, Andrew	2 + 9	1	—	—	4
Shuttleworth, Greg	3	—	—	—	—
Simpson, Andrew	6	—	—	—	—
Simpson, Frank	11 + 3	2	—	—	8
Stephenson, Nigel	6 + 4	1	1	1	7
Subritzky, Peter	5 + 1	2	—	1	9
Taylor, John	6	2	—	—	8
Thomas, Ian	22	13	3	—	58
Ventola, Roy	2 + 1	—	—	—	—
Webster, Nick	8 + 3	1	—	—	4
Wells, Trevor	2	1	—	—	4
Wilson, Mick	13 + 1	—	—	—	—
Wood, Neil	1	—	—	—	—
TOTALS:					
47 players		75	61	10	432

1988-89 MATCH ANALYSIS

Date	Competition	H/A	Opponent	Rlt	Score	Tries	Goals	Attendance	Referee
28.8.88	SD	A	Mansfield M.	L	11-24	Cooke, Sewell	Kenworthy (1, 1dg)	—	—
4.9.88	SD	H	Rochdale H.	L	16-22	Nelson, Dickinson, Taylor	Kenworthy (2)	603	Tickle
7.9.88	SD	A	Bramley	L	12-30	Johnson, Kenworthy	Kenworthy (2)	—	—
11.9.88	SD	H	Fulham	L	16-28	L. St. Hilaire, Simpson	Kenworthy (4)	379	Carter
18.9.88	YC(1)	A	Castleford	L	12-94	Taylor, Bartle	Kenworthy (2)	—	—
25.9.88	SD	A	Carlisle	L	1-40	—	Kenworthy (dg)	—	—
2.10.88	SD	H	Batley	D	19-19	Thomas (2), Nelson	Kenworthy (3), Meehan (dg)	783	Steele
9.10.88	SD	A	Workington T.	L	14-40	Ramsden, Dickinson, L. St. Hilaire	Kenworthy	—	—
16.10.88	SD	H	Dewsbury	L	12-26	Cook, Webster	Kenworthy (2)	702	Simpson
23.10.88	SD	A	Fulham	L	22-61	Thomas (2), Cook, L. St. Hilaire	Kenworthy (2), Thomas	—	—
6.11.88	SD	A	Rochdale H.	L	16-54	L. St. Hilaire, Meehan, Nelson	Kenworthy (2)	—	—
13.11.88	JPS(1)	H	Chorley B.	L	4-22	—	Kenworthy (2)	1120	Smith
20.11.88	SD	H	Sheffield E.	L	4-30	Farrell	—	572	Bowman
4.12.88	SD	A	Hunslet	W	21-18	Brooke, Kenworthy, L. St. Hilaire	Kenworthy (4, 1dg)	—	—
11.12.88	SD	A	Runcorn H.	W	25-4	Thomas (2), Farrell, Huck	Kenworthy (4), Stephenson (dg)	—	—
18.12.88	SD	A	Doncaster	L	10-18	Wells, Farrell	Kenworthy	—	—
26.12.88	SD	H	Runcorn H.	W	53-0	Farrell (3), Thomas (2), Huck (2), Mackinson, Meehan, Johnson	Kenworthy (6), Meehan (dg)	802	Whitelam
8.1.89	SD	H	Mansfield M.	W	20-10	Thomas, Mackintosh, Senior	Kenworthy (3), Thomas	1008	Holgate
15.1.89	SD	H	Carlisle	L	7-14	Dickinson	Kenworthy (1, 1dg)	1134	Simpson
22.1.89	SD	H	Bramley	W	17-14	Nelson, Stephenson, L. St. Hilaire	Kenworthy (2), Meehan (dg)	1235	Kershaw
29.1.89	CC(1)	A	Barrow	L	16-38	L. St. Hilaire, Nelson, Johnson	Kenworthy, Thomas	—	—
5.2.89	SD	H	York	L	1-17	—	Meehan (dg)	1444	Allatt
12.2.89	SD	A	York	L	4-10	Thomas	—	—	—
19.2.89	SD	A	Sheffield E.	L	0-24	—	—	—	—
26.2.89	SD	H	Whitehaven	L	2-19	—	Stephenson	518	Whitelam
12.3.89	SD	A	Batley	L	0-13	—	—	—	—
27.3.89	SD	A	Dewsbury	L	14-41	Cooper, Thomas, L. St. Hilaire	Farrell	—	—
2.4.89	SD	H	Hunslet	W	15-14	Subritzky, Simpson, L. St. Hilaire	Subritzky (dg), Farrell	703	Allatt
9.4.89	SD	A	Whitehaven	W	16-12	Thomas, Jowitt, Mackintosh	Kenworthy (2)	—	—
12.4.89	SD	H	Workington T.	W	30-3	Nelson, D. St. Hilaire, Farrell, Lee, L. St. Hilaire	L. St. Hilaire (4), Kenworthy	524	Dockray
16.4.89	SD	H	Doncaster	W	22-10	Subritzky, Nelson, Farrell, Thomas	L. St. Hilaire (3)	1433	Morris

HULL

Ground: The Boulevard
Colours: Black and white
First Season: 1895-96
Nickname: Airlie Birds
Chairman: Roy Waudby
Secretary: Ian Lockwood
Coach: Brian Smith (July 1988-)
Honours: **Championship** Winners, 1919-20, 1920-21, 1935-36, 1955-56, 1957-58
Beaten finalists, 1956-57
Division One Champions, 1982-83
Division Two Champions, 1976-77, 1978-79
Challenge Cup Winners, 1913-14, 1981-82
Beaten finalists, 1907-08, 1908-09, 1909-10, 1921-22, 1922-23, 1958-59, 1959-60, 1979-80, 1982-83, 1984-85
Yorkshire League Winners, 1918-19, 1922-23, 1926-27, 1935-36
Yorkshire Cup Winners, 1923-24, 1969-70, 1982-83, 1983-84, 1984-85
Beaten finalists, 1912-13, 1914-15, 1920-21, 1927-28, 1938-39, 1946-47, 1953-54, 1954-55, 1955-56, 1959-60, 1967-68, 1986-87
John Player Trophy Winners, 1981-82
Beaten finalists, 1975-76, 1984-85
BBC2 Floodlit Trophy Winners, 1979-80
Premiership Beaten finalists, 1980-81, 1981-82, 1982-83, 1988-89
Records: Attendance: 28,798 v. Leeds (RL Cup) 7 Mar, 1936
Season
Goals: 170 by S. Lloyd, 1978-79
Tries: 52 by J. Harrison, 1914-15
Points: 369 by S. Lloyd, 1978-79
Match
Goals: 14 by J. Kennedy v. Rochdale H., 7 Apr, 1921; S. Lloyd v. Oldham, 10 Sep, 1978
Tries: 7 by C. Sullivan v. Doncaster, 15 Apr, 1968

Points: 36 by J. Kennedy v. Keighley, 29 Jan, 1921
Highest score: 86-0 v. Elland, 1898-99
Highest against: 64-2 v. St. Helens, 1987-88

1988-89 PLAYERS' SUMMARY

	App		Tries	Goals	Dr	Pts
Blacker, Brian	15	+ 3	4	—	—	16
Boyle, David	19	+ 1	1	—	—	4
Bullock, Adrian	3		1	—	—	4
Coleman, Craig	24		3	—	2	14
Crooks, Steve	22	+ 5	—	—	1	1
Dannatt, Andy	34		2	—	—	8
Divorty, Gary	32	+ 1	8	—	—	32
Eastwood, Paul	28		7	39	—	106
Fletcher, Paul	33	+ 1	5	—	1	21
Henry, Neil	5	+ 3	1	—	—	4
Jackson, Lee	30		2	—	—	8
Khan, Paddy	1		1	—	—	4
Moon, David	25	+ 2	8	—	—	32
Nolan, Rob	1	+ 12	3	3	—	18
O'Hara, Dane	34		5	—	—	20
Patrick, Shaun	4		—	—	—	—
Pearce, Gary	23	+ 4	11	77	16	214
Price, Richard	32		13	—	—	52
Proctor, Wayne	1	+ 4	—	—	—	—
Puckering, Neil	0	+ 4	—	—	—	—
Sharp, Jon	26	+ 2	4	—	—	16
Tomlinson, Alan	6	+ 1	1	—	—	4
Welham, Paul	15	+ 14	5	—	—	20
Wilby, Tim	28	+ 5	2	—	—	8
Windley, Phil	14	+ 8	2	—	—	8

TOTALS:
25 players			89	119	20	614

Winger Paul Eastwood, a season's tally of seven tries, 39 goals and 106 points.

1988-89 MATCH ANALYSIS

Date	Competition	H/A	Opponent	Rlt	Score	Tries	Goals	Attendance	Referee
28.8.88	SBC	H	Castleford	L	8-18	Dannatt	Pearce (2)	6180	Smith
4.9.88	SBC	A	Widnes	L	6-38	Price	Eastwood	—	—
11.9.88	SBC	H	Wakefield T.	L	10-16	Fletcher	Eastwood (2), Coleman (dg), Pearce (dg)	6192	Whitfield
18.9.88	YC(1)	H	Hunslet	W	53-0	O'Hara (2), Divorty (2), Moon (2), Eastwood (2), Price	Eastwood (6), Pearce (2), Crooks (dg)	3153	Volante
25.9.88	SBC	A	Warrington	L	14-20	Eastwood, O'Hara	Eastwood (2), Pearce	—	—
27.9.88	YC(2)	H	Featherstone R.	W	18-0	Fletcher, Welham, Price	Eastwood (3)	4010	Smith
2.10.88	SBC	H	Leeds	W	14-12	Moon, Tomlinson	Eastwood (3)	7381	Holdsworth
5.10.88	YC(SF)	A	Leeds	L	8-12	Eastwood	Eastwood, Fletcher (dg), Coleman (dg)	—	—
9.10.88	SBC	A	Bradford N.	L	20-32	Price (2), Coleman	Eastwood (4)	—	—
16.6.88	SBC	A	St. Helens	W	20-9	Price, Dannatt, Moon	Eastwood (4)	—	—
6.11.88	SBC	A	Halifax	W	14-6	Eastwood, Price	Eastwood (3)	—	—
13.11.88	JPS(1)	H	Batley	W	26-10	Henry, Boyle, Moon, Khan, Divorty	Eastwood (3)	4054	Galtress
20.11.88	SBC	H	Featherstone R.	L	4-14	—	Eastwood (2)	4582	Berry
27.11.88	JPS(2)	A	St. Helens	L	13-16	Welham	Eastwood (4), Pearce (dg)	—	—
4.12.88	SBC	A	Leeds	W	13-6	Eastwood, Sharp	Eastwood, Pearce (3dg)	—	—
13.12.88	SBC	H	St. Helens	W	21-12	Sharp, Welham	Pearce (6, 1 dg)	4707	Berry
18.12.88	SBC	H	Oldham	W	11-8	Divorty	Pearce (3, 1 dg)	6119	Simpson
2.1.89	SBC	A	Hull K.R.	W	15-12	Moon, Coleman	Pearce (3, 1 dg)	—	—
8.1.89	SBC	H	Bradford N.	W	28-10	Wilby, Pearce, Price, Moon, Blacker	Pearce (4)	6628	Kendrew
11.1.89	SBC	A	Wigan	W	35-20	Moon, Coleman, Price, Fletcher, Sharp	Pearce (7, 1 dg)	—	—
18.1.89	SBC	A	Wakefield T.	W	11-2	Wilby	Pearce (3, 1 dg)	—	—
22.1.89	SBC	H	Warrington	W	10-8	Bullock	Pearce (3)	6611	Steele
28.1.89	CC(1)	H	Castleford	L	4-7	—	Pearce (2)	9194	Haigh
5.2.89	SBC	A	Salford	W	18-6	Blacker, Nolan	Pearce (5)	—	—
19.2.89	SBC	A	Oldham	L	7-9	Divorty	Pearce (1, 1 dg)	—	—
26.2.89	SBC	H	Halifax	W	24-4	Divorty (2), Pearce, Sharp	Pearce (4)	6550	Galtress
5.3.89	SBC	A	Castleford	W	23-16	Blacker (2), O'Hara, Price	Pearce (3, 1 dg)	—	—
19.3.89	SBC	H	Wigan	L	18-28	Divorty, Fletcher	Pearce (5)	9355	Tennant
24.3.89	SBC	H	Hull K.R.	W	26-2	Pearce (3), O'Hara, Price	Pearce (3)	9714	Kershaw
27.3.89	SBC	A	Featherstone R.	L	22-25	Pearce, Windley, Welham	Pearce (4, 2 dg)	—	—
5.4.89	SBC	H	Widnes	W	23-16	Pearce (2), Jackson	Pearce (5, 1 dg)	7256	Tickle
16.4.89	SBC	H	Salford	W	12-6	Divorty	Pearce (2)	7174	Whitfield
23.4.89	PT(1)	H	Castleford	W	32-6	Price (2), Pearce, Eastwood, Nolan, Windley	Nolan (3), Pearce	8409	Kershaw
7.5.89	PT(SF)	H	Featherstone R.	W	23-0	Pearce, Nolan, Fletcher	Pearce (5, 1dg)	11,028	Haigh
14.5.89	PT(F)	H Man U. F.C.	Widnes	L	10-18	Welham	Pearce (3)	(40,194)	Holdsworth

HULL KINGSTON ROVERS

● **Moved from the Holderness Road ground to a new stadium on Greatfield Estate for the start of the 1989-90 season.**

Ground: Craven Park
Colours: Red and white
First Season: 1899-1900
Nickname: Robins
Chairman: Colin Hutton
Secretary: Ron Turner
Coach: Roger Millward MBE (Mar 1977-)
Honours: **Championship** Winners, 1922-23, 1924-25
Beaten finalists, 1920-21, 1967-68
First Division Champions, 1978-79, 1983-84, 1984-85
Challenge Cup Winners, 1979-80
Beaten finalists, 1904-05, 1924-25, 1963-64, 1980-81, 1985-86
John Player Trophy Winners, 1984-85, Beaten finalists, 1981-82, 1985-86
Premiership Winners, 1980-81, 1983-84, Beaten finalists, 1984-85
Yorkshire League Winners, 1924-25, 1925-26
Yorkshire Cup Winners, 1920-21, 1929-30, 1966-67, 1967-68, 1971-72, 1974-75, 1985-86
Beaten finalists, 1906-07, 1911-12, 1933-34, 1962-63, 1975-76, 1980-81, 1984-85
BBC2 Floodlit Trophy Winners, 1977-78
Beaten finalists, 1979-80
Eastern Division Championship Winners, 1962-63
Charity Shield Beaten finalists, 1985-86
Records: Attendance: 22,282 v. Hull, 7 October, 1922. There was a crowd of 27,670 for a League match v. Hull at Hull City FC's Boothferry Park on 3 April, 1953
Season
Goals: 166 by G. Fairbairn, 1981-82
Tries: 45 by G. Prohm, 1984-85
Points: 366 by S. Hubbard, 1979-80
Match
Goals: 14 by A. Carmichael v. Merthyr Tydfil, 8 Oct, 1910
Tries: 11 by G. West v. Brookland R., 4 Mar, 1905
Points: 53 by G. West v. Brookland R., 4 Mar, 1905
Highest score: 73-5 v. Brookland R., 1904-05
Highest against: 68-0 v. Halifax, 1955-56

1988-89 PLAYERS' SUMMARY

	App	Tries	Goals	Dr	Pts
Armstrong, Colin	15 + 1	—	5	2	12
Beall, Malcolm	22 + 4	4	—	—	16
Bishop, David	25	4	1	1	19
Burton, Chris	16 + 1	1	—	—	4
Charlton, Gary	1 + 2	—	—	—	—
Clark, Garry	23	6	—	—	24
Close, Chris	24	14	—	—	56
Ema, Asuquo	16 + 3	—	—	—	—
Fairbairn, George	22	2	39	—	86
Fletcher, Mike	20 + 1	3	63	—	138
Fletcher, Paul	4 + 6	—	—	—	—
Hallas, Graeme	12 + 1	2	1	1	11
Harrison, Dave	13 + 3	4	—	—	16
Harrison, Des	16 + 14	1	—	—	4
Hogan, Phil	3	—	—	—	—
Irvine, Jimmy	9	2	—	—	8
Jones, Mark	3 + 5	2	—	1	9
Lawler, Kenny	1	—	—	—	—
Laws, David	13 + 3	3	—	—	12
Lydiat, John	12 + 2	1	—	—	4
Lyman, Paul	9 + 1	3	—	—	12
Miller, Gavin	22	5	—	—	20
O'Brien, Craig	2 + 3	—	—	—	—
Parker, Wayne	13	5	—	2	22
Porter, Mike	28 + 1	5	—	—	20
Pratt, Richard	24	5	—	—	20
Richardson, Lee	3	2	—	—	8
Robinson, Steve	9 + 2	3	—	—	12
Rudd, Chris	7 + 1	—	—	—	—
Schultz, Stuart	1 + 1	—	—	—	—
Sims, Kenny	5 + 2	1	—	—	4
Smith, Mike	27	6	—	1	25
Smith, Steve	2	—	—	—	—
Speckman, Paul	3 + 3	1	—	—	4
Stead, Ray	1 + 2	—	—	—	—
Sullivan, Tony	13	4	—	—	16
Thompson, Andy	5 + 2	2	—	—	8
Watkinson, David	11	—	—	—	—

TOTALS:
38 players | | 91 | 109 | 8 | 590

1988-89 MATCH ANALYSIS

Date	Competition	H/A	Opponent	Rlt	Score	Tries	Goals	Attendance	Referee
28.8.88	SBC	A	Salford	L	14-24	Thompson, Clark	Fletcher (3)	—	—
4.9.88	SBC	H	Featherstone R.	L	15-30	Parker (2), Clark	Fletcher, Parker (dg)	4194	Whitfield
11.9.88	SBC	A	Wigan	L	16-32	Close, Dave Harrison	Fletcher (4)	—	—
18.9.88	YC(1)	A	Keighley	W	28-22	Close, Lydiat, Laws, Parker, Miller	Fairbairn (3), Fletcher	—	—
25.9.88	SBC	H	Halifax	W	12-4	Bishop	Fletcher (4)	5986	Houghton
28.9.88	YC(2)	A	Halifax	L	2-24	—	Fletcher	—	—
2.10.88	SBC	A	Oldham	L	16-30	M. Smith (2), Close	Fletcher (2)	—	—
9.10.88	SBC	H	St. Helens	L	22-30	Jones (2), Porter	Fletcher (5)	4911	Holdsworth
16.10.88	SBC	H	Bradford N.	W	24-22	Porter, Beall, Miller	Fletcher (6)	4928	Steele
23.10.88	SBC	A	Leeds	L	8-21	Fletcher	Fletcher (2)	—	—
6.11.88	SBC	H	Wakefield T.	W	38-18	Fairbairn (2), Parker (2), Beall, Sims	Fairbairn (7)	4888	Tennant
13.11.88	JPS(1)	H	Keighley	W	40-0	Bishop, M. Smith, Clark, Pratt, Beall, Porter, Close, Dave Harrison	Fairbairn (3), Bishop	3319	Bowman
20.11.88	SBC	A	Widnes	L	6-43	Beall	Fairbairn	—	—
27.11.88	JPS(2)	A	Chorley B.	W	36-22	Close (3), Speckman, Des Harrison, Porter	Fletcher (6)	—	—
4.12.88	JPS(3)	H	Wigan	D	16-16	Close, Clark, Pratt	Fletcher (2)	7142	Whitfield
7.12.88	JPS(3) Replay	A	Wigan	L	0-30	—	—	—	—
11.12.88	SBC	A	Wakefield T.	W	12-6	Clark, Pratt	Fletcher (2)	—	—
26.12.88	SBC	A	Castleford	L	20-38	Clark, Close, Burton	Fletcher (4)	—	—
2.1.89	SBC	H	Hull	L	12-15	Close, Dave Harrison	Fairbairn (2)	8837	Tennant
8.1.89	SBC	A	Warrington	L	24-60	Irvine (2), Dave Harrison, Laws	Fairbairn (4)	—	—
15.1.89	SBC	H	Oldham	W	34-6	Robinson (2), Lyman, Laws, Close	Fairbairn (7)	5182	Kendrew
22.1.89	SBC	A	St. Helens	L	0-29	—	—	—	—
29.1.89	CC(1)	A	Rochdale H.	W	28-24	M. Smith (2), Miller, Bishop, Pratt	Fairbairn (4)	—	—
5.2.89	SBC	H	Warrington	L	7-17	Lyman	Hallas (1, 1dg)	4433	Tickle
12.2.89	CC(2)	H	Chorley B.	W	28-4	Close, M. Smith, Pratt, Lyman	Fairbairn (5), Bishop (dg), Jones (dg)	3471	Simpson
19.2.89	SBC	A	Halifax	D	12-12	Close (2)	Fairbairn (2)	—	—
26.2.89	CC(3)	H	Warrington	L	4-30	Hallas	—	7283	Tennant
5.3.89	SBC	H	Wigan	L	18-19	Robinson, Bishop	Armstrong (5)	5526	Tickle
12.3.89	SBC	A	Featherstone R.	L	6-28	Miller	Fairbairn	—	—
15.3.89	SBC	H	Leeds	L	13-18	Sullivan, Fletcher	Fletcher (2), Parker (dg)	4330	Kershaw
19.3.89	SBC	H	Salford	L	18-24	Porter, Miller	Fletcher (5)	3384	Steele
24.3.89	SBC	A	Hull	L	2-26	—	Fletcher	—	—
27.3.89	SBC	H	Castleford	W	32-30	Sullivan (3), Richardson	Fletcher (7), Armstrong (dg), M. Smith (dg)	3760	Haigh
9.4.89	SBC	H	Widnes	L	13-16	Fletcher, Hallas	Fletcher (2), Armstrong (dg)	7844	Galtress
16.4.89	SBC	A	Bradford N.	L	14-38	Richardson, Thompson	Fletcher (3)	—	—

HUNSLET

Ground: Elland Road
Colours: Myrtle, flame and white
First Season: 1895-96. Disbanded at end of 1972-73. Re-formed as New Hunslet in 1973-74. Retitled Hunslet from start of 1979-80
Chairman: Graham Lyle
Secretary: Mabel Grainger
Coaches: Nigel Stephenson (June 1988-Oct 1988) John Wolford and Jack Austin (Oct 1988-Jan 1989) David Ward (Jan 1989-May 1989)
Honours: **Challenge Cup** Winners, 1907-08, 1933-34
Beaten finalists, 1898-99, 1964-65
Championship Winners, 1907-08, 1937-38
Beaten finalists, 1958-59
Division Two Champions, 1962-63, 1986-87
Second Division Premiership Beaten finalists, 1986-87
Yorkshire Cup Winners, 1905-06, 1907-08, 1962-63
Beaten finalists, 1908-09, 1929-30, 1931-32, 1944-45, 1956-57, 1965-66
Yorkshire League Winners, 1897-98, 1907-08, 1931-32
Records: Attendance: 54,112 v. Leeds (Championship final) 30 Apr, 1938
Season
Goals: 181 by W. Langton, 1958-59
Tries: 34 by A. Snowden, 1956-57
Points: 380 by W. Langton, 1958-59
Match
Goals: 12 by W. Langton v. Keighley, 18 Aug, 1959
Tries: 7 by G. Dennis v. Bradford N., 20 Jan, 1934
Points: 27 by W. Langton v. Keighley, 18 Aug, 1959
Highest score: 75-5 v. Broughton Rec., 1896-97
Highest against: 76-8 v. Halifax, 1972-73

1988-89 PLAYERS' SUMMARY

	App	Tries	Goals	Dr	Pts
Allan, Mick	5 + 4	—	—	—	—
Bell, Mick	3	—	1	—	2
Bowden, Chris	29 + 1	6	—	—	24
Burrow, Paul	3 + 1	—	—	—	—
Coates, Jed	15 + 2	2	—	—	8
Evans, Gary	3	1	—	—	4
Gibson, Phil	15 + 1	1	—	—	4
Goodyear, George	1	—	—	—	—
Hague, Neil	25	—	—	8	8
Irvine, Jimmy	14	5	—	1	21
Jackson, Michael	4 + 1	2	—	—	8
Kay, Andy	3	—	—	—	—
Kelly, Neil	1	—	—	—	—
King, Graham	16 + 1	6	—	—	24
Lay, Steve	19 + 1	4	44	—	104
Lowes, James	8 + 3	1	—	—	4
Lumb, Tim	14 + 3	6	9	—	42
Lyons, Paddy	1 + 3	—	—	—	—
Marson, Andy	23 + 1	2	—	—	8
Mason, Keith	21	—	—	—	—
Milton, Roy	1 + 2	—	—	—	—
Mitchell, Keith	19	3	—	—	12
Moore, Herbie	19	8	—	—	32
Morgan, Paul	14 + 4	—	—	—	—
Nickle, Sonny	14	4	—	—	16
Oldroyd, Tom	0 + 1	—	—	—	—
Penola, Colin	3 + 4	—	—	—	—
Petch, Andrew	0 + 1	—	—	—	—
Pickerill, Neil	5 + 3	—	—	1	1
Price, Darren	0 + 1	—	—	—	—
Raw, Andy	9	6	—	—	24
Rollinson, Jim	1 + 2	—	—	—	—
Rowse, Gary	3 + 1	1	5	—	14
Sampson, Roy	12 + 2	1	—	—	4
Senior, Gary	0 + 1	—	—	—	—
Tate, Phil	10	3	—	—	12
Warrener, Stan	15 + 5	2	4	—	16
Whittington, Mark	17	5	—	—	20
Wilby, Simon	0 + 1	—	—	—	—
Wilkinson, Shaun	7	5	—	—	20
Wilson, Warren	22	8	8	1	49
Wood, Mark	4 + 10	—	—	—	—

TOTALS:
42 players		82	71	11	481

Neil Hague, scorer of eight drop goals in his debut campaign for Hunslet.

1988-89 MATCH ANALYSIS

Date	Competition	H/A	Opponent	Rlt	Score	Tries	Goals	Attendance	Referee
28.8.88	SD	H	Chorley B.	L	6-18	King	Lay	779	Bowman
4.9.88	SD	H	Swinton	L	10-12	King	Lay (3)	1078	Cross
11.9.88	SD	A	Dewsbury	L	5-16	—	Lay (2), Pickerill (dg)	—	—
18.9.88	YC(1)	A	Hull	L	0-53	—	—	—	—
25.9.88	SD	H	Batley	W	31-14	Tate (2), Lay, Irvine, Gibson, Moore	Lay (2), Bell, Irvine (dg)	826	Kershaw
2.10.88	SD	A	Mansfield M.	L	14-36	Bowden, King	Lay (3)	—	—
9.10.88	SD	A	Leigh	L	18-36	Wilson, Whittington, Rowse	Rowse (3)	—	—
18.10.88	SD	H	Barrow	L	0-12	—	—	541	Tidball
30.10.88	JPS(P)	A	Featherstone R.	L	2-46	—	Rowse	—	—
6.11.88	SD	H	Dewsbury	W	34-12	Moore (2), Wilson (2), King, Nickle	Lay (5)	680	Steele
20.11.88	SD	A	Doncaster	L	2-18	—	Rowse	—	—
27.11.88	SD	A	Keighley	W	19-16	Moore, Nickle	Lay (4), Hague (3 dg)	—	—
4.12.88	SD	H	Huddersfield	L	18-21	Tate, Whittington, Irvine, Lay	Lay	741	Millet (Fr)
11.12.88	SD	A	Fulham	W	16-10	Lumb, Nickle, Lay	Lay (2)	—	—
18.12.88	SD	H	Keighley	W	33-14	Irvine (3), Whittington, Mitchell, Nickle	Lay (4), Hague (dg)	803	Galtress
27.12.88	SD	A	Bramley	D	18-18	Coates, Moore, Raw	Lay (3)	—	—
1.1.89	SD	H	York	L	15-29	Coates, Lumb	Lay (3), Hague (dg)	1106	Bowman
8.1.89	SD	A	Barrow	L	0-40	—	—	—	—
15.1.89	CC(P)	A	Leeds	L	6-32	—	Lay (3)	—	—
29.1.89	SD	H	Bramley	W	27-18	Bowden (2), Lay, Moore, Lumb	Lay (3), Wilson (dg)	1011	Morris
5.2.89	SD	A	Chorley B.	W	13-10	Raw, Lumb	Lumb (2), Hague (dg)	—	—
12.2.89	SD	A	Batley	W	26-9	Raw (4), Mitchell	Lay (3)	—	—
19.2.89	SD	H	Leigh	L	16-40	Marson, Bowden, Moore	Lay (2)	1352	Whitelam
5.3.89	SD	H	Mansfield M.	W	32-15	Lumb (2), Bowden, Whittington, Wilson, Warrener	Lumb (4)	613	Carter
12.3.89	SD	A	Sheffield E.	L	10-24	Moore, Bowden	Warrener	—	—
19.3.89	SD	H	Doncaster	W	11-8	Whittington	Wilson (3), Hague (dg)	1703	Berry
26.3.89	SD	A	York	L	17-26	Wilson, Wilkinson, King	Wilson (2), King (dg)	—	—
2.4.89	SD	A	Huddersfield	L	14-15	Wilkinson (2), Marson	Lumb	—	—
9.4.89	SD	H	Fulham	W	26-21	Wilson (2), Lowes, Jackson, Wilkinson	Warrener (3)	873	Bowman
12.4.89	SD	A	Swinton	L	10-26	Wilkinson, Warrener	Wilson	—	—
16.4.89	SD	H	Sheffield E.	W	32-6	Mitchell, Sampson, King, Evans, Jackson, Wilson	Wilson (2), Lumb (2)	1150	Holgate

KEIGHLEY

Ground: Lawkholme Lane
Colours: Green, scarlet and white
First Season: 1901-02
Nickname: Lawkholmers
Chairman: Colin Farrar
Secretary: Keith Reeves
Coaches: Colin Dixon and Les Coulter
(July 1986-)
Honours: **Division Two** Champions, 1902-03
Challenge Cup Beaten finalists, 1936-37
Yorkshire Cup Beaten finalists, 1943-44, 1951-52
Records: Attendance: 14,500 v. Halifax (RL Cup) 3 Mar,.1951
Season
Goals: 155 by B. Jefferson, 1973-74
Tries: 30 by J. Sherburn, 1934-35
Points: 331 by B. Jefferson, 1973-74
Match
Goals: 11 by R. Walker v. Castleford, 13 Jan, 1906; H. Cook v. Hull K.R., 31 Oct, 1953
Tries: 5 by I. Jagger v. Castleford, 13 Jan, 1906; S. Stacey v. Liverpool C., 9 Mar, 1907
Points: 24 by J. Phillips v. Halifax, 5 Oct, 1957
Highest score: 67-0 v. Castleford, 1905-06
Highest against: 92-2 v. Leigh, 1985-86

1988-89 PLAYERS' SUMMARY

	App	Tries	Goals	Dr	Pts
Atkinson, Colin	12	4	—	—	16
Bardgett, Joe	14 + 4	4	—	—	16
Bragger, Ian	10	1	—	—	4
Butterfield, Jeff	20	5	—	—	20
Curtis, Chris	11	1	—	—	4
Dixon, Keith	23 + 1	9	41	2	120
Fairbank, Mark	21 + 1	2	—	—	8
Goodier, Frank	4 + 5	—	—	—	—
Hirst, Carl	18	2	52	—	112
Manning, Terry	31 + 1	18	—	—	72
Mason, Max	13 + 5	4	—	—	16
Moorby, Gary	28 + 2	7	—	—	28
Moses, Paul	17 + 1	4	—	2	18
O'Brien, Vince	20 + 2	5	—	—	20
Proctor, Rob	29	2	—	—	8
Ragan, Mark	15 + 6	3	7	—	26
Richardson, Peter	19 + 7	15	—	—	60
Robinson, Kevan	5 + 13	—	—	—	—
Rose, Gary	23 + 1	5	—	—	20
Rose, Kevin	15 + 1	1	—	—	4
Skerrett, Trevor	28 + 2	1	—	—	4
Tyers, Andrew	0 + 1	—	—	—	—
Waller, Vince	5 + 1	—	—	—	—
White, Brendan	23 + 4	1	—	—	4
Winterbottom, Ricky	25	10	—	—	40
TOTALS:					
25 players		104	100	4	620

Gary Moorby, seven tries in 30 appearances.

1988-89 MATCH ANALYSIS

Date	Com-petition	H/A	Opponent	Rlt	Score	Tries	Goals	Atten-dance	Referee
28.8.88	SD	H	Whitehaven	W	20-7	Moorby, Dixon, G. Rose	Hirst (4)	996	Volante
4.9.88	SD	A	York	W	18-16	Winterbottom (2), Dixon	Hirst (3)	—	—
7.9.88	SD	H	Chorley B.	W	26-12	Moorby, Fairbank, Winterbottom, Butterfield	Dixon (5)	1001	Berry
11.9.88	SD	H	Leigh	L	20-36	Manning (2), Bragger	Dixon (4)	1272	Tidball
18.9.88	YC(1)	H	Hull K.R.	L	22-28	Dixon (2), Butterfield, Hirst, Atkinson	Hirst	1596	Galtress
25.9.88	SD	A	Rochdale H.	W	28-22	Atkinson, Butterfield, G. Rose, White	Hirst (6)	—	—
2.10.88	SD	H	Workington T.	W	33-15	G. Rose, Manning, Atkinson, Moorby, Richardson	Hirst (5), Dixon (1, 1dg)	1093	Whitelam
9.10.88	SD	A	Barrow	L	16-54	Manning, G. Rose, Butterfield	Hirst (2)	—	—
16.10.88	SD	H	Carlisle	W	26-12	Richardson (3), Proctor	Hirst (5)	1076	Allatt
23.10.88	SD	A	Swinton	L	14-43	Manning (2)	Hirst (3)	—	—
6.11.88	SD	A	Sheffield E.	L	6-34	Butterfield	Hirst	—	—
13.11.88	JPS(1)	A	Hull K.R.	L	0-40	—	—	—	—
27.11.88	SD	H	Hunslet	L	16-19	O'Brien, Manning	Hirst (4)	1021	Holgate
11.12.88	SD	H	Sheffield E.	L	12-34	Manning, Richardson	Hirst (2)	714	Burke
18.12.88	SD	A	Hunslet	L	14-33	O'Brien, Atkinson	Hirst (3)	—	—
1.1.89	SD	H	Bramley	W	28-22	Mason, Manning, Winterbottom, Fairbank	Hirst (6)	1258	Tidball
8.1.89	SD	A	Chorley B.	L	6-22	—	Hirst (3)	—	—
15.1.89	SD	H	Rochdale H.	W	36-16	Richardson (2), O'Brien (2), Hirst, Manning, Ragan	Hirst (4)	1085	Houghton
22.1.89	SD	A	Leigh	L	12-20	Moorby, Ragan	Ragan (2)	—	—
29.1.89	CC(1)	A	Runcorn H.	W	28-10	Manning (2), Moorby, Richardson, Winterbottom	Ragan (4)	—	—
5.2.89	SD	A	Carlisle	L	4-20	Manning	—	—	—
12.2.89	CC(2)	A	Warrington	L	7-56	Moses	Dixon (1, 1dg)	—	—
19.2.89	SD	H	York	W	7-6	Moses	Dixon, Moses (dg)	1133	Smith
26.2.89	SD	A	Workington T.	W	14-0	Manning, O'Brien, K. Rose	Dixon	—	—
12.3.89	SD	H	Swinton	L	10-20	Winterbottom, Richardson	Dixon	1022	Morris
19.3.89	SD	H	Mansfield M.	W	38-6	Mason (2), Richardson (2), Dixon, Bardgett, Winterbottom	Dixon (5)	542	Smith
24.3.89	SD	A	Runcorn H.	W	34-6	Ragan, Dixon (2), Moses, Winterbottom, Curtis	Dixon (5)	—	—
27.3.89	SD	A	Bramley	W	29-14	Manning (2), Moorby, Skerrett	Dixon (6), Moses (dg)	—	—
2.4.89	SD	H	Barrow	W	14-10	Dixon, Richardson	Dixon (3)	851	Berry
6.4.89	SD	A	Mansfield M.	W	24-6	Bardgett (2), Manning, Moses, G. Rose	Dixon (2)	—	—
9.4.89	SD	H	Runcorn H.	W	42-4	Richardson (2), Winterbottom (2), Manning, Moorby, Bardgett, Dixon	Dixon (5)	858	Spencer
12.4.89	SD	A	Whitehaven	L	4-16	Mason	—	—	—
23.4.89	SDP(1)	A	Leigh	L	12-38	Richardson, Proctor	Ragan, Dixon	—	—

LEEDS

Ground:	Headingley
Colours:	Blue and amber
First Season:	1895-96
Nickname:	Loiners
Chairman:	Bernard Coulby
Chief Exec:	Alf Davies
Coach:	Malcolm Reilly (Aug 1988-)

Honours: **Championship** Winners, 1960-61, 1968-69, 1971-72

Beaten finalists, 1914-15, 1928-29, 1929-30, 1930-31, 1937-38, 1969-70, 1972-73

League Leaders Trophy Winners, 1966-67, 1967-68, 1968-69, 1969-70, 1971-72

Challenge Cup Winners, 1909-10, 1922-23, 1931-32, 1935-36, 1940-41, 1941-42, 1956-57, 1967-68, 1976-77, 1977-78

Beaten finalists, 1942-43, 1946-47, 1970-71, 1971-72

Yorkshire League Winners, 1901-02, 1927-28, 1930-31, 1933-34, 1934-35, 1936-37, 1937-38, 1950-51, 1954-55, 1956-57, 1960-61, 1966-67, 1967-68, 1968-69, 1969-70

Yorkshire Cup Winners, 1921-22, 1928-29, 1930-31, 1932-33, 1934-35, 1935-36, 1937-38, 1958-59, 1968-69, 1970-71, 1972-73, 1973-74, 1975-76, 1976-77, 1979-80, 1980-81, 1988-89

Beaten finalists, 1919-20, 1947-48, 1961-62, 1964-65

BBC2 Floodlit Trophy Winners, 1970-71

John Player Trophy Winners, 1972-73, 1983-84

Beaten finalists, 1982-83, 1987-88

Premiership Winners, 1974-75, 1978-79

Records: Attendance: 40,175 v. Bradford N. (League) 21 May, 1947

Season
Goals: 166 by B.L. Jones, 1956-57
Tries: 63 by E. Harris, 1935-36
Points: 431 by B.L. Jones, 1956-57

Match
Goals: 13 by B.L. Jones v. Blackpool B., 19 Aug, 1957
Tries: 8 by F. Webster v. Coventry, 12 Apr, 1913; E. Harris v. Bradford N., 14 Sep, 1931
Points: 31 by B.L. Jones v. Bradford N., 22 Aug, 1956
Highest score: 102-0 v. Coventry, 1912-13
Highest against: 71-0 v. Wakefield T., 1945-46

1988-89 PLAYERS' SUMMARY

	App	Tries	Goals	Dr	Pts
Ashton, Ray	27 + 1	3	—	2	14
Backo, Sam	8 + 10	1	—	—	4
Basnett, John	8	—	—	—	—
Bentley, John	21	15	12	—	84
Brooke-Cowden, Mark	18 + 7	2	—	—	8
Creasser, David	10 + 1	4	19	1	55
Crooks, Lee	32	7	1	—	30
Delaney, Paul	7	1	—	—	4
Dixon, Paul	11	1	—	—	4
Ettingshausen, Andrew	21	13	—	—	52
Fairbank, John	1 + 1	—	—	—	—
Fawcett, Vincent	4	3	—	—	12
Ford, Phil	17	10	—	—	40
Gibson, Carl	37	20	—	—	80
Gill, Paul	1	—	—	—	—
Gunn, Richard	4 + 2	—	—	—	—
Heron, David	33 + 1	4	—	—	16
Lord, Gary	9 + 5	—	—	—	—
Lord, Mark	1 + 1	1	—	—	4
Lyons, Cliff	23 + 1	8	—	—	32
Lyons, John	0 + 1	—	—	—	—
Maskill, Colin	33	2	—	—	8
Medley, Paul	6 + 14	10	—	—	40
Powell, Roy	36	1	—	—	4
Price, Gary	15 + 5	4	—	—	16
Schofield, Garry	30	20	12	1	105
Spencer, Gary	22 + 1	4	—	—	16
Stephenson, David	20 + 3	4	60	—	136
Vasey, Chris	0 + 1	—	—	—	—
Waddell, Hugh	24 + 7	—	—	—	—
Wilson, Mark	2 + 1	—	—	—	—

TOTALS:
31 players		138	104	4	764

1988-89 MATCH ANALYSIS

Date	Competition	H/A	Opponent	Rlt	Score	Tries	Goals	Attendance	Referee
28.8.88	SBC	A	Featherstone R.	W	32-18	Fawcett, Crooks, Price, Schofield, Medley, Stephenson	Stephenson (4)	—	—
31.8.88	YC(P)	A	Bramley	W	38-16	Fawcett (2), Crooks (2), Price, Medley, Stephenson	Stephenson (5)	—	—
4.9.88	SBC	A	Oldham	W	28-22	Schofield (2), Gibson (2), Medley	Stephenson (4)	—	—
11.9.88	SBC	H	Widnes	L	14-30	Gibson, Schofield	Stephenson (3)	12,498	Tidball
18.9.88	YC(1)	H	Bradford N.	W	24-21	Gibson, Spencer, Medley, Stephenson	Stephenson (4)	10,992	Holdsworth
25.9.88	SBC	H	St. Helens	W	32-0	Spencer (2), Schofield, Medley, Lyons	Schofield (6)	12,062	Tennant
28.9.88	YC(2)	H	Wakefield T.	W	15-10	Gibson, Medley	Schofield (3), Ashton (dg)	11,150	Kershaw
2.10.88	SBC	A	Hull	L	12-14	Heron, Gibson	Schofield (2)	—	—
5.10.88	YC(SF)	H	Hull	W	12-8	Schofield, Backo	Stephenson (2)	10,384	Tennant
9.10.88	SBC	H	Wigan	W	22-14	Schofield (4)	Stephenson (3)	15,345	Whitfield
16.10.88	YC(F)	Elland Rd, Leeds	Castleford	W	33-12	Schofield (2), Gibson (2), Medley	Stephenson (6), Schofield (dg)	(22,968)	Whitfield
23.10.88	SBC	H	Hull K. R.	W	21-8	Schofield, Ettingshausen, Brooke-Cowden, Maskill	Stephenson (2), Ashton (dg)	11,460	Kendrew
6.11.88	SBC	A	Bradford N.	W	18-10	Ettingshausen, Crooks, Lyons, Medley	Stephenson	—	—
12.11.88	JPS(1)	H	Castleford	L	12-21	Lyons, Gibson	Stephenson (2)	10,006	Simpson
20.11.88	SBC	H	Warrington	L	8-22	Lyons, Spencer	—	9752	Steele
27.11.88	SBC	A	Salford	W	24-6	Gibson (2), Ettingshausen, Schofield, Brooke-Cowden	Stephenson (2)	—	—
4.12.88	SBC	H	Hull	L	6-13	Gibson	Stephenson	9554	Carter
11.12.88	SBC	H	Featherstone R.	W	36-18	Gibson (2), Medley, Price, Ettingshausen, Lyons	Stephenson (6)	9187	Allatt
18.12.88	SBC	A	Widnes	W	20-8	Lyons, Bentley, Maskill, Ashton	Stephenson (2)	—	—
26.12.88	SBC	H	Halifax	W	34-12	Ettingshausen (2), Bentley, Heron, Gibson, Medley	Stephenson (5)	16,993	Carter
1.1.89	SBC	H	Oldham	W	48-4	Ford (3), Powell, Lyons, Price, Bentley, Ettingshausen	Bentley (8)	14,487	Whitfield
8.1.89	SBC	A	St. Helens	L	6-15	Ettingshausen	Stephenson	—	—
15.1.89	CC(P)	H	Hunslet	W	32-6	Bentley (2), Ashton, Dixon, Ford, Gibson	Stephenson (4)	9090	Tennant
22.1.89	SBC	H	Salford	W	18-16	Ettingshausen, Stephenson, Bentley	Stephenson (3)	10,135	Carter
29.1.89	CC(1)	A	York (York C. F.C.)	W	28-9	Ettingshausen (2), Crooks, Ford, Gibson, Bentley	Bentley (2)	—	—
12.2.89	CC(2)	H	Carlisle	W	24-4	Bentley (2), Ettingshausen, Ford, Ashton	Bentley (2)	9484	Steele
19.2.89	SBC	A	Wigan	L	8-16	Lyons, Bentley	—	—	—
26.2.89	CC(3)	H	Widnes	L	4-24	Crooks	—	26,303	Holdsworth
5.3.89	SBC	H	Wakefield T.	W	28-16	Ford (2), Creasser, Ettingshausen, Schofield, Bentley	Crooks, Schofield	10,333	Galtress
12.3.89	SBC	A	Wakefield T.	L	12-14	Gibson, Bentley	Creasser (2)	—	—
15.3.89	SBC	A	Hull K.R.	W	18-13	Schofield (2), Heron	Creasser (3)	—	—
19.3.89	SBC	H	Castleford	W	32-18	Bentley, Creasser, Heron, Schofield, Gibson	Creasser (6)	12,576	Whitfield
24.3.89	SBC	H	Bradford N.	W	10-7	Schofield, Crooks	Creasser	12,398	Haigh
27.3.89	SBC	A	Halifax	W	23-20	Ford, Creasser, Schofield, Bentley	Creasser (3, 1dg)	—	—
2.4.89	SBC	A	Warrington	W	10-8	Ford, Delaney	Creasser	—	—
16.4.89	SBC	A	Castleford	L	10-38	Lord, Gibson	Creasser	—	—
23.4.89	PT(1)	H	Featherstone R.	L	12-15	Bentley, Creasser	Creasser (2)	11,684	Whitfield

LEIGH

Ground:	Hilton Park
Colours:	Red and white
First Season:	1895-96
Chairman:	Bobby Hope
Secretary:	John Clark
Coach:	Billy Benyon (Dec 1986-)
Honours:	**Championship** Winners, 1905-06
	Division One Champions, 1981-82
	Division Two Champions, 1977-78, 1985-86, 1988-89
	Challenge Cup Winners, 1920-21, 1970-71
	Lancashire Cup Winners, 1952-53, 1955-56, 1970-71, 1981-82
	Beaten finalists, 1905-06, 1909-10, 1920-21, 1922-23, 1949-50, 1951-52, 1963-64, 1969-70
	BBC2 Floodlit Trophy Winners, 1969-70, 1972-73
	Beaten finalists, 1967-68, 1976-77
Records:	Attendance: 31,324 v. St. Helens (RL Cup) 14 Mar, 1953
	Season
	Goals: 173 by C. Johnson, 1985-86
	Tries: 49 by S. Halliwell, 1985-86
	Points: 400 by C. Johnson, 1985-86
	Match
	Goals: 15 by M. Stacey v. Doncaster, 28 Mar, 1976
	Tries: 6 by J. Wood v. York, 4 Oct, 1947
	Points: 38 by J. Woods v. Blackpool B., 11 Sep, 1977
	Highest score: 92-2 v. Keighley, 1985-86
	Highest against: 60-8 v. Salford, 1940

1988-89 PLAYERS' SUMMARY

	App	Tries	Goals	Dr	Pts
Burrill, Craig	11 + 7	8	—	—	32
Collier, Andy	33	4	—	—	16
Cooper, Mark	4 + 5	—	—	—	—
Cottrell, Tony	24 + 4	4	—	—	16
Dean, Mick	18 + 4	7	—	—	28
Donohue, Jason	2 + 2	—	—	—	—
Dunn, Brian	28 + 2	14	—	—	56
Earner, Adrian	7	—	—	—	—
Evans, Andy	0 + 1	—	—	—	—
Evans, David	1	—	—	—	—
Evans, Stuart	0 + 1	—	—	—	—
Henderson, John	2 + 1	1	—	—	4
Hill, David	5	—	—	—	—
Holliday, Mike	1 + 1	—	—	—	—
Jeffrey, Ian	34	20	—	—	80
Johnson, Chris	29 + 1	12	114	3	279
Johnson, Phil	31 + 3	9	28	1	93
Kerr, John	20 + 5	18	—	—	72
Knight, Mark	5 + 5	—	—	—	—
Lang, Shaun	0 + 7	1	—	—	4
Ledger, Barry	29	34	—	—	136
Mann, George	9 + 4	4	—	—	16
McCulloch, Neil	17	8	—	—	32
Mellor, Sean	0 + 1	—	—	—	—
Moimoi, Robert	20	6	—	—	24
O'Toole, David	0 + 1	—	—	—	—
Owen, Ivor	2	—	—	—	—
Peters, Steve	2 + 1	—	—	—	—
Platt, Alan	34	6	4	—	32
Ropati, Peter	21	5	—	—	20
Round, Mike	9 + 1	5	—	—	20
Ruane, David	32 + 3	23	—	—	92
Street, Tim	23 + 2	7	—	—	28
Webb, Carl	0 + 5	—	—	—	—
Westhead, John	2	1	—	—	4
TOTALS:					
35 players		197	146	4	1,084

1988-89 MATCH ANALYSIS

Date	Competition	H/A	Opponent	Rlt	Score	Tries	Goals	Attendance	Referee
28.8.88	SD	A	Workington T.	W	38-18	Dunn (2), Ledger (2), Jeffrey, Burrill, Westhead	P. Johnson (5)	—	—
4.9.88	SD	H	Runcorn H.	W	48-14	Ledger (3), Jeffrey (2), Platt, Dean, Burrill	P. Johnson (8)	2146	Whitelam
11.9.88	SD	A	Keighley	W	36-20	Ledger (3), P. Johnson (2), Henderson, Collier	P. Johnson (4)	—	—

MATCH ANALYSIS (continued)

Date	Com-petition	H/A	Opponent	Rlt	Score	Tries	Goals	Atten-dance	Referee
18.9.88	LC(1)	A	Swinton	L	14-24	Cottrell (2)	P. Johnson (3)	—	—
25.9.88	SD	H	Sheffield E.	W	12-8	Dunn, Jeffrey, McCulloch	—	1789	Bowman
2.10.88	SD	A	Carlisle	W	12-10	Platt, Ledger	P. Johnson (2)	—	—
9.10.88	SD	H	Hunslet	W	36-18	McCulloch (3), Dunn (2), Ruane, Ledger, Dean	Platt (2)	2049	Volante
16.10.88	SD	A	Sheffield E.	W	30-17	Dunn (2), Jeffrey, Street, Ruane, C. Johnson	P. Johnson (3)	—	—
23.10.88	SD	H	Whitehaven	W	56-6	Ledger (3), Ruane (2), P. Johnson (2), Moimoi (2), Dunn, Burrill	C. Johnson (6)	2213	Steele
30.12.88	SD	A	York	L	18-37	Ledger (2), P. Johnson	C. Johnson (3)	—	—
6.11.88	SD	H	Mansfield M.	W	48-2	McCulloch (3), Ruane, Moimoi, Street, Platt, Dunn, Round	C. Johnson (6)	1843	Kershaw
13.11.88	JPS(1)	H	Barrow	W	42-14	Ruane (3), Round (2), McCulloch, P. Johnson	C. Johnson (7)	3256	Tickle
20.11.88	SD	H	Bramley	W	40-8	Ledger (2), Jeffrey (2), Platt, Ropati	C. Johnson (8)	2444	Burke
27.11.88	JPS(2)	H	Doncaster	W	40-8	Ledger (3), Street (2), Cottrell, Ropati, C. Johnson	C. Johnson (4)	4321	Whitfield
4.12.88	JPS(3)	A	Bradford N.	L	0-6	—	—	—	—
11.12.88	SD	H	Carlisle	W	24-6	Kerr (2), Jeffrey, Ropati, Ledger	C. Johnson (2)	2073	Whitfield
18.12.88	SD	A	Mansfield M.	W	17-8	Street (2), Kerr	C. Johnson (2, 1 dg),	—	—
26.12.88	SD	A	Chorley B.	W	20-6	Ledger (2), P. Johnson, Moimoi	C. Johnson (2)	—	—
1.1.89	SD	H	Swinton	W	40-12	Jeffrey (3), Kerr (2), Ledger, Dunn, C. Johnson	C. Johnson (4)	3777	Dockray
4.1.89	SD	A	Barrow	L	4-22	Jeffrey	—	—	—
8.1.89	SD	H	Workington T.	W	56-1	Ledger (4), Mann (2), Collier, Ruane, Jeffrey	C. Johnson (10)	2224	Simpson
15.1.89	SD	A	Runcorn H.	W	88-2	Kerr (3), Jeffrey (3), C. Johnson (3), Ledger (2), Ruane (2), Moimoi, Lang, Dunn, Mann	C. Johnson (10)	—	—
22.1.89	SD	H	Keighley	W	20-12	Dunn (2), Ledger	P. Johnson (2), Platt (2)	2511	Morris
29.1.89	CC(1)	A	Sheffield E.	L	17-23	P. Johnson, Ruane, Ropati	C. Johnson (2), P. Johnson (dg)	—	—
5.2.89	SD	A	Rochdale H.	W	50-12	Collier (2), Kerr (2), Burrill (2), Jeffrey, Moimoi, Ruane	C. Johnson (7)	—	—
19.2.89	SD	A	Hunslet	W	40-16	Ruane (3), Platt, Jeffrey, Kerr, Ropati	C. Johnson (6)	—	—
26.2.89	SD	H	Barrow	W	26-18	Ruane (2), Kerr (2), Burrill	C. Johnson (3)	3308	Haigh
12.3.89	SD	H	Rochdale H.	W	34-3	Ruane (2), Mann, Jeffrey, Ledger, Burrill	C. Johnson (4), P. Johnson	2200	Carter
24.3.89	SD	H	Chorley B.	W	14-6	Kerr, Dean, Ruane	C. Johnson	2055	Kendrew
27.3.89	SD	A	Swinton	W	35-24	Kerr (2), Burrill, Dean, C. Johnson	C. Johnson (7, 1dg)	—	—
2.4.89	SD	A	Bramley	W	34-2	Ruane, C. Johnson, Ledger, Round, Street	C. Johnson (7)	—	—
4.4.89	SD	A	Whitehaven	W	25-16	Round, Jeffrey, C. Johnson	C. Johnson (6, 1 dg)	—	—
9.4.89	SD	H	York	W	24-14	C. Johnson (3), Dunn	C. Johnson (4)	2665	Cross
23.4.89	SDP(1)	H	Keighley	W	38-12	Dean (3), Kerr (2), P. Johnson, Platt, Ruane	C. Johnson (3)	2200	Steele
7.5.89	SDP(SF)	H	Swinton	L	8-20	Ledger, Cottrell	—	3959	Whitfield

MANSFIELD MARKSMAN

● **Moved to the Harvey Hadden Stadium in Nottingham for the start of the 1989-90 season, with a change of name to Nottingham City.**

Ground:	Alfreton Sports Stadium
Colours:	Green and yellow
First Season:	1984-85
Chairman:	Paul Tomlinson
General Manager:	David Parker
Coach:	Jim Crellin (Dec 1986-June 1988)
	Billy Platt (July 1988-Dec 1988)
	Steve Nash (Dec 1988-Feb 1989)
	Lee Greenwood (Feb 1989-)
Records:	Attendance: 2,291 v. Wakefield T. (Div. 2) 9 Sep, 1984

Season
Goals: 63 by C. Sanderson, 1984-85
Tries: 13 by S. Nicholson, K. Whiteman, 1984-85
Points: 136 by C. Sanderson, 1984-85

Match
Goals: 7 by B. Holden v. Keighley, 10 Mar, 1985; by W. Sanchez v. Hunslet, 2 Oct, 1988
Tries: 4 by K. Whiteman v. Doncaster, 4 Nov, 1984
Points: 18 by B. Holden v. Keighley, 10 Mar, 1985; M. Howarth v. Dewsbury, 17 Jan, 1988
Highest score: 54-10 v. Doncaster, 1984-85
Highest against: 76-6 v. Leigh, 1985-86

1988-89 PLAYERS' SUMMARY

	App	Tries	Goals	Dr	Pts
Andrews, Brent	19 + 1	—	—	—	—
Ashcroft, John	1 + 2	—	—	—	—
Burgess, Andy	1	—	—	—	—
Campbell, Mark	1 + 1	—	—	—	—
Chadwick, Les	12 + 1	2	—	—	8
Clayforth, Shaun	1	—	—	—	—
Cochrane, Tony	2	—	—	—	—
Cockayne, Phil	5 + 2	—	—	—	—
Davies, Paul	4	1	—	—	4
Duffy, Andy	2 + 3	—	—	—	—
Edge, Phil	17 + 4	2	—	—	8
Fakes, Ian	1	—	—	—	—
Fox, Paul	13 + 2	1	—	—	4
Hitchen, Gary	9	2	2	1	13
Hopkins, Calvin	2	—	—	—	—
Hough, Mick	28 + 2	—	—	—	—
Howarth, Mick	12 + 1	2	17	—	42
Ince, Ian	4	1	—	—	4
Janicwiez, Paul	1	—	—	—	—
Johnson, Willie	16	3	—	1	13
Kellett, Brian	26 + 3	2	—	—	8
Kilner, Shaun	4	1	2	—	8
Langton, Terry	1	1	—	—	4
Madden, Shaun	7 + 2	1	—	—	4
Maguire, Dave	11	—	—	—	—
Maher, Harry	1	—	—	—	—
McLeary, Jack	1	—	—	—	—
Moulden, Darren	25	3	—	—	12
Nash, Steve	1	—	—	—	—
Oates, David	6	1	—	—	4
O'Donnell, Damian	1	—	—	—	—
Platt, Billy	10 + 2	1	1	2	8
Powell, Paul	22	4	—	—	16
Reed, Steve	4	—	—	—	—
Roberts, Carl	2 + 3	—	—	—	—
Rudd, Neil	16 + 2	3	—	—	12
Sanchez, Wayne	11 + 2	3	14	—	40
Sanderson, Mark	11 + 3	—	15	2	32
Sealey, Camrel	5	1	—	—	4
Sheldon, Mick	12 + 4	2	—	—	8
Simpson, Colin	5 + 1	—	5	—	10
Stapleton, John	2	1	—	—	4
Stones, Chris	23 + 2	5	—	1	21
Taylor, Adrian	0 + 1	—	—	—	—
Tuffs, Simon	3	1	—	—	4
Warburton, Joe	7 + 4	2	—	—	8
Wardle, Chris	8	—	—	—	—
Whitehead, Craig	17	3	—	—	12
Woodcock, Darren	1	—	—	—	—
Woolford, Neil	1	1	—	—	4
Zilmann, Andy	8 + 3	—	—	—	—
TOTALS:					
51 players		50	56	7	319

Steve Nash, a three-month stint coaching Mansfield Marksman.

1988-89 MATCH ANALYSIS

Date	Com-petition	H/A	Opponent	Rlt	Score	Tries	Goals	Atten-dance	Referee
28.8.88	SD	H	Huddersfield	W	24-11	Stapleton, Kellett, Ince, Warburton	Simpson (4)	423	Tidball
4.9.88	SD	A	Barrow	L	6-28	Howarth	Simpson	—	—
11.9.88	SD	H	Bramley	L	0-32	—	—	442	Galtress
18.9.88	YC(1)	A	York	L	4-25	Sealey	—	—	—
21.9.88	SD	A	Sheffield E.	L	14-27	Chadwick, Stones	Howarth (3)	—	—
25.9.88	SD	A	Swinton	L	20-36	Platt, Johnson, Edge	Sanchez (4)	—	—
2.10.88	SD	H	Hunslet	W	36-14	Powell (2), Warburton, Edge, Kellett	Sanchez (7), Johnson (dg), Stones (dg)	573	Whitfield
16.10.88	SD	H	Batley	L	6-8	Moulden	Sanchez	611	Houghton
23.10.88	SD	H	Doncaster	L	10-32	Johnson, Moulden	Sanchez	1536	Bowman
30.10.88	SD	H	Swinton	L	2-24	—	Sanchez	782	Tickle
6.11.88	SD	A	Leigh	L	2-48	—	Platt (2 dg)	—	—
13.11.88	JPS(1)	A	Bramley	L	6-32	Stones	Platt	—	—
20.11.88	SD	H	Fulham	W	8-4	Chadwick	Sanderson (2)	313	Smith
27.11.88	SD	H	Dewsbury	L	6-34	Johnson	Sanderson	407	Whitelam
4.12.88	SD	A	Bramley	L	2-36	—	Sanderson	—	—
11.12.88	SD	A	Dewsbury	W	28-18	Howarth, Madden, Moulden, Stones, Sanchez	Howarth (4)	—	—
18.12.88	SD	H	Leigh	L	8-17	Whitehead	Howarth (2)	664	Haigh
26.12.88	SD	A	York	L	4-59	—	Howarth (2)	—	—
2.1.89	SD	H	Sheffield E.	L	10-50	Hitchen, Fox	Howarth	676	Galtress
8.1.89	SD	A	Huddersfield	L	10-20	Stones, Woolford	Howarth	—	—
15.1.89	SD	H	Chorley B.	D	16-16	Tuffs, Sheldon	Howarth (4)	312	Dockray
22.1.89	SD	A	York	L	12-23	Stones, Davies	Hitchen (2)	577	Smith
29.1.89	CC(1)	A	Carlisle	L	1-58	—	Hitchen (dg)	—	—
5.2.89	SD	A	Fulham	L	12-26	Oates, Sheldon	Sanderson (2)	—	—
12.2.89	SD	A	Doncaster	L	12-18	Hitchen, Sanchez	Sanderson (2)	—	—
19.2.89	SD	A	Chorley B.	L	18-28	Rudd, Sanchez, Powell	Sanderson (3)	—	—
26.2.89	SD	A	Batley	L	3-30	—	Sanderson (1, 1dg)	—	—
5.3.89	SD	A	Hunslet	L	15-32	Kilner, Rudd	Sanderson (3, 1dg)	—	—
12.3.89	SD	H	Barrow	L	12-36	Rudd, Whitehead, Powell	—	262	Simpson
19.3.89	SD	A	Keighley	L	6-38	Whitehead	Kilner	—	—
6.4.89	SD	H	Keighley	L	6-24	Langton	Kilner	264	Steele

OLDHAM

Ground: Watersheddings
Colours: Red and white
First Season: 1895-96
Nickname: Roughyeds
Chairman: Harvey Ashworth
Secretary: Anita Lees
Coach: Eric Fitzsimons (June 1987-Nov 1988)
Tony Barrow (Nov 1988-)
Honours: **Championship** Winners, 1909-10, 1910-11, 1956-57
Beaten finalists, 1906-07, 1907-08, 1908-09, 1921-22, 1954-55
Division One Champions, 1904-05
Division Two Champions, 1963-64, 1981-82, 1987-88
Second Division Premiership Winners, 1987-88
Challenge Cup Winners, 1898-99, 1924-25, 1926-27
Beaten finalists, 1906-07, 1911-12, 1923-24, 1925-26
Lancashire League Winners, 1897-98, 1900-01, 1907-08, 1909-10, 1921-22, 1956-57, 1957-58
Lancashire Cup Winners, 1907-08, 1910-11, 1913-14, 1919-20, 1924-25, 1933-34, 1956-57, 1957-58, 1958-59
Beaten finalists, 1908-09, 1911-12, 1918-19, 1921-22, 1954-55, 1966-67, 1968-69, 1986-87
Records: Attendance: 28,000 v. Huddersfield (League) 24 Feb, 1912
Season
Goals: 200 by B. Ganley, 1957-58
Tries: 49 by R. Farrar, 1921-22
Points: 412 by B. Ganley, 1957-58
Match
Goals: 14 by B. Ganley v. Liverpool C., 4 Apr, 1959
Tries: 7 by Miller v. Barry, 31 Oct, 1908
Points: 30 by A. Johnson v. Widnes, 9 Apr, 1928
Highest score: 67-6 v. Liverpool C., 1958-59
Highest against: 67-11 v. Hull K.R., 1978-79

1988-89 PLAYERS' SUMMARY

	App	Tries	Goals	Dr	Pts
Allen, Shaun	6	1	—	—	4
Atkinson, Keith	3 + 3	—	8	—	16
Bardsley, Mick	7 + 1	3	—	—	12
Bates, Ian	7 + 2	—	—	—	—
Blenheim, Graham	2 + 1	1	—	—	4
Burke, Mick	7	1	17	—	38
Casey, Leo	24 + 3	7	—	—	28
Clawson, Neil	20 + 5	—	—	—	—
Cogger, John	7	—	6	—	24
Croston, Trevor	7 + 5	—	—	—	—
Cummins, Shane	0 + 1	—	—	—	—
Fairbank, John	6 + 4	2	—	—	8
Flanagan, Neil	1	—	—	—	—
Flanagan, Terry	10 + 5	—	—	—	—
Ford, Mike	27	3	—	—	12
Foy, Des	5	2	—	—	8
Gilbert, Ashley	7 + 1	4	—	—	16
Hall, Martin	2	—	—	—	—
Hawkyard, Colin	11 + 5	4	—	—	16
Henderson, John	22	8	—	—	32
Hyde, Gary	13 + 1	4	1	—	18
Irving, Richard	4 + 1	2	—	—	8
Lord, Mark	3	—	—	—	—
Lord, Paul	12 + 3	9	—	—	36
Marsden, Bob	1 + 3	—	—	—	—
McAlister, Charlie	17 + 1	3	20	—	52
Meadows, Kevin	21 + 4	7	—	—	28
Morrison, Tony	4 + 1	—	—	—	—
Nadiole, Tom	1 + 1	—	—	—	—
Newton, Keith	13	4	—	—	16
O'Sullivan, Chris	22	5	1	4	26
Patterson, Steve	2 + 1	—	—	—	—
Platt, Duncan	15	4	41	—	98
Robinson, Steve	21 + 2	8	—	—	32
Round, Paul	29 + 1	9	—	—	36
Ruane, Andy	30	4	11	4	42
Sherratt, Ian	16 + 1	1	—	—	4
Taylor, Paul	9	1	—	—	4
Waddell, Hugh	2	—	—	—	—

TOTALS:
39 players		103	99	8	618

Paul Round, nine tries in 30 games.

1988-89 MATCH ANALYSIS

Date	Com-petition	H/A	Opponent	Rlt	Score	Tries	Goals	Atten-dance	Referee
28.8.88	SBC	A	Wigan	L	18-40	Lord, Hawkyard, Irving	McAlister (3)	—	—
4.9.88	SBC	H	Leeds	L	22-28	Meadows (2), Foy, Ford	McAlister (2), Burke	6599	Allatt
11.9.88	SBC	A	Featherstone R.	L	14-18	Casey, Taylor	Atkinson (2), McAlister	—	—
18.9.88	LC(1)	H	Workington T.	W	64-2	Meadows (3), Round, Foy, Hawkyard, Gilbert, O'Sullivan, Ford, Blenheim	Burke (10), Ruane (2)	3877	Houghton
25.9.88	SBC	A	Castleford	L	19-22	Round, Henderson, Gilbert	Ruane (3, 1dg)	—	—
28.9.88	LC(2)	H	Salford	L	2-18	—	Ruane	5497	Allatt
2.10.88	SBC	H	Hull K.R.	W	30-16	Gilbert (2), Hawkyard, Casey, Burke	Burke (4), Ruane	4298	Volante
9.10.88	SBC	A	Wakefield T.	D	12-12	Fairbank, Robinson	Burke (2)	—	—
16.10.88	SBC	A	Salford	L	20-38	Hawkyard, Robinson, Bardsley, Round	Ruane (2)	—	—
23.10.88	SBC	H	St. Helens	L	22-26	Henderson, Round, Bardsley, Sherratt, Meadows	Ruane	6658	Simpson
6.11.88	SBC	A	Warrington	L	30-32	Casey (2), Fairbank, McAlister, Henderson	McAlister (5)	—	—
13.11.88	JPS(1)	A	Warrington	L	14-21	Robinson	McAlister (5)	—	—
20.11.88	SBC	H	Halifax	L	12-14	Henderson, Round	McAlister (2)	7041	Tennant
4.12.88	SBC	A	Halifax	W	12-0	Round, McAlister	Platt (2)	—	—
11.12.88	SBC	H	Warrington	W	16-2	Platt, O'Sullivan	Platt (4)	5557	Cross
18.12.88	SBC	A	Hull	L	8-11	Bardsley	Platt, Hyde	—	—
26.12.88	SBC	H	Salford	W	23-22	Hyde, O'Sullivan, Lord	Atkinson (5), O'Sullivan (dg)	6406	Holdsworth
1.1.89	SBC	A	Leeds	L	4-48	Henderson	—	—	—
15.1.89	SBC	A	Hull K.R.	L	6-34	P. Lord	Atkinson	—	—
22.1.89	SBC	H	Bradford N.	L	14-30	Henderson (2)	Platt (3)	5932	Simpson
29.1.89	CC(1)	A	Dewsbury	W	40-9	Newton (2), Platt (2), Round, Robinson, Ruane	Platt (5), O'Sullivan	—	—
5.2.89	SBC	A	Widnes	L	14-38	O'Sullivan, Hyde	Platt (2), O'Sullivan (2dg)	—	—
12.2.89	CC(2)	A	Sheffield E.	W	32-20	O'Sullivan, Henderson, Hyde, Round, Ruane	Platt (5), Ruane (2dg)	—	—
19.2.89	SBC	H	Hull	W	9-7	Ruane	Platt (2), O'Sullivan (dg)	5155	Tennant
25.2.89	CC(3)	H	Wigan	L	4-12	Lord	—	9402	Carter
1.3.89	SBC	A	St. Helens	L	12-58	Casey, Meadows	Platt (2)	—	—
5.3.89	SBC	H	Featherstone R.	W	40-18	Cogger (3), Newton (2), Casey, Round, Robinson	Platt (4)	4752	Cross
19.3.89	SBC	H	Wakefield T.	W	24-8	Lord (2), Irving, Ford, McAlister	Platt (2)	5572	Galtress
22.3.89	SBC	H	Widnes	L	16-35	Robinson, Cogger Allen	McAlister (2)	6776	Tennant
27.3.89	SBC	H	Wigan	L	21-27	Robinson, Ruane, Lord	Platt (4), Ruane (dg)	6841	Holdsworth
9.4.89	SBC	H	Castleford	W	34-18	Cogger (2), Lord (2), Hyde, Platt	Platt (5)	4562	Haigh
12.4.89	SBC	A	Bradford N.	L	10-30	Robinson, Casey	Ruane	—	—

ROCHDALE HORNETS

Ground:	Spotland
Colours:	White, blue and red
First Season:	1895-96
Nickname:	Hornets
Chairman:	Len Stansfield
Secretary:	Paul Reynolds
Coach:	Eric Hughes (June 1987-June 1988) Jim Crellin (June 1988-)

Honours: **Challenge Cup** Winners, 1921-22
Lancashire League Winners, 1918-19
Lancashire Cup Winners, 1911-12, 1914-15, 1918-19
Beaten finalists, 1912-13, 1919-20, 1965-66
John Player Trophy Beaten finalists 1973-74
BBC2 Floodlit Trophy Beaten finalists 1971-72

Records: Attendance: 41,831 Wigan v. Oldham (RL Cup Final) 12 Apr 1924
Home: 26,664 v. Oldham (RL Cup) 25 Mar, 1922
Season
Goals: 115 by K. Harcombe, 1985-86
Tries: 30 by J. Williams, 1934-35
Points: 243 by S. Turner, 1988-89
Match
Goals: 10 by H. Lees v. Glasshoughton, 19 Feb, 1938
Tries: 5 by J. Corsi v. Barrow, 31 Dec, 1921 and v. Broughton Moor, 25 Feb, 1922; J. Williams v. St. Helens, 4 Apr, 1933; N. Brelsford v. Whitehaven, 3 Sep, 1972
Points: 27 by F. Blincow v. Normanton, 17 Oct, 1903
Highest score: 75-13 v. Broughton M., 1914-15
Highest against: 79-2 v. Hull, 1920-21

1988-89 PLAYERS' SUMMARY

	App	Tries	Goals	Dr	Pts
Bamber, Simon	15 + 1	2	—	—	8
Brierley, Craig	0 + 1	—	—	—	—
Brown, David	13 + 3	—	—	—	—
Brown, Jeff	4	1	—	—	4
Causey, Mark	14 + 1	5	—	—	20
Chadwick, Les	10	6	—	—	24
Charnock, Les	3	—	1	—	2
Clucas, Geoff	4 + 4	—	—	—	—
Cowie, Neil	31	5	—	—	20
Derbyshire, Alan	15 + 1	1	—	1	5
Dobson, Mark	1 + 2	—	—	—	—
Duffy, Andy	0 + 1	—	—	—	—
Edwards, Anthony	27	11	—	—	44
Edwards, Jeff	16 + 1	6	1	—	26
Edwards, Logan	20	9	—	—	36
Fairhurst, Alan	12 + 1	—	—	1	1
Gamble, Paul	8 + 4	—	—	—	—
Garrett, Colin	1	—	—	—	—
Garritty, Brian	15 + 1	5	—	—	20
Geldard, Steve	1	—	—	—	—
Higgins, Brian	4	—	—	—	—
Higgins, John	7 + 2	2	—	—	8
Hoare, Shaun	5 + 1	2	—	—	8
Lowe, Kevin	29	1	—	—	4
Myler, Chris	22 + 2	13	4	—	60
Nanyn, Mick	0 + 5	1	—	—	4
Sanderson, Mark	8 + 10	—	—	—	—
Sawyer, Aaron	13 + 4	8	—	1	33
Scott, Alan	13 + 1	1	4	—	12
Sealey, Camrel	17	4	—	—	16
Simcott, Stuart	13 + 4	3	—	—	12
Tupeae, Shane	1	—	—	—	—
Turner, Steve	28 + 3	9	103	1	243
Williams, Dean	22 + 1	19	—	—	76
Wilson, Walter	8	3	3	—	18
Wood, David	29 + 2	9	3	—	42

TOTALS:
	App	Tries	Goals	Dr	Pts
36 players		126	119	4	746

1988-89 MATCH ANALYSIS

Date	Com-petition	H/A	Opponent	Rlt	Score	Tries	Goals	Atten-dance	Referee
28.8.88	SD	H	Barrow	W	36-26	Williams (2), Cowie, Turner, Myler, Hoare	Turner (6)	1088	Spencer
4.9.88	SD	A	Huddersfield	W	22-16	Turner (2), Williams, Myler	Turner (3)	—	—
11.9.88	SD	H	Whitehaven	W	36-24	Williams (4), Hoare, Causey	Turner (6)	1002	Steele
18.9.88	LC(1)	H	Fulham	W	25-14	Sawyer (2), Brown, Nanyn	Turner (4), Fairhurst (dg)	645	Bowman
25.9.88	SD	H	Keighley	L	22-28	T. Edwards (2), J. Edwards, Causey	Turner (3)	1420	Burke
28.9.88	LC(2)	A	Wigan	L	4-36	Sawyer	—	—	—
2.10.88	SD	A	Whitehaven	L	8-38	J. Edwards	J. Edwards, Charnock	—	—
9.10.88	SD	A	Dewsbury	L	34-36	Wood, T. Edwards, Sawyer, Wilson (2), Cowie	Turner (5)	—	—
16.10.88	SD	H	Chorley B.	W	28-25	Sawyer, J. Edwards, Williams, Wood	Turner (3), Wood (3)	983	Whitelam
23.10.88	SD	A	Barrow	L	8-26	Sawyer	Wilson (2)	—	—
30.10.88	SD	A	Batley	L	14-39	T. Edwards, Causey	Turner (2), Wilson	—	—
6.11.88	SD	H	Huddersfield	W	54-16	Sawyer (2), Williams (2), Lowe, Wood, Simcott, T. Edwards, L. Edwards	Turner (9)	765	Carter
13.11.88	JPS(1)	H	Whitehaven	W	26-20	Sealey, Simcott, Wood, Williams, Wilson	Turner (3)	888	Morris
20.11.88	SD	A	Runcorn H.	W	28-10	Williams (2), Cowie, Myler	Turner (6)	—	—
27.11.88	JPS(2)	A	Wakefield T.	L	12-38	J. Edwards, Sealey	Turner (2)	—	—
11.12.88	SD	H	Batley	W	32-8	Williams (3), L. Edwards, J. Edwards	Turner (6)	903	Kershaw
18.12.88	SD	A	Workington T.	L	8-10	L. Edwards	Turner (2)	—	—
26.12.88	SD	H	Swinton	L	8-30	Wood, Myler	—	1480	Whitfield
1.1.89	SD	A	Fulham	W	20-10	Myler (2), J. Edwards, L. Edwards	Scott (2)	—	—
8.1.89	SD	H	Runcorn H.	W	36-6	Williams (2), T. Edwards, Simcott, Turner, Wood, L. Edwards	Myler (3), Turner	810	Tickle
15.1.89	SD	A	Keighley	L	16-36	T. Edwards (2)	Turner (4)	—	—
22.1.89	SD	A	Carlisle	L	12-44	Williams, Turner, Myler	—	—	—
29.1.89	CC(1)	H	Hull K.R.	L	24-28	L. Edwards (2), Causey (2)	Turner (3), Sawyer (dg), Derbyshire (dg)	1625	Kershaw
5.2.89	SD	H	Leigh	L	12-50	Wood, Bamber	Scott (2)	1572	Cross
19.2.89	SD	H	Workington T.	W	42-20	Garrity (2), Myler, Chadwick, Bamber, Scott, Higgins	Turner (7)	753	Morris
26.2.89	SD	A	Doncaster	W	28-18	Turner (3), Garrity	Turner (6)	—	—
5.3.89	SD	H	Dewsbury	W	32-30	T. Edwards (2), Wood, Cowie, L. Edwards, Garrity	Turner (4)	936	Tidball
12.3.89	SD	A	Leigh	L	3-34	—	Turner (1, 1dg)	—	—
24.3.89	SD	A	Swinton	L	6-26	Turner	Turner	—	—
27.3.89	SD	A	Chorley B.	W	22-15	Chadwick (2), L. Edwards, Garrity	Turner (3)	—	—
2.4.89	SD	H	Doncaster	W	44-18	Myler (4), Chadwick (2), Sealey, Wood	Turner (5), Myler	1049	Campbell (Pr)
6.4.89	SD	H	Fulham	W	26-12	Myler, T. Edwards, Chadwick, Higgins	Turner (5)	701	Bowman
16.4.89	SD	H	Carlisle	L	18-26	Cowie, Derbyshire, Sealey	Turner (3)	979	Whitelam

RUNCORN HIGHFIELD

Ground:	Canal Street
Colours:	Black
First Season:	1922-23 as Wigan Highfield. Became London Highfield in 1933-34. Became Liverpool Stanley in 1934-35 and changed to Liverpool City in 1951-52. Became Huyton in 1968-69 and changed to Runcorn Highfield in 1984-85. There was also a Liverpool City in 1906-07
Chairman:	Terry Hughes
Secretary:	Ian Swann
Coach:	Bill Ashurst (Apr 1987-Jan 1989) John Cogger (Jan 1989-Feb 1989) Geoff Fletcher (Feb 1989-Apr 1989)
Honours:	**Lancashire League** Winners, 1935-36
Records:	Attendance: 14,000 v. Widnes (Championship semi-final) 2 May, 1936 at Prescott Road

Season
Goals: 126 by P. Wood, 1984-85
Tries: 28 by J. Maloney, 1930-31
Points: 240 by P. Wood, 1984-85

Match
Goals: 11 by P. Wood v. Batley, 21 Oct, 1984
Tries: 5 by J. Maloney v. Bramley, 25 Apr, 1931
Points: 24 by T. Rose v. Workington T., 4 Oct, 1987
Highest score: 59-11 v. Bramley, 1933-34
Highest against: 92-2 v. Wigan, 1988-89

1988-89 PLAYERS' SUMMARY

	App	Tries	Goals	Dr	Pts
Ashall, Paul	4	—	—	—	—
Ashcroft, Keith	6 + 6	—	—	—	—
Ashurst, Bill	0 + 1	—	—	—	—
Barrow, Norman	1	—	1	—	2
Booth, John	16 + 1	—	—	—	—
Brogan, Mick	1	—	—	—	—
Campbell, Danny	22	—	—	—	—
Caunce, Tommy	6 + 1	—	—	—	—
Cogger, John	19 + 1	7	—	—	28
Cooney, Paul	9 + 1	—	1	—	2
Crompton, David	11 + 2	2	—	—	8
Daley, Arthur	1 + 1	—	—	—	—
Dean, Geoff	28	1	—	—	4
Dooley, Jim	16	—	—	—	—
Durnin, Paul	17	3	—	—	12
Dwyer, Mark	0 + 1	—	—	—	—
Fairclough, Dave	5	—	2	—	4
Fenney, Steve	6	1	1	—	6
Fildes, Tony	10	1	—	—	4
Fitzpatrick, Paul	11	—	—	—	—
Fraser, Paul	14 + 3	—	—	—	—
Gauchwin, Steve	11 + 1	1	—	—	4
Gerrard, Steve	5	—	—	—	—
Glover, Mick	9 + 1	—	—	—	—
Greenall, Billy	3	—	—	—	—
Gunning, Phil	7 + 3	1	3	—	10
Hammond, Gary	5	—	—	—	—
Henney, Harold	6 + 4	—	—	—	—
Hunt, David	8 + 1	1	—	—	4
Hunter, Clive	1	—	—	—	—
Jackson, Tony	11	2	1	—	10
Jones, Charles	20 + 2	1	—	—	4
Langley, Tony	1	—	—	—	—
Leadbetter, Dave	2	—	—	—	—
Lunt, Richard	1	—	—	—	—
Malloy, Frank	2	—	—	—	—
Manning, David	2	—	—	—	—
Middlehurst, Chris	7 + 1	1	12	3	31
Milner, John	6 + 3	1	—	—	4
Moffit, Ian	1	—	—	—	—
Moylan, Steve	4	—	—	—	—
Muller, Roby	4 + 1	1	—	—	4
Nanyn, Mick	5 + 1	—	—	—	—
Parkes, Brian	1	—	—	—	—
Phillips, Joe	2 + 2	—	—	—	—
Pojunas, Chris	3 + 1	1	—	—	4
Prescott, Eric	10 + 2	2	—	—	8
Rawlinson, Tom	12	—	—	—	—
Roberts, Paul	10	2	1	—	10
Rose, Terry	3	—	—	—	—
Seabrook, Derek	1 + 1	—	—	—	—
Shaw, Mark	10	3	2	1	17
Shovelton, Stuart	1	—	—	—	—
Simm, Stephen	2 + 2	—	—	—	—
Smith, Ian	7	5	1	—	22
Tinsley, Eddie	1	—	—	—	—
Walls, Dave	8 + 5	1	—	—	4
Walsh, Dave	2	—	—	—	—
Wood, Peter	4	—	9	—	18
Trialists		4	—	—	16

TOTALS:
59 players		42	34	4	240

1988-89 MATCH ANALYSIS

Date	Com-petition	H/A	Opponent	Rlt	Score	Tries	Goals	Atten-dance	Referee
28.8.88	SD	A	Dewsbury	L	20-28	Smith, Crompton, Shaw	Middlehurst (3, 1dg), Shaw (1dg)	—	—
4.9.88	SD	A	Leigh	L	14-48	Shaw, Jones, Smith	Middlehurst	—	—
11.9.88	SD	H	Batley	W	31-28	Jackson (2), Cogger, Shaw, Smith	Wood (5), Middlehurst (dg)	350	Bowman
14.9.88	SD	A	Swinton	L	2-56	—	Wood	—	—
18.9.88	LC(1)	H	Warrington	L	4-42	Prescott	—	2017	Burke
25.9.88	SD	H	Doncaster	L	10-18	Gunning	Wood (3)	321	Steele
9.10.88	SD	H	Whitehaven	L	12-28	Durnin, Pojunas	Middlehurst (2)	241	Houghton
16.10.88	SD	A	Whitehaven	L	6-16	Trialist	Shaw	—	—
23.10.88	SD	A	Carlisle	L	10-30	Crompton, Smith	Shaw	—	—
30.10.88	SD	H	Fulham	W	20-12	Hunt, Middlehurst, Trialist	Middlehurst (4)	315	Whitfield
6.11.88	SD	A	Chorley B.	L	13-22	Smith, Muller	Middlehurst (2, 1dg)	—	—
13.11.88	JPS(1)	H (Wigan)	Wigan	L	2-92	—	Fenney	(7233)	Carter
20.11.88	SD	H	Rochdale H.	L	10-28	Durnin, Cogger	Jackson	325	Haigh
4.12.88	SD	A	Batley	L	0-34	—	—	—	—
11.12.88	SD	H	Huddersfield	L	4-25	Walls	—	240	Morris
18.12.88	SD	A	Barrow	L	6-36	Cogger	Gunning	—	—
26.12.88	SD	A	Huddersfield	L	0-53	—	—	162	Haigh
1.1.89	SD	H	Chorley B.	L	2-56	—	Gunning	—	—
8.1.89	SD	A	Rochdale H.	L	6-36	Fenney	Gunning	900	Kershaw`
15.1.89	SD	H	Leigh	L	2-88	—	Roberts	200	Dockray
22.1.89	SD	H	Workington T.	D	8-8	Cogger, Fildes	—	428	Holgate
29.1.89	CC(1)	H	Keighley	L	10-28	Cogger (2)	Smith	—	—
5.2.89	SD	A	Doncaster	L	12-48	Roberts, Cogger, Gauchwin	—	414	Houghton
19.2.89	SD	H	Swinton	L	10-30	Trialist (2)	Barrow	200	Smith
26.2.89	SD	A	Fulham	L	4-28	Dean	—	—	—
5.3.89	SD	H	Carlisle	L	4-48	Prescott	—	160	Dockray
12.3.89	SD	A	Workington T.	L	0-10	—	—	200	Bowman
19.3.89	SD	H	Dewsbury	L	8-8	Durnin	Fairclough (2)	—	—
24.3.89	SD	H	Keighley	L	6-34	Milner	Cooney	150	Kendrew
9.4.89	SD	A	Keighley	L	4-42	Roberts	—		
16.4.89	SD	H	Barrow	L	0-60	—	—		

ST. HELENS

Ground: Knowsley Road
Colours: Red and white
First Season: 1895-96
Nickname: Saints
Chairman: Joe Pickavance
Secretary: Geoff Sutcliffe
Coach: Alex Murphy (Nov 1985-)
Honours: **Championship** Winners, 1931-32,
              1952-53, 1958-59, 1965-66, 1969-70,
              1970-71
              Beaten finalists, 1964-65, 1966-67,
              1971-72
              Division One Champions, 1974-75
              League Leaders Trophy Winners,
              1964-65, 1965-66
              Club Championship (Merit Table)
              Beaten finalists, 1973-74
              Challenge Cup Winners, 1955-56,
              1960-61, 1965-66, 1971-72, 1975-76
              Beaten finalists, 1896-97, 1914-15,
              1929-30, 1952-53, 1977-78, 1986-87,
              1988-89
              Lancashire Cup Winners, 1926-27,
              1953-54, 1960-61, 1961-62, 1962-63,
              1963-64, 1964-65, 1967-68, 1968-69,
              1984-85
              Beaten finalists, 1932-33, 1952-53,
              1956-57, 1958-59, 1959-60, 1970-71,
              1982-83
              Lancashire League Winners,
              1929-30, 1931-32, 1952-53, 1959-60,
              1964-65, 1965-66, 1966-67, 1968-69
              John Player Trophy Winners,
              1987-88
              Premiership Winners, 1975-76,
              1976-77, 1984-85
              Beaten finalists, 1974-75, 1987-88
              Western Division Championship
              Winners, 1963-64
              BBC2 Floodlit Trophy Winners,
              1971-72, 1975-76
              Beaten finalists, 1965-66, 1968-69,
              1970-71, 1977-78, 1978-79
Records: Attendance: 35,695 v. Wigan
              (League) 26 Dec, 1949
              Season
              Goals: 214 by K. Coslett, 1971-72
              Tries: 62 by T. Van Vollenhoven,
              1958-59
              Points: 452 by K. Coslett, 1971-72

Match
Goals: 16 by P. Loughlin v.
Carlisle, 14 Sep, 1986
Tries: 6 by A. Ellaby v. Barrow,
5 Mar, 1932; S. Llewellyn v.
Castleford, 3 Mar, 1956 and v.
Liverpool C., 20 Aug, 1956;
T. Vollenhoven v. Wakefield T.,
21 Dec, 1957 and v. Blackpool B.,
23 Apr, 1962; F. Myler v.
Maryport, 1 Sep, 1969; S. Cooper
v. Hull, 17 Feb, 1988
Points: 40 by P. Loughlin v.
Carlisle, 14 Sep, 1986
Highest score: 112-0 v. Carlisle,
1986-87
Highest against: 78-3 v.
Warrington, 1908-09

1988-89 PLAYERS' SUMMARY

	App	Tries	Goals	Dr	Pts
Allen, Shaun	6 + 8	1	—	—	4
Arkwright, Chris	0 + 4	—	—	—	—
Bailey, Mark	9 + 2	4	—	—	16
Bloor, Darren	22 + 5	7	—	1	29
Burke, Tony	35	2	—	—	8
Carrington, Mike	9	2	—	—	8
Connolly, Gary	13	1	—	—	4
Cooper, Shane	35	14	—	—	56
Cosgrove, David	4 + 3	—	—	—	—
Doherty, Paul	2 + 1	3	—	—	12
Donegan, Austin	2 + 1	1	—	—	4
Dwyer, Bernard	30 + 2	7	—	—	28
Evans, Stuart	19 + 2	2	—	—	8
Fieldhouse, John	14 + 3	1	—	—	4
Forber, Paul	21 + 3	6	2	—	28
Groves, Paul	27	2	—	—	8
Haggerty, Roy	26 + 7	2	—	2	10
Harrison, John	12 + 3	—	—	—	—
Holding, Neil	20 + 6	6	—	3	27
Hunte, Paul	8	4	—	—	16
Jones, Paul	1 + 5	—	—	—	—
Large, David	0 + 1	—	—	1	1
Lee, Mark	4	—	—	1	1
Loughlin, Paul	33	5	109	—	238
McCormick, Kevin	9	1	—	—	4
O'Connor, Michael	18	7	7	—	42
Price, Phil	0 + 1	—	—	—	—
Quirk, Les	37	24	—	—	96
Tanner, David	24 + 2	3	11	—	34
Vautin, Paul	21	4	—	—	16
Veivers, Phil	33 + 3	7	—	—	28

TOTALS:
31 players		116	129	7	729

1988-89 MATCH ANALYSIS

Date	Com- petition	H/A	Opponent	Rlt	Score	Tries	Goals	Atten- dance	Referee
28.8.88	SBC	H	Bradford N.	W	23-16	Quirk, Holding, Forber	Loughlin (5), Haggerty (dg)	7715	Whitfield
4.9.88	SBC	A	Warrington	W	25-14	Cooper (2), Bailey	Loughlin (6), Lee (dg)	—	—
11.9.88	SBC	H	Castleford	D	14-14	McCormack, Veivers	Loughlin (3)	8202	Volante
18.9.88	LC(1)	A	Widnes	L	24-32	Burke, Allen, Evans, Cooper	Loughlin (4)	—	—
25.9.88	SBC	A	Leeds	L	0-32	—	—	—	—
2.10.88	SBC	H	Wakefield T.	W	30-14	Doherty, Dwyer, Bloor, Quirk, Forber	Tanner (5)	7306	Kendrew
9.10.88	SBC	A	Hull K.R.	W	30-22	Doherty (2), Veivers, Quirk, Tanner, Vautin	Tanner (3)	—	—
16.10.88	SBC	H	Hull	L	9-20	Fieldhouse	Loughlin (2), Bloor (dg)	9036	Spencer
23.10.88	SBC	A	Oldham	W	26-22	Bloor, Dwyer, Carrington, Burke	Loughlin (5)	—	—
6.11.88	SBC	H	Salford	W	30-14	Cooper (2), Forber, Dwyer, Loughlin	Loughlin (5)	8420	Allatt
13.11.88	JPS(1)	A	York	W	14-6	Bloor, Loughlin	Loughlin (3)	—	—
20.11.88	SBC	A	Castleford	L	12-46	O'Connor, Quirk	Loughlin (2)	—	—
27.11.88	JPS(2)	H	Hull	W	16-13	Quirk, O'Connor	Loughlin (4)	7485	Volante
4.12.88	JPS(3)	H	Wakefield T.	W	34-18	Vautin, Veivers, Forber, Dwyer, Cooper	Loughlin (7)	7602	Tennant
10.12.88	JPS(SF)	Wigan	Widnes	L	18-20	Quirk (2)	Loughlin (5)	(6755)	Haigh
13.12.88	SBC	A	Hull	L	12-21	Dwyer, Carrington	Loughlin (2)	—	—
18.12.88	SBC	H	Halifax	W	50-16	O'Connor (2), Quirk (2), Loughlin, Tanner, Bloor, Cooper, Holding	O'Connor (6), Loughlin	7294	Holdsworth
26.12.88	SBC	H	Wigan	L	11-18	Haggerty	Loughlin (3), Holding (dg)	21,509	Tennant
1.1.89	SBC	A	Widnes	L	22-29	Groves, Quirk, Vautin	Loughlin (5)	—	—
8.1.89	SBC	H	Leeds	W	15-6	Quirk, O'Connor	Loughlin (3), Haggerty (dg)	11,294	Steele
15.1.89	SBC	A	Featherstone R.	L	12-13	Quirk, Evans	Loughlin (2)	—	—
22.1.89	SBC	H	Hull K.R.	W	29-0	O'Connor (2), Holding, Quirk, Cooper	Loughlin (4), Holding (dg)	7590	Haigh
29.1.89	CC(1)	A	Swinton	W	16-5	Holding, Cooper, Quirk	Loughlin, O'Connor	—	—
12.2.89	CC(2)	H	Barrow	W	28-6	Groves, Cooper, Veivers, Quirk, Forber	Loughlin (4)	8661	Kendrew
19.2.89	SBC	A	Bradford N.	W	16-12	Quirk, Bailey, Cooper	Loughlin (2)	—	—
26.2.89	CC(3)	H	Featherstone R.	W	32-3	Tanner, Veivers, Quirk, Bloor, Holding, Dwyer	Loughlin (4)	11,063	Whitfield
1.3.89	SBC	H	Oldham	W	58-12	Quirk (3), Veivers (2), Hunte (2), Holding, Bloor, Vautin, Connolly	Loughlin (7)	6690	Haigh
11.3.89	CC(SF)	Wigan	Widnes	W	16-14	Quirk (2), Bloor	Loughlin (2)	(17,119)	Holdsworth
14.3.89	SBC	A	Salford	L	4-22	—	Loughlin (2)	—	—
19.3.89	SBC	H	Featherstone R.	L	10-31	Donegan, Cooper	Loughlin	6505	Haigh
27.3.89	SBC	H	Widnes	L	16-44	Cooper	Loughlin (6)	16,009	Galtress
2.4.89	SBC	A	Wakefield T.	L	14-21	Cooper, Bailey, Quirk	Loughlin	—	—
9.4.89	SBC	H	Warrington	W	30-16	Loughlin (2), Forber, Haggerty	Loughlin (7)	8701	Holdsworth
12.4.89	SBC	A	Wigan	L	7-14	Hunte	Loughlin, Holding (dg)	—	—
16.4.89	SBC	A	Halifax	L	8-40	Hunte, Quirk	—	—	—
23.4.89	PT(1)	A	Wigan	W	4-2	—	Forber (2)	—	—
29.4.89	CC(F)	Wem- bley	Wigan	L	0-27	—	—	(78,000)	Tennant
7.5.89	PT(SF)	A	Widnes	L	14-38	Dwyer, Bailey	Tanner (3)	—	—

77

SALFORD

Ground:	The Willows
Colours:	Red and white
First Season:	1896-97
Nickname:	Red Devils
Chairman:	John Wilkinson
Secretary:	Graham McCarty
Coach:	Kevin Ashcroft (May 1984-)
Honours:	**Championship** Winners, 1913-14, 1932-33, 1936-37, 1938-39 Beaten finalists, 1933-34
	Division One Champions, 1973-74, 1975-76
	Challenge Cup Winners, 1937-38 Beaten finalists, 1899-1900, 1901-02, 1902-03, 1905-06, 1938-39, 1968-69
	Lancashire League Winners, 1932-33, 1933-34, 1934-35, 1936-37, 1938-39
	Lancashire Cup Winners, 1931-32, 1934-35, 1935-36, 1936-37, 1972-73 Beaten finalists, 1929-30, 1938-39, 1973-74, 1974-75, 1975-76, 1988-89
	Premiership Beaten finalists, 1975-76
	John Player Trophy Beaten finalists 1972-73
	BBC2 Floodlit Trophy Winners, 1974-75
Records:	Attendance: 26,470 v. Warrington (RL Cup) 13 Feb, 1937

Season
Goals: 221 by D. Watkins, 1972-73
Tries: 46 by K. Fielding, 1973-74
Points: 493 by D. Watkins, 1972-73
Match
Goals: 13 by A. Risman v. Bramley, 5 Apr, 1933 and v. Broughton R., 18 May, 1940; D. Watkins v. Keighley, 7 Jan, 1972; S. Rule v. Doncaster, 4 Sep, 1981
Tries: 6 by F. Miles v. Lees, 5 Mar, 1898; E. Bone v. Goole, 29 Mar, 1902; J. Hilton v. Leigh, 7 Oct, 1939
Points: 39 by J. Lomas v. Liverpool C., 2 Feb, 1907

Highest score: 78-0 v. Liverpool C., 1906-07
Highest against: 63-5 v. Wigan, 1924-25

1988-89 PLAYERS' SUMMARY

	App	Tries	Goals	Dr	Pts
Bentley, Keith	27 + 3	15	—	1	61
Blease, Ian	26 + 2	4	—	—	16
Bloor, Darren	2 + 1	—	—	—	—
Bragger, Ian	19	—	14	—	56
Brown, Peter	14 + 2	1	17	—	38
Bullough, David	1 + 6	—	—	—	—
Burgess, Andy	0 + 3	—	—	—	—
Cairns, David	32	2	—	2	10
Evans, Tex	20	7	—	—	28
Gibson, Steve	31	13	—	—	52
Glynn, Peter	0 + 1	—	—	—	—
Gormley, Ian	26 + 1	4	—	—	16
Hadley, Adrian	22 + 1	9	3	—	42
Herbert, Steve	32	2	—	—	8
Horo, Mark	20	4	—	—	16
Jones, Ken	14 + 5	6	22	—	68
Kerry, Steve	15 + 1	8	30	—	92
Major, David	7 + 7	—	—	—	—
McTigue, Mick	11 + 4	1	—	—	4
Mercer, Andy	5 + 5	—	—	—	—
Moran, Mark	22 + 1	2	—	—	8
O'Loughlin, Jason	0 + 2	—	—	—	—
O'Loughlin, Keiron	2 + 1	—	—	—	—
Shaw, Paul	15 + 1	2	—	—	8
Walsh, Joe	1	—	—	—	—
Whiteley, Chris	3	—	—	—	—
Williams, Peter	24	10	—	—	40
Worrall, Mick	15 + 4	2	3	2	16
Worrall, Tony	10 + 2	—	—	—	—

TOTALS:
29 players		106	75	5	579

Peter Williams, 10 tries in 24 games.

1988-89 MATCH ANALYSIS

Date	Com-petition	H/A	Opponent	Rlt	Score	Tries	Goals	Atten-dance	Referee
28.8.88	SBC	H	Hull K.R.	W	24-14	Bentley (2), Williams, Jones, Gibson	Jones (2)	3519	Haigh
4.9.88	SBC	A	Bradford N.	L	18-42	Williams (2), Jones	Jones (3)	—	—
11.9.88	SBC	H	Warrington	W	25-18	Jones, Evans, Bentley, Blease, Gibson	Jones (2), Cairns (dg)	5809	Holdsworth
18.9.88	LC(1)	H	Whitehaven	W	42-8	Evans (2), Bentley (2), Moran, Gibson, Herbert, Jones	Jones (5)	2551	Spencer
25.9.88	SBC	A	Wakefield T.	W	36-18	Bentley (3), Gibson (2), Worrall	Jones (6)	—	—
28.9.88	LC(2)	A	Oldham	W	18-2	Jones, Gibson, Gormley	Jones (3)	—	—
2.10.88	SBC	H	Widnes	W	15-12	Hadley (2), Moran	Jones, Cairns (dg)	6684	Smith
5.10.88	LC(SF)	H	Warrington	W	15-2	Bentley, Evans	Hadley (3), Bentley (dg)	7316	Allatt
9.10.88	SBC	A	Castleford	L	12-38	Gibson, Evans, Bentley	—	—	—
16.10.88	SBC	H	Oldham	W	38-20	Williams (2), Gormley, Gibson, Horo, Evans, Hadley	Brown (5)	5954	Berry
23.10.88	LC(F)	St. Helens	Wigan	L	17-22	Evans, Bentley, Herbert	Brown (2), Worrall (dg)	(19,154)	Allatt
6.11.88	SBC	A	St. Helens	L	14-30	Blease, Gibson	Worrall (3)	—	—
13.11.88	JPS(1)	A	Halifax	L	4-22	Hadley	—	—	—
20.11.88	SBC	H	Wigan	W	24-16	Horo, Jones, Shaw, Gormley	Brown (4)	8533	Cross
27.11.88	SBC	H	Leeds	L	6-24	Bragger	Brown	6025	Holdsworth
4.12.88	SBC	A	Featherstone R.	L	18-22	Blease (2), Bentley, Worrall	Brown	—	—
11.12.88	SBC	H	Bradford N.	W	33-18	Bragger (3), Cairns, Kerry, Bentley	Kerry (4), Worrall (dg)	4130	Tennant
18.12.88	SBC	H	Featherstone R.	L	8-12	Williams, Bragger	—	3126	Whitfield
26.12.88	SBC	A	Oldham	L	22-23	Hadley (2), Bragger, Bentley	Kerry (3)	—	—
8.1.89	SBC	H	Wakefield T.	W	18-8	Bragger, Shaw, Bentley	Kerry (3)	3692	Berry
15.1.89	SBC	A	Widnes	L	8-50	Williams, Hadley	—	—	—
22.1.89	SBC	A	Leeds	L	16-18	Bragger (2), Gormley	Kerry (2)	—	—
29.1.89	CC(1)	H	Widnes	L	14-18	Kerry, Gibson	Kerry (3)	7094	Kendrew
5.2.89	SBC	H	Hull	L	6-18	Cairns	Kerry	3484	Holdsworth
17.2.89	SBC	H	Castleford	L	18-20	Bragger (2), Hadley	Brown (2), Kerry	4460	Whitfield
5.3.89	SBC	A	Halifax	L	12-21	Horo, Williams	Brown (2)	—	—
14.3.89	SBC	H	St. Helens	W	22-4	Kerry (2), Horo, Brown	Kerry (3)	5003	Cross
19.3.89	SBC	A	Hull K.R.	W	24-18	Kerry (2), Williams, Hadley	Kerry (4)	—	—
27.3.89	SBC	A	Warrington	L	6-18	Gibson	Kerry	—	—
2.4.89	SBC	H	Halifax	W	22-4	Williams, Gibson, McTigue, Bragger, Kerry	Kerry	3508	Holdsworth
9.4.89	SBC	A	Wigan	L	18-28	Bragger (2), Kerry	Kerry (3)	—	—
16.4.89	SBC	A	Hull	L	6-12	Gibson	Kerry	—	—

SHEFFIELD EAGLES

Ground: Owlerton Stadium
Colours: Red and black
First Season: 1984-85
Nickname: Eagles
Managing
  Director: Gary Hetherington
Secretary: Julie Bush
Coach: Gary Hetherington (July 1986-)
Honours: **Second Division Premiership**
  Winners, 1988-89
Records: Attendance: 3,636 v. Oldham (RL
  Cup) 12 Feb, 1989
  Season
  Goals: 148 by M. Aston, 1988-89
  Tries: 28 by D. Powell, 1988-89
  Points: 307 by M. Aston, 1988-89
  Match
  Goals: 12 by R. Rafferty at Fulham,
  21 Sep, 1986
  Tries: 5 by D. Powell at Mansfield
  M., 2 Jan, 1989
  Points: 32 by R. Rafferty at Fulham,
  21 Sep, 1986
  Highest score: 80-8 v. Wigan St.
  Patricks, 1988-89
  Highest against: 62-11 v.
  Warrington, 1985-86

1988-89 PLAYERS' SUMMARY

	App		Tries	Goals	Dr	Pts
Aston, Mark	36		6	135	13	307
Bridgeman, Derek	5	+ 5	1	—	—	4
Broadbent, Paul............	27	+ 1	4	—	—	16
Cartwright, Phil..............	22	+ 3	6	—	—	24
Charlton, Gary	3		1	—	—	4
Close, David	12	+ 5	5	—	2	22
Cook, Michael	29	+ 2	6	—	—	24
Dickinson, Andy.............	30		17	—	—	68
Evans, Steve	27	+ 3	9	1	—	38
Fleming, Mark	19	+ 2	2	—	—	8
Gamson, Mark	35		12	—	—	48
Geyer, Mark	6		2	—	—	8
Gibson, Mark.................	2	+ 2	2	—	—	8
Grimoldby, Nick.............	12	+ 4	2	—	—	8
Halafihi, Nick	8	+ 7	2	—	—	8
Hale, Darren.................	3	+ 1	—	—	—	—
Idle, Graham.................	17	+ 2	—	—	—	—
Kellett, Neil	1	+ 2	—	—	—	—
Lidbury, Steve	1		—	—	—	—
McDermott, Chris...........	4	+ 4	—	—	—	—
McDermott, Paul	23	+ 10	8	—	—	32
Nelson, Dave	19	+ 2	9	—	—	36
Nickle, Sonny	6	+ 2	2	—	—	8
O'Kesene, Paul	26		9	—	—	36
Powell, Darryl	30		28	—	2	114
Solomona, Masauwee........	4		1	—	—	4
Smiles, Warren	10	+ 4	4	—	—	16
Van Bellen, Gary.............	15	+ 1	—	—	—	—
Wilders, Peter	3	+ 5	—	—	—	—
Young, Andy	33		12	—	—	48
TOTALS:						
30 players......................			150	136	17	889

1988-89 MATCH ANALYSIS

Date	Competition	H/A	Opponent	Rlt	Score	Tries	Goals	Attendance	Referee
28.8.88	SD	H	Bramley	W	13-10	Dickinson, Halafihi	Aston (2, 1dg)	700	Simpson
31.8.88	YC(P)	H	Wakefield T.	L	8-28	Aston (2)	—	1356	Holdsworth
4.9.88	SD	A	Fulham	L	20-21	Dickinson (2), Powell, McDermott	Aston (2)	—	—
11.9.88	SD	H	Barrow	D	11-11	Young	Aston (3, 1dg)	365	Berry
21.9.88	SD	H	Mansfield M.	W	27-14	Dickinson, Powell, Charlton, Nelson, McDermott	Aston (3, 1dg)	380	Burke

MATCH ANALYSIS (continued)

Date	Com-petition	H/A	Opponent	Rlt	Score	Tries	Goals	Atten-dance	Referee
25.9.88	SD	A	Leigh	L	8-12	Young	Aston (2)	—	—
9.10.88	SD	A	Chorley B.	W	14-4	McDermott, Powell	Aston (3)	—	—
16.10.88	SD	H	Leigh	L	17-30	McDermott, O'Kesene	Aston (4, 1dg)	903	Tickle
23.10.88	SD	H	Batley	L	10-17	Dickinson, Nelson	Aston	515	Spencer
26.10.88	SD	H	York	W	28-16	Aston, Fleming, Dickinson, Gamson, Evans	Aston (4)	481	Morris
6.11.88	SD	H	Keighley	W	34-6	Gamson (3), Nelson, Evans, Powell	Aston (5)	484	Smith
13.11.88	JPS(1)	H	Wigan St. Patrick	W	80-8	Nelson (3), Cook (3), Young (2), Powell (2), O'Kesene (2), Dickinson, Geyer, Solomona	Aston (10)	621	Tidball
20.11.88	SD	A	Huddersfield	W	30-4	Halafihi, Powell, Aston, Gamson, Nelson, Geyer	Aston (3)	—	—
27.11.88	JPS(2)	H	Widnes	L	9-32	O'Kesene	Aston (2, 1dg)	2716	Haigh
11.12.88	SD	A	Keighley	W	34-12	Young, Dickinson, Gamson, Broadbent, Gibson	Aston (7)	—	—
18.12.88	SD	H	Dewsbury	W	50-8	Dickinson (4), Powell (2), Evans, Cook, Broadbent, Gamson	Aston (5)	814	Dockray
26.12.88	SD	A	Doncaster	W	34-20	Powell (2), Evans, Gibson, Broadbent, Nelson	Aston (5)	—	—
2.1.89	SD	A	Mansfield M.	W	50-10	Powell (5), O'Kesene (2), Evans	Aston (9)	—	—
15.1.89	SD	A	Batley	W	42-4	Powell (2), Gamson (2), Evans (2), Grimoldby, Nelson	Aston (5)	—	—
22.1.89	SD	H	Swinton	W	23-6	Gamson, Cartwright, Young, Powell	Aston (3, 1dg)	1034	Allatt
29.1.89	CC(1)	H	Leigh	W	23-17	McDermott, O'Kesene, Gamson	Aston (4, 2dg), Powell (dg)	1898	Whitfield
5.2.89	SD	A	Bramley	L	9-13	Powell	Aston (2, 1dg)	—	—
12.2.89	CC(2)	H	Oldham	L	20-32	Dickinson, Powell, Cartwright	Aston (4)	3636	Holdsworth
19.2.89	SD	H	Huddersfield	W	24-0	Powell (2), Gamson, Young	Aston (4)	774	Berry
26.2.89	SD	A	Swinton	W	30-14	Cartwright (2), McDermott (2), Dickinson, Powell	Aston (3)	—	—
5.3.89	SD	H	Doncaster	L	25-26	Smiles, Dickinson, Cartwright	Aston (6, 1dg)	2254	Steele
12.3.89	SD	H	Hunslet	W	24-10	Evans, Smiles, Close, O'Kesene	Aston (4)	774	Bowman
19.3.89	SD	A	Barrow	W	24-20	Young, Powell, Aston, Smiles	Aston (3), Close (2dg)	—	—
24.3.89	SD	A	York	W	21-0	Young, Close, O'Kesene, Nickle	Aston, Evans, Powell (dg)	—	—
26.3.89	SD	H	Fulham	W	24-16	Close (2), Bridgeman	Aston (6)	1005	Whitelam
2.4.89	SD	H	Chorley B.	W	26-8	Evans, Grimoldby, Young, Cartwright	Aston (5)	1252	Morris
9.4.89	SD	A	Dewsbury	L	11-18	Close, Smiles	Aston (1, 1dg)	—	—
16.4.89	SD	A	Hunslet	L	6-32	Young	Aston	—	—
23.4.89	SDP(1)	H	Doncaster	W	28-10	Dickinson (2), Young, Nickle, Cook	Aston (4)	1725	Holdsworth
7.5.89	SDP(SF)	A	Barrow	W	9-6	Fleming	Aston (2, 1dg)	—	—
14.5.89	SDP(F)	Man. U. F.C.	Swinton	W	43-18	Powell (3), Aston, Broadbent, Cook, McDermott	Aston (7, 1dg)	—	Whitfield

SWINTON

Ground: Station Road
Colours: Blue and white
First Season: 1896-97
Nickname: Lions
Chairman: John Way
Secretary: Steve Moyes
Coach: Frank Barrow (Oct 1987-)
Honours: **Championship** Winners, 1926-27, 1927-28, 1930-31, 1934-35
Beaten finalists, 1924-25, 1932-33
War League Beaten finalists, 1939-40
Division One Champions, 1962-63, 1963-64
Division Two Champions, 1984-85
Second Division Premiership Winners, 1986-87
Beaten finalists, 1988-89
Challenge Cup Winners, 1899-1900, 1925-26, 1927-28
Beaten finalists, 1926-27, 1931-32
Lancashire League Winners, 1924-25, 1927-28, 1928-29, 1930-31, 1960-61
Lancashire War League Winners, 1939-40
Lancashire Cup Winners, 1925-26, 1927-28, 1939-40, 1969-70
Beaten finalists, 1910-11, 1923-24, 1931-32, 1960-61, 1961-62, 1962-63, 1964-65, 1972-73
BBC2 Floodlit Trophy Beaten finalists, 1966-67
Western Division Championship Beaten finalists, 1963-64

Records: Attendance: 44,621 Wigan v. Warrington (RL Cup SF) 7 Apr, 1951
Season
Goals: 128 by A. Blan, 1960-61
Tries: 42 by J. Stopford, 1963-64
Points: 283 by A. Blan, 1960-61

Match
Goals: 12 by K. Gowers v. Liverpool C., 3 Oct, 1959
Tries: 5 by T. Bevan v. Morecambe, 10 Sep, 1898; W. Wallwork v. Widnes, 15 Dec, 1900; J. Evans v. Bradford N., 30 Sep, 1922; H. Halsall v. St. Helens, 24 Jan, 1925; R. Cracknell v. Whitehaven Rec., 11 Feb, 1928; R. Lewis v. Keighley, 12 Jan, 1946; J. Stopford v. Bramley, 22 Dec, 1962; A. Buckley v. Salford, Apr 8, 1964
Points: 29 by B. McMahon v. Dewsbury, 15 Aug, 1959
Highest score: 76-4 v. Pontefract, 1906-07
Highest against: 76-3 v. Huddersfield, 1945-46; 76-16 v. Castleford, 1987-88

1988-89 PLAYERS' SUMMARY

	App	Tries	Goals	Dr	Pts
Ainsworth, Gary	33 + 3	11	—	—	44
Allen, John	17 + 2	—	—	—	—
Ashall, Barry	2 + 1	—	—	—	—
Bate, Derek	36 + 1	32	—	—	128
Bond, Gary	5	—	—	—	—
Brown, Andy	2	—	—	—	—
Cassidy, Frank	10 + 6	8	—	—	32
Connor, Ian	11 + 4	3	—	—	12
Edwards, Morvin	9 + 1	5	—	—	20
Forber, Gary	3	—	—	—	—
Frazer, Neil	4 + 1	—	—	—	—
Frodsham, Tommy	21 + 2	11	—	—	44
Gelling, Bryan	12 + 3	—	—	—	—
Hewitt, Tony	13 + 1	3	—	—	12
Horrocks, John	16 + 2	2	—	—	8
Howarth, Roy	5 + 2	—	—	—	—
Kinsey, Tony	4	—	—	2	2
Kuiti, Mike	18	1	16	—	36
Lee, Martin	11 + 1	2	—	—	8
Maloney, David	2 + 9	—	—	—	—
Melling, Alex	21 + 4	6	—	—	24
Mooney, Frank	13 + 2	2	—	—	8
Myler, John	18	2	36	—	80
O'Neill, Steve	27	2	—	7	15
Pickavance, Ian	1	—	—	—	—
Ranson, Scott	32	16	—	—	64
Rippon, Andy	15 + 2	1	35	—	74
Skeech, Ian	0 + 1	—	—	—	—
Smith, Dennis	5 + 2	—	—	—	—
Snape, Steve	34	8	—	—	32
Tangira, Willie	12	4	—	—	16
Topping, Paul	28	7	21	1	71
Viller, Mark	22 + 4	8	—	—	32
Wakefield, Stuart	4	—	—	—	—
Wood, John	7	—	—	—	—
Wright, Terry	8 + 2	—	—	—	—
TOTALS:					
36 players		134	108	10	762

1988-89 MATCH ANALYSIS

Date	Competition	H/A	Opponent	Rlt	Score	Tries	Goals	Attendance	Referee
28.8.88	SD	H	Carlisle	W	28-20	Bate (4), Ainsworth	Topping (4)	1404	Kershaw
4.9.88	SD	A	Hunslet	W	12-10	Frodsham, Cassidy	Topping (2)	—	—
11.9.88	SD	H	Chorley B.	L	22-28	Snape (2), Connor	Topping (4), Kinsey (2 dg)	1433	Holgate
14.9.88	SD	H	Runcorn H.	W	56-2	Bate (3), Cassidy (2), Ranson (2), Connor, Frodsham, Topping	Rippon (8)	1078	Volante
18.9.88	LC(1)	H	Leigh	W	24-14	Viller, Frodsham, Ainsworth	Rippon (6)	3225	Whitfield
25.9.88	SD	H	Mansfield M.	W	36-20	Topping (2), Ranson, Connor, Bate, Frodsham, Mooney	Rippon (4)	1398	Morris
28.9.88	LC(2)	A	Widnes	L	4-38	Ranson	—	—	—
2.10.88	SD	A	Bramley	L	22-34	Bate, Cassidy, Ranson, Topping	Rippon (3)	—	—
9.10.88	SD	H	York	L	8-26	Bate, Mooney	—	1326	Steele
16.10.88	SD	A	York	D	18-18	Ranson, Melling, Viller	Rippon (3)	—	—
23.10.88	SD	H	Keighley	W	43-14	Bate (2), Cassidy (2), Ranson, Snape, Horrocks, Hewitt	Rippon (5), Topping (dg)	1441	Carter
30.10.88	SD	A	Mansfield M.	W	24-2	Ranson, Ainsworth, Melling, Snape	Rippon (4)	—	—
6.11.88	SD	A	Barrow	L	8-30	Tangira	Rippon (2)	—	—
13.11.88	JPS(1)	H	Doncaster	L	13-16	Snape, Melling	Topping (2), O'Neill (dg)	2182	Holgate
27.11.88	SD	A	Whitehaven	D	15-15	Bate, Ranson, O'Neill	Myler, O'Neill (dg)	—	—
11.12.88	SD	H	Workington T.	W	24-10	Bate (2), Edwards, Snape	Myler (4)	1002	Berry
18.12.88	SD	A	Carlisle	W	28-6	Bate (2), Topping, Cassidy	Kuiti (6)	—	—
26.12.88	SD	A	Rochdale H.	W	30-8	Bate (2), Snape, Topping, Lee	Kuiti (2)	—	—
1.1.89	SD	A	Leigh	L	12-40	Melling, Ranson	Kuiti (2)	—	—
8.1.89	SD	H	Whitehaven	W	20-14	Ranson (2), Lee, Bate	Kuiti (2)	1173	Houghton
15.1.89	CC(P)	A	Milford	W	36-0	Bate (3), Ainsworth (2), Viller, Topping, Frodsham	Kuiti, Topping	—	—
22.1.89	SD	A	Sheffield E.	L	6-23	Ranson	Topping	—	—
29.1.89	CC(1)	H	St. Helens	L	5-16	—	Topping (2), O'Neill (dg)	5317	Cross
5.2.89	SD	H	Barrow	W	12-31	Kuiti, Ainsworth, Cassidy	—	1373	Spencer
12.2.89	SD	A	Workington T.	L	10-23	Viller, Tangira	Myler	—	—
19.2.89	SD	A	Runcorn H.	W	30-10	Edwards (3), Tangira (2), Viller	Myler (3)	—	—
26.2.89	SD	H	Sheffield E.	L	14-30	Horrocks, Edwards	Myler (2), Topping	1301	Kershaw
5.3.89	SD	A	Chorley B.	W	31-7	Bate (2), Snape, Viller, Melling	Myler (5), O'Neill (dg)	—	—
12.3.89	SD	A	Keighley	W	20-10	Bate (3), Frodsham	Myler (2)	—	—
19.3.89	SD	H	Bramley	W	16-0	Ranson, Viller, Frodsham	Myler (2)	1156	Holdsworth
24.3.89	SD	H	Rochdale H.	W	26-6	Hewitt (2), Bate, Frodsham	Myler (5)	1904	Allatt
27.3.89	SD	H	Leigh	L	24-35	Ainsworth (2), Viller, Rippon	Myler (4)	3038	Whitfield
13.4.89	SD	H	Hunslet	W	26-10	Bate (2), Frodsham (2), Ainsworth	Myler (3)	1068	Smith
23.4.89	SDP(1)	A (Castleford)	York	D	4-4	Bate	—	—	—
25.4.89	SDP(1) Replay	H	York	W	17-16	Myler (2), Ranson	Myler, Topping, O'Neill (dg)	1371	Tennant
7.5.89	SDP(SF)	A	Leigh	W	20-8	Ainsworth (2), O'Neill	Topping (3), O'Neill (2dg)	—	—
14.5.89	SDP(F)	Man U.F.C.	Sheffield E.	L	18-43	Frodsham, Melling, Ranson	Myler (3)	—	Whitfield

WAKEFIELD TRINITY

Ground:	Belle Vue
Colours:	Red, white and blue
First Season:	1895-96
Nickname:	Dreadnoughts
Chairman:	Rodney Walker
Secretary:	George Gledhill
Coach:	David Topliss (May 1987-)

Honours: **Championship** Winners, 1966-67, 1967-68
Beaten finalists, 1959-60, 1961-62
Division Two Champions, 1903-04
Challenge Cup Winners, 1908-09, 1945-46, 1959-60, 1961-62, 1962-63
Beaten finalists, 1913-14, 1967-68, 1978-79
Yorkshire League Winners, 1909-10, 1910-11, 1945-46, 1958-59, 1959-60, 1961-62, 1965-66
Yorkshire Cup Winners, 1910-11, 1924-25, 1946-47, 1947-48, 1951-52, 1956-57, 1960-61, 1961-62, 1964-65
Beaten finalists, 1926-27, 1932-33, 1934-35, 1936-37, 1939-40, 1945-46, 1958-59, 1973-74, 1974-75
John Player Trophy Beaten finalists, 1971-72

Records: Attendance: 37,906 Leeds v. Huddersfield (RL Cup SF) 21 March, 1936
Home: 28,254 v. Wigan (RL Cup) 24 Mar, 1962
Season
Goals: 163 by N. Fox, 1961-62
Tries: 38 by F. Smith, 1959-60, D. Smith, 1973-74
Points: 407 by N. Fox, 1961-62
Match
Goals: 12 by N. Fox v. Workington T., 19 Sep, 1970 and v. Batley, 26 Aug, 1967; B. Ward v. Hunslet, 6 Feb, 1971
Tries: 7 by F. Smith v. Keighley, 25 Apr, 1959; K. Slater v. Hunslet, 6 Feb, 1971
Points: 33 by N. Fox v. Batley, 26 Aug, 1967
Highest score: 78-9 v. Batley, 1967-68
Highest against: 72-6 v. Wigan, 1986-87

1988-89 PLAYERS' SUMMARY

	App		Tries	Goals	Dr	Pts
Bell, Nigel	33		8	—	—	32
Conway, Billy	26	+ 2	3	—	—	12
Conway, Mark	31	+ 2	10	20	2	82
Douglas, Ian	6		—	—	—	—
Eden, Philip	19	+ 3	8	—	—	32
Ella, Steve	20		9	32	2	102
Fletcher, Andrew	19	+ 4	8	—	—	32
Fox, Philip	13		9	—	—	36
Glancy, John	30		2	—	—	8
Graham, Mark	14		2	—	—	8
Haggerty, Gary	2	+ 6	—	—	—	—
Harcombe, Kevin	15	+ 1	—	48	1	97
Hughes, Ian	1		1	—	—	4
Hunte, Alan	1	+ 1	1	—	—	4
Jowitt, Ian	5		1	—	—	4
Kelly, Andy	16		2	—	—	8
Lazenby, Tracy	15	+ 2	4	—	—	16
Leuluai, James	24		6	—	—	24
Mallinder, Paul	14	+ 11	—	—	—	—
Mason, Andy	27		14	—	—	56
Norton, Steve	9	+ 1	3	—	—	12
Potts, Steve	2	+ 3	—	—	—	—
Price, Gary	12	+ 3	—	—	—	—
Rayne, Keith	17	+ 4	1	—	—	4
Rotherforth, Lindsay	8		2	—	—	8
Russell, Julian	6		1	—	—	4
Sheldon, Ian	3	+ 14	—	—	—	—
Slater, Richard	2	+ 1	1	—	—	4
Sygrove, Andrew	3	+ 3	—	1	—	2
Thompson, John	19	+ 1	2	—	—	8
Thornton, Gary	2	+ 1	1	—	—	4
Timmins, Jason	0	+ 1	—	—	—	—
Todd, Brent	9		—	—	—	—
Van Bellen, Gary	1		—	—	—	—
Wilson, Andy	30		10	—	—	40
Zelei, Tony	1	+ 1	—	—	—	—
TOTALS:						
36 players			109	101	5	643

TRAFFORD BOROUGH
● See also Chorley Borough

Ground:	Moss Lane, Altrincham
Colours:	Blue and crimson
First Season:	1954-55 as Blackpool Borough; changing to Springfield Borough in 1987-88 and Chorley Borough in 1988-89.
Chairman:	Mike Marsland
Secretary:	Keith Magford
Coach:	Mike Peers

1988-89 MATCH ANALYSIS

Date	Com-petition	H/A	Opponent	Rlt	Score	Tries	Goals	Atten-dance	Referee
28.8.88	SBC	H	Warrington	W	14-10	Eden (2), Ella	Ella	4495	Tennant
31.8.88	YC(P)	A	Sheffield E.	W	28-8	Conway, Fox, Rotherforth, Mason	Ella (6)	—	—
4.9.88	SBC	H	Wigan	W	25-20	Ella (2), Fox, Eden, Russell	Ella (2, 1dg)	8114	Holdsworth
11.9.88	SBC	A	Hull	W	16-10	Mason, Ella, Kelly	Ella (2)	—	—
18.9.88	YC(1)	H	Dewsbury	W	46-20	Fox (3), Graham, Hughes, Ella, M. Conway, Mason	Ella (7)	3733	Smith
25.9.88	SBC	H	Salford	L	18-36	Glancy, Wilson, Ella	Ella (3)	4276	Cross
28.9.88	YC(2)	A	Leeds	L	10-15	Glancy, Rayne	Ella	—	—
2.10.88	SBC	A	St. Helens	L	14-30	Rotherforth, Jowitt	Ella (3)	—	—
9.10.88	SBC	H	Oldham	D	12-12	Bell, Slater	Ella (2)	4744	Smith
16.10.88	SBC	A	Wigan	L	12-34	Leuluai, M. Conway	Ella, M. Conway	—	—
23.10.88	SBC	H	Widnes	L	14-28	B. Conway, Wilson	Ella (3)	5069	Volante
6.11.88	SBC	A	Hull K.R.	L	18-38	Wilson, Bell, Mason	Harcombe (3)	—	—
13.11.88	JPS(1)	H	Carlisle	W	34-14	Wilson (2), Leuluai, Graham, Mason, Norton	Harcombe (5)	2513	Houghton
20.11.88	SBC	H	Bradford N.	L	14-23	Fletcher, Thornton	Harcombe (3)	3805	Simpson
27.11.88	JPS(2)	H	Rochdale H.	W	38-12	Fletcher, Wilson, Ella, M. Conway, Norton, Leuluai, Mason	Harcombe (5)	2486	Kendrew
4.12.88	JPS(3)	A	St. Helens	L	18-34	Mason (2), Bell	Harcombe (3)	—	—
11.12.88	SBC	H	Hull K.R.	L	6-12	Mason	Sygrove	3126	Whitfield
15.12.88	SBC	A	Widnes	L	12-40	Eden, Lazenby	M. Conway (2)	—	—
26.12.88	SBC	A	Featherstone R.	W	15-14	Ella, Wilson, Thompson	Ella, M. Conway (dg)	—	—
1.1.89	SBC	H	Featherstone R.	W	19-12	Wilson, Fletcher, Mason	M. Conway (3), Ella (dg)	5638	Simpson
8.1.89	SBC	A	Salford	L	8-18	—	M. Conway (4)	—	—
15.1.89	CC(P)	H	Bramley	W	18-10	Fletcher (2), Eden	M. Conway (3)	2855	Holdsworth
18.1.89	SBC	H	Hull	L	2-11	—	Harcombe	4711	Tickle
22.1.89	SBC	A	Castleford	L	14-38	Thompson, B. Conway	Harcombe (3)	—	—
29.1.89	CC(1)	H	Batley	W	34-4	Wilson (2), Mason (2), Bell, M. Conway, Hunte	Harcombe (3)	2895	Houghton
12.2.89	CC(2)	H	Featherstone R.	L	4-10	—	Harcombe (2)	7695	Carter
19.2.89	SBC	A	Warrington	L	18-30	Ella, Fletcher	Harcombe (5)	—	—
26.2.89	SBC	H	Castleford	W	26-8	Mason, Leuluai, Fletcher, Bell, Lazenby	M. Conway (2), Harcombe	5819	Steele
5.3.89	SBC	A	Leeds	L	16-28	Norton, Fletcher, Lazenby	M. Conway (2)	—	—
12.3.89	SBC	H	Leeds	W	14-12	M. Conway, Mason	M. Conway (3)	7014	Tennant
19.3.89	SBC	A	Oldham	L	8-24	Fox, M. Conway		—	—
24.3.89	SBC	H	Halifax	W	27-10	Eden (2), Fox, Bell, M. Conway	Harcombe (3, 1dg)	5772	Cross
28.3.89	SBC	A	Bradford N.	W	28-8	M. Conway (2), Leuluai, Lazenby, Eden	Harcombe (4)	—	—
2.4.89	SBC	H	St. Helens	W	21-14	Bell, Kelly, Leuluai	Harcombe (4), M. Conway (dg)	4382	Carter
9.4.89	SBC	A	Halifax	W	22-20	Fox (2), B. Conway, Bell	Harcombe (3)	—	—

WARRINGTON

Ground: Wilderspool
Colours: Primrose and blue
First Season: 1895-96
Nickname: Wire
Chairman: Peter Higham
General
  Manager: Ron Close
Coach: Tony Barrow (Mar 1986-Nov 1988)
  Brian Johnson (Nov 1988-)
Honours: **Championship** Winners, 1947-48,
  1953-54, 1954-55
  Beaten finalists, 1925-26, 1934-35,
  1936-37, 1948-49, 1950-51, 1960-61
  League Leaders Trophy Winners,
  1972-73
  Club Championship (Merit Table)
  Winners, 1973-74
  Challenge Cup Winners, 1904-05,
  1906-07, 1949-50, 1953-54, 1973-74
  Beaten finalists, 1900-01, 1903-04,
  1912-13, 1927-28, 1932-33, 1935-36,
  1974-75
  Lancashire League Winners,
  1937-38, 1947-48, 1948-49, 1950-51,
  1953-54, 1954-55, 1955-56, 1967-68
  Lancashire Cup Winners, 1921-22,
  1929-30, 1932-33, 1937-38, 1959-60,
  1965-66, 1980-81, 1982-83
  Beaten finalists, 1906-07, 1948-49,
  1950-51, 1967-68, 1985-86, 1987-88
  John Player Trophy Winners,
  1973-74, 1977-78, 1980-81
  Beaten finalists, 1978-79, 1986-87
  Premiership Trophy Winners,
  1985-86
  Beaten finalists 1976-77, 1986-87
  Captain Morgan Trophy Winners,
  1973-74
  BBC2 Floodlit Trophy Beaten
  finalists, 1974-75
Records: Attendance: 35,000 Wigan v. Leigh
  (Lancs. Cup Final) 29 Oct, 1949
  Home: 34,304 v. Wigan (League)
  22 Jan, 1949

Season
Goals: 170 by S. Hesford, 1978-79
Tries: 66 by B. Bevan, 1952-53
Points: 363 by H. Bath, 1952-53
Match
Goals: 14 by H. Palin v. Liverpool
C., 13 Sep, 1950
Tries: 7 by B. Bevan v. Leigh,
29 Mar, 1948 and v. Bramley,
22 Apr, 1953
Points: 33 by G. Thomas v. St.
Helens, 12 Apr, 1909
Highest score: 78-3 v. St. Helens,
1908-09
Highest against: 68-14 v. Hunslet,
1927-28

1988-89 PLAYERS' SUMMARY

	App	Tries	Goals	Dr	Pts
Bacon, Mike	3	1	—	—	4
Bishop, Paul	19 + 2	6	—	2	26
Blake, Phil	25	19	—	3	79
Boyd, Les	15	—	—	—	—
Carbert, Brian	3 + 1	—	—	—	—
Carroll, Dean	4 + 1	1	—	3	7
Crompton, Martin	2 + 5	2	—	—	8
Cullen, Paul	15 + 3	2	—	—	8
Darbyshire, Paul	5	—	—	—	—
Davidson, Les	22	4	—	—	16
Drummond, Des	31	12	—	—	48
Duane, Ronnie	14 + 2	2	—	—	8
Forster, Mark	16	5	—	—	20
Gregory, Mike	25	2	—	—	8
Harmon, Neil	10 + 6	4	—	—	16
Humphries, Tony	13 + 8	1	—	—	4
Lyon, David	29	2	—	—	8
McGinty, Billy	20 + 4	4	—	—	16
Molloy, Steve	11 + 9	—	—	—	—
Muller, Roby	1	—	—	—	—
Peters, Barry	3 + 1	1	—	—	4
Rea, Kevin	0 + 1	—	—	—	—
Richards, Basil	5 + 9	2	—	—	8
Roach, Steve	20	1	—	—	4
Roberts, Mark	21 + 2	12	—	—	48
Roskell, Mark	19	1	—	—	4
Rudd, Chris	2	—	—	—	—
Sanderson, Gary	16 + 3	3	—	—	12
Sumner, Phil	2 + 1	—	—	—	—
Tamati, Kevin	11 + 2	1	—	—	4
Thomas, Mark	3	—	—	—	—
Thorniley, Tony	21 + 2	9	—	—	36
Thursfield, John	9	—	—	—	—
Turner, Robert	16 + 5	4	10	1	37
Williamson, Paul	15 + 1	8	—	—	32
Woods, John	35	12	107	—	262

TOTALS:
36 players		121	117	9	727

1988-89 MATCH ANALYSIS

Date	Competition	H/A	Opponent	Rlt	Score	Tries	Goals	Attendance	Referee
28.8.88	SBC	A	Wakefield T.	L	10-14	Woods, Turner	Woods	—	—
4.9.88	SBC	H	St. Helens	L	14-25	Forster, Drummond, Peters	Woods	7103	Smith
11.9.88	SBC	A	Salford	L	18-25	Blake (2), Forster	Woods (3)	—	—
18.9.88	LC(1)	A	Runcorn H.	W	42-4	Roberts (3), Sanderson (2), Woods, Harmon, Blake	Woods (5)	—	—
25.9.88	SBC	H	Hull	W	20-14	Blake (2), Harmon	Woods (3), Blake (2dg)	4027	Kendrew
28.9.88	LC(2)	H	Carlisle	W	34-18	Humphries, Crompton, Roberts, Davidson, Thorniley, Blake	Woods (5)	2586	Whitfield
2.10.88	SBC	A	Halifax	W	16-4	Blake, Crompton	Turner (4)	—	—
5.10.88	LC(SF)	A	Salford	L	2-15	—	Turner	—	—
9.10.88	SBC	H	Featherstone R.	W	30-22	Blake (2), Duane, Woods, Thorniley	Woods (5)	3304	Berry
16.10.88	Tour	H	France	L	6-29	Blake	Woods	3200	Tennant
23.10.88	SBC	A	Castleford	L	16-23	Thorniley, Blake, Davidson	Woods (2)	—	—
6.11.88	SBC	H	Oldham	W	32-30	Blake (2), Drummond, Davidson, Forster, Woods	Woods (4)	4388	Holdsworth
13.11.88	JPS(1)	H	Oldham	W	21-14	Blake, Woods	Woods (6), Turner (dg)	5528	Whitfield
20.11.88	SBC	A	Leeds	W	22-8	Blake, Thorniley, Drummond, Forster	Woods (3)	—	—
27.11.88	JPS(2)	H	Bramley	W	42-10	Thorniley (2), Woods, Gregory, Sanderson, Blake, Forster	Woods (7)	3274	Carter
3.12.88	JPS(3)	A	Widnes	L	7-16	Davidson	Woods, Bishop (dg)	—	—
11.12.88	SBC	A	Oldham	L	2-16	—	Woods	—	—
18.12.88	SBC	H	Castleford	L	20-26	Roberts, Bishop, Thorniley	Woods (4)	4361	Allatt
26.12.88	SBC	H	Widnes	L	8-18	Bacon	Woods (2)	6219	Simpson
1.1.89	SBC	A	Wigan	L	10-26	Duane, Blake	Woods	—	—
8.1.89	SBC	H	Hull K.R.	W	60-24	Roberts (2), Williamson, Lyon, Bishop, Thorniley, Tamati, Richards, Drummond, McGinty, Woods	Woods (8)	3945	Carter
15.1.89	SBC	A	Bradford N.	L	4-15	Drummond	—	—	—
22.1.89	SBC	A	Hull	L	8-10	Williamson, Richards	—	—	—
29.1.89	CC(1)	H	Halifax	W	25-8	Drummond, Blake, Bishop, Roberts	Woods (4), Blake (dg)	6209	Holdsworth
5.2.89	SBC	A	Hull K.R.	W	17-7	Drummond, Williamson	Woods (4), Bishop (dg)	—	—
12.2.89	CC(2)	H	Keighley	W	56-7	Roberts (3), Woods (2), Williamson (2), Drummond, Blake, Bishop, Roach	Woods (6)	4184	Haigh
14.2.89	SBC	H	Wigan	L	4-10	—	Woods (2)	7269	Kendrew
19.2.89	SBC	H	Wakefield T.	W	30-18	Drummond (2), Woods, Cullen, Bishop	Woods (5)	3816	Carter
26.2.89	CC(3)	A	Hull K.R.	W	30-4	Drummond, Roberts, Williamson, Bishop, Woods	Woods (5)	—	—
5.3.89	SBC	H	Bradford N.	L	22-23	Williamson (2), Woods, Turner	Woods (3)	4514	Whitfield
15.3.89	SBC	A	Widnes	L	4-32	Lyon	—	—	—
19.3.89	SBC	H	Halifax	W	33-4	Gregory, Drummond, Harmon, Turner	Woods (8), Carroll (dg)	5219	Tickle
25.3.89	CC(SF)	Man. C. F.C.	Wigan	L	6-13	—	Woods (3)	(26,529)	Whitfield
27.3.89	SBC	H	Salford	W	18-6	McGinty (2), Harmon	Woods (2), Carroll (2dg)	4408	Steele
2.4.89	SBC	H	Leeds	L	8-10	Turner	Woods (2)	5039	Tennant
9.4.89	SBC	A	St. Helens	L	16-30	Thorniley, Roskell, Cullen	Turner (2)	—	—
16.4.89	SBC	A	Featherstone R.	L	14-15	McGinty, Carroll	Turner (3)	—	—

87

CLUBS

WHITEHAVEN

Ground:	Recreation Ground
Colours:	Chocolate, blue and gold
First Season:	1948-49
Nickname:	Haven
Chairman:	Keith Irving
Secretary:	David Farrell
Coach:	Barry Smith (July 1988-)
Records:	Attendance: 18,500 v. Wakefield T. (RL Cup) 19 Mar, 1960

Season

Goals: 141 by J. McKeown, 1956-57

Tries: 29 by W. Smith, 1956-57

Points: 291 by J. McKeown, 1956-57

Match

Goals: 11 by W. Holliday v. Hunslet, 31 Mar, 1962

Tries: 6 by V. Gribbin v. Doncaster, 18 Nov, 1984

Points: 25 by W. Holliday v. Hunslet, 31 Mar, 1962

Highest score: 72-6 v. Fulham, 1986-87

Highest against: 74-6 v. Wigan, 1986-87

1988-89 PLAYERS' SUMMARY

	App	Tries	Goals	Dr	Pts
Ackerman, Rob	19 + 4	4	—	—	16
Amor, Martin	12 + 3	4	—	—	16
Beckwith, Mark	22 + 2	10	—	—	40
Brannan, Rob	2 + 1	—	—	—	—
Branthwaite, Steve	1 + 12	—	—	—	—
Burney, Phil	4 + 2	—	—	—	—
Burney, Steve	8 + 1	3	—	—	12
Cameron, Graham	29 + 1	6	5	7	41
D'Leny Tony	9 + 1	—	—	—	—
Dover, Peter	4	2	—	—	8
Fisher, Billy	28 + 1	6	—	—	24
Fryer, Steve	1 + 6	2	—	—	8
Hetherington, Gary	31	6	—	—	24
Hewer, Gary	7	—	—	1	1
Howland, Kevin	2 + 2	1	—	—	4
Howse, Steve	19 + 2	1	—	—	4
Huddart, Milton	9 + 1	2	—	—	8
Johnston, Frank	22 + 1	3	—	1	13
Lightfoot, David	16	3	—	1	13
Lofthouse, Norman	28 + 1	8	1	—	34
McCartney, Duncan	25 + 3	1	—	—	4
Mounsey, Gary	10	—	—	—	—
Reynolds, Graeme	15 + 2	4	—	—	16
Richardson, Willy	32	10	84	—	208
Saunders, Kevin	5 + 2	—	—	—	—
Simpson, Jeff	23 + 2	2	—	—	8
Solarie, Tony	10	2	—	—	8
Telford, Bob	0 + 1	—	—	—	—
Watson, Dave	21	9	—	1	37
Wear, Brian	0 + 1	1	—	—	4
White, Nigel	2 + 1	1	—	—	4
TOTALS:					
31 players		91	90	11	555

Milton Huddart, two tries in 10 games on his return to the Recreation Ground from Leigh.

1988-89 MATCH ANALYSIS

Date	Competition	H/A	Opponent	Rlt	Score	Tries	Goals	Attendance	Referee
28.8.88	SD	A	Keighley	L	7-20	S. Burney	Richardson, Cameron (dg)	—	—
4.9.88	SD	H	Dewsbury	W	24-2	Amor (2), S. Burney, Fisher	Richardson (4)	1332	Burke
11.9.88	SD	A	Rochdale H.	L	24-36	Beckwith (2), Huddart, Fisher, Solarie	Richardson (2)	—	—
18.9.88	LC(1)	A	Salford	L	8-42	Weir	Richardson (2)	—	—
25.9.88	SD	A	Barrow	L	6-14	White	Richardson	—	—
2.10.88	SD	H	Rochdale H.	W	38-8	Hetherington (2), Cameron (2), Solarie, Watson, Amor	Richardson (5)	1167	Galtress
9.10.88	SD	A	Runcorn H.	W	28-12	Beckwith (3), Hetherington	Richardson (6)	—	—
16.10.88	SD	H	Runcorn H.	W	16-6	Howland, S. Burney	Richardson (4)	1298	Carter
23.10.88	SD	A	Leigh	L	6-56	Beckwith	Richardson	—	—
30.10.88	JPS(P)	H	Chorley B.	W	36-14	Watson (2), Lofthouse (2), Lightfoot, McCartney, Reynolds	Richardson (4)	976	Morris
13.11.88	JPS(1)	A	Rochdale H.	L	20-26	Lightfoot, Amor, Watson	Richardson (4)	—	—
20.11.88	SD	H	Batley	D	2-2	—	Richardson	1153	Spencer
27.11.88	SD	H	Swinton	D	15-15	Lofthouse, Hetherington, Watson	Richardson, Lightfoot (dg)	1164	Kershaw
4.12.88	SD	A	Chorley B.	L	4-9	—	Richardson (2)	—	—
11.12.88	SD	H	Barrow	W	14-12	Howse, Watson, Lofthouse	Richardson	1203	Smith
26.12.88	SD	H	Workington T.	W	21-0	Cameron (2), Lofthouse, Beckwith	Richardson (2), Cameron (dg)	2234	Tickle
1.1.89	SD	A	Carlisle	L	8-9	Richardson	Richardson (2)	—	—
8.1.89	SD	A	Swinton	L	14-20	Cameron, Ackerman	Richardson (3)	—	—
15.1.89	SD	A	Fulham	W	32-16	Watson (2), Fisher, Lightfoot, Richardson	Richardson (5), Cameron (dg), Watson (dg)	—	—
22.1.89	SD	H	Doncaster	W	29-20	Richardson (2), Reynolds, Fisher, Beckwith	Richardson (2), Cameron (2, ldg)	1402	Kendrew
29.1.89	CC(1)	H	Featherstone R.	L	0-32	—	—	2729	Simpson
5.2.89	SD	A	Dewsbury	W	12-10	Simpson, Fisher	Richardson (2)	—	—
19.2.89	SD	H	Fulham	W	60-0	Hetherington (2), Reynolds (2), Beckwith (2), Huddart, Ackerman, Lofthouse, Fisher, Johnston	Richardson (8)	864	Holgate
26.2.89	SD	A	Huddersfield	W	19-2	Johnston (2), Richardson	Richardson (3), Cameron (dg)	—	—
12.3.89	SD	A	Doncaster	L	6-8	Richardson	Cameron (2 dg)	—	—
24.3.89	SD	A	Workington T.	W	12-5	Watson, Cameron	Richardson (2)	—	—
27.3.89	SD	H	Carlisle	W	30-14	Richardson (3), Ackerman, Lofthouse	Richardson (5)	1489	Simpson
4.4.89	SD	H	Leigh	L	16-25	Fryer	Richardson (6)	2000	Tidball
9.4.89	SD	H	Huddersfield	L	12-16	Richardson, Dover	Richardson (2)	1100	Burke
12.4.89	SD	H	Keighley	W	16-4	Dover, Lofthouse	Richardson (3), Lofthouse	963	Berry
16.4.89	SD	A	Batley	L	15-23	Simpson, Ackerman, Fryer	Cameron, Johnston (dg)	—	—
23.4.89	SDP(1)	A	Barrow	L	5-30	—	Cameron (2), Hewer (dg)	—	—

WIDNES

Ground:	Naughton Park
Colours:	Black and white
First Season:	1895-96
Nickname:	Chemics
Chairman:	Ray Owen
General Manager:	John Stringer
Coach:	Doug Laughton (Jan 1986-)
Honours:	**Division One** Champions, 1977-78, 1987-88, 1988-89

Championship Beaten finalists, 1935-36

Challenge Cup Winners, 1929-30, 1936-37, 1963-64, 1974-75, 1978-79, 1980-81, 1983-84 Beaten finalists, 1933-34, 1949-50, 1975-76, 1976-77, 1981-82

Lancashire League Winners, 1919-20

Lancashire Cup Winners, 1945-46, 1974-75, 1975-76, 1976-77, 1978-79, 1979-80 Beaten finalists, 1928-29, 1939-40, 1955-56, 1971-72, 1981-82, 1983-84

John Player Trophy Winners, 1975-76, 1978-79 Beaten finalists, 1974-75, 1977-78, 1979-80, 1983-84, 1988-89

Premiership Winners, 1979-80, 1981-82, 1982-83, 1987-88, 1988-89 Beaten finalists, 1977-78

BBC2 Floodlit Trophy Winners, 1978-79 Beaten finalists, 1972-73, 1973-74

Western Division Championship Beaten finalists, 1962-63

Charity Shield Winners, 1988-89

Records: Attendance: 24,205 v. St. Helens (RL Cup) 16 Feb, 1961

Season
Goals: 140 by M. Burke, 1978-79
Tries: 46 by M. Offiah, 1988-89
Points: 316 by M. Burke, 1978-79

Match
Goals: 11 by R. Whitfield v. Oldham, 28 Oct, 1965
Tries: 5 by E. Cunningham v. Doncaster, 15 Feb, 1981; J. Basnett v. Hunslet, 17 Oct, 1981 and v. Hull K.R., 2 Nov, 1986; D. Hulme v. Dewsbury, 30 Nov, 1986; A. Currier v. Featherstone R., 25 Sept, 1988; M. Offiah v. Warrington, 15 Mar, 1989
Points: 34 by A. Currie v. Featherstone R., 25 Sept, 1988
Highest score: 82-0 v. Dewsbury, 1986-87
Highest against: 60-5 v. Oldham, 1927-28

1988-89 PLAYERS' SUMMARY

	App	Tries	Goals	Dr	Pts
Ashurst, Chris	0 + 1	—	—	—	—
Currier, Andy	41	18	106	1	285
Davies, Jonathan	12 + 4	7	47	1	123
Dowd, Barry	12 + 13	1	2	—	8
Eyres, Andy	0 + 1	—	—	—	—
Eyres, Richard	38 + 3	4	—	—	16
Grima, Joe	38	7	—	—	28
Hulme, David	38 + 1	13	—	1	53
Hulme, Paul	38 + 1	3	—	—	12
Kebbie, Brima	3	2	8	—	24
Koloto, Emosi	21 + 9	7	—	—	28
Marsh, David	2 + 6	1	—	—	4
McKenzie, Phil	41	9	—	—	36
Moriarty, Paul	0 + 5	1	—	—	4
Myers, David	8	3	—	—	12
Myler, John	0 + 1	—	—	—	—
Myler, Tony	21 + 2	9	—	—	36
Newton, Ken	0 + 1	—	—	—	—
Offiah, Martin	41	58	—	—	232
O'Neill, Mike	41 + 1	9	—	—	36
O'Neill, Steve	1 + 3	—	—	1	1
Platt, Duncan	2	—	—	—	—
Pyke, Derek	22 + 9	—	—	—	—
Smith, David	1 + 2	—	—	—	—
Sorensen, Kurt	28 + 2	8	—	—	32
Sullivan, Andy	3 + 5	—	—	—	—
Tait, Alan	39	16	—	1	65
Thackray, Rick	31	16	—	—	64
Wright, Darren	37 + 1	18	—	—	72

TOTALS:
	App	Tries	Goals	Dr	Pts
29 players		210	163	5	1,171

1988-89 MATCH ANALYSIS

Date	Com-petition	H/A	Opponent	Rlt	Score	Tries	Goals	Atten-dance	Referee
21.8.88	Charity Shield	Isle of Man	Wigan	W	20-14	Offiah, Wright, McKenzie	Currier (4)	(5044)	Tennant
28.8.88	SBC	A	Halifax	L	20-26	Offiah, McKenzie, Wright, Dowd	Currier (2)	—	—
4.9.88	SBC	H	Hull	W	38-6	Offiah (4), M. O'Neill, Sorensen, Wright	Kebbie (5)	5434	Tennant
11.9.88	SBC	A	Leeds	W	30-14	Thackray (3), Tait, Sorensen, McKenzie	Dowd (2), Currier	—	—
18.9.88	LC(1)	H	St. Helens	W	32-24	Offiah (2), Wright, Tait, Sorensen, Currier	Currier (4)	10,764	Allatt
25.9.88	SBC	H	Featherstone R.	W	58-2	Currier (5), Offiah (4), D. Hulme, Tait	Currier (7)	5195	Tickle
28.9.88	LC(2)	H	Swinton	W	38-4	P. Hulme (2), Myler (2), D. Hulme, Offiah, Tait	Currier (5)	4988	Simpson
2.10.88	SBC	A	Salford	L	12-15	Offiah, Tait	Currier (2)	—	—
9.10.88	SBC	H	Halifax	W	5-4	Currier	M. O'Neill (dg)	6971	Spencer
12.10.88	LC(SF)	A	Wigan	L	10-14	M. O'Neill	Currier (3)	—	—
23.10.88	SBC	A	Wakefield T.	W	28-14	Wright (3), McKenzie, Thackray	Currier (4)	—	—
6.11.88	SBC	A	Wigan	W	24-10	Offiah, Sorensen, Tait, Wright	Currier (4)	—	—
13.11.88	JPS(1)	H	Featherstone R.	W	37-12	Offiah (3), Myler, Sorensen, D. Hulme	Currier (6), Tait (dg)	5299	Volante
20.11.88	SBC	H	Hull K.R.	W	43-6	Offiah (2), Sorensen (2), Myler (2), Tait, Grima	Currier (5), D. Hulme (dg)	5532	Holdsworth
27.11.88	JPS(2)	A	Sheffield E.	W	32-9	Offiah, Thackray, Tait, Myler, Koloto	Currier (6)	—	—
3.12.88	JPS(3)	H	Warrington	W	16-7	Offiah (2), McKenzie	Currier (2)	6449	Holdsworth
10.12.88	JPS(SF)	Wigan	St. Helens	W	20-18	Offiah (2), Currier, Eyres	Currier (2)	(6755)	Haigh
15.12.88	SBC	H	Wakefield T.	W	40-12	Currier (2), Myler, Tait, Offiah, Kebbie, D. Hulme, Koloto	Currier (4)	4060	Steele
18.12.88	SBC	H	Leeds	L	8-20	Offiah	Currier (2)	7396	Tennant
26.12.88	SBC	A	Warrington	W	18-8	M. O'Neill, Thackray, Wright	Currier (3)	—	—
1.1.89	SBC	H	St. Helens	W	29-22	Offiah, Tait, Myler, D. Hulme, Wright	Currier (4, 1dg)	11,875	Allatt
7.1.89	JPS(F)	Bolton W FC	Wigan	L	6-12	Wright	Currier	(20,709)	Holdsworth
15.1.89	SBC	H	Salford	W	50-8	Offiah (4), Grima, M. O'Neill, Myler, Thackray, Tait	Currier (7)	11,871	Haigh
29.1.89	CC(1)	A	Salford	W	18-14	M. O'Neill, D. Hulme, Offiah, Tait	Currier	—	—
5.2.89	SBC	H	Oldham	W	38-14	Myers (3), D. Hulme, M. O'Neill, McKenzie, Davies	Davies (5)	9264	Simpson
11.2.89	CC(2)	A	Castleford	W	32-18	Koloto (2), Tait, McKenzie, Grima, Offiah	Currier (4)	—	—
19.2.89	SBC	A	Featherstone R.	W	22-10	Offiah (2), D. Hulme, Thackray, M. O'Neill	Currier	—	—

(continued on page 98)

WIGAN

Ground: Central Park
Colours: Cherry and white
First Season: 1895-96
Nickname: Riversiders
Chairman: Maurice Lindsay
Secretary: Mary Charnock
Coach: Graham Lowe (Aug 1986-June 1989)

Honours: **Championship** Winners, 1908-09, 1921-22, 1925-26, 1933-34, 1945-46, 1946-47, 1949-50, 1951-52, 1959-60
Beaten finalists, 1909-10, 1910-11, 1911-12, 1912-13, 1923-24, 1970-71
League Leaders Trophy Winners, 1970-71
Division One Champions 1986-87
Challenge Cup Winners, 1923-24, 1928-29, 1947-48, 1950-51, 1957-58, 1958-59, 1964-65, 1984-85, 1987-88, 1988-89
Beaten finalists, 1910-11, 1919-20, 1943-44, 1945-46, 1960-61, 1962-63, 1965-66, 1969-70, 1983-84
Lancashire League Winners, 1901-02, 1908-09, 1910-11, 1911-12, 1912-13, 1913-14, 1914-15, 1920-21, 1922-23, 1923-24, 1925-26, 1945-46, 1946-47, 1949-50, 1951-52, 1958-59, 1961-62, 1969-70
Lancashire War League Winners, 1940-41
Lancashire Cup Winners, 1905-06, 1908-09, 1909-10, 1912-13, 1922-23, 1928-29, 1938-39, 1946-47, 1947-48, 1948-49, 1949-50, 1950-51, 1951-52, 1966-67, 1971-72, 1973-74, 1985-86, 1986-87, 1987-88, 1988-89
Beaten finalists, 1913-14, 1914-15, 1925-26, 1927-28, 1930-31, 1934-35, 1935-36, 1936-37, 1945-46, 1953-54, 1957-58, 1977-78, 1980-81, 1984-85
John Player Trophy Winners, 1982-83, 1985-86, 1986-87, 1988-89
Premiership Winners 1986-87
BBC2 Floodlit Trophy Winners, 1968-69
Beaten finalists, 1969-70
Charity Shield Winners, 1985-86, 1987-88
Beaten finalists, 1988-89

War League Championship Winners, 1943-44
Beaten finalists, 1940-41
Records: Attendance: 47,747 v. St. Helens (League) 27 Mar, 1959
Season
Goals: 176 by F. Griffiths, 1958-59
Tries: 62 by J. Ring, 1925-26
Points: 394 by F. Griffiths, 1958-59
Match
Goals: 22 by J. Sullivan v. Flimby & Fothergill, 14 Feb, 1925
Tries: 7 by J. Ring v. Flimby & Fothergill, 14 Feb, 1925; v. Salford, 13 Apr, 1925 and v. Pemberton R., 12 Feb, 1927; G. Ratcliffe v. Liverpool S., 23 Aug, 1947; W. Boston v. Dewsbury, 20 Aug, 1955 and v. Salford, 30 Apr. 1962; G. Vigo v. St. Helens, 21 Aug, 1976
Points: 44 by J. Sullivan v. Flimby & Fothergill, 14 Feb, 1925
Highest score: 116-0 v. Flimby & Fothergill, 1924-25
Highest against: 58-3 v. Leeds, 1972-73

1988-89 PLAYERS' SUMMARY

	App	Tries	Goals	Dr	Pts
Bell, Dean	31 + 2	15	—	—	60
Betts, Dennis	24 + 15	9	1	—	38
Byrne, Ged	28 + 4	8	—	—	32
Case, Brian	12 + 4	1	—	—	4
Clark, Phil	0 + 1	—	—	—	—
Dermott, Martin	15 + 1	1	—	—	4
Edwards, Shaun	31 + 1	15	—	—	60
Frost, Steve	2 + 1	1	—	—	4
Gildart, Ian	4 + 6	—	—	—	—
Gill, Henderson	4 + 1	1	1	—	6
Goodway, Andy	27 + 6	4	—	—	16
Goulding, Bobby	2	1	—	—	4
Gregory, Andy	25 + 3	2	6	3	23
Hampson, Steve	34	7	7	—	42
Hanley, Ellery	38	25	—	1	101
Ingram, Dave	0 + 1	—	—	—	—
Iro, Kevin	24 + 1	20	29	—	138
Iro, Tony	38 + 1	15	—	—	60
Kiss, Nicky	26	2	—	—	8
Lucas, Ian	29 + 6	2	—	—	8
Lydon, Joe	29	13	77	4	210
Marshall, David	1 + 1	—	—	—	—
O'Donnell, Augustine	2	—	—	—	—
Platt, Andy	32 + 3	6	—	—	24
Potter, Ian	19 + 2	—	—	—	—
Preston, Mark	24 + 5	15	—	—	60
Russell, Richard	4 + 1	—	—	—	—
Shelford, Adrian	40	4	—	—	16
Tyrer, Shaun	6	—	15	—	30
Wane, Shaun	8 + 5	—	—	—	—
TOTALS:					
30 players		167	136	8	948

1988-89 MATCH ANALYSIS

Date	Competition	H/A	Opponent	Rlt	Score	Tries	Goals	Attendance	Referee
21.8.88	Charity Shield	Isle of Man	Widnes	L	14-20	T. Iro (2), Lydon	Lydon	(5044)	Tennant
28.8.88	SBC	H	Oldham	W	40-18	Bell (3), Gill, Betts, Byrne, Goodway	Lydon (6)	14,701	Tickle
4.9.88	SBC	A	Wakefield T.	L	20-25	Preston (2), Hampson, Goodway	Lydon (2)	—	—
11.9.88	SBC	H	Hull K.R.	W	32-16	T. Iro (2), Bell, Lydon, Platt, Byrne	Lydon (4)	12,537	Tennant
18.9.88	LC(1)	A	Barrow	W	24-10	Hampson, Lydon, Bell, Platt, Byrne	Lydon (2)	—	—
25.9.88	SBC	A	Bradford N.	W	20-17	Bell (3), T. Iro	Tyrer (2)	—	—
28.9.88	LC(2)	H	Rochdale H.	W	36-4	Hanley (2), Edwards, Preston, Kiss, Byrne, Bell, Platt	Tyrer, Betts	7719	Houghton
2.10.88	SBC	H	Castleford	L	12-20	Preston, Hanley	Gill, Lydon	13,275	Allatt
9.10.88	SBC	A	Leeds	L	14-22	Hanley, Lucas, Frost	Gregory	—	—
12.10.88	LC(SF)	H	Widnes	W	14-10	Dermott	Tyrer (5)	17,813	Houghton
16.10.88	SBC	H	Wakefield T.	W	34-12	T. Iro (2), Hanley (2), Betts (2), Edwards, K. Iro	Tyrer	13,342	Holdsworth
23.10.88	LC(F)	St. Helens	Salford	W	22-17	T. Iro (2), Shelford, Bell	K. Iro (3)	(19,154)	Allatt
6.11.88	SBC	H	Widnes	L	10-24	T.Iro	Tyrer (3)	16,595	Berry
13.11.88	JPS(1)	A (Wigan)	Runcorn H.	W	92-2	K. Iro (4), T. Iro (3), Hampson (2), Hanley (2), Preston (2), Byrne, Bell, Betts, Lucas, Platt	K. Iro (9), Hampson	(7233)	—
20.11.88	SBC	A	Salford	L	16-24	Shelford, T. Iro, Hanley	K. Iro (2)	—	—
26.11.88	JPS(2)	H	Halifax	W	20-16	Preston (2), Lydon	K. Iro (3), Lydon	10,826	Allatt
4.12.88	JPS(3)	A	Hull K.R.	D	16-16	K. Iro (2), Case	K. Iro (2)	—	—
7.12.88	JPS(3) Replay	H	Hull K.R.	W	30-0	Preston (2), K. Iro, Hampson, Platt	Lydon (5)	13,278	Whitfield
11.12.88	SBC	A	Halifax	W	20-16	Preston, Goulding, Lydon, K. Iro	Lydon (2)	—	—
17.12.88	JPS(SF)	Leeds	Bradford N.	W	16-5	Hanley, T. Iro, Lydon	Lydon (2)	(6809)	Carter
26.12.88	SBC	A	St. Helens	W	18-11	K. Iro, Lydon, Edwards	Lydon (3)	—	—
1.1.89	SBC	H	Warrington	W	26-10	Hanley (2), K. Iro, Edwards	Lydon (5)	18,162	Holdsworth
7.1.89	JPS(F)	Bolton W. F.C.	Widnes	W	12-6	K. Iro, Hanley	Lydon (2)	(20,709)	Holdsworth
11.1.89	SBC	H	Hull	L	20-35	Bell, Hanley, Betts, Preston	Gregory (2)	11,521	Tennant
15.1.89	SBC	H	Halifax	W	26-12	K. Iro (2), Edwards (2), Shelford	Tyrer (3)	16,258	McCallum (Aus)
29.1.89	CC(1)	A	Doncaster	W	38-6	Lydon (4), Betts, T. Iro, Edwards	K. Iro (5)	—	—
12.2.89	CC(2)	A	Bradford N.	W	17-4	Edwards, Kiss, Byrne	K. Iro (2), Lydon (dg)	—	—
14.2.89	SBC	A	Warrington	W	10-4	Preston, Hanley	Lydon	—	—
19.2.89	SBC	H	Leeds	W	16-8	Bell, Hanley	Lydon (4)	19,775	Cross
25.2.89	CC(3)	A	Oldham	W	12-4	Edwards, K. Iro	Lydon (2)	—	—
1.3.89	SBC	A	Featherstone R.	W	24-19	Hampson, Edwards, Hanley	Lydon (5, 1dg), Gregory (1dg)	—	—
5.3.89	SBC	A	Hull K.R.	W	19-18	Edwards, Hanley, Byrne	K. Iro (3), Hanley (dg)	—	—
12.3.89	SBC	H	Bradford N.	W	20-13	Hanley, Gregory	Lydon (6)	11,745	—
19.3.89	SBC	A	Hull	W	28-18	Byrne, K. Iro, Hanley, Betts	Lydon (6)	—	—
25.3.89	CC(SF)	Man C. F.C.	Warrington	W	13-6	Lydon, Edwards	Lydon (2, 1dg)	(26,529)	Whitfield

(continued on page 98)

WORKINGTON TOWN

Ground: Derwent Park
Colours: Blue and white
First Season: 1945-46
Nickname: Town
Chairman: Kevin Gorge
Secretary: John Bell
Coach: Maurice Bamford (July 1988-Dec 1988)
Phil Kitchin (Dec 1988-)
Honours: **Championship** Winners, 1950-51
Beaten finalists, 1957-58
Challenge Cup Winners, 1951-52
Beaten finalists, 1954-55, 1957-58
Lancashire Cup Winners, 1977-78
Beaten finalists, 1976-77, 1978-79, 1979-80
Western Division Championship Winners, 1962-63
Records: Attendance: 17,741 v. Wigan (RL Cup) 3 Mar, 1965. There was a crowd of 20,403 at Borough Park for a RL Cup-tie v. St. Helens on 8 Mar, 1952
Season
Goals: 186 by L. Hopkins, 1981-82
Tries: 49 by J. Lawrenson, 1951-52
Points: 438 by L. Hopkins, 1981-82
Match
Goals: 11 by I. MacCorquodale v. Blackpool B., 6 Jan, 1973
Tries: 7 by I. Southward v. Blackpool B., 17 Sep, 1955
Points: 33 by I. Southward v. Blackpool B., 17 Sep, 1955
Highest score: 62-15 v. Hunslet, 1963-64
Highest against: 68-0 at Wigan, 1986-87

1988-89 PLAYERS' SUMMARY

	App	Tries	Goals	Dr	Pts
Beck, David	24	6	—	—	24
Bower, Ian	2 + 2	—	—	—	—
Burgess, Glen	3 + 6	—	—	—	—
Falcon, Colin	12 + 1	3	—	—	12
Gorge, Paul	24 + 2	—	—	—	—
Higgins, Michael	16	5	—	—	20
Johnson, Robert	1	—	—	—	—
Key, Andrew	1	1	—	—	4
Lamb, Keith	2 + 2	—	—	—	—
Law, Andrew	15	2	—	—	8
Law, Michael	8	—	—	—	—
Lowden, David	28	4	60	4	140
Lynch, Keith	7 + 5	1	—	—	4
Mawson, Mark	26	5	—	—	20
McMullen, Alan	6	—	—	—	—
Morley, Martin	4	—	—	—	—
Newall, John	11 + 2	4	—	—	16
Nixon, Gary	20 + 1	3	—	—	12
Penrice, Paul	15 + 5	2	—	—	8
Phillips, Graham	4 + 1	1	—	—	4
Pickering, Brendan	1 + 1	—	—	—	—
Platt, Billy	4	—	—	—	—
Priestley, Stephen	2	—	—	—	—
Rea, Geoff	11 + 1	4	—	—	16
Riley, Peter	16 + 2	—	—	—	—
Rooney, Neil	9 + 1	1	—	—	4
Shearman, Robert	1	—	—	—	—
Shuttleworth, Greg	16	—	—	1	1
Smith, Gary	29 + 1	5	7	2	36
Stoddart, Peter	1 + 7	—	—	—	—
Sullivan, Joe	21 + 1	3	—	—	12
Tabern, Ray	13 + 1	—	—	—	—
Thornton, Peter	0 + 3	—	—	—	—
Torley, Ian	1	—	—	—	—
Tubman, Keith	19	5	—	—	20
Vannett, Paul	20 + 2	4	—	—	16
Walker, William	1	—	—	—	—
Ward, David	9 + 1	—	—	—	—
TOTALS: 38 players		59	67	7	377

Maurice Bamford, coach of Workington Town for seven months.

1988-89 MATCH ANALYSIS

Date	Competition	H/A	Opponent	Rlt	Score	Tries	Goals	Attendance	Referee
28.8.88	SD	H	Leigh	L	18-38	Penrice, Falcon, Sullivan	Lowden (3)	1534	Carter
4.9.88	SD	A	Chorley B.	W	22-8	Lowden, Vannett, Beck, Higgins	Lowden (2), G. Smith	—	—
11.9.88	SD	H	Carlisle	L	10-11	Higgins	Lowden (3)	1389	Simpson
18.9.88	LC(1)	A	Oldham	L	2-64	—	Lowden	—	—
25.9.88	SD	H	Chorley B.	W	25-4	Rae (2), Smith, Nixon	Lowden (4), Shuttleworth (dg)	697	Holdsworth
2.10.88	SD	A	Keighley	L	15-33	Falcon, Higgins	Lowden (3, ldg)	—	—
9.10.88	SD	H	Huddersfield	W	40-14	Beck (3), Mawson (2), Rae, Smith, Higgins	Lowden (4)	657	Kendrew
16.10.88	SD	A	Doncaster	L	16-34	Falcon, Vannett, Higgins	Lowden (2)	—	—
30.10.88	JPS(P)	H	Castleford	L	2-28	—	Lowden	1502	Dockray
6.11.88	SD	H	Doncaster	W	22-14	Vannett, Sullivan, Beck	Lowden (5)	991	Haigh
20.11.88	SD	A	Dewsbury	L	20-22	Smith, Penrice, Key	Lowden (4)	—	—
4.12.88	SD	H	Fulham	L	16-17	Phillips, Mawson, Rae	Lowden (2)	505	Galtress
11.12.88	SD	A	Swinton	L	10-24	Lowden, Beck	Lowden	—	—
18.12.88	SD	H	Rochdale H.	W	10-8	Mawson	Lowden (3)	562	Holgate
26.12.88	SD	A	Whitehaven	L	0-21	—	—	—	—
1.1.89	SD	H	Barrow	L	4-20	Rooney	—	545	Spencer
8.1.89	SD	A	Leigh	L	1-56	—	Lowden (dg)	—	—
15.1.89	CC(P)	A	York	L	8-35	Tubman	Smith (2)	—	—
22.1.89	SD	A	Runcorn H.	L	8-8	Lowden	Lowden (2)	—	—
5.2.89	SD	H	Batley	W	6-5	Law	Lowden	344	Burke
12.2.89	SD	H	Swinton	W	23-10	Sullivan, Smith, Newall	Lowden (5, ldg)	589	Berry
19.2.89	SD	A	Rochdale H.	L	20-42	Law, Smith, Newall, Mawson	Lowden (2)	—	—
26.2.89	SD	H	Keighley	L	0-14	—	—	447	Houghton
5.3.89	SD	A	Fulham	L	19-21	Tubman (2), Newall	Lowden (3, ldg)	—	—
12.3.89	SD	H	Runcorn H.	W	10-0	Tubman (2)	Lowden	389	Burke
19.3.89	SD	A	Batley	L	14-25	Vannett, Lowden, Newall	Lowden	—	—
24.3.89	SD	H	Whitehaven	L	5-12	—	Lowden (2), Smith (dg)	1669	Steele
27.3.89	SD	A	Barrow	L	0-32	—	—	—	—
2.4.89	SD	H	Dewsbury	W	10-2	—	Lowden (5)	402	Holgate
9.4.89	SD	A	Carlisle	L	18-24	Nixon (2), Lynch	Smith (3)	—	—
12.4.89	SD	A	Huddersfield	L	3-30	—	Smith (1, ldg)	—	—

YORK

● **Moved to Monks Cross Stadium, Ryedale, at the start of the 1989-90 season, with a change of name to Ryedale-York.**

Ground: Wiggington Road
Colours: Amber and black
First Season: 1901-02
Nickname: Wasps
Chairman: Ted Tebbutt
Secretary: Ian Clough
Coach: Gary Stephens (Apr 1988-)
Honours: **Division Two** Champions, 1980-81
Challenge Cup Beaten finalists, 1930-31
Yorkshire Cup Winners, 1922-23, 1933-34, 1936-37
Beaten finalists, 1935-36, 1957-58, 1978-79
Records: Attendance: 14,689 v. Swinton (RL Cup) 10 Feb, 1934
Season
Goals: 146 by V. Yorke, 1957-58
Tries: 35 by J. Crossley, 1980-81
Points: 318 by G. Steadman, 1984-85
Match
Goals: 11 by V. Yorke v. Whitehaven, 6 Sep, 1958; C. Gibson v. Dewsbury, 28 Sep, 1980
Tries: 6 by R. Hardgrave v. Bramley, 5 Jan, 1935
Points: 26 by G. Steadman v. Batley, 25 Nov, 1984
Highest score: 60-0 v. Barrow, 1971-72; 60-10 v. Workington T., 1986-87
Highest against: 75-3 v. Warrington 1950-51

1988-89 PLAYERS' SUMMARY

	App	Tries	Goals	Dr	Pts
Atkins, Gary	29 + 1	14	—	—	56
Atkins, Paul...................	9	3	—	—	12
Bleakley, Steve	26 + 1	4	—	—	16
Carlyle, Brendan	2 + 1	2	—	—	8
Crossley, John	0 + 7	2	—	—	8
Dobson, Steve	10 + 8	3	—	4	16
Ellis, St. John	29	10	38	—	116
Fletcher, Ian	21 + 3	5	—	—	20
Hague, Neil....................	1	—	—	—	—
Hammerton, Chris	13 + 3	5	1	2	24
Harrison, Chris...............	7 + 2	—	—	—	—
Hayes, Richard...............	3 + 1	—	—	—	—
Horton, Stuart................	29 + 2	4	—	6	22
Hughes, Ian...................	7 + 4	—	—	—	—
Macklin-Shaw, Chris........	16 + 2	4	13	—	42
Miles, Paul	8 + 2	1	—	—	4
Mulherin, Paul	27	6	—	—	24
Olsen, Steve..................	9 + 5	1	—	—	4
Paver, Ian	32 + 2	6	—	—	24
Payne, Phil	20 + 1	5	—	—	20
Pryce, Geoff..................	20	11	—	—	44
St. Hilaire, Darren	22 + 1	5	—	—	20
Scott, Mick...................	8 + 1	—	—	—	—
Shillito, Alan.................	4 + 2	—	—	—	—
Smith, Steve	2	—	—	—	—
Stephens, Gary	14 + 1	2	—	1	9
Sullivan, Graham	25 + 3	5	58	1	137
Timson, Andy	2	—	—	—	—
Wheatley, Steve	6 + 2	2	—	—	8
White, Paul	21	4	—	—	16
Wigglesworth, Iain	25	10	—	—	40
Willey, Sean..................	2 + 2	—	—	—	—
Williams, Dean...............	6 + 1	1	—	—	4
TOTALS:					
33 players......................		115	110	14	694

York player-coach Gary Stephens, who made 15 appearances.

1988-89 MATCH ANALYSIS

Date	Competition	H/A	Opponent	Rlt	Score	Tries	Goals	Attendance	Referee
26.8.88	SD	H	Batley	W	24-15	Macklin-Shaw (2), White, St. Hilaire	Macklin-Shaw (4)	1567	Holgate
4.9.88	SD	H	Keighley	L	16-18	Macklin-Shaw, St. Hilaire, Fletcher	Macklin-Shaw, Sullivan	1872	Spencer
11.9.88	SD	A	Doncaster	L	10-23	Wigglesworth, Wheatley	Macklin-Shaw	—	—
18.9.88	YC(1)	H	Mansfield M.	W	25-4	Sullivan (2), Wheatley, Fletcher	Macklin-Shaw (4), Dobson (dg)	1370	Whitelam
25.9.88	SD	H	Dewsbury	L	12-14	Wigglesworth, G. Atkins	Macklin-Shaw (2)	1536	Spencer
28.9.88	YC(2)	A	Castleford	L	14-40	Paver, St. Hilaire	Sullivan (2), Macklin-Shaw	—	—
9.10.88	SD	A	Swinton	W	26-8	Bleakley, Ellis, G. Atkins	Sullivan (6), Dobson (2dg)	—	—
16.10.88	SD	H	Swinton	D	18-18	Wigglesworth, Pryce	Sullivan (4, 1dg), Dobson (1dg)	1785	Kendrew
23.10.88	SD	A	Dewsbury	W	45-6	Pryce (3), G. Atkins (2), Ellis, Wigglesworth, Paver	Sullivan (6), Stephens (dg)	—	—
26.10.88	SD	A	Sheffield E.	L	16-28	Miles, Ellis, Horton	Sullivan (2)	—	—
30.10.88	SD	H	Leigh	W	37-18	Wigglesworth (2), Pryce, Atkins, Mulherin	Sullivan (8), Horton (dg)	2305	Allatt
13.11.88	JPS(1)	H	St. Helens	L	6-14	—	Sullivan (3)	3082	Cross
20.11.88	SD	H	Barrow	L	12-18	Pryce, Dobson	Sullivan (2)	1621	Houghton
27.11.88	SD	A	Fulham	W	22-8	Wigglesworth, G. Atkins, Pryce, Payne	Sullivan (3)	—	—
4.12.88	SD	H	Doncaster	W	20-10	Fletcher, Mulherin, Crossley	Sullivan (4)	2337	Dockray
11.12.88	SD	H	Chorley B.	W	30-6	Ellis, Payne, Mulherin, Crossley, Paver	Ellis (5)	1531	Tickle
18.12.88	SD	H	Bramley	L	11-20	Payne, Horton	Ellis, Horton (dg)	2108	Kendrew
26.12.88	SD	H	Mansfield M.	W	59-4	Wigglesworth (2), Fletcher (2), Pryce (2), Payne, Macklin-Shaw, G. Atkins, Ellis, Paver	Ellis (6), Hammerton, Horton (dg)	1706	Burke
1.1.89	SD	A	Hunslet	W	29-15	Ellis, Paver, Bleakley, White	Ellis (6), Horton (dg)	—	—
15.1.89	CC(P)	H	Workington T.	W	35-8	Ellis (2), St. Hilaire, Hammerton, Horton, Carlyle	Ellis (5), Horton (dg)	1959	Allatt
22.1.89	SD	A	Mansfield M.	W	23-12	Hammerton, White, G. Atkins, Ellis	Ellis (3), Hammerton (dg)	—	—
29.1.89	CC(1)	H (York C. F.C.)	Leeds	L	9-28	Horton	Ellis (2), Horton (dg)	(11,347)	Tennant
5.2.89	SD	A	Huddersfield	W	17-1	Pryce (2), White	Ellis (2), Hammerton (dg)	—	—
12.2.89	SD	H	Huddersfield	W	10-4	St. Hilaire, Hammerton	Ellis	2089	Galtress
19.2.89	SD	A	Keighley	L	6-7	Ellis	Ellis	—	—
5.3.89	SD	A	Barrow	W	26-12	P. Atkins (2), Payne, Bleakley, Hammerton	Ellis (2), Sullivan	—	—
12.3.89	SD	H	Fulham	W	30-10	Sullivan (2), G. Atkins (2), P. Atkins, Dobson	Ellis (3)	1877	Crashley (Pr)
19.3.89	SD	A	Chorley B.	W	6-4	Olsen	Sullivan	—	—
24.3.89	SD	H	Sheffield E.	L	0-21	—	—	2809	Galtress
26.3.89	SD	H	Hunslet	W	26-17	Wigglesworth, G. Atkins, Mulherin, Paver, Williams	Sullivan (3)	2904	Morris
2.4.89	SD	A	Batley	W	20-19	G. Atkins (2), Sullivan, Mulherin	Sullivan (2)	—	—
9.4.89	SD	A	Leigh	L	14-24	Hammerton, G. Atkins	Sullivan (2), Ellis	—	—
16.4.89	SD	A	Bramley	L	20-23	Carlyle, Stephens, Bleakley	Sullivan (4)	—	—
23.4.89	SDP (1)	H (Castleford)	Swinton	D	4-4	—	Sullivan (2)	1000	Tennant
25.4.89	SD(1) Replay	A	Swinton	L	16-17	Mulherin, Dobson, Stephens	Sullivan (2)	—	—

WIDNES MATCH ANALYSIS (continued)

Date	Competition	H/A	Opponent	Rlt	Score	Tries	Goals	Attendance	Referee
26.2.89	CC(3)	A	Leeds	W	24-4	Grima (2), Eyres, Currier, Offiah	Currier (2)	—	—
11.3.89	CC(SF)	Wigan	St. Helens	L	14-16	Wright, D. Hulme	Currier (3)	(17,119)	Holdsworth
15.3.89	SBC	H	Warrington	W	32-4	Offiah (5), Tait	Currier (4)	8947	Tennant
19.3.89	SBC	A	Bradford N.	D	16-16	Wright (2), Currier	Currier (2)	—	—
22.3.89	SBC	A	Oldham	W	35-16	Davies (2), Wright (2), Offiah, Thackray	Davies (5, ldg)	—	—
27.3.89	SBC	A	St. Helens	W	44-16	Offiah (3), Currier, Eyres, Davies, D. Hulme	Davies (8)	—	—
30.3.89	SBC	H	Castleford	W	36-4	D. Hulme (3), Offiah (2), Currier	Davies (6)	11,024	Steele
2.4.89	SBC	H	Bradford N.	L	12-22	Currier, M. O'Neill	Currier (2)	9537	Cross
5.4.89	SBC	A	Hull	L	16-23	Davies, Tait	Davies (4)	—	—
9.4.89	SBC	A	Hull K.R.	W	16-13	Currier, Koloto, Tait	Davies (2)	—	—
12.4.89	SBC	A	Castleford	W	24-22	Koloto (2), Currier, Offiah	Currier (4)	—	—
16.4.89	SBC	H	Wigan	W	32-18	Offiah (3), McKenzie, Sorensen, P. Hulme	Davies (4)	17,323	Holdsworth
23.4.89	PT(1)	H	Bradford N.	W	30-18	Offiah (3), Thackray, McKenzie	Currier (5)	8483	Haigh
7.5.89	PT(SF)	H	St. Helens	W	38-14	Offiah (2), Thackray (2), Eyres, O'Neill, Wright	Davies (5)	12,484	Holdsworth
14.5.89	PT(F)	Man U. F.C.	Hull	W	18-10	Wright, Currier, Offiah	Davies (3)	40,194	Holdsworth
27.5.89	Euro' Champ	Arles	St. Esteve	W	60-6	Thackray (4), Davies (2), Grima (2), Marsh, Kebbie, Moriarty	Davies (5), Kebbie (3)	350	Tennant

WIGAN MATCH ANALYSIS (continued)

Date	Competition	H/A	Opponent	Rlt	Score	Tries	Goals	Attendance	Referee
27.3.89	SBC	A	Oldham	W	27-21	Edwards (3), Betts, T. Iro	Gregory (3, 1dg)	—	—
2.4.89	SBC	A	Castleford	W	17-4	Hanley, Bell	Lydon (4, 1dg)	—	—
5.4.89	SBC	H	Featherstone R.	W	14-10	Preston, Bell, Goodway	Lydon	10,124	Cross
9.4.89	SBC	H	Salford	W	28-18	Hanley, Lydon, Shelford, Betts, Preston	Lydon (4)	—	Kershaw
12.4.89	SBC	H	St. Helens	W	14-7	Hanley	Hampson (5)	21,076	Whitfield
16.4.89	SBC	A	Widnes	L	18-32	Platt, Goodway, Hanley	Lydon (3)	—	—
23.4.89	PT(1)	H	St. Helens	L	2-4	—	Hampson	17,542	Carter
29.4.89	CC(F)	Wembley	St. Helens	W	27-0	K. Iro (2), Hanley, Gregory, Hampson	Lydon (3), Gregory (dg)	78,000	Tennant

1988-89 top goals and points scorer, Sheffield Eagles stand off Mark Aston.

RECORDS

LEADING SCORERS FOR 1988-89

TOP TEN TRIES

1. Martin Offiah (Widnes) 60
2. Barry Ledger (Leigh) 34
3. Derek Bate (Swinton)................................. 32
4. Ellery Hanley (Wigan)................................ 29
5. Peter Lister (Bramley)................................ 28
   Darryl Powell (Sheffield E.) 28
7. Peter Lewis (Bramley)................................ 26
8. Les Quirk (St. Helens)............................... 24
   Grant Anderson (Castleford) 24
   Paul Burns (Barrow) 24
● Others with 20 or more: David Ruane (Leigh) 23;
Garry Schofield (Leeds), Paul Gearey (Batley) 22; Steve
McGowan (Bradford N.) 21; Karl Fairbank (Bradford
N.), Carl Gibson (Leeds), Kevin Iro (Wigan), Ian Jeffrey
(Leigh), Neil Turner (Doncaster), Dean Williams
(Rochdale H. and York) 20.

TOP TEN GOALS
(Including drop goals)

1. Mark Aston (Sheffield E.) 148
2. Martin Ketteridge (Castleford)..................... 129
3. David Hobbs (Bradford N.)......................... 118
4. Chris Johnson (Leigh) 117
5. Dean Marwood (Barrow) 115
6. Paul Loughlin (St. Helens) 113
7. David Noble (Doncaster)........................... 110
8. John Woods (Warrington) 107
   Andy Currier (Widnes) 107
10. Steve Turner (Rochdale H.)....................... 104
● Also 100 goals or more: Barry Vickers (Carlisle) 102.

TOP FIVE DROP GOALS

1. Gary Pearce (Hull) 16
2. John Stainburn (Batley) 13
   Mark Aston (Sheffield E.) 13
4. Simon Wilson (Batley) 11
5. Deryck Fox (Featherstone R.) 9

TOP FIVE POINTS

	T	G	DG	Pts
1. Mark Aston (Sheffield E.)..	6	135	13	307
2. Andy Currier (Widnes)......	19	106	1	289
3. Chris Johnson (Leigh).......	12	114	3	279
4. David Hobbs (Bradford N.)	10	113	5	271
5. Martin Ketteridge (Cas'd)..	3	129	0	270

Key:
SBC .... Stones Bitter Championship
SD............... Second Division
SDP............. Second Division Premiership
LC............... Lancashire Cup
YC............... Yorkshire Cup
JPS.............. John Player Special Trophy
CC............... Challenge Cup
PT.............. Premiership Trophy
NA .... Non-appearance

OUTSTANDING SCORING FEATS IN 1988-89

INDIVIDUAL

Most tries in a match:
5 by Andy Currier (Widnes) v. Featherstone R... SBC
   Darryl Powell (Sheffield E) at Mansfield M   SD
   Martin Offiah (Widnes) v. Warrington .... SBC

Most goals in a match:
13 by Martin Ketteridge (Castleford) v.
Huddersfield .... YC
11 by Steve Guyett (Fulham) v. Huddersfield..... SD
10 by Mick Burke (Oldham) v. Workington T.... LC
   Mark Aston (Sheffield E.) v.
   Wigan St. Patricks............................... JPS
   Dean Marwood (Barrow) at Runcorn H .... SD
   Chris Johnson (Leigh) v. Workington T.... SD
   Chris Johnson (Leigh) v. Runcorn H........ SD
   Chris Wilkinson (Dewsbury) v.
   Huddersfield .... SD

Most points in a match:
34 by Andy Currier (Widnes) v. Featherstone R . SD
   Kevin Iro (Wigan) v. Runcorn H .... JPS
   Martin Ketteridge (C'ford) v. Huddersfield YC
32 by Chris Johnson (Leigh) at Runcorn H........ SD
28 by Dean Marwood (Barrow) at Runcorn H .... SD

TEAM

Highest score:
Castleford 94 v. Huddersfield 12...................... YC
● There was a total of 29 matches in which a team scored
50 points or more, compared with 22 in the previous
season. The other 60-plus scores were:

Home:
Wigan 92 v. Runcorn H 2.............................. JPS
Sheffield E 80 v. Wigan St. Patricks 8.............. JPS
Oldham 64 v. Workington T 2....................... LC
Bramley 62 v. Dewsbury 14........................... SD
Fulham 61 v. Huddersfield 22.......................... SD
Warrington 60 v. Hull K.R. 24........................ SBC
Whitehaven 60 v. Fulham 0............................ SD

Away:
Runcorn H 2 v. Leigh 88............................... SD
Runcorn H 0 v. Barrow 60............................. SD

Highest score by losing team:
Dewsbury 36 v. Rochdale H 34....................... SD
● There was a total of 64 matches in which a team scored
20 points or more and lost, compared with 54 the
previous season.

High-scoring draws:
None in which both teams scored 20 or more points,
compared with four the previous season.

● From the start of the 1983-84 season, the value of a try was raised from three points to four points. It was decided officially that records for most points in a match, season or career would subsequently include the four-point try and that no attempt would be made to adjust existing records featuring the three-point try. This rule applies to all other changes in scoring values.
● Substitute appearances do not count towards players' full appearance records.

RECORD-BREAKING FEATS 1988-89

MARTIN OFFIAH scored a Widnes record 58 tries in a season, including a club record-equalling five in one match. He also raced to the fastest century of career tries.

DARRYL POWELL scored a Sheffield Eagles record 28 tries in a season, including a club record five in one match. He also extended the club career record to 59 tries. ANDY DICKINSON briefly held the match record with four tries.

NEIL TURNER equalled the Doncaster record of 20 tries in a season set by himself.

ELLERY HANLEY of Wigan finished the season with a Division One career record 178 tries.

MARK ASTON scored a Sheffield Eagles record 148 goals and 307 points in a season while joining the few players who have scored in every match throughout a season.

STEVE TURNER scored a Rochdale Hornets record of 243 points in a season.

JOHN WOODS of Warrington finished the season with a Division One career record 854 goals.

WAYNE SANCHEZ scored a record-equalling seven goals in a match for Mansfield Marksman.

STEVE GUYETT scored a record 11 goals in a match for Fulham.

CHRIS WILKINSON scored a record equalling 10 goals in a match for Dewsbury.

DAVID STEPHENSON of Leeds scored a record six goals in a Yorkshire Cup final.

BARRY VICKERS scored a record-breaking 22 points in a match for Carlisle and equalled the club record of nine goals in a match.

ANDY CURRIER scored a Widnes record 34 points in a match, including a club record-equalling five tries in a match.

DAVID NOBLE scored a Doncaster record-equalling 20 points in a match.

John Woods, Division One career goals record holder.

DEAN MARWOOD scored a record-equalling 28 points in a match for Barrow.

CASTLEFORD scored a club record 94-12 victory which was also Huddersfield's biggest defeat and the highest score in a Yorkshire Cup-tie.

FULHAM ran up their highest score with a 61-22 defeat of Huddersfield.

BRAMLEY ran up their highest score with a 62-14 defeat of Dewsbury.

SHEFFIELD EAGLES had a club record 80-8 victory over Wigan St. Patricks.

CHORLEY BOROUGH's 56-2 win at Runcorn Highfield was a club record.

CARLISLE had a club record 58-1 victory over Mansfield Marksman which beat the 52-10 defeat of Fulham earlier in the season.

LEIGH scored a Division Two record away win of 88-2 at Runcorn Highfield.

WIGAN ran up a 92-2 record John Player Special Trophy score which was Runcorn Highfield's biggest defeat.

ROCHDALE HORNETS scored most points by a losing side in a Division Two match when they lost 36-34 at Dewsbury.

NEW RECORDS IN DETAIL . . .

MARTIN OFFIAH broke the Widnes tries in a season record for the second successive season and equalled the match record of five touchdowns. The former Rosslyn Park Rugby Union winger followed his record-breaking first season in even more remarkable style as he scored 58 tries for Widnes — 16 more than he had scored in 1987-88.

Offiah reached the old record of 42 tries with the last of his club record-equalling five tries in the 32-4 Stones Bitter championship home defeat of Warrington on 15 March.

He beat the season's record with a try in a 35-16 league win at Oldham on 23 March.

Including representative scores, and a tour Down Under, Offiah claimed the fastest-ever century of tries with the first of his two in a 22-10 Stones Bitter Championship win at Featherstone Rovers on 19 February. It came 17½ months after making his Rugby League debut at home to Halifax on 30 August 1987.

The previous fastest century was in 18½ months by South African Tom Van Vollenhoven of St. Helens from 26 October 1957 to 15 May 1959.

The record century in fewest matches played remains with Billy Boston who did it in 68 matches for Wigan and representative teams after his debut in 1953-54. Offiah's century came in his 80th match including two substitute appearances on the 1988 tour of Australia. Offiah, who finished with 60, became the first winger to score 50 or more in a season since Boston got 51 in 1961-62.

His match-by-match record in 1988-89 was as follows:

Widnes

		Tries
Wigan (Charity Shield)	(IOM)	1
Halifax	(A)	1
Hull	(H)	4
Leeds	(A)	0
St. Helens (LC)	(H)	2
Featherstone R	(H)	4
Swinton (LC)	(H)	1
Salford	(A)	1
Halifax	(H)	0
Wigan (LC)	(A)	0
Wakefield T	(A)	0
Wigan	(A)	1
Featherstone R. (JPS)	(H)	3
Hull K.R.	(H)	2
Sheffield E (JPS)	(A)	1
Warrington (JPS)	(H)	2
St. Helens (JPS)	(Wigan)	2
Wakefield T	(H)	1
Leeds	(H)	1
Warrington	(A)	0
St. Helens	(H)	1
Wigan (JPS)	(Bolton)	0
Salford	(H)	4
Salford (CC)	(A)	1
Oldham	(H)	NA
Castleford (CC)	(A)	1
Featherstone R	(A)	2
Leeds (CC)	(A)	1
St. Helens (CC)	(Wigan)	0
Warrington	(H)	5
Bradford N	(A)	0
Oldham	(A)	1
St. Helens	(A)	3
Castleford	(H)	2
Bradford N	(H)	0
Hull	(A)	0
Hull K.R.	(A)	0
Castleford	(A)	1
Wigan	(H)	3
Bradford N. (PT)	(H)	3
St. Helens (PT)	(H)	2
Hull (PT)	(Man. U.)	1
St. Esteve (Euro Challenge)	(A)	NA

Great Britain

Rest of the World	(H)	1
France	(H)	1
France	(A)	0
Total		**60**

DARRYL POWELL broke three club records at Sheffield Eagles with 28 tries in a season, five in a match and a career total of 59.

ANDY DICKINSON, Powell's co-centre, had become the first Sheffield player to score more than three tries in a match when he touched down four times in the 50-8 Division Two home win over Dewsbury on 18 December. But the record lasted only two weeks before Powell smashed it with five tries in a 50-10 league win at Mansfield Marksman on 2 January.

Two more tries in the next match — a 42-4 win at Sheffield on 15 January — took the centre past the season's record, winger Steve Lidbury having set the record with 17 in 1986-87. A hat-trick in Sheffield's 43-18 Division Two Premiership final win over Swinton at Old Trafford gave Powell a season's total of 28, three of his tries coming in a six-match spell as loose forward at the start of the season.

The Division Two Player of the Year finished the season with a club record 59 career tries, having shared the old record of 31 with Lidbury.

A former Redhill, Castleford, junior player, Powell made his professional debut in Sheffield's first-ever game on 2 September 1984 when they beat Rochdale Hornets 29-10.

Powell's career total of 59, which includes a five-try feat and one other hat-trick, is made up as follows:

Sheffield E.

1984-85	5
1985-86	9
1986-87	8
1987-88	9
1988-89	28
Total	**59**

Powell's record-breaking season went as follows:

		Tries
Bramley	(H)	NA
Wakefield T. (YC)	(H)	NA
Fulham	(A)	1
Barrow	(H)	0
Mansfield M.	(H)	1
Leigh	(A)	0
Chorley B	(A)	1
Leigh	(H)	0
Batley	(H)	0
York	(H)	0
Keighley	(H)	1
Wigan St. Patricks (JPS)	(H)	2
Huddersfield	(A)	1
Widnes (JPS)	(H)	0
Keighley	(A)	0
Dewsbury	(H)	2
Doncaster	(A)	2
Mansfield M.	(A)	5
Batley	(A)	2
Swinton	(H)	1
Leigh (CC)	(H)	0
Bramley	(A)	1
Oldham (CC)	(H)	1
Huddersfield	(H)	2
Swinton	(A)	1
Doncaster	(H)	0
Hunslet	(H)	NA
Barrow	(A)	1
York	(A)	0
Fulham	(H)	0
Chorley B	(H)	NA
Dewsbury	(A)	NA
Hunslet	(A)	NA
Doncaster (SDP)	(H)	0
Barrow (SDP)	(A)	0
Swinton (SDP)	(Man. U.)	3
Total		**28**

NEIL TURNER equalled the Doncaster record of 20 tries in a season which he had set in 1985-86. The winger equalled the record with a try in the closing minutes of the last match of the season, a 28-10 defeat at Sheffield Eagles in the Division Two Premiership first round on 23 April.

He played in 30 matches, compared with 35 in 1985-86.

Turner's match-by-match figures were:

		Tries
Fulham	(H)	1
Bramley	(A)	0
York	(H)	0
Featherstone R. (YC)	(A)	0
Runcorn H.	(A)	0
Dewsbury	(H)	2
Carlisle	(A)	1
Workington T.	(H)	1

Mansfield M.	(A)	3
Workington T.	(A)	0
Swinton (JPS)	(A)	1
Hunslet	(H)	0
Leigh (JPS)	(A)	0
York	(A)	0
Bramley	(H)	0
Huddersfield	(H)	1
Sheffield E.	(H)	1
Dewsbury	(A)	1
West Hull (CC)	(A)	2
Whitehaven	(A)	1
Wigan (CC)	(H)	0
Runcorn H.	(H)	3
Mansfield M.	(H)	NA
Batley	(A)	NA
Rochdale H.	(H)	0
Sheffield E.	(A)	NA
Whitehaven	(H)	0
Hunslet	(A)	0
Fulham	(A)	0
Batley	(H)	NA
Rochdale H.	(A)	1
Carlisle	(H)	0
Huddersfield	(A)	0
Sheffield E. (SDP)	(A)	1
Total		**20**

ELLERY HANLEY of Wigan finished the season with a Division One career record of 178 tries. The old record of 165 was scored by former Salford winger Keith Fielding from 1973-74 to 1980-81.

Hanley equalled the record with a try at Salford on 20 November when Wigan lost 24-16 and beat it with the first of two tries in a 26-10 home win over Warrington on 1 January.

The Great Britain Test star also holds the record for most Division One tries in a season with 44 for Wigan in 1986-87, having set the record with 40 for Bradford Northern in 1984-85.

He equalled the Division One record of five in a match for Wigan against Bradford on 1 March 1987. Although that was beaten by Shane Cooper's six for St. Helens, Hanley's five is still the best by a forward.

Hanley turned professional with Bradford as a 17-year-old on 2 June 1978 from Corpus Christi amateurs in Leeds and made a tryscoring debut as a substitute in a 30-18 Division One home defeat of Rochdale Hornets on 26 November 1978.

He was then absent for a period and did not make his full debut until 16 August 1981 when he scored a try playing centre in a Yorkshire Cup tie at Halifax. His full Division One debut followed on 30 August when he scored a try at stand off in an 11-12 home defeat against Widnes.

Wigan signed him in a then world record £150,000 deal on 16 September 1985 and he made his debut in the centre in a 32-10 Division One home win over Widnes on 22

September 1985.

After playing as a centre or stand off, Hanley switched to loose forward in February 1987. Three times he has finished as Division One's top tryscorer and has totalled 18 league hat-tricks including four four-try feats and five once.

His season-by-season Division One totals are as follows:

Bradford N.

1978-79	1
1979-80	0
1980-81	0
1981-82	12
1982-83	8
1983-84	11
1984-85	40

Wigan

1985-86	22
1986-87	44
1987-88	22
1988-89	18

Totals

Bradford N.	72
Wigan	106

GRAND TOTAL 178

MARK ASTON scored a Sheffield Eagles record 148 goals and 307 points in a season while joining the few players who have scored in every match throughout a season. The half back's totals included 13 drop goals and six tries.

The old Sheffield records were by winger Roy Rafferty in 1985-86 with 79 goals and 186 points, including seven tries.

Aston broke the goals record with the last of five in a 42-4 Division Two win at Batley on 15 January and the points record went when he scored 10 points in a 23-17 Silk Cut Challenge Cup first round home defeat of Leigh on 29 January.

A 19-point haul in the 43-18 Division Two Premiership final defeat of Swinton at Old Trafford completed Aston's record-breaking season by becoming only the 11th player to score in every match throughout a season.

Aston's match-by-match tally was as follows:

		T	G	DG	Pts
Bramley	(H)	0	2	1	5
Wakefield T. (YC)	(H)	2	0	0	8
Fulham	(A)	0	2	0	4
Barrow	(H)	0	3	1	7
Mansfield M.	(H)	0	3	1	7
Leigh	(A)	0	2	0	4
Chorley B.	(A)	0	3	0	6
Leigh	(H)	0	4	1	9
Batley	(H)	0	1	0	2
York	(H)	1	4	0	12

Keighley	(H)	0	5	0	10
Wigan St. Patricks (JPS)	(H)	0	10	0	20
Huddersfield	(A)	1	3	0	10
Widnes (JPS)	(H)	0	2	1	5
Keighley	(A)	0	7	0	14
Dewsbury	(H)	0	5	0	10
Doncaster	(A)	0	5	0	10
Mansfield M.	(A)	0	9	0	18
Batley	(A)	0	5	0	10
Swinton	(H)	0	3	1	7
Leigh (CC)	(H)	0	4	2	10
Bramley	(A)	0	2	1	5
Oldham (CC)	(H)	0	4	0	8
Huddersfield	(H)	0	4	0	8
Swinton	(A)	0	3	0	6
Doncaster	(H)	0	6	1	13
Hunslet	(H)	0	4	0	8
Barrow	(A)	1	3	0	10
York	(A)	0	1	0	2
Fulham	(H)	0	6	0	12
Chorley B.	(H)	0	5	0	10
Dewsbury	(A)	0	1	1	3
Hunslet	(A)	0	1	0	2
Doncaster (SDP)	(H)	0	4	0	8
Barrow (SDP)	(A)	0	2	1	5
Swinton (SDP)	(Man. U)	1	7	1	19
Totals					
36 appearances		6	135	13	307

STEVE TURNER scored a club record 243 points in a season for Rochdale Hornets, made up of 104 goals, including a drop, and nine tries. He beat the old record of 235 points by utility back Graham Starkey, who scored 98 goals and 13 tries in 1966-67.

Turner passed Starkey's figure with the last of his five goals in a 26-12 Division Two home defeat of Fulham on 6 April.

It was Turner's first season back with Rochdale after a spell in amateur rugby. He played mostly at stand off but occasionally centre, wing and loose forward.

Turner's record-breaking season went as follows:

		T	G	DG	Pts
Barrow	(H)	1	6	0	16
Huddersfield	(A)	2	3	0	14
Whitehaven	(H)	0	6	0	12
Fulham (LC)	(H)	0	4	0	8
Keighley	(H)	0	3	0	6
Wigan (LC)	(A)	0	0	0	0
Whitehaven	(A)	NA			
Dewsbury	(A)	0	5	0	10
Chorley B.	(H)	0	3	0	6
Barrow	(A)	NA			
Batley	(A)	0	2	0	4
Huddersfield	(A)	0	9	0	18
Whitehaven (JPS)	(H)	0	3	0	6

Runcorn H. .... (A)	0	6	0	12
Wakefield T. (JPS) .... (A)	0	2	0	4
Batley .... (H)	0	6	0	12
Workington T. .... (A)	0	2	0	4
Swinton .... (H)	0	0	0	0
Fulham .... (A)★	0	0	0	0
Runcorn H. .... (H)★	1	1	0	6
Keighley .... (A)	0	4	0	8
Carlisle .... (A)★	1	0	0	4
Hull K.R. (CC) .... (H)	0	3	0	6
Leigh .... (H)	0	0	0	0
Workington T. .... (H)	0	7	0	14
Doncaster .... (A)	3	6	0	24
Dewsbury .... (H)	0	4	0	8
Leigh .... (A)	0	1	1	3
Swinton .... (A)	1	1	0	6
Chorley B. .... (A)	0	3	0	6
Doncaster .... (H)	0	5	0	10
Fulham .... (H)	0	5	0	10
Carlisle .... (H)	0	3	0	6

★ substitute appearance

Totals

Appearances 28 + 3	9	103	1	243

Leigh

1976-77	62	(2)
1977-78 .... In Division Two		
1978-79	72	(1)
1979-80	55	(2)
1980-81	62	(1)
1981-82	110	(1)
1982-83	44	(1)
1983-84	102	(1)
1984-85	56	(1)

Bradford N.

1985-86	84	
1986-87	48	

Warrington

1987-88	95	(4)
1988-89	64	

Totals

Leigh	563	(10)
Bradford N.	132	
Warrington	159	(4)
GRAND TOTAL	854	**(14)**

( ) Drop goals included in total

JOHN WOODS of Warrington finished the season with a Division One career record 854 goals. The previous holder was former Warrington player Steve Hesford who kicked 845, including 35 drop goals, between 1975 and 1985. Woods broke the record with eight goals in a 33-4 home defeat of Halifax on 19 March. Woods' total included 14 drop goals and is made up of 563 for Leigh, 132 for Bradford Northern and 159 for Warrington.

He made his debut for Leigh in a Division One 18-8 home win over Barrow on 5 September 1976 when he scored a try but did not kick a goal. Leigh were relegated to Division Two the following season but returned after one season and Woods has remained a Division One player.

The former Test player was transferred to Bradford during the 1985 close season for £65,000, then a record fee for both clubs. Woods kicked a goal on his Northern debut in a 32-7 league defeat at Warrington on 1 September 1985.

After two seasons Woods moved to Warrington for about £40,000 and made his debut with nine goals in a 54-4 home league defeat of Hunslet on 30 August 1987.

Woods has twice finished at the top of the Division One goalscoring list with 110 in 1981-82 and 95 in 1987-88. His best Division One match tally is 10 against York in a 56-6 home victory on 28 March 1982.

Woods is also the record holder of most Division One career points with 2,130 and holds the record for most points in a season with 295 for Leigh in 1983-84.

His Division One goals totals, which do not include six scored in two abandoned matches that were replayed, are as follows:

WAYNE SANCHEZ scored a record-equalling seven goals in a match for Mansfield Marksman in a Division Two home win of 36-14 over Hunslet on 2 October. It was only the Australian scrum half's third match for Mansfield, including one as substitute. Barry Holden set the record with seven goals in a 54-10 Division Two home defeat of Doncaster on 10 March 1985.

STEVE GUYETT kicked a club record 11 goals for Fulham in a 61-22 Division Two home defeat of Huddersfield on 23 October. The full back's tally included a drop goal and beat the eight, including a drop, by Ian MacCorquodale, also against Huddersfield, in a 30-7 Division Two home win on 12 October 1980.

CHRIS WILKINSON scored a club record-equalling 10 goals for Dewsbury when they beat Huddersfield 41-14 in a Division Two home game on 27 March. It was the former Fulham stand off's seventh match for Dewsbury. He shares the record with Jim Ledgard, who kicked 10 goals in a 53-2 Yorkshire Cup first round defeat of Yorkshire Amateurs on 13 September 1947 and Nigel Stephenson's 10 against Blackpool Borough in a 41-13 home league win on 28 August 1972.

DAVID STEPHENSON of Leeds kicked a Yorkshire Cup final record six goals in the 33-12 defeat of Castleford at Elland Road on 16 October. The previous best of five goals had been achieved 12 times. Stephenson also shares the Lancashire Cup final record with seven for Wigan against Warrington in 1985.

BARRY VICKERS equalled the Carlisle record of nine goals in a match, the full back adding a try for a club record 22 points in the 58-1 Silk Cut Challenge Cup first round defeat of Mansfield Marksman on 29 January. Dean Carroll also kicked nine goals, including a drop, against Mansfield in a Division Two 45-13 home win on 16 March 1986. The half back added a try to set the old points record of 21 which he equalled with seven goals, including a drop, plus two tries in a 41-22 Division Two victory at Fulham on 2 May 1986.

ANDY CURRIER scored a Widnes record 34 points in a match, including a record-equalling five tries, in a 58-2 Stones Bitter Championship home defeat of Featherstone Rovers on 25 September. The centre, who also kicked seven goals, beat the points record of 27 by Harry Dawson, who scored nine goals and three tries in a 45-0 League home defeat of Liverpool City on 22 April 1957. Other Widnes players to score five tries in a match are: Eddie Cunningham v. Doncaster, 15 February 1982; John Basnett v. Hunslet, 17 October 1981 and Hull K.R. 2 November 1986; David Hulme v. Dewsbury, 30 November 1986.

DAVID NOBLE scored a Doncaster record-equalling 20 points in a match with the prop scoring eight goals and a try in a 48-19 Division Two home defeat of Dewsbury on 2 October. The record was set by scrum half Kevin Jones, who scored six goals and two tries in a 40-12 Division Two home defeat of Whitehaven on 13 March 1988.

DEAN MARWOOD scored a record-equalling 28 points for Barrow, who won 60-0 v. Runcorn Highfield in a Division Two game on 16 April. The scrum half's total was made up of 10 goals and two tries. He shares the record with centre Keith Jarrett (11 goals, two tries) v. Doncaster on 25 August 1970 and full back Steve Tickle (12 goals, one try) at Kent Invicta on 8 April 1984.

CASTLEFORD ran up a club and Yorkshire Cup record score with their 94-12 first round home defeat of Huddersfield on 18 September. It was also Huddersfield's biggest defeat.

Ironically, Huddersfield had set the Yorkshire Cup record with a 79-5 defeat of Yorkshire Amateurs in the first round on 11 September 1948 when they scored 19 tries.

Castleford's previous highest score was when they beat Millom amateurs 88-5 in the first round of the Player's No. 6 Trophy on 16 September 1973. They scored 18 tries compared with 17 in their new record score. The 1973 result remains Castleford's widest winning margin.

Huddersfield's previous biggest defeat was 64-17 at Leeds in the first round of the Yorkshire Cup on 30 September 1958 when they conceded 16 tries.

FULHAM produced their highest score with a 61-22 Division Two home defeat of Huddersfield on 23 October. They scored 10 tries compared with 12 when they ran up their previous highest score of 50-5 in a Division Two win at Huyton on 5 December 1982.

BRAMLEY achieved their highest score when they had a 62-14 Division Two home win over Dewsbury on 30 October. They scored 12 tries against the 10 when setting the previous record of 52-17 in a Yorkshire Cup first round home tie versus Doncaster on 1 September 1974.

SHEFFIELD EAGLES scored a club record 80-8 victory at home to Wigan St. Patricks in the first round of the John Player Special Trophy on 13 November. The Eagles scored 15 tries compared with the 11 when they ran up the old record of 68-14 in a Division Two match at Fulham on 21 September 1986.

CHORLEY BOROUGH registered a club record 56-2 win at Runcorn Highfield on 1 January. They scored 11 tries compared with 10 when, as Blackpool Borough, they won 54-0 in a Division Two home win against Carlisle on 26 December 1985.

CARLISLE twice beat the club's record score of 47-18 which was set at Fulham in a Division Two match on 6 October 1984 when they scored eight tries. That score was surpassed with a nine-try 52-10 Division Two home defeat of Fulham on 8 January. Carlisle then raised the record as they beat Mansfield Marksman 58-1 in the first round of the Silk Cut Challenge Cup at home on 29 January.

LEIGH ran up a Division Two record away score and winning margin of 88-2 at Runcorn Highfield on 15 January, including 17 tries. The previous best was Barrow's 14-try 80-6 victory at Kent Invicta on 8 April 1984. Leigh already held the Division Two home record with a 92-2 defeat of Keighley on 30 April 1986.

WIGAN rattled up a 92-2 John Player Special Trophy score against RUNCORN HIGHFIELD, who suffered their worst defeat after conceding home advantage in the Cup draw and including nine amateurs because of a players' dispute. They were also reduced to 12 men when coach Bill Ashurst, coming out of retirement, was sent off in the 11th minute. The tie on 13 November produced 18 Wigan tries. Castleford also scored 18 tries when they ran up the previous John Player record of 88-5 at home to Millom amateurs on 16 September 1973. Runcorn's previous heaviest defeat was 73-0 at Warrington in the first round second leg of the Lancashire Cup on 13 September 1950 when, as Liverpool Stanley, they conceded 15 tries.

ROCHDALE HORNETS scored the most points by a losing side in a Division Two match when they lost 36-34 at Dewsbury on 9 October. The previous record was 32 by Blackpool Borough who lost 38-32 at Hunslet on 22 September 1985 and Carlisle were beaten 33-32 by Blackpool on 27 October 1985.

MILESTONES . . .

JOHN WOODS of Warrington passed the 200-try career mark and became the first player to tot up 2,000 Division One points. The former Test back's total of 203 tries at the end of the season was made up of 135 for Leigh, 21 Bradford Northern, 25 Warrington, plus 22 in representative matches. His Division One points total stood at 2,130 with 1,440 for Leigh, 320 Bradford and 370 Warrington. He is the only player to total both 100 tries and 500 goals in Division One.

Woods scored the 200th try of his career with two in Warrington's 56-7 Silk Cut Challenge Cup second round home win over Keighley on 11 February.

He passed the 2,000 Division One points mark with five goals and a try in the 30-22 home defeat of Featherstone Rovers on 9 October.

Woods' most prolific tryscoring season was 1983-84 .when he scored 27 tries to finish fourth in the try chart, the only time he has finished in the top ten. His best match feat was five tries for Bradford at home to Swinton on 13 October 1985, which was then a Division One record. He has also scored four in a match twice and seven other hat-tricks.

Woods holds the record for most points in a Division One season with 295 for Leigh in 1983-84. His best match tally is 36 points against Swinton in 1985 which was then a Division One record. Woods' season-by-season try totals are as follows:

Leigh

1976-77	5	
1977-78	16	+ 2 GB Under-24s; 2 Lancs.
1978-79	10	+ 1 England
1979-80	22	+ 1 Lancs.
1980-81	14	+ 1 England; 2 Lancs.
1981-82	18	+ 1 Britain
1982-83	12	
1983-84	27	
1984-85	11	

Bradford N.

1985-86	13
1986-87	8

Warrington

1987-88	13
1988-89	12

Totals

Leigh	135
Bradford N.	21
Warrington	25
Britain	1
1979 Tour	12
GB Under-24s	2
England	2
Lancashire	5

GRAND TOTALS 203

Woods' Division One totals, which do not include six goals in two abandoned matches, are as follows:

Leigh	T	G	DG	Pts
1976-77	5	60	2	137
1977-78	In Division Two			
1978-79	7	71	1	164
1979-80	18	53	2	162
1980-81	10	61	1	153
1981-82	14	109	1	261
1982-83	10	43	1	117
1983-84	23	101	1	295
1984-85	10	55	1	151
Bradford N.				
1985-86	10	84	0	208
1986-87	4	48	0	112
Warrington				
1987-88	8	91	4	218
1988-89	6	64	0	152
Totals				
Leigh	97	553	10	1,440
Bradford N.	14	132	0	320
Warrington	14	155	4	370
GRAND TOTALS	**125**	**840**	**14**	**2,130**

DES DRUMMOND of Warrington took his career tries total past 200 during the season and also notched a century of Division One touchdowns.

The Test winger scored his 200th career try with the only one in Warrington's 15-4 Stones Bitter Championship home defeat at Bradford Northern on 15 January. Drummond's 100th Division One try followed when he scored one in a 17-7 win at Hull K.R. on 5 February.

At the end of the season Drummond's career total stood at 207 made up of 141 for Leigh, 38 Warrington and 28 in representative matches.

His Division One total of 103 consists of 75 for Leigh and 28 for Warrington. At Leigh he played two seasons in Division Two. Drummond made his senior debut for Leigh in a 23-9 Division One defeat at Hull K.R. on 27 December 1976. After 10 seasons he was transferred to Warrington for £40,000, making his debut with a try in a 31-10 Division One home defeat of Bradford on 8 February 1987.

Drummond has twice finished in the top ten try chart, being seventh with 20 in 1980-81 and second with 26 the following season. His best match feat was a then John Player record-equalling five for Leigh at Carlisle on 20 November 1983. He scored nine other hat-tricks for Leigh, one for Warrington and another for Great Britain Under-24s.

Drummond's season-by-season totals are as follows:

Leigh

1976-77	1	(1)
1977-78	19	In Division Two
1978-79	13	(12)
1979-80	13	(9) + 2 GB U-24
1980-81	17	(14) + 2 GB; 1 GB U-24
1981-82	16	(12) + 2 GB; 1 Eng.; 4 GB U-24; 3 Lancs.
1982-83	19	(15)
1983-84	17	(8)
1984-85	5	(4)
1985-86	21	In Div. 2 + 1 GB

Warrington

1986-87	8	(6)
1987-88	18	(13) + 1 GB
1988-89	12	(9)

Totals

Leigh	141	(75)
Warrington	38	(28)
Great Britain	8	
1984 Tour	9	(Not inc. 2 in Tests)
GB Under-24s	7	
England	1	
Lancashire	3	

GRAND TOTALS 207 (103)

( ) Division One tries included in totals.

GRAHAM STEADMAN of Featherstone Rovers scored the 100th try and 1,000th point of his career during the season.

The stand off's try century came with the second of two touchdowns in Featherstone's 30-15 Stones Bitter Championship win at Hull K.R. on 4 September. At the end of the season his total of 111 was made up of 63 for York and 48 Featherstone.

Steadman reached the 1,000 points mark with a try and drop goal in Featherstone's 21-17 Stones Bitter Championship home defeat of Halifax on 16 October. He finished the season with a total of 1,112, with 762 for York and 350 Featherstone. His total of 449 goals included 20 drop goals.

An amateur from the Featherstone area, Steadman made his senior professional debut for York at Hull K.R. as an unnamed trialist stand off on 24 March 1982. York lost the Division One match 36-7 but Steadman played in the next match before being signed.

Steadman was transferred to Featherstone in February 1986 for £50,000, a record for both clubs. He made his debut for Featherstone at Leeds on 16 February 1986 when he scored the try and goal in a 44-6 Division One defeat. Steadman's most prolific tryscoring season was 1983-84 when he scored 25 for York and was seventh in the try chart, the only time he has finished in the top ten. His career total includes four hat-tricks, three of them for York.

He still holds the York records for most points in a season, 318 in 1984-85, and in a match, 26, Steadman scoring club record match figures three times in an eight-month spell. Twice in a week he beat the old record of 22 points with 24 and then set the existing figure of 26 with nine goals and two tries in a 54-4 Division Two home defeat of Batley on 25 November 1984.

Steadman's season-by-season totals are as follows:

York	T	G	DG	Pts
1981-82	1	4	0	11
1982-83	9	12	0	51
1983-84	25	71	7	249
1984-85	20	116	6	318
1985-86	8	50	1	133
Featherstone R.				
1985-86	5	17	0	54
1986-87	12	1	1	51
1987-88	17	12	2	94
1988-89	14	46	3	151
Totals				
York	63	253	14	762
Featherstone R.	48	76	6	350
GRAND TOTALS ...	**111**	**329**	**20**	**1,112**

JOE LYDON of Wigan scored the 100th try and 1,000th point of his career during the season.

The Great Britain utility back's try century came with a touchdown in Wigan's 24-10 win at Barrow in the first round of the Grunhalle Lager Lancashire Cup on 18 September. He finished the season with 111 made up of 54 for Widnes, 45 Wigan and 12 in representative matches.

Lydon reached the 1,000 points mark with the first of four tries in a 38-6 win at Doncaster in the first round of the Silk Cut Challenge Cup on 28 January. His total at the end of the season was 1,112 from 435 for Widnes, 500 Wigan and 177 in representative matches. A total of 446 goals includes nine drop goals.

Lydon made his senior professional debut for Widnes on 29 October 1982 when they lost 10-9 in a Division One match at home to Leigh. He moved to Wigan for a then world record £100,000 and made his debut for them at stand off on 2 March 1986 when he scored a try in the 44-6 Division One home defeat of Hull.

Lydon's most prolific tryscoring season was 1983-84 when he finished second in the try chart with 28. His only other final top ten place was in 1986-87 when he was ninth with 24. Lydon scored two hat-tricks with Widnes and a four-try feat for Wigan. His best points tally in a match was 22 from seven goals and two tries in Wigan's 60-6 Division One home win over Bradford Northern on 1 March 1987. Lydon's most prolific season was 1983-84 when he totalled 244 points.

His season-by-season totals were as follows:

Graham Steadman, who registered his career 100th try and 1,000th point.

Widnes	T	G	DG	Pts	
1982-83	14	42	0	126	+ 1t,3g Britain
1983-84	27	54	0	216	+ 1t,12g Britain Under-24s
1984-85	6	8	0	40	
1985-86	7	12	1	53	+ 1t, 6g Britain
Wigan					
1985-86	2	13	1	35	
1986-87	22	36	3	163	+ 2t,14g Britain
1987-88	8	30	0	92	+ 1t,1g Lancs.; 1t Britain
1988-89	13	77	4	210	+ 1t,3g Britain
Totals					
Widnes	54	116	1	435	
Wigan	45	156	8	500	
1984 tour	4	26	0	68	
Britain	6	26	0	75	
Lancashire	1	1	0	6	
Under-24s	1	12	0	28	
GRAND TOTALS	**111**	**337**	**9**	**1,112**	

DAVID HULME reached a career century of tries when he scored one in Widnes' 38-14 Stones Bitter Championship home win over Oldham on 5 February. Apart from one on Great Britain's 1988 tour of Australia, all of Hulme's tries have been scored for Widnes for whom he reached his club century with a try in a 22-10 Stones Bitter Championship win at Featherstone Rovers on 19 February.

He is the co-holder of the Widnes match record with five in the 82-0 home defeat of Dewsbury in the first round of the John Player Special Trophy on 30 November 1986. He has scored two other hat-tricks and his most prolific season was 1986-87 with 19 tries.

Widnes signed him from amateur side Halton Hornets and he made his first team debut as a 16-year-old substitute in a Lancashire Cup second round 22-20 home victory over St. Helens on 24 August 1980. His next and first full appearance was at scrum half in a 24-7 Division One home defeat of Castleford on 8 November 1981.

Hulme did not score on his one substitute appearance in 1980-81 but since then his season-by-season account is as follows:

Widnes	Tries
1981-82	6
1982-83	12
1983-84	15
1984-85	12
1985-86	12
1986-87	19
1987-88	16
1988-89	13
Total	**105**
1988 tour	1
GRAND TOTAL	**106**

DEREK BATE scored the 100th try of his career with the second of two touchdowns in Swinton's 30-8 Division Two win at Rochdale Hornets on 26 December. At the end of the season the winger's total stood at 113, all for Swinton for whom he made a one try debut as an unnamed trialist in a 14-10 Division Two home win over Batley on 28 August 1983.

Last season was his most prolific as he finished third in the charts with 32, one more than 1986-87 when he was fourth, his only other top ten placing. Bate's best match feat is four tries and he has scored seven other hat-tricks.

His season-by-season totals are as follows:

1983-84	13
1984-85	21
1985-86	9
1986-87	31
1987-88	7
1988-89	32
Total	**113**

LES QUIRK scored the 100th try of his career with the first of two vital touchdowns in St. Helens' surprise 16-14 defeat of Widnes in the Silk Cut Challenge Cup semi-final at Wigan on 11 March. They also gave him a club record of 10 successive tryscoring matches. At the end of the season Quirk's career total was 103, having scored 63 for Barrow and 40 for St. Helens.

A former Dalton amateur, Quirk signed for Barrow in November 1982 and made a tryscoring debut on the wing in a 22-13 Division One defeat at Leigh on 13 March 1983. He moved to St. Helens for £55,000 — then a record for a winger — and made another tryscoring debut in a 14-12 Division One defeat at Halifax on 4 October 1987. He has scored four hat-tricks, including one for Barrow. Last season was his best as he finished eighth with 24 tries, his only other top ten finish being the previous campaign when he was 10th with 20.

His season-by-season try totals are as follows:

Barrow	Tries
1982-83	4
1983-84	11
1984-85	14
1985-86	17
1986-87	13
1987-88	4
St. Helens	
1987-88	16
1988-89	24
Totals	
Barrow	63
St. Helens	40
GRAND TOTAL	**103**

TONY MARCHANT scored the 100th try of his career with one in the Stones Bitter Championship defeat at Leeds on 19 March. The centre finished the season with a total of 103, made up of 98 for Castleford and five in representative matches.

After gaining youth international honours, Marchant signed for Castleford and less than two months later made his debut at centre in a 25-7 Division One home defeat against Hull on 17 March 1982. Marchant's most prolific tryscoring season was 1985-86 when he totalled 22, including one for Great Britain on his Test debut. He has never finished in the top ten. His total of 103 tries includes a four-try feat and two other hat-tricks.

Marchant's season-by-season totals are as follows:

Castleford

1981-82	2	
1982-83	16	
1983-84	16	
1984-85	12	
1985-86	21	+ 1 Great Britain
1986-87	8	+ 1 Yorkshire
1987-88	10	+ 2 Yorkshire
1988-89	13	+ 1 Yorkshire

Totals

Castleford	98
Great Britain	1
Yorkshire	4

GRAND TOTAL...... 103

MARTIN OFFIAH raced to a fastest-ever century of tries with the first of two touchdowns in Widnes's 22-10 Stones Bitter Championship win at Featherstone Rovers on 19 February.

The former Rosslyn Park RU winger's century came only 17½ months after making his Rugby League debut on 30 August 1987 in a 28-6 Stones Bitter Championship home defeat of Halifax. His feat was aided by 19 tries on Great Britain's 1988 Down Under tour.

The previous fastest century was 18½ months by St. Helens' former South African international RU winger Tom Van Vollenhoven from 26 October 1957 to 15 May 1959.

Offiah's 100th try came in his 80th club and represent-ative match including two matches as substitute on tour, thus leaving Wigan's Billy Boston with the record for a century in fewest matches — 68 from his debut in 1953-54.

Offiah reached his century of tries for Widnes with a vital touchdown in the 18-10 Stones Bitter Premiership final defeat of Hull at Old Trafford on 14 May.

Offiah had a remarkable first season in Rugby League, breaking the Widnes club record with 42 tries and going even better last term when he scored 58 for the club, plus two for Great Britain. It was the first time a winger had reached the half-century since Boston's 51 in 1961-62.

Tony Marchant, a ton-up career try scorer.

Offiah also equalled the Widnes match record with five tries in a 32-4 Stones Bitter Championship home defeat of Warrington on 15 March. He has scored 13 other hat-tricks including four four-try feats. Two of his hat-tricks and a four-try feat were on Britain's 1988 tour.

Offiah's total of 123 tries is made up as follows:

Widnes

1987-88	42	+ 1 Britain;
		1 President's XIII
1988-89	58	+ 2 Britain
1988-tour	17	(Not inc. 2 in Tests)

Totals

Widnes	100
Britain	5
President's XIII	1
Tour	17 (Not inc. 2 in Tests)

GRAND TOTAL...... 123

GARRY SCHOFIELD of Leeds reached a century of Division One tries by scoring all four in the 22-14 home defeat of Wigan on 9 October. He finished the season with 108, made up of 31 for Leeds and 77 Hull.

The Test centre reached his league century in only his sixth season, having topped the Division One chart in his first season with 28 in 1983-84 when he was only 18 years old.

A former Hunslet Parkside Junior, Schofield signed for Hull soon after captaining the Great Britain amateur youth squad to New Zealand in 1983. He made his professional debut in a 22-22 Division One home draw against Warrington on 21 August 1983. Hull transferred Schofield to Leeds for a world record £155,000 and he scored two debut tries for his home town club in a 29-25 defeat by Auckland on 25 October 1987. Schofield scored five Division One hat-tricks, including two four-try feats.

His Division One totals are as follows:

Hull

1983-84	28
1984-85	15
1985-86	11
1986-87	23

Leeds

1987-88	14
1988-89	17

Totals

Hull	77
Leeds	31
GRAND TOTAL	**108**

STEVE TICKLE scored the 1,000th point of his career with the first of three goals in Barrow's 28-6 Division Two home defeat of Mansfield Marksman on 4 September. At the end of the season the full back had totalled 1,029 all for Barrow apart from four goals for Cumbria. His points total was made up of 65 tries and 407 goals, including 18 drop goals.

The former Waterloo RU player made his debut for Barrow on 22 October 1978 when he kicked three goals in a 40-12 Division One defeat at Hull K.R.

Tickle equalled two Barrow records with 12 goals and 28 points in an 80-8 Division Two win at Kent Invicta on 8 April 1984. It was the only time he has kicked 10 or more goals in a match and he has scored just one try hat-trick. His most prolific season was 1985-86 when he totalled 207 points.

Tickle's season-by-season figures are as follows:

Barrow	T	G	DG	Pts	
1978-79	7	13	0	47	
1979-80	9	20	0	67	
1980-81	5	5	0	25	
1981-82	5	28	0	71	+ 4g Cumbria
1982-83	1	70	1	144	
1983-84	8	78	13	201	
1984-85	1	30	1	65	
1985-86	13	77	1	207	
1986-87	7	27	1	83	
1987-88	5	27	0	74	
1988-89	4	10	1	37	

Totals

	T	G	DG	Pts
Barrow	65	385	18	1,021
Cumbria	0	4	0	8
GRAND TOTALS	**65**	**389**	**18**	**1,029**

DAVID CREASSER of Leeds scored the 1,000th point of his career in the 32-18 Stones Bitter Championship home defeat of Castleford on 19 March. The centre or stand off finished the season with 1,035 points from 72 tries and 374 goals, including one drop goal. All the points have been scored for Leeds, apart from 40 in representative matches.

A former Hunslet Parkside Junior, Creasser signed for his home town club after touring with the Great Britain youth squad to New Zealand in 1983. He made his debut for Leeds as a substitute in a 30-14 Yorkshire Cup first round win at Batley on 4 September 1983, his first full senior game coming in the second round 24-16 win at York when he played centre on 14 September 1983.

Creasser's most prolific season was 1984-85 when he totalled 252 points, including 34 in representative matches. His best match tally was 28 points from 10 goals and two tries in a 60-6 Division One home defeat of Salford on 27 September 1987. He has also scored 22 and 24 points in a match.

Creasser's season-by-season totals are as follows:

Leeds	T	G	Pts	
1983-84	16	76	216	
1984-85	12	85	218	+ 9g GB;
				8g GB-
				Under-21s
1985-86	12	84	216	
1986-87	13	48	148	
1987-88	14	43	142	1t Yorks.;
				1g GB
1988-89	4	20(1)	55	

Totals

	T	G	Pts
Leeds	71	356(1)	995
Britain	0	10	20
GB Under-21	0	8	16
Yorkshire	1	0	4
GRAND TOTALS	**72**	**374(1)**	**1,035**

( ) Drop goals included in total

LEADING SCORERS 1895-1971

	TRIES	GOALS	POINTS
1895-96	Hurst (Oldham) 28	Lorimer (Manningham) 35	Cooper (Bradford)..........106
			Lorimer (Manningham)...106
1896-97	Hannah (Hunslet)............19	Goldthorpe (Hunslet) 26	Rigg (Halifax) 112
		Sharpe (Liversedge) 26	
1897-98	Hoskins (Salford) 30	Goldthorpe (Hunslet) 66	Goldthorpe (Hunslet)......135
1898-99	Williams (Oldham) 39	Goldthorpe (Hunslet) 67	Jaques (Hull) 169
1899-00	Williams (Oldham) 36	Cooper (Bradford) 39	Williams (Oldham).........108
1900-01	Williams (Oldham) 47	Goldthorpe (Hunslet) 44	Williams (Oldham).........141
1901-02	Wilson (Broughton R.).....38	James (Broughton R.) 75	Lomas (Salford)............172
1902-03	Evans (Leeds).................27	Goldthorpe (Hunslet) 48	Davies (Batley)..............136
1903-04	Hogg (Broughton R.) 34	Lomas (Salford) 66	Lomas (Salford)............222
1904-05	Dechan (Bradford)...........31	Ferguson (Oldham)..........50	Lomas (Salford)............146
1905-06	Leytham (Wigan) 40	Ferguson (Oldham)..........49	Leytham (Wigan)...........160
1906-07	Eccles (Halifax)...............41	Lomas (Salford) 86	Lomas (Salford)............280
1907-08	Leytham (Wigan) 44	Goldthorpe (Hunslet)......101	Goldthorpe (Hunslet)......217
1908-09	Miller (Wigan)................49	Lomas (Salford) 88	Lomas (Salford)............272
	Williams (Halifax) 49		
1909-10	Leytham (Wigan) 48	Carmichael (Hull K.R.) 78	Leytham (Wigan)...........232
1910-11	Kitchen (Huddersfield).....40	Carmichael (Hull K.R.)...129	Carmichael (Hull K.R.)...261
	Rosenfeld (Huddersfield) ..40		
	Miller (Wigan)................40		
1911-12	Rosenfeld (Huddersfield) ..78	Carmichael (Hull K.R.)...127	Carmichael (Hull K.R.)...254
1912-13	Rosenfeld (Huddersfield) ..56	Carmichael (Hull K.R.) 93	Thomas (Wigan)............198
1913-14	Rosenfeld (Huddersfield) ..80	Holland (Huddersfield) ...131	Holland (Huddersfield) ...268
1914-15	Rosenfeld (Huddersfield) ..56	Gronow (Huddersfield) ...136	Gronow (Huddersfield) ...284

● Competitive matches suspended during war years

	TRIES	GOALS	POINTS
1918-19	Francis (Hull).................25	Kennedy (Hull) 54	Kennedy (Hull) 135
1919-20	Moorhouse (Huddersfield).39	Gronow (Huddersfield) ...148	Gronow (Huddersfield) ...332
1920-21	Stone (Hull) 41	Kennedy (Hull) 108	Kennedy (Hull) 264
1921-22	Farrar (Oldham) 49	Sullivan (Wigan)............100	Farrar (Oldham) 213
1922-23	Ring (Wigan) 41	Sullivan (Wigan)............161	Sullivan (Wigan)............349
1923-24	Ring (Wigan) 49	Sullivan (Wigan)............158	Sullivan (Wigan)............319
1924-25	Ring (Wigan) 54	Sullivan (Wigan)............138	Sullivan (Wigan)............282
1925-26	Ring (Wigan) 63	Sullivan (Wigan)............131	Sullivan (Wigan)............274
1926-27	Ellaby (St. Helens) 55	Sullivan (Wigan)............149	Sullivan (Wigan)............322
1927-28	Ellaby (St. Helens) 37	Thompson (Leeds).........106	Thompson (Leeds).........233
1928-29	Brown (Wigan) 44	Sullivan (Wigan)............107	Sullivan (Wigan)............226
	Mills (Huddersfield)........44		
1929-30	Ellaby (St. Helens) 39	Thompson (Leeds).........111	Thompson (Leeds).........243
1930-31	Harris, E. (Leeds)...........58	Sullivan (Wigan)............133	Sullivan (Wigan)............278
1931-32	Mills (Huddersfield)........50	Sullivan (Wigan)............117	Sullivan (Wigan)............249
1932-33	Harris, E. (Leeds)...........57	Sullivan (Wigan)............146	Sullivan (Wigan)............307
1933-34	Brown (Salford) 45	Sullivan (Wigan)............193	Sullivan (Wigan)............404

	TRIES	GOALS	POINTS
1934-35	Morley (Wigan) 49	Sullivan (Wigan).............165	Sullivan (Wigan)............348
1935-36	Harris, E. (Leeds)...........63	Sullivan (Wigan).............117	Sullivan (Wigan)............246
1936-37	Harris, E. (Leeds)...........40	Sullivan (Wigan).............120	Sullivan (Wigan)............258
1937-38	Harris, E. (Leeds)...........45	Sullivan (Wigan).............135	Sullivan (Wigan)............285
1938-39	Markham (Huddersfield)...39	Sullivan (Wigan).............124	Risman (Salford)............267

● For the next six seasons emergency war-time competitions resulted in a reduction of matches and players were allowed to 'guest' for other clubs

	TRIES	GOALS	POINTS
1939-40	Batten (Hunslet) 38	Hodgson (Swinton)..........98	Hodgson (Swinton) 208
1940-41	Walters (Bradford N.) 32	Lockwood (Halifax) 70	Belshaw (Warrington) 174
1941-42	Francis (Barrow)...............30	Lockwood (Halifax) 91	Lockwood (Halifax)........185
1942-43	Batten (Hunslet) 24	Lockwood (Halifax) 65	Lockwood (Halifax)........136
1943-44	Lawrenson (Wigan) 21	Horne (Barrow) 57	Horne (Barrow)..............144
1944-45	Batten (Bradford N.)........41	Stott (Wakefield T.).........51	Stott (Wakefield T.) 129

● Normal peace-time rugby resumed

	TRIES	GOALS	POINTS
1945-46	Batten (Bradford N.)........35	Ledgard (Dewsbury)........89	Bawden (Huddersfield) ...239
1946-47	Bevan (Warrington) 48	Miller (Hull)..................103	Bawden (Huddersfield) ...243
1947-48	Bevan (Warrington) 57	Ward (Wigan) 141	Ward (Wigan) 312
1948-49	Cooper (Huddersfield) 60	Ward (Wigan) 155	Ward (Wigan) 361
1949-50	Nordgren (Wigan) 57	Gee (Wigan) 133	Palin (Warrington) 290
		Palin (Warrington) 133	
1950-51	Bevan (Warrington) 68	Cook (Leeds) 155	Cook (Leeds) 332
1951-52	Cooper (Huddersfield) 71	Ledgard (Leigh) 142	Horne (Barrow).............313
1952-53	Bevan (Warrington) 72	Bath (Warrington)..........170	Bath (Warrington)..........379
1953-54	Bevan (Warrington) 67	Metcalfe (St. Helens)......153	Metcalfe (St. Helens)......369
		Bath (Warrington)..........153	
1954-55	Cooper (Huddersfield) 66	Ledgard (Leigh) 178	Ledgard (Leigh) 374
1955-56	McLean (Bradford N.) 61	Ledgard (Leigh) 155	Bath (Warrington)..........344
1956-57	Boston (Wigan)...............60	Jones (Leeds).................194	Jones (Leeds).................496
1957-58	Sullivan (Wigan) 50	Ganley (Oldham) 219	Ganley (Oldham) 453
1958-59	Vollenhoven (St. Helens) ..62	Ganley (Oldham) 190	Griffiths (Wigan) 394
1959-60	Vollenhoven (St. Helens) ..54	Rhodes (St. Helens) 171	Fox (Wakefield T.) 453
		Fox (Wakefield T.) 171	
1960-61	Vollenhoven (St. Helens) ..59	Rhodes (St. Helens) 145	Rhodes (St. Helens) 338
1961-62	Boston (Wigan)...............51	Fox (Wakefield T.) 183	Fox (Wakefield T.) 456
1962-63	Glastonbury (Work'ton T.)41	Coslett (St. Helens)........156	Coslett (St. Helens)........321
1963-64	Stopford (Swinton) 45	Coslett (St. Helens)........138	Fox (Wakefield T.) 313
1964-65	Lake (Wigan) 40	Kellett (Hull K.R.)........150	Killeen (St. Helens)........360
1965-66	Killeen (St. Helens) 32	Killeen (St. Helens)........120	Killeen (St. Helens)........336
	Lake (Wigan) 32		
1966-67	Young (Hull K.R.)..........34	Risman (Leeds) 163	Killeen (St. Helens)........353
	Howe (Castleford) 34		
1967-68	Millward (Hull K.R.)........38	Risman (Leeds) 154	Risman (Leeds) 332
1968-69	Francis (Wigan) 40	Risman (Leeds) 165	Risman (Leeds) 345
1969-70	Atkinson (Leeds).............38	Tyrer (Wigan)...............167	Tyrer (Wigan)...............385
1970-71	Haigh (Leeds) 40	Coslett (St. Helens) 183	Coslett (St. Helens) 375
1971-72	Atkinson (Leeds).............36	Costlett (St. Helens) 214	Watkins (Salford)..........473
	Lamb (Bradford N.) 36		

LEADING SCORERS 1972-88

TRIES

1972-73

Atkinson (Leeds)..39
Richards (Salford)...38
Charlton (Salford)...33
Topliss (Wakefield T.)..30
Lowe (Hull K.R.)..29
Hardisty (Leeds)..28
A. Smith (Leeds)...28
Dunn (Hull K.R.)...27
D. Redfearn (Bradford N.).....................................27
N. Stephenson (Dewsbury)....................................26
Mathias (St. Helens)...26

1973-74

Fielding (Salford)...49
Mathias (St. Helens)...40
D. Smith (Wakefield T.)..38
Eckersley (St. Helens)...26
Fleay (Swinton)..26
Jones (St. Helens)..25
Wilson (St. Helens)...25
Watkins (Salford)...24
Atkinson (Leeds)...23
Lamb (Bradford N.)..22
A. Smith (Leeds)...22
Bevan (Warrington)..22
Ayres (Wigan)...22

1974-75

Dunn (Hull K.R.)...42
Fielding (Salford)...35
Bevan (Warrington)..31
A. Smith (Leeds)...30
Millward (Hull K.R.)...30
Atkinson (Leeds)...29
Richards (Salford)...28
Sullivan (Hull K.R.)..28
Mathias (St. Helens)...27
Dyl (Leeds)..26

1975-76

Richards (Salford)...37
Fielding (Salford)...33
Jones (St. Helens)..31
Briggs (Leigh)...27
D. Smith (Wakefield T.)..26
Burton (Castleford)...25
Clark (Hull)..23
Wright (Workington T.)..22
Barends (York)...21
Boxall (Hull)..21
Holmes (Leeds)..21
Mathias (St. Helens)...21
Butler (Salford)..21

1976-77

Wright (Widnes)...31
Burton (Castleford)...29
D. Smith (Leeds)...28
Fielding (Salford)...27
Dunn (Hull K.R.)...26
Cunningham (St. Helens).......................................26
Topliss (Wakefield T.)..24
Richards (Salford)...23
Mathias (St. Helens)...23
Barends (York)...22

1977-78

Wright (Widnes)...33
Fielding (Salford)...31
Cunningham (St. Helens).......................................30
Bevan (Warrington)..30
Fenton (Castleford)...30
Vigo (Wigan)..29
Glynn (St. Helens)...28
D. Smith (Leeds)...28
T. Morgan (York)..27
Burton (Castleford)...27

1978-79

Hartley (Hull K.R.)..35
Wright (Widnes)...28
Barends (Bradford N.)..25
Lowe (Hull K.R.)...25
Prendiville (Hull)..25
Fielding (Salford)...24
D. Redfearn (Bradford N.).....................................23
Mathias (St. Helens)...22
Bray (Hull)..21
O'Loughlin (Wigan)...21
Sullivan (Hull K.R.)..21

1979-80

Fielding (Salford)...30
Hubbard (Hull K.R.)...30
Munro (Oldham)...29
Ball (Barrow)...27
Bentley (Widnes)..27
Glynn (St. Helens)...27
Mathias (St. Helens)...27
Bevan (Warrington)..26
D. Redfearn (Bradford N.).....................................26
D. Smith (Leeds)...24

1980-81

Crossley (York)	35
Richardson (Castleford)	28
Hubbard (Hull K.R.)	25
Hartley (Hull K.R.)	23
McDermott (York)	23
Slater (Huddersfield)	23
Drummond (Leigh)	20
Ball (Barrow)	19
Bevan (Warrington)	19
Cramp (Huddersfield)	19
Hyde (Castleford)	19
Ramsdale (Wigan)	19

1981-82

Jones (Workington T.)	31
Drummond (Leigh)	26
Basnett (Widnes)	26
Ashton (Oldham)	26
Morgan (Carlisle)	25
Hartley (Hull K.R.)	23
Hopkins (Workington T.)	23
Day (Hull)	23
Evans (Hull)	22
D. Hobbs (Featherstone R.)	21
Moll (Keighley)	21

1982-83

Eccles (Warrington)	37
Evans (Hull)	28
Crossley (Fulham)	27
David (Cardiff C.)	26
Topliss (Hull)	24
M'Barki (Fulham)	23
Hyde (Castleford)	22
McDermott (York)	22
Leuluai (Hull)	21
Phil Ford (Warrington)	20
Clark (Hull K.R.)	20

1983-84

Schofield (Hull)	38
Lydon (Widnes)	28
King (Hunslet)	28
Woods (Leigh)	27
Basnett (Widnes)	26
Gibson (Batley)	26
Herbert (Barrow)	25
Steadman (York)	25
Prohm (Hull K.R.)	25
Clark (Hull K.R.)	24

1984-85

Hanley (Bradford N.)	55
Prohm (Hull K.R.)	45
Gill (Wigan)	34
Ledger (St. Helens)	30
Meninga (St. Helens)	28
Gibbin (Whitehaven)	27
Gibson (Batley)	26
G. Peacham (Carlisle)	25
Byrne (Salford)	25
Evans (Hull)	24
Ferguson (Wigan)	24

1985-86

Halliwell (Leigh)	49
Hanley (Wigan)	38
Lister (Bramley)	34
Henderson (Leigh)	31
Frodsham (Blackpool B.)	30
Fox (Leigh)	29
Williams (Barrow)	27
Garrity (Runcorn H.)	24
Gibson (Leeds)	23
Beck (Workington T.)	23

1986-87

Hanley (Wigan)	63
Schofield (Hull)	37
Gill (Wigan)	32
Bate (Swinton)	31
Ford (Bradford N.)	30
Henderson (Leigh)	27
Edwards (Wigan)	26
Johnson (Warrington)	25
Lydon (Wigan)	24
Dunn (Rochdale H.)	23
Ledger (St. Helens)	23
McCormack (St. Helens)	23

1987-88

Offiah (Widnes)	44
Hanley (Wigan)	36
Schofield (Leeds)	25
Gibson (Leeds)	24
Goodway (Wigan)	23
Pape (Carlisle)	23
Edwards (Wigan)	21
Foy (Oldham)	21
Smith (Featherstone R.)	21
Bibb (Featherstone R.)	20
M. Conway (Wakefield T.)	20
Elia (St. Helens)	20
Quirk (St. Helens)	20

GOALS
(including drop goals)

1972-73

Watkins (Salford) 221
Coslett (St. Helens) 162
Tees (Bradford N.)...160
Stephenson (Dewsbury) 149
C. Kellett (Featherstone R.) 139
Fox (Wakefield T.)...138
Whitehead (Warrington) 136
Larder (Oldham)...127
Jefferson (Keighley)......................................120
Quinn (York) 107

1973-74

Watkins (Salford) 183
Whitehead (Warrington) 168
Jefferson (Keighley)......................................165
Coslett (St. Helens) 134
Mumby (Bradford N.).....................................131
Dutton (Widnes)...129
Lloyd (Castleford) 121
Quinn (York) 112
Fiddler (Leigh)..111
Holliday (Rochdale H.) 107

1974-75

Fox (Hull K.R.) 146
Coslett (St. Helens) 129
Dutton (Widnes)...122
Lloyd (Castleford) 112
Quinn (York) 112
Hartley (Huddersfield) 110
MacCorquodale (Workington T.) 107
Marshall (Leeds)..107
Mumby (Bradford N.)...................................... 96
Fiddler (Salford, Leigh)................................... 85

1975-76

Watkins (Salford) 175
Pimblett (St. Helens) 149
Lloyd (Castleford) 149
Dutton (Widnes)...148
Fairbairn (Wigan)...146
Stacey (Leigh) 137
MacCorquodale (Workington T.) 130
Fox (Hull K.R., York)......................................102
Marshall (Leeds) 101
Gaitley (New Hunslet).....................................100

1976-77

Lloyd (Castleford) 163
Quinn (Featherstone R.)..................................152
Pimblett (St. Helens) 152
Hesford (Warrington).....................................132
MacCorquodale (Workington T.) 128
Watkins (Salford) 125
Stephenson (Dewsbury) 106
Fairbairn (Wigan)...105
Dutton (Widnes).. 97
Woods (Leigh)... 90

1977-78

Pimblett (St. Helens) 178
Hesford (Warrington).....................................158
Woods (Leigh)...149
MacCorquodale (Workington T.) 138
Woods (Widnes)...122
Watkins (Salford) 110
Mumby (Bradford N.).....................................107
Lloyd (Castleford) 104
Fox (Bradford N.)... 95
Oulton (Leeds) 80

1978-79

Lloyd (Hull) 172
Hesford (Warrington).....................................170
Burke (Widnes)..140
MacCorquodale (Workington T.) 114
Pimblett (St. Helens) 105
Beale (Keighley)... 96
Woods (Leigh).. 96
Birts (Halifax) 86
Fairbairn (Wigan).. 86
Norton (Castleford).. 82

1979-80

Quinn (Featherstone R.)..................................163
Hubbard (Hull K.R.).......................................138
Rule (Salford)..134
Hesford (Warrington).....................................128
Burke (Widnes)..127
Ball (Barrow)...119
Diamond (Wakefield T.)..................................116
Fitzsimons (Oldham)......................................108
Parrish (Hunslet)... 98
Birts (Halifax) 97

1980-81

Hesford (Warrington).....................................147
Quinn (Featherstone R.)..................................123
Diamond (Wakefield T.)..................................112
Burke (Widnes) 110
Hubbard (Hull K.R.).......................................109
Ball (Barrow)...104
Birts (Halifax)..100
Beale (Keighley)... 97
Parrish (Oldham) 95
Fairbairn (Wigan).. 94

1981-82

Hopkins (Workington T.) 190
Fairbairn (Hull K.R.) 168
Parrish (Oldham) 164
Woods (Leigh)..158
Rule (Salford) 130
Dick (Leeds) 125
Quinn (Featherstone R.) 120
Agar (Halifax) 119
Crooks (Hull) 118
Hesford (Warrington)...................................116

1982-83

Diamond (Fulham)......................................136
Fitzsimons (Hunslet).....................................121
Crooks (Hull)...120
R. Beardmore (Castleford)...............................117
Hesford (Warrington)....................................113
Fenwick (Cardiff C.).....................................111
Jones (Swinton)..110
Whitfield (Wigan).......................................104
Kilner (Bramley)..104
Quinn (Featherstone R.)................................. 98

1983-84

Hesford (Warrington)....................................142
R. Beardmore (Castleford)...............................142
Hallett (Cardiff C.).......................................140
Fitzsimons (Hunslet).....................................131
Woods (Leigh)..124
Whitfield (Wigan).......................................122
Ball (Barrow)...104
Parrish (Oldham) 101
Agar (Halifax) 94
Tickle (Barrow) 91

1984-85

Day (St. Helens)..157
Fairbairn (Hull K.R.) 141
Wood (Runcorn H.)......................................126
Steadman (York) 122
Griffiths (Salford)......................................118
Parrish (Oldham).......................................117
Schofield (Hull)..105
Creasser (Leeds).......................................102
Agar (Halifax) 87
Jones (Swinton) 87

1985-86

C. Johnson (Leigh)......................................173
Stephenson (Wigan)....................................128
Noble (Doncaster) 118
Harcombe (Rochdale H.) 115
Kilner (Bramley).......................................110
Dorahy (Hull K.R.)......................................101
Woods (Bradford N.)................................... 98
Creasser (Leeds)...................................... 84
Carroll (Carlisle)...................................... 83
Smith (Workington T.).................................. 83

1986-87

Loughlin (St. Helens) 190
Bishop (Warrington) 117
Noble (Doncaster) 114
Whitfield (Halifax) 109
Platt (Hunslet)...102
Topping (Swinton).....................................100
C. Johnson (Leigh)..................................... 86
Ketteridge (Castleford) 80
Wood (Rochdale H.).................................... 80
Quinn (Featherstone R.)................................ 77

1987-88

Woods (Warrington) 152
Quinn (Featherstone R.) 128
Harcombe (Wakefield T.) 116
Loughlin (St. Helens) 114
Pearce (Hull)...111
Smith (Springfield B.).................................. 98
Stephenson (Leeds).................................... 95
M. Fletcher (Hull K.R.)................................. 94
Hobbs (Bradford N.) 83
Jones (Salford)....................................... 79

DROP GOALS

1974-75 Seabourne (Bradford N.) 10
1975-76 Hancock (Hull)...............................10
1976-77 N. Stephenson (Dewsbury)....................16
1977-78 Fiddler (Bramley, Leigh) 10
1978-79 Turley (Blackpool B.) 18
1979-80 Dean (Hunslet) 18
1980-81 Walker (Whitehaven) 22
1981-82 Agar (Halifax).................................17
       Donlan (Leigh) 17
1982-83 Pinner (St. Helens).............................13
1983-84 Hallett (Cardiff C.).............................29
1984-85 Wood (Runcorn H.) 28
1985-86 Bishop (Warrington) 13
1986-87 Platt (Mansfield M.)...........................18
1987-88 W. Parker (Hull K.R.)..........................15

POINTS

1972-73 Watkins (Salford).............................493
1973-74 Watkins (Salford).............................438
1974-75 Fox (Hull K.R.)................................333
1975-76 Watkins (Salford).............................385
1976-77 Lloyd (Castleford).............................341
1977-78 Pimblett (St. Helens)..........................381
1978-79 Lloyd (Hull)..................................373
1979-80 Quinn (Featherstone R.).......................375
1980-81 Hesford (Warrington).........................310
1981-82 Hopkins (Workington T.).......................446
1982-83 Diamond (Fulham) 308
1983-84 Woods (Leigh) 355
1984-85 Day (St. Helens) 362
1985-86 C. Johnson (Leigh) 400
1986-87 Loughlin (St. Helens) 424
1987-88 Woods (Warrington) 351

ALL TIME RECORDS

Most goals in a match:
22 by Jim Sullivan (Wigan) v. Flimby & Fothergill (Challenge Cup), 14th February 1925

Most goals in a season:
DAVID WATKINS holds the record for most goals in a season with 221 — all for Salford — in 1972-73. Watkins played and scored a goal in every match that season as follows:

1972			
Aug. 19	Leeds ....(H)	5
23	Featherstone R. ....(A)	3
26	Whitehaven..........................(A)	4
28	Swinton ....(H)	1
Sept. 1	Oldham ....(LC) (H)	10
9	Leeds..............................(A)	2
15	Rochdale H. ....(LC) (H)	11
17	Leigh ....(A)	6
24	Barrow..........................(JP) (A)	4
29	Huyton ....(H)	10
Oct. 3	Oldham.........................(FT) (A)	4
6	Wigan.......................(LC) (A)	4
8	Blackpool B. ....(A)	5
13	Blackpool B. ....(H)	8
21	Swinton ....(LCF)	5
Nov. 5	Huyton ....(A)	8
10	Rochdale H. ....(H)	6
17	Warrington ....(A)	4
19	New Zealand........................(H)	10
24	Dewsbury ....(JP) (H)	4
26	Workington T. ....(H)	6
Dec. 1	Barrow.............................(H)	9
10	Bradford N. ....(JP) (H)	9
13	Oldham.............................(A)	4
15	Leigh ....(H)	3
24	Bradford N. ....(A)	5
26	Workington T. ....(A)	3
30	Hull K.R. ....(JP) (A)	5
1973			
Jan. 3	Bradford N.........................(H)	6
7	Rochdale H. ....(A)	2
12	Featherstone R. ....(H)	4
28	Featherstone R..........(RL Cup) (A)	4
Feb. 2	Whitehaven.........................(H)	4
11	Barrow.............................(A)	5
23	St. Helens ....(H)	3
Mar. 7	Widnes.............................(A)	3
9	Dewsbury ....(H)	3
16	St. Helens ....(A)	2
24	Leeds.........................(JP Final)	2
30	Warrington ....(H)	1
Apr. 6	Widnes.............................(A)	4
13	Oldham.............................(H)	3
15	Dewsbury ....(A)	2

17	Wigan.............................(A)	3
20	Swinton...........................(A)	7
23	Wigan.............................(H)	3
29	Rochdale H. ....(top 16) (H)	2

	App	Gls
League	34	147
Lancs Cup..............................	4	30
John Player............................	5	24
Tour match	1	10
RL Cup	1	4
Floodlit Cup	1	4
Top 16	1	2
Totals	**47**	**221**

Fastest goals century:
Three players share the record of scoring the fastest 100 goals from the start of a season in terms of number of matches played. They are Bernard Ganley, David Watkins and Steve Quinn, who achieved the century in 18 matches.

Ganley reached 100 goals on 16 November 1957, after playing 17 matches for Oldham and one for Great Britain.

Watkins scored his 100th goal on 17 November 1972, all for Salford.

Quinn scored his 100th goal on 16 December 1979, all for Featherstone Rovers.

Most goals in a career:
JIM SULLIVAN holds the record for most goals in a career with 2,867 between 1921-22 and 1945-46. He scored a century of goals in every season after leaving Welsh Rugby Union for Wigan until the War interrupted the 1939-40 campaign.

The Test full back played all of his club rugby for Wigan apart from War-time appearances with Bradford Northern, Dewsbury and Keighley.

Sullivan's total includes 441 in representative matches, including three tours of Australasia. These figures are accepted by the Record Keepers' Club following research by James Carter and Malcolm Bentley.

Most one-point drop goals in a match:
5 by Danny Wilson (Swinton) v. Hunslet (John Player Special), 6 November 1983.
    Peter Wood (Runcorn H.) v.Batley, 21 October 1984.
    Paul Bishop (Warrington) at Wigan (Premiership semi-final), 11 May 1986.

Most one-point drop goals in a season:
29 by Lyn Hallett (Cardiff C.)....................1983-84

Most one-point drop goals in a career:
85 by Norman Turley (Warrington, Runcorn H., Swinton, Blackpool B., Rochdale H., Barrow, Workington T.) 1974-88

Most tries in a match:
11 by George West (Hull K.R.) v Brookland Rovers
Challenge Cup ....4 March 1905

Most tries in a career:
BRIAN BEVAN holds the record for most tries in a career
with 796 between 1946 and 1964. His season-by-season
record is:

1946-47	48
1947-48	57
1948-49	56
1949-50	33
1950-51	68
1951-52	51
1952-53	72
1953-54	67
1954-55	63
1955-56	57
1956-57	17
1957-58	46
1958-59	54
1959-60	40
1960-61	35
1961-62	15
1962-63	10
1963-64	7

Totals

Warrington	740
Blackpool Borough	17
Other Nationalities	26
Other representative matches	13
Grand Total	**796**

The Australian winger played his first game for
Warrington on 17 November 1945 and his last on 23 April
1962 before having two seasons at Blackpool Borough.
His last match for Borough was on 22 February, 1964.

Most tries in a season:
ALBERT ROSENFELD holds the record for most tries
in a season with 80 — all for Huddersfield — in 1913-14.

Rosenfeld's match-by-match record:
1913

Sept.	6	York	(A)	4
	8	Warrington	(H)	2
	13	Leeds	(H)	5
	20	Halifax	(A)	1
	27	Batley	(A)	0
Oct.	4	Oldham	(H)	2
	11	Rochdale H.	(A)	0
	18	Bramley	(YC) (H)	2
	25	Dewsbury	(A)	4
Nov.	1	Halifax	(YC) (A)	2
	8	Wigan	(A)	1
	15	Dewsbury	(YC) (H)	3

	19	Bradford N.	(H)	3
	22	Leeds	(A)	3
	29	Bradford N.	(Halifax, YCF)	1
Dec.	3	Halifax	(H)	3
	6	Hunslet	(A)	2
	13	Rochdale H.	(H)	3
	20	Hull K.R.	(A)	2
	25	Hull	(A)	1
	26	Wakefield T.	(H)	3
	27	Hunslet	(H)	0
1914				
Jan.	1	St. Helens	(A)	0
	3	Warrington	(A)	0
	10	York	(H)	3
	17	Keighley	(A)	2
	24	Dewsbury	(A)	1
	31	Batley	(H)	0
Feb.	7	Oldham	(A)	0
	14	Bramley	(H)	5
	21	Wigan	(H)	3
	28	Swinton Park R.	(RL Cup) (H)	7
Mar.	7	Wakefield T.	(A)	2
	14	Hull K.R.	(RL Cup) (A)	2
	18	Bramley	(A)	3
	21	Widnes	(RL Cup) (H)	0
	25	Keighley	(H)	3
	28	Hull K.R.	(H)	1
	30	Bradford N.	(A)	1
Apr.	4	Hull	(Leeds, RL Cup SF)	0
	11	Hull	(H) did not play	
	13	St. Helens	(H)	0
	20	Hull	(Play-off) (H) did not play	
	25	Salford	(Leeds, Championship final)	0

	App	Tries
League	33	63
Yorks Cup	4	8
RL Cup	4	9
Play Off	1	0
Totals	**42**	**80**

Most points in a season:
LEWIS JONES holds the record for most points in a
season with 496 from 194 goals and 36 tries for Leeds and
representative teams in 1956-57.

Jones' match-by-match record:

For Leeds
1956

				Gls	Tries	Pts
Aug.	17	Halifax	(H)	3	0	6
	22	Bradford N.	(A)	11	3	31
	25	Wigan	(A)	4	0	8
	27	Featherstone R.	(H)	4	1	11
Sept.	1	Wakefield	(YC) (A)	3	1	9
	8	Dewsbury	(A)	6	0	12
	15	Warrington	(H)	7	0	14
	22	Huddersfield	(A)	3	0	6
	29	York	(H)	6	0	12

Oct.	6	Batley.........................(A)	4	2	14
	13	Australia...................(H)	Did not play		
	20	Hull K.R. ....(A)	Did not play		
	27	Wigan ....(H)	2	0	4
Nov.	3	Hunslet ....(A)	1	0	2
	10	Barrow ....(H)	3	2	12
	17	Halifax ....(A)	4	0	8
	24	Keighley....................(H)	3	3	15
Dec.	1	Barrow ....(A)	4	0	8
	8	Bramley.......................(A)	5	0	10
	15	Doncaster ....(H)	1	2	8
	22	Bradford N (abandoned) (H)	1	1	5
	25	Batley.......................(H)	8	1	19
	29	Keighley ....(A)	3	0	6
1957					
Jan.	5	Hull ....(H)	5	2	16
	12	Warrington.................(A)	0	3	9
	19	St. Helens...................(H)	5	1	13
	26	Doncaster....................(A)	Did not play		
Feb.	2	Huddersfield ....(H)	6	0	12
	9	Wigan ....(RL Cup) (H)	2	1	7
	16	York ....(A)	7	1	17
	23	Warrington...(RL Cup) (A)	5	1	13
	27	Castleford ....(H)	4	1	11
Mar.	9	Halifax ....(RL Cup) (A)	5	0	10
	16	Wakefield T. ....(H)	5	1	13
	20	Bradford N ....(H)	5	1	13
	23	Hull...........................(A)	2	0	4
	30	Whitehaven			
		..........(Odsal, RL Cup SF)	1	0	2
Apr.	3	Wakefield T. ....(A)	3	0	6
	6	St. Helens...................(A)	0	0	0
	12	Hull K.R. ....(H)	Did not play		
	13	Dewsbury ....(H)	6	2	18
	19	Hunslet ....(H)	5	2	16
	20	Featherstone R.............(A)	2	0	4
	22	Castleford...................(A)	2	0	4
	23	Bramley.......................(H)	7	1	17
May	4	Oldham ....(Play-off) (A)	3	0	6
	11	Barrow			
		...(Wembley, RL Cup final)	0	0	0

Representative matches
For Great Britain:

Jan.	26	France..............(at Leeds)	9	1	21
Mar.	3	France..........(at Toulouse)	5	1	13
Apr.	10	France.........(at St. Helens)	7	1	17

For The Rest:

Oct.	3	Britain XIII .....(at Bradford)	4	0	8

For RL XIII:

Oct.	29	Australia................(Leigh)	3	0	6

	App	Gls	Tries	Pts
League	36	147	30	384
RL Cup.............................	5	13	2	32
Yorks Cup..........................	1	3	1	9
Play-off.............................	1	3	0	6
Representative.....................	5	28	3	65
Totals	**48**	**194**	**36**	**496**

Most points in a match:
53 (11t, 10g) by George West (Hull K.R.) v. Brookland Rovers (RL Cup)...............................4 March, 1905

Most points in a career:
NEIL FOX holds the record for most points in a career with 6,220 between 1956 and 1979. This total does not include points scored during a spell of club rugby in New Zealand.

Fox was a month short of his 17th birthday when he made his debut for Wakefield Trinity on 10 April, 1956. Apart from a brief time at Bradford Northern Fox had 19 seasons at Wakefield before moving to a succession of clubs in later years.

After a long career as an international centre Fox moved into the forwards and played his last professional match for Bradford in their opening fixture of the 1979-80 season, on 19 August. That match enabled him to join the elite few who have played first team rugby at 40 years of age.

Fox's season-by-season tally is as follows:

	Gls	Tries	Pts
1955-56............................	6	0	12
1956-57............................	54	10	138
1957-58............................	124	32	344
1958-59............................	148	28	380
1959-60............................	171	37	453
1960-61............................	94	20	248
1961-62............................	183	30	456
1962 Tour			
Australasia.........................	85	19	227
South Africa	19	4	50
1962-63............................	125	14	292
1963-64............................	125	21	313
1964-65............................	121	13	281
1965-66............................	98	11	229
1966-67............................	144	16	336
1967-68............................	98	18	250
1968-69............................	95	9	217
1969-70............................	17	5	49
1970-71............................	110	12	256
1971-72............................	84	6	186
1972-73............................	138	8	300
1973-74............................	62	8	148
1974-75............................	146(1)	14	333
1975-76............................	102(1)	4	215
1976-77............................	79(1)	6	175
1977-78............................	95(1)	9	216
1978-79............................	50	4	112
1979-80............................	2	0	4

A breakdown of Fox's club and representative totals is as follows:

	App	Gls	Tries	Pts
Wakefield T.	574	1,836	272	4,488
Bradford N.	70	85(1)	12	205
Hull K.R..................	59	212(2)	16	470
York	13	42	2	90
Bramley..................	23	73	6	164
Huddersfield..............	21	73(1)	5	160
Club Totals	**760**	**2,321(4)**	**313**	**5,577**
				(cont)

Yorkshire..................	17	60	9	147
Britain v. Australia	8	26	3	61
New Zealand.	4	11	1	25
France.........	17	56	10	142
Other representative				
games including tour	22	101	22	268
Representative Totals.	**68**	**254**	**45**	**643**
Grand Totals	**828**	**2,575(4)**	**358**	**6,220**

( ) Figures in brackets are one point drop goals included in total.

Score-a-match:
The following players have appeared and scored in all of their club's matches in one season:

Jim Hoey (Widnes) 1932-33
Billy Langton (Hunslet) 1958-59
Stuart Ferguson (Leigh) 1970-71
David Watkins (Salford)............................1972-73
David Watkins (Salford).............................1973-74
John Woods (Leigh)...................................1977-78
Steve Quinn (Featherstone R.) 1979-80
Mick Parrish (Hunslet) 1979-80
John Gorton (Swinton)..............................1980-81
Mick Parrish (Oldham) 1981-82
Peter Wood (Runcorn H.) 1984-85
David Noble (Doncaster)...........................1986-87
Mark Aston (Sheffield E.) 1988-89

Longest scoring run:
DAVID WATKINS holds the record for the longest scoring run, playing and scoring in 92 consecutive matches for Salford from 19 August 1972 to 25 April 1974. He totalled 403 goals, 41 tries and 929 points.

Longest run of appearances:
KEITH ELWELL holds the record for the longest run of appearances with one club with a total of 239 for Widnes. The consecutive run started at Wembley in the 1977 Challenge Cup final against Leeds on 7 May, and ended after he played in a Lancashire Cup-tie at home to St. Helens on 5 September 1982. He was dropped for the match at Featherstone Rovers a week later. Although he went on as a substitute the record refers to full appearances only.
Elwell played as a substitute in the next match and then made a full appearance before his run of all appearances ended at 242.

Highest score:
Huddersfield 119 v. Swinton Park 2 (RL Cup)
.......28 February 1914

Most points in all matches in a season:
1,436 by Leigh from 43 matches in 1985-86 as follows:
34 Division Two matches 1,156
2 Lancashire Cup 54
4 John Player Special Trophy 161
3 RL Challenge Cup 65

1,000 points in a League season:
1,156 by Leigh from 34 Division Two matches in 1985-86.
1,126 by Barrow from 34 Division Two matches in 1983-84.
1,005 by St. Helens from 38 matches in one-league system in 1958-59.

Longest winning run:
29 by Wigan from February to October, 1987, as follows:
20 Division One, 3 Premiership, 4 Lancashire Cup, Charity Shield and World Club Challenge.

Longest unbeaten run:
38 Cup and League matches by Huddersfield in 1914-15, including three draws. After the interruption by the First World War Huddersfield won their next five competitive matches — 4 Yorkshire Cup ties in 1918-19 and the opening league match of 1919-20.

Longest winning run in the League:
31 matches by Wigan. Last 8 matches of 1969-70 and first 23 of 1970-71.
● In 1978-79 Hull won all of their 26 Division Two matches, the only time a club has won all its league matches in one season.

Longest League losing run:
40 Division Two matches by Doncaster between November 1975 and April 1977. This period included a run of 37 Cup and League defeats.
● In 1906-07 Liverpool City lost all 30 of their league matches, the only time a team playing more than 12 league matches has lost them all. Liverpool also lost their two cup ties and dropped out after only one season. Liverpool did manage a home league draw against Bramley but when they were unable to fulfil a return fixture the match was expunged from league records.

Wigan captain Ellery Hanley with the Silk Cut Challenge Cup.

CUPS

RUGBY LEAGUE CHALLENGE CUP

1989 Final

Peerless Wigan retained the Silk Cut Challenge Cup and set off back to Central Park fired with a new ambition . . . to become the first club to lift the coveted trophy for a third successive time.

The Riversiders became the ninth side to retain the Cup — and the second to do it twice — their 27-0 whitewash of arch rivals St. Helens surpassing their impressive 32-12 hammering of Halifax a year earlier.

The Saints became the first side to be nilled at Wembley since 1951 when Wigan beat Barrow 10-0, while the scoreline was the widest margin for 29 years.

That St. Helens failed to contribute to the Wembley showpiece was as much a credit to the professional, almost clinical, defence of Wigan as to the non-activity in the Saints ranks.

It was all Wigan in a contest which disappointed the new lower capacity crowd of 78,000 — paying a record £1,121,293. Skipper Ellery Hanley rounded off a memorable 12 months at international and domestic level by being awarded the Lance Todd Trophy, to add to the British Man of the Series title in the 1988 Tests in Australia and the Man of the Match award in the 1989 John Player Special Trophy final.

He was pushed in the Press voting by New Zealand Test centre Kevin Iro, who touched down twice for a second successive year to take his tally to a Wembley record total of four and equal the best in all Challenge Cup finals. Also in contention was stand off Shaun Edwards and second row man Andy Platt.

That a St. Helens player was not even in the reckoning says it all. Only Great Britain hooker Paul Groves and, to a lesser extent, scrum half Neil Holding made notable contributions to a mistake-ridden Saints'

display. The £20,000 exercise of flying back from Sydney Manly duo Michael O'Connor and Paul Vautin — captain for the day — proved to be an expensive flop as neither Australian Test man made any impact on the committed Wigan rearguard.

Amid speculation on his departure from Central Park for an Australian club post, Wigan coach Graham Lowe masterminded his 10th trophy success during his three-year reign, adding the Silk Cut Challenge Cup to his 1988-89 haul of the John Player Special Trophy and the Grunhalle Lager Lancashire Cup, plus runners-up spot in the Stones Bitter Championship.

The comfortable victory continued Wigan's rewriting of the Challenge Cup annals. Extending their record of appearances in the final to 19, the Riversiders equalled Leeds' record of 10 triumphs, including a record nine at Wembley.

Playing in the unfamiliar colours of blue and white, having lost the toss to decide, Wigan broke the deadlock as early as the third minute when 20-year-old Kiwi centre Kevin Iro burst onto an astute pass from Hanley to power his way down the right flank and crash his way over for a try. He left in his wake 17-year-old full back Gary Connolly, believed to be the first amateur player to feature in a Cup final at Wembley, whose nightmare had already begun with the first downfield kick of the game which he knocked on. His only redeeming action of a nervous afternoon was a beautifully timed touchline tackle on Joe Lydon late in the game.

But the youngster was not on his own in the Saints ranks as their error rate of lost balls was 21, many committed at a pedestrian pace with second row man Roy Haggerty the biggest culprit with six spilled possessions. Wigan lost the ball 16 times.

Weak defence contributed to Iro's opening touchdown, Lydon hitting a penalty goal before Hanley produced one of the great Wembley touchdowns. His 45-yard solo effort was an amazing, weaving run which combined skill and power to leave four defenders stranded in his wake for a 26th minute score to which Lydon added the goal for a 12-0 half-time lead.

Playing his first game for a month after an ankle injury, scrum half Andy Gregory sent over a drop goal three minutes after the break before gaining confidence to extend his running game and create a highly productive half back unit with Edwards. After Kevin Iro had chosen to power his way over for a 47th minute try when a pass to his brother Tony would have been simpler, Gregory popped up to take the final tryscoring pass from Edwards after a brilliant run, Lydon's goal extending the Wigan supremacy to 23-0.

Wigan's cool, professional dismissal of a club which had won both the previous Wembley meetings, in 1961 and 1966, was given a fairy tale ending with four minutes left. Lydon provided the pass which sent Steve Hampson diving over for a try which helped compensate for the Great Britain full back missing Wigan's previous three Wembley visits with a broken leg in 1984 and a broken arm in both 1985 and 1988.

Livewire Gregory became the sixth player to share the record of figuring in four Cup winning sides at Wembley, the Widnes draw with Hull in 1982 extending his unbeaten run to a record-equalling five matches. Wigan substitute Denis Betts became the sixth player to tread the sacred turf having previously featured in an under-11 schoolboy curtain raiser, for Salford in 1981.

Wigan's Kevin Iro gets to grips with St. Helens' Australian winger Michael O'Connor.

SILK CUT CHALLENGE CUP FINAL

29 April   **Wembley**

WIGAN 27   **ST. HELENS 0**

Steve Hampson	1.	Gary Connolly
Tony Iro	2.	Michael O'Connor
Kevin Iro	3.	Phil Veivers
Dean Bell	4.	Paul Loughlin
Joe Lydon	5.	Les Quirk
Shaun Edwards	6.	Shane Cooper
Andy Gregory	7.	Neil Holding
Ian Lucas	8.	Tony Burke
Nicky Kiss	9.	Paul Groves
Adrian Shelford	10.	Paul Forber
Andy Platt	11.	Bernard Dwyer
Ian Potter	12.	Roy Haggerty
Ellery Hanley, Capt.	13.	Paul Vautin, Capt.
Denis Betts	14.	Darren Bloor
Andy Goodway	15.	Stuart Evans

T: K. Iro (2), Hanley, Gregory, Hampson
G: Lydon (3), Gregory (dg)
Substitutions:
Goodway for Potter (66 min.)
Betts for Kiss (72 min.)

Substitutions:
Evans for Dwyer (45 min.)
Bloor for Loughlin (63 min.)
Half-time: 12-0
Referee: Ray Tennant (Castleford)
Attendance: 78,000
Receipts: £1,121,293

Scorechart

Minute	Score		Wigan	St. Helens
3:	K. Iro (T)		4	0
19:	Lydon (P)		6	0
26:	Hanley (T)			
	Lydon (G)		12	0
43:	Gregory (DG)		13	0
47:	K. Iro (T)		17	0
65:	Gregory (T)			
	Lydon (G)		23	0
76:	Hampson (T)		27	0
		Scrums	12	8
		Penalties	4	11

Wigan tryscorer Steve Hampson.

1989 Round by Round

In the six-tie preliminary round, Leeds beat derby rivals Hunslet 32-6 at Headingley, late tries from Phil Ford and Carl Gibson providing a flattering scoreline, Hunslet stand off Neil Hague being impressive on his return to his former club. Across the city at Bramley's McLaren Field, local amateurs Milford went down 36-0 to Second Division Swinton, who led only 10-0 at half-time before hooker Gary Ainsworth orchestrated a series of tryscoring moves, plus touching down twice to earn the Man of the Match award. Amateurs West Hull entertained Doncaster at the Boulevard, the senior side gaining a comfortable 48-2 success with Kevin Jones and Neil Turner each bagging two tries. Visitors Workington Town led 8-6 before York scored either side of the interval, adding three further tries in a 35-8 victory. Wakefield Trinity struggled to lead only 2-0 at half-time to visitors Bramley before involving the backs more, winger Andy Fletcher scoring two tries and centre Phil Eden one en route to an 18-10 success. In an all-amateur tie at Barrow's Craven Park, Barrow Island went down 18-11 to St. Helens side Thatto Heath, who scored four tries to one.

In the first round, Hull's televised home tie with league leaders Castleford was a defence orientated encounter settled by Kiwi winger Shane Horo scoring the only try, amid controversy, as Castleford registered a hard-earned 7-4 victory. Record Rugby Union signing Jonathan Davies added a further 14 minutes to his League education in Widnes's 18-14 triumph at Salford. The Chemics led 18-10 before Salford full back Steve Gibson touched down four minutes from time. Halifax's bid for a third successive Wembley appearance floundered at Warrington where a Steve Roach-inspired Wire recorded a 25-8 success. Second Division pacesetters Leigh went down 23-17 at Sheffield Eagles, Kiwi Paul O'Kesene sealing victory with a last

ditch try, Mark Aston contributing four goals and two drop goals to break the club's points scoring record of 186 in a season. Bradford Northern opened an 8-0 lead after only five minutes at Fulham, before centre Steve McGowan scored a hat-trick of tries in a comfortable 28-10 victory.

Holders Wigan travelled to Doncaster, the Second Division side holding the big spenders to 8-6 until 10 minutes after the break. The world class style of centre Joe Lydon demolished the Dons in a second half romp, the Great Britain star claiming four tries and Kiwi Kevin Iro adding five goals as the Riversiders ran home 38-6 winners. York City's soccer stadium housed a five-figure crowd as visitors Leeds registered a 28-9 success over York, who trailed only 10-9 after 53 minutes before Australian Andrew Ettingshausen inspired a Loiners' success to finish with a tally of two tries. Thatto Heath came close to ending an 80-year drought of success for amateurs in the Challenge Cup, going down only 8-4 at Chorley Borough. The St. Helens side lacked pace in the backs, exposed by Borough whose stand off Steve Griffiths sealed victory with two touchdowns.

Two try-saving tackles by amateur international Under-19 full back Gary Connolly in only his second full game paved the way for a 16-5 success by St. Helens at Swinton. The Saints scored three tries to lead 14-5 at the break. Relegation-haunted Hull K.R. trailed 17-6 at half-time away to Second Division Rochdale Hornets before staging a rally of three tries in a 10-minute spell to secure an unimpressive 28-24 victory. Two tries from teenage centre Paul Newlove were the highlight of Featherstone Rovers' 32-0 win at Whitehaven, his second touchdown being a superb 50-yard solo effort as the Colliers ran in a total of seven tries. After an even first half, visitors Keighley led Runcorn Highfield 8-6 before taking advantage of the slope to win 28-10. Oldham stormed into a 30-5 half-time lead at Dewsbury before coasting to a 40-9 victory, hallmarked by a Man of the Match performance from loose forward Keith Newton, former Widnes clubmate Duncan Platt also contributing two tries and five goals.

Carlisle rewrote the club record books in a 58-1 hammering of Mansfield Marksman, the home side running up a record points tally and full back Barry Vickers scoring a record nine goals and 22 points. The 10-try rout was marred by the dismissal of Tony Catton, plus Mansfield's Brent Andrews and Mick Howarth. Batley's hard working defence thwarted Wakefield Trinity until the last quarter when the home side ran in three tries in a 10-minute spell to seal a 34-4 success, one touchdown coming from amateur international Alan Hunte. Barrow played host to Huddersfield who were unlucky not to be in the lead at half-time having had two tries disallowed. The Cumbrians pulled away 38-16 with five second half tries, one from Man of the Match Cavill Heugh.

In the second round, Widnes produced a five-star performance to take a 22-0 lead in as many minutes at league leaders Castleford. Castleford staged a second half rally but could not catch up on the Chemics' brilliant opening spell, tryscorer Emosi Koloto taking the Silk Cut Award in a 32-18 victory. Wigan proved to be a cup side for all seasons by combating wind and rain to gain a 17-4 success at Bradford Northern. Leading 7-4 at the break, the Riversiders sealed victory when hooker Nicky Kiss battled over in the 65th minute, Kevin Iro adding his second goal. Hull K.R. cast aside the pressure of relegation battles to dispose of Second Division visitors Chorley Borough 28-4, Man of the Match Paul Lyman adding the only second half touchdown after the Robins had a 20-4 interval lead. Carlisle visited Leeds with a six-match winning run under their belts. Although below par, the Loiners finished up 24-4 victors, their lacklustre performance being reflected by the Silk Cut Award going to busy Carlisle hooker Malcolm Thomason.

Sheffield Eagles' hopes of a giant killing act dwindled when First Division visitors Oldham scored two tries in the opening minutes, adding a further three touchdowns in a 32-20 success, the Eagles' consolation being Aston's recording of his 200th point of the season. St. Helens progressed into the third round for the 10th time in 14 seasons by disposing of Second Division title challengers Barrow by 28-6 at Knowsley Road. The Cumbrians, seeking to end a 43-year lack of success at St. Helens, led 6-0 before tailing 14-6 at the break. Featherstone Rovers gained handsome revenge for a Christmas holiday double defeat at the hands of Wakefield Trinity by winning 10-4 at Belle Vue, Man of the Match Graham Steadman scoring the only try of the tie. Keighley's only try of the afternoon came from scrum half Paul Moses as the Yorkshiremen went down 56-7 at Warrington, Woods scoring 20 points from two tries and six goals to take the Silk Cut Award, Mark Roberts grabbing a hat-trick of tries.

The highlight of the third round was a crowd of 26,282 witnessing the Widnes defeat of Leeds by 24-4 at Headingley. Bargain buy Joe Grima scored two tries as the Chemics' pack power laid the foundation for an impressive victory, Leeds only score coming from a try from hardworking skipper Lee Crooks. Warrington's Australian import Phil Blake marked his farewell performance with a Silk Cut Award winning display at Hull K.R., creating all but one of the Wire's five tries in the 30-4 victory. Neil Holding came on as a 35th minute substitute to earn Man of the Match rating as St. Helens turned a 3-0 deficit into a 32-3 triumph over visitors Featherstone Rovers. Holding rounded off a superb display by scoring a top class individual try. In the televised tie, injury-hit Oldham defended valiantly to hold Wigan to 12-4 at a snowbound Watersheddings. Half back Andy Gregory provided the springboard for success, being instrumental in Wigan's two tries by Edwards and Kevin Iro, while

Oldham were inspired by Paul Lord's try and the work rate of hooker and Man of the Match, Andy Ruane.

The first semi-final, at Wigan, saw injury-hit Saints tear up the form book by registering a last ditch 16-14 success over in-form Widnes. Former Barrow winger Les Quirk opened the scoring with his 100th career try, creating a St. Helens club record by touching down in his 10th successive match, then adding the winning try four minutes from time. The turning point in a classic encounter was the dismissal of Widnes packman Richard Eyres in the 20th minute for a trip, the lead changing hands five times. Two weeks later, injury-weakened Warrington almost repeated the shock treatment. A dramatic 61-yard drop goal from Joe Lydon in the 73rd minute put Wigan 7-6 ahead and then Ellery Hanley kicked ahead for Shaun Edwards to touch down in the dying seconds for a flattering 13-6 final scoreline. Warrington's John Woods, in the unfamiliar role of scrum half, sought his Wembley debut and was outstanding, kicking three goals but being robbed of the Silk Cut Award by Lydon, who also added a try and two goals. The Maine Road, Manchester, crowd of 26,523 was the best Challenge Cup semi-final gate for 20 years, the receipts of £144,056 the best outside Wembley.

1989 PRIZES

Round	Per Round	Total
Preliminary	12 × £1,300	£15,600
First	16 × £1,300	£20,800
Second	8 × £2,000	£16,000
Third	4 × £3,250	£13,000
Semi-Finals	2 × £5,500	£11,000
Runners-up	1 × £11,000	£11,000
Winners	1 × £20,000	£20,000
Total Prize Money		£107,400
Capital Development Fund		£62,600
Grand Total		£170,000

1989 RESULTS

Preliminary Round

Barrow Island	11	Thatto Heath	18
Leeds	32	Hunslet	6
Milford	0	Swinton	36
Wakefield T.	18	Bramley	10
West Hull	2	Doncaster	48
York	35	Workington T.	8

First Round

Barrow	38	Huddersfield	16
Carlisle	58	Mansfield M.	1
Chorley B.	8	Thatto Heath	4
Dewsbury	9	Oldham	40
Doncaster	6	Wigan	38
Fulham	10	Bradford N.	28
Hull	4	Castleford	7
Rochdale H.	24	Hull K.R.	28
Runcorn H.	10	Keighley	28
Salford	14	Widnes	18
Sheffield E.	23	Leigh	17
Swinton	5	St. Helens	16
Wakefield T.	34	Batley	4
Warrington	25	Halifax	8
Whitehaven	0	Featherstone R.	32
York	9	Leeds	28

Second Round

Bradford N.	4	Wigan	17
Castleford	18	Widges	32
Hull K.R.	28	Chorley B.	4
Leeds	24	Carlisle	4
St. Helens	28	Barrow	6
Sheffield E.	20	Oldham	32
Wakefield T.	4	Featherstone R.	10
Warrington	56	Keighley	7

Third Round

Hull K.R.	4	Warrington	30
Leeds	4	Widnes	24
Oldham	4	Wigan	12
St. Helens	32	Featherstone R.	3

Semi-Finals

St. Helens	16	Widnes	14
(at Wigan)			
Wigan	13	Warrington	6
(at Man. C. FC)			

Final

Wigan	27	St. Helens	0
(at Wembley)			

CHALLENGE CUP ROLL OF HONOUR

Year	Winners		Runners-up		Venue	Attendance	Receipts
1897	Batley	10	St Helens	3	Leeds	13,492	£624.17.7
1898	Batley	7	Bradford	0	Leeds	27,941	£1,586.3.0
1899	Oldham	19	Hunslet	9	Manchester	15,763	£946.16.0
1900	Swinton	16	Salford	8	Manchester	17,864	£1,100.0.0
1901	Batley	6	Warrington	0	Leeds	29,563	£1,644.16.0
1902	Broughton R.	25	Salford	0	Rochdale	15,006	£846.11.0
1903	Halifax	7	Salford	0	Leeds	32,507	£1,834.8.6
1904	Halifax	8	Warrington	3	Salford	17,041	£936.5.6
1905	Warrington	6	Hull K.R.	0	Leeds	19,638	£1,271.18.0
1906	Bradford	5	Salford	0	Leeds	15,834	£920.0.0
1907	Warrington	17	Oldham	3	Broughton	18,500	£1,010.0.0
1908	Hunslet	14	Hull	0	Huddersfield	18,000	£903.0.0
1909	Wakefield T.	17	Hull	0	Leeds	23,587	£1,490.0.0
1910	Leeds	7	Hull	7	Huddersfield	19,413	£1,102.0.0
Replay	Leeds	26	Hull	12	Huddersfield	11,608	£657.0.0
1911	Broughton R.	4	Wigan	0	Salford	8,000	£376.0.0
1912	Dewsbury	8	Oldham	5	Leeds	15,271	£853.0.0
1913	Huddersfield	9	Warrington	5	Leeds	22,754	£1,446.9.6
1914	Hull	6	Wakefield T.	0	Halifax	19,000	£1,035.5.0
1915	Huddersfield	37	St. Helens	3	Oldham	8,000	£472.0.0
1920	Huddersfield	21	Wigan	10	Leeds	14,000	£1,936.0.0
1921	Leigh	13	Halifax	0	Broughton	25,000	£2,700.0.0
1922	Rochdale H.	10	Hull	9	Leeds	32,596	£2,964.0.0
1923	Leeds	28	Hull	3	Wakefield	29,335	£2,390.0.0
1924	Wigan	21	Oldham	4	Rochdale	41,831	£3,712.0.0
1925	Oldham	16	Hull K.R.	3	Leeds	28,335	£2,879.0.0
1926	Swinton	9	Oldham	3	Rochdale	27,000	£2,551.0.0
1927	Oldham	26	Swinton	7	Wigan	33,448	£3,170.0.0
1928	Swinton	5	Warrington	3	Wigan	33,909	£3,158.1.11
1929	Wigan	13	Dewsbury	2	Wembley	41,500	£5,614.0.0
1930	Widnes	10	St. Helens	3	Wembley	36,544	£3,102.0.0
1931	Halifax	22	York	8	Wembley	40,368	£3,908.0.0
1932	Leeds	11	Swinton	8	Wigan	29,000	£2,479.0.0
1933	Huddersfield	21	Warrington	17	Wembley	41,874	£6,465.0.0
1934	Hunslet	11	Widnes	5	Wembley	41,280	£6,686.0.0
1935	Castleford	11	Huddersfield	8	Wembley	39,000	£5,533.0.0
1936	Leeds	18	Warrington	2	Wembley	51,250	£7,070.0.0
1937	Widnes	18	Keighley	5	Wembley	47,699	£6,704.0.0
1938	Salford	7	Barrow	4	Wembley	51,243	£7,174.0.0
1939	Halifax	20	Salford	3	Wembley	55,453	£7,681.0.0
1940	*No competition*						
1941	Leeds	19	Halifax	2	Bradford	28,500	£1,703.0.0
1942	Leeds	15	Halifax	10	Bradford	15,250	£1,276.0.0
1943	Dewsbury	16	Leeds	9	Dewsbury	10,470	£823.0.0
	Dewsbury	0	Leeds	6	Leeds	16,000	£1,521.0.0
	Dewsbury won on aggregate 16-15						
1944	Bradford	0	Wigan	3	Wigan	22,000	£1,640.0.0
	Bradford	8	Wigan	0	Bradford	30,000	£2,200.0.0
	Bradford won on aggregate 8-3						
1945	Huddersfield	7	Bradford N.	4	Huddersfield	9,041	£1,184.3.7
	Huddersfield	6	Bradford N.	5	Bradford	17,500	£2,050.0.0
	Huddersfield won on aggregate 13-9						

Year	Winners		Runners-up		Venue	Attendance	Receipts
1946	Wakefield T.	13	Wigan	12	Wembley	54,730	£12,013.13.6
1947	Bradford N.	8	Leeds	4	Wembley	77,605	£17,434.5.0
1948	Wigan	8	Bradford N.	3	Wembley	91,465	£21,121.9.9
1949	Bradford N.	12	Halifax	0	Wembley	*95,050	£21,930.5.0
1950	Warrington	19	Widnes	0	Wembley	94,249	£24,782.13.0
1951	Wigan	10	Barrow	0	Wembley	94,262	£24,797.19.0
1952	Workington T.	18	Featherstone R.	10	Wembley	72,093	£22,374.2.0
1953	Huddersfield	15	St. Helens	10	Wembley	89,588	£30,865.12.3
1954	Warrington	4	Halifax	4	Wembley	81,841	£29,706.7.3
Replay	Warrington	8	Halifax	4	Bradford	102,569	£18,623.7.0
1955	Barrow	21	Workington T.	12	Wembley	66,513	£27,453.16.0
1956	St. Helens	13	Halifax	2	Wembley	79,341	£29,424.7.6
1957	Leeds	9	Barrow	7	Wembley	76,318	£32,671.14.3
1958	Wigan	13	Workington T.	9	Wembley	66,109	£33,175.17.6
1959	Wigan	30	Hull	13	Wembley	79,811	£35,718.19.9
1960	Wakefield T.	38	Hull	5	Wembley	79,773	£35,754.16.0
1961	St. Helens	12	Wigan	6	Wembley	94,672	£38,479.11.9
1962	Wakefield T.	12	Huddersfield	6	Wembley	81,263	£33,390.18.4
1963	Wakefield T.	25	Wigan	10	Wembley	84,492	£44,521.17.0
1964	Widnes	13	Hull K.R.	5	Wembley	84,488	£44,840.19.0
1965	Wigan	20	Hunslet	16	Wembley	89,016	£48,080.4.0
1966	St. Helens	21	Wigan	2	Wembley	*98,536	£50,409.0.0
1967	Featherstone R.	17	Barrow	12	Wembley	76,290	£53,465.14.0
1968	Leeds	11	Wakefield T.	10	Wembley	87,100	£56,171.16.6
1969	Castleford	11	Salford	6	Wembley	*97,939	£58,848.1.0
1970	Castleford	7	Wigan	2	Wembley	95,255	£89,262.2.0
1971	Leigh	24	Leeds	7	Wembley	85,514	£84,452.15
1972	St. Helens	16	Leeds	13	Wembley	89,495	£86,414.30
1973	Featherstone R.	33	Bradford N.	14	Wembley	72,395	£125,826.40
1974	Warrington	24	Featherstone R.	9	Wembley	77,400	£132,021.05
1975	Widnes	14	Warrington	7	Wembley	85,098	£140,684.45
1976	St. Helens	20	Widnes	5	Wembley	89,982	£190,129.40
1977	Leeds	16	Widnes	7	Wembley	80,871	£241,488.00
1978	Leeds	14	St. Helens	12	Wembley	*96,000	£330,575.00
1979	Widnes	12	Wakefield T.	3	Wembley	94,218	£383,157.00
1980	Hull K.R.	10	Hull	5	Wembley	*95,000	£448,202.90
1981	Widnes	18	Hull K.R.	9	Wembley	92,496	£591,117.00
1982	Hull	14	Widnes	14	Wembley	92,147	£684,500.00
Replay	Hull	18	Widnes	9	Elland Rd., L'ds	41,171	£180,525.00
1983	Featherstone R.	14	Hull	12	Wembley	84,969	£655,510.00
1984	Widnes	19	Wigan	6	Wembley	80,116	£686,171.00
1985	Wigan	28	Hull	24	Wembley	*97,801	£760,322.00
1986	Castleford	15	Hull K.R.	14	Wembley	82,134	£806,676.00
1987	Halifax	19	St. Helens	18	Wembley	91,267	£1,009,206.00
1988	Wigan	32	Halifax	12	Wembley	*94,273	£1,102,247.00
1989	Wigan	27	St. Helens	0	Wembley	*78,000	£1,121,293.00

*Indicates a capacity attendance, the limit being fixed annually taking into account variable factors.

RUGGBY LEAGUE CHALLENGE CUP ....
A REVIEW
1966-67
Featherstone R. 17 Wrigglesworth; Thomas (1t),
Cotton, Jordan, Greatorex; M. Smith, Dooler (1g);
Tonks, Harris, Dixon, A. Morgan (1t),
Thompson (1t), Smales (1t, 3g)
Barrow 12 Tees (1g); Burgess, Challinor,
Hughes, Murray; Brophy (1t), G. Smith; Kelland,
Redhead, Hopwood, Sanderson, Delooze (2g),
Watson (1t)
Referee: E. Clay (Leeds)
1967-68
Leeds 11 Risman (4g); Alan Smith, Hynes,
Watson, Atkinson (1t); Shoebottom, Seabourne;
Clark, Crosby, K. Eyre, Ramsey, A. Eyre, Batten
Wakefield T. 10 Cooper, Hirst (2t), Brooke,
Coetzer, Batty; Poynton, Owen; Jeanes,
Shepherd, D. Fox (2g); Haigh, McLeod, Hawley
Referee: J.P. Hebblethwaite (York)
1968-69
Castleford 11 Edwards; Briggs, Howe (1t),
Thomas, Lowndes; Hardisty (1t), Hepworth (1t);
Hartley, C. Dickinson, J. Ward, Redfearn (1g),
Lockwood, Reilly
Salford 6 K. Gwilliam; Burgess, Whitehead,
Hesketh, Jackson; Watkins, Brennan; Ogden,
Dickens, Bott, Coulman, Dixon, Hill (3g)
Referee: D.S. Brown (Preston)
1969-70
Castleford 7 Edwards; Briggs, Thomas, Stenton,
Lowndes (1t); Hardisty (Hargrave), Hepworth;
Hartley, C. Dickinson, Redfearn (2g), Kirkbride,
Lockwood, Reilly
Wigan 2 Tyrer (1g) (C. Hill); Jones, Francis,
Rowe, Kevin O'Loughlin; D. Hill, Parr;
Ashcroft, Burdell, Hogan, Ashurst, D. Robinson,
Laughton
Referee: G.F. Lindop (Wakefield)
1970-71
Leigh 24 Eckersley (1t, 1g); Ferguson (5g),
Dorrington (1t), Collins, Walsh; A. Barrow,
Murphy (2g) (L. Chisnall); Watts, Ashcroft,
Fiddler (1g), Grimes, Clarkson, Smethurst
Leeds 7 Holmes (2g); Langley, Hynes, Cowan
(Dyl), Atkinson; Wainwright (1t), Seabourne;
J. Burke, Fisher, Barnard, Hick, Haigh, Ramsey
Referee: W.H. Thompson (Huddersfield)
1971-72
St. Helens 16 G. Pimblett; L. Jones (1t), Benyon,
Walsh, Wilson; K. Kelly, Heaton; Rees (1t),
Greenall, J. Stephens, Mantle, E. Chisnall,
Coslett (1g)
Leeds 13 Holmes; Alan Smith, Hynes (Langley),
Dyl, Atkinson; Hardisty, Hepworth; Clawson
(5g), Fisher, Ramsey, Cookson (1t), Haigh, Batten
Referee: E. Lawrinson (Warrington)

1972-73
Featherstone R. 33 C. Kellett (8g); Coventry,
M. Smith (1t) (Hartley) (1t), Newlove (2t),
K. Kellett; Mason, Nash (1g); Tonks, Bridges,
Farrar (1t), Rhodes (Hollis), Thompson, Stone
Bradford N. 14 Tees (4g); Lamb, Stockwell,
Watson, D. Redfearn (1t); Blacker (Treasure),
Seabourne; Hogan, Dunn, Earl (Long), Joyce,
W. Pattinson, Fearnley (1t)
Referee: M.J. Naughton (Widnes)
1973-74
Warrington 24 Whitehead (7g); M. Philbin,
Noonan, Whittle, Bevan; Murphy (2g) (Pickup),
Gordon; D. Chisnall, Ashcroft (1t), Brady
(Wanbon), Wright, Nicholas (1t), B. Philbin
Featherstone R. 9 Box (3g); Dyas, M. Smith,
Hartley, Bray; Newlove (1t), Nash; Tonks,
Bridges, Harris, Rhodes (Busfield), Thompson
(Stone), Bell
Referee: S. Shepherd (Oldham)
1974-75
Widnes 14 Dutton (5g, 1dg); A. Prescott, George,
Aspey, Anderson; Hughes, Bowden; Mills (1t),
Elwell, Sheridan, Foran, Adams, Laughton
Warrington 7 Whitehead (2g); M. Philbin,
Noonan, Reynolds (W. Briggs), Bevan (1t);
Whittle, Gordon; D. Chisnall, Ashcroft, Wanbon,
Conroy, Martyn (Nicholas), B. Philbin
Referee: P. Geraghty (York)
1975-76
St. Helens 20 G. Pimblett (3g, 2dg); L. Jones,
Cunningham (1t), Noonan, Mathias; Benyon
(Glynn 2t), Heaton (1t); Mantle (James),
A. Karalius, Coslett, Nicholls, E. Chisnall, Hull
Widnes 5 Dutton (2g); A. Prescott (D. O'Neill),
Hughes, George, Jenkins; Eckersley, Bowden;
Nelson, Elwell (1dg), Wood, Foran (Sheridan),
Adams, Laughton
Referee: R. Moore (Wakefield)
1976-77
Leeds 16 Murrell; Alan Smith (D. Smith),
Hague, Dyl (1t), Atkinson (1t); Holmes,
Dick (1t, 3g, 1dg); Harrison, Ward, Pitchford,
Eccles, Cookson, Fearnley (Dickinson)
Widnes 7 Dutton (2g); S. Wright (George),
Aspey (1t), Eckersley, D. O'Neill; Hughes,
Bowden; Ramsey, Elwell, Mills, Dearden
(Foran), Adams, Laughton
Referee: V. Moss (Manchester)
1977-78
Leeds 14 Oulton (1g); D. Smith (1t), Hague, Dyl,
Atkinson (1t); Holmes (1dg), J. Sanderson (Dick);
Harrison (Dickinson), Ward (2dg), Pitchford,
Cookson (1t), Eccles, Crane
St. Helens 12 G. Pimblett (3g), L. Jones,
Noonan, Glynn, Mathias; Francis (1t),
K. Gwilliam; D. Chisnall, Liptrot (1t), James,
Nicholls, Cunningham, Pinner
Referee: W.H. Thompson (Huddersfield)

1978-79
Widnes 12 Eckersley (1dg); S. Wright (1t),
Aspey, George (Hull), Burke (2g); Hughes (1t),
Bowden; Mills, Elwell (1dg), Shaw, Adams,
Dearden (M. O'Neill), Laughton
Wakefield T. 3 Sheard; Fletcher (1t), K. Smith,
Diamond, Juliff; Topliss, Lampkowski; Burke,
McCurrie, Skerrett, Ashurst, Keith Rayne, Idle
Referee: J.E. Jackson (Pudsey)
1979-80
Hull K.R. 10 Hall; Hubbard (3g, 1t) (Hogan),
M. Smith, Hartley, Sullivan; Millward (1dg),
Agar; Holdstock, Watkinson, Lockwood, Lowe,
Rose (Millington), Casey
Hull 5 Woods; Bray, Walters, Wilby (1t),
Prendiville; Newlove (Hancock), Pickerill;
Tindall, Wileman, Stone (Farrar), Birdsall,
Lloyd (1g), Norton
Referee: G.F. Lindop (Wakefield)
1980-81
Widnes 18 Burke (4g, 1t); S. Wright, George (1t),
Cunningham (J. Myler), Bentley; Hughes,
Gregory (1t); M. O'Neill (Shaw), Elwell,
Lockwood, L. Gorley, E. Prescott, Adams (1dg)
Hull K.R. 9 Hall; Hubbard (3g), M. Smith,
Hogan, Muscroft; Hartley, Harkin; Holdstock
(Millington), Watkinson, Crooks (Proctor), Lowe,
Burton (1t), Casey
Referee: D.G. Kershaw (Easingwold)
1981-82
Hull 14 Kemble; O'Hara (1t), Day, S. Evans,
Prendiville; Topliss, Harkin; Skerrett, Wileman,
Stone, Crane (Crooks), Lloyd (4g), Norton (1t)
Widnes 14 Burke (1g), (A. Myler); S. Wright (1t),
Keiron O'Loughlin, Cunningham (2t), Basnett;
Hughes, Gregory (1g); M. O'Neill, Elwell (1dg),
Lockwood (S. O'Neill), L. Gorley, E. Prescott,
Adams
Referee: G.F. Lindop (Wakefield)
Replay
Hull 18 Kemble (1t); Sullivan, Leuluai, S. Evans,
Prendiville; Topliss (2t), Dean; Tindall, Duke,
Stone, Skerrett, Crooks (1t, 3g), Norton (Crane)
Widnes 9 Burke (3g); S. Wright (1t), Keiron
O'Loughlin, Cunningham, Basnett; Hughes,
Gregory; M. O'Neill, Elwell, Lockwood,
L. Gorley, E. Prescott, Adams
Referee: G.F. Lindop (Wakefield)
1982-83
Featherstone R. 14 N. Barker; Marsden,
Quinn (4g), Gilbert (Lyman), K. Kellett;
A. Banks, Hudson; Gibbins, Handscombe,
Hankins, D. Hobbs (2t), Slatter (Siddall), Smith
Hull 12 Kemble; O'Hara, S. Evans, Leuluai (1t),
Prendiville; Topliss, Harkin (Day), (Crane);
Skerrett, Bridges, Stone, Rose, Crooks (1t, 3g),
Norton
Referee: M.R. Whitfield (Widnes)

1983-84
Widnes 19 Burke (3g); D. Wright, Hughes
(D. Hulme), Lydon (2t), Basnett;
Keiron O'Loughlin (1t), Gregory; S. O'Neill
(1dg), Elwell, K. Tamati, L. Gorley, M. O'Neill
(Whitfield), Adams
Wigan 6 Edwards; Ramsdale, Stephenson,
Whitfield (1g), (Elvin), Gill; Cannon, Stephens;
Hemsley (1t), H. Tamati, Case (Juliff), West,
Scott, Pendlebury
Referee: W.H. Thompson (Huddersfield)
1984-85
Wigan 28 Edwards (1t); Ferguson (2t),
Stephenson (1g), Donlan, Gill (1t, 3g);
Kenny (1t), M. Ford; Courtney, Kiss, Case
(Campbell), West, Dunn, Potter
Hull 24 Kemble; James (1t), S. Evans (1t),
Leuluai (2t), O'Hara (Schofield); Ah Kuoi,
Sterling; Crooks (2g), Patrick, Puckering
(Divorty 1t), Muggleton, Rose, Norton
Referee: R. Campbell (Widnes)
1985-86
Castleford 15 Lord (Roockley); Plange,
Marchant (1t), Hyde, Sandy (1t); Joyner,
R. Beardmore (1t, 1dg); Ward, K. Beardmore
(Horton), Johnson, England, Ketteridge (1g),
French
Hull K.R. 14 Fairbairn; Clark, M. Smith,
Prohm (2t), Laws; Dorahy (1g), Harkin; P.
Johnston, Watkinson, Ema, Kelly (G. Smith),
Des Harrison (Lydiat 1t), Miller
Referee: R. Whitfield (Widnes)
1986-87
Halifax 19 Eadie (1t); Wilson, Whitfield (3g),
Rix, George (1t); C. Anderson (Juliff), Stephens;
Beevers (James), McCallion (1t), Neller, Dixon,
Scott, Pendlebury (1dg)
St. Helens 18 Veivers; Ledger, Loughlin (1t, 3g),
Elia (1t), McCormack; Clark, Holding; Burke,
Liptrot, Fieldhouse, Platt, Haggerty (Round 1t),
Arkwright
Referee: J. Holdsworth (Kippax)
1987-88
Wigan 32 Lydon (1t, 1g); T. Iro (1t), K. Iro (2t),
Bell (1t); Gill (1t); Edwards (Byrne), Gregory
(1g); Case, Kiss, Shelford, Goodway, Potter
(Wane), Hanley (1t)
Halifax 12 Eadie; Meredith, T. Anderson (1t),
Wilkinson, Whitfield (2g); Grogan, Robinson
(Fairbank); James (1t), McCallion, Neller,
Holliday (Scott), Dixon, Pendlebury.
Referee: G. F. Lindop (Wakefield)

THE LANCE TODD TROPHY

The Lance Todd Trophy is presented to the Man of the Match in the Rugby League Challenge Cup Final, the decision being reached by a ballot of members of the Rugby League Writers' Association present at the game.

Lance Todd made his name in Britain as a player with Wigan and as manager of Salford. His untimely death in a road accident on the return journey from a game at Oldham was commemorated by the introduction of the Lance Todd Trophy.

The award was instituted by Australian-born Harry Sunderland, Warrington director Bob Anderton and Yorkshire journalist John Bapty.

Around 1950, the Red Devils' Association at Salford, comprising players and officials who had worked with Todd, raised sufficient funds to provide a trophy and replica for each winner.

Gerry Helme, of Warrington, is the only player to win the trophy twice; Len Killeen, of St. Helens, is the only winger to earn the title; Hull's Tommy Harris the only hooker; and Ray Ashby and Brian Gabbitas the only players to share the honour.

Following the 1954 replay, it was decided by the Red Devils that in future the trophy would be awarded for the Wembley game. In 1954, Gerry Helme had received the trophy for his performance in the Odsal replay. In the 1982 replay at Elland Road, Leeds, the Man of the Match award went to Hull skipper David Topliss, the Lance Todd Trophy having been awarded to Eddie Cunningham, of Widnes, in the drawn Wembley tie.

The 1989 winner was Wigan skipper and loose forward Ellery Hanley.

The Lance Todd Trophy Roll of Honour

Year	Winner	Team	Position
1946	Billy Stott	Wakefield Trinity (v Wigan)	Centre
1947	Willie Davies	Bradford Northern (v Leeds)	Stand off
1948	Frank Whitcombe	Bradford Northern (v Wigan)	Prop
1949	Ernest Ward	Bradford Northern (v Halifax)	Centre
1950	Gerry Helme	Warrington (v Widnes)	Scrum half
1951	Cec Mountford	Wigan (v Barrow)	Stand off
1952	Billy Ivison	Workington T. (v Featherstone R.)	Loose forward
1953	Peter Ramsden	Huddersfield (v St. Helens)	Stand off
1954	Gerry Helme	Warrington (v Halifax)	Scrum half
1955	Jack Grundy	Barrow (v Workington Town)	Second row
1956	Alan Prescott	St. Helens (v Halifax)	Prop
1957	Jeff Stevenson	Leeds (v Barrow)	Scrum half
1958	Rees Thomas	Wigan (v Workington Town)	Scrum half
1959	Brian McTigue	Wigan (v Hull)	Second row
1960	Tommy Harris	Hull (v Wakefield Trinity)	Hooker
1961	Dick Huddart	St. Helens (v Wigan)	Second row
1962	Neil Fox	Wakefield Trinity (v Huddersfield)	Centre
1963	Harold Poynton	Wakefield Trinity (v Wigan)	Stand off
1964	Frank Collier	Widnes (v Hull K.R.)	Prop

1965	Ray Ashby	Wigan	Full back
	Brian Gabbitas	Hunslet	Stand off
1966	Len Killeen	St. Helens (v Wigan)	Winger
1967	Carl Dooler	Featherstone Rovers (v Barrow)	Scrum half
1968	Don Fox	Wakefield Trinity (v Leeds)	Prop
1969	Malcolm Reilly	Castleford (v Salford)	Loose forward
1970	Bill Kirkbride	Castleford (v Wigan)	Second row
1971	Alex Murphy	Leigh (v Leeds)	Scrum half
1972	Kel Coslett	St. Helens (v Leeds)	Loose forward
1973	Steve Nash	Featherstone R. (v Bradford N.)	Scrum half
1974	Derek Whitehead	Warrington (v Featherstone Rovers)	Full back
1975	Ray Dutton	Widnes (v Warrington)	Full back
1976	Geoff Pimblett	St. Helens (v Widnes)	Full back
1977	Steve Pitchford	Leeds (v Widnes)	Prop
1978	George Nicholls	St. Helens (v Leeds)	Second row
1979	David Topliss	Wakefield Trinity (v Widnes)	Stand off
1980	Brian Lockwood	Hull K.R. (v Hull)	Prop
1981	Mick Burke	Widnes (v Hull K.R.)	Full back
1982	Eddie Cunningham	Widnes (v Hull)	Centre
1983	David Hobbs	Featherstone Rovers (v Hull)	Second row
1984	Joe Lydon	Widnes (v Wigan)	Centre
1985	Brett Kenny	Wigan (v Hull)	Stand off
1986	Bob Beardmore	Castleford (v Hull K.R.)	Scrum half
1987	Graham Eadie	Halifax (v St. Helens)	Full back
1988	Andy Gregory	Wigan (v Halifax)	Scrum half
1989	Ellery Hanley	Wigan (v St. Helens)	Loose forward

1989 Lance Todd Trophy winner Ellery Hanley on the attack.

CHALLENGE CUP RECORDS

ALL ROUNDS

TEAM
Highest score:
Huddersfield 119 v. *Swinton Park 2 1914

INDIVIDUAL

Most goals in a match:
22 by Jim Sullivan (Wigan) v. *Flimby and Fothergill
. . . . 1925

Most tries in a match:
11 by George West (Hull K.R.) v. *Brookland Rovers
. . . . 1905

Most points in a match:
53 (11t,10g) by George West (Hull K.R.) as above.

*Amateur teams

FINAL RECORDS

TEAM

Most wins: 10 by Leeds, Wigan

Most finals: 19 by Wigan

Highest score:
Wakefield T. 38 v. Hull 5 1960

Widest margin:
Huddersfield 37 v. St. Helens 3 1915

Biggest attendance:
102,569 Warrington v. Halifax (Replay) at Bradford
. . . . 1954

INDIVIDUAL

Most goals:
8 by Cyril Kellett (Featherstone R.) v. Bradford N.
. . . . 1973

Most tries:
3 by Bob Wilson (Broughton R.) v. Salford. . . . 1902
Stan Moorhouse (Huddersfield) v. Warrington. 1913
Tom Holliday (Oldham) v. Swinton. 1927

Most points:
20 (7g,2t) by Neil Fox (Wakefield T.) v. Hull. . . 1960

WEMBLEY FACTS

WIGAN made a record 15th appearance at Wembley in the 1989 final against St. Helens, recording a record ninth victory at the stadium.

A RECORD 10 overseas players trod the Wembley turf in 1985. Hull fielded six — a record for one club. The Airlie Birds sextet were Australians Peter Sterling and John Muggleton, plus New Zealanders Gary Kemble, James Leuluai, Dane O'Hara and Fred Ah Kuoi. Wigan added Australians John Ferguson and Brett Kenny together with New Zealanders Graeme West and Danny Campbell, who went on as substitute. South African Nick Du Toit was substitute back but did not play.

THE 1985 aggregates of 10 tries and 52 points were both record totals for a Challenge Cup final with Hull's 24 points the most by a losing side. There were also 10 tries in the 1915 final when Huddersfield beat St. Helens 37-3, which is the widest margin. Wakefield Trinity ran up the highest Cup final score when they beat Hull 38-5 in 1960.

WORLD RECORD receipts of £1,121,293 were taken at the 1989 Final between Wigan and St. Helens from a capacity crowd of 78,000.

SIX players share the record of playing in four Cup-winning sides at Wembley — Alex Murphy, Brian Lockwood, Eric Hughes, Keith Elwell, Mick Adams and Andy Gregory.
Murphy was in St. Helens' victorious side of 1961 and as captain led St. Helens (1966), Leigh (1971) and Warrington (1974) to victory. He played in three different positions — stand off, centre and scrum half. Murphy was a scorer in each final with a total of five drop goals and a try.
Brian Lockwood was in the winning final teams of Castleford (1969 and 1970), Hull K.R. (1980) and Widnes (1981). He also appeared with Widnes in the drawn final of 1982.
Hughes, Elwell and Adams each played in the Widnes teams that won the Cup in 1975, 1979, 1981 and 1984. They also appeared in the drawn final of 1982.
Gregory was in the Widnes sides of 1981 and 1984, plus Wigan's victorious teams in 1988 and 1989. His appearance for Widnes in the 1982 drawn final takes his Wembley unbeaten record to five games.

THE Widnes trio of Eric Hughes, Keith Elwell and Mick Adams also hold the record for most appearances at Wembley...seven. In addition to the five finals mentioned above they were on the losing side in 1976 and 1977.

ERIC ASHTON captained a record six teams at Wembley — Wigan in 1958, 1959, 1961, 1963, 1965 and 1966. His record of three wins (in 1958, 1959, 1965) is shared with Derek Turner (Wakefield Trinity 1960, 1962, 1963) and Alex Murphy (St. Helens 1966, Leigh 1971 and Warrington 1974).

THE YOUNGEST player to appear in a Wembley Cup final was Shaun Edwards who was 17 years, 6 months and 19 days when he played full back for Wigan against Widnes in 1984. He was also the youngest captain at Wembley, leading Wigan to success in the 1988 final against Halifax at the age of 21 years, 6 months and 14 days.

ALEX MURPHY has been a record six times to Wembley as a coach. He was a winner as player-coach with Leigh (1971) and Warrington (1974), but losing each time when confined to the bench with Warrington (1975), Wigan (1984) and St. Helens (1987 and 1989). Murphy also went twice solely as a player, with St. Helens in 1961 and 1966.

MOST WINS as a coach at Wembley is three, by Jim Sullivan (Wigan 1948, 1951 and St. Helens 1956), Joe Egan (Wigan 1958, 1959 and Widnes 1964) and Ken Traill (Wakefield T. 1960, 1962 and 1963).

THE OLDEST player at Wembley was Gus Risman, who at 41 years 29 days led Workington Town to victory over Featherstone Rovers in 1952. He played full back.

THE TALLEST player at Wembley was New Zealand Test star Graeme West who captained Wigan in the 1984 and 1985 finals. He measured 6ft. 5in.

SCHOOLBOYS who have appeared in an Under-11 curtain-raiser at Wembley and gone on to play in the major final at the stadium are Joe Lydon, David Hulme, Mike Ford, Neil Puckering, David Plange and Denis Betts. Lydon became the first to achieve the feat with Widnes in the 1984 final against Wigan, followed by Hulme who went on as a 72nd minute substitute. Both had played in the first schoolboys' curtain-raiser in 1975 — Lydon for Wigan, and Hulme for Widnes. Ford played scrum half for Wigan in the 1985 final having represented Oldham in the 1977 curtain-raiser. Puckering played for Hull in the 1977 curtain-raiser and for his home town club in the Challenge Cup final of 1985. Plange was in the Hull Schools team of 1976 and played for Castleford in the 1986 final, while Betts was in the beaten Salford schools side in 1981, before coming on as a substitute for Wigan in the 1989 Cup Final.

CYRIL KELLETT holds the record for most goals in a Challenge Cup final with his eight for Featherstone Rovers in 1973.

In the most remarkable exhibition of kicking seen at Wembley, the veteran full back was successful with every one of his attempts as Bradford Northern crashed 33-14.

Nine years earlier he scored only one for Hull Kingston Rovers in the 13-5 defeat by Widnes.

NEIL FOX — the record aggregate points scorer of all time — piled up the most points in a Challenge Cup final in 1960. His 20 points helped Wakefield Trinity to a 38-5 defeat of Hull. Fox's points came from two tries and seven goals.

His three drop goals for Trinity in the 12-6 victory over

Huddersfield two years later was another extraordinary feat in the days when the drop goal was a rarity.

NO player has scored a hat-trick of tries at Wembley, the feat being achieved only three times in the preceding era.

The last to do it was Oldham winger Tom Holliday in the 26-7 defeat of Swinton in 1927.

Bob Wilson, the Broughton Rangers centre and captain, was the first to score three tries, in the 25-0 victory over Salford in 1902.

In between, Stan Moorhouse's three-try feat accounted for all of Huddersfield's points when they beat Warrington 9-5 in 1913. Moorhouse was winger to Harold Wagstaff, recognised as the greatest centre of all time.

MANY great players have gone through an entire career without achieving their ambition of playing at Wembley. Hull's Mike Smith achieved it in his first senior game.

Smith made one of the most remarkable debuts in sporting history when he played in the second row of an injury-hit Boulevard side against Wakefield Trinity in 1960.

In contrast, Freddie Miller signed for Hull in 1932 and did not play at Wembley until 1952…two years after joining Featherstone Rovers.

A NOTABLE Wembley captain was Gus Risman who led two clubs to victory…14 years apart.

He was captain of Salford when they beat Barrow in 1938. At 41, he led Workington Town to their triumph over Featherstone Rovers in 1952.

PROBABLY the unluckiest Challenge Cup finalist was Dai Davies who appeared in four finals and was on the losing side each time. Three of those occasions were at Wembley with different clubs. He was a loser with Warrington (1933), Huddersfield (1935) and Keighley (1937). Before the Wembley era he was also in Warrington's beaten team of 1928.

Steve Norton has played at Wembley four times and has yet to be on the winning side. He was in the beaten Hull teams of 1980, 1983 and 1985 in addition to playing in the 1982 drawn final. In 1970 he was a non-playing substitute for Castleford who won the Cup.

Bill Ramsey was on the losing side in four Wembley finals but gained a winner's medal with Leeds in 1968. He picked up losers' medals with Hunslet (1965), Leeds (1971 and 1972) and Widnes (1977).

A TOTAL of 13 current clubs, excluding newcomers Chorley, have yet to play at Wembley …Batley, Bramley, Carlisle, Doncaster, Fulham, Mansfield Marksman, Oldham, Rochdale Hornets, Runcorn Highfield, Sheffield Eagles, Swinton, Trafford Borough and Whitehaven.

Fate seems to be against Swinton and Oldham. In the five years preceding the move to Wembley, one or the other appeared in the final, twice meeting each other. Oldham played in four successive finals in that period. Swinton's run of three finals ended when the first Wembley took place in 1929. They got through to the final three years later …only for it to be played at Wigan!

137

CHALLENGE CUP

Wembley Era Semi-Finals

It is generally felt that it is better to have played at Wembley and lost than never to have played there at all. This makes the semi-final stage of the RL Challenge Cup almost as important as the final with no consolation for the losers.

Of the 13 current clubs who have never appeared at Wembley four have been beaten semi-finalists. They are Oldham (four times), Swinton, Rochdale Hornets (twice) and Whitehaven.

Probably the unluckiest are Oldham. They have reached the penultimate stage four times without being able to realise their ambition. Oldham almost made it in 1964. After drawing 5-5 with Hull K.R. they were winning 17-14 in extra time of the replay when bad light stopped play and they were beaten in the third game.

Swinton did win a semi-final in 1932 but the final that year was switched from Wembley to Wigan!

There have been three occasions when Yorkshire has provided all four semi-finalists in one year — in 1962, 1973 and 1983. Twice

have all four semi-finalists come from west of the Pennines — in 1930 and 1989.

Until 1962 the two semi-finals were always played on the same Saturday, but with four Yorkshire clubs competing for the first time it was decided to play one mid-week. Both matches were played at Odsal Stadium, Bradford. The first was on a Wednesday evening — without floodlights — when 43,625 saw Wakefield Trinity beat Featherstone Rovers and on the following Saturday there were 31,423 to see Huddersfield beat Hull K.R.

The following year both semi-finals were again played on the same Saturday, but since then they have been staged on different Saturdays.

Some semi-final facts during the Wembley era are:

Biggest attendance: 69,898 Warrington v. Leeds at Bradford in 1950

Biggest aggregate: 104,453 in 1939 (Only other six-figure aggregate was 102,080 in 1951)

Record receipts: £144,056 Warrington v. Wigan at Maine Road, Manchester in 1989

Lowest attendance: 7,971 Featherstone R. v. Leigh at Leeds in 1974

Highest score and widest margin: Wigan 34 v. Salford 4 in 1988

CHALLENGE CUP SEMI-FINALS

Year	Winners		Runners-up		Venue	Attendance	Receipts
1929	Dewsbury	9	Castleford	3	Huddersfield	25,000	£1,562
	Wigan	7	St. Helens Recs.	7	Swinton	31,000	£2,209
Replay	Wigan	13	St. Helens Recs.	12	Leigh	21,940	£1,437
1930	Widnes	10	Barrow	3	Warrington	25,500	£1,630
	St. Helens	5	Wigan	5	Swinton	37,169	£2,666
Replay	St. Helens	22	Wigan	10	Leigh	24,000	£1,657
1931	Halifax	11	St. Helens	2	Rochdale	21,674	£1,498
	York	15	Warrington	5	Leeds	32,419	£2,329
1932	Leeds	2	Halifax	2	Huddersfield	31,818	£2,456
Replay	Leeds	9	Halifax	2	Wakefield	21,000	£1,417
	Swinton	7	Wakefield T.	4	Rochdale	21,273	£1,369
●	*Final was played at Wigan, not Wembley*						
1933	Huddersfield	30	Leeds	8	Wakefield	36,359	£2,299
	Warrington	11	St. Helens	5	Swinton	30,373	£2,055
1934	Hunslet	12	Huddersfield	7	Wakefield	27,450	£1,797
	Widnes	7	Oldham	4	Swinton	17,577	£1,050

Year	Winners		Runners-up		Venue	Attendance	Receipts
1935	Castleford	11	Barrow	5	Swinton	24,469	£1,534
	Huddersfield	21	Hull	5	Leeds	37,111	£2,753
1936	Leeds	10	Huddersfield	5	Wakefield	37,906	£2,456
	Warrington	7	Salford	2	Wigan	41,538	£2,796
1937	Keighley	0	Wakefield T.	0	Leeds	39,998	£2,793
Replay	Keighley	5	Wakefield T.	3	Huddersfield	14,400	£1,052
	Widnes	13	Wigan	9	Warrington	29,260	£1,972
1938	Barrow	4	Halifax	2	Huddersfield	31,384	£2,431
	Salford	6	Swinton	0	Belle Vue, Manchester	31,664	£2,396
1939	Halifax	10	Leeds	4	Bradford	64,453	£3,645
	Salford	11	Wigan	2	Rochdale	40,000	£2,154
●	*During the war the semi-finals were two-legged and the finals were not played at Wembley*						
1946	Wakefield T.	7	Hunslet	3	Leeds	33,000	£4,991
	Wigan	12	Widnes	5	Swinton	36,976	£4,746
1947	Bradford N.	11	Warrington	7	Swinton	33,474	£4,946
	Leeds	21	Wakefield T.	0	Huddersfield	35,136	£6,339
1948	Bradford N.	14	Hunslet	7	Leeds	38,125	£7,437
	Wigan	11	Rochdale H.	0	Swinton	26,004	£4,206
1949	Bradford N.	10	Barrow	0	Swinton	26,572	£4,646
	Halifax	11	Huddersfield	10	Bradford	61,875	£8,638
1950	Warrington	16	Leeds	4	Bradford	69,898	£9,861
	Widnes	8	Bradford N.	0	Wigan	25,390	£3,936
1951	Barrow	14	Leeds	14	Bradford	57,459	£8,248
Replay	Barrow	28	Leeds	13	Huddersfield	31,078	£5,098
	Wigan	3	Warrington	2	Swinton	44,621	£7,358
1952	Featherstone R.	6	Leigh	2	Leeds	35,621	£6,494
	Workington T.	5	Barrow	2	Wigan	31,206	£4,782
1953	Huddersfield	7	Wigan	0	Bradford	58,722	£10,519
	St. Helens	9	Warrington	3	Swinton	38,059	£7,768
1954	Halifax	18	Hunslet	3	Bradford	46,961	£8,243
	Warrington	8	Leeds	4	Swinton	36,993	£7,596
1955	Barrow	9	Hunslet	6	Wigan	25,493	£4,671
	Workington T.	13	Featherstone R.	2	Leeds	33,499	£7,305
1956	Halifax	11	Wigan	10	Bradford	51,889	£9,054
	St. Helens	5	Barrow	5	Swinton	38,897	£7,793
Replay	St. Helens	10	Barrow	5	Wigan	44,731	£7,750
1957	Barrow	2	Leigh	2	Wigan	34,628	£6,340
Replay	Barrow	15	Leigh	10	Swinton	28,081	£5,695
	Leeds	10	Whitehaven	9	Bradford	49,094	£8,987
1958	Wigan	5	Rochdale H.	3	Swinton	28,597	£6,354
	Workington T.	8	Featherstone R.	2	Bradford	31,517	£6,325
1959	Wigan	5	Leigh	0	Swinton	27,906	£6,068
	Hull	15	Featherstone R.	5	Bradford	52,131	£9,776
1960	Wakefield T.	11	Featherstone R.	2	Bradford	55,935	£10,390
	Hull	12	Oldham	9	Swinton	27,545	£6,093
1961	St. Helens	26	Hull	9	Bradford	42,935	£9,231
	Wigan	19	Halifax	10	Swinton	35,118	£7,557
1962	Wakefield T.	9	Featherstone R.	0	Bradford	43,625	£8,496
	Huddersfield	6	Hull K.R.	0	Bradford	31,423	£6,685

139

Year	Winners		Runners-up		Venue	Attendance	Receipts
1963	Wakefield T.	5	Warrington	2	Swinton	15,565	£3,530
	Wigan	18	Hull K.R.	4	Leeds	21,420	£6,029
1964	Widnes	7	Castleford	7	Swinton	25,603	£5,541
Replay	Widnes	7	Castleford	5	Wakefield	28,739	£5,313
	Hull K.R.	5	Oldham	5	Leeds	28,823	£7,411
Replay	Hull K.R.	14	Oldham	17	Swinton	27,209	£5,929

● *Score after 80 minutes was 14-14, then bad light caused match to be abandoned after 12 minutes of extra time with Oldham winning 17-14*

Year	Winners		Runners-up		Venue	Attendance	Receipts
Second Replay	Hull K.R.	12	Oldham	2	Huddersfield	28,732	£6,183
1965	Wigan	25	Swinton	10	St. Helens	26,658	£6,384
	Hunslet	8	Wakefield T.	0	Leeds	21,262	£6,090
1966	St. Helens	12	Dewsbury	5	Swinton	13,046	£3,102
	Wigan	7	Leeds	2	Huddersfield	22,758	£5,971
1967	Featherstone R.	16	Leeds	8	Huddersfield	20,052	£6,276
	Barrow	14	Dewsbury	9	Swinton	13,744	£4,560
1968	Leeds	25	Wigan	4	Swinton	30,058	£9,845
	Wakefield T.	0	Huddersfield	0	Bradford	21,569	£6,196
Replay	Wakefield T.	15	Huddersfield	10	Leeds	20,983	£6,425
1969	Castleford	16	Wakefield T.	10	Leeds	21,497	£8,477
	Salford	15	Warrington	8	Wigan	20,600	£7,738
1970	Castleford	6	St. Helens	3	Swinton	18,913	£7,171
	Wigan	19	Hull K.R.	8	Leeds	18,495	£7,862
1971	Leeds	19	Castleford	8	Bradford	24,464	£9,120
	Leigh	10	Huddersfield	4	Wigan	14,875	£5,670
1972	St. Helens	10	Warrington	10	Wigan	19,300	£8,250
Replay	St. Helens	10	Warrington	6	Wigan	32,380	£12,604
	Leeds	16	Halifax	3	Bradford	16,680	£6,851
1973	Featherstone R.	17	Castleford	3	Leeds	15,369	£9,454
	Bradford N.	23	Dewsbury	7	Leeds	14,028	£9,221
1974	Warrington	17	Dewsbury	7	Wigan	11,789	£6,821
	Featherstone R.	21	Leigh	14	Leeds	7,971	£4,461
1975	Widnes	13	Wakefield T.	7	Bradford	9,155	£5,856
	Warrington	11	Leeds	4	Wigan	13,168	£9,581
1976	Widnes	15	Featherstone R.	9	Swinton	13,019	£9,078
	St. Helens	5	Keighley	4	Huddersfield	9,829	£6,113
1977	Leeds	7	St. Helens	2	Wigan	12,974	£11,379
	Widnes	14	Hull K.R.	5	Leeds	17,053	£16,068
1978	Leeds	14	Featherstone R.	9	Bradford	12,824	£11,322
	St. Helens	12	Warrington	8	Wigan	16,167	£13,960
1979	Widnes	14	Bradford N.	11	Swinton	14,324	£16,363
	Wakefield T.	9	St. Helens	7	Leeds	12,393	£14,195
1980	Hull K.R.	20	Halifax	7	Leeds	17,910	£31,650
	Hull	10	Widnes	5	Swinton	18,347	£29,415
1981	Widnes	17	Warrington	9	Wigan	12,624	£20,673
	Hull K.R.	22	St. Helens	5	Leeds	17,073	£30,616
1982	Hull	15	Castleford	11	Leeds	21,207	£41,867
	Widnes	11	Leeds	8	Swinton	13,075	£25,796
1983	Featherstone R.	11	Bradford N.	6	Leeds	10,784	£22,579
	Hull	14	Castleford	7	Elland Rd., L'ds	26,031	£65,498

Year	Winners		Runners-up		Venue	Attendance	Receipts
1984	Wigan	14	York	8	Elland Rd., L'ds	17,156	£52,888
	Widnes	15	Leeds	4	Swinton	14,046	£37,183
1985	Wigan	18	Hull K.R.	11	Elland Rd., L'ds	19,275	£70,192
	Hull	10	Castleford	10	Leeds	20,982	£64,163
Replay	Hull	22	Castleford	16	Leeds	20,968	£65,005
1986	Castleford	18	Oldham	7	Wigan	12,430	£38,296
	Hull K.R.	24	Leeds	24	Elland Rd., L'ds	23,866	£83,757
Replay	Hull K.R.	17	Leeds	0	Elland Rd., L'ds	32,485	£113,345
1987	St. Helens	14	Leigh	8	Wigan	13,105	£48,627
	Halifax	12	Widnes	8	Leeds	16,064	£61,260
1988	Wigan	34	Salford	4	Bolton W. FC	20,783	£95,876
	Halifax	0	Hull	0	Leeds	20,534	£82,026
Replay	Halifax	4	Hull	3	Elland Rd., L'ds	25,117	£113,679
1989	St. Helens	16	Widnes	14	Wigan	17,119	£70,411
	Wigan	13	Warrington	6	Man. C. FC	26,529	£144,056

NON-LEAGUE CLUBS IN THE CHALLENGE CUP

AMATEUR clubs were invited to compete in the 1986 Rugby League Challenge Cup after a five-year break. The League asked for two of the three county cup competition winners to enter the preliminary round. Cumbria Cup winners Kells were given a bye into the draw for the preliminary round, while Yorkshire victors Dudley Hill met Lancashire winners Simms Cross at Bramley in an eliminator, the White Rose side going through.

The League later decided that from 1987 the Silk Cut Challenge Cup campaign would feature 38 teams, four amateur clubs joining the professionals for a preliminary round of six ties.

In the early years of the Northern Union Challenge Cup — as it was then called — the line between professional and amateur was less clearly defined.

A variety of Leagues also make it difficult to set non-League clubs apart. Fifty-six clubs appeared in the inaugurating first round of 1897 and four others received byes. The complications continued until 1904 when the League format settled down and non-League clubs had to qualify for the first round.

Between 1904 and 1907 there was a preliminary round of up to 14 ties involving mostly non-league clubs. In 1906-07 SAVILLE GREEN beat Bramley 10-0, and NEWINGTON ROVERS drew 3-3 and 13-13 with York before losing 14-5.

Not since 1909 when BEVERLEY beat Ebbw Vale 7-2 has a senior team been knocked out by a non-League club although amateur teams twice had victories in the two-leg era of 1946-54.

RECORDS OF NON-LEAGUE CLUBS IN THE RUGBY LEAGUE CHALLENGE CUP SINCE 1904

(Excluding preliminary rounds before 1908)
Non-League Clubs in Capitals

Victories over Senior Clubs

1905-06
*FEATHERSTONE ROVERS 23 v. Widnes 2
(second round)

1907-08
WHITEHAVEN RECREATION 13 v. St. Helens 8
(Lost 33-5 at Merthyr Tydfil in second round)

1908-09
BEVERLEY 7 v. Ebbw Vale 2
(Lost 53-2 at Halifax in second round)

1945-46
SHARLSTON 12 v. Workington Town 7
(1st leg) (Workington Town won 2nd leg 16-2)

1947-48
RISEHOW and GILLHEAD 10 v. Keighley 2 (2nd leg)
(Keighley won 1st leg 11-0)

*FEATHERSTONE ROVERS are the only non-League club to appear in the third round when they lost 3-0 at Keighley. In the first round they beat BROOKLAND ROVERS 16-5.

There have been several other instances of non-League clubs meeting in the first round. The last occasion was in 1960 when WALNEY CENTRAL beat LOCK LANE 10-5 before losing at Oldham 55-4 in the second round.

In 1964 THAMES BOARD MILLS received a bye when Bradford Northern disbanded, but lost 48-8 at Blackpool Borough in the second round.

CHALLENGE CUP PROGRESS CHART

A 20-year review ....

Key: W — Winners. F — Beaten finalists. SF — Semi-final. P — Preliminary round.

	1988-89	1987-88	1986-87	1985-86	1984-85	1983-84	1982-83	1981-82	1980-81	1979-80	1978-79	1977-78	1976-77	1975-76	1974-75	1973-74	1972-73	1971-72	1970-71	1969-70
BARROW	2	1	2	2	P	1	2	2	1	2	3	1	2	1	1	1	1	2	1	2
BATLEY	1	1	1	1	1	1	1	2	1	1	1	1	1	1	1	1	1	1	1	1
BRADFORD N.	2	1	2	3	3	3	SF	3	1	3	SF	3	3	2	3	3	F	2	1	1
BRAMLEY	P	P	1	2	3	1	1	1	1	1	2	1	1	1	2	1	3	3	2	
CARLISLE	2	1	2	1	1	P	1	1												
CASTLEFORD	2	1	1	W	SF	3	SF	SF	2	2	3	3	3	1	1	1	SF	2	SF	W
CHORLEY B.	2	2	1	2	1	1	1	1	1	1	1	1	1	1	1	1	1	1	1	1
DEWSBURY	1	1	1	1	1	1	1	1	2	1	2	1	3	1	SF	SF	1	2	1	
DONCASTER	1	3	1	2	P	2	1	1	1	1	1	1	2	1	1	1	1	1	3	
FEATHERSTONE R.	3	2	1	1	P	1	W	P	3	1	1	SF	2	SF	1	F	W	2	2	1
FULHAM	1	1	1	1	1	2	2	2	1											
HALIFAX	1	F	W	1	2	1	2	3	2	SF	1	1	1	1	1	1	1	SF	1	1
HUDDERSFIELD	1	P	1	1	1	1	1	1	2	3	3	1	1	1	1	1	2	SF	2	
HULL	1	SF	3	1	F	2	F	W	2	F	3	2	2	1	2	1	2	2	3	1
HULL K.R.	3	3	3	F	SF	3	1	2	F	W	2	1	SF	2	3	2	2	1	1	SF
HUNSLET	P	1	2	1	3	2	3	1	1	1	1	2	1	2	3	1	2	1	2	1
KEIGHLEY	2	2	2	1	1	1	1	1	2	1	2	1	1	SF	1	1	1	1	2	1
LEEDS	3	2	3	SF	1	SF	2	SF	1	2	1	W	W	3	SF	3	1	F	F	3
LEIGH	1	1	SF	3	2	1	1	3	2	1	2	1	1	3	2	SF	2	2	W	3
MANSFIELD M.	1	2	2	P	1															
OLDHAM	3	1	2	SF	1	2	1	2	3	2	2	2	1	3	3	1	3	1	1	2
ROCHDALE H.	1	2	1	2	2	1	1	2	1	2	2	1	2	1	2	2	2	1	1	2
RUNCORN H.	1	1	1	1	2	1	2	1	1	1	1	1	1	1	2	1	1	1	2	
ST. HELENS	F	3	F	2	1	3	3	1	SF	2	SF	F	SF	W	2	3	2	W	2	SF
SALFORD	1	SF	1	1	2	1	2	1	3	3	1	2	2	2	2	1	1	3	3	
SHEFFIELD E.	2	2	1	1	1															
SWINTON	1	1	P	P	1	P	2	1	1	1	1	2	2	1	2	1	3	3	2	
WAKEFIELD T.	2	1	2	1	2	2	2	3	3	3	F	2	2	1	SF	1	3	3	1	1
WARRINGTON	SF	2	1	2	2	2	3	1	SF	3	1	SF	1	3	F	W	3	SF	2	2
WHITEHAVEN	1	P	3	1	1	1	1	1	1	1	1	1	1	1	1	1	1	1	1	1
WIDNES	SF	3	SF	3	3	W	1	F	W	SF	W	3	F	F	W	2	2	1	2	1
WIGAN	W	W	1	3	W	F	1	2	1	1	2	2	2	2	3	3	2	2	F	
WORKINGTON T.	P	1	P	1	2	2	3	2	2	1	1	2	3	2	2	2	1	1	1	
YORK	1	1	P	2	1	SF	1	1	2	2	1	1	1	2	2	1	1	3	1	1

JOHN PLAYER SPECIAL TROPHY

1988-89 Final

Newly-recruited record Rugby Union signing Jonathan Davies sat in the stand to witness a world-class performance from Wigan skipper Ellery Hanley which inspired the Central Park outfit to a record fourth John Player Special Trophy haul.

Hanley walked off with the trophy and the Man of the Match award to emphasise to Davies the standard of individual performance demanded in the modern 13-a-side game.

The Widnes capture of the Welsh RU captain dominated the build up to the final, staged at Bolton's Burnden Park for the second time. But after the kick-off it was Wigan who grabbed the spotlight and the £18,000 winners' cheque. Determined not be to overshadowed, Wigan overcame the late withdrawals of hooker Nicky Kiss and prop Ian Lucas through injury to beat the favourites more emphatically than the 12-6 scoreline suggested. The victory, added to successes in 1983, 1986 and 1987, was a testament to Wigan's strength in depth, professionalism and superb organisation.

It was also a personal triumph for Great Britain skipper Hanley, a one-man inspiration with his non-stop contribution on attack and defence, sealing the hard-earned victory with a try 11 minutes from the final whistle.

Widnes, extending their record appearances in the final to seven and seeking a record-equalling third success, were never allowed to move into gear. Winger Martin Offiah entered the tie needing a try to establish a competition record of touching down in every round, but Wigan's excellent cover defence coupled with the Chemics' poor handling, denied him a decent chance.

While the Widnes fans were still celebrating the pre-match parade of new signing Davies, Wigan began in style, Shaun Edwards opening the defence for Ged Byrne to send Kiwi centre Kevin Iro powering through for a sixth minute try. Wigan's line was breached only once during a performance of industry and discipline, prop Adrian Shelford blotting an otherwise impeccable display by sending out a careless pass for Widnes centre Darren Wright to intercept and race 40 yards for a 13th minute try to which Andy Currier added the goal.

Joe Lydon struck a 21st minute penalty goal after a foul by Emosi Koloto to level the scores at 6-6, the stalemate continuing up to the interval.

Wigan adapted better to the greasy pitch, dulling the attacking forces of Widnes half back David Hulme and Tony Myler, while the Chemics did not help their own cause by spilling so much ball with double their opponents' error rate.

Two minutes after the break, a second piece of indiscipline by Koloto was again punished by a Lydon penalty success, the Tongan from New Zealand Rugby Union looking very raw in his first major final.

Hanley clinched the match in the 69th minute by taking an Andy Gregory pass to lunge over near the corner, his vital try taking the final score to 12-6.

In a final packed with personal aims, Hanley showed Davies that he was not willing to relinquish his crown as the top player; Wigan's full back Steve Hampson outshone Great Britain rival Alan Tait; while Wigan half back Andy Gregory went on as substitute after a week-long transfer dispute to confirm his world-class rating.

The rain-affected encounter attracted a crowd of 20,709 — the third 20,000 plus gate in five years — who paid a competition record £94,874.

JOHN PLAYER SPECIAL TROPHY FINAL

7 January   **Bolton Wanderers FC**

WIGAN 12   **WIDNES 6**

Steve Hampson	1.	Alan Tait
Dean Bell	2.	Rick Thackray
Kevin Iro	3.	Andy Currier
Joe Lydon	4.	Darren Wright
Tony Iro	5.	Martin Offiah
Ged Byrne	6.	Tony Myler
Shaun Edwards	7.	David Hulme
Adrian Shelford	8.	Kurt Sorensen, Capt.
Martin Dermott	9.	Phil McKenzie
Shaun Wane	10.	Joe Grima
Dennis Betts	11.	Mike O'Neill
Ian Potter	12.	Emosi Koloto
Ellery Hanley, Capt.	13.	Richard Eyres
Andy Gregory	14.	Barry Dowd
Andy Goodway	15.	Paul Hulme

T: K. Iro, Hanley   T: Wright
G: Lydon (2)   G: Currier
Substitutions: Substitution:
Goodway for Shelford (20min.)   P. Hulme for Koloto (44 min.)
Gregory for Lydon (51 min.)   Half-time: 6-6
Referee: John Holdsworth (Kippax)   Attendance: 20,709

A champagne shampoo for triumphant skipper Ellery Hanley as Wigan celebrate their record fourth John Player Special Trophy haul.

1988-89 Round by Round

Bramley were the high scorers of the four-tie preliminary round, running in three tries in the opening 10 minutes on the way to a 56-10 success over visitors Fulham, failing by six points to equal the club record established a week earlier. Featherstone Rovers enjoyed a runaway nine-try home victory over Hunslet, Graham Steadman, Chris Bibb and Paul Newlove each collecting two tries in a 46-2 success, Hunslet's sole reply being a Gary Rowse penalty goal. League leaders Castleford travelled to Second Division outpost Workington Town to record a 28-2 triumph with Grant Anderson gaining two touchdowns and Town's packman Paul Vannet collecting the Man of the Match award. The two amateur entrants, Wigan St. Patricks and Elland, of Halifax, met at Wigan's Central Park, with the local side earning a 36-2 success featuring six tries.

The first round was marked by a strike-hit Runcorn Highfield conceding home advantage to mighty Wigan, the weakened outfit going down to a competition record defeat of 92-2, out-of-retirement coach Bill Ashurst being sent off 12 minutes after coming on as a substitute. Wigan ran in 18 tries, with Kevin Iro tallying 34 points from four tries and nine goals. Welsh Rugby Union convert David Bishop was chosen as Man of the Match in the Hull K.R.-Keighley tie despite being substituted at half-time, scoring the first try after only three minutes and setting up three of the next four touchdowns in the Robins' 40-0 victory. Across the city, Hull registered a 26-10 success over Batley after visiting second row man Paul Gearey had scored two tries to threaten the Airlie Birds, who showed superior fitness to run in four tries in the last quarter. Veteran back row man Steve Norton came out of retirement to inspire Wakefield Trinity to a 34-14 victory over Carlisle in a contest marred by the

sending off of Trinity's Andy Mason and the visiting Mark Doyle, two other players being sin-binned.

Doncaster winger Neil Turner shone on attack and defence to steer Doncaster to a 16-13 success at Swinton. His powerful try-saving tackle on Swinton paceman Derek Bate was a first half highlight before grabbing a solo 50-yard touchdown 24 minutes after the break. Great Britain winger Martin Offiah registered a hat-trick against Featherstone Rovers for the second time in the season as Widnes secured a 37-12 home victory, his first two tries coming almost inside a minute of each other and the third only 30 seconds before the final whistle. A sparkling display by David Ruane laid the foundations for Leigh's 42-14 home victory over Barrow, his hat-trick of tries being upstaged only by his creation of a superb long range try for winger Neil McCulloch. Halifax ended a run of five successive defeats by beating visitors Salford 22-4, hooker Seamus McCallion setting up the first three tries with Salford's only score being a try from former Welsh RU star Adrian Hadley.

Warrington's 21-14 home victory over Oldham was followed by the resignation of coach Tony Barrow. A superb try by Australian Phil Blake sealed victory, to add to six goals and a try from John Woods and a Robert Turner drop goal. Second Division hosts York held trophy holders St. Helens to a four-point lead with only five minutes left before the Saints clinched a 14-6 win with a Paul Loughlin try. Without finding the fluid form of recent weeks, Bramley gained a 32-6 home win over Mansfield Marksman, having built a 24-0 lead featuring two exhilarating Peter Lewis tries. After conceding 141 points in their last three league matches, visitors Dewsbury proved to be obstinate opponents for Bradford Northern with Chris Vasey and Gary Cocks outstanding, while Northern's Karl Fairbank recorded a hat-trick of tries in the 34-18 victory.

The dismissal of second row man Dave Nelson after only 24 minutes left Huddersfield with too great a task against Chorley Borough at Fartown, their biggest crowd of the season to date witnessing a 22-4 reversal. Unbeaten league leaders Castleford hit back from a 12-6 half-time deficit to register a 21-12 success in the televised tie at Leeds, Australian full back Gary Belcher earning the Man of the Match award and scrum half Bob Beardmore being involved in a controversial trip on Leeds centre Garry Schofield. Sheffield Eagles ran up a club record score of 80-8 over amateurs Wigan St. Patricks with 15 tries and 10 goals after the visitors opened the scoring with a penalty goal inside two minutes. The Eagles collected nine tries in the last 25 minutes before the interval. Rochdale Hornets served up their best display of the season to score five tries to Whitehaven's three in the 26-20 home success.

Bradford Northern provided the shock of the second round by winning at top-of-table Castleford 19-18. Skipper Paul Harkin and veteran Keith Mumby were outstanding for Northern who endured a late comeback by Castleford, a Giles Boothroyd try and Martin Ketteridge goal two minutes from the end leaving only a one-point margin. But Ketteridge's last ditch drop goal was hopelessly off target. Sheffield Eagles attracted a record crowd of 2,716 for the visit of Widnes, who ran in five tries plus six goals from Andy Currier in a 32-9 success. Australian Test back row forward Gavin Miller took the Man of the Match award in the scrum half role as Hull K.R. won 36-22 at Chorley Borough, Rovers' import Chris Close claiming a hat-trick of tries. Doncaster's bid to reach the last eight for the first time failed at Leigh who ran in 40 points or more for the fourth successive match, scoring four tries to lead 18-0 at half-time. Barry Ledger completed a hat-trick of touchdowns after the break, as Leigh eased to a 40-8 win.

With Welshman Gary Pearce in superb kicking form, Hull led 10-8 at the interval at St. Helens before Australian Test star Michael O'Connor raced in for a try to seal a hard-earned 16-13 victory for the Saints. Rochdale Hornets crashed 38-12 at Wakefield Trinity after trailing only 10-4 at half-time. Bramley showed outstanding commitment to restrict Warrington to a 14-6 lead at the break before the home side's superior pace took them to a 42-10 win, Woods claiming 18 points with a try and seven goals. In the televised tie, Halifax players were each rewarded with a £250 bonus after going down 20-16 at Wigan. Halifax were leading 14-2 after 24 minutes before the Riversiders pulled level at 16-apiece, winger Mark Preston snatching victory with a 70-yard solo effort five minutes before the final whistle.

The television cameras travelled to Widnes for the third round tie where Warrington gained a 6-0 half-time lead with packmen Steve Roach, Les Davidson and Mark Roberts outstanding. The Chemics staged a second half comeback with Offiah registering two touchdowns in a hard fought 16-7 victory. Lowly Wakefield Trinity took a shock 18-2 lead after 22 minutes in the tie at St. Helens with tries from Andy Mason (2) and Nigel Bell, before Australian Test forward Paul Vautin gave a Man of the Match performance to inspire the Saints to a 34-18 success. Leigh's prolific scoring machine was halted at a rainswept Odsal Stadium, where Bradford Northern claimed a 6-0 victory. Entering the tie with a scoring average of 33 points per match, Leigh conceded a try and goal to Great Britain packman David Hobbs. A last ditch drop goal attempt from scrum half Bishop went narrowly wide to deny Hull K.R. the shock result of the round, having to settle for a 16-16 home draw with Wigan, for whom New Zealand Kevin Iro scored two tries and two goals. In the replay three days later Wigan romped home 30-0 in a one-sided contest against a Rovers side severely weakened by injuries. Inspired by Andy Gregory, Wigan led 18-0 after half an hour, the Robins battling valiantly throughout.

The semi-finals were highlighted by a superb contest at Wigan between Widnes and holders St. Helens, the Chemics coming back to win 20-18. The Saints were 18-10 in front with 11 minutes left when Currier touched down before full back Alan Tait put Richard Eyres in for a try to which Currier coolly added the goals to extend Widnes' record final appearance tally to seven.

Bradford Northern were not disgraced in going down 16-5 against Wigan at Headingley in the other semi-final. But lack of pace meant all their hard work failed to produce a try, while Wigan ran in three. Barry Seabourne's post-match criticism of the referee, Dave Carter of Widnes, led to Northern's coach being eventually severely reprimanded by the Rugby League.

1988-89 PRIZES

Round		Per Team		Total
Preliminary	8 ×	£1,250		£10,000
First	16 ×	£1,250		£20,000
Second	8 ×	£1,850		£14,800
Third	4 ×	£3,175		£12,700
Semi-Finals	2 ×	£5,250		£10,500
Runners-up	1 ×	£10,000		£10,000
Winners	1 ×	£18,000		£18,000

Total Prize Money		£96,000
Capital Development Fund		£74,000
Grand Total		£170,000

RESULTS 1988-89

Preliminary Round

Bramley	56	Fulham	10
Featherstone R.	46	Hunslet	2
St. Patricks (Wigan)	36	Elland (Halifax)	2
Workington T.	2	Castleford	28

First Round

Bradford N.	34	Dewsbury	18
Bramley	32	Mansfield M.	6
Halifax	22	Salford	4
Huddersfield	4	Chorley B.	22
Hull	26	Batley	10
Hull K.R.	40	Keighley	0
Leeds	12	Castleford	21
Leigh	42	Barrow	14
Rochdale H.	26	Whitehaven	20
Sheffield E.	80	St. Patricks (Wigan)	8
Swinton	13	Doncaster	16
Wakefield T.	34	Carlisle	14
Warrington	21	Oldham	14
Widnes	37	Featherstone R.	12
*Wigan	92	Runcorn H.	2
York	6	St. Helens	14

* Runcorn H. forfeited home advantage

Second Round

Castleford	18	Bradford N.	19
Chorley B.	22	Hull K.R.	36
Leigh	40	Doncaster	8
St. Helens	16	Hull	13
Sheffield E.	9	Widnes	32
Wakefield T.	38	Rochdale H.	12
Warrington	42	Bramley	10
Wigan	20	Halifax	16

Third Round

Bradford N.	6	Leigh	0
Hull K.R.	16	Wigan	16
St. Helens	34	Wakefield T.	18
Widnes	16	Warrington	7

Replay

Wigan	30	Hull K.R.	0

Semi-Finals

Widnes (at Wigan)	20	St. Helens	18
Wigan (at Leeds)	16	Bradford N.	5

Final

Wigan (at Bolton W. FC)	12	Widnes	6

JOHN PLAYER SPECIAL TROPHY ROLL OF HONOUR

Season	Winners		Runners-up		Venue	Attendance	Receipts
1971-72	Halifax	22	Wakefield T.	11	Bradford	7,975	£2,545
1972-73	Leeds	12	Salford	7	Huddersfield	10,102	£4,563
1973-74	Warrington	27	Rochdale H.	16	Wigan	9,347	£4,380
1974-75	Bradford N.	3	Widnes	2	Warrington	5,935	£3,305
1975-76	Widnes	19	Hull	13	Leeds	9,035	£6,275
1976-77	Castleford	25	Blackpool B.	15	Salford	4,512	£2,919
1977-78	Warrington	9	Widnes	4	St. Helens	10,258	£8,429
1978-79	Widnes	16	Warrington	4	St. Helens	10,743	£11,709
1979-80	Bradford N.	6	Widnes	0	Leeds	9,909	£11,560
1980-81	Warrington	12	Barrow	5	Wigan	12,820	£21,020
1981-82	Hull	12	Hull K.R.	4	Leeds	25,245	£42,987
1982-83	Wigan	15	Leeds	4	Elland Rd, Leeds	19,553	£49,027
1983-84	Leeds	18	Widnes	10	Wigan	9,510	£19,824
1984-85	Hull K.R.	12	Hull	0	Hull City FC	25,326	£69,555
1985-86	Wigan	11	Hull K.R.	8	Elland Rd, Leeds	17,573	£66,714
1986-87	Wigan	18	Warrington	4	Bolton W. FC	21,144	£86,041
1987-88	St. Helens	15	Leeds	14	Wigan	16,669	£62,232
1988-89	Wigan	12	Widnes	6	Bolton W.FC	20,709	£94,874

JOHN PLAYER SPECIAL FINAL ....
A REVIEW
1971-72
Halifax 22 Hepworth; Rayner, Davies (1t), Willicombe (1t), Kelly (1t); Burton (5g), Baker (Sanderson); Dewhirst, Hawksley, Callon (1t), (Reeves), Fogerty, J. Martin, Halmshaw
Wakefield T. 11 Wraith (Ward); Slater (1t), Marston, Hegarty, Major; Topliss (1t), Harkin; Jeanes, Morgan, Lyons, Harrison (Spencer), Valentine (1t), N. Fox (1g)
Referee: S. Shepherd (Oldham)
1972-73
Leeds 12 Holmes (1g); Alan Smith, Hynes, Dyl, Atkinson (2t); Hardisty, Hepworth; Clawson (2g) (Ward), Fisher (Pickup), Jeanes, Haigh, Cookson, Eccles
Salford 7 Charlton; Colloby, Watkins (2g), Hesketh, Richards; Gill (P. Ward), Banner; Ramshaw, J. Ward, Mackay, Grice (Davies), Kirkbride, Dixon (1t)
Referee: W.H. Thompson (Huddersfield)
1973-74
Warrington 27 Whitehead (6g, 1t); M. Philbin, Noonan (2t), Reynolds (Pickup), Bevan (1t); Whittle, Gordon; D. Chisnall, (Nicholas 1t), Ashcroft, Brady, Wright, Wanbon, B. Philbin

Rochdale H. 16 Crellin; Brelsford (2t), Brophy (1t), Taylor (1t), Aspinall; Butler (Wood), Gartland; Holliday (2g), Harris, Whitehead, Fogerty, Sheffield, Halmshaw
Referee: D.G. Kershaw (York)
1974-75
Bradford N. 3 Carlton (1t); Francis, Ward, Gant, D. Redfearn; Blacker, Seabourne; Earl, Jarvis, Jackson, Joyce, Trotter, Fearnley
Widnes 2 Dutton (1g); A. Prescott, D.O'Neill, Aspey, Anderson; Hughes, Bowden; Mills, Elwell, Sheridan, Adams, Blackwood, Laughton
Referee: G.F. Lindop (Wakefield)
1975-76
Widnes 19 Dutton (3g); A. Prescott, George, Aspey, Jenkins (2t); Hughes, Bowden (1t, 1dg); Mills, Elwell, Wood, Foran, Sheridan, Adams (1t)
Hull 13 Stephenson; A. Macklin, Clark, Portz, Hunter (1t); Hancock, Foulkes (Davidson); Ramsey, Flanagan, Wardell, Boxall (2g), Walker, Crane (2t)
Referee: J.V. Moss (Manchester)
1976-77
Castleford 25 Wraith (1t); Fenton, Joyner (1t), P. Johnson (1t), Briggs; Burton (1t), Stephens (1t); Khan, Spurr, A. Dickinson, Reilly, Lloyd (5g), S. Norton

Blackpool B 15 Reynolds; Robinson, Heritage, Machen (1t), Pitman (Lamb); Marsh, Newall; Hamilton, Allen (1t), Egan (3g, 1t), Gamble, Groves (Hurst), M. Pattinson
Referee: M. J. Naughton (Widnes)
1977-78
Warrington 9 Finnegan; Hesford (3g), Benyon, Wilson, Bevan (1t); K. Kelly, Gordon; Lester, Dalgreen, Nicholas, Martyn, B. Philbin, Potter
Widnes 4 Eckersley; Wright, Aspey, George, Woods (2g); Hughes, Bowden; Ramsey, Elwell, Shaw (Dearden), Adams, Hull, Laughton
Referee: W.H. Thompson (Huddersfield)
1978-79
Widnes 16 Eckersley; Wright (1t), Aspey, Hughes, Burke (3g); Moran, Bowden; Mills, Elwell (2dg), Shaw, Dearden, Hull (1t), Adams (2dg)
Warrington 4 Finnegan; M. Kelly, Hesford (2g), Benyon, Sutton; K. Kelly, (Hunter), Gordon; Lester, Waller, Nicholas, Case, Martyn, A. Gwilliam
Referee: G.F. Lindop (Wakefield)
1979-80
Bradford N. 6 Mumby (1g); Barends, D. Redfearn, D. Parker (1t), Gant; Stephenson (1dg), A. Redfearn; Thompson, Bridges, Forsyth (I. Van Bellen), Grayshon, G. Van Bellen (Ferres), Casey
Widnes 0 Eckersley; Wright, Aspey, George, Burke; Hughes, Bowden; Hogan (Mills), Elwell, Shaw, L. Gorley, Hull, Adams
Referee: W.H. Thompson (Huddersfield)
1980-81
Warrington 12 Hesford (2g, 2dg); Thackray, I. Duane, Bevan (2t), M. Kelly; K. Kelly, A. Gwilliam; Courtney, Waller, Case, Martyn, Potter, Hunter (Eccles)
Barrow 5 Elliott; McConnell, French, Ball (1g), Wainwright; Mason (1t), Cairns; D. Chisnall, Allen (Szymala), Flynn, K. James, Kirkby, Hadley
Referee: W.H. Thompson (Huddersfield)
1981-82
Hull 12 Banks; O'Hara, Harrison, Leuluai, Prendiville; Day, Dean (1dg) (K. Harkin); Skerrett, Wileman (1t), Stone, Crane, L. Crooks (4g), Norton
Hull K.R. 4 Fairbairn (2g); Hubbard, M. Smith, Hogan, Muscroft; Hartley, P. Harkin (Burton); Holdstock (Millington), Watkinson, S. Crooks, Lowe, Casey, Hall
Referee: G.F. Lindop (Wakefield)
1982-83
Wigan 15 Williams; Ramsdale, Stephenson, Whitfield (4g, 1dg), Gill (1t) (Juliff 1t); M. Foy, Fairhurst; Shaw, Kiss, Campbell, West (Case), Scott, Pendlebury

Leeds 4 Hague; Campbell, Wilkinson, Dyl, Andy Smith; Holmes, Dick (2g); Dickinson, Ward, Burke, Sykes, W. Heron, D. Heron
Referee: R. Campbell (Widnes)
1983-84
Leeds 18 Wilkinson; Prendiville, Creasser (5g), D. Bell, Andy Smith; Holmes (1t), Dick (1t); Keith Rayne, Ward (Squire), Kevin Rayne, Moorby, Laurie, Webb
Widnes 10 Burke (1g); Wright, Keiron O'Loughlin, Lydon (1t), Linton (1t); Hughes, Gregory; S. O'Neill, Elwell, K. Tamati, L. Gorley, Whitfield, Adams
Referee: W.H. Thompson (Huddersfield)
1984-85
Hull K.R. 12 Fairbairn; Clark (1t), Robinson, Prohm (1t), Laws; M. Smith, Harkin; Broadhurst, Watkinson, Ema, Burton, Hogan (1t), Miller
Hull 0 Kemble (Schofield); S. Evans, Ah Kuoi, Leuluai, O'Hara; Topliss, Sterling; Edmonds (Dannatt), Patrick, Rose, L. Crooks, Proctor, Divorty
Referee: S. Wall (Leigh)
1985-86
Wigan 11 Hampson; Mordt, Stephenson (1g), Hanley, Gill (Edwards); Ella, M. Ford (1t); Dowling (1dg), Kiss, Wane (1t), West, Goodway, Potter (Du Toit)
Hull K.R. 8 Lydiat (1t); Clark, M. Smith, Dorahy, Laws (1t); G. Smith, Harkin; P. Johnston (Robinson), Watkinson, Ema, Burton, Kelly, Miller
Referee: J. Holdsworth (Kippax)
1986-87
Wigan 18 Hampson; Stephenson, Lydon, Bell (1t), Gill (2t, 1g); Hanley, Edwards; West, Dermott, Case, Roberts, Potter, Goodway (1t)
Warrington 4 Johnson; Meadows, Cullen, Ropati, Forster (1t); K. Kelly, Peters (Duane); Boyd, K. Tamati (Rathbone), Jackson, Sanderson, Roberts, M. Gregory
Referee: J. Holdsworth (Kippax)
1987-88
St. Helens 15 Veivers; Tanner, Loughlin (2t, 3g), Elia, Quirk; Cooper, Holding (1dg); Burke, Groves, Souto (Evans), Forber, Haggerty, Platt
Leeds 14 Gurr; Morris, Schofield, Jackson (1t), Basnett (Gibson); Creasser (1t, 3g), Ashton; Tunks, Maskill, Kevin Rayne (Fairbank), Powell, Medley, D. Heron
Referee: G.F. Lindop (Wakefield)

JOHN PLAYER SPECIAL MAN OF THE MATCH

Season	Winner	Team	Position
1971-72	Bruce Burton	Halifax (v. Wakefield T.)	Stand off
1972-73	Keith Hepworth	Leeds (v. Salford)	Scrum half
1973-74	Kevin Ashcroft	Warrington (v. Rochdale H.)	Hooker
1974-75	Barry Seabourne	Bradford N. (v. Widnes)	Scrum half
1975-76	Reg Bowden	Widnes (v. Hull)	Scrum half
1976-77	Gary Stephens	Castleford	Scrum half
	Howard Allen	Blackpool B.	Hooker
1977-78	Steve Hesford	Warrington (v. Widnes)	Winger
1978-79	David Eckersley	Widnes (v. Warrington)	Full back
1979-80	Len Casey	Bradford N. (v. Widnes)	Loose forward
1980-81	Tommy Martyn	Warrington (v. Barrow)	Second row
1981-82	Trevor Skerrett	Hull (v. Hull K.R.)	Prop
1982-83	Martin Foy	Wigan (v. Leeds)	Stand off
1983-84	Mark Laurie	Leeds (v. Widnes)	Second row
1984-85	Paul Harkin	Hull K.R. (v. Hull)	Scrum half
1985-86	Paul Harkin	Hull K.R. (v. Wigan)	Scrum half
1986-87	Andy Goodway	Wigan (v. Warrington)	Loose forward
1987-88	Paul Loughlin	St. Helens (v. Leeds)	Centre
1988-89	Ellery Hanley	Wigan (v. Widnes)	Loose forward

JOHN PLAYER SPECIAL TROPHY RECORDS

ALL ROUNDS

TEAM
Highest score: Wigan 92 v. Runcorn H. 2 (1988-89)
Biggest attendance: 25,326 Hull v. Hull K.R.
(at Hull C. FC)....... Final 1984-85

INDIVIDUAL
Most tries: 6 by Vince Gribbin (Whitehaven) v. Doncaster 1984-85
*Most goals: 17 by Sammy Lloyd (Castleford)
*Most points: 43 (17g,3t) by Sammy Lloyd (Castleford)
*The above records were achieved in the Castleford v. Millom first round tie in 1973-74.

JOHN PLAYER SPECIAL TROPHY FINAL RECORDS

Most final appearances: 7 by Widnes
Most wins: 4 by Wigan
Most tries: No player has scored 3 or more
Most goals: 6 by Derek Whitehead (Warrington) v.
Rochdale H............................ 1973-74
Most points: 15 (6g,1t) by Derek Whitehead (Warrington)
v. Rochdale H........................ 1973-74
Highest score: Warrington 27 v. Rochdale H. 16 1973-74
Widest margin win: Wigan 18 v. Warrington 4 1986-87
Biggest attendance: 25,326 Hull v. Hull K.R.
(at Hull C. FC).............. 1984-85
Biggest receipts: £94,874 Widnes v. Wigan
(at Bolton W. FC).............. 1988-89

●*BEFORE 1977-78 the competition was known as the Player's No. 6 Trophy, then the John Player Trophy. In 1983-84 it became the John Player Special Trophy, renamed the Regal Trophy in 1989-90. It was not until 1979-80 that semi-finals were played at neutral venues.*

NON-LEAGUE CLUBS IN THE
JOHN PLAYER SPECIAL TROPHY

Amateur clubs have entered the John Player tournament in every season apart from a period between 1981 and 1984. Two figured in the first round up to 1979-80 and one the following season. They were then left out from 1981-82 because the number of professional clubs had grown beyond the mathematically suitable 32.

But the amateurs returned in 1984-85 with two clubs joining the professionals in a small preliminary round.

The fate of the amateurs has varied from the record 88-5 hammering Millom received at Castleford to victories by Cawoods and Myson over Halifax and Batley respectively.

The full list of amateur clubs' results — all first round matches except where stated (P) Preliminary (2) Second Round — is:

Season							Attendance
1971-72		Wigan	33	v	Ace Amateurs (Hull)	9	2,678
		Thames Board Mill (Warr.)	7	v	Huddersfield	27	1,175
1972-73		Bramley	26	v	Pilkington Recs. (St. Helens)	5	616
		Dewsbury	22	v	Dewsbury Celtic	4	1,897
1973-74		Whitehaven	26	v	Dewsbury Celtic	3	1,276
		Castleford	88	v	Millom (Cumbria)	5	1,031
1974-75		Whitehaven	32	v	Lock Lane (Castleford)	6	537
		Doncaster	15	v	Kippax White Swan	6	453
1975-76		Salford	57	v	Mayfield (Rochdale)	3	3,449
		Barrow	16	v	Pilkington Recs. (St. Helens)	9	612
1976-77		Halifax	24	v	Ovenden (Halifax)	4	3,680
		Salford	39	v	Ace Amateurs (Hull)	15	3,037
1977-78		N.D.L.B. (Hull)	4	v	New Hunslet	18	3,845
		Halifax	8	v	Cawoods (Hull)	9	1,168
	(2)	Wakefield T.	31	v	Cawoods (Hull)	7	3,380
1978-79		Leigh Miners Welfare	9	v	Halifax	21	1,621
		Milford (Leeds)	5	v	Dewsbury	38	3,129
1979-80		Pilkington Recs. (St. Helens)	9	v	Wigan	18	6,707
		Blackpool B.	6	v	West Hull	3	555
1980-81		Castleford	30	v	Pilkington Recs. (St. Helens)	17	2,823
1984-85	(P)	Myson (Hull)	2	v	Dewsbury	8	1,572
	(P)	Keighley	24	v	Dudley Hill (Bradford)	10	1,570
1985-86	(P)	Keighley	24	v	Jubilee (Featherstone)	6	1,007
	(P)	West Hull	10	v	Castleford	24	2,500
1986-87	(P)	Batley	2	v	Myson (Hull)	8	687
	(P)	Millom (Cumbria)	4	v	Wakefield T.	18	2,000
		Myson (Hull)	11	v	Swinton	18	1,648
1987-88	(P)	Featherstone R.	34	v	Thatto Heath (St. Helens)	16	1,045
	(P)	Heworth (York)	5	v	Swinton	32	1,063
1988-89	(P)	Wigan St. Patricks	36	v	Elland (Halifax)	2	2,510
		Sheffield E.	80	v	Wigan St. Patricks	8	621

151

JOHN PLAYER SPECIAL TROPHY PROGRESS CHART

Key: W — Winners. F — Beaten finalists. SF — Semi-final. P — Preliminary round.

	1988-89	1987-88	1986-87	1985-86	1984-85	1983-84	1982-83	1981-82	1980-81	1979-80	1978-79	1977-78	1976-77	1975-76	1974-75	1973-74	1972-73	1971-72
BARROW	1	1	3	2	1	2	3	3	F	1	1	1	1	2	1	1	1	3
BATLEY	1	2	P	1	1	P	1	1	1	1	1	1	1	2	1	1	2	1
BRADFORD N.	SF	1	3	2	2	1	3	2	1	W	SF	SF	2	1	W	1	3	1
BRAMLEY	2	P	1	1	3	*	1	1	1	1	2	1	1	2	1	2	SF	2
CARLISLE	1	1	2	P	P	2	2	2										
CASTLEFORD	2	2	2	1	2	1	1	2	SF	3	3	2	W	SF	1	2	1	2
CHORLEY B.	2	3	2	1	1	1	2	P	2	2	1	1	F	1	1	1	1	3
DEWSBURY	1	2	1	1	3	1	1	1	1	1	1	2	1	1	1	3	2	1
DONCASTER	2	1	2	2	1	1	1	1	1	1	1	1	1	1	2	1	1	1
FEATHERSTONE R.	1	1	2	P	2	3	1	2	2	2	2	3	2	1	1	1	2	1
FULHAM	P	P	1	1	1	1	1	1	2									
HALIFAX	2	2	2	1	SF	1	1	1	3	1	2	1	2	1	1	2	1	W
HUDDERSFIELD	1	1	P	1	1	2	2	2	2	1	1	3	1	3	1	1	2	2
HULL	2	3	SF	3	F	2	2	W	SF	1	2	1	3	F	1	1	3	3
HULL K.R.	3	2	1	F	W	2	3	F	2	1	SF	1	1	3	SF	1	SF	2
HUNSLET	P	1	1	2	P	1	1	1	2	1	1	2	1	2	1	1	1	1
KEIGHLEY	1	1	1	2	1	2	1	2	1	2	3	2	1	2	3	1	2	2
LEEDS	1	F	1	1	SF	W	F	3	1	2	1	1	3	2	3	3	W	SF
LEIGH	3	2	3	SF	1	SF	2	1	3	3	3	3	SF	2	1	2	2	1
MANSFIELD M.	1	2	1	1	1													
OLDHAM	1	SF	1	2	2	1	1	SF	1	1	1	2	2	2	2	1	1	1
ROCHDALE H.	2	1	1	1	2	1	2	1	1	1	1	1	1	1	1	F	1	2
RUNCORN H.	1	1	1	1	2	2	P	1	1	1	1	1	1	1	2	1	1	1
ST. HELENS	SF	W	3	SF	3	SF	2	1	1	2	2	2	2	3	1	SF	SF	SF
SALFORD	1	3	1	2	1	2	3	3	2	SF	2	2	2	SF	3	2	F	1
SHEFFIELD E.	2	1	2	1	1													
SWINTON	1	1	2	1	1	3	1	SF	1	1	1	1	1	1	3	1	3	1
WAKEFIELD T.	3	2	2	2	P	1	1	1	1	SF	3	SF	1	2	2	3	2	F
WARRINGTON	3	3	F	3	1	2	SF	2	W	3	F	W	1	1	3	W	1	1
WHITEHAVEN	1	1	1	1	2	P	1	1	3	1	1	1	1	1	SF	2	1	2
WIDNES	F	1	SF	3	3	F	SF	3	3	F	W	F	SF	W	F	1	3	1
WIGAN	W	SF	W	W	2	3	W	1	1	2	2	3	2	2	2	2	1	3
WORKINGTON T.	P	1	1	1	1	1	1	2	1	3	2	2	3	3	1	2	1	1
YORK	1	1	P	3	1	1	2	1	2	2	1	1	3	1	2	2	2	2

*Bramley withdrew from the Trophy while in liquidation, opponents Hull K.R. receiving a bye.

PREMIERSHIP TROPHY

1989 Final

Champions Widnes sank Hull with three high speed touchdowns to extend their Premiership Trophy records to five wins in six final appearances.

A record crowd of 40,194 — paying a record £264,242 — saw the Chemics register two long range tries and a typical Martin Offiah effort to stave off the brave challenge of the Airlie Birds, who led 8-6 up to a minute before half-time.

Widnes clinched the trophy and £10,000 prize money with an 18-10 victory in the third — and most successful — Stones Bitter Premiership doubleheader at Manchester United's Old Trafford. The Naughton Park club became the first to retain the Premiership and Championship titles in successive seasons.

The Chemics struck their first long distance blow in the 11th minute when Tongan second row man Emosi Koloto cleared the way for Test centre Darren Wright to romp half the length of the field for a try behind the posts, former Welsh RU skipper Jonathan Davies adding the goal for a 6-0 lead.

But the Boulevarders displayed the fighting spirit which had dragged them out of the relegation zone to a top four spot and pulled level within five minutes. In an unspectacular movement, a couple of forward lunges were followed by loose forward Gary Divorty skipping a tackle before handing on for second row man Paul Welham to drop over the line. Welshman Gary Pearce added the goal and 20 minutes later put Hull ahead with a penalty.

The Yorkshiremen were looking confident of holding that 8-6 lead at the break, despite the loss of scrum half Phil Windley after 20 minutes with a blow to the head, when Widnes grabbed a freak try. A minute before half-time the Airlie Birds were putting Widnes under pressure when centre Richard Price tried a sharp kick through on the last tackle.

The ball jabbed straight into the hands of Andy Currier and the Widnes centre sprinted 95 yards down the right touchline for a stunning try. Hull went in trailing 10-8.

Within a minute of the restart, the Chemics' high speed strike force again devastated the Hull defence. Great Britain winger Offiah ghosted in from the left behind his threequarters as Widnes won the ball from a scrum on Hull's 25-yard line before taking the ball and wafting through for his 100th try for Widnes. Davies tagged on the goal, plus a penalty 14 minutes later, to put the game out of Hull's reach without being able to add to their score, Pearce hitting a penalty goal for Hull on the hour.

Windley returned in the second half without being as effective as in past weeks, while Widnes softened the blow of losing newly crowned First Division Player of the Year David Hulme in the 38th minute by bringing on another Test stand off in Tony Myler, who produced a steady supply of astute passes.

Ex-Scotland RU cap Alan Tait made a series of long, clearing breaks in addition to slipping out the pass that put Offiah away for his try in a brilliant, if not faultless, full back display that made him the clear winner of the Harry Sunderland Trophy as Man of the Match.

Hull, bidding to end a record of three Premiership final defeats, battled to the end with hooker Lee Jackson being denied a try through a forward pass and captain Dane O'Hara also going close to scoring before being bundled over near the corner flag by a fast covering Widnes defence.

Widnes prop Joe Grima was sent to the sin bin in the 21st minute but there were few other fouls in a 12-10 penalty count to Hull, who won the scrums 9-8.

STONES BITTER PREMIERSHIP FINAL

14 May   Old Trafford, Manchester

WIDNES 18		HULL 10
Alan Tait	1.	Paul Fletcher
Jonathan Davies	2.	Paul Eastwood
Andy Currier	3.	Brian Blacker
Darren Wright	4.	Richard Price
Martin Offiah	5.	Dane O'Hara, Capt.
David Hulme	6.	Gary Pearce
Paul Hulme	7.	Phil Windley
Kurt Sorensen, Capt.	8.	Andy Dannatt
Phil McKenzie	9.	Lee Jackson
Joe Grima	10.	Steve Crooks
Mike O'Neill	11.	Paul Welham
Emosi Koloto	12.	Jon Sharp
Richard Eyres	13.	Gary Divorty
Tony Myler	14.	Rob Nolan
Derek Pyke	15.	Tim Wilby

T: Wright, Currier, Offiah   T: Welham
G: Davies (3)   G: Pearce (3)
Substitutions: Substitutions:
Myler for D. Hulme (38 min.)   Nolan for Windley (20 min.)
Pyke for Currier (49 min.)   Wilby for Price (67 min.)
Half-time: 10-8   Attendance: 40,194
Referee: John Holdsworth (Kippax)   Receipts: £264,242

1989 Round by Round

A week before their Wembley meeting, arch rivals Wigan and St. Helens clashed in the Premiership first round at Central Park, the Saints recording a shock 4-2 success. Paul Forber registered his first two goals of the season as the visitors deserved their victory on a saturated pitch, Wigan replying with a penalty goal from Steve Hampson. Champions Widnes blasted Bradford Northern with Martin Offiah's eighth hat-trick of the season, racing to a 20-4 lead before tries from Kelvin Skerrett and Phil Cornforth helped make the final scoreline a more respectable 30-18. Third-placed Leeds suffered a shock defeat at the hands of Featherstone Rovers, substitute forward Glenn Booth scoring a sensational try three minutes from the end to

clinch a deserved 15-12 victory for former Headingley coach Peter Fox. After topping the table for much of the season, Castleford finished on a low note with a six-try defeat at Hull, winger Chris Chapman scoring a consolation try in a 32-6 hammering, Hull centre Richard Price grabbing two tries.

In heatwave semi-finals, Widnes produced another super show to record seven tries in the 38-14 home defeat of Wembley runners-up St. Helens, wingers Offiah and Rick Thackray each scoring two tries. Hull disposed of Featherstone Rovers by 23-0 at the Boulevard, stand off Gary Pearce earning the Man of the Match award with five goals, a drop goal and a try, plus the creation of another, his selection having been in doubt after a loss of goalkicking form.

1989 Results

First Round

Hull	32	Castleford	6
Leeds	12	Featherstone R.	15
Widnes	30	Bradford N.	18
Wigan	2	St. Helens	4

Semi-Finals

Hull	23	Featherstone R.	0
Widnes	38	St. Helens	14

Final

Widnes	18	Hull	10

(at Old Trafford, Manchester)

1989 Prizes:

Winners	£10,000
Runners-up	£4,000

History

With the reintroduction of two divisions in 1973-74 there was no longer a need for a play-off to decide the championship.

However, it was decided to continue the tradition of an end-of-season play-off, the winners to receive the newly instituted Premiership Trophy.

In the first season of the Premiership, 1974-75, the top 12 Division One clubs and the top four from Division Two went into a first round draw, the luck of the draw operating through to the final, played on a neutral venue.

The following season the play-off was reduced to the top eight clubs in the First Division, the ties being decided on a merit basis i.e. 1st v. 8th, 2nd v. 7th etc. At the semi-final stage the highest placed clubs had the option of when to play at home in the two-legged tie.

In 1978-79 the two-leg system was suspended because of fixture congestion and the higher placed clubs had home advantage right through to the neutrally staged final. Two legs returned the following season, but were finally abolished from 1980-81.

A Second Division Premiership tournament was introduced for the first time in 1986-87, Manchester United's Old Trafford being selected as a new fixed venue for a doubleheader final.

PREMIERSHIP ROLL OF HONOUR

Year	Winners	Runners-up	Venue	Attendance	Receipts
1975	Leeds 26	St. Helens 11	Wigan 14,531		£7,795
1976	St. Helens 15	Salford 2	Swinton 18,082		£13,138
1977	St. Helens 32	Warrington.........20	Swinton 11,178		£11,626
1978	Bradford N. 17	Widnes............. 8	Swinton 16,813		£18,677
1979	Leeds 24	Bradford N. 2	Huddersfield.................19,486		£21,291
1980	Widnes 19	Bradford N. 5	Swinton 10,215		£13,665
1981	Hull K.R. 11	Hull................. 7	Leeds 29,448		£47,529
1982	Widnes 23	Hull................. 8	Leeds 12,100		£23,749
1983	Widnes 22	Hull.................10	Leeds 17,813		£34,145
1984	Hull K.R. 18	Castleford...........10	Leeds 12,515		£31,769
1985	St. Helens 36	Hull K.R. 16	Elland Rd, Leeds...........15,518		£46,950
1986	Warrington.........38	Halifax 10	Elland Rd, Leeds...........13,683		£50,879
1987	Wigan 8	Warrington......... 0	Old Trafford, Man'r......38,756		£165,166
1988	Widnes 38	St. Helens 14	Old Trafford, Man'r......35,252		£202,616
1989	Widnes 18	Hull.................10	Old Trafford, Man'r......40,194		£264,242

PREMIERSHIP FINAL .... A REVIEW

1974-75

Leeds 26 Holmes (2g) (Marshall 3g); Alan Smith (1t), Hynes (1t, 1dg) (Eccles), Dyl, Atkinson (2t), Mason (1t), Hepworth; Dickinson, Ward, Pitchford, Cookson, Batten, Haigh
St. Helens 11 G. Pimblett; L. Jones (1t), Wilson, Hull, Mathias (1t); Walsh, Heaton (1t); Warlow (Cunningham), A. Karalius, Mantle (K. Gwilliam), E. Chisnall, Nicholls, Coslett (1g)
Referee: W.H. Thompson (Huddersfield)

1975-76

St. Helens 15 G. Pimblett (3g); L. Jones, Glynn (1t), Noonan, Mathias; Benyon, Heaton (K. Gwilliam); Mantle, A. Karalius (1t), James, Nicholls, E. Chisnall (1t), Coslett
Salford 2 Watkins (2dg); Fielding, Richards, Hesketh, Graham; Butler, Nash; Coulman, Raistrick, Sheffield, Knighton (Turnbull), Dixon, E. Prescott
Referee: M. J. Naughton (Widnes)

1976-77
St. Helens 32 G. Pimblett (7g, 1t); L. Jones,
Benyon (1t), Cunningham (1t), Mathias (1t),
Glynn (Ashton); K. Gwilliam (1t); D. Chisnall,
Liptrot, James (1t), Nicholls (A. Karalius),
E. Chisnall, Pinner
Warrington 20 Finnegan; Curling, Bevan
(Cunliffe), Hesford (4g), M. Kelly; A. Gwilliam
(1t), Gordon (1t); Weavill (1t), Price, Case,
Martyn (Peers), Lester, B. Philbin (1t)
Referee: G.F. Lindop (Wakefield)

1977-78
Bradford N. 17 Mumby (2g); Barends (1t),
Roe (1t), Austin, D. Redfearn (1t); Wolford (1dg),
A. Redfearn; I. Van Bellen (Fox), Raistrick,
Thompson, Joyce (Forsyth), Trotter, Haigh (1t)
Widnes 8 Eckersley; Wright, Hughes, Aspey (2t),
Woods (1g); Gill, Bowden; Mills, Elwell, Shaw
(Ramsey) (George), Adams, Hull, Laughton
Referee: J.E. Jackson (Pudsey)

*1989 Harry Sunderland Trophy winner, Widnes full back
Alan Tait.*

Hull's sole try scorer, second row man Paul Welham.

156

1978-79
Leeds 24 Hague; Alan Smith (1t), D. Smith (1t),
Dyl (Fletcher), Atkinson; Dick (7g, 1dg);
J. Sanderson, Harrison, Ward (1t), Pitchford,
Joyce, Eccles (Adams), Cookson
Bradford N. 2 Mumby; D. Parker, Okulicz,
Gant, Spencer; Ferres (1g), A. Redfearn;
Thompson, Bridges, Forsyth (I. Van Bellen),
Trotter (Mordue), Grayshon, Casey
Referee: W.H. Thompson (Huddersfield)
1979-80
Widnes 19 Burke (1g); Wright (1t), George,
Aspey (1t), Bentley (1t); Eckersley (1dg),
Bowden; Shaw, Elwell (1t, 1dg), M. O'Neill,
L. Gorley (1t), Hull (Hogan), Adams
Bradford N. 5 Mumby (1g); MacLean (Ferres),
D. Redfearn (1t), D. Parker, Gant; Stephenson,
A. Redfearn; Thompson, Bridges, Forsyth,
Clarkson (G. Van Bellen), Grayshon, Hale
Referee: W.H. Thompson (Huddersfield)
1980-81
Hull K.R. 11 Proctor; Hubbard (1g), M. Smith
(1t), Hogan (1t), Muscroft; Hartley (1t), Harkin;
Holdstock, Watkinson, Millington, Lowe, Casey,
Hall (Burton)
Hull 7 Woods (2g); Peacham, Elliott, Wilby,
Prendiville; Banks, Dean; Tindall, Wileman,
Stone, Skerrett (Madley), Crane (1t), Norton
Referee: J. Holdsworth (Leeds)
1981-82
Widnes 23 Burke (4g, 1t); Wright (1t), Kieron
O'Loughlin, Cunningham (A. Myler), Basnett
(1t); Hughes (1t), Gregory; M. O'Neill, Elwell,
Lockwood (Whitfield), L. Gorley, E. Prescott,
Adams (1t)
Hull 8 Kemble; O'Hara (Day), Leuluai,
S. Evans, Prendiville; Topliss, Harkin; Tindall,
Wileman (Lloyd), Stone, Skerrett, Crooks
(1t, 2g, 1dg), Norton
Referee: S. Wall (Leigh)
1982-83
Widnes 22 Burke; Linton, Hughes, Lydon (5g),
Basnett (2t); A. Myler (1t), Gregory (1t) (Hulme);
M. O'Neill, Elwell, L. Gorley, Whitfield
(S. O'Neill), Prescott, Adams
Hull 10 Kemble; O'Hara (1t), Day (Solal),
Leuluai, S. Evans; Topliss (1t), Dean; Skerrett,
Bridges, Stone, Rose, Crooks (2g), Norton
(Crane)
Referee: F. Lindop (Wakefield)

1983-84
Hull K.R. 18 Fairbairn; Clark, M. Smith (1t),
Prohm (1t), Laws (1t); Dorahy (1t, 1g), Harkin;
Holdstock, Rudd, Millington (Robinson),
Burton (Lydiat), Broadhurst, Hall
Castleford 10 Roockley; Coen, Marchant, Hyde,
Kear (1t); Robinson, R. Beardmore (3g); Ward,
Horton, Connell, Crampton, Atkins, Joyner
Referee: R. Campbell (Widnes)
1984-85
St. Helens 36 Veivers (1t); Ledger (2t), Peters,
Meninga (2t) (Allen), Day (4g); Arkwright,
Holding; Burke (Forber), Ainsworth (1t),
P. Gorley, Platt, Haggerty, Pinner (1t)
Hull K.R. 16 Fairbairn (1t, 2g); Clark,
Robinson (1t), Prohm, Laws (1t); M. Smith,
G. Smith (Harkin); Broadhurst, Watkinson,
Ema (Lydiat), Kelly, Hogan, Hall
Referee: S. Wall (Leigh)
1985-86
Warrington 38 Paul Ford (Johnson 1t);
Forster (1t), Cullen, R. Duane, Carbert;
Bishop (1t, 5g), A. Gregory; Boyd (2t),
Tamati (1t), Jackson (1t), Sanderson (McGinty),
Roberts, M. Gregory
Halifax 10 Whitfield (3g) (Smith); Riddlesden,
T. Anderson, C. Anderson (1t), Wilson;
Crossley, Stephens; Scott, McCallion, Robinson,
Juliff, James (Bond), Dixon
Referee: F. Lindop (Wakefield)
1986-87
Wigan 8 Hampson; Gill (1g), Stephenson (1g),
Bell, Lydon (1t) (Russell); Edwards, Gregory;
Case, Kiss, Wane (West), Goodway, Potter,
Hanley
Warrington 0 Johnson; Drummond, Ropati, B.
Peters, Forster; Cullen, Bishop; Tamati, Roberts
(Eccles), Jackson, Humphries (Gregory),
Sanderson, Duane
Referee: K. Allatt (Southport)
1987-88
Widnes 38 Platt (1g); Thackray (Tait, 1t),
Currier (4g), Wright (2t), Offiah; Dowd,
D. Hulme (2t); Sorensen (1t), McKenzie (1t),
Grima (S. O'Neill),M. O'Neill, P. Hulme, Eyres
St. Helens 14 Loughlin (3g); Ledger (1t),
Tanner, Elia, Quirk; Bailey, Holding; Burke,
Groves, Evans (Dwyer), Forber, Fieldhouse
(Allen), Haggerty (1t)
Referee: J. Holdsworth (Kippax)

THE HARRY SUNDERLAND TROPHY

The trophy, in memory of the famous
Queenslander, a former Australian Tour
Manager, broadcaster and journalist, is
presented to the Man of the Match in the end
of season Championship or Premiership final.

The award is donated and judged by the
Rugby League Writers' Association and is
sponsored by Stones Bitter.

The Harry Sunderland Trophy Roll of Honour

Year	Winner	Team	Position
1965	Terry Fogerty	Halifax (v. St. Helens)	Second row
1966	Albert Halsall	St. Helens (v. Halifax)	Prop
1967	Ray Owen	Wakefield T. (v. St. Helens)	Scrum half
1968	Gary Cooper	Wakefield T. (v. Hull K.R.)	Full back
1969	Bev Risman	Leeds (v. Castleford)	Full back
1970	Frank Myler	St. Helens (v. Leeds)	Stand off
1971	Bill Ashurst	Wigan (v. St. Helens)	Second row
1972	Terry Clawson	Leeds (v. St. Helens)	Prop
1973	Mick Stephenson	Dewsbury (v. Leeds)	Hooker
1974	Barry Philbin	Warrington (v. St. Helens)	Loose forward
1975	Mel Mason	Leeds (v. St. Helens)	Stand off
1976	George Nicholls	St. Helens (v. Salford)	Second row
1977	Geoff Pimblett	St. Helens (v. Warrington)	Full back
1978	Bob Haigh	Bradford N. (v. Widnes)	Loose forward
1979	Kevin Dick	Leeds (v. Bradford N.)	Stand off
1980	Mal Aspey	Widnes (v. Bradford N.)	Centre
1981	Len Casey	Hull K.R. (v. Hull)	Second row
1982	Mick Burke	Widnes (v. Hull)	Full back
1983	Tony Myler	Widnes (v. Hull)	Stand off
1984	John Dorahy	Hull K.R. (v. Castleford)	Stand off
1985	Harry Pinner	St. Helens (v. Hull K.R.)	Loose forward
1986	Les Boyd	Warrington (v. Halifax)	Prop
1987	Joe Lydon	Wigan (v. Warrington)	Winger
1988	David Hulme	Widnes (v. St. Helens)	Scrum half
1989	Alan Tait	Widnes (v. Hull)	Full back

PREMIERSHIP RECORDS First staged 1975

ALL ROUNDS

TEAM

Highest score: Hull K.R. 54 v. Leeds 0 1984
(Also widest margin)
Biggest attendance: 40,194 Hull v. Widnes
..........Final at Old Trafford 1989

INDIVIDUAL

Most goals:
9 by Andy Gregory (Widnes) v. Leeds...Round 1 1982
Most points:
22 (7g, 2t) by John Dorahy (Hull K.R.) v. Leeds
.............Round 1 1984
Most tries:
4 by David Hall (Hull K.R.) v. Castleford
.............Round 1 1983
4 by Phil Ford (Wigan) v. Hull...........Round 1 1985
4 by Ellery Hanley (Wigan) v. Hull K.R.
.............Round 1 1986

PREMIERSHIP FINAL

TEAM

Most appearances: 6 by Widnes
Most wins: 5 by Widnes
Highest score:
Warrington 38 v. Halifax 10 (widest margin).......1986
Widnes 38 v. St. Helens 14 1988
Biggest attendance:
40,194 Hull v. Widnes
(at Old Trafford, Man'r) 1989

INDIVIDUAL

Most tries:
No player has scored 3 or more
Most goals:
8 by Kevin Dick (Leeds) v. Bradford N.............1979
Most points: 17 (7g, 1t) by Geoff Pimblett (St. Helens)
v. Warrington..........1977

SECOND DIVISION PREMIERSHIP TROPHY

1989 Final

High flying Sheffield Eagles crowned only their fifth season by swooping for a first-ever trophy, carrying off the Second Division Premiership title in thrilling style.

The 43-18 disposal of Swinton, inaugural Second Division trophy winners two years earlier, was just reward for the hard work and enterprise by club founder Gary Hetherington, whose players responded to the occasion with superb teamwork, plus several outstanding individual performances.

The brightest star was half back Mark Aston who collected the Tom Bergin Man of the Match award with a 19-point haul from a try, seven goals and a drop goal. He also produced the final pass for two tries and set up another with a well-placed kick over the Swinton line in a marvellous all-round display featuring a switch from stand off to scrum half when David Close went off in the 39th minute.

Aston entered the tension-filled Old Trafford stadium with the added pressure of needing to score to record the 13th feat of playing and scoring in every match throughout a season. The extra burden was soon lifted when he sent over a third minute drop goal to open the scoring. His overall tally established Aston's leadership of the season's goals and points charts with 148 and 307 respectively.

Skipper Darryl Powell contributed a hat-trick of tries to take his club record for the season to 28, the centre twice supporting Aston to go over before completing the scoring with a last minute try from substitute Steve Evans' long pass.

Swinton were the early pacesetters, leading 8-1 after 20 minutes with a try from hooker Alex Melling and two goals from captain John Myler. Sheffield replied with Powell's first touchdown to trail 8-5 before the 33rd minute dismissal of prop forward Steve O'Neill for alleged tripping.

The Eagles earned a half-time 13-8 lead when Aston linked with full back Mark Gamson to send in hooker Mick Cook, Aston adding the goal. But their lead lasted only four minutes into the second half, stand off Tommy Frodsham nipping over for a try, Myler adding the goal for a one-point advantage. A thrilling finish looked in prospect to maintain the traditional high standard of entertainment in the Second Division showpiece when Aston restored Sheffield's lead with a penalty goal two minutes later.

But the last half hour belonged to the soaring Eagles as they ran in a further five tries, interrupted by only one from Swinton. The procession of touchdowns started with one from substitute forward Paul McDermott after a tremendous midfield break by Australian loose forward Warren Smiles, an early season recruit from Bramley.

Aston added the goal and continued his domination as he opened the way for Powell to go over before snatching a try himself, tagging on the goal each time, plus another when forward Paul Broadbent touched down from close range.

Opposing half back Frodsham was Swinton's best player as he tried desperately to swing the game back in favour of the Lions. In addition to scoring his early first half try, he cut out another with a long pass to Scott Ranson after Sheffield had raced 33-14 ahead.

While Swinton won the scrums 9-5, the penalty count favoured Sheffield 9-6, only two awarded for fouls in a fast moving, well-disciplined game. The sending off of O'Neill was a major blow for Swinton, but the Eagles had already begun to recover from a slow start led by recent £20,000 recruit from Hunslet, second row man Sonny Nickle, who always took a lot of stopping before going off with a swollen eye in the 64th minute.

SECOND DIVISION PREMIERSHIP FINAL

14 May   **Old Trafford, Manchester**

SHEFFIELD EAGLES 43   **SWINTON 18**

Mark Gamson	1.	Paul Topping
Phil Cartwright	2.	Scott Ranson
Andy Dickinson	3.	Mark Viller
Darryl Powell, Capt.	4.	Steve Snape
Andy Young	5.	Derek Bate
Mark Aston	6.	Tommy Frodsham
David Close	7.	Tony Hewitt
Paul Broadbent	8.	Frank Mooney
Mick Cook	9.	Alex Melling
Gary Van Bellen	10.	Steve O'Neill
Sonny Nickle	11.	Gary Ainsworth
Mark Fleming	12.	John Allen
Warren Smiles	13.	John Myler, Capt.
Steve Evans	14.	Dave Maloney
Paul McDermott	15.	John Horrocks

T: Powell (3), Broadbent, Aston,
Cook, McDermott
G: Aston (7, 1dg)
Substitutions:
McDermott for Fleming (20 min.)
Evans for Close (39 min.)
Referee: Robin Whitfield (Widnes)

T: Frodsham, Melling, Ranson
G: Myler (3)
Substitutions:
Maloney for Viller (56 min.)
Horrocks for Allen (72 min.)
Half-time: 13-8

1989 Round by Round

Second Division Champions Leigh secured their 10th successive victory with a 38-12 home success over eighth-placed Keighley, hooker Mick Dean registering a hat-trick of tries and David Ruane scoring his 23rd touchdown of the season. Runners-up Barrow disposed of fellow Cumbrians Whitehaven 30-5 at Craven Park, Paul Burns scoring twice in the last 10 minutes to confirm supremacy. Promoted Sheffield Eagles overcame South Yorkshire rivals Doncaster 28-10 at Owlerton Stadium, Eagle Mark Aston maintaining his ever present scoring run with four goals, while Doncaster full back Neil Turner grabbed a late try to equal his own club record of 20 tries in a season. Having sold their Wiggington Road ground, York hired Castleford's Wheldon Road to stage their home tie with Swinton. York led 4-0 through two David Sullivan goals before Swinton winger Derek Bate scored an equalising try, disputed by opposition players who claimed he had stepped in touch. In the Station Road replay, Swinton won 17-16 after a late scare when Sullivan was unable to add the goal to coach Gary Stephens' last ditch try.

In the semi-finals, Sheffield travelled to Barrow to register a 9-6 success, Aston again scoring while dictating play with some astute tactical kicking. Barrow had taken the lead after only six minutes with a Paul Crearey try and Dean Marwood goal. In the second half, Aston kicked two goals and a drop goal to add to Mark Fleming's try. Champions Leigh also fell at home in a shock 20-8 defeat against fifth-placed Swinton, second row man Gary Ainsworth contributing two tries and prop Steve O'Neill a try and two drop goals, Leigh having taken an early lead with a 40-yard try from winger Barry Ledger.

Sheffield Eagles' skipper Darryl Powell, on his way to an Old Trafford hat-trick of tries.

Eagles' latest recruit Sonny Nickle, outstanding until his 64th minute eye injury.

1989 Results

First Round

Barrow	30	Whitehaven	5
Leigh	38	Keighley	12
Sheffield E.	28	Doncaster	10
York	4	Swinton	4

Replay

Swinton	17	York	16

Semi-Finals

Barrow	6	Sheffield E.	9
Leigh	8	Swinton	20

Final

Sheffield E.	43	Swinton	18

(at Old Trafford, Manchester)

1989 Prizes:

Winners	£5,000
Runners-up	£2,000

SECOND DIVISION PREMIERSHIP . . . A REVIEW

1986-87

Swinton 27 Viller; Bate (1t), Topping (Ratcliffe), Brown, Rippon (3g); Snape, Lee (1t); Grima (1t), Ainsworth (1t), Muller, Derbyshire (1t), M. Holliday (Allen), L. Holliday (1dg)

Hunslet 10 Kay; Tate, Penola, Irvine, Wilson; Coates, King; Sykes, Gibson (Senior), Bateman (2t), Platt (1g) (Mason), Bowden, Jennings

Referee: J. McDonald (Wigan)

1987-88

Oldham 28 Burke (Irving); Round, D. Foy (2t), McAlister (4g), Meadows (1t); Walsh (1t), Ford; Sherratt (Warnecke), Sanderson, Waddell, Hawkyard, Graham, Flanagan (1t)

Featherstone R. 26 Quinn (5g); Bannister (1t), Sykes (1t), Banks, Marsh (Crossley); Steadman (2t), Fox; Siddall (Bastian), K. Bell, Harrison, Hughes, Smith, Lyman

Referee: R. Whitfield (Widnes)

SECOND DIVISION PREMIERSHIP ROLL OF HONOUR

Year	Winners		Runners-up		Venue
1987	Swinton	27	Hunslet	10	Old Trafford, Manchester
1988	Oldham	28	Featherstone R.	26	Old Trafford, Manchester
1989	Sheffield E.	43	Swinton	18	Old Trafford, Manchester

THE TOM BERGIN TROPHY

The trophy, in honour of the President of the Rugby League Writers' Association and former Editor of the *Salford City Reporter*, is presented to the Man of the Match in the end of season Second Division Premiership final. The award is donated and judged by the Association and sponsored by Stones Bitter.

The Tom Bergin Trophy Roll of Honour

Year	Winner	Team	Position
1987	Gary Ainsworth	Swinton (v. Hunslet)	Hooker
1988	Des Foy	Oldham (v. Featherstone R.)	Centre
1989	Mark Aston	Sheffield E. (v. Swinton)	Stand off

LANCASHIRE CUP

1988 Final

Three tries in a five-minute spell late in the second half secured Wigan's retention of the Grunhalle Lager Lancashire Cup for a fourth consecutive year, leaving a valiant Salford still seeking their first county triumph in 16 years.

The Knowsley Road, St. Helens, confrontation confirmed the Red Devils' re-emergence and showed the determination which had maintained their First Division status in recent relegation battles. Even when a Wigan side back to near full strength with 10 Test players on duty led 22-9 with only five minutes left, Salford showed depth of character with two late tries presenting a respectable scoreline.

The absence of suspended Australian full back Steve Gibson and the departure of their influential captain Peter Williams with concussion were handicaps for Salford in their first county final since 1975. But the Willows outfit gave a commendable display and had it not been for poor marksmanship by New Zealand Test import Peter Brown, who managed only two successes from seven attempts, they could have embarrassed a Wigan side unable to find top gear while extending their Lancashire Cup final record to 20 victories in 34 appearances.

Salford should have gained an ideal start after a mere 37 seconds but Brown missed a penalty goal attempt. After an intense, finely balanced opening quarter, Wigan full back Steve Hampson was sent to the sin bin for the first time in his career after a tackle on Australian stand off Paul Shaw in the 23rd minute, Brown this time being successful with his shot at goal.

A drop goal from former Oldham packman Mick Worrall on the half hour maintained their initiative before Wigan struck back after a scrum near the Salford line, scrum half Andy Gregory's neat pass creating an easy run-in for Kevin Iro. Two goals from the Kiwi extended Wigan's lead but Salford refused to buckle under with top class tackling by New Zealand Test forward Mark Horo and safe handling from fellow countryman Brown.

The Red Devils finally broke the Wigan cover in the 50th minute with a move involving hooker Mark Moran, scrum half David Cairns and Worrall to provide former Swinton winger Tex Evans with the touchdown. When Brown kicked a penalty five minutes later to give them a 9-8 lead, the destiny of the Red Rose trophy was in the balance.

Wigan managed to draw on their vast cup experience and Gregory again provided the vital tryscoring pass as New Zealand Test prop Adrian Shelford went over in the 67th minute. Williams, Salford's ex-England RU star, was forced to leave the field a minute later and while they were still reorganising, Wigan substitute Dennis Betts set up Kevin Iro for their third try 11 minutes before the end.

Within a further three minutes, the game was beyond Salford as Great Britain half back Shaun Edwards hoisted a high ball and skipper Ellery Hanley's tackle forced Ken Jones to drop the ball which ran invitingly for Kiwi centre Dean Bell to touch down and for Kevin Iro to add his third goal

To their credit, Salford kept their heads up and Brown sent in Keith Bentley with three minutes left. Brown made up for his poor goalkicking by again providing the ball for an injury time touchdown by prop forward Steve Herbert.

Salford's attitude and fitness were admirable and they provided the Man of the Match in stand off Shaw whose blistering pace was sometimes even too quick for his team-mates. He became the fourth successive half back to win the award and the third Australian recipient.

GRUNHALLE LAGER LANCASHIRE CUP FINAL

23 October   St. Helens

WIGAN   22   **SALFORD   17**

Steve Hampson	1.	Peter Williams, Capt.
Tony Iro	2.	Tex Evans
Kevin Iro	3.	Keith Bentley
Dean Bell	4.	Ken Jones
Joe Lydon	5.	Adrian Hadley
Shaun Edwards	6.	Paul Shaw
Andy Gregory	7.	David Cairns
Ian Lucas	8.	Steve Herbert
Martin Dermott	9.	Mark Moran
Adrian Shelford	10.	Peter Brown
Andy Platt	11.	Ian Gormley
Andy Goodway	12.	Mick Worrall
Ellery Hanley, Capt.	13.	Mark Horo
Ged Byrne	14.	Ian Blease
Dennis Betts	15.	Mick McTigue

T: K. Iro (2) Shelford, Bell   T: Evans, Bentley, Herbert
G: K. Iro (3)   G: Brown (2), Worrall (dg)
Substitutions: Substitutions:
Betts for Lucas (49 min.)   Blease for Williams (68 min.)
Byrne for Lydon (76 min.)   McTigue for Horo (74 min.)
Half-time: 8-3   Attendance: 19,154
Referee: Kevin Allatt (Southport)

1988 Round by Round

Holders Wigan travelled to Barrow in the first round, six men being dismissed to the sin bin in a scrappy game. The Riversiders scored five tries in the 24-10 win with Australian prop forward Cavill Heugh scoring Barrow's only touchdown eight minutes from time. Carlisle opened their home tie with Chorley Borough at a fierce pace rattling up 16 points without reply in the first 20 minutes and leading 17-6 at the interval, the only second half contribution being a Mike Smith drop goal for Chorley. Oldham winger Kevin Meadows notched a hat-trick in a 10-try 64-2 rout of visitors Workington Town, Mick Burke adding 10 goals and hooker Andy Ruane two. Level 2-2 at half-time, Rochdale Hornets ran in four of the six second half tries to secure a 25-14 victory over visitors Fulham, Aaron Sawyer touching down twice.

A Mark Roberts hat-trick of tries and a 16-point haul by stand off John Woods were the main features of Warrington's 42-4 victory at Runcorn Highfield, the visitors leading 24-4 at the break. Having never won in 29 previous visits to Salford, Whitehaven again went down, 42-8, the Red Devils celebrating a hat-trick of tries by debutant Paul Shaw despite the loss of Peter Williams after only seven minutes. Swinton maintained their unbeaten Lancashire Cup record over visitors Leigh with a 24-14 home victory, six Andy Rippon goals being a decisive factor. In a Merseyside derby, Widnes led St. Helens 22-0 at half-time and held out to win 32-24 after a second half revival by the visitors.

In the second round, Salford travelled to Oldham and showed their new-found resilience on an energy-sapping pitch. The Red Devils scored two tries in the opening 10 minutes, hooker Ian Gormley sealing an 18-2 victory with a 77th minute touchdown.

Warrington were made to work hard for a

34-18 victory over Second Division visitors Carlisle, the Cumbrians staging a second half comeback to trail only 22-18 before the Wire's class and fitness paid dividends. Widnes coasted to a comfortable 38-4 success over Swinton, who made John Wood skipper for the day on his return to Naughton Park. Swinton found the pace of the Chemics too decisive, Tony Myler and Alan Tait both collecting two tries. Wigan also coasted through 36-4 against Second Division Rochdale Hornets at Central Park despite being without seven regulars and losing Test forward Andy Goodway after only 13 minutes. The Riversiders qualified for a fifth successive semi-final by scoring eight tries.

Rejuvenated Salford reached their first major final with a 15-2 home win over Warrington in the semi-final. Salford always led the previous year's runners-up who were without 10 regulars, the Red Devils' points coming from tries from Keith Bentley and Tex Evans, plus three Adrian Hadley goals and a Bentley drop goal. Wigan reached the final for the fifth consecutive season by disposing of visiting Widnes 14-10 in a semi-final thriller, the Chemics being without skipper Kurt Sorensen on World Cup duty with New Zealand. Young full back Sean Tyrer, son of former Wigan player Colin — now on the coaching staff at Widnes — kicked five goals from seven attempts for Wigan.

Wigan second row man Andy Platt subjected to a double Salford tackle by Steve Herbert (left) and Ian Gormley.

1988 RESULTS

First Round

Barrow	10	Wigan	24
Carlisle	17	Chorley B.	7
Oldham	64	Workington T.	2
Rochdale H.	25	Fulham	14
Runcorn H.	4	Warrington	42
Salford	42	Whitehaven	8
Swinton	24	Leigh	14
Widnes	32	St. Helens	24

Second Round

Oldham	2	Salford	18
Warrington	34	Carlisle	18
Widnes	38	Swinton	4
Wigan	36	Rochdale H.	4

Semi-Finals

Salford	15	Warrington	2
Wigan	14	Widnes	10

Final

Wigan	22	Salford	17
(at St. Helens)			

1988 Man of the Match winner, Australian Paul Shaw.

LANCASHIRE CUP ROLL OF HONOUR

Season	Winners		Runners-up		Venue	Attendance	Receipts
1905-06	Wigan	0	Leigh	0	Broughton	16,000	£400
(replay)	Wigan	8	Leigh	0	Broughton	10,000	£200
1906-07	Broughton R.	15	Warrington	6	Wigan	14,048	£392
1907-08	Oldham	16	Broughton R.	9	Rochdale	14,000	£340
1908-09	Wigan	10	Oldham	9	Broughton	20,000	£600
1909-10	Wigan	22	Leigh	5	Broughton	14,000	£296
1910-11	Oldham	4	Swinton	3	Broughton	14,000	£418
1911-12	Rochdale H.	12	Oldham	5	Broughton	20,000	£630
1912-13	Wigan	21	Rochdale H.	5	Salford	6,000	£200
1913-14	Oldham	5	Wigan	0	Broughton	18,000	£610
1914-15	Rochdale H.	3	Wigan	2	Salford	4,000	£475
1915-16 to 1917-18 *Competition suspended*							
1918-19	Rochdale H.	22	Oldham	0	Salford	18,617	£1,365
1919-20	Oldham	7	Rochdale H.	0	Salford	19,000	£1,615
1920-21	Broughton R.	6	Leigh	3	Salford	25,000	£1,800
1921-22	Warrington	7	Oldham	5	Broughton	18,000	£1,200
1922-23	Wigan	20	Leigh	2	Salford	15,000	£1,200
1923-24	St. Helens Recs.	17	Swinton	0	Wigan	25,656	£1,450
1924-25	Oldham	10	St. Helens Recs.	0	Salford	15,000	£1,116
1925-26	Swinton	15	Wigan	11	Broughton	17,000	£1,115
1926-27	St. Helens	10	St. Helens Recs.	2	Warrington	19,439	£1,192
1927-28	Swinton	5	Wigan	2	Oldham	22,000	£1,275
1928-29	Wigan	5	Widnes	4	Warrington	19,000	£1,150
1929-30	Warrington	15	Salford	2	Wigan	21,012	£1,250
1930-31	St. Helens Recs.	18	Wigan	3	Swinton	16,710	£1,030
1931-32	Salford	10	Swinton	8	Broughton	26,471	£1,654
1932-33	Warrington	10	St. Helens	9	Wigan	28,500	£1,675

Season	Winners		Runners-up		Venue	Attendance	Receipts
1933-34	Oldham	12	St. Helens Recs.	0	Swinton	9,085	£516
1934-35	Salford	21	Wigan	12	Swinton	33,544	£2,191
1935-36	Salford	15	Wigan	7	Warrington	16,500	£950
1936-37	Salford	5	Wigan	2	Warrington	17,500	£1,160
1937-38	Warrington	8	Barrow	4	Wigan	14,000	£800
1938-39	Wigan	10	Salford	7	Swinton	27,940	£1,708
1939-40*	Swinton	5	Widnes	4	Widnes	5,500	£269
	Swinton	16	Widnes	11	Swinton	9,000	£446

Swinton won on aggregate 21-15

1940-41 to 1944-45 *Competition suspended during war-time*

Season	Winners		Runners-up		Venue	Attendance	Receipts
1945-46	Widnes	7	Wigan	3	Warrington	28,184	£2,600
1946-47	Wigan	9	Belle Vue R.	3	Swinton	21,618	£2,658
1947-48	Wigan	10	Belle Vue R.	7	Warrington	23,110	£3,043
1948-49	Wigan	14	Warrington	8	Swinton	39,015	£5,518
1949-50	Wigan	20	Leigh	7	Warrington	35,000	£4,751
1950-51	Wigan	28	Warrington	5	Swinton	42,541	£6,222
1951-52	Wigan	14	Leigh	6	Swinton	33,230	£5,432
1952-53	Leigh	22	St. Helens	5	Swinton	34,785	£5,793
1953-54	St. Helens	16	Wigan	8	Swinton	42,793	£6,918
1954-55	Barrow	12	Oldham	2	Swinton	25,204	£4,603
1955-56	Leigh	26	Widnes	9	Wigan	26,507	£4,090
1956-57	Oldham	10	St. Helens	3	Wigan	39,544	£6,274
1957-58	Oldham	13	Wigan	8	Swinton	42,497	£6,918
1958-59	Oldham	12	St. Helens	2	Swinton	38,780	£6,933
1959-60	Warrington	5	St. Helens	4	Wigan	39,237	£6,424
1960-61	St. Helens	15	Swinton	9	Wigan	31,755	£5,337
1961-62	St. Helens	25	Swinton	9	Wigan	30,000	£4,850
1962-63	St. Helens	7	Swinton	4	Wigan	23,523	£4,122
1963-64	St. Helens	15	Leigh	4	Swinton	21,231	£3,857
1964-65	St. Helens	12	Swinton	4	Wigan	17,383	£3,393
1965-66	Warrington	16	Rochdale H.	5	St. Helens	21,360	£3,800
1966-67	Wigan	16	Oldham	13	Swinton	14,193	£3,558
1967-68	St. Helens	2	Warrington	2	Wigan	16,897	£3,886
(replay)	St. Helens	13	Warrington	10	Swinton	7,577	£2,485
1968-69	St. Helens	30	Oldham	2	Wigan	17,008	£4,644
1969-70	Swinton	11	Leigh	2	Wigan	13,532	£3,651
1970-71	Leigh	7	St. Helens	4	Swinton	10,776	£3,136
1971-72	Wigan	15	Widnes	8	St. Helens	6,970	£2,204
1972-73	Salford	25	Swinton	11	Warrington	6,865	£3,321
1973-74	Wigan	19	Salford	9	Warrington	8,012	£2,750
1974-75	Widnes	6	Salford	2	Wigan	7,403	£2,833
1975-76	Widnes	16	Salford	7	Wigan	7,566	£3,880
1976-77	Widnes	16	Workington T.	11	Wigan	8,498	£6,414
1977-78	Workington T.	16	Wigan	13	Warrington	9,548	£5,038
1978-79	Widnes	15	Workington T.	13	Wigan	10,020	£6,261
1979-80	Widnes	11	Workington T.	0	Salford	6,887	£7,100
1980-81	Warrington	26	Wigan	10	St. Helens	6,442	£8,629
1981-82	Leigh	8	Widnes	3	Wigan	9,011	£14,029
1982-83	Warrington	16	St. Helens	0	Wigan	6,462	£11,732
1983-84	Barrow	12	Widnes	8	Wigan	7,007	£13,160
1984-85	St. Helens	26	Wigan	18	Wigan	26,074	£62,139
1985-86	Wigan	34	Warrington	8	St. Helens	19,202	£56,030
1986-87	Wigan	27	Oldham	6	St. Helens	20,180	£60,329
1987-88	Wigan	28	Warrington	16	St. Helens	20,237	£67,339
1988-89	Wigan	22	Salford	17	St. Helens	19,154	£71,879

*Emergency War-time competition

LANCASHIRE CUP FINAL .... A REVIEW

1966-67
Wigan 16 Ashby; Boston (1t), Ashton (1t),
Holden, Lake; C. Hill, Parr; Gardiner,
Clarke (1t), J. Stephens, Lyon, Gilfedder
(2g, 1t), Major
Oldham 13 McLeod; Dolly, McCormack,
Donovan (1t), Simms; Warburton (5g),
Canning; Wilson, Taylor, Fletcher, Smethurst,
Irving, Mooney
Referee: P. Geraghty (York)
1967-68
St. Helens 2 F. Barrow; Vollenhoven, Whittle,
Benyon, A. Barrow; Douglas, Bishop; Warlow,
Sayer, Watson, Hogan, Mantle, Coslett (1g)
Warrington 2 Affleck; Coupe, Melling, Harvey
(Pickavance), Glover; Aspinall (1g), Gordon;
Ashcroft, Harrison, Brady, Parr, Briggs, Clarke
Referee: G.F. Lindop (Wakefield)
Replay
St. Helens 13 F. Barrow; Vollenhoven, Smith,
Benyon, Jones (1t); Douglas (Houghton 2g),
Bishop; Warlow (1t), Sayer, Watson,
E. Chisnall (1t), Mantle, Coslett (Egan)
Warrington 10 Conroy; Coupe, Melling (1t),
Allen (2g), Glover; Scahill, Gordon (1t);
Ashcroft, Harrison, Price, Parr, Briggs, Clarke
Referee: G.F. Lindop (Wakefield)
1968-69
St. Helens 30 Rhodes; F. Wilson (2t), Benyon,
Myler, Williams (1t); Whittle, Bishop (1t);
Warlow, Sayer, Watson, Rees (1t), E. Chisnall
(1t) Coslett (6g)
Oldham 2 Murphy; Elliott, Larder,
McCormack, Whitehead; Briggs (1g), Canning;
K. Wilson, Taylor, Fletcher (Maders), Irving,
McCourt, Hughes
Referee: W.H. Thompson (Huddersfield)
1969-70
Swinton 11 Gowers; Gomersall, Fleet, Buckley,
M. Philbin (1t); Davies, Kenny (4g); Bate,
D. Clarke, Mackay, Holliday, Smith, Robinson
Leigh 2 Grainey; Tickle, Warburton, Collins,
Stringer (Brown); Eckersley, Murphy (1g);
D. Chisnall, Ashcroft, Watts, Welding, Lyon,
Fiddler
Referee: E. Clay (Leeds)
1970-71
Leigh 7 Ferguson (2g); Tickle (Canning),
L. Chisnall, Collins, Walsh; Eckersley (1t),
Murphy; D. Chisnall, Ashcroft, Watts, Grimes,
Clarkson, Mooney
St. Helens 4 F. Barrow; L. Jones, Benyon,
Walsh, Wilson; Myler, Whittle; Halsall,
A. Karalius, Rees (Prescott), Mantle,
E. Chisnall, Coslett (2g)
Referee: W.H. Thompson (Huddersfield)

1971-72
Wigan 15 Tyrer (3g); Eastham (1t), Francis (1t),
Fuller, Wright (Gandy); D. Hill, Ayres (1t);
Ashcroft, Clarke, Fletcher, Ashurst, Kevin
O'Loughlin, Laughton
Widnes 8 Dutton; Brown, McLoughlin, Aspey
(1g), Gaydon (1t); D. O'Neill (1t), Bowden;
Warlow, Foran, Doughty, Kirwan, Walsh
(Lowe), Nicholls
Referee: W.H. Thompson (Huddersfield)
1972-73
Salford 25 Charlton (1t); Eastham (1t),
Watkins (1t, 5g), Hesketh, Richards (1t); Gill,
Banner (1t); Mackay, Walker, Ward,
Whitehead, Dixon, Prescott
Swinton 11 Jackson; Fleay (1t), Cooke,
Buckley, Gomersall; Kenny (1g) (M. Philbin),
Gowers (3g); Halsall, Evans, Bate, R. Smith
(Holliday), Hoyle, W. Pattinson
Referee: W.H. Thompson (Huddersfield)
1973-74
Wigan 19 Francis; Vigo, D. Hill, Keiron
O'Loughlin (2t), Wright (1t); Cassidy,
Ayres (1g); Smethurst, Clarke, Gray (4g),
Irving, D. Robinson, Cunningham
Salford 9 Charlton; Fielding, Watkins (1t, 3g),
Hesketh, Holland; Gill, Banner; Mackay,
Walker, Davies (Grice), Dixon, Kear
(Knighton), E. Prescott
Referee: W.H. Thompson (Huddersfield)
1974-75
Widnes 6 Dutton (1g); George (1t),
D. O'Neill, Aspey, A. Prescott; Hughes (1dg),
Bowden; Mills, Elwell, J. Stephens, Adams,
Blackwood, Laughton
Salford 2 Charlton; Fielding (1g), Dixon,
Graham, Richards; Taylor, Banner; Mackay,
Devlin, Grice, Knighton, Coulman, E. Prescott
Referee: G.F. Lindop (Wakefield)
1975-76
Widnes 16 Dutton (3g, 1dg); A. Prescott (1t),
George (1t), Aspey (1t), Jenkins; Hughes (1t),
Bowden; Mills, Elwell, Nelson, Foran,
Fitzpatrick (Sheridan), Adams
Salford 7 Charlton; Fielding, Butler,
Hesketh, Richards (1t); Gill, Nash; Fiddler,
Hawksley, Dixon (Mackay), Turnbull,
Knighton, E. Prescott
Referee: W.H. Thompson (Huddersfield)
1976-77
Widnes 16 Dutton (4g, 1dg); Wright (1t),
Aspey, George (1t), A. Prescott; Eckersley,
Bowden (1dg); Ramsey, Elwell, Nelson,
Dearden, Adams, Laughton
Workington T. 11 Charlton; Collister,
Wilkins (1t), Wright, MacCorquodale (4g);
Lauder, Walker; Mills, Banks, Calvin,
Bowman, L. Gorley, W. Pattinson (P. Gorley)
Referee: W.H. Thompson (Huddersfield)

1977-78
Workington T. 16 Charlton (Atkinson);
Collister, Risman, Wright (1t), MacCorquodale
(4g); Wilkins (1t), Walker (2dg); Watts, Banks,
Bowman, L. Gorley, W. Pattinson, P. Gorley
Wigan 13 Swann; Vigo, Davies (Burke 1g),
Willicombe (1t), Hornby; Taylor, Nulty (1t, 1g);
Hogan, Aspinall, Irving, Ashurst (1t),
Blackwood, Melling (Regan)
Referee: W.H. Thompson (Huddersfield)
1978-79
Widnes 15 Eckersley; Wright (1t), Aspey,
George, Burke (3g); Hughes, Bowden; Mills,
Elwell, Shaw, Adams, Dearden (Hull),
Laughton (2t)
Workington T. 13 Charlton; Collister, Risman,
Wilkins (1t), MacCorquodale (1t, 2g), McMillan,
Walker; Beverley, Banks, Bowman, Blackwood,
P. Gorley, W. Pattinson (L. Gorley 1t)
Referee: W.H. Thompson (Huddersfield)
1979-80
Widnes 11 Eckersley; Wright, Aspey, Hughes
(George), Burke (2g); Moran (1t), Bowden;
Hogan, Elwell (1dg), Shaw, L. Gorley, Dearden,
Adams (1t)
Workington T. 0 Charlton; MacCorquodale,
Maughan, Thompson, Beck; Rudd, Walker
(Roper); Beverley, Banks, Wallbanks (Varty),
W. Pattinson, Lewis, Dobie
Referee: W.H. Thompson (Huddersfield)
1980-81
Warrington 26 Finnegan; Thackray (1t),
I. Duane, Bevan (1t), Hesford (7g, 1t);
K. Kelly, A. Gwilliam; Courtney, Waller, Case,
Martyn (1t), Eccles (Potter), Hunter
Wigan 10 Fairbairn (1t, 2g); Ramsdale (1t),
Willicombe, Davies, Hornby; M. Foy, Bolton
(Coyle); Breheny, Pendlebury (M. Smith),
S. O'Neill, Melling, Clough, Hollingsworth
Referee: D. G. Kershaw (York)
1981-82
Leigh 8 Hogan; Drummond, Bilsbury (1t),
Donlan (1dg), Worgan; Woods (2g), Green;
Wilkinson, Tabern, Cooke, Martyn (Platt),
Clarkson, McTigue
Widnes 3 Burke; George, Hughes,
Cunningham, Bentley (1t); Moran, Gregory;
M. O'Neill, Elwell, Lockwood, L. Gorley,
E. Prescott, Adams
Referee: W.H. Thompson (Huddersfield)
1982-83
Warrington 16 Hesford (2g); Fellows (1t),
R. Duane, Bevan, M. Kelly (1t); Cullen,
K. Kelly (1t); Courtney, Webb, Cooke
(D. Chisnall), Eccles (1t), Fieldhouse, Gregory

St. Helens 0 Parkes (Smith); Ledger,
Arkwright, Haggerty, Litherland; Peters,
Holding; James, Liptrot, Bottell (Mathias),
Moorby, P. Gorley, Pinner
Referee: J. Holdsworth (Leeds)
1983-84
Barrow 12 Tickle (1dg); Moore, Whittle,
Ball (3g, 1dg), Milby; McConnell (1t), Cairns;
Hodkinson, Wall, McJennett, Herbert, Szymala,
Mossop
Widnes 8 Burke; Lydon (1t, 2g), Hughes,
Keiron O'Loughlin, Basnett; A. Myler,
Gregory; S. O'Neill, Elwell, K. Tamati,
Whitfield, E. Prescott, Adams
Referee: K. Allatt (Southport)
1984-85
St. Helens 26 Veivers (Haggerty 1t); Ledger,
Allen, Meninga (2t), Day (1t, 5g); Arkwright,
Holding; Burke, Liptrot, P. Gorley, Platt,
Round, Pinner
Wigan 18 Edwards; Ferguson, Stephenson,
Whitfield (3g), Gill (1t) (Pendlebury); Cannon,
Fairhurst; Courtney, Kiss (1t), Case, West (1t),
Wane, Potter
Referee: R. Campbell (Widnes)
1985-86
Wigan 34 Edwards (1t); Henley-Smith
(Hampson), Stephenson (7g), Hanley (1t),
Whitfield; Ella (2t), M. Ford; Dowling, Kiss
(1t), Wane (Case), Du Toit, Goodway, Potter
Warrington 8 Johnson (1t); Carbert (2g), Cullen,
Blake (Forster), Thackray; Kelly, A. Gregory;
Eccles, Webb, Jackson, Boyd (Tamati),
M. Gregory, Rathbone
Referee: J. Holdsworth (Kippax)
1986-87
Wigan 27 Edwards (2t); Lydon (1t, 1dg),
Stephenson, Bell, Gill (5g); Hanley, M. Ford
(1t); West, Dermott, Case, Roberts (Louw),
Potter, Goodway
Oldham 6 M'Barki; Sherman, Bridge (1t),
Warnecke, Taylor; Topliss, Kirwan; Clark,
Flanagan, Hobbs (1g), Nadiole, Worrall, Raper
(Hawkyard)
Referee: J.E. Smith (Halifax)
1987-88
Wigan 28 Hampson; Russell, Stephenson (1g)
(Bell), Lydon (5g), Gill (1t); Edwards, A.
Gregory; Case, Kiss, Wane (West, 1t),
Goodway, Potter, Hanley (2t)
Warrington 16 Johnson; Drummond, Forster
(2t), Peters, Carbert; Woods (2g), Holden;
K. Tamati, Webb (Harmon), Humphries,
Sanderson, Roberts, M. Gregory (1t)
Referee: G.F. Lindop (Wakefield)

MAN OF THE MATCH AWARDS

An award for the adjudged man of the match in the Lancashire Cup final was first presented in 1974-75. For four years the award was sponsored by the *Rugby Leaguer* newspaper. From 1978-85 the trophy was presented by Burtonwood Brewery, then from 1986 by Greenall Whitley, as part of their sponsorship of the Lancashire Cup. Under the auspices of the *Rugby Leaguer*, the choice was made by the Editor, while the breweries invited a panel of the Press to make the decision.

Season	Winner	Team	Position
1974-75	Mike Coulman	Salford (v. Widnes)	Second row
1975-76	Mick George	Widnes (v. Salford)	Centre
1976-77	David Eckersley	Widnes (v. Workington T.)	Stand off
1977-78	Arnold Walker	Workington T. (v. Wigan)	Scrum half
1978-79	Arnold Walker	Workington T. (v. Widnes)	Scrum half
1979-80	Mick Adams	Widnes (v. Workington T.)	Loose forward
1980-81	Tony Waller	Warrington (v. Wigan)	Hooker
1981-82	Ray Tabern	Leigh (v. Widnes)	Hooker
1982-83	Steve Hesford	Warrington (v. St. Helens)	Full back
1983-84	David Cairns	Barrow (v. Widnes)	Scrum half
1984-85	Mal Meninga	St. Helens (v. Wigan)	Centre
1985-86	Steve Ella	Wigan (v. Warrington)	Stand off
1986-87	Mike Ford	Wigan (v. Oldham)	Scrum half
1987-88	Shaun Edwards	Wigan (v. Warrington)	Stand off
1988-89	Paul Shaw	Salford (v. Wigan)	Stand off

LANCASHIRE CUP FINAL RECORDS

TEAM

Most appearances: 34 by Wigan
Most wins: 20 by Wigan
Highest score: Wigan 34 v. Warrington 8 1985
Widest margin: St. Helens 30 v. Oldham 2 1968
Biggest attendance:
42,793 St. Helens v. Wigan (at Swinton) 1953

INDIVIDUAL

Most tries:
4 by Brian Nordgren (Wigan) v. Leigh 1949
Most goals:
7 by Jim Ledgard (Leigh) v. Widnes 1955
　　Steve Hesford (Warrington) v. Wigan 1980
　　David Stephenson (Wigan) v. Warrington .. 1985
Most points:
17 (7g, 1t) by Steve Hesford (Warrington) v. Wigan
　　　　　　　　　　　　　　　　　　........ 1980

Wigan's Ellery Hanley vies for the ball with an in-flight Ken Jones, of Salford.

YORKSHIRE CUP

1988 Final

Leeds' record-breaking investment in the transfer market paid a first dividend with the capture of the John Smiths Yorkshire Cup in a magnificent final at Elland Road, Leeds, in front of an enthralled 23,000 crowd.

An intriguing 50 minutes had seen the Loiners hold an uncertain 15-12 lead before Great Britain tourist Carl Gibson scored two spectacular touchdowns to determine the destiny of the county trophy as Leeds opened a 27-12 lead against an unbeaten, table-topping Castleford outfit.

Australian stand off Cliff Lyons figured prominently in the final burst of high speed action by a Leeds side extending the record number of county final wins to 17 out of a record 21 appearances. He was awarded the White Rose Trophy as Man of the Match, being closely run by Test centre Garry Schofield and outstanding packmen Lee Crooks and Roy Powell.

The first half belonged to Schofield who deprived Castleford of a deserved half-time advantage by twice shocking them with tries and sending over a drop goal. After only four minutes, an all-out scoring raid by Castleford suddenly evaporated as Schofield intercepted and raced 90 yards to touch down. David Stephenson added the goal and a penalty in reply to one from Martin Ketteridge before Schofield popped over his drop goal.

Centre Giles Boothroyd finished off a breathtaking move to score the try Castleford had threatened so often as they began to get well on top . . . until Schofield struck again. Skipper Crooks — back to form with a non-stop series of charges and deft ball handling — broke from his own half to feed the supporting Gary Spencer who did well to hand on to the ever-alert Schofield. Captain John Joyner calmed Castleford's nerves with

a try after interpassing with winger David Plange, Ketteridge's touchline goal leaving them only a point behind until Stephenson hit another penalty.

The second half opened in identical nightmare fashion for Castleford, contesting their fifth county final in seven years. Just as they looked like scoring, winger Gibson nipped in to intercept and race 90 yards for a try between the posts, Stephenson's goal providing a flattering 21-12 scoreline after 52 minutes. A tremendous example of centre play from Stephenson six minutes later gave Gibson the sort of break wingers dream of and the former Batley threequarter went away in classic fashion to step out of Australian Gary Belcher's tackle and curve in towards the post for Stephenson to add the goal.

Having come on as a 53rd minute substitute, Paul Medley wrapped up the afternoon's memorable try tally after a long pass from Lyons, the third time in the competition that the Great Britain tourist had touched down after going on as a late replacement.

Stephenson rounded off the scoring with a last minute penalty goal after a Keith England tackle which broke his nose. The sixth successful shot gave him a Yorkshire Cup final record to go with the Lancashire Cup final record of seven he scored for Wigan in 1985.

The epic final, played at breakneck pace, produced a string of top-class performances. A full 80 minutes of power play from Crooks was counterbalanced in the first hour by Castleford's tower of strength Kevin Ward. In the backs, Castleford's Plange caught the eye of Great Britain coach Malcolm Reilly on the eve of selection for the Rest of the World Challenge encounter, playing a role in both their tries and making a dynamic midfield run in the second half.

The crowd of 22,968 was the second best attendance at a Yorkshire Cup final for 29 years.

JOHN SMITHS YORKSHIRE CUP FINAL

16 October   **Elland Road, Leeds**

LEEDS 33   CASTLEFORD 12

Leeds	No.	Castleford
Gary Spencer	1.	Gary Belcher
Andrew Ettingshausen	2.	David Plange
Garry Schofield	3.	Tony Marchant
David Stephenson	4.	Giles Boothroyd
Carl Gibson	5.	Chris Chapman
Cliff Lyons	6.	Grant Anderson
Ray Ashton	7.	Bob Beardmore
Lee Crooks, Capt.	8.	Kevin Ward
Colin Maskill	9.	Kevin Beardmore
Hugh Waddell	10.	Keith England
Roy Powell	11.	Martin Ketteridge
Mark Brooke-Cowden	12.	Ron Gibbs
David Heron	13.	John Joyner, Capt.
Paul Medley	14.	David Roockley
Sam Backo	15.	Dean Sampson

T: Schofield (2), Gibson (2),
Medley
G: Stephenson (6), Schofield (dg)
Substitutions:
Medley for Brooke-Cowden (53 min.)
Backo for Waddell (64 min.)
Referee: Robin Whitfield (Widnes)

T: Boothroyd, Joyner
G: Ketteridge (2)
Substitutions:
Roockley for Chapman (46 min.)
Sampson for Roockley (59 min.)
Half-time: 15-12
Attendance: 22,968

YORKSHIRE CUP

1988 Round by Round

In a two-tie preliminary round, Wakefield Trinity secured a 28-8 success at Sheffield Eagles, new Australian import Steve Ella kicking six goals from seven attempts and packman John Glancy impressing on his first return to Owlerton Stadium since his summer transfer. Bramley entertained First Division neighbours Leeds, who ran in seven tries to the home side's three, the Loiners' tally featuring four touchdowns in a 12-minute spell to give them a 38-16 win.

In the first round, Castleford played hosts to trouble-torn Huddersfield and ran up a club record score of 94-12. Having scored three tries in the opening six minutes, the Glassblowers went on to total 17 touchdowns with hat-tricks for Chris Chapman, David Plange and Kevin Beardmore, with Martin Ketteridge adding 13 goals. Featherstone Rovers led only 10-8 with 23 minutes left at home to Doncaster before a late scoring burst brought a 38-8 victory and a hat-trick for Paul Lyman, Rovers having lost debutant New Zealander Trevor Clark, injured after only seven minutes. Despite the incentive of a pounds-for-points bonus, Halifax struggled to dispose of Second Division Batley, the home side working hard for a 36-14 victory, Man of the Match hooker Seamus McCallion scoring two tries. Hull and Hunslet entered their tie each without a league win, the former running in nine tries in a 53-0 home success hallmarked by the form of Australian scrum half Craig Coleman and prop Andy Dannatt, winger Paul Eastwood contributing a 20-point haul.

Visitors Hull K.R. led Keighley 18-0 at quarter-time before the visitors rallied to equal the Robins' tally of five tries before going down 28-22. Keighley's three missed goal attempts proved fatal. Paul Medley fully justified the over-used tag of 'super-sub' in the Leeds' home clash with Bradford Northern. Northern were leading 21-8 when Medley came on in the 57th minute to set up a try for Gary Spencer and then score himself in the space of 10 minutes, finally combining with Dave Heron to set up David Stephenson's winning try in a 24-21 success, earning Man of the Match rating for a remarkable 23-minute performance. Lowly Dewsbury, victims of a fire in their stand during the week, received a pre-match standing ovation at Wakefield. There was no sympathy after the kick-off with Trinity sealing a 46-20 victory with an 18-point scoring burst in the last 10 minutes of the first half. Mansfield Marksman travelled to York to be well served by Willie Johnson and Darren Moulden in a 25-4 defeat at the hands of a much improved Wasps outfit for whom Graham Sullivan scored two tries.

In the second round, Hull scrum half Coleman brightened up a dour contest with visitors Featherstone Rovers, having a hand in all three tries in an 18-0 success over a side badly missing stand off Graham Steadman. Man of the Match Bob Grogan scored Halifax's fifth and final try in a 24-2 victory over a lethargic Hull K.R. side whose only points came from a Mike Fletcher penalty goal. Leeds substitute Medley again came on to clinch victory, being on the field for only 13 minutes before kicking ahead and winning a 40-yard chase for a spectacular, vital touchdown in a 15-10 home success against a Wakefield Trinity side hampered by Ella having missed two easy kicks at goal. Castleford, aiming for their sixth county final in eight years, led 14-0 in the early stages before York skipper Steve Dobson inspired a comeback by the visitors who scored the try of the tie through Darren St. Hilaire before the Wheldon Road side pulled away with five tries in the last quarter to win 40-14.

In the semi-finals Halifax entertained Castleford, who secured their "fourth successive final appearance with a 12-8 victory, highlighted by a sparkling try from Great Britain centre Tony Marchant as the only score in the second half. Hull travelled to Headingley where Leeds overcame their semi-final hoodoo to reach the county final for the first time since 1980 with a 12-8 victory. Hull built an 8-0 lead before centre Garry Schofield launched a Loiners' rally with a try, Australian prop Sam Backo coming on with only eight minutes left to clinch a final place with a dramatic late try.

Leeds scrum half Ray Ashton in full flight in the Elland Road final.

1988 RESULTS

Preliminary Round					Second Round			
Bramley	16	Leeds	38		Castleford	40	York	14
Sheffield E.	8	Wakefield T.	28		Halifax	24	Hull K.R.	2
					Hull	18	Featherstone R.	0
First Round					Leeds	15	Wakefield T.	10
Castleford	94	Huddersfield	12					
Featherstone R.	38	Doncaster	8		**Semi-Finals**			
Halifax	36	Batley	14		Halifax	8	Castleford	12
Hull	53	Hunslet	0		Leeds	12	Hull	8
Keighley	22	Hull K.R.	28					
Leeds	24	Bradford N.	21		**Final**			
Wakefield T.	46	Dewsbury	20		Leeds	33	Castleford	12
York.	25	Mansfield M.	4		(at Elland Rd, Leeds)			

YORKSHIRE CUP ROLL OF HONOUR

Year	Winners		Runners-up		Venue	Attendance	Receipts
1905-06	Hunslet	13	Halifax	3	Bradford P.A.	18,500	£465
1906-07	Bradford	8	Hull K.R.	5	Wakefield	10,500	£286
1907-08	Hunslet	17	Halifax	0	Leeds	15,000	£397
1908-09	Halifax	9	Hunslet	5	Wakefield	13,000	£356
1909-10	Huddersfield	21	Batley	0	Leeds	22,000	£778
1910-11	Wakefield T.	8	Huddersfield	2	Leeds	19,000	£696
1911-12	Huddersfield	22	Hull K.R.	10	Wakefield	20,000	£700
1912-13	Batley	17	Hull	3	Leeds	16,000	£523
1913-14	Huddersfield	19	Bradford N.	3	Halifax	12,000	£430
1914-15	Huddersfield	31	Hull	0	Leeds	12,000	£422
1918-19	Huddersfield	14	Dewsbury	8	Leeds	21,500	£1,309
1919-20	Huddersfield	24	Leeds	5	Halifax	24,935	£2,096
1920-21	Hull K.R.	2	Hull	0	Leeds	20,000	£1,926
1921-22	Leeds	11	Dewsbury	3	Halifax	20,000	£1,650
1922-23	York	5	Batley	0	Leeds	33,719	£2,414
1923-24	Hull	10	Huddersfield	4	Leeds	23,300	£1,728
1924-25	Wakefield T.	9	Batley	8	Leeds	25,546	£1,912
1925-26	Dewsbury	2	Huddersfield	0	Wakefield	12,616	£718
1926-27	Huddersfield	10	Wakefield T.	3	Leeds	11,300	£853
1927-28	Dewsbury	8	Hull	2	Leeds	21,700	£1,466
1928-29	Leeds	5	Featherstone R.	0	Wakefield	13,000	£838
1929-30	Hull K.R.	13	Hunslet	7	Leeds	11,000	£687
1930-31	Leeds	10	Huddersfield	2	Halifax	17,812	£1,405
1931-32	Huddersfield	4	Hunslet	2	Leeds	27,000	£1,764
1932-33	Leeds	8	Wakefield T.	0	Huddersfield	17,685	£1,183
1933-34	York	10	Hull K.R.	4	Leeds	22,000	£1,480
1934-35	Leeds	5	Wakefield T.	5	Dewsbury	22,598	£1,529
Replay	Leeds	2	Wakefield T.	2	Huddersfield	10,300	£745
Replay	Leeds	13	Wakefield T.	0	Hunslet	19,304	£1,327
1935-36	Leeds	3	York	0	Halifax	14,616	£1,113
1936-37	York	9	Wakefield T.	2	Leeds	19,000	£1,294
1937-38	Leeds	14	Huddersfield	8	Wakefield	22,000	£1,508
1938-39	Huddersfield	18	Hull	10	Bradford	28,714	£1,534
1939-40	Featherstone R.	12	Wakefield T.	9	Bradford	7,077	£403
1940-41	Bradford N.	15	Dewsbury	5	Huddersfield	13,316	£939
1941-42	Bradford N.	24	Halifax	0	Huddersfield	5,989	£635

Year	Winners		Runners-up		Venue	Attendance	Receipts
1942-43	Dewsbury	7	Huddersfield	0	Dewsbury	11,000	£680
	Huddersfield	2	Dewsbury	0	Huddersfield	6,252	£618
	Dewsbury won on aggregate 7-2						
1943-44	Bradford N.	5	Keighley	2	Bradford	10,251	£757
	Keighley	5	Bradford N.	5	Keighley	8,993	£694
	Bradford N. won on aggregate 10-7						
1944-45	Hunslet	3	Halifax	12	Hunslet	11,213	£744
	Halifax	2	Hunslet	0	Halifax	9,800	£745
	Halifax won on aggregate 14-3						
1945-46	Bradford N.	5	Wakefield T.	2	Halifax	24,292	£1,934
1946-47	Wakefield T.	10	Hull	0	Leeds	34,300	£3,718
1947-48	Wakefield T.	7	Leeds	7	Huddersfield	24,344	£3,461
Replay	Wakefield T.	8	Leeds	7	Bradford	32,000	£3,251
1948-49	Bradford N.	18	Castleford	9	Leeds	31,393	£5,053
1949-50	Bradford N.	11	Huddersfield	4	Leeds	36,000	£6,365
1950-51	Huddersfield	16	Castleford	3	Leeds	28,906	£5,152
1951-52	Wakefield T.	17	Keighley	3	Huddersfield	25,495	£3,347
1952-53	Huddersfield	18	Batley	8	Leeds	14,705	£2,471
1953-54	Bradford N.	7	Hull	2	Leeds	22,147	£3,833
1954-55	Halifax	22	Hull	14	Leeds	25,949	£4,638
1955-56	Halifax	10	Hull	10	Leeds	23,520	£4,385
Replay	Halifax	7	Hull	0	Bradford	14,000	£2,439
1956-57	Wakefield T.	23	Hunslet	5	Leeds	30,942	£5,609
1957-58	Huddersfield	15	York	8	Leeds	22,531	£4,123
1958-59	Leeds	24	Wakefield T.	20	Bradford	26,927	£3,833
1959-60	Featherstone R.	15	Hull	14	Leeds	23,983	£4,156
1960-61	Wakefield T.	16	Huddersfield	10	Leeds	17,456	£2,937
1961-62	Wakefield T.	19	Leeds	9	Bradford	16,329	£2,864
1962-63	Hunslet	12	Hull K.R.	2	Leeds	22,742	£4,514
1963-64	Halifax	10	Featherstone R.	0	Wakefield	13,238	£2,471
1964-65	Wakefield T.	18	Leeds	2	Huddersfield	13,527	£2,707
1965-66	Bradford N.	17	Hunslet	8	Leeds	17,522	£4,359
1966-67	Hull K.R.	25	Featherstone R.	12	Leeds	13,241	£3,482
1967-68	Hull K.R.	8	Hull	7	Leeds	16,729	£5,515
1968-69	Leeds	22	Castleford	11	Wakefield	12,573	£3,746
1969-70	Hull	12	Featherstone R.	9	Leeds	11,089	£3,419
1970-71	Leeds	23	Featherstone R.	7	Bradford	6,753	£1,879
1971-72	Hull K.R.	11	Castleford	7	Wakefield	5,536	£1,589
1972-73	Leeds	36	Dewsbury	9	Bradford	7,806	£2,659
1973-74	Leeds	7	Wakefield T.	2	Leeds	7,621	£3,728
1974-75	Hull K.R.	16	Wakefield T.	13	Leeds	5,823	£3,090
1975-76	Leeds	15	Hull K.R.	11	Leeds	5,743	£3,617
1976-77	Leeds	16	Featherstone R.	12	Leeds	7,645	£5,198
1977-78	Castleford	17	Featherstone R.	7	Leeds	6,318	£4,528
1978-79	Bradford N.	18	York	8	Leeds	10,429	£9,188
1979-80	Leeds	15	Halifax	6	Leeds	9,137	£9,999
1980-81	Leeds	8	Hull K.R.	7	Huddersfield	9,751	£15,578
1981-82	Castleford	10	Bradford N.	5	Leeds	5,852	£10,359
1982-83	Hull	18	Bradford N.	7	Leeds	11,755	£21,950
1983-84	Hull	13	Castleford	2	Elland Rd, Leeds	14,049	£33,572
1984-85	Hull	29	Hull K.R.	12	Hull C. FC	25,237	£68,639
1985-86	Hull K.R.	22	Castleford	18	Leeds	12,686	£36,327
1986-87	Castleford	31	Hull	24	Leeds	11,132	£31,888
1987-88	Bradford N.	12	Castleford	12	Leeds	10,947	£40,283
Replay	Bradford N.	11	Castleford	2	Elland Rd, Leeds	8,175	£30,732
1988-89	Leeds	33	Castleford	12	Elland Rd, Leeds	22,968	£76,658

YORKSHIRE CUP FINAL .... A REVIEW

1967-68
Hull K.R. 8 Kellett (1g); Young, Moore, Elliott, A. Burwell (1t); Millward (1t), Cooper; Holliday, Flanagan, Mennell, Lowe, Hickson (Foster), Major
Hull 7 Keegan; Oliver, Doyle-Davidson, Maloney (1g), Stocks; Devonshire, Davidson (1t, 1g); Harrison, McGlone, Broom, Edson, J. Macklin, Sykes
Referee: D.T.H. Davies (Manchester)
1968-69
Leeds 22 Risman (5g); Alan Smith (1t), Hynes, Watson (1t), Atkinson (1t); Shoebottom, Seabourne; Clark, Crosby, K. Eyre, Ramsey (Hick 1t), A. Eyre, Batten
Castleford 11 Edwards; Howe, Hill (1t, 2g), Thomas, Stephens; Hardisty (2g), Hargrave; Hartley, C. Dickinson, Ward, Small, Lockwood (Redfearn), Reilly
Referee: J. Manley (Warrington)
1969-70
Hull 12 Owbridge; Sullivan (1t), Gemmell, Maloney (2g), A. Macklin; Hancock, Davidson; Harrison, McGlone, J. Macklin (1t), Kirchin, Forster, Brown (1g)
Featherstone R. 9 C. Kellett (3g); Newlove, Jordan, M. Smith, Hartley (T. Hudson); D. Kellett, Nash (1t); Tonks, Farrar, Lyons, A. Morgan, Thompson, Smales
Referee: R.L. Thomas (Oldham)
1970-71
Leeds 23 Holmes; Alan Smith (2t), Hynes (4g), Cowan, Atkinson (1t); Wainwright (Langley), Shoebottom; J. Burke, Dunn (1t), Cookson, Ramsey (1t), Haigh, Batten
Featherstone R. 7 C. Kellett (2g); M. Smith, Cotton, Newlove, Hartley (1t); Harding (Coventry), Hudson; Windmill, D. Morgan, Lyons, Rhodes, Thompson, Farrar
Referee: D.S. Brown (Preston)
1971-72
Hull K.R. 11 Markham; Stephenson, Coupland, Kirkpatrick, Longstaff (1t); Millward (4g), Daley; Wiley, Flanagan, Millington, Wallis, Palmer (Cooper), Brown
Castleford 7 Edwards; Foster (1t), S. Norton, Worsley, Lowndes; Hargrave, Stephens; Hartley, Miller, I. Van Bellen (Ackroyd 2g), A. Dickinson, Lockwood, Blakeway
Referee: A. Givvons (Oldham)
1972-73
Leeds 36 Holmes (3t); Alan Smith, Hynes (1g), Dyl (2t), Atkinson (1t); Hardisty (1t), Hepworth (Langley); Clawson (5g) (Fisher), Ward, Ramsey, Cookson, Eccles (1t), Batten

Dewsbury 9 Rushton; Ashcroft (1t), Childe, Day, Yoward; Agar (3g), A. Bates; Bell (Beverley), M. Stephenson, Lowe, Grayshon, J. Bates (Lee), Hankins
Referee: M.J. Naughton (Widnes)
1973-74
Leeds 7 Holmes; Langley (1t) (Marshall 1g), Hynes (1g), Dyl, Atkinson; Hardisty, Hepworth; Jeanes (Ramsey), Ward, Clarkson, Eccles, Cookson, Batten
Wakefield T. 2 Wraith (Sheard); D. Smith, Crook (1g), Hegarty, B. Parker; Topliss, Bonnar; Valentine, Morgan, Bratt, Knowles (Ballantyne), Endersby, Holmes
Referee: M.J. Naughton (Widnes)
1974-75
Hull K.R. 16 Smithies; Sullivan (Dunn 1t), Watson (2t), Coupland, Kirkpatrick (1t); Millward, Stephenson; Millington, Heslop, Rose, Wallis, N. Fox (2g) (Madley), Brown
Wakefield T. 13 Sheard; D. Smith (1t), Crook (2g), Hegarty (1t), Archer; Topliss, Bonnar; Ballantyne, Handscombe, Bratt (1t), Skerrett, A. Tonks (Goodwin), (Holmes), Morgan
Referee: M.J. Naughton (Widnes)
1975-76
Leeds 15 Marshall; Alan Smith, Hague, Dyl (1t), Atkinson; Holmes (4g, 1dg), Hynes; Harrison, Payne, Pitchford, (Dickinson), Eccles, Batten, Cookson (1t)
Hull K.R. 11 Wallace; Dunn, A. Burwell, Watson, Sullivan (1t); Turner, Millward (1dg); Millington, Dickinson, Lyons, Rose, N. Fox (2g, 1t), Hughes (Holdstock)
Referee: J.V. Moss (Manchester)
1976-77
Leeds 16 Marshall (2g); Hague, Hynes, Dyl (2t), D. Smith; Holmes, Banner; Dickinson, Ward, Pitchford, Eccles (1t), Burton, Cookson (1t)
Featherstone R. 12 Box; Bray (1t), Coventry, Quinn (3g), K. Kellett; Newlove, Fennell; Gibbins, Bridges, Farrar, Stone, P. Smith (1t), Bell (Spells)
Referee: M.J. Naughton (Widnes)
1977-78
Castleford 17 Wraith; Richardson, Joyner, P. Johnson, Fenton; Burton (2t, 1dg), Pickerill (Stephens); Fisher (Woodall), Spurr, Weston, Huddlestone, Reilly, Lloyd (5g)
Featherstone R. 7 Marsden; Evans, Gilbert, Quinn (1g) (N. Tuffs), K. Kellett; Newlove, Butler; Townend (1g), Bridges, Farrar, Gibbins, Stone (P. Smith 1t), Bell
Referee: M.J. Naughton (Widnes)

1978-79
Bradford N. 18 Mumby; Barends, Gant (1t),
D. Parker (1t), D. Redfearn; Slater (Wolford),
A. Redfearn (1t); Thompson, Fisher, Forsyth
(Joyce), Fox (3g), Trotter, Haigh (1t)
York 8 G. Smith (1t); T. Morgan, Day
(Crossley), Foster, Nicholson; Banks (2g),
Harkin; Dunkerley, Wileman, Harris, Rhodes,
Hollis (1dg) (Ramshaw), Cooper
Referee: M.J. Naughton (Widnes)
1979-80
Leeds 15 Hague; Alan Smith (2t), D. Smith
(1t), Dyl, Atkinson; Holmes (J. Sanderson),
Dick (3g); Dickinson, Ward, Pitchford, Eccles,
D. Heron (Adams), Cookson
Halifax 6 Birts (3g); Howard (Snee), Garrod,
Cholmondeley, Waites; Blacker, Langton;
Jarvis (Callon), Raistrick, Wood, Scott, Sharp,
Busfield
Referee: M.J. Naughton (Widnes)
1980-81
Leeds 8 Hague; Alan Smith (1t), D. Smith,
Atkinson, Oulton; Holmes, Dick (2g, 1dg);
Harrison, Ward, Pitchford, Eccles, Cookson
(Carroll), D. Heron
Hull K.R. 7 Robinson; McHugh (1t),
M. Smith, Hogan (2g); Youngman; Hall,
Harkin; Holdstock, Price, Crooks (Rose),
Lowe, Casey, Crane
Referee: R. Campbell (Widnes)
1981-82
Castleford 10 Claughton; Richardson, Fenton,
Hyde (1t), Morris; Joyner (1t), R. Beardmore;
Hardy (P. Norton), Spurr, B. Johnson, Finch
(2g), Ward, Timson
Bradford N. 5 Mumby; Barends, Hale,
A. Parker (1t), Gant; Hanley (1g), A. Redfearn;
Grayshon, Noble, Sanderson (D. Redfearn),
G. Van Bellen (Jasiewicz), Idle, Rathbone
Referee: M.R. Whitfield (Widnes)
1982-83
Hull 18 Kemble; S. Evans (1t), Day, Leuluai,
Prendiville (1t); Topliss, Harkin; Skerrett,
Bridges, Stone, Rose (2t), L. Crooks (2g, 2dg),
Crane (Norton)
Bradford N. 7 Mumby; Barends, Gant,
A. Parker, Pullen (Smith); Whiteman (1t),
Carroll (1g, 2dg); Grayshon, Noble, G. Van
Bellen (Sanderson), Idle, Jasiewicz, Hale
Referee: S. Wall (Leigh)
1983-84
Hull 13 Kemble; Solal, Schofield, Leuluai,
O'Hara (1t); Topliss, Dean; Edmonds,
Wileman, Skerrett, Proctor (1t), L. Crooks,
Crane (1t, 1dg)

Castleford 2 Coen; Fenton, Marchant, Hyde
(Orum), Kear; Joyner, R. Beardmore (1g);
Connell, Horton, Reilly, Timson, James,
England
Referee: W.H. Thompson (Huddersfield)
1984-85
Hull 29 Kemble (2t); Leuluai, Schofield (4g,
1dg), S. Evans (1t), O'Hara; Ah Kuoi,
Sterling; Edmonds, Patrick, L. Crooks (1t),
Norton (1t), Proctor, Divorty (Rose)
Hull K.R. 12 Fairbairn (1t); Clark, Robinson
(1t), Prohm, Laws; M. Smith, Harkin (Rudd);
Broadhurst, Watkinson, Ema (Hartley),
Burton, Kelly, Hall (1t)
Referee: G.F. Lindop (Wakefield)
1985-86
Hull K.R. 22 Fairbairn (Lydiat); Clark (1t),
Dorahy (5g), Prohm, Laws; G. Smith, Harkin;
Des Harrison, Watkinson, Ema, Burton, Hogan
(Kelly), Miller (2t)
Castleford 18 Lord; Plange, Marchant (2t),
Hyde, Spears; Diamond (1g), R. Beardmore
(1t, 2g); Ward, K. Beardmore, B. Johnson,
England, Ketteridge, Joyner
Referee: R. Campbell (Widnes)
1986-87
Castleford 31 Scott; Plange, Marchant, Johns,
Hyde (Lord); Joyner, R. Beardmore (1dg);
Ward (1t), K. Beardmore (2t), B. Johnson,
Ketteridge (1t, 5g), Atkins (1t) (Shillito),
England
Hull 24 Kemble; Brand (2t), Schofield, O'Hara
(2t), Eastwood; Ah Kuoi, Windley; Brown
(Puckering), S. Patrick, Dannatt, Norton
(Divorty), L. Crooks (4g), Sharp
Referee: J. McDonald (Wigan)
1987-88
Bradford N. 12 Mercer; Ford, McGowan,
Simpson, Francis; Mumby (2g), Harkin;
Grayshon (Hobbs 2g), Noble, Hill, Skerrett,
Fairbank (1t), Holmes (Roebuck)
Castleford 12 Roockley; Plange (1t), Marchant,
Beattie, Hyde; Joyner, R. Southernwood;
Shillito (R. Beardmore), K. Beardmore
(Sampson), Ward, Ketteridge (2g), Fifita,
Lindner (1t)
Referee: K. Allatt (Southport)
Replay
Bradford N. 11 Mumby; Ford, McGowan,
Mercer, Simpson; Stewart, Harkin; Hobbs (1g,
1dg), Noble, Hill (1t), Skerrett, Fairbank,
Heron (1t)
Castleford 2 Roockley; Plange, Marchant,
Beattie, Hyde; R. Southernwood, R.
Beardmore; Ward, Hill, Fifita (Sampson),
Ketteridge (1g), England (Boothroyd), Joyner
Referee: K. Allatt (Southport)

THE WHITE ROSE TROPHY

First awarded in 1966, the trophy is presented to the adjudged man of the match in the Yorkshire Cup final.

Donated by the late T.E. Smith, of York, the award is organised by the Yorkshire Federation of Rugby League Supporters' Clubs and judged by a panel of the Press.

The trophy is not awarded in replays, although Bradford Northern's Brendan Hill was named Man of the Match in the second game against Castleford in 1987.

Season	Winner	Team	Position
1966-67	Cyril Kellett	Hull K.R. (v. Featherstone R.)	Full back
1967-68	Chris Davidson	Hull (v. Hull K.R.)	Scrum half
1968-69	Barry Seabourne	Leeds (v. Castleford)	Scrum half
1969-70	Joe Brown	Hull (v. Featherstone R.)	Loose forward
1970-71	Syd Hynes	Leeds (v. Featherstone R.)	Centre
1971-72	Ian Markham	Hull K.R. (v. Castleford)	Full back
1972-73	John Holmes	Leeds (v. Dewsbury)	Full back
1973-74	Keith Hepworth	Leeds (v. Wakefield T.)	Scrum half
1974-75	Roger Millward	Hull K.R. (v. Wakefield T.)	Stand off
1975-76	Neil Fox	Hull K.R. (v. Leeds)	Second row
1976-77	Les Dyl	Leeds (v. Featherstone R.)	Centre
1977-78	Bruce Burton	Castleford (v. Featherstone R.)	Stand off
1978-79	Bob Haigh	Bradford N. (v. York)	Loose forward
1979-80	Alan Smith	Leeds (v. Halifax)	Winger
1980-81	Kevin Dick	Leeds (v. Hull K.R.)	Scrum half
1981-82	Barry Johnson	Castleford (v. Bradford N.)	Prop
1982-83	Keith Mumby	Bradford N. (v. Hull)	Full back
1983-84	Mick Crane	Hull (v. Castleford)	Loose forward
1984-85	Peter Sterling	Hull (v. Hull K.R.)	Scrum half
1985-86	Gavin Miller	Hull K.R. (v. Castleford)	Loose forward
1986-87	Kevin Beardmore	Castleford (v. Hull)	Hooker
1987-88	Paul Harkin	Bradford N. (v. Castleford)	Scrum half
1988-89	Cliff Lyons	Leeds (v. Castleford)	Stand Off

YORKSHIRE CUP FINAL RECORDS

TEAM
Most appearances: 21 Leeds
Most wins: 17 Leeds
Highest score: Leeds 36 v. Dewsbury 9............ 1972
Widest margin win: Huddersfield 31 v. Hull 0... 1914
Biggest attendance:
36,000 Bradford N. v. Huddersfield (at Leeds).. 1949

INDIVIDUAL
Most tries:
4 by Stan Moorhouse (Huddersfield) v. Leeds.... 1919
Most points:
14 (5g, 1t) by Martin Ketteridge (Castleford)
  v. Hull 1986
Most goals:
6 by David Stephenson (Leeds) v. Castleford.......1988

Leeds skipper Lee Crooks with the Yorkshire Cup.

1988 CHARITY SHIELD

Widnes collected their first piece of silverware in the barrel shape of the Isle of Man Breweries Charity Shield by performing the task which eluded them four times during their Stones Bitter Championship and Premiership double campaign ... beating Wigan.

The Chemics laid their Wigan hoodoo after failing to topple the cherry-and-whites in four meetings during the previous season. Widnes led 20-4 after an hour, before the Silk Cut Challenge Cup holders restored respectability with two late Tony Iro tries.

A record Charity Shield crowd of 5,044 — in what was to be the last annual event on the island — saw Wigan take the lead against the run of play after 16 minutes when stand off Ged Byrne and centre Dean Bell combined to put Joe Lydon over for a try. Great Britain replacement tourist Andy Currier hit a penalty goal four minutes later and Widnes then took a lead they were never to surrender.

The scorer was the man who had dominated the tryscoring scene for the past year, Great Britain winger Martin Offiah, top of the try chart with 44 the previous season and leading scorer on the summer tour Down Under with 19 touchdowns. Offiah struck in the 26th minute, slicing through the Wigan defence and beating four men on the way to the line, Currier adding the goal.

Lacking four of their Wembley side, including skipper Ellery Hanley on Sydney Premiership duty with Balmain, Wigan struggled to find their traditional cohesion in a bid to maintain an unbeaten record on their third Charity Shield appearance.

A determined Chemics side provided a killer blow on the stroke of half-time when centre Darren Wright went over for a try, Currier adding the goal to open up a 14-4 scoreline.

Nine minutes into the second half Australian hooker Phil McKenzie scored a top-class try to virtually seal victory for Widnes. The former Rochdale Hornets number nine offered an outrageous dummy to Great Britain full back Steve Hampson and drifted over untouched, Currier again obliging with his fourth successful kick at goal from five attempts to take the score to 20-4.

Wigan coach Graham Lowe then reaped the benefit of a tactical substitution which saw Great Britain Under-21 prop Ian Lucas come on for winger Mark Preston, allowing New Zealander Tony Iro to return to his customary wing role after a first half experimental spell in the second row.

Relishing the familiar surroundings, Iro used his strong running to touch down in the 59th and 75th minutes, Lydon adding the goal to the first try, his only success in four attempts.

But Wigan's valiant comeback ran out of time and Widnes took the Isle of Man Breweries Charity Shield and a £6,000 prize cheque at their first attempt. The Jack Bentley Memorial Trophy for the Man of the Match went to Widnes hooker McKenzie, the previous three recipients being stand offs.

Widnes tryscorer Darren Wright.

ISLE OF MAN BREWERIES CHARITY SHIELD

21 August   **Douglas Bowl, Isle of Man**

WIDNES 20		WIGAN 14
Alan Tait	1.	Steve Hampson
Rick Thackray	2.	Henderson Gill
Andy Currier	3.	Joe Lydon
Darren Wright	4.	Dean Bell
Martin Offiah	5.	Mark Preston
Barry Dowd	6.	Ged Byrne
David Hulme	7.	Andy Gregory
Kurt Sorensen, Capt.	8.	Adrian Shelford
Phil McKenzie	9.	Nicky Kiss
Joe Grima	10.	Brian Case
Mike O'Neill	11.	Tony Iro
Paul Hulme	12.	Shaun Wane
Richard Eyres	13.	Andy Goodway
Steve O'Neill	14.	Dennis Betts
Derek Pyke	15.	Ian Lucas

T: Offiah, Wright, McKenzie
G: Currier (4)
Substitution:
Pyke for Grima (63 min.)
Half Time: 14-4
Referee: Ray Tennant (Castleford)

T: Iro (2), Lydon
G: Lydon
Substitutions:
Lucas for Preston (45 min.)
Betts for Shelford (66 min.)
Attendance: 5,044

CHARITY SHIELD ROLL OF HONOUR

Year	Winners		Runners-up		Attendance
1985-86	Wigan	34	Hull K.R.	6	4,066
1986-87	Halifax	9	Castleford	8	3,276
1987-88	Wigan	44	Halifax	12	4,804
1988-89	Widnes	20	Wigan	14	5,044

CHARITY SHIELD .... A REVIEW

1985-86
Wigan 34 Hampson; P. Ford, Stephenson (7g), Donlan (2t), Gill (2t); Edwards, M. Ford (1t); Courtney (Mayo), Kiss, Campbell, West (Lucas), Du Toit, Wane
Hull K.R. 6 Fairbairn (Lydiat 1g); Clark (1t), Robinson, Prohm, Laws; M. Smith, G. Smith; Des Harrison, Watkinson, Ema, Kelly (Rudd), Burton, Hogan
Referee: R. Campbell (Widnes)

1986-87
Halifax 9 Smith (Wilson); Riddlesden, Whitfield (1t), Hague (1dg), George (1t); C. Anderson, Stephens; Dickinson, McCallion, Juliff, Scott (James), Bell, Dixon

Castleford 8 Roockley; Plange, Lord (1t), Irwin (R. Southernwood), Spears; Joyner (Fletcher), R. Beardmore; Ward, K. Beardmore, Johnson, Ketteridge (2g), Mountain, England
Referee: G. F. Lindop (Wakefield)

1987-88
Wigan 44 Hampson (2t); Stephenson (8g), Byrne (Russell), Bell (2t), Gill (1t); Edwards (2t), Gregory; West, Kiss, Case, Gildart (Wane), Potter, Goodway
Halifax 12 Eadie (2g); Taylor, Wilson, T. Anderson, George; Simpson (Juliff, 1t), Stephens; Dickinson, Pendlebury, Beevers, James, Scott (Bell), Dixon (1t)
Referee: J. Holdsworth (Kippax)

MAN OF THE MATCH AWARDS

Season	Winner	Team	Position
1985-86	Shaun Edwards	Wigan (v. Hull K.R.)	Stand off
1986-87	Chris Anderson	Halifax (v. Castleford)	Stand off
1987-88	Shaun Edwards	Wigan (v. Halifax)	Stand off
1988-89	Phil McKenzie	Widnes (v. Wigan)	Hooker

● From 1987 it became the Jack Bentley Trophy in memory of the former Daily Express Rugby League journalist.

EUROPEAN CLUB CHAMPIONSHIP

Widnes were crowned European Champions in the final act of a French farce. The Chemics' encounter with their French counterparts was originally conceived after their 1988 title success as the European sector of a World Club Championship. The home-and-away Northern Hemisphere leg was scheduled for March but was cancelled when the International Board scrapped plans for the World tournament and a final to be staged in Japan. The League bowed to a French request for the Euro-title to be decided with a one-off meeting at Le Pontet at the end of the season even though the 1989 champions would have been decided. Ironically, Widnes retained their crown but three days before the 27 May fixture, Le Pontet withdrew after having Marc Palanque stripped of his captaincy and hooker Christian Macalli banned for six months for their part in the assault of the referee in the Championship final with St. Esteve 10 days earlier. New Champions St. Esteve accepted the invitation to meet Widnes at the new venue of Arles after more than a week of celebrations. The Anglo-French title decider was then boycotted by the French public and media, a crowd of 350 consisting almost wholly of Widnes fans with another two coachloads arriving after the final whistle and more than 200 stranded at Newhaven after missing their ferry.

27 May — **Arles**

WIDNES 60		ST. ESTEVE 6
David Marsh	1.	Jean Philippe Pougeau
Rick Thackray	2.	Hugues Ratier
Jonathan Davies	3.	Brian Coles
Darren Wright	4.	Michel Roses
Brimah Kebbie	5.	Jean-Luc Tene
Tony Myler	6.	Roger Palisses
Paul Hulme	7.	Bruno Castany
Kurt Sorensen	8.	David Barker
Phil McKenzie	9.	Mathieu Khedimi
Joe Grima	10.	Abet Baklouch
Mike O'Neill	11.	Morio Femia
Emosi Koloto	12.	Bernard Cartier
Richard Eyres	13.	Steve Robinson
Derek Pyke	14.	Dernard Guasch
Paul Moriarty	15.	Patrick Alberola

T: Thackray (4), Davies (2), Grima (2), Kebbie, Marsh, Moriarty
G: Davies (5), Kebbie (3)
Substitutions:
Moriarty for Sorensen (Half-time)
Pyke for Grima (48 min.)
Referee: Ray Tennant (Castleford)

T: Pougeau
G: Coles
Substitutions:
Alberola for Pougeau (35 min.)
Guasch for Femia (36 min.)
Half-time: 32-0
Attendance: 350

BBC-2 FLOODLIT TROPHY

The BBC-2 Floodlit Trophy competition was launched in 1965. Eight clubs competed in the first year and the total had grown to 22 by 1980 when the competition was abolished as part of the BBC's financial cut-backs.

For 15 years the matches became a regular television feature on Tuesday evenings throughout the early winter months.

Although the format changed slightly over the years, it was basically a knockout competition on the lines of the Challenge Cup.

In 1966 the Floodlit Competition was used to introduce the limited tackle rule, then four tackles, which proved such a great success it was adopted in all other matches before the end of the year.

BBC-2 FLOODLIT TROPHY FINALS
(Only the 1967, at Leeds, and 1972, at Wigan, finals were played on neutral grounds)

Season	Winners		Runners-up		Venue	Attendance	Receipts
1965-66	Castleford	4	St. Helens	0	St. Helens	11,510	£1,548
1966-67	Castleford	7	Swinton	2	Castleford	8,986	£1,692
1967-68	Castleford	8	Leigh	5	Leeds	9,716	£2,099
1968-69	Wigan	7	St. Helens	4	Wigan	13,479	£3,291
1969-70	Leigh	11	Wigan	6	Wigan	12,312	£2,854
1970-71	Leeds	9	St. Helens	5	Leeds	7,612	£2,189
1971-72	St. Helens	8	Rochdale H.	2	St. Helens	9,300	£2,493
1972-73	Leigh	5	Widnes	0	Wigan	4,691	£1,391
1973-74	Bramley	15	Widnes	7	Widnes	4,422	£1,538
1974-75	Salford	0	Warrington	0	Salford	4,473	£1,913
Replay	Salford	10	Warrington	5	Warrington	5,778	£2,434
1975-76	St. Helens	22	Dewsbury	2	St. Helens	3,858	£1,747
1976-77	Castleford	12	Leigh	4	Leigh	5,402	£2,793
1977-78	Hull K.R.	26	St. Helens	11	Hull K.R.	10,099	£6,586
1978-79	Widnes	13	St. Helens	7	St. Helens	10,250	£7,017
1979-80	Hull	13	Hull K.R.	3	Hull	18,500	£16,605

BBC2 FLOODLIT TROPHY . . . . A REVIEW
1965-66
Castleford 4 Edwards; C. Battye, M. Battye, Willett (2g), Briggs; Hardisty, Millward; Terry, J. Ward, C. Dickinson, Bryant, Taylor, Small
St. Helens 0 F. Barrow; Vollenhoven, Wood, Benyon, Killeen; Murphy, Prosser; French, Dagnall, Watson, Hicks, Mantle, Laughton
Referee: L. Gant (Wakefield)
1966-67
Castleford 7 Edwards; Howe, Stenton, Willett (1g), Austin (1t); Hardisty, Hepworth (1g); Hartley, C. Dickinson, McCartney, Bryant, Small, Walker
Swinton 2 Gowers; Whitehead (1g), Gomersall, Buckley, Davies; Fleet, G. Williams; Halliwell, D. Clarke, Scott (Cummings), Rees, Simpson, Robinson
Referee: J. Manley (Warrington)
1967-68
Castleford 8 Edwards; Harris, Thomas, Stenton, Willett (4g); Hardisty, Hepworth; Hartley, J. Ward, Walton, Bryant (C. Dickinson), Redfearn, Reilly

Leigh 5 Grainey; Tickle (1t), Lewis, Collins, Walsh; Entwistle, A. Murphy; Whitworth, Ashcroft, Major, Welding, M. Murphy, Gilfedder (1g)
Referee: G.F. Lindop (Wakefield)
1968-69
Wigan 7 Tyrer (2g); Francis, Ashton, Ashurst, Rowe; C. Hill (1t), Jackson; J. Stephens, Clarke, Mills, Fogerty (Lyon), Kevin O'Loughlin, Laughton
St. Helens 4 Williams; Wilson, Benyon, Myler, Wills; Whittle, Bishop; Warlow, Sayer, Watson, Mantle, Hogan, Coslett (2g)
Referee: E. Clay (Leeds)
1969-70
Leigh 11 Ferguson (3g) (Lewis); Tickle (1t), Dorrington, Collins, Walsh; Eckersley, Murphy (1g); D. Chisnall, Ashcroft, Watts, Welding, Grimes, Lyon
Wigan 6 C. Hill; Wright, Francis (2g), Rowe, Kevin O'Loughlin; D. Hill (1g), Jackson; J. Stephens, Clarke, Ashcroft, Ashurst, Mills, Laughton
Referee: W.H. Thompson (Huddersfield)

1970-71
Leeds 9 Holmes (2g); Alan Smith, Hynes (1t, 1g), Cowan, Atkinson; Wainwright, Shoebottom; J. Burke, Fisher, Barnard, Haigh, Ramsey, Batten
St. Helens 5 F. Barrow; L. Jones (1t), Benyon, Walsh, Wilson; Whittle, Heaton; Rees, A. Karalius, E. Chisnall, Mantle, E. Prescott, Coslett (1g)
Referee: E. Lawrinson (Warrington)
1971-72
St. Helens 8 G. Pimblett; L. Jones, Benyon, Walsh, Wilson; Kelly, Heaton; Rees, A. Karalius, E. Chisnall, E. Prescott, Mantle, Coslett (4g)
Rochdale H. 2 Chamberlain (1g); Brelsford, Crellin, Taylor, Glover; Myler, Gartland; Birchall, P. Clarke, Brown, Welding, Sheffield (Hodkinson), Delooze
Referee: E. Clay (Leeds)
1972-73
Leigh 5 Hogan; Lawson (1t) (Lester), Atkin, Collins, Stacey; A. Barrow, Sayer (Ryding); Grimes, D. Clarke, Fletcher, Fiddler (1g), F. Barrow, Martyn
Widnes 0 Dutton; A. Prescott, Aspey, Blackwood, McDonnell; Lowe, Ashton; Mills, Elwell, Warlow, Foran, Sheridan, Nicholls
Referee: G.F. Lindop (Wakefield)
1973-74
Bramley 15 Keegan; Goodchild (1t), Bollon, Hughes, Austin (1t); T. Briggs, Ward (1g) (Ashman); D. Briggs, Firth, Cheshire, D. Sampson (1t), Idle, Wolford (2g)
Widnes 7 Dutton (2g); D. O'Neill, Hughes, Aspey, Macko (1t); Warburton, Bowden; Hogan, Elwell, Nelson, Sheridan, Blackwood (Foran) Laughton
Referee: D. G. Kershaw (York)

1974-75
Salford 0 Charlton; Fielding, Hesketh, Graham, Richards; Brophy (Taylor), Banner; Coulman, Devlin, Grice, Knighton, Dixon, E. Prescott
Warrington 0 Whitehead; Sutton, Cunliffe (Lowe), Whittle, Bevan; Briggs, Gordon; D. Chisnall, Ashcroft, Wright, Gaskell, Conroy, B. Philbin (Jewitt)
Referee: W.H. Thompson (Huddersfield)
Replay
Salford 10 Stead; Fielding (1t), Watkins (2g), Hesketh, Richards (1t); Gill, Banner; Grice, Walker, Mackay, Dixon, Knighton, E. Prescott

Warrington 5 Cunliffe; Whitehead (1g), Pickup, Whittle, Bevan (1t); Noonan (Briggs), Gordon; D. Chisnall, Ashcroft, Wanbon, Conroy, Nicholas (Brady), B. Philbin
Referee: W.H. Thompson (Huddersfield)
1975-76
St. Helens 22 G. Pimblett (2g); L. Jones, Benyon (1t), Hull (1t), Mathias (2t); Wilson (1t), Heaton (1dg); Mantle, A. Karalius, James, Nicholls, E. Chisnall, Coslett (1g)
Dewsbury 2 Langley; Hegarty, Chalkley, Simpson, Mitchell; N. Stephenson (1g) (Lee), A. Bates; Beverley, Price, Hankins, Halloran (Artis), Bell, Grayshon
Referee: W.H. Thompson (Huddersfield)
1976-77
Castleford 12 Wraith; Fenton, Joyner, P. Johnson, Walsh (1t); Burton (1t), Stephens; Khan, Spurr, A. Dickinson, Reilly, Lloyd (3g), S. Norton
Leigh 4 Hogan; A. Prescott, Stacey, Woods, Walsh (1t); Taylor, Sayer; D. Chisnall, Ashcroft (1dg), Fletcher, Macko, Grimes, Boyd
Referee: J.E. Jackson (Pudsey)
1977-78
Hull K.R. 26 Hall (4g); Dunn (2t), M. Smith (1t), Watson, Sullivan (1t); Hartley (1t), Millward; Millington, Watkinson, Cunningham (Hughes), Lowe, Rose (1t), Casey
St. Helens 11 G. Pimblett (Platt); L. Jones (Courtney), Noonan, Cunningham (1t), Glynn (2t, 1g); Francis, K. Gwilliam; D. Chisnall, Liptrot, James, Hope, A. Karalius, Pinner
Referee: M. J. Naughton (Widnes)
1978-79
Widnes 13 Eckersley; Wright (2t), Hughes, Aspey, P. Shaw; Burke (2g, 1t), Bowden; Hogan, Elwell, Mills, Adams, Dearden, Laughton
St. Helens 7 G. Pimblett (2g), L. Jones, Glynn, Cunningham, Mathias; Francis, Holding; D. Chisnall (1t), Liptrot, James, Nicholls, Knighton (E. Chisnall), Pinner
Referee: J. McDonald (Wigan)
1979-80
Hull 13 Woods; Bray, G. Evans (1t), Coupland, Dennison (1t, 2g); Newlove, Hepworth; Tindall, Wileman, Farrar, Stone, Boxall (Birdsall 1t), Norton
Hull K.R. 3 Robinson; Hubbard (1t), M. Smith, Watson, Sullivan; Hall, Agar; Holdstock, Tyreman, Lockwood, Clarkson (Hartley), Lowe, Hogan (Millington)
Referee: W.H. Thompson (Huddersfield)

CAPTAIN MORGAN TROPHY

This sponsored competition, with a winners' prize of £3,000, lasted only one season. Entry was restricted to the 16 clubs who won their Yorkshire and Lancashire Cup first round ties. The Lancashire contingent was made up to eight by including the side which lost their first round county Cup-tie by the narrowest margin. The first round of the Captain Morgan Trophy was zoned with clubs being drawn against those in their own county. The remainder of the competition was integrated. The final was on a neutral ground as follows:

1973-74	Warrington	4	Featherstone R.	0	Salford	5,259	£2,265

1973-74
Warrington 4 Whitehead (2g); M. Philbin, Noonan, Reynolds (Pickup), Bevan; Whittle, Gordon; D. Chisnall, Ashcroft, Brady, Wanbon (Price), Wright, Mather

Featherstone R. 0 Box; Coventry, M. Smith, Hartley, Bray; Mason, Wood; Tonks, Bridges, Harris, Gibbins (Stone), Rhodes, Bell
Referee: G.F. Lindop (Wakefield)

Tongan Emosi Koloto, an outstanding new recruit from New Zealand Rugby Union for 1988-89 Stones Bitter Champions, Widnes.

LEAGUE

1988-89 CHAMPIONSHIP

Widnes and Wigan met in a title showdown at Naughton Park on the last day of an eight-month campaign to determine the destiny of the Stones Bitter Championship Trophy and a record prize cheque for £25,000. Corals had quoted Wigan as pre-season 7-4 title favourites with Widnes next at 4-1.

Needing only a draw, the Chemics lifted the coveted trophy by running in six tries in a 32-18 victory, highlighted by a Martin Offiah hat-trick and witnessed by a capacity crowd of 17,323 – a Division One record for Widnes.

They became the fourth club to retain the First Division title, emulating Swinton, Bradford Northern and Hull K.R.

Wigan received a consolation prize cheque for £10,000 as runners-up, big spenders Leeds missing out on second spot by crashing 38-10 at Castleford on the same afternoon.

Castleford had been title pacesetters for most of the season after Wakefield Trinity held top spot in the opening weeks by winning their opening three games, having been promoted from third place in the Second Division. Under new Australian coach Darryl Van de Velde, Castleford took over the leadership on 25 September and did not relinquish it until 19 March.

They lost only one and drew one of their first 16 Championship fixtures, going down 21-12 at Halifax and levelling 14-apiece at St. Helens. After a second round exit from the Silk Cut Challenge Cup, Castleford had a disastrous run-in to their bid for a first Championship success, winning only one and drawing one of their last 10 league matches.

Leeds took over the number one position one point ahead of Widnes, having played four more matches. The Loiners enjoyed pole place for only 11 days before the Chemics made up their backlog to lead by one point with three matches in hand. During one four-day spell in March, Castleford, Leeds and Widnes exchanged the leadership.

Wigan, meanwhile, were entering the final frame by losing only one Championship match in 15 between mid-December and mid-April, including a run of 11 consecutive league wins, which complemented a run-in to a Wembley appearance.

At the bottom of the 14-club table Halifax and Hull K.R., both recent champions, were shock relegation victims, along with Oldham, promoted as Second Division Champions 12 months earlier.

Halifax's new Australian team manager, Ross Strudwick, began with a 26-20 home win over champions Widnes before the slump began. The club was embroiled in a row over the stepping down as coach of 1987 Lance Todd Trophy winner Graham Eadie before the season began and his subsequent axing from the overseas quota allocation. While the off-the-field unrest ensued, the Thrum Hallers won only two of their next 15 fixtures up to the start of February.

With relegation looming, Strudwick was sacked and former Great Britain half back Alan Hardisty promoted from physiotherapist to caretaker coach for the last eight matches which produced two wins.

Gloom struck twice in East Hull, where the Robins were relegated at the end of their last season at the old Craven Park ground before moving to a new stadium on the Greatfield Estate. With Roger Millward in his 12th full season as coach, Rovers lost their opening three games and when the pressure was on in the final third of the campaign could muster only one victory in their last eight matches to repeat the drop of 15 years earlier.

The two other sides promoted a year earlier, Featherstone Rovers and Wakefield Trinity, battled hard for Championship survival, Rovers reaching an impressive sixth position despite starting as 100-1 outsiders for the title. Under coach Peter Fox, Rovers found increased confidence as the season progressed, taking 11 points from their last seven matches.

Trinity opened in style with a hat-trick of league victories at home to Warrington and Wigan and away at Hull which put them on top. Then relegation began to haunt them as they collected only five points from a possible 30 before securing six victories in their last eight games to finish ninth. The early departure of overseas Test players Mark Graham, Steve Ella and Brent Todd were unexpected blows for Trinity.

One of the success stories in the dramatic title chase was the influence of new Australian coach Brian Smith at the Boulevard where Hull had finished the previous campaign in 10th position and were restricted by a limited budget. The former Illawara coach brought over three Australians — David Boyle, Craig Coleman and David Moon — but started his British career with four successive league defeats. The Airlie Birds laid the foundations for their top four spot with only three defeats in their next 17 league matches, including nine victories on the trot.

In the Second Division, 7-4 favourites Leigh took the Championship Bowl for the third time. Promotion was their fourth up-or-down movement in the league in five years and their table-topping feat was sealed with only two defeats in the 28-match campaign, highlighted by a run-in of 12 successive victories from 8 January onwards to earn a £12,000 Stones Bitter prize cheque.

Barrow were also promoted, as runners-up nine points behind Leigh, their 11th switch of divisions in 14 seasons. Sheffield Eagles gained promotion in only their fifth season, inspired by the losing of only two matches out of 18 between the end of October and the final days of March, featuring a run of nine consecutive wins. Mainstays of the high-flying Eagles were founder and coach Gary Hetherington plus skipper Darryl Powell, voted Greenalls Second Division Player of the Year.

Elsewhere in the division, Doncaster opened with a club record eight successive victories and staked a promotion claim before

falling away with only one success in their last six games. Huddersfield started the campaign with one point from 11 matches before being taken over by new management to finish the season with four consecutive wins. Batley were also subject to boardroom changes and the new regime celebrated with seven wins in the last eight games.

Troubled Runcorn Highfield finished bottom, collecting only five points in a season when Bill Ashurst, John Cogger and Geoff Fletcher took turns in holding the coaching reins.

Widnes skipper Kurt Sorensen lifts the 1989 Stones Bitter Championship Trophy.

Chris Johnson, top goal and points scorer for Second Division Champions Leigh.

The 1988-89 Stones Bitter Second Division Champions Leigh with the prized Bowl.

FINAL TABLES 1988-89

STONES BITTER CHAMPIONSHIP

	P.	W.	D.	L.	Dr.	FOR Gls.	FOR Trs.	FOR Pts.	Dr.	AGAINST Gls.	AGAINST Trs.	AGAINST Pts.	Pts.
Widnes	26	20	1	5	4	99	131	726	5	62	54	345	41
Wigan	26	19	0	7	5	83	93	543	8	75	69	434	38
Leeds	26	18	0	8	2	72	96	530	6	61	63	380	36
Hull	26	17	0	9	15	86	60	427	5	59	58	355	34
Castleford	26	15	2	9	1	102	99	601	6	83	77	480	32
Featherstone R.	26	13	1	12	8	81	78	482	9	74	97	545	27
St. Helens	26	12	1	13	7	89	82	513	5	88	87	529	25
Bradford N.	26	11	1	14	7	97	86	545	2	86	86	518	23
Wakefield T.	26	11	1	14	5	66	69	413	4	74	97	540	23
Salford	26	11	0	15	3	61	86	469	6	94	83	526	22
Warrington	26	10	0	16	6	73	76	456	9	81	71	455	20
Oldham	26	8	1	17	6	66	81	462	4	94	110	632	17
Halifax	26	6	1	19	5	49	58	335	5	79	93	535	13
Hull K.R.	26	6	1	19	6	83	59	408	6	97	109	636	13

Corals pre-season betting for the 1988-89 Championship: 7-4 Wigan; 4-1 Widnes; 5-1 St. Helens; 7-1 Leeds; 10-1 Warrington; 12-1 Bradford N; 16-1 Castleford, Halifax; 20-1 Hull K.R.; 25-1 Hull; 50-1 Oldham, Salford, Wakefield T; 100-1 Featherstone R.

SECOND DIVISION

	P.	W.	D.	L.	Dr.	FOR Gls.	FOR Trs.	FOR Pts.	Dr.	AGAINST Gls.	AGAINST Trs.	AGAINST Pts.	Pts.
Leigh	28	26	0	2	3	127	167	925	6	64	51	338	52
Barrow	28	21	1	6	4	107	127	726	4	47	57	326	43
Sheffield E.	28	19	1	8	11	103	113	669	12	55	60	362	39
York	28	17	1	10	11	89	99	585	11	62	62	383	35
Swinton	28	16	2	10	5	88	110	621	12	75	80	482	34
Doncaster	28	17	0	11	7	104	96	599	8	78	75	464	34
Whitehaven	28	15	2	11	10	82	87	522	8	61	62	378	32
Keighley	28	16	0	12	3	92	91	551	7	81	89	525	32
Rochdale H.	28	15	0	13	1	107	110	655	3	107	115	677	30
Bramley	28	14	1	13	6	89	104	600	12	85	83	514	29
Carlisle	28	14	1	13	6	91	81	512	7	71	73	441	29
Batley	28	13	3	12	27	63	77	461	10	59	72	416	29
Dewsbury	28	13	0	15	12	93	80	518	8	101	104	626	26
Hunslet	28	12	1	15	11	67	82	473	10	89	88	540	25
Fulham	28	10	0	18	10	77	75	464	8	95	113	650	20
Chorley B.	28	9	1	18	8	60	70	408	7	93	85	533	19
Workington T.	28	9	1	18	7	63	58	365	9	80	95	549	19
Huddersfield	28	9	1	18	10	55	70	400	9	91	106	615	19
Mansfield M.	28	4	1	23	6	55	48	308	7	107	137	769	9
Runcorn H.	28	2	1	25	4	32	39	224	4	143	177	998	5

Corals pre-season betting for the 1988-89 Championship: 7-4 Leigh; 7-2 Swinton; 9-2 Hunslet; 8-1 Barrow; 10-1 York; 14-1 Sheffield E.; 20-1 Chorley B., Whitehaven; 25-1 Workington T.; 33-1 Carlisle, Mansfield M.; 50-1 Runcorn H.; 66-1 Bramley, Dewsbury, Doncaster; 100-1 Fulham, Rochdale H.; 150-1 Batley; 200-1 Huddersfield.

TWO DIVISION CHAMPIONSHIP ROLL OF HONOUR

	FIRST DIVISION	SECOND DIVISION
1902-03	Halifax	Keighley
1903-04	Bradford	Wakefield Trinity
1904-05	Oldham	Dewsbury
1962-63	Swinton	Hunslet
1963-64	Swinton	Oldham
1973-74	Salford	Bradford Northern
1974-75	St. Helens	Huddersfield
1975-76	Salford	Barrow
1976-77	Featherstone Rovers	Hull
1977-78	Widnes	Leigh
1978-79	Hull Kingston Rovers	Hull
1979-80	Bradford Northern	Featherstone Rovers
1980-81	Bradford Northern	York
1981-82	Leigh	Oldham
1982-83	Hull	Fulham
1983-84	Hull Kingston Rovers	Barrow
1984-85	Hull Kingston Rovers	Swinton
1985-86	Halifax	Leigh
1986-87	Wigan	Hunslet
1987-88	Widnes	Oldham
1988-89	Widnes	Leigh

THE UPS AND DOWNS OF TWO DIVISION FOOTBALL
Since re-introduction of two divisions in 1973-74.

● Figure in brackets indicates position in division.

	RELEGATED	PROMOTED
1973-74	Oldham (13)	Bradford Northern (1)
	Hull K.R. (14)	York (2)
	Leigh (15)	Keighley (3)
	Whitehaven (16)	Halifax (4)
1974-75	York (13)	Huddersfield (1)
	Bramley (14)	Hull K.R. (2)
	Rochdale Hornets (15)	Oldham (3)
	Halifax (16)	Swinton (4)
1975-76	Dewsbury (13)	Barrow (1)
	Keighley (14)	Rochdale Hornets (2)
	Huddersfield (15)	Workington T. (3)
	Swinton (16)	Leigh (4)

1976-77	Rochdale Hornets (13)	Hull (1)
	Leigh (14)	Dewsbury (2)
	Barrow (15)	Bramley (3)
	Oldham (16)	New Hunslet (4)
1977-78	Hull (13)	Leigh (1)
	New Hunslet (14)	Barrow (2)
	Bramley (15)	Rochdale Hornets (3)
	Dewsbury (16)	Huddersfield (4)
1978-79	Barrow (13)	Hull (1)
	Featherstone Rovers (14)	New Hunslet (2)
	Rochdale Hornets (15)	York (3)
	Huddersfield (16)	Blackpool Borough (4)
1979-80	Wigan (13)	Featherstone Rovers (1)
	Hunslet (14)	Halifax (2)
	York (15)	Oldham (3)
	Blackpool Borough (16)	Barrow (4)
1980-81	Halifax (13)	York (1)
	Salford (14)	Wigan (2)
	Workington T. (15)	Fulham (3)
	Oldham (16)	Whitehaven (4)
1981-82	Fulham (13)	Oldham (1)
	Wakefield T. (14)	Carlisle (2)
	York (15)	Workington T. (3)
	Whitehaven (16)	Halifax (4)
1982-83	Barrow (13)	Fulham (1)
	Workington T. (14)	Wakefield T. (2)
	Halifax (15)	Salford (3)
	Carlisle (16)	Whitehaven (4)
1983-84	Fulham (13)	Barrow (1)
	Wakefield T. (14)	Workington T. (2)
	Salford (15)	Hunslet (3)
	Whitehaven (16)	Halifax (4)
1984-85	Barrow (13)	Swinton (1)
	Leigh (14)	Salford (2)
	Hunslet (15)	York (3)
	Workington T. (16)	Dewsbury (4)
1985-86	York (14)	Leigh (1)
	Swinton (15)	Barrow (2)
	Dewsbury (16)	Wakefield T. (3)
1986-87	Oldham (13)	Hunslet (1)
	Featherstone R. (14)	Swinton (2)
	Barrow (15)	
	Wakefield T. (16)	
1987-88	Leigh (12)	Oldham (1)
	Swinton (13)	Featherstone R. (2)
	Hunslet (14)	Wakefield T. (3)
1988-89	Oldham (12)	Leigh (1)
	Halifax (13)	Barrow (2)
	Hull K.R. (14)	Sheffield E. (3)

FIRST DIVISION RECORDS
Since reintroduction in 1973

INDIVIDUAL

Match records

Most tries:
6 Shane Cooper (St. Helens) v. Hull Feb 17, 1988

Most goals: 13 Geoff Pimblett (St. Helens) v. Bramley
Mar 5, 1978

Most points: 38 (11g, 4t) Bob Beardmore (Castleford) v.
Barrow Mar 22, 1987

Season records

Most tries: 44 Ellery Hanley (Wigan) 1986-87
Most goals: 130 Steve Hesford (Warrington) 1978-79
Most points: 295 (101g, 1dg, 23t) John Woods (Leigh)
1983-84

TEAM

Highest score: Castleford 76 v. Swinton 16 Mar 16, 1988

Biggest away win and widest margin: Wakefield T. 6 v.
Wigan 72 Mar 29, 1987

Most points by losing team: Hunslet 40 v. Barrow 41
Sep 9, 1984

Scoreless draw: Wigan 0 v. Castleford 0 Jan 26, 1974

Highest score draw: Hunslet 32 v. Swinton 32
Sep 20, 1987

Best opening sequence: 13 wins then a draw by Widnes
1981-82

Longest winning run: 25 by St. Helens
Won last 13 of 1985-86 and first 12 of 1986-87.
(Also longest unbeaten run.)

Longest losing run: 20 by Whitehaven 1983-84

Longest run without a win: 23, including 3 draws, by
Whitehaven 1981-82 (Also worst opening sequence)

Biggest attendance: 23,809 Wigan v. St. Helens
Dec 27, 1987

100 Division One tries
178 Ellery Hanley (Bradford N., Wigan)
165 Keith Fielding (Salford)
144 David Smith (Wakefield T., Leeds, Bradford N.)
139 Stuart Wright (Wigan, Widnes)
136 Roy Mathias (St. Helens)
130 John Bevan (Warrington)
129 John Joyner (Castleford)
126 Steve Hartley (Hull K.R.)
126 David Topliss (Wakefield T., Hull, Oldham)
125 John Woods (Leigh, Bradford N., Warrington)
122 Maurice Richards (Salford)
122 Steve Evans (Featherstone R., Hull, Wakefield T.,
Bradford N.)
113 David Redfearn (Bradford N.)
108 Phil Ford (Warrington, Wigan, Bradford N., Leeds)
108 Garry Schofield (Hull, Leeds)
105 Gary Hyde (Castleford, Oldham)
103 Keiron O'Loughlin (Wigan, Workington T.,
Widnes, Salford)
103 Henderson Gill (Bradford N., Wigan)
103 Des Drummond (Leigh, Warrington)

500 Division One goals
854 John Woods (Leigh, Bradford N., Warrington)
845 Steve Hesford (Warrington)
818 Steve Quinn (Featherstone R.)
811 George Fairbairn (Wigan, Hull K.R.)
586 Sammy Lloyd (Castleford, Hull)
574 Colin Whitfield (Salford, Wigan, Halifax)

1,000 Division One points
2,130 John Woods (Leigh, Bradford N.)
1,814 George Fairbairn (Wigan, Hull K.R.)
1,768 Steve Quinn (Featherstone R.)
1,756 Steve Hesford (Warrington)
1,396 Colin Whitfield (Salford, Wigan, Halifax)
1,264 Sammy Lloyd (Castleford, Hull)
1,127 Mick Burke (Widnes, Oldham)
1,115 Keith Mumby (Bradford N.)
1,103 Bob Beardmore (Castleford)

20 Division One tries in a season

Season	No.	Player
1973-74	36	Keith Fielding (Salford)
	29	Roy Mathias (St. Helens)
	21	David Smith (Wakefield T.)
1974-75	21	Maurice Richards (Salford)
	21	Roy Mathias (St. Helens)
1975-76	26	Maurice Richards (Salford)
	20	David Smith (Wakefield T.)
1976-77	22	David Topliss (Wakefield T.)
	21	Keith Fielding (Salford)
	21	Ged Dunn (Hull K.R.)
	20	David Smith (Leeds)
	20	Stuart Wright (Widnes)
1977-78	26	Keith Fielding (Salford)
	25	Steve Fenton (Castleford)
	24	Stuart Wright (Widnes)
	20	David Smith (Leeds)
	20	Bruce Burton (Castleford)
	20	John Bevan (Warrington)
1978-79	28	Steve Hartley (Hull K.R.)
1979-80	24	Keith Fielding (Salford)
	21	Roy Mathias (St. Helens)
	21	Steve Hubbard (Hull K.R.)
	20	David Smith (Leeds)
1980-81	20	Steve Hubbard (Hull K.R.)
1981-82		David Hobbs (Featherstone R.) was top scorer with 19 tries.
1982-83	22	Bob Eccles (Warrington)
	20	Steve Evans (Hull)
1983-84	28	Garry Schofield (Hull)
	23	John Woods (Leigh)
	20	James Leuluai (Hull)
1984-85	40	Ellery Hanley (Bradford N.)
	34	Gary Prohm (Hull K.R.)
	23	Henderson Gill (Wigan)
	22	Barry Ledger (St. Helens)
	22	Mal Meninga (St. Helens)
1985-86	22	Ellery Hanley (Wigan)
1986-87	44	Ellery Hanley (Wigan)
	24	Phil Ford (Bradford N.)
	24	Henderson Gill (Wigan)
	23	Garry Schofield (Hull)
	21	John Henderson (Leigh)
1987-88	33	Martin Offiah (Widnes)
	22	Ellery Hanley (Wigan)
1988-89	37	Martin Offiah (Widnes)
	20	Grant Anderson (Castleford)

Top Division One goalscorers

1973-74 126 David Watkins (Salford)
1974-75 96 Sammy Lloyd (Castleford)
1975-76 118 Sammy Lloyd (Castleford)
1976-77 113 Steve Quinn (Featherstone R.)
1977-78 116 Steve Hesford (Warrington)
1978-79 130 Steve Hesford (Warrington)
1979-80 104 Steve Hubbard (Hull K.R.)
1980-81 96 Steve Diamond (Wakefield T.)
1981-82 110 Steve Quinn (Featherstone R.)
        John Woods (Leigh)
1982-83 105 Bob Beardmore (Castleford)
1983-84 106 Steve Hesford (Warrington)
1984-85 114 Sean Day (St. Helens)
1985-86 85 David Stephenson (Wigan)
1986-87 120 Paul Loughlin (St. Helens)
1987-88 95 John Woods (Warrington)
1988-89 95 David Hobbs (Bradford N.)

Top Division One pointscorer 1988-89
214 (91g, 4dg, 7t) David Hobbs (Bradford N.)

SECOND DIVISION RECORDS
Since reintroduction in 1973

INDIVIDUAL

Match records

Most tries: 6 Ged Dunn (Hull K.R.) v. New Hunslet Feb 2, 1975

Most goals: 15 Mick Stacey (Leigh) v. Doncaster Mar 28, 1976

Most points: 38 (13g, 4t) John Woods (Leigh) v. Blackpool B. Sep 11, 1977

Season records

Most tries: 48 Steve Halliwell (Leigh) 1985-86

Most goals: 166 Lynn Hopkins (Workington T.) 1981-82

Most points: 395 (163g, 3dg, 22t) Lynn Hopkins (Workington T.) 1981-82

TEAM

Highest score: Leigh 92 v. Keighley 2 Apr 30, 1986 (Also widest margin)

Highest away: Runcorn H. 2 v. Leigh 88 Jan 15, 1989 (Also widest margin)

Most points by losing team:
Dewsbury 36 v. Rochdale H. 34 Oct 9, 1988

Highest score draw: Huddersfield B. 32 v. Keighley 32 Apr 17, 1986

Scoreless draw: Dewsbury 0 v. Rochdale H. 0. Jan 30, 1983

Longest winning run: 30 by Leigh in 1985-86. Hull won all 26 matches in 1978-79

Longest losing run: 40 by Doncaster (16 in 1975-76 and 24 in 1976-77)

Biggest attendance: 12,424 Hull v. New Hunslet May 18, 1979

1988-89 Top Division Two scorers

Most tries: 30 Barrie Ledger (Leigh)

Most goals: 110 Mark Aston (Sheffield E.)

Most points: 243 (98g, 3dg, 11t) Chris Johnson (Leigh)
NB. Division One and Two records do not include scores in abandoned matches that were replayed.

TWO DIVISION SCORING
The following tables show the scoring totals for each two-division season:

DIVISION ONE

Season	Matches each club played	Goals	1-Point drop goals	Tries	Pts
1973-74	30	1,508	—	1,295	6,901
1974-75	30	1,334	48	1,261	6,499
1975-76	30	1,498	53	1,331	7,042
1976-77	30[1]	1,435	91	1,423	7,230
1977-78	30[2]	1,402	99	1,443	7,232
1978-79	30	1,367	119	1,448	7,197
1979-80	30	1,389	131	1,349	6,956
1980-81	30	1,439	147	1,342	7,051
1981-82	30	1,486	132	1,354	7,166
1982-83	30	1,369	64	1,386	6,960
1983-84	30	1,472	108	1,479	8,968
1984-85	30	1,464	84	1,595	9,392
1985-86	30	1,296	80	1,435	8,412
1986-87	30	1,412	90	1,607	9,342
1987-88	26	1,070	75	1,170	6,895
1988-89	26	1,107	80	1,154	6,910

[1] Salford & Leeds played 29 matches — their final match was abandoned and not replayed. This match was expunged from league records.

[2] Featherstone R. & Bradford N. played 29 matches — their final match was cancelled following Featherstone's strike.

DIVISION TWO

Season	Matches each club played	Goals	1-Point drop goals	Tries	Pts
1973-74	26	1,054	—	955	4,973
1974-75	26	992	36	919	4,777
1975-76	26	1,034	49	963	5,006
1976-77	26	942	78	1,046	5,100
1977-78	26	976	86	1,020	5,098
1978-79	26	971	114	972	4,972
1979-80	26	1,046	106	1,069	5,405
1980-81	28	1,133	123	1,220	6,049
1981-82	32	1,636	152	1,589	8,189
1982-83	32	1,510	103	1,648	8,067
1983-84	34	1,782	254	1,897	11,406
1984-85	28[1]	1,542	226	1,666	9,974
1985-86	34	1,722	130	2,021	11,658
1986-87	28[1]	1,323	112	1,496	8,742
1987-88	28[2]	1,443	125	1,543	9,183
1988-89	28	1,644	162	1,784	10,586

[1] The 20 clubs played 28 matches each.

[2] The 18 clubs played 28 matches each.

SIXTEEN-SEASON TABLE

Widnes took over from St. Helens as the most successful Division One side since the reintroduction of two divisions in 1973 in terms of most points gained. After their second successive title-winning campaign they head the 16-season table with 622 points from 472 matches.

St. Helens, however, remain the only club to have finished in the top eight in each season although their only championship success was in 1974-75. In addition to St. Helens only Widnes, Castleford, Leeds and Warrington have remained in Division One.

Three clubs have spent the entire 16 seasons in Division Two — Batley, Doncaster and Runcorn Highfield.

Bradford Northern, Hull and Leigh were all Division Two champions who went on to win the Division One title a few seasons after being promoted, while Hull Kingston Rovers, Halifax and Wigan are other former lower grade clubs who later won the major championship.

The highest place gained by a newly-promoted club is third by Hull in 1979-80 after winning the Division Two championship with a 100 per cent record the previous season.

Division One champions who were relegated a few seasons after winning the Division One title were Salford, Featherstone Rovers, Leigh, Halifax and Hull K.R.

The records of the five clubs who have appeared in Division One throughout the 16 seasons are as follows:

Roger Millward MBE, a player and coach at Hull K.R. throughout their First Division career before relegation last year.

	P.	W.	D.	L.	F.	A.	Pts
1. Widnes	472	302	18	152	8,537	5,979	622
2. St. Helens	472	300	19	153	9,648	6,354	619
3. Leeds	471	272	19	180	8,641	6,928	563
4. Warrington	472	260	17	195	8,022	6,734	537
5. Castleford	472	239	25	208	8,654	7,544	503

● Although Bradford Northern and Hull Kingston Rovers have had only 15 seasons in Division One their records compare more favourably with some of the above. Three times champions Rovers have gained 526 points and twice champions Northern 508.

CHAMPIONSHIP PLAY-OFFS

Following the breakaway from the English Rugby Union, 22 clubs formed the Northern Rugby Football League. Each club played 42 matches and Manningham won the first Championship as league leaders in 1895-96.

This format was then abandoned and replaced by the Yorkshire Senior and Lancashire Senior Combination leagues until 1901-02 when 14 clubs broke away to form the Northern Rugby League with Broughton Rangers winning the first Championship.

The following season two divisions were formed with the Division One title going to Halifax (1902-03), Bradford (1903-04), who won a play-off against Salford 5-0 at Halifax after both teams tied with 52 points, and Oldham (1904-05).

In 1905-06 the two divisions were merged with Leigh taking the Championship as league leaders. They won the title on a percentage basis as the 31 clubs did not play the same number of matches. The following season the top four play-off was introduced as a fairer means of deciding the title.

The top club played the fourth-placed, the second meeting the third, with the higher club having home advantage. The final was staged at a neutral venue.

It was not until 1930-31 that all clubs played the same number of league matches, but not all against each other, the top four play-off being a necessity until the reintroduction of two divisions in 1962-63.

This spell of two division football lasted only two seasons and the restoration of the Championship table brought about the introduction of a top-16 play-off, this format continuing until the reappearance of two divisions in 1973-74.

Since then the Championship Trophy has been awarded to the leaders of the First Division, with the Second Division champions receiving a silver bowl.

Slalom Lager launched a three-year sponsorship deal of the Championship and the Premiership in 1980-81 in a £215,000 package, extending the deal for another three years from 1983-84 for £270,000. From 1986-87, the sponsorship was taken over by brewers Bass, under the Stones Bitter banner, in a new £400,000 three-year deal, renewed for a further three years from 1989-90 for £750,000.

CHAMPIONSHIP PLAY-OFF FINALS

Season	Winners		Runners-up		Venue	Attendance	Receipts
Top Four Play-Offs							
1906-07	Halifax	18	Oldham	3	Huddersfield	13,200	£722
1907-08	Hunslet	7	Oldham	7	Salford	14,000	£690
Replay	Hunslet	12	Oldham	2	Wakefield	14,054	£800
1908-09	Wigan	7	Oldham	3	Salford	12,000	£630
1909-10	Oldham	13	Wigan	7	Broughton	10,850	£520
1910-11	Oldham	20	Wigan	7	Broughton	15,543	£717
1911-12	Huddersfield	13	Wigan	5	Halifax	15,000	£591
1912-13	Huddersfield	29	Wigan	2	Wakefield	17,000	£914
1913-14	Salford	5	Huddersfield	3	Leeds	8,091	£474
1914-15	Huddersfield	35	Leeds	2	Wakefield	14,000	£750
COMPETITION SUSPENDED DURING WAR TIME							
1919-20	Hull	3	Huddersfield	2	Leeds	12,900	£1,615
1920-21	Hull	16	Hull K.R.	14	Leeds	10,000	£1,320
1921-22	Wigan	13	Oldham	2	Broughton	26,000	£1,825
1922-23	Hull K.R.	15	Huddersfield	5	Leeds	14,000	£1,370
1923-24	Batley	13	Wigan	7	Broughton	13,729	£968
1924-25	Hull K.R.	9	Swinton	5	Rochdale	21,580	£1,504
1925-26	Wigan	22	Warrington	10	St. Helens	20,000	£1,100
1926-27	Swinton	13	St. Helens Recs.	8	Warrington	24,432	£1,803
1927-28	Swinton	11	Featherstone R.	0	Oldham	15,451	£1,136
1928-29	Huddersfield	2	Leeds	0	Halifax	25,604	£2,028
1929-30	Huddersfield	2	Leeds	2	Wakefield	32,095	£2,111
Replay	Huddersfield	10	Leeds	0	Halifax	18,563	£1,319
1930-31	Swinton	14	Leeds	7	Wigan	31,000	£2,100
1931-32	St. Helens	9	Huddersfield	5	Wakefield	19,386	£943
1932-33	Salford	15	Swinton	5	Wigan	18,000	£1,053
1933-34	Wigan	15	Salford	3	Warrington	31,564	£2,114
1934-35	Swinton	14	Warrington	3	Wigan	27,700	£1,710
1935-36	Hull	21	Widnes	2	Huddersfield	17,276	£1,208

Season	Winners		Runners-up		Venue	Attendance	Receipts
1936-37	Salford	13	Warrington	11	Wigan	31,500	£2,000
1937-38	Hunslet	8	Leeds	2	Elland Rd., Leeds	54,112	£3,572
1938-39	Salford	8	Castleford	6	Man. City FC	69,504	£4,301

WAR-TIME EMERGENCY PLAY-OFFS
For the first two seasons the Yorkshire League and Lancashire League champions met in a two-leg final as follows:

Season	Winners		Runners-up		Venue	Attendance	Receipts
1939-40	Swinton	13	Bradford N.	21	Swinton	4,800	£237
	Bradford N.	16	Swinton	9	Bradford	11,721	£570
	Bradford N. won 37-22 on aggregate						
1940-41	Wigan	6	Bradford N.	17	Wigan	11,245	£640
	Bradford N.	28	Wigan	9	Bradford	20,205	£1,148
	Bradford N. won 45-15 on aggregate						

For the remainder of the War the top four in the War League played-off as follows:

Season	Winners		Runners-up		Venue	Attendance	Receipts
1941-42	Dewsbury	13	Bradford N.	0	Leeds	18,000	£1,121
1942-43	Dewsbury	11	Halifax	3	Dewsbury	7,000	£400
	Halifax	13	Dewsbury	22	Halifax	9,700	£683

Dewsbury won 33-16 on aggregate but the Championship was declared null and void because they had played an ineligible player

Season	Winners		Runners-up		Venue	Attendance	Receipts
1943-44	Wigan	13	Dewsbury	9	Wigan	14,000	£915
	Dewsbury	5	Wigan	12	Dewsbury	9,000	£700
	Wigan won 25-14 on aggregate						
1944-45	Halifax	9	Bradford N.	2	Halifax	9,426	£955
	Bradford N.	24	Halifax	11	Bradford	16,000	£1,850
	Bradford N. won 26-20 on aggregate						
1945-46	Wigan	13	Huddersfield	4	Man. C. FC	67,136	£8,387
1946-47	Wigan	13	Dewsbury	4	Man. C. FC	40,599	£5,895
1947-48	Warrington	15	Bradford N.	5	Man. C. FC	69,143	£9,792
1948-49	Huddersfield	13	Warrington	12	Man. C. FC	75,194	£11,073
1949-50	Wigan	20	Huddersfield	2	Man. C. FC	65,065	£11,500
1950-51	Workington T.	26	Warrington	11	Man. C. FC	61,618	£10,993
1951-52	Wigan	13	Bradford N.	6	Huddersfield Town FC	48,684	£8,215
1952-53	St. Helens	24	Halifax	14	Man. C. FC	51,083	£11,503
1953-54	Warrington	8	Halifax	7	Man. C. FC	36,519	£9,076
1954-55	Warrington	7	Oldham	3	Man. C. FC	49,434	£11,516
1955-56	Hull	10	Halifax	9	Man. C. FC	36,675	£9,179
1956-57	Oldham	15	Hull	14	Bradford	62,199	£12,054
1957-58	Hull	20	Workington T.	3	Bradford	57,699	£11,149
1958-59	St. Helens	44	Hunslet	22	Bradford	52,560	£10,146
1959-60	Wigan	27	Wakefield T.	3	Bradford	83,190	£14,482
1960-61	Leeds	25	Warrington	10	Bradford	52,177	£10,475
1961-62	Huddersfield	14	Wakefield T.	5	Bradford	37,451	£7,979

TWO DIVISIONS 1962-63 and 1963-64

Top Sixteen Play-Offs

Season	Winners		Runners-up		Venue	Attendance	Receipts
1964-65	Halifax	15	St. Helens	7	Swinton	20,786	£6,141
1965-66	St. Helens	35	Halifax	12	Swinton	30,634	£8,750
1966-67	Wakefield T.	7	St. Helens	7	Leeds	20,161	£6,702
Replay	Wakefield T.	21	St. Helens	9	Swinton	33,537	£9,800
1967-68	Wakefield T.	17	Hull K.R.	10	Leeds	22,586	£7,697
1968-69	Leeds	16	Castleford	14	Bradford	28,442	£10,130
1969-70	St. Helens	24	Leeds	12	Bradford	26,358	£9,791
1970-71	St. Helens	16	Wigan	12	Swinton	21,745	£10,200
1971-72	Leeds	9	St. Helens	5	Swinton	24,055	£9,513
1972-73	Dewsbury	22	Leeds	13	Bradford	18,889	£9,479

CHAMPIONSHIP FINAL . . . . A 10-YEAR REVIEW

1961-62 HUDDERSFIELD 14 Dyson (4g); Breen, Deighton, Booth, Wicks (1t); Davies, Smales (1t); Slevin, Close, Noble, Kilroy, Bowman, Ramsden
WAKEFIELD T. 5 Round; F. Smith, Skene, N. Fox (1t, 1g), Hirst; Poynton, Holliday; Wilkinson, Kosanovic, Firth, Briggs, Vines, Turner
Referee: N. T. Railton (Wigan)

TWO DIVISIONS — NO PLAY-OFFS 1963 and 1964

1964-65 HALIFAX 15 James (3g); Jackson (1t), Burnett (2t), Kellett, Freeman; Robinson, Daley; Roberts, Harrison, Scroby, Fogerty, Dixon, Renilson
ST. HELENS 7 F. Barrow; Harvey, Vollenhoven, Northey, Killeen (1t, 2g); Murphy, Smith; Tembey (Warlow), Dagnall, Watson, French, Mantle, Laughton
Referee: D. S. Brown (Dewsbury)

1965-66 ST. HELENS 35 F. Barrow; A. Barrow (1t), Murphy (1g), Benyon, Killeen (3t, 6g); Harvey; Bishop; Halsall (3t), Sayer, Watson, French, Warlow (Hitchen), Mantle
HALIFAX 12 Cooper (3g); Jones, Burnett, Dixon, Freeman; Robinson, Baker (1t); Roberts, Harrison, Scroby, Ramshaw (Duffy), Fogerty (1t), Renilson
Referee: J. Manley (Warrington)

1966-67 WAKEFIELD T. 7 Cooper; Hirst, Brooke, N. Fox (2g), Coetzer; Poynton, Owen (1t); Bath, Prior, Campbell, Clarkson, Haigh, D. Fox
ST. HELENS 7 F. Barrow; Vollenhoven, A. Barrow, Smith, Killeen (2g); Douglas, Bishop; Warlow, Sayer, Watson (1t), French, Hogan (Robinson), Mantle
Referee: G. Philpott (Leeds)

Replay: WAKEFIELD T. 21 Cooper; Hirst (1t), Brooke (2t), N. Fox (3g), Coetzer; Poynton (1t), Owen (1t); Bath, Prior, Campbell, Clarkson, Haigh, D. Fox
ST. HELENS 9 F. Barrow; Vollenhoven (1t), A. Barrow, Smith, Killeen (2g); Douglas, Bishop (1g); Warlow, Sayer, Watson, French, Hogan, Mantle
Referee: J. Manley (Warrington)

1967-68 WAKEFIELD T. 17 G. Cooper; Coetzer, Brooke, N. Fox (1t, 2g), Batty; Poynton (1g), Owen (1t); Jeanes (1t), Shepherd, D. Fox (1g), Haigh, McLeod, Hawley
HULL K.R. 10 Wainwright; C. Young, Moore (1t), A. Burwell, Longstaff (1t); Millward (2g), C. Cooper; L. Foster, Flanagan, Mennell, Lowe, Major, F. Foster
Referee: D. S. Brown (Preston)

1968-69 LEEDS 16 Risman (4g); Cowan (1t), Hynes, Watson, Atkinson (1t); Shoebottom, Seabourne (Langley); Clark (Hick), Crosby, K. Eyre, Joyce, Ramsey (1g), Batten
CASTLEFORD 14 Edwards; Briggs, Howe, Thomas, Lowndes; Hardisty (1t, 1g), Hepworth; Hartley, C. Dickinson (1t), J. Ward, Redfearn (3g), Lockwood, Reilly (Fox)
Referee: W. H. Thompson (Huddersfield)

1969-70 ST. HELENS 24 F. Barrow; L. Jones, Benyon, Walsh (1t, 2g), E. Prescott (2t), Myler, Heaton; Halsall, Sayer (1t), Watson, Mantle, E. Chisnall, Coslett (4g)
LEEDS 12 Holmes (3g); Alan Smith (1t), Hynes, Cowan (1t), Atkinson; Shoebottom, Seabourne; J. Burke, Crosby, A. Eyre, Ramsey (Hick), Eccles, Batten
Referee: W. H. Thompson (Huddersfield)

1970-71 ST. HELENS 16 Pimblett; L. Jones, Benyon (1t), Walsh, Blackwood (1t); Whittle, Heaton; J. Stephens, A. Karalius, Rees (Wanbon), Mantle, E. Chisnall, Coslett (5g)
WIGAN 12 Tyrer (1g); Kevin O'Loughlin; Francis, Rowe, Wright; D. Hill, Ayres; Hogan, Clarke, Fletcher, Ashurst (1t, 2g), Robinson (1t) (Cunningham), Laughton
Referee: E. Lawrinson (Warrington)

1971-72 LEEDS 9 Holmes (Hick); Alan Smith, Langley, Dyl, Atkinson (1t); Hardisty, Barham; Clawson (3g), Ward, Fisher (Pickup), Cookson, Eccles, Batten
ST. HELENS 5 Pimblett; L. Jones (Whittle), Benyon, Walsh (1g), Wilson; Kelly, Heaton; Rees, Greenall (1t), J. Stephens, Mantle, E. Chisnall, Coslett
Referee: S. Shepherd (Oldham)

1972-73 DEWSBURY 22 Rushton; Ashcroft, Clark, N. Stephenson (5g, 1t), Day; Agar (1t), A. Bates; Beverley (Taylor), M. Stephenson (2t), Lowe, Grayshon, J. Bates, Whittington
LEEDS 13 Holmes; Alan Smith, Hynes (1g), Dyl (1t), Atkinson; Hardisty, Hepworth; Clawson (1g), Fisher (Ward), Clarkson (Langley), Cookson (1t), Eccles (1t), Haigh
Referee: H. G. Hunt (Prestbury)

LEAGUE LEADERS TROPHY

While the top 16 play-off decided the Championship between 1964 and 1973 it was decided to honour the top club in the league table with a League Leaders Trophy. The winners were:

1964-65	St. Helens
1965-66	St. Helens
1966-67	Leeds
1967-68	Leeds
1968-69	Leeds
1969-70	Leeds
1970-71	Wigan
1971-72	Leeds
1972-73	Warrington

CLUB CHAMPIONSHIP (Merit Table)

With the reintroduction of two divisions, a complicated merit table and Division Two preliminary rounds system produced a 16 club play-off with the Club Championship finalists as follows:

Season	Winners		Runners-up		Venue	Attendance	Receipts
1973-74	Warrington	13	St. Helens	12	Wigan	18,040	£10,032

This format lasted just one season and was replaced by the Premiership.

CLUB CHAMPIONSHIP FINAL . . . . A REVIEW

1973-74 WARRINGTON 13 Whitehead (2g); M. Philbin (1t), Noonan (1t), Pickup (Lowe), Bevan; Whittle, A. Murphy; D. Chisnall, Ashcroft, Brady (1t), Wanbon (Gaskell), Mather, B. Philbin

ST. HELENS 12 Pimblett; Brown, Wills, Wilson (2t), Mathias; Eckersley, Heaton; Mantle, Liptrot, M. Murphy, E. Chisnall (Warlow), Nicholls, Coslett (3g)

Referee: P. Geraghty (York)

PREMIERSHIP

With the further reintroduction of two divisions in 1973-74, it was declared that the title of Champions would be awarded to the leaders of the First Division.

However, it was also decided to continue the tradition of an end-of-season play-off, the winners to receive the newly instituted Premiership Trophy.

*For full details of the Premiership Trophy see the CUPS section.

COUNTY LEAGUE

In the early seasons of the code the Lancashire Senior and Yorkshire Senior Competitions, not to be confused with the later reserve leagues, were major leagues. The winners were:

	Lancashire SC	Yorkshire SC
1895-96	Runcorn	Manningham
1896-97	Broughton Rangers	Brighouse Rangers
1897-98	Oldham	Hunslet
1898-99	Broughton Rangers	Batley
1899-00	Runcorn	Bradford
1900-01	Oldham	Bradford
1901-02	Wigan	Leeds

With the introduction of two divisions in 1902-03, the county league competitions were scrapped until they reappeared as the Lancashire League and Yorkshire League in 1907-08. Clubs from the same county played each other home and away to decide the titles. These games were included in the main championship table along with inter-county fixtures. The county leagues continued until 1970, with the exception of war-time interruptions and two seasons when regional leagues with play-offs operated during the 1960s two division era. They were then abolished when a more integrated fixture formula meant clubs did not play all others from the same county, this system later being replaced by the present two division structure.

Welshman John Bevan, left winger for Club Championship winners Warrington.

LEAGUE LEADERS .... A REVIEW

The following is a list of the League leaders since the formation of the Northern Union, with the exception of the three eras of two-division football — 1902-05, 1962-64 and 1973-85 — which are comprehensively featured earlier in this section. From 1896 to 1901, the League was divided into a Lancashire Senior Competition and a Yorkshire Senior Competition, winners of both leagues being listed for those seasons. From 1905 to 1930 not all the clubs played each other, the League being determined on a percentage basis.

LSC — Lancashire Senior Competition
LL — Lancashire League
YSC — Yorkshire Senior Competition
YL — Yorkshire League
WEL — War Emergency League
★ Two points deducted for breach of professional rules
† Decided on a percentage basis after Belle Vue Rangers withdrew shortly before the start of the season.

		P.	W.	D.	L.	F.	A.	Pts.	
1895-96	Manningham	42	33	0	9	367	158	66	
1896-97	Broughton R.	26	19	5	2	201	52	43	LSC
	Brighouse R.	30	22	4	4	213	68	48	YSC
1897-98	Oldham	26	23	1	2	295	94	47	LSC
	Hunslet	30	22	4	4	327	117	48	YSC
1898-99	Broughton R.	26	21	0	5	277	74	42	LSC
	Batley	30	23	2	5	279	75	48	YSC
1899-00	Runcorn	26	22	2	2	232	33	46	LSC
	Bradford	30	24	2	4	324	98	50	YSC
1900-01	Oldham	26	22	1	3	301	67	45	LSC
	Bradford	30	26	1	3	387	100	51★	YSC
1901-02	Broughton R.	26	21	1	4	285	112	43	
1902-05	Two Divisions								
1905-06	Leigh	30	23	2	5	245	130	48	80.00%
1906-07	Halifax	34	27	2	5	649	229	56	82.35%
1907-08	Oldham	32	28	2	2	396	121	58	90.62%
1908-09	Wigan	32	28	0	4	706	207	56	87.50%
1909-10	Oldham	34	29	2	3	604	184	60	88.23%
1910-11	Wigan	34	28	1	5	650	205	57	83.82%
1911-12	Huddersfield	36	31	1	4	996	238	63	87.50%
1912-13	Huddersfield	32	28	0	4	732	217	56	87.50%
1913-14	Huddersfield	34	28	2	4	830	258	58	85.29%
1914-15	Huddersfield	34	28	4	2	888	235	60	88.24%
1915-18	Competitive matches suspended during First World War								
1918-19	Rochdale H.	12	9	0	3	92	52	18	75.00% LL
	Hull	16	13	0	3	392	131	26	81.25% YL
1919-20	Huddersfield	34	29	0	5	759	215	58	85.29%
1920-21	Hull K.R.	32	24	1	7	432	233	49	76.56%
1921-22	Oldham	36	29	1	6	521	201	59	81.94%
1922-23	Hull	36	30	0	6	587	304	60	83.33%
1923-24	Wigan	38	31	0	7	824	228	62	81.57%
1924-25	Swinton	36	30	0	6	499	224	60	83.33%
1925-26	Wigan	38	29	3	6	641	310	61	80.26%
1926-27	St. Helens R.	38	29	3	6	544	235	61	80.26%
1927-28	Swinton	36	27	3	6	439	189	57	79.16%

		P.	W.	D.	L.	F.	A.	Pts.	
1928-29	Huddersfield	38	26	4	8	476	291	56	73.68%
1929-30	St. Helens	40	27	1	12	549	295	55	68.75%
1930-31	Swinton	38	31	2	5	504	156	64	
1931-32	Huddersfield	38	30	1	7	636	368	61	
1932-33	Salford	38	31	2	5	751	165	64	
1933-34	Salford	38	31	1	6	715	281	63	
1934-35	Swinton	38	30	1	7	468	175	61	
1935-36	Hull	38	30	1	7	607	306	61	
1936-37	Salford	38	29	3	6	529	196	61	
1937-38	Hunslet	36	25	3	8	459	301	53	
1938-39	Salford	40	30	3	7	551	191	63	
1939-40	Swinton	22	17	0	5	378	158	34	WEL LL
	Bradford N.	28	21	0	7	574	302	42	WEL YL
1940-41	Wigan	16	15	1	0	297	71	31	WEL LL
	Bradford N.	25	23	1	1	469	126	47	WEL YL
1941-42	Dewsbury	24	19	1	4	431	172	39	81.25% WEL
1942-43	Wigan	16	13	0	3	301	142	26	81.25% WEL
1943-44	Wakefield T.	22	19	0	3	359	97	38	86.36% WEL
1944-45	Bradford N.	20	17	0	3	337	69	34	85.00% WEL
1945-46	Wigan	36	29	2	5	783	219	60	
1946-47	Wigan	36	29	1	6	567	196	59	
1947-48	Wigan	36	31	1	4	776	258	63	
1948-49	Warrington	36	31	0	5	728	247	62	
1949-50	Wigan	36	31	1	4	853	320	63	
1950-51	Warrington	36	30	0	6	738	250	60	
1951-52	Bradford N.	36	28	1	7	758	326	57	
1952-53	St. Helens	36	32	2	2	769	273	66	
1953-54	Halifax	36	30	2	4	538	219	62	
1954-55	Warrington	36	29	2	5	718	321	60	
1955-56	Warrington	34	27	1	6	712	349	55	80.88% †
1956-57	Oldham	38	33	0	5	893	365	66	
1957-58	Oldham	38	33	1	4	803	415	67	
1958-59	St. Helens	38	31	1	6	1,005	450	63	
1959-60	St. Helens	38	34	1	3	947	343	69	
1960-61	Leeds	36	30	0	6	620	258	60	
1961-62	Wigan	36	32	1	3	885	283	65	
1962-64	Two Divisions								
1964-65	St. Helens	34	28	0	6	621	226	56	
1965-66	St. Helens	34	28	1	5	521	275	57	
1966-67	Leeds	34	29	0	5	704	373	58	
1967-68	Leeds	34	28	0	6	720	271	56	
1968-69	Leeds	34	29	2	3	775	358	60	
1969-70	Leeds	34	30	0	4	674	314	60	
1970-71	Wigan	34	30	0	4	662	308	60	
1971-72	Leeds	34	28	2	4	750	325	58	
1972-73	Warrington	34	27	2	5	816	400	56	

St. Helens coach Alex Murphy celebrates victory over Widnes in the 1989 Silk Cut Challenge Cup semi-final at Wigan.

COACHES

COACHES

Between June 1988 and June 1989 a total of 18 clubs made first team coaching changes, some more than once. Thirteen new coaches had their first senior appointments bringing the total of coaches since the start of the 1974-75 season to 207.

This chapter is a compilation of those appointments, featuring a club-by-club coaches register, an index, plus a detailed dossier of the 1988-89 coaches.

CLUB-BY-CLUB REGISTER

The following is a list of coaches each club has had since the start of the 1974-75 season.

BARROW
Frank Foster	May 73 - Apr. 83
Tommy Dawes	May 83 - Feb. 85
Tommy Bishop	Feb. 85 - Apr. 85
Ivor Kelland	May 85 - Feb. 87
Dennis Jackson	Feb. 87 - Nov. 87
Rod Reddy	Nov. 87 -

BATLEY
Don Fox	Nov. 72 - Oct. 74
Alan Hepworth	Nov. 74 - Apr. 75
Dave Cox	May 75 - June 75
Trevor Walker	June 75 - June 77
Albert Fearnley	June 77 - Oct. 77
Dave Stockwell	Oct. 77 - June 79
*Tommy Smales	June 79 - Oct. 81
Trevor Lowe	Oct. 81 - May 82
Terry Crook	June 82 - Nov. 84
George Pieniazek	Nov. 84 - Nov. 85
Brian Lockwood	Nov. 85 - May 87
Paul Daley	July 87 -

*Ex-forward

BRADFORD NORTHERN
Ian Brooke	Jan. 73 - Sept. 75
Roy Francis	Oct. 75 - Apr. 77
Peter Fox	Apr. 77 - May 85
Barry Seabourne	May 85 -

BRAMLEY
Arthur Keegan	May 73 - Sept. 76
Peter Fox	Sept. 76 - Apr. 77
*Tommy Smales	May 77 - Dec. 77
Les Pearce	Jan. 78 - Oct. 78
Don Robinson	Oct. 78 - May 79
Dave Stockwell	June 79 - June 80
Keith Hepworth	June 80 - May 82
Maurice Bamford	May 82 - Oct. 83
Peter Jarvis	Oct. 83 - Apr. 85
Ken Loxton	Apr. 85 - Dec. 85
Allan Agar	Dec. 85 - Apr. 87
Chris Forster	June 87 - Nov. 87
Tony Fisher	Nov. 87 - Feb. 89
Barry Johnson	Mar. 89 -

*Ex-forward

CARLISLE
Allan Agar	May 81 - June 82
Mick Morgan	July 82 - Feb. 83
John Atkinson	Feb. 83 - Feb. 86
Alan Kellett	Feb. 86 - May 86
Roy Lester	June 86 - Nov. 88
Tommy Dawes	Dec. 88 -

Barry Seabourne, coach at Bradford Northern since May 1985.

CASTLEFORD

Dave Cox	Apr. 74 - Nov. 74
*Malcolm Reilly	Dec. 74 - May 87
Dave Sampson	May 87 - Apr. 88
Darryl Van de Velde	July 88 -

Shortly after his appointment Reilly returned to Australia to fulfil his contract before resuming at Castleford early the next season.

CHORLEY BOROUGH

Tommy Blakeley	Aug. 74 - Apr. 76
Jim Crellin	May 76 - Mar. 77
Joe Egan Jnr.	Mar. 77 - Oct 77
Albert Fearnley (Mgr)	Nov. 77 - Apr. 79
Bakary Diabira	Nov. 78 - June 79
Graham Rees	June 79 - Mar. 80
Geoff Lyon	July 80 - Aug. 81
Bob Irving	Aug. 81 - Feb. 82
John Mantle	Feb. 82 - Mar. 82
Tommy Dickens	Mar. 82 - Nov. 85
*Stan Gittins	Nov. 85 - June 88
*Mike Peers	June 88 -

Joint coaches Aug. 87 - June 88

DEWSBURY

Maurice Bamford	June 74 - Oct. 74
Alan Hardisty	Oct. 74 - June 75
Dave Cox	June 75 - July 77
Ron Hill	July 77 - Dec. 77
Lewis Jones	Dec. 77 - Apr. 78
Jeff Grayshon	May 78 - Oct. 78
Alan Lockwood	Oct. 78 - Oct. 80
Bernard Watson	Oct. 80 - Oct. 82
Ray Abbey	Nov. 82 - Apr. 83
*Tommy Smales	May 83 - Feb. 84
Jack Addy	Feb. 84 - Jan. 87
Dave Busfield	Jan. 87 - Apr. 87
Terry Crook	Apr. 87 - Dec. 88
Maurice Bamford	Dec. 88 -

Ex-forward

DONCASTER

Ted Strawbridge	Feb. 73 - Apr. 75
Derek Edwards	July 75 - Nov. 76
Don Robson	Nov. 76 - Sept. 77
Trevor Lowe	Sept. 77 - Apr. 79
*Tommy Smales	Feb. 78 - Apr. 79
Billy Yates	Apr. 79 - May 80
Don Vines	Sept. 79 - Jan. 80
Bill Kenny	June 80 - May 81
Alan Rhodes	Aug. 81 - Mar. 83
Clive Sullivan M.B.E.	Mar. 83 - May 84
John Sheridan	June 84 - Nov. 87
Graham Heptinstall	Nov. 87 - Jan. 88
John Sheridan	Jan. 88 - Apr. 89
Dave Sampson	May 89 -

Ex-forward, who shared the coaching post with Trevor Lowe for just over a year.

FEATHERSTONE ROVERS

*Tommy Smales	July 74 - Sept. 74
Keith Goulding	Sept. 74 - Jan. 76
†Tommy Smales	Feb. 76 - May 76
Keith Cotton	June 76 - Dec. 77
Keith Goulding	Dec. 77 - May 78
Terry Clawson	July 78 - Nov. 78
†Tommy Smales	Nov. 78 - Apr. 79
Paul Daley	May 79 - Jan. 81
Vince Farrar	Feb. 81 - Nov. 82
Allan Agar	Dec. 82 - Oct. 85
George Pieniazek	Nov. 85 - Nov. 86
Paul Daley	Nov. 86 - Apr. 87
Peter Fox	May 87 -

Ex-forward
†Ex-scrum half

FULHAM

Reg Bowden	July 80 - June 84
Roy Lester	June 84 - Apr. 86
Bill Goodwin	Apr. 86 - May 88
*Bev Risman	May 88 - Feb. 89
Phil Sullivan	Feb. 89 - Mar. 89
Bill Goodwin	Mar. 89 - Apr 89

*Team manager

HALIFAX

Derek Hallas	Aug. 74 - Oct. 74
Les Pearce	Oct. 74 - Apr. 76
Alan Kellett	May 76 - Apr. 77
Jim Crellin	June 77 - Oct. 77
Harry Fox	Oct. 77 - Feb. 78
Maurice Bamford	Feb. 78 - May 80
Mick Blacker	June 80 - June 82
Ken Roberts	June 82 - Sept. 82
Colin Dixon	Sept. 82 - Nov. 84
Chris Anderson	Nov. 84 - May 88
Graham Eadie	May 88 - Aug 88
Ross Strudwick	Aug. 88 - Feb. 89
Alan Hardisty	Feb. 89 - Apr. 89

HUDDERSFIELD

Brian Smith	Jan. 73 - Mar. 76
Keith Goulding	Mar. 76 - Dec. 76
Bob Tomlinson	Jan. 77 - May 77
Neil Fox	June 77 - Feb. 78
*Roy Francis	-
Keith Goulding	May 78 - July 79
Ian Brooke	July 79 - Mar. 80
Maurice Bamford	May 80 - May 81
Les Sheard	June 81 - Nov. 82
Dave Mortimer	Nov. 82 - Aug. 83
Mel Bedford	Aug. 83 - Nov. 83
Brian Lockwood	Nov. 83 - Feb. 85
Chris Forster	Feb. 85 - Dec. 86
Jack Addy	Jan. 87 - Mar. 88
Allen Jones ⎫ Neil Whittaker ⎭	Mar. 88 - Nov. 88
Nigel Stephenson	Nov. 88 -

*Although Roy Francis was appointed he was
unable to take over and Dave Heppleston stood
in until the next appointment.*

HULL

David Doyle-Davidson	May 74 - Dec. 77
Arthur Bunting	Jan. 78 - Dec. 85
Kenny Foulkes	Dec. 85 - May 86
Len Casey	June 86 - Mar. 88
Tony Dean ⎫ Keith Hepworth ⎭	Mar. 88 - Apr. 88
Brian Smith	July 88 -

HULL KINGSTON ROVERS

Arthur Bunting	Feb. 72 - Nov. 75
Harry Poole	Dec. 75 - Mar. 77
Roger Millward M.B.E.	Mar. 77 -

HUNSLET

Paul Daley	Apr. 74 - Aug. 78
Bill Ramsey	Aug. 78 - Dec. 79
Drew Broatch	Dec. 79 - Apr. 81*
Paul Daley	Apr. 81 - Nov. 85
*Peter Jarvis	Nov. 85 - Apr. 88
*David Ward	July 86 - Apr. 88
Nigel Stephenson	Jun. 88 - Oct. 88
Jack Austin ⎫ John Wolford ⎭	Oct. 88 - Jan. 89
David Ward	Jan. 89 - May 89

Joint coaches from July 1986.

KEIGHLEY

Alan Kellett	Jan. 73 - May 75
Roy Sabine	Aug. 75 - Oct. 77
Barry Seabourne	Nov. 77 - Mar. 79
Albert Fearnley (Mgr)	Apr. 79 - Aug. 79
Alan Kellett	Apr. 79 - Apr. 80
Albert Fearnley	May 80 - Feb. 81
Bakary Diabira	Feb. 81 - Sept. 82
Lee Greenwood	Sept. 82 - Oct. 83
Geoff Peggs	Nov. 83 - Sept. 85
Peter Roe	Sept. 85 - July 86
Colin Dixon ⎫ Les Coulter ⎭	July 86 -

LEEDS

Roy Francis	June 74 - May 75
Syd Hynes	June 75 - Apr. 81
Robin Dewhurst	June 81 - Oct. 83
Maurice Bamford	Nov. 83 - Feb. 85
Malcolm Clift	Feb. 85 - May 85
Peter Fox	May 85 - Dec. 86
Maurice Bamford	Dec. 86 - Apr. 88
Malcolm Reilly	Aug. 88 -

LEIGH

Eddie Cheetham	May 74 - Mar. 75
Kevin Ashcroft	June 75 - Jan. 77
Bill Kindon	Jan. 77 - Apr. 77
John Mantle	Apr. 77 - Nov. 78
Tom Grainey	Nov. 78 - Dec. 80
*Alex Murphy	Nov. 80 - June 82
*Colin Clarke	June 82 - Dec. 82
Peter Smethurst	Dec. 82 - Apr. 83
Tommy Bishop	June 83 - June 84
John Woods	June 84 - May 85
Alex Murphy	Feb. 85 - Nov. 85
Tommy Dickens	Nov. 85 - Dec. 86
Billy Benyon	Dec. 86 -

From Dec. 80 to June 82 Clarke was officially appointed coach and Murphy manager

MANSFIELD MARKSMAN

Mick Blacker	May 84 - Oct. 85
Bill Kirkbride	Nov. 85 - Mar. 86
Steve Dennison	Apr. 86 - Dec. 86
Jim Crellin	Dec. 86 - June 88
Billy Platt	July 88 - Dec. 88
Steve Nash	Dec. 88 - Feb. 89
Lee Greenwood	Feb. 89 -

OLDHAM

Jim Challinor	Aug. 74 - Dec. 76
Terry Ramshaw	Jan. 77 - Feb. 77
Dave Cox	July 77 - Dec. 78
Graham Starkey (Mngr)	Jan. 79 - May 81
Bill Francis	June 79 - Dec. 80
Frank Myler	May 81 - Apr. 83
Peter Smethurst	Apr. 83 - Feb. 84
Frank Barrow	Feb. 84 - Feb. 84
Brian Gartland	Mar. 84 - June 84
Frank Myler	June 84 - Apr. 87
*Eric Fitzsimons	June 87 - Nov. 88
*Mal Graham	June 87 - Apr. 88
Tony Barrow	Nov. 88 -

Joint coaches June 87 - Apr. 88

ROCHDALE HORNETS

Frank Myler	May 71 - Oct. 74
Graham Starkey	Oct. 74 - Nov. 75
Henry Delooze	Nov. 75 - Nov. 76
Kel Coslett	Nov. 76 - Aug. 79
Paul Longstaff	Sept. 79 - May 81
Terry Fogerty	May 81 - Jan. 82
Dick Bonser	Jan. 82 - May 82
Bill Kirkbride	June 82 - Sept. 84
Charlie Birdsall	Sept. 84 - Apr. 86
Eric Fitzsimons	June 86 - June 87
Eric Hughes	June 87 - June 88
Jim Crellin	June 88 -

RUNCORN HIGHFIELD

Terry Gorman	Aug. 74 - May 77
Geoff Fletcher	Aug. 77 - June 86
Frank Wilson	July 86 - Nov. 86
Arthur Daley Paul Woods }	Nov. 86 - Apr. 87
Bill Ashurst	Apr. 87 - Jan. 89
John Cogger	Jan. 89 - Feb. 89
Geoff Fletcher	Feb. 89 - Apr. 89

ST. HELENS

Eric Ashton M.B.E.	May 74 - May 80
Kel Coslett	June 80 - May 82
Billy Benyon	May 82 - Nov. 85
Alex Murphy	Nov. 85 -

SALFORD

Les Bettinson	Dec. 73 - Mar. 77
Colin Dixon	Mar. 77 - Jan. 78
Stan McCormick	Feb. 78 - Mar. 78
Alex Murphy	May 78 - Nov. 80
Kevin Ashcroft	Nov. 80 - Mar. 82
Alan McInnes	Mar. 82 - May 82
Malcolm Aspey	May 82 - Oct. 83
Mike Coulman	Oct. 83 - May 84
Kevin Ashcroft	May 84 -

SHEFFIELD EAGLES

Alan Rhodes	Apr. 84 - May 86
Gary Hetherington	July 86 -

SWINTON

Austin Rhodes	June 74 - Nov. 75
Bob Fleet	Nov. 75 - Nov. 76
John Stopford	Nov. 76 - Apr. 77
Terry Gorman	June 77 - Nov. 78
Ken Halliwell	Nov. 78 - Dec. 79
Frank Myler	Jan. 80 - May 81
Tom Grainey	May 81 - Oct. 83
Jim Crellin	Nov. 83 - May 86
Bill Holliday ⎫ Mike Peers ⎭	June 86 - Oct. 87
Frank Barrow	Oct. 87 -

WAKEFIELD TRINITY

Peter Fox	June 74 - May 76
Geoff Gunney M.B.E.	June 76 - Nov. 76
Brian Lockwood	Nov. 76 - Jan. 78
Ian Brooke	Jan. 78 - Jan. 79
Bill Kirkbride	Jan. 79 - Apr. 80
Ray Batten	Apr. 80 - May 81
Bill Ashurst	June 81 - Apr. 82
Ray Batten	May 82 - July 83
Derek Turner	July 83 - Feb. 84
Bob Haigh	Feb. 84 - May 84
Geoff Wraith	May 84 - Oct. 84
David Lamming	Oct. 84 - Apr. 85
Len Casey	Apr. 85 - June 86
Tony Dean	June 86 - Dec. 86
Trevor Bailey	Dec. 86 - Apr. 87
David Topliss	May 87 -

WARRINGTON

Alex Murphy	May 71 - May 78
Billy Benyon	June 78 - Mar. 82
Kevin Ashcroft	Mar. 82 - May 84
Reg Bowden	June 84 - Mar. 86
Tony Barrow	Mar. 86 - Nov. 88
Brian Johnson	Nov. 88 -

WHITEHAVEN

Jeff Bawden	May 72 - May 75
Ike Southward	Aug. 75 - June 76
Bill Smith	Aug. 76 - Oct. 78
Ray Dutton	Oct. 78 - Oct. 79
Phil Kitchin	Oct. 79 - Jan. 82
Arnold Walker	Jan. 82 - May 82
Tommy Dawes	June 82 - May 83
Frank Foster	June 83 - June 85
Phil Kitchin	June 85 - Oct. 87
John McFarlane	Oct. 87 - May 88
Barry Smith	July 88 -

WIDNES

Vince Karalius	Jan. 72 - May 75
Frank Myler	May 75 - May 78
Doug Laughton	May 78 - Mar. 83
Harry Dawson ⎫ Colin Tyrer ⎭	Mar. 83 - May 83
*Vince Karalius ⎫ Harry Dawson ⎭	May 83 - May 84
Eric Hughes	June 84 - Jan. 86
Doug Laughton	Jan. 86 -

Dawson quit as coach in March 1984 with Karalius continuing as team manager.

WIGAN

Ted Toohey	May 74 - Jan. 75
Joe Coan	Jan. 75 - Sept. 76
Vince Karalius	Sept. 76 - Sept. 79
Kel Coslett	Oct. 79 - Apr. 80
George Fairbairn	Apr. 80 - May 81
Maurice Bamford	May 81 - May 82
Alex Murphy	June 82 - Aug. 84
Colin Clarke ⎫ Alan McInnes ⎭	Aug. 84 - May 86
Graham Lowe	Aug. 86 - June 89

Former Great Britain skipper David Topliss, in charge at Wakefield Trinity for two seasons.

WORKINGTON TOWN

Ike Southward	Aug. 73 - June 75
Paul Charlton	June 75 - June 76
Ike Southward	June 76 - Feb. 78
Sol Roper	Feb. 78 - Apr. 80
Keith Irving	Aug. 80 - Oct. 80
Tommy Bishop	Nov. 80 - June 82
Paul Charlton	July 82 - Dec. 82
Dave Cox	Mar. 83 - Mar. 83
Harry Archer/Bill Smith	May 83 - June 84
Bill Smith	June 84 - Apr. 85
Jackie Davidson	Apr. 85 - Jan. 86
Keith Davies	Feb. 86 - Mar. 87
Norman Turley	Mar. 87 - Apr. 88
Maurice Bamford	July 88 - Dec. 88
Phil Kitchin	Dec. 88 -

YORK

Keith Goulding	Nov. 73 - Sept. 74
Gary Cooper	Dec. 74 - Sept. 76
Mal Dixon	Sept. 76 - Dec. 78
Paul Daley	Jan. 79 - May 79
David Doyle-Davidson	July 79 - July 80
Bill Kirkbride	Aug. 80 - Apr. 82
Alan Hardisty	May 82 - Jan. 83
Phil Lowe	Mar. 83 - Mar. 87
Danny Sheehan	Mar. 87 - Apr. 88
Gary Stephens	Apr. 88 -

REPRESENTATIVE REGISTER

The following is a list of international and county coaches since 1974-75.

GREAT BRITAIN

Jim Challinor	Dec. 71 - Aug. 74
	(Inc. tour)
David Watkins	1977 World Championship
Peter Fox	1978
Eric Ashton	1979 tour
Johnny Whiteley	Aug. 80 - Nov. 82
Frank Myler	Dec. 82 - Aug. 84
	(Inc. tour)
Maurice Bamford	Oct. 84 - Dec. 86
Malcolm Reilly	Jan. 87 -
	(Inc. tour)

ENGLAND

Alex Murphy	Jan. 75 - Nov. 75
	(Inc. World Championship tour)
Peter Fox	1976-77
Frank Myler	1977-78
Eric Ashton	1978-79 & 1979-80
Johnny Whiteley	1980-81 & 1981-82
Reg Parker	1984-85
(Mngr)	

WALES

Les Pearce	Jan. 75 - Nov. 75
	(Inc. World Championship tour)
David Watkins	1976-77
Bill Francis	
Kel Coslett	1977-78
Bill Francis	
Kel Coslett	1978-79 to 1981-82
David Watkins	1982-83, 1984-85

GREAT BRITAIN UNDER-24s

Johnny Whiteley	1976-82
Frank Myler	1983-84

GREAT BRITAIN UNDER-21s

Maurice Bamford	Oct. 84 - Dec. 86
Malcolm Reilly	1986-87 to 1987-88
David Topliss	1988-89

CUMBRIA

Ike Southward	1975-76
Frank Foster	1976-77 & 1977-78
Sol Roper	1978-79
Frank Foster	1979-80
Phil Kitchin	1980-81 to 1981-82
Frank Foster	1982-83
Jackie Davidson	1985-86
Phil Kitchin	1986-87 to 1988-89

LANCASHIRE

Alex Murphy	1973-74 to 1977-78
Eric Ashton M.B.E.	1978-79 to 1979-80
Tom Grainey	1980-81 to 1981-82
Doug Laughton	1982-83 & 1988-89
Alex Murphy	1985-86 to 1987-88

YORKSHIRE
Johnny Whiteley 1970-71 to 1979-80
Arthur Keegan 1980-81
Johnny Whiteley 1981-82 to 1982-83
Peter Fox 1985-86 to 1988-89

OTHER NATIONALITIES
Dave Cox 1974-75 to 1975-76

INDEX OF COACHES
The following is an index of the 207 coaches who have held first team coaching posts since the start of the 1974-75 season with the alphabetical listing of British clubs they coached in this period.

Ray Abbey (Dewsbury)
Jack Addy (Dewsbury, Huddersfield B.)
Allan Agar (Bramley, Carlisle, Featherstone R.)
Dave Alred (Bridgend)
Chris Anderson (Halifax)
Harry Archer (Workington T.)
Kevin Ashcroft (Leigh, Salford, Warrington)
Eric Ashton M.B.E. (St. Helens)
Bill Ashurst (Runcorn H., Wakefield T.)
Mal Aspey (Salford)
Jack Austin (Hunslet)
John Atkinson (Carlisle)

Trevor Bailey (Wakefield T.)
Maurice Bamford (Bramley, Dewsbury, Halifax, Huddersfield, Leeds, Wigan, Workington T.)
Frank Barrow (Oldham, Swinton)
Tony Barrow (Oldham, Warrington)
Ray Batten (Wakefield T.)
Jeff Bawden (Whitehaven)
Mel Bedford (Huddersfield)
Billy Benyon (Leigh, St. Helens, Warrington)
Les Bettinson (Salford)
Charlie Birdsall (Rochdale H.)
Tommy Bishop (Barrow, Leigh, Workington T.)
Mick Blacker (Halifax, Mansfield M.)
Tommy Blakeley (Blackpool B.)
Dick Bonser (Rochdale H.)
Reg Bowden (Fulham, Warrington)
Drew Broatch (Hunslet)
Ian Brooke (Bradford N., Huddersfield, Wakefield T.)
Arthur Bunting (Hull, Hull K.R.)
Dave Busfield (Dewsbury)

Len Casey (Hull, Wakefield T.)
Jim Challinor (Oldham)
Paul Charlton (Workington T.)
Eddie Cheetham (Leigh)
Colin Clarke (Leigh, Wigan)
Terry Clawson (Featherstone R.)
Malcolm Clift (Leeds)
Joe Coan (Wigan)
John Cogger (Runcorn H.)
Gary Cooper (York)
Kel Coslett (Rochdale H., St. Helens, Wigan)
Keith Cotton (Featherstone R.)
Mike Coulman (Salford)
Les Coulter (Keighley)
Dave Cox (Batley, Castleford, Dewsbury, Huyton, Oldham, Workington T.)
Jim Crellin (Blackpool B., Halifax, Mansfield M., Rochdale H., Swinton)
Terry Crook (Batley, Dewsbury)

Arthur Daley (Runcorn H.)
Paul Daley (Batley, Featherstone R., Hunslet, York)
Jackie Davidson (Workington T.)
Keith Davies (Workington T.)
Tommy Dawes (Barrow, Carlisle, Whitehaven)
Harry Dawson (Widnes)
Tony Dean (Wakefield T., Hull)
Henry Delooze (Rochdale H.)
Steve Dennison (Mansfield M.)
Robin Dewhurst (Leeds)
Bakary Diabira (Blackpool B., Keighley)
Tommy Dickens (Blackpool B., Leigh)
Colin Dixon (Halifax, Keighley, Salford)
Mal Dixon (York)
David Doyle-Davidson (Hull, York)
Ray Dutton (Whitehaven)

Graham Eadie (Halifax)
Derek Edwards (Doncaster)
Joe Egan Jnr. (Blackpool B.)

George Fairbairn (Wigan)
Vince Farrar (Featherstone R.)
Albert Fearnley (Batley, Blackpool B., Keighley)
Tony Fisher (Bramley)
Eric Fitzsimons (Rochdale H., Oldham)
Bob Fleet (Swinton)
Geoff Fletcher (Huyton, Runcorn H.)
Terry Fogerty (Rochdale H.)
Chris Forster (Huddersfield B., Bramley)
Frank Foster (Barrow, Whitehaven)
Kenny Foulkes (Hull)

Don Fox (Batley)
Harry Fox (Halifax)
Neil Fox (Huddersfield)
Peter Fox (Bradford N., Bramley, Featherstone R.,
    Leeds, Wakefield T.)
Bill Francis (Oldham)
Roy Francis (Bradford N., Huddersfield, Leeds)

Brian Gartland (Oldham)
Stan Gittins (Blackpool B.)
Bill Goodwin (Fulham, Kent Invicta)
Terry Gorman (Huyton, Swinton)
Keith Goulding (Featherstone R., Huddersfield,
    York)
Mal Graham (Oldham)
Tom Grainey (Leigh, Swinton)
Jeff Grayshon (Dewsbury)
Lee Greenwood (Keighley, Mansfield M.)
Geoff Gunney M.B.E.(Wakefield T.)
Bob Haigh (Wakefield T.)
Derek Hallas (Halifax)
Ken Halliwell (Swinton)
Alan Hardisty (Dewsbury, Halifax, York)
Graham Heptinstall (Doncaster)
Alan Hepworth (Batley)
Keith Hepworth (Bramley, Hull)
Gary Hetherington (Sheffield E.)
Ron Hill (Dewsbury)
Bill Holliday (Swinton)
Eric Hughes (Widnes, Rochdale H.)
Syd Hynes (Leeds)

Bob Irving (Blackpool B.)
Keith Irving (Workington T.)

Dennis Jackson (Barrow)
Peter Jarvis (Bramley, Hunslet)
Brian Johnson (Warrington)
Allen Jones (Huddersfield B.)
Lewis Jones (Dewsbury)

Vince Karalius (Widnes, Wigan)
Arthur Keegan (Bramley)
Ivor Kelland (Barrow)
Alan Kellett (Carlisle, Halifax, Keighley)
Bill Kenny (Doncaster)
Bill Kindon (Leigh)
Bill Kirkbride (Mansfield M., Rochdale H.,
    Wakefield T., York)
Phil Kitchin (Whitehaven, Workington T.)

*Doug Laughton, winner of 12 trophies while coach of Widnes
in two separate spells.*

Dave Lamming (Wakefield T.)
Steve Lane (Kent Invicta)
Doug Laughton (Widnes)
Roy Lester (Carlisle, Fulham)
Alan Lockwood (Dewsbury)
Brian Lockwood (Batley, Huddersfield,
    Wakefield T.)
Paul Longstaff (Rochdale H.)
Graham Lowe (Wigan)
Phil Lowe (York)
Trevor Lowe (Batley, Doncaster)
Ken Loxton (Bramley)
Geoff Lyon (Blackpool B.)

John Mantle (Blackpool B., Cardiff C., Leigh)
Stan McCormick (Salford)
John McFarlane (Whitehaven)
Alan McInnes (Salford, Wigan)
Roger Millward M.B.E. (Hull K.R.)
Mick Morgan (Carlisle)
David Mortimer (Huddersfield)
Alex Murphy (Leigh, St. Helens, Salford,
    Warrington, Wigan)
Frank Myler (Oldham, Rochdale H., Swinton,
    Widnes)

Steve Nash (Mansfield M.)

Les Pearce (Bramley, Halifax)
Mike Peers (Chorley B., Swinton)
Geoff Peggs (Keighley)
George Pieniazek (Batley, Featherstone R.)
Billy Platt (Mansfield M.)
Harry Poole (Hull K.R.)

Bill Ramsey (Hunslet)
Terry Ramshaw (Oldham)
Rod Reddy (Barrow)
Graham Rees (Blackpool B.)
Malcolm Reilly (Castleford)
Alan Rhodes (Doncaster, Sheffield E.)
Austin Rhodes (Swinton)
Bev Risman (Fulham)
Ken Roberts (Halifax)
Don Robinson (Bramley)
Don Robson (Doncaster)
Peter Roe (Keighley)
Sol Roper (Workington T.)

Roy Sabine (Keighley)
Dave Sampson (Castleford, Doncaster)
Barry Seabourne (Bradford N., Keighley)
Les Sheard (Huddersfield)
Danny Sheehan (York)
John Sheridan (Doncaster)
Tommy Smales [*Scrum-half*] (Featherstone R.)
Tommy Smales [*Forward*] (Batley, Bramley,
   Dewsbury, Doncaster, Featherstone R.)
Peter Smethurst (Leigh, Oldham)
Barry Smith (Whitehaven)
Bill Smith (Whitehaven, Workington T.)
Brian Smith (Huddersfield)
Brian Smith (Hull)
Ike Southward (Whitehaven, Workington T.)
Graham Starkey (Oldham, Rochdale H.)
Gary Stephens (York)
Nigel Stephenson (Hunslet, Huddersfield)
Dave Stockwell (Bramley, Batley)
John Stopford (Swinton)
Ted Strawbridge (Doncaster)
Ross Strudwick (Halifax)
Clive Sullivan M.B.E. (Doncaster, Hull)
Phil Sullivan (Fulham)

Bob Tomlinson (Huddersfield)
Ted Toohey (Wigan)
David Topliss (Wakefield T.)
Norman Turley (Workington T.)
Derek Turner (Wakefield T.)
Colin Tyrer (Widnes)

Australian coach Darryl Van de Velde, who joined Castleford in the summer of 1988 from Brisbane club football.

Darryl Van de Velde (Castleford)
Don Vines (Doncaster)

Arnold Walker (Whitehaven)
Trevor Walker (Batley)
David Ward (Hunslet)
John Warlow (Bridgend)
David Watkins (Cardiff C.)
Bernard Watson (Dewsbury)
Neil Whittaker (Huddersfield B.)
Frank Wilson (Runcorn H.)
John Wolford (Hunslet)
Jeff Woods (Bridgend)
John Woods (Leigh)
Paul Woods (Runcorn H.)
Geoff Wraith (Wakefield T.)

Billy Yates (Doncaster)

DOSSIER OF 1988-89 COACHES

The following is a dossier of the coaching and playing careers of coaches holding first team posts from June 1988 to the end of May 1989. BF — beaten finalist.

KEVIN ASHCROFT
Leigh:	June 75 - Jan. 77 (Promotion, Floodlit Trophy BF)
Salford:	Nov. 80 - Mar. 82
Warrington:	Mar. 82 - May 84 (Lancs. Cup winners, BF)
Salford:	May 84 - (Promotion)

Played for: Dewsbury, Rochdale H., Leigh, Warrington, Salford

BILL ASHURST
Wakefield T.:	June 81 - Apr. 82
Runcorn H.:	Apr. 87 - Jan. 89

Played for: Wigan, Penrith (Aus.), Wakefield T.

JACK AUSTIN
Hunslet	Oct. 88 - Jan. 89

Played for: Castleford, Bramley, Bradford N.

MAURICE BAMFORD
Dewsbury:	Aug. - Oct. 74
Halifax:	Feb. 78 - May 80 (Yorks. Cup BF., Promotion)
Huddersfield:	May 80 - May 81
Wigan:	May 81 - May 82
Bramley:	May 82 - Oct. 83
Leeds:	Nov. 83 - Feb. 85 (John Player winners)
Leeds:	Dec. 86 - Apr. 88 (John Player BF)
Workington T:	July 88 - Dec. 88
Dewsbury:	Dec. 88 -
Great Britain & Under-21s:	Oct. 84 - Dec. 86

Played for: Dewsbury, Hull, Batley

FRANK BARROW
Oldham:	Feb. 84 - Feb. 84
Swinton:	Oct. 87 - (Div 2 Premier BF)

Played for: St. Helens, Leigh

TONY BARROW
Warrington:	Mar. 86 - Nov. 88 (Premier winners and BF, John Player BF., Lancs. Cup BF)
Oldham:	Nov. 88 -

Played for: St. Helens, Leigh

BILLY BENYON
Warrington:	June 78 - Mar. 82 (Lancs. Cup winners, John Player winners and BF)
St. Helens:	May 82 - Nov. 85 (Lancs. Cup winners and BF, Premier winners)
Leigh:	Dec. 86 - (Div. 2 champs)

Played for: St. Helens, Warrington

JOHN COGGER
Runcorn H:	Jan. 89 - Feb. 89

Played for: Runcorn H., Oldham

LES COULTER
Keighley:	July 86 -

Non-professional player

JIM CRELLIN
Blackpool B.:	May 76 - Mar. 77 (John Player BF)
Halifax:	June 77 - Oct. 77
Swinton:	Nov. 83 - May 86 (Div. 2 champs)
Mansfield M.:	Dec. 86 - June 88
Rochdale H:	June 88 -

Played for: Workington T., Oldham, Rochdale H.

TERRY CROOK
Batley:	June 82 - Nov. 84
Dewsbury:	Apr. 87 - Dec. 88

Played for: Wakefield T., Bramley, Batley

PAUL DALEY
New Hunslet:	Apr. 74 - Aug. 78 (Promotion)
York:	Jan. 79 - May 79 (Promotion)
Featherstone R.:	May 79 - Jan. 81 (Div. 2 champs)
Hunslet:	Apr. 81 - Nov. 85 (Promotion)
Featherstone R.:	Nov. 86 - Apr. 87
Batley:	July 87 -

Played for: Halifax, Bradford N., Hull K.R., Hunslet

TOMMY DAWES
Whitehaven: June 82 - May 83 (Promotion)
Barrow: May 83 - Feb. 85 (Lancs. Cup
     Winners, Div. 2 champs)
Carlisle: Dec. 88 -
Played for: Barrow

COLIN DIXON
Salford: Mar. 77 - Jan. 78
Halifax: Sept. 82 - Nov. 84 (Promotion)
Keighley: July 86 -
Played for: Halifax, Salford, Hull KR

GRAHAM EADIE
Halifax: May 88 - Aug. 88
Played for: Manly (Aust.), Halifax

TONY FISHER
Bramley: Nov. 87 - Feb. 89
Played for: Bradford N., Leeds, Castleford

ERIC FITZSIMONS
Rochdale H.:   June 86 - June 87
Oldham: June 87 - Nov. 88
     (Div. 2 champs, Div. 2 Premier
     winners)
Played for: Oldham, Hunslet, Rochdale H.

GEOFF FLETCHER
Runcorn H: Aug. 77 - June 86
Runcorn H: Feb. 89 - Apr. 89
Played for: Leigh, Oldham, Wigan, Workington T.,
Runcorn H.

PETER FOX
Featherstone R.:   Jan. 71 - May 74
     (RL Cup winners & BF)
Wakefield T.:   June 74 - May 76
     (Yorks. Cup BF)
Bramley: Sept. 76 - Apr. 77 (Promotion)
Bradford N.:   Apr. 77 - May 85 (Div. 1
     champs (2), Yorks. Cup winners
     and BF (2), Premier winners
     and BF (2), John Player winners)
Leeds: May 85 - Dec. 86
Featherstone R.:   May 87 - (Promotion, Div. 2
     Premier BF)
England: 1977 (2 matches)
Great Britain: 1978 (3 Tests v. Australia)
Yorkshire: 1985-86 to 1988-89
Played for: Featherstone R., Batley, Hull K.R.,
Wakefield T.

STAN GITTINS
Springfield B.:   Nov. 85 - June 88
Played for: Batley, Swinton

BILL GOODWIN
Kent Invicta: Apr. 83 - Nov. 83
Kent Invicta: Aug. 84 - May 85
Fulham: Apr. 86 - Apr. 89
Played for: Doncaster, Featherstone R., Batley

LEE GREENWOOD
Keighley: Sept. 82 - Oct. 83
Mansfield M: Feb. 89 -
Played for: Halifax, Keighley

ALAN HARDISTY
Dewsbury: Oct. 74 - June 75
York: May 82 - Jan 83
Halifax: Feb. 89 - Apr. 89
Played for: Castleford, Leeds

GARY HETHERINGTON
Sheffield E.:   July 86 - (Promotion, Div. 2
     Premier winners)
Played for: York, Leeds, Kent I., Sheffield E.

ERIC HUGHES
Widnes: June 84 - Jan. 86
Rochdale H.:   June 87 - June 88
Played for: Widnes, St. Helens, Rochdale H.

BRIAN JOHNSON
Warrington: Nov. 88 -
Played for: Warrington, St. George (Aus.)

ALLEN JONES
Huddersfield B.:   Mar. 88 - Nov. 88
Played for: Warrington, Rochdale H., Leigh,
Oldham

PHIL KITCHIN
Whitehaven: Oct. 79 - Jan. 82 (Promotion)
Whitehaven: June 85 - Oct. 87
Workington T: Dec. 88 -
Cumbria: 1980-81, 1981-82, 1986-87,
     1987-88
Played for: Whitehaven, Workington T.

DOUG LAUGHTON

Widnes:	May 78 - Mar. 83 (RL Cup winners (2) and BF, Lancs. Cup winners (2) and BF, John Player winners and BF, Premier winners (2))
Widnes:	Jan. 86 - (Div. 1 champs (2), Premier winners (2), Charity Shield winners, John Player BF)
Lancashire:	1982-83 & 1988-89

Played for: Wigan, St. Helens, Widnes

ROY LESTER

Fulham:	June 84 - Apr. 86
Carlisle:	June 86 - Nov. 88

Played for: Warrington, Leigh, Fulham

GRAHAM LOWE

Wigan:	Aug. 86 - June 89 (RL Cup winners (2), Lancs. Cup winners (3), John Player winners (2), Div. 1 champs, Premier winners, Charity Shield winners and BF)

Played for: Othuhu (NZ)

ROGER MILLWARD M.B.E.

Hull K.R.:	Mar. 77 - (Div. 1 champs (3), RL Cup winners and BF (2), John Player winners and BF (2), Premier winners (2) and BF, Yorks. Cup winners and BF (2), Floodlit Trophy winners and BF, Charity Shield BF)

Played for: Castleford, Hull K.R., Cronulla (Aus.)

ALEX MURPHY

Leigh:	Nov. 66 - May 71 (RL Cup winners, Lancs. Cup winners and BF, Floodlit Trophy winners and BF)
Warrington:	May 71 - May 78 (League Leaders, Club Merit winners, RL Cup winners and BF, John Player winners (2), Floodlit Trophy BF, Capt. Morgan winners, Premier BF)
Salford:	May 78 - Nov. 80
Leigh:	Nov. 80 - June 82 (Div. 1 champs, Lancs. Cup winners)

Wigan:	June 82 - Aug. 84 (John Player winners, RL Cup BF)
Leigh:	Feb. 85 - Nov. 85
St. Helens:	Nov. 85 - (RL Cup BF (2), John Player winners, Premier BF)
Lancashire:	1973-74 to 1977-78 Champions (2); 1985-86 to 1987-88
England:	1975 (including World Championship (European Champions))

Played for: St. Helens, Leigh, Warrington

STEVE NASH

Mansfield M:	Dec. 88 - Feb. 89

Played for: Featherstone R., Salford, Rochdale H., Mansfield M.

MIKE PEERS

Swinton:	June 86 - Oct. 87 (Promotion, Div. 2 Premier winners)
Chorley B.:	Aug. 87 -

Played for: Warrington, Swinton

BILLY PLATT

Mansfield M:	July 88 - Dec. 88

Played for: St. Helens, Leigh, Rochdale H., Huddersfield, Mansfield M.

ROD REDDY

Centrals (Aus.):	Feb. 86 - Sep. 87
Barrow:	Nov. 87 - (Promotion)

Played for: St. George, Illawarra, Centrals (All Aus.), Barrow

MALCOLM REILLY

Castleford:	Dec. 74 - May 87 (Yorks. Cup winners (3) and BF (2), Floodlit Trophy winners, John Player winners, Premier BF, RL Cup winners, Charity Shield BF)
Leeds:	Aug. 88 - (Yorks. Cup winners)
Great Britain:	Jan. 87 -
Under-21s:	Jan. 87 - Apr. 88

Played for: Castleford, Manly (Aus.)

BEV RISMAN

Fulham:	May 88 - Feb. 89

Played for: Leigh, Leeds

BARRY SEABOURNE

Keighley:	Nov. 77 - Mar. 79
Bradford N.:	May 85 - (Yorks. Cup winners)

Played for: Leeds, Bradford N., Keighley

JOHN SHERIDAN
Doncaster: June 84 - Nov. 87
Doncaster: Jan. 88 - Apr. 89
Played for: Castleford

BARRY SMITH
Whitehaven: July 88 -
Played for: Whitehaven

BRIAN SMITH
Hull: July 88 - (Premier. BF)
Played for: St. George, Souths (both Aus.)

GARY STEPHENS
York: Apr. 88 -
Played for: Castleford, Wigan, Leigh, Halifax,
Leeds, Manly (Aus.)

NIGEL STEPHENSON
Hunslet: June - Oct 88
Huddersfield: Nov. 88 -
Played for: Dewsbury, Bradford N., Carlisle,
Wakefield T., York, Huddersfield

PHIL SULLIVAN
Fulham: Jan - Feb. 89
Played for: Penrith (Aus.)

DAVID TOPLISS
Wakefield T.:   May 87 - (Promotion)
Under-21s: 1988-89
Played for: Wakefield T., Hull, Oldham

DARRYL VAN DE VELDE
Castleford: July 88 - (Yorks. Cup BF)
Played for: Easts, Souths, Redcliffe (All Brisbane,
Aus.)

DAVID WARD
Hunslet: July 86 - Apr. 88 (Div. 2
                champs, Div. 2 Premier BF)
Hunslet: Jan. 89 - May 89
Played for: Leeds, Workington T.

NEIL WHITTAKER
Huddersfield B.: Mar. 88 - Nov. 88
Played for: Huddersfield

JOHN WOLFORD
Hunslet: Oct 88 - Jan. 89
Played for: Bramley, Bradford N., Dewsbury,
Hunslet

David Ward, who left the Hunslet coaching post in May 1989 to join Leeds as assistant to Malcolm Reilly.

New Zealand's Dean Bell supported by loose forward Hugh McGahan in the first Test against Great Britain at Leeds in 1985.

NEW ZEALAND

NEW ZEALAND

The following is a list of Test matches involving New Zealand. For matches against Great Britain see the GREAT BRITAIN section.

New Zealand v. Australia Tests

Date		Score	Venue
9 May 1908	W	11-10	Sydney
30 May 1908	W	24-12	Brisbane
6 Jun. 1908	L	9-14	Sydney
12 Jun. 1909	W	19-11	Sydney
26 Jun. 1909	L	5-10	Brisbane
3 July 1909	L	5-25	Sydney
23 Aug. 1919	L	21-44	Wellington
30 Aug. 1919	W	26-10	Christchurch
6 Sept. 1919	L	23-34	Auckland
13 Sept. 1919	L	2-32	Auckland
28 Sept. 1935	W	22-14	Auckland
2 Oct. 1935	L	8-29	Auckland
5 Oct. 1935	L	8-31	Auckland
7 Aug. 1937	L	8-12	Auckland
14 Aug. 1937	W	16-15	Auckland
29 May 1948	W	21-19	Sydney
12 Jun. 1948	L	4-13	Brisbane
17 Sept. 1949	W	26-21	Wellington
8 Oct. 1949	L	10-13	Auckland
9 Jun. 1952	L	13-25	Sydney
28 Jun. 1952	W	49-25	Brisbane
2 July 1952	W	19-9	Sydney
27 Jun. 1953	W	25-5	Christchurch
4 July 1953	W	12-11	Wellington
18 July 1953	L	16-18	Auckland
9 Jun. 1956	L	9-12	Sydney
23 Jun. 1956	L	2-8	Brisbane
30 Jun. 1956	L	14-31	Sydney
13 Jun. 1959	L	8-9	Sydney
27 Jun. 1959	L	10-38	Brisbane
4 July 1959	W	28-12	Sydney
1 July 1961	W	12-10	Auckland
8 July 1961	L	8-10	Auckland
8 Jun. 1963	L	3-7	Sydney
22 Jun. 1963	W	16-13	Brisbane
29 Jun. 1963	L	0-14	Sydney
19 Jun. 1965	L	8-13	Auckland
26 Jun. 1965	W	7-5	Auckland
10 Jun. 1967	L	13-22	Sydney
1 July 1967	L	22-35	Brisbane
8 July 1967	L	9-13	Sydney
1 Jun. 1969	L	10-20	Auckland
7 Jun. 1969	W	18-14	Auckland
26 Jun. 1971	W	24-3	Auckland
8 July 1972	L	11-36	Sydney
15 July 1972	L	7-31	Brisbane
24 Jun. 1978	L	2-24	Sydney
15 July 1978	L	7-38	Brisbane
22 July 1978	L	16-33	Sydney
1 Jun. 1980	L	6-27	Auckland
15 Jun. 1980	L	6-15	Auckland
3 July 1982	L	8-11	Brisbane
17 July 1982	L	2-20	Sydney
12 Jun. 1983	L	4-16	Auckland
9 July 1983	W	19-12	Brisbane
18 Jun. 1985	L	20-26	Brisbane
30 Jun. 1985	L	6-10	Auckland
*7 July 1985	W	18-0	Auckland
6 July 1986	L	8-22	Auckland
19 July 1986	L	12-29	Sydney
*29 July 1986	L	12-32	Brisbane
21 July 1987	W	13-6	Brisbane

*Also World Cup

	P	W	D	L	F	A
TOTALS	62	21	0	41	800	1,139

New Zealand v. Australia World Cup

Date		Score	Venue
7 Nov. 1954	L	15-34	Marseilles
15 Jun. 1957	L	5-25	Brisbane
1 Oct. 1960	L	15-21	Leeds
1 Jun. 1968	L	12-31	Brisbane
21 Oct. 1970	L	11-47	Wigan
1 Nov. 1972	L	5-9	Paris
1 Jun. 1975	L	8-36	Brisbane
27 Sep. 1975	L	8-24	Auckland
29 May 1977	L	12-27	Auckland
9 Oct 1988	L	12-25	Auckland

● Tests on 7 July 1985 and 29 July 1986 also World Cup matches.

New Zealand v. Australia other matches

Date		Score	Venue
19 Nov. 1954	L	5-18	Leigh

New Zealand v. France Tests

28 Dec. 1947	W	11-7	Paris
25 Jan. 1948	L	7-25	Bordeaux
4 Aug. 1951	W	16-15	Auckland
23 Dec. 1951	L	3-8	Paris
30 Dec. 1951	L	7-17	Bordeaux
6 Aug. 1955	L	9-19	Auckland
15 Aug. 1955	W	11-6	Auckland
8 Jan. 1956	L	7-24	Toulouse
15 Jan. 1956	W	31-22	Lyons
21 Jan. 1956	L	3-24	Paris
23 Jul. 1960	W	9-2	Auckland
6 Aug. 1960	W	9-3	Auckland
11 Nov. 1961	D	6-6	Bordeaux
18 Nov. 1961	W	23-2	Perpignan
9 Dec. 1961	D	5-5	St. Ouen
25 Jul. 1964	W	24-16	Auckland
1 Aug. 1964	W	18-8	Christchurch
15 Aug. 1964	W	10-2	Auckland
14 Nov. 1965	L	3-14	Marseilles
28 Nov. 1965	L	2-6	Perpignan
12 Dec. 1965	L	5-28	Toulouse
11 Nov. 1971	W	27-11	Perpignan
21 Nov. 1971	W	24-2	Carcassonne
28 Nov. 1971	D	3-3	Toulouse
22 Nov. 1980	L	5-6	Perpignan
7 Dec. 1980	W	11-3	Toulouse
7 Jun. 1981	W	26-3	Auckland
21 Jun. 1981	W	25-2	Auckland
23 Nov. 1985	W	22-0	Marseilles
*7 Dec. 1985	W	22-0	Perpignan

*Also World Cup

	P	W	D	L	F	A
TOTALS	30	17	3	10	384	289

New Zealand v. France World Cup

30 Oct. 1954	L	13-22	Paris
17 Jun. 1957	L	10-14	Brisbane
8 Oct. 1960	W	9-0	Wigan
25 May 1968	L	10-15	Auckland
25 Oct. 1970	W	16-15	Hull
28 Oct. 1972	L	9-20	Marseilles
15 Jun. 1975	W	27-0	Christchurch
17 Oct. 1975	D	12-12	Marseilles
19 Jun. 1977	W	28-20	Auckland

●Second Test in 1985 also World Cup.

New Zealand v. France other matches

13 Oct. 1960	L	11-22	Paris
15 Nov. 1970	L	2-16	Carcassonne

New Zealand v. Great Britain Tests
see GREAT BRITAIN section

New Zealand v. Great Britain World Cup

11 Nov. 1954	L	6-26	Bordeaux
25 Jun. 1957	W	29-21	Sydney
24 Sept. 1960	L	8-23	Bradford
8 Jun. 1968	L	14-38	Sydney
31 Oct. 1970	L	17-27	Swinton
4 Nov. 1972	L	19-53	Pau
12 Jun. 1977	L	12-30	Christchurch

●The Third Test in 1985 and one in 1988 were also World Cup matches.

New Zealand v. Papua New Guinea Tests

25 Jul. 1982	W	56-5	Port Moresby
2 Oct. 1983	W	60-20	Auckland
10 Aug. 1986	W	36-26	Goroka
*17 Aug. 1986	L	22-24	Port Moresby
12 Jul. 1987	W	36-22	Port Moresby
*10 Jul. 1988	W	66-14	Auckland

*Also World Cup

New Zealand v. Papua New Guinea other matches

30 Jul. 1978	W	30-21	Port Moresby

New Zealand v. England World Cup

21 Jun. 1975	D	17-17	Auckland
25 Oct. 1975	L	12-27	Bradford

New Zealand v. England other matches

11 Jan. 1908	L	16-18	Wigan

New Zealand v. Wales World Cup

28 Jun. 1975	W	13-8	Auckland
2 Nov. 1975	L	24-25	Swansea

New Zealand v. Wales other matches

1 Jan. 1908	L	8-9	Aberdare
4 Dec. 1926	L	8-34	Pontypridd
18 Oct. 1947	W	28-20	Swansea
7 Dec. 1951	W	15-3	Bradford

New Zealand v. other international sides

23 Jan. 1952	British Empire	L	2-26	Chelsea
7 Dec. 1955	RL XIII	L	11-24	Bradford
12 Dec. 1955	RL XIII (Charity)	W	28-15	Castleford
8 July 1957	Northern Hemisphere	L	31-34	Auckland
20 Sep. 1961	RL XIII	L	20-22	Manchester
10 Aug. 1963	South Africa	L	3-4	Auckland
18 Aug. 1965	Commonwealth XIII	W	15-7	Crystal Palace
5 Nov. 1980	Britain Under-24	W	18-14	Fulham
9 Oct. 1985	Britain Under-21	W	16-12	Bradford

NEW ZEALAND TEAMS . . .

A 20-year review

The following is a compendium of New Zealand Test and World Cup teams since 1969. Only playing substitutes are included on the teamsheets.

Key: *: Captain (WC): World Cup t: try g: goal dg: drop goal

1969 Australia	**1969 Australia**	**1970 Great Britain**
Auckland: 1 June	Auckland: 7 June	Auckland: 11 July
Lost 10-20	Won 18-14	Lost 15-19
Ladner 5g	Ladner 6g	Ladner 6g
Key	Orchard, P. 1t	Orchard, P. 1t
Wilson, R.	Clark	Christian
Rolleston	Christian	Lowther
Brereton	Brereton	Brereton
Patrick	Woollard	Bailey
Cooksley	Cooksley	Patrick
Danielson	Danielson	Orchard, R.
*O'Neil	*O'Neil	*O'Neil
Noonan	Gailey	Gailey
Hibbs	Deacon	Hibbs
Kriletich	Noonan 1t	Deacon
Walker	Kriletich	Kriletich
		Sub: Walker

1970 Great Britain
Christchurch: 19 July
Lost 9-23
Ladner 3g
Orchard, P.
Christian 1t
Bailey
Brereton
Schuster
Carson
Orchard, R.
*O'Neil
Gailey
Hibbs
Deacon
Kriletich

1970 France (WC)
Hull: 25 Oct.
Won 16-15
Ladner 5g
Whittaker
*Christian
Lowther
Brereton 1t
Woollard
Cooksley 1t
Greengrass
O'Neil
Gailey
Smith, Gary
Kereopa
Kriletich
Subs: Graham, L.
        Deacon

1971 Great Britain
Salford: 25 Sept.
Won 18-13
Whittaker 1t
Orchard, P. 1t
*Christian
Lowther
Brereton
Williams, Dennis 1t
Stirling
Tatanah 3g
Fisher, J.
Gailey
Smith, Gary
Greengrass
Kriletich
Subs: Cooksley
        Orchard, R. 1t

1970 Great Britain
Auckland: 25 July
Lost 16-33
Ladner 5g
Lowther
Christian
Redmond
Brereton
Bailey 1t
Carson
Orchard, R. 1t
*O'Neil
Gailey
Deacon
Dixon
Kriletich
Sub: R. Williams

1970 Great Britain (WC)
Swinton: 31 Oct.
Lost 17-27
Ladner 4g
Whittaker
*Christian 1t
Lowther
Brereton
Woollard
Cooksley
Greengrass
O'Neil
Kereopa
Smith, Gary 1t
Heatley
Kriletich 1t
Sub: Graham, L.

1971 Great Britain
Castleford: 16 Oct.
Won 17-14
Whittaker
Orchard, P. 2t
Lowther
*Christian
Brereton
Williams, Dennis
Stirling
Tatanah 1t,4g
Fisher, J.
Gailey
Greengrass
Smith, Gary
Kriletich
Subs: Woollard
        Orchard, R.

1970 Australia (WC)
Wigan: 21 Oct.
Lost 11-47
Ladner 4g
McGuinn
*Christian
Lowther
Brereton
Woollard
Cooksley
Smith, Gary 1t
O'Neil
Gailey
Deacon
Heatley
Kriletich
Subs: Greengrass
        Graham, L.

1971 Australia
Auckland: 26 June
Won 24-3
McClennan
Whittaker 2t
Lowther
*Christian
Brereton 1t
Woollard
Stirling
Orchard, R. 1t
O'Neil
Tatanah 6g
Kriletich
Smith, Gary
Heatley

1971 Great Britain
Leeds: 6 Nov.
Lost 3-12
Whittaker
McGuinn
*Christian
Williams, Dennis
Brereton
Woollard
Stirling
Tatanah
Fisher, J.
Orchard, R.
Smith, Gary
Greengrass 1t
Kriletich
Sub: Eade

1971 France
Perpignan: 11 Nov.
Won: 27-11
Whittaker
Orchard, P. 3t
*Christian 1t
Williams, Dennis
Brereton
Woollard
Stirling
Tatanah 6g
Fisher, J.
Gailey
Smith, Gary
Greengrass
Kriletich
Subs: Orchard, R. 1t
     McGuinn

1971 France
Carcassonne: 21 Nov.
Won 24-2
Whittaker
Orchard, P. 2t
*Christian
Williams, Dennis 1dg
Brereton
Woollard 1t
Stirling
Tatanah 4g
Fisher, J.
Gailey
Smith, Gary 1t
Orchard, R.
Kriletich 1t

1971 France
Toulouse: 28 Nov.
Drew 3-3
Whittaker
Orchard, P.
Williams, Dennis
*Christian
Brereton
Woollard 1t
Stirling
Tatanah
Smith, Gary
Gailey
Orchard, R.
Fisher, J.
Kriletich

1972 Australia
Sydney: 8 July
Lost 11-36
Whittaker 1t
Orchard, P.
*Christian
Williams, Dennis
Brereton
Sorensen, Dave
Stirling
Gailey
Fisher, J.
Orchard, R. 4g
Eade
Greengrass
Kriletich
Sub: O'Sullivan

1972 Australia
Sydney: 15 July
Lost 7-31
Collicoat 2g
Orchard, P.
*Christian
O'Sullivan
Brereton
Williams, Dennis
Dowsett
Paul
Fisher, J.
Gailey
Eade 1t
Greengrass
Kriletich
Sub: Bolton

1972 France (WC)
Marseilles: 28 Oct.
Lost 9-20
Whittaker
Orchard, P. 2t
O'Sullivan
*Christian
Brereton 1t
Williams, Dennis
Tracey
Mohi
Burgoyne
Paul
Gailey
Gurnick
Eade
Subs: Cooksley
     Coll

1972 Australia (WC)
Paris: 1 Nov.
Lost 5-9
Wilson, J. 1g
Orchard, P.
Brereton
*Christian
Whittaker 1t
Williams, Dennis
Tracey
Mann
Burgoyne
Gailey
Eade
Paul
Gurnick
Sub: Walker

1972 Great Britain (WC)
Pau: 4 Nov.
Lost 19-53
Wilson, J. 2g
Orchard, P.
Brereton
*Christian
Whittaker 1t
Williams, Dennis 1t
Tracey
Mann
Burgoyne 1t
Gailey
Eade 1t
Coll 1t
Gurnick
Subs: Collicoat
     Walker

1974 Great Britain
Auckland: 27 July
Won 13-8
Collicoat 5g
Brereton
Johnsen
Kerrigan
O'Sullivan
Williams, Dennis
*Stirling 1t
Proctor
Burgoyne
Gailey
Coll
Greengrass
Eade
Sub: Robertson

1974 Great Britain

Christchurch: 4 Aug.

Lost 8-17

Collicoat 4g
Brereton
O'Sullivan
Johnsen
Kerrigan
Williams, Dennis
*Stirling
Gailey
Hibbs
Greengrass
Coll
Robertson
Eade
Sub: Mann

1974 Great Britain

Auckland: 10 Aug.

Lost 0-20

Collicoat
Brereton
Johnsen
O'Sullivan
Kerrigan
Williams, Dennis
*Stirling
Gailey
Hibbs
Mann
Robertson
Greengrass
Eade
Subs: Jarvis
     Gurnick

1975 Australia (WC)

Brisbane: 1 June

Lost 8-36

Collicoat 1g
Brereton
O'Sullivan
Whittaker 1t
Orchard, P.
Williams, Dennis
*Stirling 1t
West
Conroy
Hibbs
Coll
Baxendale
Eade
Sub: Jarvis

1975 France (WC)

Christchurch: 15 June

Won 27-0

Whittaker
Orchard, P.
O'Sullivan
Williams, Dennis
Munro
Jarvis 2t
*Stirling 1t
Greengrass
Conroy 1t
Sorensen, Dane 6g
Coll
Baxendale
Eade 1t
Subs: Collicoat
     Proctor

1975 England (WC)

Auckland: 21 June

Drew 17-17

Whittaker
Orchard, P. 1t
O'Sullivan
Williams, Dennis 2t
Munro
Jarvis
*Stirling
Greengrass
Conroy
Sorensen, Dane 4g
Coll
Baxendale
Eade
Subs: Collicoat
     Proctor

1975 Wales (WC)

Auckland: 28 June

Won 13-8

Collicoat 5g
Orchard, P. 1t
O'Sullivan
Williams, Dennis
Munro
Jarvis
*Stirling
Proctor
Conroy
Sorensen, Dane
Coll
Baxendale
Eade

1975 Australia (WC)

Auckland: 27 Sept.

Lost 8-24

Collicoat 4g
Orchard, P.
Matete
Williams, Dennis
Ah Kuoi
Jarvis
*Stirling
Greengrass
Conroy
Sorensen, Dane
Coll
Baxendale
Eade
Subs: Smith, J.
     Sorensen, K.

1975 France (WC)

Marseilles: 17 Oct

Drew 12-12

Collicoat 3g
Orchard, P.
Williams, Dennis
Smith, J.
Dickison
Jarvis 1t
*Stirling
Greengrass
Conroy
Proctor 1t
Coll
Baxendale
Gurnick
Sub: Gordon

1975 England (WC)

Bradford: 25 Oct.

Lost 12-27

Collicoat 2g
Orchard, P.
Smith, J. 1t
Williams, Dennis
Dickison
Jarvis
*Stirling
Proctor
Conroy
Greengrass
Baxendale
Coll
Eade
Subs: Gordon 1t,1g
     Gurnick

1975 Wales (WC)
Swansea: 2 Nov.
Lost 24-25
Collicoat 1g
Orchard, P. 1t
Ah Kuoi
*Williams, Dennis
Gordon 1t,5g
Jarvis
Smith, J.
Sorensen, Dane
Conroy
Greengrass 1t
Sorensen, K.
Coll 1t
Gurnick
Subs: Proctor
      Dickison

1977 Australia (WC)
Auckland: 29 May
Lost 12-27
Collicoat 3g
O'Hara
Filipaina
Jordan
Fisher, K.
Williams, Dennis
Smith, J. 1t
Henry, Whetu
Rushton 1t
Sorensen, Dane
Sorensen, K.
*Coll
Henry, Whare

1977 Great Britain (WC)
Christchurch: 12 June
Lost 12-30
Collicoat 3g
Fisher, K. 1t
Ah Kuoi
Filipaina
Whittaker 1t
Williams, Dennis
Smith, J.
Proctor
Rushton
Henry, Whetu
Sorensen, K.
*Coll
Henry, Whare
Sub: Graham, M.

1977 France (WC)
Auckland: 19 June
Won 28-20
O'Donnell
Fisher, K. 1t
Ah Kuoi
Williams, Dennis
Whittaker
Jordan 1t,8g
Smith, J. 1t
Proctor
Rushton
Henry, Whetu
*Coll
Sorensen, K.
Graham, M. 1t

1978 Australia
Sydney: 24 June
Lost 2-24
Jordan 1g
Ah Kuoi
Filipaina
Williams, Dennis
O'Hara
Smith, J.
*Stirling
Baxendale
Rushton
Proctor
Coll
Taylor, G.
Eade
Sub: Prohm

1978 Australia
Brisbane: 15 July
Lost 7-38
Jordan 2g
Varley
Filipaina
Williams, Dennis
O'Hara 1t
Smith, J.
*Stirling
Baxendale
Rushton
Proctor
Prohm
Coll
Graham, M.
Sub: Henry, Whetu

1978 Australia
Sydney: 22 July
Lost 16-33
Jordan 1t,5g
Ah Kuoi
Filipaina
Williams, Dennis
O'Hara 1t
Smith, J.
*Stirling
Bell, I.
Rushton
Proctor
Prohm
Coll
Graham, M.

1979 Great Britain
Auckland: 21 July
Lost 8-16
Collicoat 1g
Uluave 1t
Leuluai
Filipaina
O'Hara
Ah Kuoi 1t
Smith, Gordon
Broadhurst
Tamati, H.
Sorensen, Dane
*West
Tamati, K.
Coll

1979 Great Britain
Christchurch: 5 Aug.
Lost 7-22
Leuluai
O'Hara
Filipaina 1t,2g
Hudson
Uluave
Ah Kuoi
Smith, Gordon
Broadhurst
Tamati, H.
Sorensen, Dane
Tamati, K.
*West
Coll

1979 Great Britain
Auckland: 11 Aug.
Won 18-11
Leuluai 1t
Fisher, K. 1t
Filipaina 3g
Hudson
O'Hara 1t
*Ah Kuoi
Varley
Broadhurst
Tamati, H.
Tamati, K.
Edkins
Coll
Graham, M. 1t
Sub: Smith, J.
Ravlich

1980 Great Britain
Wigan: 18 Oct.
Drew 14-14
O'Donnell
Fisher, K.
Leuluai
Dickison
O'Hara
Ah Kuoi 1t
Smith, G. 4g
Broadhurst
Rushton
Tamati, K.
West
Coll 1t
*Graham, M.
Sub: Baxendale

1980 France
Perpignan: 22 Nov.
Lost 5-6
Kemble
Prohm 1t
O'Donnell
Whittaker
O'Hara
Ah Kuoi
Smith, G. 1g
Broadhurst
Rushton
Tamati, K.
West
Baxendale
*Graham, M.
Subs: Dickison
Tamati, H.

1980 Australia
Auckland: 1 June
Lost 6-27
O'Donnell 3g
Fisher, K.
Filipaina
Leuluai
*O'Hara
Smith, G.
Varley
Broadhurst
Tamati, H.
Te Ariki
Tamati, K.
Edkins
Graham, M.

1980 Great Britain
Bradford: 2 Nov.
Won 12-8
O'Donnell 1t
Prohm
Whittaker
Leuluai
O'Hara 1t
Ah Kuoi
Smith, G. 3g
Broadhurst
Rushton
Tamati, K.
West
Coll
*Graham, M.
Sub: Baxendale

1980 France
Toulouse: 7 Dec.
Won 11-3
O'Donnell
Prohm 1t
Whittaker
Leuluai
O'Hara 1t
Ah Kuoi
Smith, G. 1t,1g
Broadhurst
Tamati, H.
Tamati, K.
West
Coll
*Graham, M.

1980 Australia
Auckland: 15 June
Lost 6-15
O'Donnell 3g
Fisher, K.
Filipaina
Leuluai
*O'Hara
Williams, Dennis
Smith, G.
Broadhurst
Tamati, H.
Tamati, K.
Coll
Edkins
Graham, M.

1980 Great Britain
Leeds: 15 Nov.
Lost 2-10
O'Donnell
Prohm
Whittaker
Dickison
O'Hara
Ah Kuoi
Smith, G. 1g
Broadhurst
Rushton
Tamati, K.
West
Edkins
*Graham, M.
Sub: Tamati, H.

1981 France
Auckland: 7 June
Won 26-3
O'Donnell 1t
Prohm 1t
Williams, Dennis 4g
Leuluai 1t
O'Hara
Ah Kuoi
Varley 1t
Broadhurst
Rushton
Tamati, K.
Coll 1t
West
*Graham, M. 1t

1981 France
Auckland: 21 June
Won 25-2
O'Donnell
Prohm
Filipaina 5g
Leuluai 1t
O'Hara 1t
Ah Kuoi 1t
Varley
Broadhurst
Rushton
Baxendale
Coll
West
*Graham, M. 1t
Sub: Tamati, H. 1t
    Wilson, W.

1982 Australia
Brisbane: 3 July
Lost 8-11
Kemble
Prohm
Filipaina
Leuluai
O'Hara
Ah Kuoi
Smith, G. 4g
Broadhurst
Tamati, H.
Tamati, K.
West
Gall
*Graham, M.
Sub: Whittaker

1982 Australia
Sydney: 17 July
Lost 2-20
Kemble
Prohm
Filipaina
Leuluai
O'Hara
Ah Kuoi
Smith, G. 1g
Broadhurst
Tamati, H.
Tamati, K.
West
Gall
*Graham, M.
Subs: Whittaker
    McGahan

1982 Papua New Guinea
Port Moresby: 25 July
Won 56-5
Leuluai 2t
Fisher, K. 2t
Prohm 1t
Whittaker
O'Hara
Smith, G. 9g
Friend 1t
Broadhurst
Tamati, H. 1t
Tamati, K. 1t
*West 1t
Gall 1t
McGahan 2t
Subs: Wright, O.
    Coll 1g

1983 Australia
Auckland: 12 June
Lost 4-16
Kemble
Ropati, J.
Leuluai 1t
O'Regan
Bell, D.
Ah Kuoi
Smith, G.
Broadhurst
Tamati, H.
Sorensen, Dane
*Graham, M.
Sorensen, K.
Prohm
Subs: Varley
    West

1983 Australia
Brisbane: 9 July
Won 19-12
Wright, N. 3g,1dg
Ropati, J. 1t
Leuluai 1t
Ah Kuoi
Bell, D.
Smith, G.
Varley
Broadhurst
Tamati, H.
Sorensen, Dane
*West 1t
Sorensen, K.
Prohm
Subs: O'Regan
    Bell, I.

1983 Papua New Guinea
Auckland: 2 Oct.
Won 60-20
Wright, N. 8g
Alfeld
Bell, D. 3t
O'Regan
Crequer 1t
Varley
Friend
Tinitelia
*Tamati, H.
Bell, I.
Wright, O. 1t
Sorensen, K.
McGahan 6t
Subs: Orr
    Ackland

1984 Great Britain
Auckland: 14 July
Won 12-0
Kemble
Bell, D.
Leuluai 1t
*Ah Kuoi 1t
O'Hara
Filipaina 2g
Varley
Tamati, K.
Tamati, H.
Sorensen, Dane
Wright, O.
Sorensen, K.
McGahan
Sub: Friend

1984 Great Britain
Christchurch: 22 July
Won 28-12
Kemble
Bell, D. 1t
Leuluai 1t
*Ah Kuoi 1t
O'Hara 2t
Filipaina 4g
Varley
Tamati, K.
Tamati, H.
Sorensen, Dane
Wright, O.
Sorensen, K.
McGahan
Subs: Friend
    Cowan

1984 Great Britain
Auckland: 28 July
Won 32-16
Kemble
Bell, D.
Leuluai 2t
*Ah Kuoi
O'Hara 1t
Filipaina 6g
Varley
Tamati, K.
Tamati, H.
Sorensen, Dane
Wright, O.
Sorensen, K.
McGahan
Subs: Friend 2t
Cowan

1985 Australia (Also WC)
Auckland: 7 July
Won 18-0
Kemble
Bell, D.
Prohm
Leuluai 1t
O'Hara
Filipaina 3g
Friend 2t
Sorensen, K.
Tamati, H.
Tamati, K.
*Graham, M.
Wright, O.
McGahan
Subs: Ropati, J.
Cowan

1985 Great Britain (Also WC)
Elland Rd, Leeds: 9 Nov.
Drew 6-6
Kemble
Williams, Darrell
Leuluai
Bell, D.
O'Hara
Ah Kuoi
Friend
Tamati, K.
Wallace
Sorensen, Dane 1g
*Graham, M. 1t
Sorensen, K.
Prohm
Subs: Filipaina
McGahan

1985 Australia
Brisbane: 18 June
Lost 20-26
Kemble
Bell, D. 1t
Prohm
Leuluai
O'Hara
Filipaina 1t,4g
Friend
Wright, O.
Tamati, H.
Tamati, K.
*Graham, M.
Sorensen, K.
McGahan 1t
Subs: Elia
Cowan

1985 Great Britain
Leeds: 19 Oct.
Won 24-22
Leuluai 1t
Bell, D. 1t
Ah Kuoi
Prohm
O'Hara 1t
Filipaina 2g
Friend
Sorensen, K. 1t
Tamati, H.
Sorensen, Dane
*Graham, M. 1t
Wright, O.
McGahan
Subs: Kemble
Tamati, K.

1985 France
Marseilles: 23 Nov.
Won 22-0
Kemble
Williams, Darrell
Leuluai
Bell, D.
O'Hara 1t
Cooper
Friend
Sorensen, Dane 2g
Wallace
Sorensen, K. 2t
Wright, O.
Goulding
*McGahan 1t
Subs: Ah Kuoi
Filipaina 1g

1985 Australia
Auckland: 30 June
Lost 6-10
Kemble
Bell, D.
Prohm
Leuluai 1t
O'Hara
Filipaina 1g
Friend
Wright, O.
Tamati, H.
Tamati, K.
*Graham, M.
Sorensen, K.
McGahan
Subs: Ropati, J.
Cowan

1985 Great Britain
Wigan: 2 Nov.
Lost 8-25
Kemble
Bell, D. 1t
Leuluai
Prohm
O'Hara
*Filipaina 2g
Friend
Sorensen, K.
Tamati, H.
Sorensen, Dane
West
Stewart
McGahan
Subs: Ah Kuoi
Cowan

Goalkicking Kiwi forward Dane Sorensen.

225

1985 France (Also WC)
Perpignan: 7 Dec.
Won 22-0
Kemble 1t
Bell, D.
Leuluai
Ah Kuoi
O'Hara
Filipaina 3g
Friend
Sorensen, Dane
Wallace
Sorensen, K. 1t
*McGahan 2t
Wright, O.
O'Regan
Subs: Elia
      Todd

1986 Australia
Auckland: 6 July
Lost 8-22
Williams, Darrell
Ropati, J.
Bell, D. 1t
Leuluai
O'Hara
Filipaina 2g
Cooper
Wright, O.
Wallace
Sorensen, K.
*Graham, M.
McGahan
Prohm
Subs: Elia
      O'Regan

1986 Australia
Sydney: 19 July
Lost 12-29
Kemble
Bell, D.
Ropati, J.
Elia
O'Hara 1t
Filipaina 1t,2g
Freeman,
Wright, O.
Harvey
Sorensen, K.
*Graham, M.
McGahan
Prohm
Sub: Cooper

1986 Australia (Also WC)
Brisbane: 29 July
Lost 12-32
Kemble
Williams, Darrell 2t
Ropati, J.
Prohm
O'Hara
Filipaina 2g
Freeman
Todd
Harvey
Sorensen, K.
*Graham, M.
McGahan
O'Regan
Subs: Cooper
      Wright, O.

1986 Papua New Guinea
Goroka: 10 Aug.
Won 36-26
Kemble
Ropati, J. 1t,3g
Williams, Darrell
Elia 1t
O'Hara 1t
Leuluai
Freeman 1t
Shelford
Wallace
Brown 2t,1g
Wright, O.
*McGahan 1t
O'Regan
Subs: Crequer
      Stewart

1986 Papua New Guinea (Also WC)
Port Moresby: 17 Aug.
Lost 22-24
Kemble
Crequer
Williams, Darrell
Ropati, J. 1t
O'Hara
Cooper
Freeman
Shelford
Wallace 1t
Brown 1t,3g
Wright, O.
*McGahan 1t
O'Regan
Subs: Leuluai
      Stewart

1987 Papua New Guinea
Port Moresby: 12 July
Won 36-22
Mercer
Elia 2t
Iro, K. 3t,4g
*Bell, D. 2t
Horo, S.
Freeman
Friend
Taylor, R.
Wallace
Todd
Shelford
Horo, M.
Cooper
Subs: Stewart
      Lonergan

1987 Australia
Brisbane: 21 July
Won 13-6
Williams, Darrell
Elia
Iro, K. 2g
Bell, D.
Mercer 1t
Cooper 1dg
Friend
Taylor, R. 1t
Wallace
Shelford
Horo, M.
Stewart
*McGahan
Subs: Freeman
      Lonergan

Prop forward Ross Taylor, a tryscorer against Australia in July 1987.

1988 Papua New Guinea (Also WC)
Auckland: 10 July
Won 66-14
Williams, Darrell 1t
Horo, S. 3t
*Bell, D.
Iro, K. 3t
Mercer 2t
Cooper
Friend
Brown 9g
Wallace 1t
Shelford 1t
Graham, M. 1t
Stewart
Horo, M.
Subs: Freeman
Faimalo

1988 Great Britain (Also WC)
Christchurch: 17 July
Won 12-10
Williams, Darrell
Horo, S.
*Bell, D.
Iro, K.
Mercer
Cooper
Friend
Brown 2g
Wallace
Shelford
Graham, M.
Stewart
Horo, M.
Sub: Freeman 2t

1988 Australia (WC)
Auckland: 9 Oct.
Lost 12-25
Mercer
Iro, T. 1t
*Bell, D.
Iro, K. 1t
Elia
Freeman
Friend
Brown 2g
Wallace
Shelford
Sorensen, K.
Graham, M.
Horo, M.
Subs: Cooper
Stewart

NEW ZEALAND REGISTER . . .
1969-89

The following is an index of players who have appeared for New Zealand, toured or been members of a World Cup squad from 1969 to 1 June 1989.

Appearances refer to Test and World Cup matches only. World Cup matches are given in bold letters. Substitute appearances are in lower case letters.

Key: A — Australia, B — Britain, E — England, F — France, P — Papua New Guinea, W — Wales.

ACKLAND, John
Appearances: 1983 p
AH KUOI, Fred
Appearances: 1975 **A,W;** 1977 **B,F;** 1978 A2; 1979 B3; 1980 B3, F2; 1981 F2; 1982 A2; 1983 A2; 1984 B3; 1985 B2b, Ff
Tours: 1978 A,P; 1980 B; 1982 A,P
World Cup: 1975, 1977
ALFELD, Robin
Appearances: 1983 P

BAILEY, Roger
Appearances: 1970 B3
BARRY, Kevin
Tours: 1975 A
World Cup: 1975

BAXENDALE, Ray
Appearances: 1975 **A2,F2,E2,W;** 1978 A2; 1980 b2,F; 1981 F
Tours: 1975 A; 1978 A,P; 1980 B
World Cup: 1975, 1977
BEEHRE, Les
World Cup: 1975
BELL, Dean
Appearances: 1983 A2,P; 1984 B3; 1985 A3,B3,F2; 1986 A2; 1987 P,A; 1988 P,B,**A**
Tours: 1985 B; 1986 A,P; 1987 A,P
BELL, Ian
Appearances: 1978 A; 1983 a,P
Tours: 1978 A,P
BOLTON, Dick
Appearances: 1972 a
Tours: 1972 A
BOURNEVILLE, Mark
Tours: 1985 B
BRERETON, Maurice
Appearances: 1969 A2; 1970 B3,**A,F,B;** 1971 A,B3,F3; 1972 A2, **F,A,B;** 1974 B3; 1975 **A**
Tours: 1971 B; 1972 A; 1975 A
World Cup: 1970, 1972, 1975
BROADHURST, Mark
Appearances: 1979 B3; 1980 A2,B3,F2; 1981 F2; 1982 A2,P; 1983 A2
Tours: 1980 B; 1982 A,P
BROWN, Peter
Appearances: 1986 A2; 1988 P,B,**A**
Tours: 1986 A,P; 1987 A,P

BURGOYNE, William
Appearances: 1972 **F,A,B**; 1974 B
Tours: 1971 B
World Cup: 1970, 1972

CAMPBELL, Danny
Tours: 1980 1 guest app. while with Wigan
CARSON, Eric
Appearances: 1970 B2
World Cup: 1970
CHRISTIAN, Roy
Appearances: 1969 A; 1970 B3,**A,F,B**; 1971 A,B3,F3;
    1972 A2,**F,A,B**
Tours: 1971 B; 1972 A
World Cup: 1970, 1972
CLARK, Brian
Appearances: 1969 A
COLL, Tony
Appearances: 1972 **f,B**; 1974 B2; 1975 **A2,F2,E2,W2**;
    1977 **A,B,F**; 1978 A3; 1979 B3; 1980 A,B2,F;
    1981 F2; 1982 p
Tours: 1975 A; 1978 A,P; 1980 B; 1982 A,P
World Cup: 1972, 1975, 1977
COLLICOAT, Warren
Appearances: 1972 A,**b**; 1974 B3; 1975 **A2,fF,eE,W2**; 1977
    A,B; 1979 B
Tours: 1972 A; 1975 A
World Cup: 1972, 1975, 1977
CONROY, Tom
Appearances: 1975 **A2,F2,E2,W2**
Tours: 1975 A
World Cup: 1975
COOKSLEY, Graeme
Appearances: 1969 A2; 1970 **A,F,B**; 1971 b; 1972 **f**
Tours: 1971 B
World Cup: 1970, 1972
COOPER, Shane
Appearances: 1985 F; 1986 Aa2,P; 1987 P,A; 1988 P,B,**a**
Tours: 1985 B; 1986 A,P; 1987 A,P
COWAN, Ricky
Appearances: 1984 b2; 1985 a3,b
Tours: 1985 B
CREQUER, Marty
Appearances: 1983 P; 1986 Pp
Tours: 1985 B, 1986 A,P

DANIELSON, Oscar
Appearances; 1969 A2
DEACON, William
Appearances: 1969 A; 1970 B3,**A,f**
Tours: 1971 B
World Cup: 1970
DICKISON, Bruce
Appearances: 1975 **F,E,W**; 1980 B2,f
Tours: 1980 B
World Cup: 1975

DIXON, Kevin
Appearances: 1970 B
DONALDSON, Glen
Tours: 1986 A,P
DOWSETT, Shane
Appearances: 1972 A
Tours: 1971 B; 1972 A
DWYER, Wayne
Tours: 1982 A,P
DYER, Barrie
Tours: 1975 A
World Cup: 1975

EADE, Murray
Appearances: 1971 b; 1972 A2, **F,A,B,** 1974 B3; 1975
    A2,F,E2,W; 1978 A
Tours: 1971 B; 1972 A; 1975 A; 1978 A,P
World Cup: 1972, 1975
EDKINS, Barry
Appearances: 1979 B; 1980 A2,B
Tours: 1978 A,P; 1980 B
ELIA, Mark
Appearances: 1985 a,f; 1986 aA,P; 1987 P,A; 1988 **A**
Tours: 1985 B; 1986 A,P; 1987 A,P

FAIMALO, Esene
Appearances: 1988 p
FEPULEAI, Toa
Tours: 1978 A,P
FIELD, David
Tours: 1982 A,P
FILIPAINA, Olsen
Appearances: 1977 **A,B;** 1978 A3; 1979 B3; 1980 A2;
    1981 F; 1982 A2; 1984 B3; 1985 A3,B2b,Ff; 1986
    A3
Tours: 1978 A,P; 1982 A,P; 1985 B; 1986 A,P
World Cup: 1977
FISHER, James
Appearances: 1971 B3, F3; 1972 A2
Tours: 1971 B; 1972 A; 1982 A,P
FISHER, Kevin
Appearances: 1977 **A,F,B;** 1979 B; 1980 A2,B; 1982 P
Tours: 1980 B; 1982 A,P
World Cup: 1977
FREEMAN, Gary
Appearances: 1986 A2,P2; 1987 P,a; 1988 p,b,**A**
Tours: 1986 A,P; 1987 A,P
FRIEND, Clayton
Appearances: 1982 P; 1983 P; 1984 b3; 1985
    A3,B3,F2; 1987 P,A; 1988 P,B,**A**
Tours: 1982 A,P; 1985 B; 1987 A,P

GAILEY, Doug
Appearances: 1969 A; 1970 B3,**A,F;** 1971 B2, F3; 1972
    A2 **F,A,B;** 1974 B3
Tours: 1971 B; 1972 A
World Cup: 1970, 1972

GALL, Bruce
Appearances: 1982 A2,P
Tours: 1980 B; 1982 A,P
GIBB, Glen
Tours: 1985 B
GILLESPIE, Mark
Tours: 1982 A,P
GORDON, Tony
Appearances: 1975 **f,e,W**
World Cup: 1975
GOULDING, James
Appearances: 1985 F
Tours: 1985 B; 1986 A,P
GRAHAM, Lummy
Appearances: 1970 **a,f,b**
World Cup: 1970
GRAHAM, Mark
Appearances: 1977 **b,F**; 1978 A2; 1979 B; 1980
  A2,B3,F2; 1981 F2; 1982 A2; 1983 A; 1985
  A3,B2; 1986 A3; 1988 P,B,**A**
Tours: 1978 A,P; 1980 B; 1982 A,P; 1985 B; 1986
  A,P
World Cup: 1977
GREEN, Bernard
Tours: 1980 B
GREENGRASS, John
Appearances: 1970 **a,F,B**; 1971 B3,F; 1972 A2; 1974
  B3; 1975 **F2,E2,A,W**
Tours: 1971 B; 1972 A
World Cup: 1970, 1975
GRIFFIN, John
Tours: 1982 A,P
GURNICK, Peter
Appearances: 1972 **F,A,B**; 1974 b; 1975 **F,e,W**
Tours: 1975 A
World Cup: 1972, 1975

HARVEY, Barry
Appearances: 1986 A2
Tours: 1986 A,P; 1987 A,P
HEATLEY, Eddie
Appearances: 1970 **A,B**; 1971 A
World Cup: 1970
HENRY, Whare
Appearances: 1977 **A,B**
World Cup: 1977
HENRY, Whetu
Appearances: 1977 **A,B,F**; 1978 a
Tours: 1978 A,P
World Cup: 1977
HIBBS, John
Appearances: 1969 A; 1970 B2; 1974 B2; 1975 **A**
Tours: 1975 A
World Cup: 1975
HORO, Mark
Appearances: 1987 P; 1987 A; 1988 P,B,**A**
Tours: 1987 A,P

HORO, Shane
Appearances: 1987 P; 1988 P,B
Tours: 1985 B; 1987 A,P
HUDSON, Lewis
Appearances: 1979 B2
Tours: 1982 A,P

IRO, Kevin
Appearances: 1987 P,A; 1988 P,B,**A**
Tours: 1987 A,P
IRO, Tony
Appearances: 1988 **A**

JARVIS, Robert
Appearances: 1974 b; 1975 **F2,E2,W2,A**
Tours: 1975 A
World Cup: 1975
JOHNSEN, Bill
Appearances: 1974 B3
JORDAN, Chris
Appearances: 1977 **A,F**; 1978 A3
Tours: 1978 A,P
World Cup: 1977

KELLS, Bill
Tours: 1980 B
KEMBLE, Gary
Appearances: 1980 F; 1982 A2; 1983 A; 1984 B3;
  1985 A3,B2b,F2; 1986 A2,P2
Tours: 1980 B; 1982 A,P; 1986 A,P
KEREOPA, Elliot
Appearances: 1970 **F,B**
World Cup: 1970
KERRIGAN, Eddie
Appearances: 1974 B3
KEY, Dennis
Appearances: 1969 A
KRILETICH, Tony
Appearances: 1969 A2; 1970 B3,**A,F,B**: 1971 A,B3,F3;
  1972 A2
Tours: 1971 B; 1972 A
World Cup: 1970

LADNER, Don
Appearances: 1969 A2; 1970 B3, **A,F,B**
World Cup: 1970
LAJPOLD, George
Tours: 1987 A,P
LEULUAI, James
Appearances: 1979 B3; 1980 A2,B2,F; 1981 F2; 1982
  A2,P; 1983 A2; 1984 B3; 1985 A3,B3,F2; 1986
  A,Pp
Tours: 1978 A,P; 1980 B; 1982 A,P; 1986 A,P
LIAVAA, Josh
Tours: 1975 A
World Cup: 1975

LONERGAN, Dean
Appearances: 1987 p,a
Tours: 1986 A,P: 1987 A,P
LOWTHER, Bernard
Appearances: 1970 B2, **A,F,B;** 1971 A,B2
Tours: 1971 B
World Cup: 1970

MANN, Donald
Appearances: 1972 **A,B;** 1974 Bb
Tours: 1971 B
World Cup: 1972
MATETE, Paul
Appearances; 1975 **A**
World Cup: 1975
McGAHAN, Hugh
Appearances: 1982 a,P; 1983 P; 1984 B3; 1985
    A3,B2,F2; 1986 A3,P2; 1987 A
Tours: 1982 A,P; 1985 B: 1986 A,P; 1987 A,P
McGREGOR, Steve
Tours: 1978 A,P
McGUINN, Robert
Appearances: 1970 **A;** 1971 B,f
Tours: 1971 B
World Cup: 1970
McLENNAN, Michael
Appearances: 1971 A
Tours: 1971 B
MELLARS, Peter
Tours: 1982 A,P
MERCER, Gary
Appearances: 1987 P,A; 1988 P,B,**A**
Tours: 1986 A,P: 1987 A,P
MOHI, Mita
Appearances: 1972 **F**
World Cup: 1972
MUNRO, Don
Appearances: 1975 **F,E,W**
Tours: 1975 A
World Cup: 1975
MURU, Rick
Tours: 1980 B

NOONAN, Bill
Appearances: 1969 A2

O'CALLAGHAN, Vaun
Tours: 1985 B
O'DONNELL, Michael
Appearances: 1977 **F**; 1980 A2; 1980 B3,F2; 1981 F2
Tours: 1978 A,P; 1980 B
World Cup: 1977
O'HARA, Dane
Appearances: 1977 **A;** 1978 A3; 1979 B3; 1980
    A2,B3,F2; 1981 F2; 1982 A2, P; 1984 B3; 1985
    A3,B3,F2; 1986 A3,P2
Tours: 1978 A,P; 1980 B; 1982 A,P; 1986 A,P
World Cup: 1977

O'NEIL, Colin
Appearances: 1969 A2; 1970 B3, **A,F,B;** 1971 A
World Cup: 1970
ORCHARD, Phil
Appearances: 1969 A; 1970 B2; 1971 B2,F3;
    1972 A,**F,A,B:** 1975 **A2,F2,E2,W2**
Tours: 1971 B; 1972 A; 1975 A
World Cup: 1972, 1975
ORCHARD, Robert
Appearances: 1970 B3; 1971 A,Bb2,F2f; 1972 A2
Tours: 1971 B; 1972 A
O'REGAN, Ron
Appearances: 1983 Aa,P; 1985 F; 1986 Aa,P2
Tours: 1985 B; 1986 A,P
ORR, Dean
Appearances: 1983 p
O'SULLIVAN, John
Appearances: 1969 A; 1972 aA,**F**; 1974 B3; 1975
    A,F,E,W
Tours: 1971 B; 1972 A; 1975 A
World Cup: 1972, 1975

PANAPA, Sam
Tours: 1987 A,P
PATRICK, Trevor
Appearances: 1970 B
PAUL, Bob
Appearances: 1972 A2,**F,A**
Tours: 1972 A
World Cup: 1972
POTTER, Kevin
Tours: 1975 A
World Cup: 1975
PROCTOR, Lyndsey
Appearances: 1974 B; 1975 **Ff,Ee,Ww;** 1977 **B,F;** 1978
    A3
Tours: 1978 A,P; 1975 A
World Cup: 1975, 1977
PROHM, Gary
Appearances: 1978 aA2; 1980 B2, F2; 1981 F2; 1982
    A2,P; 1983 A2; 1985 A3, B3; 1986 A3
Tours: 1978 A,P; 1980 B; 1982 A,P; 1986 A,P

RAVLICH, Paul
Appearances: 1971 b
REDMOND, Wayne
Appearances: 1970 B
ROBERTSON, Wayne
Appearances: 1974 B2b
ROLLESTON, Sam
Appearances: 1969 A
ROPATI, Joe
Appearances: 1983 A2; 1985 a2; 1986 A3,P2
Tours: 1985 B; 1986 A,P; 1987 A,P
ROPATI, Tea
Tours: 1986 A,P

RUSHTON, Alan
Appearances: 1977 **A,B,F;** 1978 A3; 1980 B3,F; 1981 F2
Tours: 1978 A,P; 1980 B
World Cup: 1977

SCHUSTER, Fred
Appearances: 1970 B

SHELFORD, Adrian
Appearances: 1986 P2; 1987 P,A; 1988 P,B,**A**
Tours: 1985 B; 1986 A,P; 1987 A,P

SMITH, Gary
Appearances: 1970 **A,F,B;** 1971 A,B3,F3
Tours: 1971 B
World Cup: 1970

SMITH, Gordon
Appearances: 1979 B2; 1980 A2,B3,F2; 1982 A2,P; 1983 A
Tours: 1980 B; 1982 A,P

SMITH, John
Appearances: 1975 **a,F,E,W;** 1977 **A,B,F:** 1978 A3; 1979 b
Tours: 1978 A,P
World Cup: 1975, 1977

SORENSEN, Dane
Appearances: 1975 **F,E,W2,A;** 1977 **A;** 1979 B2; 1983 A2; 1984 B3; 1985 B3,F2
Tours: 1985 B
World Cup: 1975, 1977

SORENSEN, Dave
Appearances: 1972 A
Tours: 1971 B; 1972 A

SORENSEN, Kurt
Appearances: 1975 **a,W;** 1977 **A,B,F;** 1983 A2,P; 1984 B3; 1985 A3,B3,F2; 1986 A3; 1988 **A**
Tours: 1985 B; 1986 A,P
World Cup: 1975, 1977

The most famous of the Sorensen family, 23-cap forward Kurt, about to tackle Britain's Harry Pinner in the first 1985 Test at Leeds.

STEWART, Sam
Appearances: 1985 B; 1986 p2; 1987 p,A; 1988 P,B,**a**
Tours: 1985 B; 1986 A,P; 1987 A,P
STIRLING, Ken
Appearances: 1971 A,B3,F3; 1972 A; 1974 B3;
1975 **A2,F2,E2,W**; 1978 A3
Tours: 1971 B; 1972 A; 1975 A; 1978 A,P
World Cup: 1975
STOKES, Gerard
Tours: 1982 A,P

TAMATI, Howie
Appearances: 1979 B3; 1980 A2,b,Ff; 1981 f; 1982 A2,P;
1983 A2,P; 1984 B3; 1985 A3,B2
Tours: 1980 B; 1982 A,P; 1985 B
TAMATI, Kevin
Appearances: 1979 B3; 1980 A2,B3,F2; 1981 F; 1982 A2,P;
1984 B3; 1985 A3,Bb
Tours: 1980 B; 1982, A,P
TATANAH, Henery
Appearances: 1971 A,B3,F3
Tours: 1971 B
TAYLOR, Glen
Appearances: 1978 A
Tours: 1978 A,P
TAYLOR, Ross
Appearances: 1987 P,A
Tours: 1985 B; 1987 A,P
TE ARIKI, Paul
Appearances: 1980 A
Tours: 1980 B
THOMPSON, Angus
Tours: 1972 A
TINITELIA, Frank
Appearances: 1983 P
TODD, Brent
Appearances: 1985 f; 1986 A; 1987 P
Tours: 1985 B; 1986 A,P; 1987 A,P
TRACEY, Brian
Appearances: 1972 **F,A,B**
World Cup: 1972
TUPAEA, Nolan
Tours: 1980 B

ULUAVE, Dick
Appearances; 1979 B2

VARLEY, Shane
Appearances: 1978 A; 1979 B; 1980 A; 1981 F2; 1983 aA,P;
1984 B3
Tours: 1978 A,P; 1980 B; 1982 A,P

WALKER, Rodney
Appearances: 1969 A; 1970 b; 1972 **a,b**
World Cup: 1972
WALLACE, Wayne
Appearances: 1985 B,F2; 1986 A,P2; 1987 P,A; 1988
P,B,A
Tours: 1985 B; 1986 A,P; 1987 A,P
WEST, Graeme
Appearances: 1975 **A;** 1979 B2; 1980 B3,F2; 1981 F2;
1982 A2,P; 1983 aA; 1985 B
Tours: 1975 A; 1980 B; 1982 A,P
World Cup: 1975
WHITTAKER, John
Appearances: 1970 **F,B;** 1971 A,B3,F3; 1972 A,**F,A,B;**
1975 **A,F,E;** 1977 **B,F;** 1980 B2,F2; 1982 a2,P
Tours: 1971 B; 1972 A; 1975 A; 1980 B; 1982 A,P
World Cup: 1970, 1972, 1975, 1977
WILLIAMS, Darrell
Appearances: 1985 B,F: 1986 A2,P2; 1987 A; 1988 P,B
Tours: 1985 B; 1986 A,P; 1987 A,P
WILLIAMS, Dennis
Appearances: 1971 B3,F3; 1972 A2,**F,A,B;** 1974 B3;
1975 **A2,F2,E2,W2;** 1977 **A,B,F;** 1978 A3; 1980 A;
1981 F
Tours: 1971 B; 1972 A; 1975 A; 1978 A,P
World Cup: 1972, 1975, 1977
WILLIAMS, Ray
Appearances: 1970 b
Tours: 1971 B
WILSON, John
Appearances: 1972 **A,B**
World Cup: 1972
WILSON, Ray
Appearances: 1969 A
Tours: 1972 A
WILSON, Wally
Appearances: 1981 f
WINTER, Warren
Tours: 1978 A,P
WOOLLARD, Gary
Appearances: 1969 A; 1970 **A,F,B;** 1971 ABb,F3
Tours: 1971 B
World Cup: 1970
WRIGHT, John
Tours: 1975 A; 1978 A,P
World Cup: 1975
WRIGHT, Murray
Tours: 1975 A
World Cup: 1975
WRIGHT, Nick
Appearances: 1983 A,P
Tours: 1978 A,P
WRIGHT, Owen
Appearances: 1982 p; 1983 P; 1984 B3; 1985 A3,B,F2;
1986 A2a,P2
Tours: 1982 A,P; 1985 B; 1986 A,P

NEW ZEALAND TOURS OF BRITAIN

1907-08 TOUR

MATCH RESULTS

Bramley	W	25-6	6,000
Huddersfield	W	19-8	9,000
Widnes	W	26-11	7,000
Broughton R.	W	20-14	24,000
Wakefield T.	D	5-5	5,800
Leeds	W	8-2	12,321
St. Helens	W	24-5	8,000
Merthyr Tydfil	W	27-9	7,000
Keighley	W	9-7	8,000
Wigan	L	8-12	30,000
Barrow	L	3-6	7,500
Hull	W	18-13	12,000
Leigh	L	9-15	8,000
Oldham	L	7-8	12,000
Runcorn	L	0-9	4,500
Dewsbury & Batley	W	18-8	7,000
Swinton	W	11-2	4,000
Rochdale H.	W	19-0	8,000
Bradford N.	L	2-7	2,000
Halifax	L	4-9	11,000
Yorkshire (Wakefield)	**W**	**23-4**	**3,000**
Warrington	L	7-8	8,000
Hunslet	D	11-11	19,000
Salford	W	9-2	12,000
Wales (Aberdare)	**L**	**8-9**	**15,000**
Hull K.R.	W	6-3	10,000
Cumberland (Workington)	**L**	**9-21**	**4,000**
England (Wigan)	**L**	**16-18**	**10,000**
Lancashire (Oldham)	**L**	**4-20**	**6,500**
GREAT BRITAIN (Leeds)	**L**	**6-14**	**8,182**
York	L	3-5	4,500
Ebbw Vale	W	3-2	8,000
GREAT BRITAIN (Chelsea)	**W**	**18-6**	**14,000**
GREAT BRITAIN (Cheltenham)	**W**	**8-5**	**4,000**
St. Helens	W	21-10	4,000

SUMMARY

Played 35 Won 19 Drew 2 Lost 14

For
Tries 90 Goals 72 Points 414

Against
Tries 70 Goals 42 Points 294

Won Test series 2-1

TOUR PARTY

Manager: H. J. Palmer Captain: H. R. Wright

	App	Tries	Gls	Pts
A. H. Baskerville	1	1	0	3
C. A. Byrne	17	2	0	6
A. Callum	1	0	0	0
T. W. Cross	29	2	0	6
C. Dunning	7	0	0	0
D. Gilchrist	24	0	0	0
J. G. Gleeson	2	0	0	0
W. Johnston	30	7	0	21
A. F. Kelly	12	1	0	3
J. A. Lavery	8	2	0	6
A. Lile	14	1	0	3
D. McGregor	6	2	0	6
W. Mackrell	10	0	0	0
H. H. Messenger	29	7	60	141
C. J. Pearce	30	0	0	0
H. F. Rowe	24	10	0	30
G. W. Smith	24	7	0	21
L. B. Todd	22	10	0	30
W. M. Trevarthen	16	1	0	3
H. S. Turtill	33	1	5	13
W. T. Tyler	15	4	0	12
H. Tyne	9	2	0	6
E. Wrigley	31	7	7	35
H. R. Wright	21	5	0	15
R. J. Wynard	31	15	0	45
W. T. Wynard	9	3	0	9

MEMO

First match on 9 October, last match on 22 February.

The first-ever tour by any country 12 years after the game was born. Organised by Albert H. Baskerville and made up of Rugby Union players, including four of the New Zealand RU squad which toured Britain in 1905. Regarded as mercenaries by RU authorities who labelled them the *All Golds*, the breakaway group were the pioneers of Rugby League in New Zealand.

They also helped to found the game in Australia, playing matches there en route to Britain and on their return. The great Australian player Dally Messenger joined the squad as a guest player and did much to make the tour a success.

Several tourists signed for British clubs, including Lance Todd who joined Wigan and later became manager of Salford.

Tragedy hit the squad on the way home when Baskerville died of pneumonia, aged 25.

The first-ever tour game was at Bramley on Wednesday 9 October.

NEW ZEALAND

1926-27 TOUR

MATCH RESULTS

Dewsbury	W	13-9	13,000
Leigh	W	23-16	12,000
Halifax	L	13-19	13,000
Rochdale H.	W	11-9	7,590
Barrow	W	19-16	5,500
Widnes	W	15-5	6,000
GREAT BRITAIN (Wigan)	**L**	**20-28**	**14,500**
York	W	19-11	3,099
Warrington	L	5-17	5,000
Bramley	W	35-12	
Hull	W	15-13	13,000
Bradford N.	W	38-17	4,000
Oldham	L	10-15	16,000
Leeds	W	13-11	4,000
St. Helens Rec.	L	14-28	6,000
Salford	W	18-10	3,500
Huddersfield	L	10-12	5,000
GREAT BRITAIN (Hull)	**L**	**11-21**	**7,000**
Wigan Highfield	W	14-2	2,000
Batley	L	17-19	3,000
Keighley	W	21-3	3,861
Swinton	L	14-16	12,000
Wales (Pontypridd)	**L**	**8-34**	**18,000**
St. Helens	L	12-22	2,000
Wigan	L	15-36	9,000
Yorkshire (Huddersfield)	**L**	**16-17**	**3,000**
Hunslet	L	12-13	
Pontypridd	W	17-8	
Broughton R.	W	32-8	5,000
Wakefield T.	W	29-24	6,000
Hull K. R.	L	15-20	7,500
Lancashire (Leigh)	**L**	**3-28**	**7,000**
Cumberland (Workington)	**W**	**18-3**	**4,200**
GREAT BRITAIN (Leeds)	**L**	**17-32**	**6,000**

SUMMARY

Played 34 Won 17 Lost 17

For
Tries 132 Goals 83 Points 562

Against
Tries 126 Goals 88 Points 554

Lost Test series 3-0

TOUR PARTY

Manager: G. H. Ponder Team Manager: E. H. Mair
Captain: H. Avery

	App	Tries	Gls	Pts
H. Avery	29	23	0	69
H. Brisbane	27	6	0	18
L. Brown	27	15	0	45
A. Carroll	17	3	0	9
H. Cole	14	1	0	3
B. Davidson	23	14	0	42
F. Delgrosso	20	4	6	24
W. L. Desmond	15	8	0	24
W. W. Devine	9	2	0	6
C. Dufty	19	2	42	90
G. Gardiner	20	10	10	50
E. C. Gregory	15	0	6	12
A. W. Hall	22	4	0	12
F. Henry	12	2	0	6
E. Herring	30	6	0	18
J. Kirwan	18	5	0	15
L. Mason	26	8	3	30
J. Menzies	12	1	0	3
N. Mouat	10	3	16	41
J. Parkes	17	5	0	15
L. Peterson	8	2	0	6
J. Sanders	15	5	0	15
A. Singe	6	1	0	3
H. Thomas	18	2	0	6
C. Webb	7	0	0	0
J. Wright	6	0	0	0

MEMO

First match on 11 September, last match on 15 January.

Following their 2-1 Test series defeat of the 1924 British Lions, New Zealand replaced Australia as the 1926 tourists to Britain. But the high hopes were dashed by a long-running dispute between players and management which resulted in seven tourists being sent home in December.

At the centre of the dispute was the coach-manager E. H. Mair, an Australian with revolutionary playing tactics who was a strict disciplinarian.

The players were all amateurs receiving only expenses and this led to further protests when the English Rugby League gave the suspended players £10 to assist them on their passage home.

Despite the disputes Bert Avery was a worthy captain with the forward's 23 tries still a record for a New Zealand tourist in Britain.

All three Tests against Britain were lost and only half of the 34 tour games won with a big financial loss also reported.

1939 TOUR

MATCH RESULTS

St. Helens	W	19-3	4,000
Dewsbury	W	22-10	6,200

SUMMARY
Played 2   Won 2

For
Tries 7   Goals 10   Points 41

Against
Tries 3   Goals 2   Points 13

MEMO
The tour was abandoned because of the outbreak of the Second World War the day after the first match was played at St. Helens on 2 September.

While arrangements were being made to send the squad home safely a second game was played against Dewsbury on 9 September.

Both games were won which suggests that the tour would have been one of their best.

Lou Brown, who signed for Wigan after the 1926-27 tour, returned with the tourists and played in one of the matches to complete a span of 13 years between tours.

This was the first tour on which the New Zealanders adopted the Kiwis title, having previously been the All Blacks.

TOUR PARTY
Managers: J. A. Redwood and R. Doble
Captain: R. King

	App	Tries	Gls	Pts
J. Banham	2	1	0	3
G. Beadle	1	1	0	3
G. Ballaney	1	0	0	0
L. Brown	1	0	0	0
J. Campbell	1	0	0	0
T. Chase	1	0	0	0
J. Clark	1	0	0	0
J. Cootes	0	0	0	0
C. Davidson	0	0	0	0
J. Hemi	2	0	10	20
R. Jones	2	1	0	3
A. Kay	1	1	0	3
R. King	1	1	0	3
B. Leatherbarrow	1	1	0	3
A. McInnarney	0	0	0	0
H. Mataira	1	0	0	0
H. Milliken	2	0	0	0
L. Mills	1	0	0	0
G. Mitchell	0	0	0	0
G. Orman	1	0	0	0
P. Ririnui	1	0	0	0
V. Scott	0	0	0	0
J. Smith	1	0	0	0
D. Solomon	2	1	0	3
I. Sterling	1	0	0	0
W. Tittleton	1	0	0	0

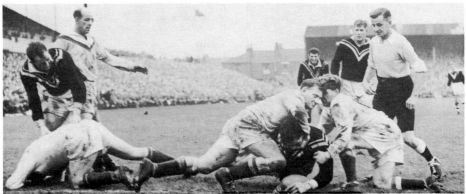

Prop forward Maxwell bulldozes over for a New Zealand try in the first 1955 Test at Swinton, despite the attentions of British duo Wilkinson (left) and Foster.

1947-48 TOUR

MATCH RESULTS

St. Helens	W	11-5	22,000
Swinton	L	6-8	12,148
York	W	29-0	4,500
GREAT BRITAIN (Leeds)	**L**	**10-11**	**28,445**
Castleford	W	17-3	11,000
Hull K.R.	L	7-13	12,000
Bradford N.	W	17-7	17,519
Leigh	W	10-5	15,000
Wales (Swansea)	**W**	**28-20**	**18,283**
Wigan	W	10-8	24,089
Oldham	W	18-8	17,239
Hunslet	L	10-18	5,533
Hull	L	7-13	16,113
Batley	L	18-19	3,510
GREAT BRITAIN (Swinton)	**W**	**10-7**	**29,031**
Leeds	W	23-16	8,864
Warrington	L	5-7	20,682
Halifax	W	21-5	5,276
Huddersfield	L	7-12	8,872
Widnes	L	0-7	11,900
Dewsbury	W	24-5	7,270
Workington T.	W	12-7	10,722
Barrow	D	2-2	5,565
Wakefield T.	W	30-3	11,595
Bramley	W	31-3	3,100
Belle Vue R.	W	19-3	10,000
GREAT BRITAIN (Bradford)	**L**	**9-25**	**42,680**

SUMMARY
Played 27 Won 16 Drew 1 Lost 10

For
Tries 83   Goals 71   Points 391

Against
Tries 52   Goals 42   Points 240

Lost Test series 2-1

TOUR PARTY

Managers: J. A. Redwood and L. Hunter
Captain: P. A. Smith   Coach: T. A. McClymont

	App	Tries	Gls	Pts
H. D. Anderson	15	8	0	24
R. Aynsley	13	3	0	9
D. A. Richard	13	3	0	9
R. J. Clark	14	1	2	7
S. W. Clarke	19	2	52	110
R. Cunningham	10	1	0	3
W. G. Davidson	9	1	0	3
J. A. Forrest	18	9	0	27
A. E. C. Gillman	10	1	0	3
A. H. Graham	2	0	0	0
J. S. Haig	7	0	0	0
C. C. Hancox	9	1	0	3
T. H. Hardwick	18	7	0	21
J. J. Johnson	16	0	0	0
L. R. Jordan	19	10	0	30
C. McBride	20	5	0	15
R. G. McGregor	18	8	0	24
A. J. McInnarney	15	4	0	12
A. W. McKenzie	5	0	0	0
K. Mountford	19	3	0	9
J. Newton	19	7	0	21
R. Nuttall	7	0	16	32
L. R. Pye	14	2	1	8
M. W. Robertson	21	6	0	18
P. A. Smith	21	1	0	3

MEMO
First match on 25 September, last match on 20 December.

A dock strike in Auckland delayed the tourists' departure by three weeks, forcing them to open with four matches in 10 days, including the first Test on 4 October.

Another setback was Sandy Hurndell being taken ill en route and the second row forward returned home without being replaced.

The post-war boom was at its height and over 375,000 saw the 27 matches with 42,680 at Bradford for the third Test, which remains a record for a New Zealand game in this country.

Arthur McInnarney was the only player from the war-hit 1939 squad to return for a full tour.

For the first time the New Zealanders extended their tour to France and played eight matches including two Tests in a four-week trip.

Ten tries in 19 appearances for L.R. Jordan.

1951-52 TOUR

MATCH RESULTS

Rochdale H.	W	13-9	4,000
Halifax	L	12-18	15,000
Workington T.	W	17-15	8,935
Oldham	L	18-21	15,174
Castleford	W	10-9	6,600
GREAT BRITAIN (Bradford)	**L**	**15-21**	**37,475**
Huddersfield	W	34-12	9,859
Warrington	W	19-13	18,889
Batley	W	20-13	5,087
Bramley	W	24-20	2,100
St. Helens	W	33-10	17,000
Leigh	W	31-5	9,000
Barrow	L	5-9	13,319
Bradford N.	L	8-13	29,072
Wigan	W	15-8	13,500
York	W	15-12	4,183
GREAT BRITAIN (Swinton)	**L**	**19-20**	**29,938**
Wakefield T.	W	26-18	8,850
Leeds	W	19-4	16,000
Lancashire (Warrington)	**L**	**12-13**	**7,313**
Belle Vue R.	L	5-7	5,000
Hull	W	28-8	9,000
Salford	W	27-12	10,000
Yorkshire (Wakefield)	**W**	**10-3**	**2,910**
Wales (Bradford)	**W**	**15-3**	**8,568**
Cardiff	W	18-10	2,000
GREAT BRITAIN (Leeds)	**L**	**12-16**	**18,649**
British Empire (Chelsea)	**L**	**2-26**	**6,800**

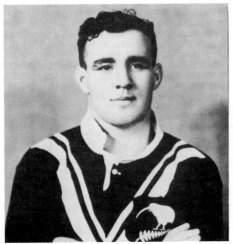

Joint top number of appearances for C. McBride, scorer of six tries.

SUMMARY
Played 28   Won 18   Lost 10

For
Tries 110   Goals 76   Points 482

Against
Tries 72   Goals 66   Points 348

Lost Test series 3-0

TOUR PARTY

Managers: D. A. Wilkie and T. F. McKenzie
Captain: M. W. Robertson   Coach: T. A. McClymont

	App	Tries	Gls	Pts
A. J. Atkinson	19	5	0	15
D. A. Barchard	16	1	0	3
T. O. Baxter	20	9	0	27
A. Berryman	5	3	0	9
D. L. Blanchard	12	1	0	3
G. J. Burgoyne	6	1	0	3
R. J. Cranch	7	2	0	6
J. J. Curtain	7	1	0	3
W. G. Davidson	20	2	0	6
J. F. Dodd	8	4	0	12
C. A. Eastlake	18	9	6	39
J. R. Edwards	14	6	0	18
K. English	10	3	0	9
J. A. Forrest	10	7	0	21
J. S. Haig	14	3	3	15
B. K. Hough	19	12	0	36
C. R. Johnson	19	7	0	21
C. McBride	22	6	0	18
W. R. McLennan	20	2	0	6
G. Menzies	7	1	0	3
F. G. Mulcare	19	4	0	12
D. Richards-Jolley	7	1	0	3
B. E. Robertson	14	13	0	39
M. W. Robertson	22	4	0	12
W. Sorensen	7	1	4	11
D. H. White	22	2	63	132

MEMO

First match on 18 September, last match on 23 January.

The second Test at Swinton made history as the first to be televised, Britain winning 20-19 with a late penalty goal by Jim Ledgard.

Des White was New Zealand's goalkicking star with 63, which remains a Kiwi record for a tour of Britain.

A young squad arrived with great expectations after a series of good performances against Australia, France and Britain, but never fully recovered from a poor start.

All three Test matches were lost and after making a 12-match trip to France the Kiwis ended their Britain tour with a 26-2 defeat against a British Empire side at Chelsea soccer ground.

237

1955 TOUR

MATCH RESULTS

Blackpool B.	D	24-24	12,015
York	L	16-20	8,174
Halifax	L	17-18	12,492
Yorkshire (Hull K.R.)	**W**	**33-17**	**7,907**
Wigan	L	15-17	19,386
Hull	W	17-12	10,167
Barrow	L	13-17	7,098
Workington T.	W	26-16	11,043
GREAT BRITAIN (Swinton)	**L**	**6-25**	**21,937**
Lancashire (Warrington)	**W**	**17-15**	**6,887**
Leeds	W	18-16	15,738
Featherstone R.	W	7-6	5,100
Huddersfield	L	16-25	11,271
St. Helens	L	8-16	14,000
Oldham	W	15-13	15,000
Leigh	L	13-14	3,400
Warrington	L	15-22	14,462
GREAT BRITAIN (Bradford)	**L**	**12-27**	**24,443**
Castleford	W	31-7	2,440
Rochdale H.	W	17-16	9,300
Bradford N.	W	11-6	5,271
Salford	W	21-5	4,000
Wakefield T.	W	27-16	4,838
Rugby League XIII (Bradford)	**L**	**11-24**	**3,643**
Keighley	D	11-11	4,200
GREAT BRITAIN (Leeds)	**W**	**28-13**	**10,438**

SUMMARY
Played 26   Won 13   Drew 2   Lost 11

For
Tries 95   Goals 80   Points 445

Against
Tries 94   Goals 68   Points 418

Lost Test series 2-1

TOUR PARTY

Managers: H. Tetlow and C. Siddle
Captain: T. O. Baxter

	App	Tries	Gls	Pts
A. Atkinson	19	11	0	33
V. Bakalich	21	20	0	60
T. O. Baxter	22	1	0	3
S. E. Belsham	2	1	0	3
D. L. Blanchard	13	1	0	3
J. E. Bond	6	1	0	3
J. R. Butterfield	13	1	0	3
P. J. Creedy	18	1	5	13
N. L. Denton	6	3	0	9
I. N. Grey	7	2	0	6
R. Haggie	18	6	48	114
R. P. Hawes	6	3	0	9
T. T. Kilkelly	10	0	0	0
H. D. Maxwell	19	4	0	12
G. S. MacDonald	20	0	0	0
B. McLennan	18	2	2	10
R. J. McKay	16	4	7	26
L. J. McNicol	11	8	0	24
G. Menzies	14	3	0	9
R. L. Moore	6	1	17	37
R. W. Percy	18	10	1	32
J. Riddell	5	0	0	0
N. K. Roberts	10	2	0	6
B. E. Robertson	9	4	0	12
W. Sorensen	22	5	0	15
J. E. Yates	9	1	0	3

MEMO

First match on 10 September, last match on 17 December.

The Kiwis flew to Britain for the first time but were slow to find form, opening with a draw at Blackpool Borough and losing their next two matches.

But after being well beaten in the first two Test matches New Zealand finished the tour with a shock 28-13 win over a complacent Great Britain at Headingley.

During the game at Castleford home prop Dennis Norton complained of chest pains and died 12 days later. A benefit game was played at Castleford in aid of Norton's dependants.

The tourists, with Halifax's Tony Lynch making a guest appearance, beat an RL XIII 28-15 but the game is not included in tour records.

Tour manager H. Tetlow.

1961 TOUR

MATCH RESULTS

Widnes-Liverpool	L	6-9	9,050
Manchester XIII	L	7-19	6,926
Castleford-Featherstone	W	31-20	5,744
Leeds XIII	W	24-9	7,085
Oldham-Rochdale H.	L	8-10	8,795
Yorkshire (Hull K.R.)	**L**	**11-21**	**6,750**
Barrow	W	36-11	6,647
Lancashire (Warrington)	**L**	**13-15**	**9,332**
Huddersfield-Halifax	W	31-11	7,251
Rugby-League XIII			
(Manchester)	**L**	**20-22**	**5,271**
Warrington	W	21-9	8,959
GREAT BRITAIN (Leeds)	**W**	**29-11**	**16,540**
Hull-Hull K.R.	L	6-17	8,125
Wigan	L	6-28	25,483
Cumberland (Whitehaven)	**W**	**10-9**	**4,970**
St. Helens	L	10-25	21,680
GREAT BRITAIN (Bradford)	**L**	**10-23**	**19,980**
Leigh	W	15-4	6,584
Wakefield T.	L	7-20	16,558
GREAT BRITAIN (Swinton)	**L**	**19-35**	**22,536**

SUMMARY

'Played 20   Won 8   Lost 12

For
Tries 60   Goals 70   Points 320

Against
Tries 62   Goals 71   Points 328

Lost Test series 2-1

Top goals and points scorer, J.E. Fagan.

TOUR PARTY

Manager: C. Siddle   Coach: W. Telford
Captain: R. D. Hammond

	App	Tries	Gls	Pts
A. N. Amer	10	5	0	15
G. R. Bailey	3	0	0	0
R. W. Bailey	15	12	0	36
J. A. Bond	14	5	0	15
J. R. Butterfield	17	1	0	3
B. E. Castle	11	4	0	12
M. I. Cooke	13	3	0	9
R. S. Cooke	16	4	24	60
R. H. G. Duffy	5	1	0	3
S. K. Edwards	15	2	0	6
H. K. Emery	17	0	0	0
J. E. Fagan	14	1	43	89
G. S. Farrar	8	2	0	6
J. P. Ford	5	0	0	0
B. T. Hadfield	9	6	0	18
R. D. Hammond	14	2	0	6
R. W. Harrison	6	0	0	0
W. R. Harrison	6	0	0	0
R. G. Hart	3	0	0	0
G. M. Kennedy	7	0	3	6
B. S. Lee	11	1	0	3
K. R. McCracken	5	1	0	3
J. G. Patterson	5	0	0	0
B. T. Reidy	15	9	0	27
W. L. Snowden	13	1	0	3
N. T. Tiller	3	0	0	0

MEMO

First match on 19 August, last match on 4 November.

The shortest tour so far with the schedule cut to just 20 matches with seven of them against combined club sides such as Swinton and Salford. None of these matches attracted attendances of 10,000 or more.

They finished with the worst record of all, still being the only Kiwi squad to lose more matches than they won. Yet the tourists shocked Great Britain by winning the first Test 29-11, which remains their highest Test score in this country.

Britain made seven changes for the next Test which they won 23-10 and clinched the series with a 35-15 final Test win, which was their biggest home score over New Zealand.

1965 TOUR

MATCH RESULTS

Commonwealth XIII (Crystal Palace)	**W**	**15-7**	**1,200**
Bradford N.	L	15-28	8,373
Warrington	W	14-7	8,162
Halifax	W	24-12	6,730
Oldham	W	5-2	13,021
Wigan	W	17-12	12,853
Widnes	L	3-8	9,450
Hull K.R.	W	21-11	7,540
St. Helens	L	7-28	11,270
Leeds	W	28-13	5,782
Yorkshire (Castleford)	**L**	**8-15**	**14,814**
GREAT BRITAIN (Swinton)	**L**	**2-7**	**8,541**
Leigh	W	10-5	4,840
Barrow	W	20-10	5,081
Whitehaven	L	7-12	3,208
Castleford	W	7-6	5,702
Hull	W	11-8	6,591
Lancashire (St. Helens)	**W**	**21-10**	**8,781**
Rochdale H.	W	10-4	7,075
GREAT BRITAIN (Bradford)	**L**	**9-15**	**15,740**
Swinton	L	7-14	8,345
Wakefield T.	L	4-16	7,484
GREAT BRITAIN (Wigan)	**D**	**9-9**	**7,919**

SUMMARY
Played 23   Won 13   Drew 1   Lost 9

For
Tries 48   Goals 65   Points 274

Against
Tries 41   Goals 68   Points 259

Lost Test series 2-0, one drawn

TOUR PARTY

Managers: W. L. O'Callaghan and T. Wellsmore
Captain: W. L. Snowden   Coach: W. Telford

	App	Sub	Tries	Gls	Pts
R. W. Bailey	18	0	5	0	15
L. P. Brown	6	1	2	0	6
R. F. Christian	14	0	2	0	6
W. G. Deacon	13	0	2	0	6
J. K. Dixon	9	0	2	0	6
S. K. Edwards	15	1	0	0	0
H. R. Emery	18	0	7	0	21
J. E. Fagan	12	1	0	28	56
R. D. Hammond	14	1	2	0	6
R. S. Irvine	8	2	1	0	3
G. M. Kennedy	19	0	1	7	17
B. W. Langton	8	0	1	0	3
G. Mattson	11	1	5	0	15
E. Moore	12	0	1	0	3
C. O'Neil	10	0	1	0	3
R. I. Orchard	10	1	2	0	6
B. T. Reidy	15	1	5	0	15
R. O. Scholefield	7	0	0	0	0
P. Shultz	12	0	3	0	9
W. T. Shultz	13	0	1	0	3
W. L. Snowden	13	0	0	0	0
R. Strong	8	0	0	0	0
R. Tait	14	1	3	30	69
J. D. M. Walshe	6	1	1	0	3
J. L. White	6	0	0	0	0
P. M. White	8	0	1	0	3

MEMO
First match on 18 August, last match on 6 November.

The tour opened with a 15-7 victory over a Commonwealth XIII at Crystal Palace, London. There was a crowd of only 1,200 with the receipts going to the Central Council for Physical Recreation.

Another disappointing tour with the Kiwis' lack of flair reflected in a total of only 48 tries scored in 23 matches and no player scoring more than seven.

It was the last tour under the old unlimited play-the-ball rule and Britain clinched a dull Test series with two wins and then a draw.

The slump in New Zealand rugby continued in France where they lost all three Test matches.

Top scorer of goals and points, Roger Tait.

1971 TOUR

MATCH RESULTS

Rochdale H.	W	23-8	2,374
St. Helens	L	8-18	8,169
Hull K.R.	L	10-12	5,746
Widnes	W	18-15	5,787
Castleford	L	8-25	5,889
Warrington	L	2-13	6,295
GREAT BRITAIN (Salford)	**W**	**18-13**	**3,764**
Barrow	W	25-15	4,839
Whitehaven	W	21-8	3,105
Swinton	L	15-26	3,280
Wigan	W	24-10	12,187
GREAT BRITAIN			
(Castleford)	**W**	**17-14**	**4,108**
Huddersfield	L	10-11	3,495
Leigh	L	5-10	4,012
Salford	L	30-31	7,127
Wakefield T.	W	23-12	5,367
Oldham	W	24-13	2,172
Bradford N.	W	30-23	6,362
York	L	5-11	2,803
GREAT BRITAIN (Leeds)	**L**	**3-12**	**5,479**

SUMMARY

Played 20   Won 10   Lost 10

For

Tries 68   Goals 57   Drop goal 1   Points 319

Against

Tries 62   Goals 55   Drop goals 4   Points 300

Won Test series 2-1

Tour captain Roy Christian.

TOUR PARTY

Managers: W. O'Callaghan and J. Williams
Captain: R. F. Christian   Coach: D. I. Blanchard

	App	Sub	Tries	Gls	Pts
M. P. Brereton	12	2	10	0	30
W. J. Burgoyne	9	0	0	0	0
R. F. Christian	13	0	4	0	12
G. R. Cooksley	7	1	1	0	3
W. G. Deacon	9	1	0	6	12
D. S. Dowsett	1	0	0	0	0
M. K. Eade	9	1	2	0	6
J. H. Fisher	11	1	0	0	0
D. Gailey	9	1	1	0	3
J. Greengrass	11	0	3	0	9
A. P. Kriletich	14	2	2	0	6
B. R. Lowther	9	0	2	0	6
M. J. McLennan	9	0	1	0	3
R. C. McGuinn	11	1	1	0	3
D. K. Mann	4	1	0	0	0
R. I. Orchard	10	3	2	5	16
P. C. Orchard	14	1	20	0	60
J. C. O'Sullivan	8	3	2	0	6
G. M. Smith	12	1	1	0	3
Dave Sorensen	6	0	1	0	3
K. L. Stirling	9	1	1	0	3
H. Tatanah	15	0	4	46	104
J. A. Whittaker	16	0	3	0	9
Dennis Williams	13	1	6	(1)	19
R. F. Williams	7	1	1	0	3
G. F. Woollard	12	3	0	0	0

(1) Drop goal — one point

MEMO

First match on 4 September, last match on 6 November.

Before travelling north, the Kiwis played two matches against Southern Amateur XIIIs, winning 67-6 on 29 August and 66-0 the following day, but these games are not included in the tour records.

Although the Kiwis showed only modest form against club sides they made it a memorable tour by winning the Test series 2-1, the first time they had achieved it since the inaugural tour of 1907.

The squad was captained by Roy Fletcher Christian, who had toured in 1965 and gained additional publicity as a direct descendant of Fletcher Christian of *Mutiny on the Bounty* fame.

Success on the field was not reflected in attendances with a total of fewer than 14,000 seeing the three Test matches.

1980 TOUR

MATCH RESULTS

Blackpool B.	W	23-5	1,312
Hull	W	33-10	15,945
Cumbria (Whitehaven)	**L**	**3-9**	**4,070**
St. Helens	L	6-11	6,000
Bradford N.	L	10-15	4,553
GREAT BRITAIN (Wigan)	**D**	**14-14**	**7,031**
Hull K.R.	W	20-12	9,516
Leeds	W	25-5	5,662
Warrington	L	7-11	5,680
GREAT BRITAIN (Bradford)	**W**	**12-8**	**10,946**
Great Britain Under-24s			
(Fulham)	**W**	**18-14**	**2,397**
Widnes	L	7-14	6,416
Leigh	W	22-5	3,166
GREAT BRITAIN (Leeds)	**L**	**2-10**	**8,210**

SUMMARY

Played 14   Won 7   Drew 1   Lost 6

For
Tries 42   Goals 38   Points 202

Against
Tries 23   Goals 35   Drop goals 4   Points 143

Drew Test series 1-1, one drawn

Tour captain Mark Graham.

TOUR PARTY

Manager-coach: C. Mountford.
Business Manager: W. Nesbitt
Captain: M. Graham

	App	Sub	Tries	Gls	Pts
F. Ah Kuoi	9	0	1	0	3
R. Baxendale	6	3	1	0	3
M. Broadhurst	9	0	0	0	0
T. Coll	6	0	4	0	12
B. Dickison	8	0	2	0	6
B. Edkins	7	0	0	9	18
K. Fisher	6	1	0	0	0
B. Gall	7	1	3	0	9
M. Graham	6	0	4	0	12
B. Green	5	0	2	0	6
B. Kells	4	0	0	0	0
G. Kemble	7	0	2	9	24
J. Leuluai	9	0	3	0	9
R. Muru	4	1	1	0	3
M. O'Donnell	8	0	1	5	13
D. O'Hara	9	2	6	0	18
G. Prohm	8	1	0	0	0
A. Rushton	7	1	1	0	3
G. Smith	7	0	1	15	33
H. Tamati	8	1	1	0	3
K. Tamati	8	0	1	1	3
P. Te Ariki	4	2	0	0	0
N. Tupaea	6	0	3	0	9
S. Varley	6	1	1	0	3
G. West	9	0	2	0	6
J. Whittaker	8	1	2	0	6

D. Campbell (Wigan) played one game on loan, a non-scorer.

MEMO

First match on 29 September, last match on 15 November.

The tour programme was cut to 14 matches and though the Kiwis won only half of them several players emerged who were to have a long stay on the international scene.

Hull signed three of them in one of the biggest-ever signing coups — Gary Kemble, James Leuluai and Dane O'Hara. Many more were to join other clubs as restrictions on overseas signings were lifted.

The Test series was drawn for the first time in this country with New Zealand's second Test win their first-ever at Bradford.

Although attendances for Test matches were well above those of 1971 they were still disappointing and the biggest crowd was 15,945 for the match against Hull at Hull City's soccer ground.

1985 TOUR

MATCH RESULTS

Wigan	L	8-14	12,856	
Great Britain Under-21s				
(Bradford)	**W**	**16-12**	**2,285**	
Hull K.R.	**W**	**20-10**	**6,630**	
Cumbria (Whitehaven)	**W**	**32-6**	**5,212**	
GREAT BRITAIN (Leeds)	**W**	**24-22**	**12,591**	
Yorkshire (Bradford)	**L**	**8-18**	**3,745**	
St. Helens	**W**	**46-8**	**7,897**	
Leeds	**W**	**16-10**	**4,829**	
GREAT BRITAIN (Wigan)	**L**	**8-25**	**15,506**	
Widnes	**W**	**32-12**	**5,181**	
GREAT BRITAIN				
(Elland Rd, Leeds)	**D**	**6-6**	**22,209**	
Hull	**W**	**33-10**	**8,406**	

SUMMARY
Played 12   Won 8   Drew 1   Lost 3

For
Tries 42   Goals 40   Drop goals 1   Points 249

Against
Tries 20   Goals 35   Drop goals 3   Points 153

Drew Test series 1-1, one drawn

MEMO
First match on 6 October, last match on 17 November.

The shortest tour on record was reduced even further when the game against Lancashire at Oldham was postponed because of frost.

Interest in the 12 remaining matches, however, produced the best Kiwi tour attendances for 20 years.

After an opening defeat at Wigan, the tourists won all five of their other club matches.

They ran up their highest-ever score on tour with a 46-8 defeat of St. Helens, including a record nine goals by Olsen Filipaina.

A late equalising penalty goal by Britain's Lee Crooks in the third Test squared the series.

The squad of 24 tourists was strengthened by the use of several British-based New Zealanders, mostly for the Test matches.

TOUR PARTY
Coach: G. Lowe Manager: J. Campbell.
Business Manager: T. McKeown Captain: M. Graham

	App	Sub	Tries	Gls	Pts
D. Bell	7	1	2	0	8
M. Bourneville	9	0	3	0	12
S. Cooper	5	3	3	0	12
R. Cowan	5	1	0	0	0
M. Crequer	1	0	1	0	4
M. Elia	8	0	8	0	32
O. Filipaina	7	2	0	20	40
C. Friend	8	0	3	0	12
G. Gibb	3	0	0	0	0
J. Goulding	6	0	0	0	0
M. Graham	4	0	3	0	12
S. Horo	5	0	3	0	12
H. McGahan	7	1	3	0	12
V. O'Callaghan	3	0	1	7	18
R. O'Regan	5	2	1	0	4
J. Ropati	5	1	0	8	16
A. Shelford	4	3	2	0	8
Dane Sorensen	5	1	0	1	2
K. Sorensen	6	1	2	0	8
S. Stewart	7	0	4	0	16
H. Tamati	6	0	0	0	0
R. Taylor	3	0	1	0	4
*B. Todd	0	1	0	0	0
W. Wallace	6	0	0	0	0
Darrell Williams	8	0	0	0	0
O. Wright	6	2	0	4(1)	9
British-based players					
F. Ah Kuoi (Hull)	2	1	0	0	0
G. Kemble (Hull)	2	1	0	0	0
J. Leuluai (Hull)	3	0	1	0	4
D. O'Hara (Hull)	3	0	1	0	4
G. Prohm (Hull K.R.)	3	0	0	0	0
K. Tamati (Warrington)	2	1	0	0	0
G. West (Wigan)	2	0	0	0	0

*Replacement
()drop goal — one point

NEW ZEALAND APPENDIX

In addition to full tours, World Cup squads made occasional appearances against club sides as follows, Kiwis' score first:

1960

| Halifax | W | 18-12 | 1,960 |

1970

Salford	W	8-7	2,226
Bradford N.	W	28-17	2,542
Barrow	W	14-10	5,118

1972

Leeds	L	6-11	3,510
Huddersfield	W	32-2	1,069
Salford	L	4-50	3,572

1975

| Barrow | W | 24-0 | 4,150 |
| Keighley | W | 20-8 | 2,125 |

RECORDS AGAINST CLUB SIDES

Highest score: 46-8 v. St. Helens in 1985
(Also *widest margin win*)
Biggest defeat: 4-50 v. Salford (1972 World Cup tour)
Biggest attendance: 30,000 v. Wigan in 1907-08

INDIVIDUAL RECORDS

(Club and representative matches)
Most tries on tour: 23 by Bert Avery in 1926-27
Most goals on tour: 63 by Des White in 1951-52
Most points on tour: 141 (60g, 7t) by Herbert Messenger in 1907-08
Most appearances on tour: 33 by H. Turtill in 1907-08
Most tries in a match: 5 by Bert Avery v. Broughton Rangers in 1926-27
Most goals in a match: 9 by Olsen Filipaina v. St. Helens in 1985
Most points in a match: 18 by Olsen Filipaina v. St. Helens in 1985

NEW ZEALAND TOURS OF AUSTRALIA

	P	W	D	L	F	A
1907-08	13	9	1	3	275	131
1909	10	5	0	5	181	182
1911	8	5	0	3	94	67
1912	7	4	0	3	84	83
1913	9	5	0	4	199	161
1919	11	5	0	6	211	187
1921	7	2	0	5	103	147
1925	12	5	0	7	223	230
1930	13	6	0	7	211	276
1938	9	5	1	3	182	161
1948	8	6	0	2	118	99
1952	13	10	0	3	368	149
1956	15	9	0	6	353	244
1959	15	13	0	2	488	205
1963	16	12	0	4	258	157
1967	17	11	0	6	369	216
1972	3	0	0	3	28	93
1975*	6	3	0	3	154	124
1978	16	10	0	6	358	241
1982	8	3	0	5	145	147
1986	6	3	0	3	138	105
1987	3	3	0	0	79	34

*Including one World Cup match.

NEW ZEALAND TOURS OF PAPUA NEW GUINEA

	P	W	D	L	F	A
1978	2	2	0	0	79	33
1982	3	3	0	0	136	30
1986	4	2	0	2	104	82
1987	1	1	0	0	36	22

NEW ZEALAND TOURS OF FRANCE

Each tour immediately followed trip to Britain.

	P	W	D	L	F	A
1947-48	8	4	1	3	118	104

Drew Test series 1-1

| 1951-52 | 12 | 7 | 1 | 4 | 181 | 93 |

Lost Test series 2-0

| 1955-56 | 8 | 3 | 1 | 4 | 107 | 143 |

Lost Test series 2-1

| 1961 | 9 | 6 | 2 | 1 | 150 | 57 |

Won 1 Test, drew 2

| 1965 | 8 | 3 | 1 | 4 | 67 | 80 |

Lost Test series 3-0

| 1971 | 6 | 5 | 1 | 0 | 108 | 43 |

Won Test series 2-0, one drawn

| 1980 | 7 | 6 | 1 | 0 | 119 | 34 |

Drew Test series 1-1

| 1985 | 7 | 7 | 0 | 0 | 192 | 41 |

Won Test series 2-0

● Two World Cup squads also played extra matches. In 1970 New Zealand played twice, winning and losing. The defeat was 16-2 against France in an unofficial Test. In 1975 they won two and drew one of three matches.

NEW ZEALAND TOUR SQUADS TO AUSTRALIA

Captains in bold

New Zealand's first tour was by A. H. Baskerville's famous *All Golds* of **1907-08** who played three matches in Australia en route to Britain and 10 more on their return. For squad see Tours of Britain.

1909

B. King

J. Barber
E Buckland
C. Byrne
A. Carlaw
D. Fraser
P. George
G. Hooker
T. Houghton
A. House
B. King
H. Knight
A. Lile
R. McDonald
H. Rowe
G. Spencer
J. Spencer
C. Sullivan
W. Trevarthen

Manager: D. Fraser

1911

C. Dunning

E. Asher
E. Buckland
H. Cotterill
C. Dunning
S. Feary
A. Francis
G. Gillett
E. Hughes
S. Kean
F. Mason
R. McDonald
W. Milne
F. Morse
J. Rukutai
C. Savoury
G. Seager
R. Shragne
G. Siddells
G. Smith
A. Stannaway
F. Woodward

Managers: E.W. Watts
A.J. Powley

1912

A. Francis

J. Barber
C. Bradley
T. Brownlee
A. Carlaw
W. Curran
W. Dervan
C. Dunning
D. Evans
A. Francis
J. Gilmour
A. Hardgrave
H. Hayward
R. Irvine
W. Kelly
D. Kenealy
C. King
C. Moir
J. Rukutai
C. Webb
S. Weston

Managers: T.A. MacReynolds
B. Brigham

1913

H. Hayward

A. Asher
J. Auld
G. Bradley
C. Byrne
L. Campbell
A. Carlaw
J. Clark
H. Devrall
H. Hayward
J. Hogan
K. Ifwerson
A. Jackson
W. Kelly
C. King
C. Manning
W. Miller
R. Mitchell
W. Mitchell
R. Probestal
R. Reke
A. Shadbolt
S. Walters

Managers: Dr. H.T.J. Thacker
S. Brice

1919

W. Mitchell

J. Brown
J. Clark
W. Cloke
W. Davidson
E. Herring
K. Ifwerson
B. Laing
A. Matthews
N. McCarthy
T. McClymont
A. McGregor
W. Mitchell
J. Parker
J. Rukutai
W. Somers
I. Stewart
H. Tancred
W. Waddell
W. Walsh
S. Walters
W. Williams
W. Wilson

Managers: H. Oakley
N.B. Levien

1921

H. Tancred

A. Avery
N. Bass
P. Burrows
W. Davidson
F. Delgrono
B. Laing
T. McClymont
C. McElwie
I. Meadows
H. Nunn
G. Paki
C. Polson
J. Saunders
A. Shadbolt
W. Somers
H. Tancred
S. Walters
W. Williams
W. Wilson
C. Wooley

Managers: R.J. Stirling
J. Rukutai

1925
B. Laing
H. Avery
H. Brisbane
L. Brown
E. Carroll
F. Delgrono
H. Dixon
C. Dufty
J. Ellis
A Green
C. Gregory
F. Henry
E. Herring
J. Kirwan
B. Laing
N. Monatt
J. O'Brien
J. Parkes
J. Sanders
H. Thomas
M. Weatherill
C. Webb
W. Wilson-Hall
Managers: N. Culpan
 J.D. Wingham
Coach: C.J. Pearce

1930
C. Gregory
E. Abbott
J. Amos
L. Barchard
H. Brisbane
J. Calder
S. Clarke
C. Dobbs
J. Dodds
C. Dufty
A. Eckhoff
C. Gregory
N. Griffiths
J. Jones
E. Meyer
J. Pearce
L. Seagar
R. Stephenson
T. Timms
G. Tittleton
R. Trounettor
S. Watene
M. Weatherill
Managers: J.A. Ferguson
 W.J. Taylor
Coach: A. Hennessy

1938
W. McNeight
J. Anderson
W. Brimble
J. Broderick
R. Brown
R. Chase
J. Cootes
A. Gault
W. Glynn
R. Grotte
J. Hemi
D. Herring
A. Kay
J. McLeod
W. McNeight
G. McNeil
G. Midgley
G. Orman
J. Satherley
J. Smith
H. Tetley
W. Tittleton
Managers: J.A. Redwood
 W.D. Carlaw
Coach: T.A. McClymont

1948
P. Smith
D. Anderson
R. Aynsley
D. Barchard
V. Belsham
W. Clarke
R. Cunningham
J. Duke
J. Forrest
A. Graham
A. Hambleton
C. Hurndell
J. Johnson
A. Laird
C. McBride
W. McKenzie
J. Newton
D. Redmond
M. Rich
M. Roberston
P. Smith
A. Wiles
Managers: W.A. Swift
 M.V. Simpson

1952
T. Harwick
A. Atkinson
T. Baxter
L. Blanchard
G. Davidson
C. Eastlake
J. Edwards
J. Haig
C. Harris
T. Harwick
B. Hough
H. Kreyl
R. McKay
W. McKenzie
W. McLennan
G. Menzies
R. Moore
F. Mulcare
R. Neilson
R. O'Donnell
J. Ratima
A. Riechelmann
R. Roff
J. Russell-Green
D. White
Managers: W.A. Swift
Coach: J.E. Amos

1956
T. Baxter
R. Ackland
V. Bakalich
T. Baxter
S. Belsham
J. Bond
O. Butt
J. Butterfield
P. Creedy
C. Eastlake
A. Green
R. Griffiths
T. Hadfield
C. Johnson
J. Lasher
H. Maxwell
D. McRae
G. Menzies
G. Moncur
F. Mulcare
J. Murray
R. Percy
J. Riccell
K. Roberts
W. Sorensen
D. White
J. Yates
Managers: R.G. McGregor
Coach: W. Telford

1959
C. Johnson
R. Ackland
E. Anderson
J. Butterfield
B. Campbell
M. Cooke
N. Denton
C. Eastlake
R. Griffiths
T. Hadfield
B. Hallaway
D. Hammond
C. Johnson
G. Kennedy
T. Kilkelly
H. Maxwell
G. Menzies
M. Paterson
R. Percy
G. Phillips
J. Ratima
B. Reidy
N. Roberts
W. Schultz
W. Snowden
G. Turner
P. Turner
Managers: W.F. Moyle
 A. Chapman
Coach: T. Hardwick

1963
M. Cooke
R. Ackland
R. Bailey
G. Blacker
J. Bond
J. Butterfield
M. Cooke
N. Denton
S. Edwards
D. Ellwood
H. Emery
J. Fagan
J. Fisher
K. George
R. Griffiths
D. Hammond
G. Kennedy
B. Lee
K. McCracken
C. McMaster
G. Phillips
B. Reidy
R. Sinel
W. Snowden
J. Sparnon
F. White
G. Woollard
Managers: C.G. Plant
          W. C. Desmond
Coach: W. Telford

1978 (Including Papua NG)
K. Stirling
F. Ah Kuoi
R. Baxendale
I. Bell
A. Coll
M. Eade
B. Edkins
T. Fepuleai
O. Filipaina
M. Graham
Whetu Henry
C. Jordan
S. McGregor
M. O'Donnell
D. O'Hara
L. Proctor
G. Prohm
A. Rushton
J. Smith
K. Stirling
G. Taylor
S. Varley
Dennis Williams
W. Winter
J. Wright
N. Wright
Managers:
W. O'Callaghan, A. Bernard
Coach: R. Ackland

1967
B. Castle
R. Bailey
E. Baker
R. Ballantyne
G. Brown
R. Carey
B. Castle
R. Christian
O. Danielson
W. Deacon
K. Dixon
D. Ellwood
R. Irvine
A. Kriletich
L. Mills
L. Morgan
W. Noonan
C. O'Neil
R. Orchard
P. Schultz
R. Sinel
G. Smith
W. Southorn
R. Tait
H. Tatanah
W. White
G. Woollard
Managers: M.A. Goe
          C.R. Mountford
Coach: D.L. Blanchard

1982 (Including Papua NG)
G. West
F. Ah Kuoi
M. Broadhurst
A. Coll
W. Dwyer
D. Field
O. Filipaina
K. Fisher
C. Friend
B. Gall
M. Gillespie
M. Graham
J. Griffin
L. Hudson
G. Kemble
J. Leuluai
H. McGahan
P. Mellars
D. O'Hara
G. Prohm
Gordon Smith
G. Stokes
H. Tamati
K. Tamati
S. Varley
G. West
J. Whittaker
O. Wright
Manager: J. Campbell
Coach: C.R. Mountford

1972
R. Christian
B. Bolton
M. Brereton
R. Christian
W. Collicoat
S. Dowsett
M. Eade
J. Fisher
D. Gailey
J. Greengrass
A. Kriletich
P. Orchard
R. Orchard
J. O'Sullivan
R. Paul
Dave Sorensen
K. Stirling
A. Thompson
J. Whittaker
Dennis Williams
R. Wilson
Manager: J. Williams
Coach: D.L. Blanchard

For 1975 see World Cup squads

1986 (Including Papua NG)
R. O'Regan
D. Bell
P. Brown
S. Cooper
M. Crequer
G. Donaldson
M. Elia
O. Filipaina
G. Freeman
J. Goulding
M. Graham
B. Harvey
G. Kemble
J. Leuluai
D. Lonergan
H. McGahan
G. Mercer
D. O'Hara
R. O'Regan
G. Prohm
J. Ropati
T. Ropati
A. Shelford
K. Sorensen
S. Stewart
B. Todd
W. Wallace
Darrell Williams
O. Wright
Manager: T. McKeown
Coach: G. Lowe

247

NEW ZEALAND

1987 (Including Papua NG)

D. Bell

D. Bell
P. Brown
S. Cooper
M. Elia
G. Freeman
C. Friend
B. Harvey
M. Horo
S. Horo
K. Iro
G. Lajpold
D. Lonergan
H. McGahan
G. Mercer
S. Panapa
J. Ropati
A. Shelford
S. Stewart
R. Taylor
B. Todd
W. Wallace
Darrell Williams

Manager: J. Bray
Coach: T. Gordon

New Zealand 1987 tourists to Australia and Papua New Guinea, second row man Sam Stewart, left, and hooker Wayne Wallace.

NEW ZEALAND WORLD CUP SQUADS

Captains in bold

1954 in France

C. Eastlake

H. Anderson
A. Atkinson
J. Austin
D. Blanchard
J. Bond
J. Butterfield
N. Denton
C. Eastlake
J. Edwards
L. Erikson
I. Grey
C. Johnson
G. McDonald
R. McKay
W. McLennan
G. Menzies
W. Sorensen
J. Yates

Manager: T. McKenzie
Coach: J. Amos

1957 in Australia

C. Johnson

R. Ackland
V. Bakalich
K. Bell
S. Belsham
J. Butterfield
P. Creedy
R. Griffiths
B. Hadfield
C. Johnson
W. McLennan
H. Maxwell
G. Menzies
K. Pearce
R. Percy
J. Riddell
W. Sorensen
G. Turner
J. Yates

Manager: K. Blow
Coach: W. Telford

1960 in England

C. Johnson

R. Ackland
J. Butterfield
M. Cooke
R. Cooke
N. Denton
C. Eastlake
R. Griffiths
B. Hadfield
C. Johnson
T. Kilkelly
H. Maxwell
G. Menzies
L. Oliff
G. Phillips
T. Reid
N. Roberts
W. Sorensen
G. Turner

Managers: G. Platt
T. Skinner
Coach: T. Hardwick

1968 in Australia and New Zealand

J. Bond

J. Bond
E. Carson
J. Clarke
O. Danielson
J. Dixon
S. Dunn
J. Ellwood
A. Kriletich
B. Lee
C. McMaster
R. Mincham
C. O'Neil
D. Parkinson
P. Schultz
H. Sinel
Gary Smith
R. Tait
H. Tatanah
E. Wiggs

Manager: D. Wilson
Coach: B. Barchard

1970 in England

R. Christian

M. Brereton
W. Burgoyne
E. Carson
F. Christian
G. Cooksley
W. Deacon
D. Gailey
L. Graham
J. Greengrass
E. Heatley
E. Kereopa
A. Kriletich
D. Ladner
B. Lowther
R. McGuinn
C. O'Neil
Gary Smith
J. Whittaker
G. Woollard

Manager: C. Mountford
Coach: L. Blanchard

1972 in France

R. Christian

M. Brereton
W. Burgoyne
F. Christian
A. Coll
W. Collicoat
G. Cooksley
M. Eade
D. Gailey
P. Gurnick
D. Mann
M. Mohi
P. Orchard
J. O'Sullivan
R. Paul
B. Tracey
R. Walker
J. Whittaker
Dennis Williams
J. Wilson

Manager: T. Wellsmore
Coach: D. Barchard

1975 First phase in Australia

K. Stirling

K. Barry
R. Baxendale
M. Brereton
T. Coll
W. Collicoat
T. Conroy
B. Dyer
M. Eade
P. Gurnick
J. Hibbs
R. Jarvis
S. Liavaa
D. Munro
P. Orchard
J. O'Sullivan
K. Potter
L. Proctor
K. Stirling
G. West
J. Whittaker
Dennis Williams
J. Wright
M. Wright

Manager: B. Watson
Coach: G. Menzies

1975 Second phase in Britain and France

K. Stirling

F. Ah Kuoi
P. Baxendale
L. Beehre
T. Coll
W. Collicoat
T. Conroy
B. Dickison
M. Eade
A. Gordon
J. Greengrass
P. Gurnick
R. Jarvis
P. Orchard
L. Proctor
J. Smith
Dane Sorensen
K. Sorensen
K. Stirling
Dennis Williams

Manager: B. Watson
Coach: G. Menzies

1977 in Australia and New Zealand

T. Coll

F. Ah Kuoi
R. Baxendale
T. Coll
W. Collicoat
O. Filipaina
K. Fisher
M. Graham
Whare Henry
Whetu Henry
C. Jordan
M. O'Donnell
D. O'Hara
L. Proctor
A. Rushton
J. Smith
Dane Sorensen
K. Sorensen
J. Whittaker
Dennis Williams

Manager: D. Barchard
Coach: R. Ackland

● The following players appeared in 1975 World Cup games in New Zealand but did not tour Australia: F. Ah Kuoi, J. Greengrass, P. Matete, J. Smith, Dane Sorensen, K. Sorensen.

RECORDS IN TEST AND WORLD CUP MATCHES

For New Zealand

Highest score: 66-14 v. Papua New Guinea, Test and World Cup match at Auckland 10 July 1988 (Also *widest margin win*)

Most tries in a match: 6 by Hugh McGahan v. Papua New Guinea Test at Auckland 2 Oct. 1983

Most points in a match: 24 by Hugh McGahan (As above)

Most goals in a match: 11 by Des White v. Australia, Second Test at Brisbane 28 June 1952

Most appearances: 36 by Jock Butterfield (1954-63)

Most career tries: 15 by Phil Orchard (1969-75)

Most career goals: 62 by Des White (1950-56)

Most career points: 130 by Des White (1950-56)

Biggest attendance: 47,363 v. Australia, World Cup final at Eden Park, Auckland 9 October 1988

Against New Zealand

Highest score: 53-19 v. Great Britain, World Cup at Pau 4 November 1972

Widest margin: 47-11 v. Australia, World Cup at Wigan 21 October 1970

Most tries in a match: 4 by Billy Boston (Britain) First Test at Auckland 24 July 1954
4 by Garry Schofield (Britain) Second Test at Wigan 2 November 1985

Most goals in a match: 10 by John Holmes (Britain) World Cup at Pau 4 November 1972

Most points in a match: 26 (10g,2t) by John Holmes (Britain) as above

Phil Orchard, holder of New Zealand record for most tries in an international career.

One of the great successes of the 1988 Lions Tour, Warrington skipper Mike Gregory.

1988 LIONS TOUR

1988 LIONS TOUR

1988 TOUR REVIEW

Great Britain's dream of wresting the Ashes from Australia for the first time since 1970 while qualifying for the World Cup final turned into a nightmare.

Mass withdrawals and long-term injuries decimated the most intensive preparations for a Lions tour, the 18th Australasian trip being hallmarked by a catalogue of casualties.

Four of the original squad withdrew before departure and six more returned home injured during the tour. The ins and outs of the jinxed tour squad were:

IN came 23 players, plus 10 on stand-by and Joe Lydon as a mid-tour arrival after his degree examinations, as coach Malcolm Reilly named his squad at the start of April, three remaining players to be added by the end of the month.

OUT went full back Steve Hampson with a broken arm which failed to mend in time to join the party midway through the tour.

OUT went back row forward Andy Goodway, withdrawing to concentrate on a proposed new restaurant business.

IN came his replacement, St. Helens utility man Roy Haggerty, from the stand-by squad.

IN came stand-bys Lee Crooks and Des Drummond, after passing medical tests, and prop forward Hugh Waddell.

IN came utility back Ian Wilkinson to replace Hampson, thus completing the 26-man squad.

OUT go Lydon and Drummond, withdrawn by the League for being involved in legal proceedings alleging assaults on spectators.

IN came Leeds threequarter Carl Gibson to stand in for Drummond despite not being in the shadow line-up, joining the party in Australia along with Andy Platt who had been left at home to recover from an ankle injury.

IN came Widnes centre Darren Wright a fortnight after the tour set off, joining the squad in Sydney as cover for Shaun Edwards, a knee injury victim only seven minutes into the first match.

OUT went Edwards, jetting home on 4 June to recuperate from a knee cartilage operation.

OUT went Leeds duo Garry Schofield and Paul Medley, flying home on 21 June with a broken cheekbone and neck injury respectively.

IN came Widnes pair Andy Currier and Paul Hulme as replacements two days later.

OUT went packmen Crooks, never fully fit after a six-month lay off with a shoulder injury, and Platt, nursing a broken wrist, on a 1 July flight.

IN flew Richard Eyres, a fourth Widnes replacement, and John Joyner, for a record-equalling third tour, 48 hours later.

OUT went homeward-bound Halifax forward Paul Dixon with a broken thumb in plaster.

Great Britain were always judged to have a mountain to climb to regain the Ashes after an 18-year Australian stranglehold featuring a run of 13 consecutive victories. The ever-growing rota of absentees made the task Everest-like.

It resulted in a list of unwanted records. Seven defeats from 16 matches in Australia and New Zealand was the worst percentage since tours to these countries began. They also lost three successive matches for the first time and the 30-0 defeat at Manly was the only time the Lions have been nilled in Australia outside the Tests. Finally, the last Test was played before the lowest-ever crowd for a Test involving Britain in Australia, 15,994.

But the bare facts do not reflect the spirit in adversity which was fostered.

That never-say-die attitude fully blossomed on 9 July when Great Britain added a another chapter to the annals of historic Lions' victories, rescuing the tour from becoming the most unsuccessful on record. Having sent six players home injured, the British camp took time from being pilloried by the hostile Sydney Press to count a new crop of injuries.

On the eve of the third Australian Test, a World Cup-rated encounter, regular hooker Kevin Beardmore was already a casualty with a shoulder injury sustained in mid-week. His understudy, Paul Groves, failed a fitness test, as did his replacement, Widnes back row forward Eyres. Fellow Chemic Paul Hulme was brought in to join namesake David — only the fourth set of brothers to be Lions — in the Test line-up as fourth choice hooker.

Tour legends were rewritten as the new Sydney Football Stadium staged a 26-12 British victory to be judged alongside the 1914 Rorke's Drift Test and the 1958 Battle of Brisbane. Amid scenes of intense emotion, Britain's new found heroes salvaged an ill-fated tour and suddenly found themselves on top of the protracted World Cup table with a place in the autumn final beckoning.

The crunch came in Christchurch a week later with the Lions needing only a draw to qualify for a clash with Australia scheduled for Manchester United's Old Trafford in October. The fairytale ending never materialised as New Zealand secured a 12-10 victory in rainswept mud amid British laments of a disallowed try, missed goalkicks, unawarded penalty kicks at goals and two blunders which led to a brace of tries for 13th minute substitute Gary Freeman.

Not all Britain's problems were on the field. The 10-week itinerary ranked as an obstacle course in the race for both playing and financial returns. Leaving the day after the Stones Bitter Premiership finals, the squad spent nearly three days reaching Papua New Guinea for a three-day acclimatisation for the opening fixture, a World Cup qualifying Test match.

The Australian authorities acceded to Britain's request for higher grade fixtures and then sited the premier games with Grand Final winners Manly and the President's XIII — an Australian B side — only days before a Test. In between were a string of country fixtures which provided long distance travel and limited gate returns. The tour jinx even struck the match accounts with the only three rainy days of the trip falling on lucrative match dates! In New Zealand, the tourists were compelled to fulfil a fixture in Wellington four days before the vital Kiwi Test having rejected the game in the planning stages of the tour.

The tour was an ordeal-cum-triumph for coach Reilly, himself a 1970 Ashes-winning tourist. The former Castleford coach refused to buckle under the pressure of losing key personnel on a regular basis, undermining the months of intensive preparation masterminded with his assistant Phil Larder and team manager Les Bettinson.

On the day of the third tour fixture in Cairns, Leeds announced his appointment as their new coach, to take up the Headingley role at the end of his Great Britain duties in July.

The third Test success in Sydney simply confirmed calls for the system to be changed back to the policy of allowing a club coach to take the national post part-time, thus maintaining Reilly's control of the Test team.

Another record to be proud of is that not one player was sent off during the tour, although there were seven instances of British players being sent to the sin bin.

The tour recorded a profit of £12,000, having paid out first-ever Test bonuses of £10,000 for the Papua victory and £15,000 for the historic third Australian Test success, and despite the Australians' lack of celebration of the first Test being the 100th Anglo-Aussie meeting.

TOUR RESULTS

Date	Result	Score	Opposition	Venue	Attendance
In Papua New Guinea					
May 22	W	42-22	*PAPUA NEW GUINEA	Port Moresby	12,107
24	W	36-18	Nthn/Highland Zones	Lae	3,270
In Australia					
27	W	66-16	North Queensland	Cairns	5,500
June 1	W	28-12	Newcastle Knights	Newcastle	6,649
5	L	12-36	Northern Division	Tamworth	2,192
7	L	0-30	Manly	Manly	11,131
11	L	6-17	AUSTRALIA	Sydney	24,202
15	W	28-14	Combined Brisbane	Brisbane	1,810
17	W	64-8	Central Queensland	Rockhampton	4,418
22	W	28-12	Toowoomba	Toowoomba	3,874
25	W	14-0	Wide Bay	Gympie	2,310
28	L	14-34	AUSTRALIA	Brisbane	27,103
July 3	W	28-26	Western Division	Orange	3,520
5	L	16-24	President's XII	Canberra	6,037
9	W	26-12	*AUSTRALIA	Sydney	15,994
In New Zealand					
13	W	24-18	Wellington	Wellington	4,428
17	L	10-12	*NEW ZEALAND	Christchurch	8,525
19	L	14-30	Auckland	Auckland	8,000

* World Cup-rated

TOUR SUMMARY

	P	W	D	L	T	G	Dr	Pts	T	G	Dr	Pts
					FOR				AGAINST			
In Papua New Guinea	2	2	0	0	13	13	0	78	7	6	0	40
In Australia	13	8	0	5	59	47	0	330	42	36	1	241
In New Zealand	3	1	0	2	8	8	0	48	10	10	0	60
Tour totals	18	11	0	7	80	68	0	456	59	52	1	341

TEST SUMMARY

	P	W	D	L	T	G	Dr	Pts	T	G	Dr	Pts
					FOR				AGAINST			
In Papua New Guinea	1	1	0	0	7	7	0	42	4	3	0	22
In Australia	3	1	0	2	8	7	0	46	11	9	1	63
In New Zealand	1	0	0	1	2	1	0	10	2	2	0	12
Test totals	5	2	0	3	17	15	0	98	17	14	1	97

It's mine ... Great Britain's Phil Ford takes to the air against Combined Brisbane at Lang Park.

TOUR RECORDS

Biggest attendance: 27,103, second Test at Lang Park, Brisbane

Highest score: 66-16 v. North Queensland

Widest margin: 64-8 v. Central Queensland

Highest score against: Lost to Northern Division 36-12

Widest margin defeat: Lost to Manly 30-0

Most tries in a match: 4 by Martin Offiah v. North Queensland

Most goals and points in a match: 10 goals and 20 points by Paul Loughlin v. Central Queensland

Most tries on tour: 19 by Martin Offiah

Most goals on tour: 43 by Paul Loughlin

Most points on tour: 90 (43 goals and one try) by Paul Loughlin

Most appearances: 14 (including two as substitute) by Roy Powell

Most full appearances: 13 by Phil Ford

Sin bin: Mike Ford v. Northern/Highland Zones; Paul Groves v. Northern Division; Roy Haggerty v. Manly; Paul Dixon v. Toowoomba; Andy Gregory v. Australia, second Test; Carl Gibson v. Western Division; Mike Gregory v. Auckland.

Opponents' sin bin: Dallas Dalley (North Queensland); Mark Brokenshire (Manly)

TOUR MANAGEMENT

Manager: Les Bettinson

Business Manager: David Howes

Coach: Malcolm Reilly

Captain: Ellery Hanley

Assistant Coach: Phil Larder

Doctor: Forbes Mackenzie

Physiotherapist: Geoff Plummer

TOUR PARTY

Player	Club	IN PAPUA NEW GUINEA					IN AUSTRALIA					IN NEW ZEALAND					TOUR TOTALS				
		App	Sub	T	G	Pts	App	Sub	T	G	Pts	App	Sub	T	G	Pts	App	Sub	T	G	Pts
BEARDMORE, Kevin	Castleford	1	—	—	—	—	6	—	—	—	—	2	—	—	—	—	9	—	—	—	—
CASE, Brian	Wigan	1	—	—	—	—	5	1	—	—	—	1	—	—	—	—	7	1	—	—	—
†CURRIER, Andy	Widnes	1	—	—	—	—	3	—	2	4	16	1	—	1	1	6	5	—	3	5	22
*CROOKS, Lee	Leeds	1	—	—	5	10	2	2	—	—	—	—	—	—	—	—	3	2	—	5	10
*DIXON, Paul	Halifax	1	—	—	—	—	5	2	1	—	4	—	—	—	—	—	6	2	1	—	4
EDWARDS, Shaun	Wigan	—	—	—	—	—	1	—	—	—	—	—	—	—	—	—	1	—	—	—	—
†EYRES, Richard	Widnes	1	—	1	—	4	1	—	—	—	—	1	1	—	—	—	3	1	1	—	4
FAIRBANK, Karl	Bradford N.	1	—	—	—	—	7	1	4	—	16	1	—	2	—	8	9	1	6	—	24
FORD, Mike	Oldham	1	—	—	—	—	5	—	4	—	16	1	—	1	—	4	7	—	5	—	20
FORD, Phil	Bradford N.	2	—	2	—	8	9	—	7	1	30	2	—	—	—	—	13	—	9	1	38
●GIBSON, Carl	Leeds	1	—	—	—	—	8	1	2	—	8	—	—	—	—	—	9	1	2	—	8
GILL, Henderson	Wigan	1	—	2	—	8	7	—	5	—	20	2	2	—	—	—	10	2	7	—	28
GREGORY, Andy	Wigan	1	—	—	—	—	5	—	—	—	—	2	—	—	—	—	8	—	—	—	—
GREGORY, Mike	Warrington	1	—	1	—	4	7	—	4	—	16	2	—	—	—	—	10	—	5	—	20
GROVES, Paul	St. Helens	1	—	—	—	—	6	2	1	—	4	1	—	—	—	—	8	2	1	—	4
HAGGERTY, Roy	St. Helens	1	—	—	—	—	3	1	—	—	—	1	—	—	—	—	5	1	—	—	—
HANLEY, Ellery	Wigan	1	—	1	—	4	8	—	7	—	28	1	—	—	—	—	10	—	8	—	32
HULME, David	Widnes	1	—	—	—	—	9	1	1	—	4	1	—	—	—	—	11	1	1	—	4
†HULME, Paul	Castleford	—	—	—	—	—	3	2	—	—	—	1	1	—	—	—	4	3	—	—	—
†JOYNER, John	Castleford	—	—	—	—	—	1	—	—	—	—	2	—	—	—	—	3	—	—	—	—
LOUGHLIN, Paul	St. Helens	1	—	—	7	14	8	1	1	28	60	2	1	—	8	16	11	2	1	43	90
*MEDLEY, Paul	Leeds	2	—	1	—	4	3	2	2	—	8	—	—	—	—	—	5	2	3	—	12
OFFIAH, Martin	Widnes	1	—	3	—	12	9	2	16	—	64	1	—	—	—	—	11	2	19	—	76
●*PLATT, Andy	St. Helens	—	—	—	—	—	5	1	—	—	—	—	—	—	—	—	5	1	—	—	—
POWELL, Roy	Leeds	1	—	—	—	—	10	2	1	—	4	1	—	—	—	—	12	2	1	—	4
*SCHOFIELD, Garry	Leeds	2	—	3	1	14	3	—	2	—	8	—	—	—	—	—	5	—	5	1	22
STEPHENSON, David	Leeds	1	—	1	—	4	7	—	—	12	24	3	—	—	1	2	11	—	1	13	30
WADDELL, Hugh	Oldham	1	—	—	—	—	6	3	—	—	—	3	—	—	—	—	10	3	—	—	—
WARD, Kevin	Castleford	1	—	—	—	—	7	—	1	—	4	2	—	—	—	—	10	—	1	—	4
WILKINSON, Ian	Halifax	1	—	—	—	—	4	—	—	—	—	1	—	—	—	—	6	—	—	—	—
†WRIGHT, Darren	Widnes	—	—	—	—	—	6	1	—	—	—	1	—	—	—	—	7	1	—	—	—

● Joined squad in Cairns (25 May).

* Sent home injured: Edwards (4 June), Medley and Schofield (21 June), Crooks and Platt (1 July), Dixon (5 July).

† Arrived as replacement: Wright (29 May), Currier and P. Hulme (23 June), Eyres and Joyner (3 July).

Great Britain 1988 Lions: (left to right, back row) Roy Haggerty, Garry Schofield, Karl Fairbank, Paul Dixon, David Stephenson, Paul Loughlin, Lee Crooks, Kevin Ward, Paul Medley, Ian Wilkinson; (middle row) Geoff Plummer (Physiotherapist), Brian Case, Phil Ford, Andy Platt, Hugh Waddell, Roy Powell, Mike Gregory, Henderson Gill, *Steve Hampson, Martin Offiah, Paul Groves, Forbes Mackenzie (Doctor); (front row) Phil Larder (Asst Coach), Mike Ford, Andy Gregory, David Hulme, Les Bettinson (Manager) Ellery Hanley (Captain), Malcolm Reilly (Coach), Shaun Edwards, *Des Drummond, Kevin Beardmore, David Howes (Business Manager). *withdrew before departure.

TEST v. PAPUA NEW GUINEA

For Great Britain coach Malcolm Reilly this 42-22 victory was the ideal start to a demanding 18-match tour. For British stand off Shaun Edwards it was the premature end of a projected 10-week trip through three countries, a knee injury halting his first tour after only seven minutes.

Defeat at the Lloyd Robson Oval in the searing heat of the Pacific would have killed off public interest in the 18th British Lions tour Down Under. As it was, Britain, having to open a tour with a Test match — carrying World Cup qualifying status — and with some players not having played for up to three weeks, faced the task with great character, surviving a second half comeback. Heat exhaustion proved as great a threat as the Kumuls themselves.

Edwards, recognised as one of the key players in the 26-man squad, twisted round on the bone-hard Port Moresby pitch with the Test only seven minutes old and fell to the ground, having to be carried off. He was flown to Sydney for a knee operation which was to force his early return home.

The Lions were already 12-0 up when Edwards collapsed with nobody near him. Wigan teammate and half back partner Andy Gregory was the kingpin in a series of early raids, part of the British game plan to build as big a lead as possible before the high temperature took its toll. Gregory created a try for centre Garry Schofield in the third minute, followed two minutes later by Gregory carving out a touchdown for second row man Paul Medley, full back Paul Loughlin adding both goals.

The British camp's three days of intensive preparation, featuring a full programme of medical advice on heat exhaustion and afternoon training sessions to acclimatise to match conditions, paid dividends in the first half as winger Henderson Gill added a further try in the 10th minute to take the visitors into a comfortable 16-0 lead.

Papuan full back Dairi Kovae, on Sydney Premiership duty with North Sydney, stepped out of three tackles to score a solo try after 25 minutes, captain Bal Numapo adding the goal.

Britain soon returned to their scoring ways with second row man Mike Gregory crossing the line in the 32nd minute and Schofield touching down for the second time six minutes later, Loughlin adding both goals to provide the Lions with a 28-6 interval lead.

The visitors' dressing room at half-time almost proved to be the turning point of the World Cup-rated Test encounter as British players struggled to catch their breath, some being physically sick, while changing their sweat-sodden playing strip.

The second half was nearly a mirror-image of the first with Papua New Guinea, urged on by 12,000 partisan fans in the stadium and hundreds more perched in trees in nearby streets, pulling themselves back into the game. First Arnold Krewanty scored a delightful left wing try in the 48th minute, leaving Phil Ford and skipper Ellery Hanley floundering in his wake, Numapo adding the goal.

Then Kovae set off on a spectacular run up the right wing to register his second touchdown in the 53rd minute, Loughlin replying with a penalty goal nine minutes later. But inside 60 seconds Papua were within reach of a shock success when prop Isaac Rop ran through Kevin Ward's token challenge to leave Numapo a simple goal kick to take the scoreline to 30-22 with 17 minutes left.

Hanley, having made two superb try saving tackles, sent out a long pass to the non-stop Schofield who handed on to centre partner David Stephenson for a 73rd minute try which virtually sealed success for the Lions. Gill ran in his second try to provide ultimate relief, Loughlin sending over both goals for a 20-point victory margin.

TEST (World Cup-rated)

22 May   **Port Moresby**

PAPUA NEW GUINEA 22		GREAT BRITAIN 42
Dairi Kovae (North Sydney)	1.	Paul Loughlin
Kepi Saea (Port Moresby)	2.	Phil Ford
Mea Morea (Port Moresby)	3.	Garry Schofield
Bal Numapo (Kundialea) Capt.	4.	David Stephenson
Arnold Krewanty (Port Moresby)	5.	Henderson Gill
Darius Haili (Kimbe)	6.	Shaun Edwards
Tony Kila (Port Moresby)	7.	Andy Gregory
Isaac Rop (Port Moresby)	8.	Kevin Ward
Michael Matmillo (Port Moresby)	9.	Kevin Beardmore
Yer Bom (Port Moresby)	10.	Brian Case
Mathias Kombra (Mendi)	11.	Paul Medley
Tuiyo Evei (Goroka)	12.	Mike Gregory
Haoda Kouoru (Port Moresby)	13.	Ellery Hanley, Capt.
Thomas Rombuk	14.	David Hulme
Ngala Lapan	15.	Paul Dixon

T: Kovae (2), Krewanty, Rop
G: Numapo (3)
Substitutions:
Rombuk for Bom (59 min.)
Lapan for Kombra (77 min.)
Half-time: 6-28
Referee: Greg McCallum (Australia)
Attendance: 12,107

T: Schofield (2), Gill (2), Medley,
M. Gregory, Stephenson
G: Loughlin (7)
Substitutions:
D. Hulme for Edwards (7 min.)
Dixon for Case (36 min.)

Scorechart

Minute	Score	PNG	GB
3:	Schofield (T)		
	Loughlin (G)	0	6
5:	Medley (T)		
	Loughlin (G)	0	12
10:	Gill (T)	0	16
25:	Kovae (T)		
	Numapo (G)	6	16
32:	M. Gregory (T)		
	Loughlin (G)	6	22
38:	Schofield (T)		
	Loughlin (G)	6	28
48:	Krewanty (T)		
	Numapo (G)	12	28
53:	Kovae (T)	16	28
62:	Loughlin (PG)	16	30
63:	Rop (T)		
	Numapo (G)	22	30
73:	Stephenson (T)		
	Loughlin (G)	22	36
75:	Gill (T)		
	Loughlin (G)	22	42
	Scrums	10	14
	Penalties	12	7

24 May

Lae

NORTHERN/HIGHLAND ZONES 18
GREAT BRITAIN 36

1. Wilkinson (Hanley, 44 min.)
2. P. Ford
3. Schofield, Capt.
4. Medley
5. Offiah
6. D. Hulme
7. M. Ford
8. Waddell
9. Groves
10. Crooks
11. Powell
12. Fairbank
13. Haggerty (Dixon, 67 min.)

T: Offiah (3), P. Ford (2), Schofield
G: Crooks (5), Schofield

Northern/Highland Zones:
Naea (Halala); Pokana, Kool, Kamiak, Yapi; Moi, Kiarara; Seeto, Kemutafe, Kairat, Kin, Kuno, Launa (Kawage)

T: Kool (2), Pokana
G: Kamiak (3)

Half-time: 6-12

Referee: Graham Ainui (Port Moresby)
Attendance: 3,270

Prop forward Crooks played his first full game for six months to break through the psychological barrier of a serious shoulder injury sustained back on 12 December. The Leeds packman contributed a steady performance and five goals in the 36-18 success, the Whitbread Trophy Man of the Match award going to fellow prop Waddell with a relentless show of punishing runs in the humid conditions.

On his tour debut, winger Offiah gave an enigmatic display combining some basic errors with a hat-trick of tries, while on the other flank Phil Ford overcame a troublesome ankle to touch down twice.

But it was the introduction of substitute Hanley four minutes after the interval which turned the game after the divisional side had levelled the scores at 12-apiece. In the 53rd minute, the tour captain carved out a huge gap for Schofield to score a try and set the Lions en route to a further three touchdowns.

27 May

Cairns

NORTH QUEENSLAND 16
GREAT BRITAIN 66

1. P. Ford
2. Medley
3. Gibson
4. Stephenson
5. Offiah
6. D. Hulme
7. M. Ford, Capt.
8. Case
9. Groves
10. Powell
11. Fairbank (Haggerty, 66 min.)
12. Dixon
13. Platt

T: Offiah (4), M. Ford (3), P. Ford (2), Medley (2), Dixon
G: Stephenson (8), P. Ford

North Queensland:
Namok; Gagai, Taylor (Ernest), Turia, Curry; Worth (Conlan), Filosi; Colwell, Bax, McAskill, House, Dalley, Greenwood

T: Filosi (2), House
G: Worth, Conlan

Half-time: 10-18

Referee: Barry Gomersall (Mackay)
Attendance: 5,500

Australian Rugby League fans enjoyed their first sight of Widnes flier Offiah as he raced in for four tries in an impressive British success littered with personal triumphs.

Recently arrived loose forward Platt showed no signs of jetlag with a powerful display which earned Whitbread Trophy Man of the Match rating, while Mike Ford celebrated captaincy by registering a hat-trick of tries.

David Hulme revelled in the stand off role to give coach Reilly a viable Test alternative to Hanley, while Phil Ford linked well from full back to score two fine tries, as did makeshift winger Medley.

The impressive 12-try rout formed a double celebration for coach Reilly on the day that he announced his acceptance of the post of coach of Leeds from the end of the tour.

Great Britain's skipper Ellery Hanley dives over for the opening try in the 100th Anglo-Aussie Test in Sydney.

Castleford's Kevin Ward prepares to off load despite the attentions of Wally Lewis and Greg Conescu (below).

1 June

Newcastle

NEWCASTLE KNIGHTS 12
GREAT BRITAIN 28

1. Loughlin
2. Gill
3. Gibson
4. Wright
5. Offiah
6. Hanley, Capt.
7. A. Gregory
8. Ward
9. Beardmore
10. Waddell
11. M. Gregory
12. Dixon
13. Platt

T: Offiah (2), Hanley (2), Ward
G: Loughlin (4)

Newcastle Knights:
Frendo (Walters); Clarke, Doyle, Kemp, Miller; McCormack, Fulmer; Shore, Townsend (Carter), Thorne, McKiernan, Stewart, Glanville

T: Shore, Kemp, Miller

Half-time: 4-12

Referee: Greg McCallum (Sydney)
Attendance: 6,649

Facing their toughest fixture to date on their debut in the Sydney area, the Lions produced a sterling performance to defeat Sydney Premiership side Newcastle Knights by a 16-point margin.

Scrum half Andy Gregory earned the Whitbread Trophy Man of the Match award with a hand in everything after Shore had put the Knights into an 11th minute lead with a try. Gregory and prop Ward stormed back, the pack-man scoring a 26th minute touchdown before combining with Gregory to send Offiah flying over, two Loughlin goals opening up a 12-4 lead.

The Knights levelled the scores with fine tries from Kemp and Miller before a confident Britain pulled away with two tries from skipper Hanley and a second from Offiah, Loughlin contributing two more goals.

5 June

Tamworth

NORTHERN DIVISION 36
GREAT BRITAIN 12

1. Loughlin
2. P. Ford
3. Schofield, Capt.
4. Stephenson
5. Gill
6. D. Hulme
7. M. Ford
8. Case
9. Groves
10. Crooks
11. Powell
12. Medley (Fairbank)
13. Haggerty

T: Gill, Schofield
G: Loughlin (2)

Northern Division:
Spinks; Plater, Gardner (McCormack), Ryan, French; Laurie, McGrady; McCann, Masters, Cotter, Cumming, Lavender (Briggs), Maynes

T: McGrady (2), Cumming, Plater, Maynes
G: Spinks (8)

Half-time: 22-12

Referee: Barry Priest (Orange)
Attendance: 2,192

Coach Reilly locked the dressing room door for a 30-minute verbal lashing of a team which had conceded what was to become the highest points tally of the tour in the biggest defeat against a non-Test side for 68 years.

Northern Division had not beaten the Lions since 1966, this five-try hammering coming after four succcessive victories for the tourists and only a week before the first Test.

Full back Spinks missed only one goal kick from nine attempts in a non-contest which saw the country amateurs race in to a 22-6 lead after 36 minutes. Schofield's typical long-range interception try on the stroke of half-time raised hopes of a comeback but the second half was all Northern Division, who added 14 points without reply to bring the buoyant Lions firmly down to earth.

7 June

Manly

MANLY	**30**
GREAT BRITAIN	**0**

1. P. Ford (Crooks, 55 min.)
2. Gibson
3. Wilkinson
4. Wright
5. Offiah
6. Stephenson
7. D. Hulme
8. Waddell
9. Groves
10. Powell
11. Fairbank
12. Medley (Haggerty, 31 min.)
13. Platt, Capt.

Manly:
Dwyer; Davis, Ropati, Williams, Austin; Lyons, Toovey (Shaw); Gateley, Haggett, Brokenshire (Ryan), Pocock, Cleal, Hasler

T: Gateley, Pocock, Toovey, Haggett, Lyons
G: Dwyer (5)

Half-time: 18-0

Referee: Francis Desplas (France)
Attendance: 11,131

Five days before the Centenary Test, the Lions crashed to a humiliating defeat at the hands of Grand Final winners Manly. It was the first time any British tour side had failed to score in Australia outside of Test matches.

The Sydney Premiers ran in five tries and wasted a further three scoring chances, although they were well under full strength.

Full back Dwyer kicked five goals from five attempts as Manly steadily built on their opening try by prop Gateley after only six minutes.

Captain for the night, Platt was Britain's sole star although half backs David Hulme and Stephenson worked hard behind a beaten pack, second row man Medley retiring with a neck injury.

Britain introduced a physical presence, mainly in the shape of substitutes Crooks and Haggerty, the latter earning a a spell in the sin bin after Manly's Brokenshire had received the same punishment.

David Hulme, who filled the Lions' stand off role against Australia and New Zealand.

FIRST TEST v. AUSTRALIA

With Australia's bicentennial in full swing and Sydney critics forecasting a 30-point hammering, Great Britain suddenly threatened to spoil their celebrations.

The 100th Anglo-Aussie Test, staged in the new, controversial Sydney Football Stadium, was sadly lacking in atmosphere until the spirited Lions turned on a determined controlled performance to lead 6-0 at the interval.

Highly-charged Britain cast aside the shadow of Australia's 13-match winning run against them and the 66 points conceded in two humiliating defeats during the previous week and took the green-and-golds on head-to-head.

With David Hulme making his first full Test appearance and charged with marking the inimitable Wally Lewis, plus Paul Dixon in the new role of prop forward, Britain set out to smash Australia's attack before it gathered momentum.

The success of the basic plan worked and forced the confident Kangaroos to dig deep into their vast resources. Inevitably, it was maestro Lewis and half back partner Peter Sterling who steered the floundering Australians back on course.

Rookie full back Paul Loughlin had booted Britain into a 12th minute lead with a penalty goal. Two minutes before half-time the Lions converted their superiority into points when skipper Ellery Hanley produced a dummy, a shuffle then a pile-driving hand off on Sterling before powering his way over for their only touchdown.

The 6-0 interval scoreline boosted Britain's confidence, but also stirred Australia's fighting spirit. The home side came out to throw the ball about immediately in a more accustomed display of high-speed support play.

Sterling's value was emphasised by coach Don Furner pleading with him to take the field despite a first half shoulder injury.

Within 10 minutes of the restart, the former Hull scrum half had sent giant prop Sam Backo crashing through for their opening try before paving the way for the first of Peter Jackson's two tries, Michael O'Connor adding both goals.

Lewis strode through the second half with an air of superiority, opening a vital seven-point gap with a 69th minute drop goal, before Jackson completed the scoring with a try seven minutes from the end.

The British camp would not be consoled by the high praise bestowed on them by the Australian factions. Man of the Match Kevin Ward reluctantly received the award, stone-faced with disappointment, mirroring the mood of the Lions.

Britain's heartwarming display was packed with positive influences. Ward was an outstanding cornerstone of a pack which never stopped working, Andy Platt topping the tackle count with 35, ahead of Paul Dixon (32) and hooker Kevin Beardmore with 30. The Castleford number nine also took the scrums 9-6 with three against the head.

Australia's second half comeback was tinted with fortune as Backo's opening try owed a lot to Sterling miskicking before snapping up the ball to feed the big prop, while Jackson's first touchdown featured a hint of obstruction.

Then shortly before Lewis sent over his drop goal — the only one of the tour — the Lions were denied an equalising score when Ward's pass to Andy Gregory was ruled forward by French referee Francis Desplas.

Malcolm Reilly's men had earned new-found respect, the admiration of their opponents and the affection of Rugby League followers...but not the 100th Test scalp they so desperately sought.

Unfortunately, the loss brought them another unwanted record — the first time a British squad had lost three successive matches on tour.

FIRST TEST

11 June Sydney Football Stadium

AUSTRALIA 17		GREAT BRITAIN 6
Garry Jack (Balmain)	1.	Paul Loughlin
Andrew Ettingshausen (Cronulla)	2.	Phil Ford
Michael O'Connor (Manly)	3.	Garry Schofield
Peter Jackson (Canberra)	4.	David Stephenson
Tony Currie (Canterbury)	5.	Martin Offiah
Wally Lewis (Brisbane Broncos) Capt.	6.	David Hulme
Peter Sterling (Parramatta)	7.	Andy Gregory
Phil Daley (Manly)	8.	Kevin Ward
Greg Conescu (Brisbane Broncos)	9.	Kevin Beardmore
Sam Backo (Canberra)	10.	Paul Dixon
Wally Fullerton-Smith (St. George)	11.	Mike Gregory
Paul Vautin (Manly)	12.	Andy Platt
Bob Lindner (Parramatta)	13.	Ellery Hanley, Capt.
Gary Belcher (Canberra)	14.	Henderson Gill
Steve Folkes (Canterbury)	15.	Roy Powell

T: Jackson (2), Backo
G: O'Connor (2), Lewis (dg)
Substitutions:
Folkes for Vautin (69 min.)
Belcher for Sterling (71 min.)
Half-time: 0-6
Attendance: 24,202

T: Hanley
G: Loughlin
Substitutions:
Powell for M. Gregory (69 min.)
Gill for Loughlin (77 min.)
Referee: Francis Desplas (France)

Scorechart

Minute	Score	Aus	GB
12:	Loughlin (PG)	0	2
38:	Hanley (T)	0	6
50:	Backo (T)		
	O'Connor	6	6
62:	Jackson (T)		
	O'Connor (G)	12	6
69:	Lewis (DG)	13	6
73:	Jackson (T)	17	6
	Scrums	6	9
	Penalties	13	13

British hooker Kevin Beardmore, who won the scrums 9-6

15 June

Brisbane

| COMBINED BRISBANE | 14 |
| GREAT BRITAIN | 28 |

1. P. Ford
2. Gill
3. Schofield (Offiah, 20 min.)
4. Stephenson
5. Gibson
6. Hanley, Capt.
7. M. Ford
8. Case (Waddell, 70 min.)
9. Groves
10. Crooks
11. Powell
12. Fairbank
13. Dixon

T: Offiah (2), Schofield, Fairbank, M. Ford
G: Stephenson (4)

Combined Brisbane:
Hegarty (Langer); Egan, McCarthy, Cherry, Barwick; Coyne, Daunt; McIntyre, Holmes, Ponting, Haggath, Stains, Smith (White)

T: McCarthy, Egan, Barwick
G: Coyne

Half-time: 4-20

Referee: David Manson (Brisbane)
Attendance: 1,810

After scoring the opening try in the eighth minute, centre Schofield suffered a broken cheekbone 13 minutes later ruling the ace try scorer out of the rest of the tour. The score of 17 tries in 19 Tests, Schofield also returned home early from the 1984 tour.

Britain were also hit by a Mike Ford hand injury, Stephenson's damaged knee ligaments and Case having six stitches in a head wound. All on a dismal night before one of the lowest ever tour crowds of 1,810. They saw a disappointing contest highlighted by flashes of brilliance from Phil Ford and skipper Hanley.

Ironically, Schofield's replacement, Offiah, scored two tries to take his tally to 11 as the Lions built a 20-4 half-time lead.

17 June

Rockhampton

| CENTRAL QUEENSLAND | 8 |
| GREAT BRITAIN | 64 |

1. Loughlin
2. Gibson
3. Wilkinson
4. Wright
5. Offiah
6. Hanley, Capt.
7. Hulme
8. Ward (Crooks, 49 min.) (Gill, 59 min.)
9. Beardmore
10. Waddell
11. Powell
12. Fairbank
13. Haggerty

T: Offiah (3), Fairbank (3), Gibson(2), Hanley (2), Powell
G: Loughlin (10)

Central Queensland:
Crow (Gilbert); Miller, Peter White, Paul White, Hinricks; Iles (Morgan), Upkett; Olsson, Emmert, Weinert, Leisha, Duff, Brazier

T: Leisha
G: Weinert (2)

Half-time: 2-24

Referee: L. Crane (Brisbane)
Attendance: 4,418

Britain's demolition of Central Queensland was marred by a recurrence of Crooks' shoulder injury. The Leeds prop forward came on as a 49th minute substitute for fellow prop Ward only to last just seven minutes before hurting the shoulder in a tackle, ending hopes of a return for the Test in Brisbane.

The rampaging Lions ran in 11 tries, Loughlin adding 10 goals, to record the widest winning margin since the 1962 tour.

Whitbread Trophy Man of the Match Bradford Northern packman Fairbank grabbed three tries while winger Offiah registered a genuine hat-trick of touchdowns between the 53rd and 66th minutes. Skipper Hanley was in commanding form, scoring twice, as did Leeds back Gibson.

22 June

Toowoomba

TOOWOOMBA	**12**	
GREAT BRITAIN	**28**	

1. Loughlin
2. Gill
3. Stephenson (Gibson, 30 min.)
4. P. Ford
5. Offiah
6. Hanley, Capt.
7. D. Hulme
8. Ward
9. Beardmore
10. Dixon
11. Fairbank
12. Powell (Waddell, 63 min.)
13. M. Gregory

T: Hanley (2), M. Gregory (2), P. Ford
G: Loughlin (4)

Toowoomba:
Weribone (T. Cook); Clevin, Blake, Pratt, Stower; Clancy, Smith; Dwyer, M. Cook, Sutton, Buckle, Johnson, Sullivan (Neale)

T: Clancy, Johnson
G: Dwyer (2)

Half-time: 0-18

Referee: Tim Bliss (Toowoomba)
Attendance: 3,874

Biased refereeing was blamed for tour defeats at the hands of Toowoomba in both 1979 and 1984. This time coach Reilly took the safeguard of fielding a near-Test strength side which was sufficient to counter the referee's 18-7 penalty count in favour of the home side.

For the first hour, the Lions gave one of their most impressive displays of the tour to hold a 22-0 lead before relaxing to allow Toowoomba to touch down twice.

Skipper Hanley finished the match as he started by scoring a try, being a commanding figure in between. Phil Ford showed potential in his first outing in the centre, while Whitbread Trophy Man of the Match Mike Gregory also touched down twice.

The frustration with the referee's decisions led to two second half brawls, Britain's Dixon spending 10 minutes in the sin bin.

25 June

Gympie

WIDE BAY	**0**	
GREAT BRITAIN	**14**	

1. Wilkinson (Loughlin, 20 min.)
2. Gibson (Offiah, 56 min.)
3. Currier
4. Wright
5. Gill
6. M. Ford, Capt.
7. P. Hulme
8. Case
9. Groves
10. Waddell
11. Powell
12. Fairbank
13. Haggerty

T: Currier, Offiah, M. Ford
G: Loughlin

Wide Bay:
Ovens; Templeman (Graving), Kirby, Lalli, Kinsela; Jones, Ward; Reddacliff, Gerrard, McGrath (Ryan), Sempf, Schulte, March

Half-time: 0-4

Referee: Russell Leis (Gympie)
Attendance: 2,310

Gympie provided the low spot of the Queensland section of the tour with the Lions' second string providing a dismal display and the lowest Lions score against a Wide Bay outfit.

Britain struggled to score their three tries and at one stage were in danger of going down to another embarrassing defeat, leading only 4-0 with 15 minutes left.

Then Offiah came on as a 56th minute substitute for Gibson and showed his class to beat three players on a 60-yard sprint for Britain's second try.

Skipper Mike Ford brought further relief with a late try goalled by Loughlin, who had replaced Wilkinson, suffering a bruised shoulder.

SECOND TEST v. AUSTRALIA

Australia retained the Ashes they have held since 1973 as Great Britain's newly-built hopes of Test glory were sent crashing.

At the centre of the demolition job was skipper Wally Lewis who strutted through the Lang Park Test with arrogant ease. The Brisbane Bronco set up two of their six tries and scored one himself in a masterful stand off display that fully deserved Man of the Match rating.

Not only were Britain subjected to waves of Australian attacks inspired by pack supremacy, but also a barrage of post-match criticism for an indisciplined performance, both with the ball and on defence.

The Lions were branded 'headhunters' and ironically scrum half Andy Gregory was chosen as Britain's Whitbread Trophy Man of the Match while serving the last six minutes of the match in the sin bin for a high tackle on winger Andrew Ettingshausen. The Lions paid the ultimate price for their wayward style by going down to a 20-point margin after re-asserting their international standing in the first Test.

Britain's injury jinx struck again with second row man Andy Platt no longer being able to disguise his broken wrist and having to come off after 50 minutes and pack partner Paul Dixon suffering a broken thumb. Despite the injury, Dixon topped Britain's tackle count with 38 and ran strongly on attack.

As in several of the now 15 successive defeats against Australia, Britain could again claim the most spectacular touchdowns, some consolation to the 1,000-plus Anglos in the 27,103 crowd. Both British touchdowns were 60-yard scores involving their often brilliantly unorthodox threequarters.

Britain had taken the lead for the only time with a fourth minute penalty goal by Paul Loughlin before Michael O'Connor touched down in the corner, adding a touchline conversion. Lewis collected his own deflected kick off a British defender to put Peter Jackson in for his third try in two successive Tests. Then Lewis was a central figure in a combination of passes which ended with Ettingshausen clearing Martin Offiah's mis-tackle to score a try two minutes from half-time, O'Connor obliging with the goal, Britain's only response being a second Loughlin penalty goal.

Britain registered their first touchdown eight minutes after the break. Skipper Ellery Hanley — wasted in the centre position — made his mark by setting up the try with a superb break from inside his own half before switching inside to co-centre Phil Ford who sprinted clear to the posts for Loughlin to add the goal and reduce the arrears to eight points.

Australia's response to the Lions' faint hopes of a shock comeback was to run in three further tries, two of them converted by O'Connor, to set up victory at 34-10 with 11 minutes left. The fifth try went to Canberra prop Sam Backo, an outstanding figure in the totally dominant Kangaroo pack, while the final Australian touchdown went, fittingly, to the inspirational Lewis.

But the last score of the evening went to Britain winger Offiah, desperate to justify his growing reputation despite a nervous introduction to Australian Test football in Sydney. Three minutes before the final whistle the Widnes flier received the ball from clubmate and acting scrum half Paul Hulme, a Test debutant as a 50th minute substitute for Platt. From 60 yards out, the winger slipped easily through Gary Belcher's fingers and then high-stepped away from full back Garry Jack to go in for a classic try.

Defensive lapses at the play-the-ball, an old failing, had allowed Backo and the reinstated Wayne Pearce to squeeze in for soft second half tries, while the indiscipline in ball handling allowed Australia to enjoy possession for a crucial 70 per cent of the match.

SECOND TEST

28 June   **Lang Park, Brisbane**

AUSTRALIA 34		GREAT BRITAIN 14
Garry Jack (Balmain)	1.	Paul Loughlin
Andrew Ettingshausen (Cronulla)	2.	Henderson Gill
Michael O'Connor (Manly)	3.	Phil Ford
Peter Jackson (Canberra)	4.	Ellery Hanley, Capt.
Tony Currie (Canterbury)	5.	Martin Offiah
Wally Lewis (Brisbane Broncos) Capt.	6.	David Hulme
Peter Sterling (Parramatta)	7.	Andy Gregory
Phil Daley (Manly)	8.	Kevin Ward
Greg Conescu (Brisbane Broncos)	9.	Kevin Beardmore
Sam Backo (Canberra)	10.	Roy Powell
Wally Fullerton-Smith (St. George)	11.	Paul Dixon
Paul Vautin (Manly)	12.	Andy Platt
Wayne Pearce (Balmain)	13.	Mike Gregory
Gary Belcher (Canberra)	14.	Darren Wright
Bob Lindner (Parramatta)	15.	Paul Hulme

T: O'Connor, Jackson, Ettingshausen, Backo, Pearce, Lewis
G: O'Connor (5)
Substitutions:
Lindner for Conescu (68 min.)
Belcher for Ettingshausen (75 min.)
Half-time: 18-4

T: Ford, Offiah
G: Loughlin (3)
Substitutions:
P. Hulme for Platt (50 min.)
Wright for Ford (71 min.)
Referee: Francis Desplas (France)
Attendance: 27,103

Scorechart

Minute	Score	Aus	GB
4:	Loughlin (PG)	0	2
6:	O'Connor (T)		
	O'Connor (G)	6	2
14:	Loughlin (PG)	6	4
17:	O'Connor (PG)	8	4
20:	Jackson (T)		
	O'Connor (G)	14	4
38:	Ettingshausen (T)	18	4
48:	P. Ford (T)		
	Loughlin (G)	18	10
59:	Backo (T)		
	O'Connor (G)	24	10
66:	Pearce (T)	28	10
69:	Lewis (T)		
	O'Connor (G)	34	10
77:	Offiah (T)	34	14
	Scrums	10	10
	Penalties	9	8

British Man of the Match, Andy Gregory.

3 July

Orange

WESTERN DIVISION	26
GREAT BRITAIN	28

1. Wilkinson
2. Gibson
3. Currier
4. Wright
5. Offiah
6. Hanley, Capt.
7. M. Ford
8. Case
9. Groves
10. Waddell
11. Fairbank
12. P. Hulme
13. M. Gregory (D. Hulme, 62 min.)

T: Offiah (2), Groves, Hanley, Currier
G: Currier (4)

Western Division:
Frail (Stammers); Williams, Casey, Smith, Newman; Clark, Douglas; Gibson, Luke, McAnally, Fitzgerald (Batty), Peachy, Moy

T: Moy, Peachy, Smith, Williams
G: Clark (5)

Half-time: 4-10

Referee: Phil Robinson (Moree)
Attendance: 3,520

Britain came dangerously close to losing their unbeaten record against Western Division after squandering a 22-4 lead built in 50 minutes.

Then the dismal Lions conceded four tries, all but one converted, relying on Offiah's second try — his 18th of the tour — and a Currier penalty goal to give them a two-point safety margin.

This time Britain could not blame the referee for their plight — either of them. Phil Robinson retired with a pulled muscle in the 52nd minute to be replaced by a touch judge, Peter Ryan, the final penalty count being 9-7 in the visitors' favour.

The only highlight for the Lions was Offiah's first try in the 41st minute, beating several defenders on a weaving crossfield run, while Gibson had a hand in both first half tries by Groves and Hanley before a 61st-minute trip to the sin bin.

5 July

Canberra

PRESIDENT'S XIII	24
GREAT BRITAIN	16

1. P. Ford
2. Gibson
3. Loughlin
4. Wright
5. Currier
6. D. Hulme
7. A. Gregory, Capt. (Waddell, 55 min.)
8. Ward
9. Beardmore (P. Hulme, 10 min.)
10. Powell
11. M. Gregory
12. Eyres
13. Joyner

T: P. Ford (2), M. Gregory
G: Loughlin (2)

President's XIII:
Blake; O'Brien, Meninga, Bradley, O'Neil (Robinson); Florimo, Alexander; Lazarus, Fenech (Capt.), Gillespie (Gately), Miller, Geyer, Trewhella

T: O'Brien, Lazarus, Alexander, Meninga, Bradley
G: Meninga (2)

Half-time: 14-8

Referee: Eddie Ward (Sydney)
Attendance: 6,037

Australia's boast of being able to field three Test teams to beat Britain's best was given credence by the President's XIII, containing only one international player, beating a British side featuring eight current Test regulars.

The contest was staged in wet and muddy conditions, theoretically suited to the British, although in practice the Australians adapted better to run in five tries to three, two of the British tries going to Phil Ford in a first-class display of attacking full back play.

The other try-scorer was Britain's Whitbread Trophy Man of the Match Mike Gregory as the Lions pulled back to trail only 18-16 with 15 minutes left, the home outfit sealing victory with a try seven minutes from the end by Penrith centre Bradley, Meninga adding his second goal.

Shoulder-troubled Lee Crooks piledrives into the combined Brisbane defence, one of only five tour appearances.

THIRD TEST v. AUSTRALIA

A patched up Great Britain side, minus seven or eight first choice players and fielding a fourth choice makeshift hooker, rewrote the Rugby League history books with an emotional victory of epic proportions.

The staggering success at the Sydney Football Stadium, to be ranked alongside the famous Rorke's Drift Test of 1914 and Alan Prescott's Brisbane heroics in 1958:

★ Ended a record run of 15 consecutive Australian victories over Britain
★ Recorded Britain's first win on Australian soil for 14 years
★ Gained the first British success over Australia for a decade
★ Won Britain the race to register a 50th Anglo-Aussie success
★ Put the Lions at the top of the World Cup table with only one point needed from the last fixture with New Zealand to reach the final

The 26-12 victory was a personal triumph for coach Malcolm Reilly. Only 24 hours before the kick-off of the World Cup-rated encounter, the British injury hoodoo struck again with stand-in hooker Paul Groves being ruled out, plus third choice replacement Richard Eyres crying off his Test debut. The hooking role fell to Widnes back row forward Paul Hulme in a side featuring Phil Ford at full back, his third position in three Tests, and Hugh Waddell making his first Test appearance on the tour.

Blasted by the Australian Press pundits, the Lions entered the sparsely populated stadium earmarked for the slaughter. Reilly and his backroom staff had refused to relax their high standards of pre-match preparation, the final call being for a show of old-fashioned Bulldog spirit.

Australia were swamped as the tide turned for Britain. Full back Ford was denied what appeared to be a perfectly good try before the outstanding Andy Gregory and prop Kevin Ward combined yet again to send Martin Offiah in for a 16th minute try. Five minutes later Ford confirmed his rating as a top-class tourist by weaving his way past four mesmerised defenders to touch down at the posts, Paul Loughlin adding the goal for a 10-0 lead.

Memories of the first Test at the same ground came flooding back as Australian skipper Wally Lewis came out for the second half determined to put the green-and-golds back into the contest. One difference was the lack of his half back partner Peter Sterling, injured and substituted by Gary Belcher in the 33rd minute. It was Lewis who twisted out of Ford's tackle to touch down under the posts two minutes after half-time, O'Connor adding the goal to cut the deficit to only four points.

This time Britain were not to be denied their long-awaited victory. The irrepressible Andy Gregory created a try for Henderson Gill with a cunningly disguised grubber kick, Loughlin obliging with the goal to re-open the 10-point gap. Kangaroo prop Sam Backo maintained his record of having scored a try in each Test with a 61st minute touchdown, O'Connor again adding the goal.

The Lions pulled away again when centre Loughlin strode majestically down the right flank to send Gill streaking past Garry Jack to score at the corner and perform his now famous post-try wiggle.

The seal of success came with a stunning length of the field try. Andy Gregory, fully justifying his Man of the Match rating, eluded four defenders and sent namesake Mike clear from Britain's 25-yard line. Both Gregorys would normally have been ruled out by injury except for the crisis, but Mike ignored the speedier Offiah on his outside to race the 70 yards to the posts, pursued in vain by skipper Lewis and Wayne Pearce. Loughlin added the simple goal as every Briton in the stadium waited those final nine minutes to celebrate the end of an era of Australian domination.

THIRD TEST (World Cup-rated)

9 July   **Sydney Football Stadium**

AUSTRALIA 12		GREAT BRITAIN 26
Garry Jack (Brisbane)	1.	Phil Ford
Andrew Ettingshausen (Cronulla)	2.	Henderson Gill
Michael O'Connor (Manly)	3.	David Stephenson
Peter Jackson (Canberra)	4.	Paul Loughlin
Tony Currie (Canterbury)	5.	Martin Offiah
Wally Lewis (Brisbane Broncos) Capt.	6.	David Hulme
Peter Sterling (Parramatta)	7.	Andy Gregory
Martin Bella (North Sydney)	8.	Kevin Ward
Greg Conescu (Brisbane Broncos)	9.	Paul Hulme
Sam Backo (Canberra)	10.	Hugh Waddell
Wally Fullerton-Smith (St. George)	11.	Mike Gregory
Paul Vautin (Manly)	12.	Roy Powell
Wayne Pearce (Balmain)	13.	Ellery Hanley, Capt.
Gary Belcher (Canberra)	14.	Darren Wright
Bob Lindner (Parramatta)	15.	Brian Case

T: Lewis, Backo
G: O'Connor (2)
Substitutions:
Belcher for Sterling (33 min.)
Lindner for Fullerton-Smith (64 min.)
Half-time: 0-10

T: Gill (2), Offiah, P. Ford,
M. Gregory
G: Loughlin (3)
Substitution:
Case for Waddell (64 min.)
Referee: Francis Desplas (France)
Attendance: 15,994

Scorechart

Minute	Score	Aus	GB
16:	Offiah (T)	0	4
21:	P. Ford (T)		
	Loughlin (G)	0	10
42:	Lewis (T)		
	O'Connor (G)	6	10
48:	Gill (T)		
	Loughlin (G)	6	16
61:	Backo (T)		
	O'Connor (G)	12	16
64:	Gill (T)	12	20
71:	M. Gregory (T)		
	Loughlin (G)	12	26
	Scrums	8	7
	Penalties	9	4

Two-try hero Henderson Gill.

Australian captain Wally Lewis faces a three-man British reception committee, from the left, Paul Hulme, Paul Dixon and Kevin Beardmore, in the second Test in Brisbane.

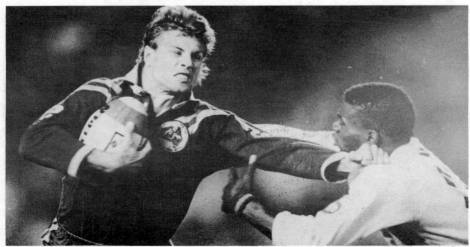

Top tryscoring Lion Martin Offiah on the defensive against Australian opposite wingman Andrew Ettingshausen in the third Test at Sydney.

Top goals and points scorer on the tour, St. Helens full back or centre Paul Loughlin.

13 July

Wellington

WELLINGTON   18
GREAT BRITAIN   24

1. Wilkinson
2. Gibson
3. Stephenson (Loughlin, 20 min.)
4. Wright
5. Currier
6. Joyner
7. M. Ford, Capt. (Powell, 53 min.)
8. Case
9. Groves
10. Waddell
11. Fairbank
12. Haggerty
13. Eyres

T: Fairbank (2), Eyres, Currier
G: Loughlin (2), Currier, Stephenson

Wellington:
Edwards; W. Tangira, Ewe, Paikea, Aramoana; Leuluai, G; Tangira (Rolleston), Piva, Harvey, Makaori, Henry, Williams (Bristowe), Kuiti

T: Leuluai (2), Kuiti
G: Ewe (3)

Half-time: 14-12

Referee: Des O'Sullivan (Wellington)
Attendance: 4,428

The Lions had to produce a late, late show which brought three tries in the last 14 minutes to avoid an embarrassing defeat only four days before the World Cup-rated Test with New Zealand.

Wellington, coached by ex-Wigan hooker Howie Tamati, hustled the British into a catalogue of errors for the first hour, building an 18-12 lead. The main inspiration came from veteran Kiwi stand off Leuluai, formerly with Hull and Leigh, the scorer of two tries.

Aided by some barnstorming runs from Britain's Whitbread Trophy Man of the Match Waddell, the Lions found form in the last quarter to register two tries from back row forward Fairbank and one from Currier to open a six-point victory margin.

TEST v. NEW ZEALAND

Great Britain's dreams of capping an historic Test victory over Australia by reaching the final of the protracted World Cup competition slithered away in the rainswept mud of the Addington Showgrounds in Christchurch.

The Lions, seeking to salvage an ill-fated tour in style, needed only to draw to meet Australia in an Old Trafford, Manchester, World Cup final. A controversial disallowed try, three misses at goal and a couple of defensive blunders contributed to a two-point defeat which proved to be as dampening as the weather.

Australian referee Mick Stone denied Britain's claim for a try in the 25th minute when prop Kevin Ward fed scrum half Andy Gregory in a runaround move which sent the scrum half scooting over the line, the pass being ruled forward.

Only days after being voted the best tourist by his fellow British Lions, Paul Loughlin failed to find his markmanship form and missed two kickable chances before co-centre David Stephenson took over, only to be unsuccessful with his attempt.

The defensive lapses allowed substitute back Gary Freeman to snatch two tries, his first from an outrageous dummy and the second, on the stroke of half-time, coming from a British knock on and a missed opportunity to snap up the resultant loose ball.

Sydney whistler Stone also upset the British camp for failing to penalise a New Zealand boot which forced skipper Ellery Hanley to leave the field with a serious eye injury 10 minutes from the end.

But the Lions could not hive off all the blame. Match statistics proved that Kevin Beardmore had supplied a 18-9 scrum advantage and most of the game had been played in the Kiwi half.

Britain set off to an ideal start when Loughlin scored in the first minute after pressurising opposite number Kevin Iro into a mistake over his own line. Kicking into the stiff wind, the St. Helens threequarter could not add the goal, missing a penalty goal shot from a better position minutes later.

After nine minutes Britain were caught offside and prop Peter Brown hit the target. Seven minutes later, the Lions were behind, a misunderstanding between Andy Gregory and Roy Powell providing the possession for New Zealand to feed substitute Freeman, Britain paying the full price for buying his dummy. Brown missed the goal but made amends five minutes later by sending over a penalty goal to extend the Kiwi lead to 8-4.

With the half-time whistle only two minutes away Britain levelled the scores, Hanley feeding stand off David Hulme for his first touchdown of the tour. As Britain began to contemplate a second half with the wind behind them and a stalemate scoreline, the Kiwis struck a killer blow.

From the restart to Hulme's hard fought try, full back Phil Ford knocked on. With New Zealand winning the scrum and Britain missing a chance to regain possession, Freeman again crossed the line to give the home side a four-point interval advantage.

The New Zealanders — and Mr Stone — did not present Britain with a penalty goal opportunity during a dour second half and the Lions rarely looked like creating their own scoring chance as they sought the draw which would guarantee a World Cup final spot.

The final whistle brought an end to Britain's dream of a World Cup clash at Old Trafford and the start of New Zealand's preparations for an October meeting with Australia at Auckland's Rugby Union stonghold, Eden Park.

TEST (World Cup-rated)

17 July   **Christchurch**

NEW ZEALAND 12   GREAT BRITAIN 10

Darrel Williams (Manly)	1.	Phil Ford
Shane Horo (Northcote)	2.	Henderson Gill
Dean Bell (Wigan) Capt.	3.	David Stephenson
Kevin Iro (Mt. Albert & Wigan)	4.	Paul Loughlin
Gary Mercer (Pikiao)	5.	Martin Offiah
Shane Cooper (Mangere East)	6.	David Hulme
Clayton Friend (North Sydney)	7.	Andy Gregory
Peter Brown (Te Atatu)	8.	Kevin Ward
Wayne Wallace (Linwood)	9.	Kevin Beardmore
Adrian Shelford (Wigan)	10.	Hugh Waddell
Mark Graham (North Sydney)	11.	Mike Gregory
Sam Stewart (Newcastle)	12.	Roy Powell
Mark Horo (Te Atatu)	13.	Ellery Hanley, Capt.
Gary Freeman (Balmain)	14.	Darren Wright
Esene Faimalo (Sydenham)	15.	Paul Hulme

T: Freeman (2)

G: Brown (2)

Substitution:

Freeman for M. Horo (13 min.)

Half-time: 12-8

Attendance: 8,525

T: Loughlin, D. Hulme,

G: Loughlin

Substitution:

P. Hulme for Hanley (70 min.)

Referee: Mick Stone (Australia)

Scorechart

Minute	Score	NZ	GB
1:	Loughlin (T)	0	4
9:	Brown (PG)	2	4
16:	Freeman (T)	6	4
21:	Brown (PG)	8	4
38:	D. Hulme (T)	8	8
40:	Freeman (T)	12	8
44:	Loughlin (PG)	12	10
	Scrums	9	18
	Penalties	3	7

Tenth Test cap for centre David Stephenson.

19 July

Auckland

AUCKLAND   30
GREAT BRITAIN   14

1. P. Ford
2. Gill
3. Stephenson
4. Loughlin
5. Currier
6. Joyner
7. A. Gregory, Capt.
8. Ward
9. Beardmore
10. Waddell
11. Eyres
12. P. Hulme
13. M. Gregory

T: Gill (2)
G: Loughlin (3)

Auckland:
Tuimavave; Bourneville, Patton, Watson, Horo; K. Shelford, Bancroft; Brown, Mann, Solomona, Timoko (Hiley), Leota, Hansen

T: Shelford (2), Tuimavave, Brown, Leota
G: Brown (3), Bancroft (2)

Half-time: 14-4

Referee: Bill Shrimpton (Auckland)
Attendance: 8,000

Auckland continued their tradition of end-of-tour victories, the 30-14 success being their fourth against the last five visiting parties.

Britain's seventh defeat of an 18-match tour was always on the cards after former Swinton back Tuimavave opened their try account after 16 minutes, crowning an outstanding display at full back.

Shoddy handling ruined any chances of a Lions' comeback despite two good tries from Gill in the 50th and 77th minutes, their frustration boiling over on the hour when Mike Gregory spent 10 minutes in the sin bin for dissent.

Auckland's five tries to two success left the tourists looking tired and downhearted, the management ready to recommend that the Auckland fixture no longer be the end of the tour, a Test being the ideal finish.

Australia's World Cup winning skipper, Wally Lewis, victim of a broken arm in the Eden Park final.

WORLD CUP

WORLD CUP

Rugby League's longest running World Cup competition — spread over more than three years — reached its climax in October 1988 with Australia retaining the title of world champions for the third successive tournament.

Launched at Carlaw Park, Auckland, back in July 1985, the final of the World Cup was staged in the same New Zealand city but at a prestigious new venue. Eden Park, home of Rugby Union, housed 47,363 fans for the meeting of the top two sides in the qualifying table, Australia and New Zealand.

Despite skipper Wally Lewis suffering a broken arm in the first half, the Australians continued their domination of world football with a convincing 25-12 success, inspired by two-try scrum half Allan Langer.

The elongated tournament, devised by the French, was based on the principle of a World Cup rating being attached to the last match of a Test series during the four-year tour cycle operated by the five International Board countries, thus meeting home and away.

The formula was disrupted by the French themselves who cried off their tour Down Under in the summer of 1987. The International Board ruled that France's World Cup-rated completed fixtures would count towards the final table with the three antipodean countries each receiving two points in lieu of the unfulfilled French away fixtures.

1988 WORLD CUP FINAL

9 October   Eden Park, Auckland

AUSTRALIA 25		NEW ZEALAND 12
Garry Jack	1.	Gary Mercer
Dale Shearer	2.	Tony Iro
Andrew Farrar	3.	Kevin Iro
Mark McGaw	4.	Dean Bell, Capt.
Michael O'Connor	5.	Mark Elia
Wally Lewis, Capt.	6.	Gary Freeman
Allan Langer	7.	Clayton Friend
Paul Dunn	8.	Peter Brown
Ben Elias	9.	Wayne Wallace
Steve Roach	10.	Adrian Shelford
Paul Sironen	11.	Mark Graham
Gavin Miller	12.	Kurt Sorensen
Wayne Pearce	13.	Mark Horo
Terry Lamb	14.	Shane Cooper
David Gillespie	15.	Sam Stewart

T: Langer (2), Shearer, Miller
G: O'Connor (4), Elias (1dg)
Substitutions:
Lamb for Lewis
Gillespie for Roach
Coach: Don Furner
Referee: Graham Ainui (Papua New Guinea)

T: K. Iro, T. Iro
G: Brown (2)
Substitutions:
Cooper for Mercer
Stewart for Shelford
Coach: Tony Gordon
Attendance: 47,363

QUALIFYING MATCHES

NEW ZEALAND 18   AUSTRALIA 0
Auckland: 7 July 1985   19,000
New Zealand: Kemble; Bell, Prohm, Leuluai (1t), O'Hara; Filipaina (3g), Friend (2t); Wright, H. Tamati, K. Tamati, Graham, K. Sorensen, McGahan. Subs: Ropati, Cowan
Australia: Jack; Ribot, Meninga, Ella, Ferguson; Lewis, Hasler; Tunks, Elias, Roach, Vautin, Wynn, Pearce. Subs: Close, Dowling
Referee: J. Rascagneres (France)

GREAT BRITAIN 6   NEW ZEALAND 6
Elland Road, Leeds: 9 November 1985
22,209
Britain: Burke (Widnes); Drummond (Leigh), Schofield (Hull), Edwards (Wigan), Lydon (Widnes); Hanley (Wigan), Fox (Featherstone R.); Grayshon (Leeds), Watkinson (Hull KR), Fieldhouse (Widnes), Goodway (Wigan), Potter (Wigan), Pinner (St. Helens). Subs: L. Crooks (Hull, 3g), Arkwright (St. Helens)
New Zealand: Kemble; Williams, Bell, Leuluai, O'Hara; Ah Kuoi, Friend; K. Tamati, Wallace, D. Sorensen (1g), Graham (1t), K. Sorensen, Prohm. Subs: Filipaina, McGahan
Referee: B. Gomersall (Australia)

Two-try Australian scrum half Allan Langer, Man of the Match in the October 1988 World Cup final.

FRANCE 0   NEW ZEALAND 22
Perpignan: 7 December 1985   5,000
France: Pallares; Ratier, Berge, Palisses, Couston; Espugna, Guasch; Chantal, Bernabe, Titeux, Montgaillard, Palanque, G. Laforgue. Subs: Perez, Rabot
New Zealand: Kemble (1t); Bell, Ah Kuoi, Leuluai, O'Hara; Filipaina (3g), Friend; K. Sorensen (1t), Wallace, D. Sorensen, McGahan (2t), Wright, O'Regan. Subs: Elia, Todd
Referee: R. Campbell (England)

FRANCE 10   GREAT BRITAIN 10
Avignon: 16 February 1986   4,000
France: Dumas (1t,3g); Couston, Maury, Fourquet, Laroche; Espugna, Entat; Chantal, Baco, Titeux, G. Laforgue, Palanque, Bernabe. Subs: Rabot, Berge
Britain: Burke (Widnes); Drummond (Leigh), Schofield (Hull), Hanley (Wigan, 1t), Gill (Wigan); A. Myler (Widnes), Fox (Featherstone R.); L. Crooks (Hull, 3g), Watkinson (Hull KR), Wane (Wigan), Potter (Wigan), Fieldhouse (Widnes), Pinner (St. Helens). Sub: Platt (St. Helens)
Referee: K. Roberts (Australia)

AUSTRALIA 32   NEW ZEALAND 12
Brisbane: 29 July 1986   22,811
Australia: Jack; O'Connor (1t,4g), Miles (1t), Kenny (2t), Kiss; Lewis (1t), Sterling (1t); Roach, Simmons, Tunks, Cleal, Folkes, Pearce. Subs: Lamb, Niebling
New Zealand: Kemble; Williams (2t), Ropati, Prohm, O'Hara; Filipaina (2g), Freeman; Todd, Harvey, K. Sorensen, Graham, McGahan, O'Regan. Subs: Cooper, Wright
Referee: R. Whitfield (England)

PAPUA NEW GUINEA 24
NEW ZEALAND 22
Port Moresby: 17 August 1986   15,000
Papua New Guinea: Kovae (4g); Katsir, Atoi (1t), Numapo, Kerekere; Haili (2t), Kila; Tep, Heni, Loitive, Ako (1t), Waketsi, Taumaku. Subs: Lomutopa, Peter
New Zealand: Kemble; Crequer, Williams, Ropati (1t), O'Hara; Cooper, Freeman; Shelford, Wallace (1t), Brown (1t,3g), Wright, McGahan (1t), O'Regan. Subs: Leuluai, Stewart
Referee: K. Roberts (Australia)

281

PAPUA NEW GUINEA 12 AUSTRALIA 62
Port Moresby: 4 October 1986 17,000

Papua New Guinea: Kovae (2g); Katsir, Atoi, Numapo (2t), Kerekere; Haili, Kila; Tep, Heni, Lomutopa, Ako, Waketsi, Taumaku. Subs: Saea, Andy
Australia: Jack (1t); O'Connor (2t,7g), Miles, C. Mortimer (1t), Kiss (2t); Lewis (1t), Hasler (1t); Roach (1t), Simmons, Niebling, Dunn, Cleal (2t), Lindner (1t). Subs: Meninga, Sironen
Referee: N. Kesha (New Zealand)

GREAT BRITAIN 15 AUSTRALIA 24
Wigan: 22 November 1986 20,169

Britain: Lydon (Wigan, 2g); Gill (Wigan, 1g), Schofield (Hull, 2t,dg), Stephenson (Wigan), Basnett (Widnes); A. Myler (Widnes), A. Gregory (Warrington); Ward (Castleford), Watkinson (Hull KR), L. Crooks (Hull), Burton (Hull KR), Goodway (Wigan), Pinner (Widnes). Sub: Potter (Wigan)
Australia: Jack; Shearer (1t), Kenny, Miles (1t), O'Connor (4g); Lewis (1t), Sterling; Dowling, Simmons, Dunn, Meninga, Niebling, Lindner (1t). Subs: Davidson, Lamb
Referee: J. Rascagneres (France)

FRANCE 0 AUSTRALIA 52
Carcassonne: 13 December 1986 3,000

France: Wozniack; Rodriguez, Fourquet, F. Laforgue, Ratier; Palisses, Scicchitano; Chantal, Bernabe, Titeux, G. Laforgue, Verdes, Gestas. Subs: Dumas, Storer
Australia: Jack (3t); Shearer (4t), Kenny, Miles, O'Connor (1t,6g); Lewis, Sterling; Dowling, Simmons, Dunn, Folkes (1t), Niebling (1t), Lindner. Subs: Lamb, Davidson
Referee: G. F. Lindop (England)

GREAT BRITAIN 52 FRANCE 4
Leeds: 24 January 1987 6,567

Britain: Lydon (Wigan, 1t,8g); Forster (Warrington, 1t), Schofield (Hull), Stephenson (Wigan), Gill (Wigan); Hanley (Wigan, 2t), Edwards (Wigan, 2t); Hobbs (Oldham), K. Beardmore (Castleford), L. Crooks (Hull), Goodway (Wigan, 1t), Haggerty (St. Helens), M. Gregory (Warrington, 2t). Subs: Creasser (Leeds), England (Castleford)
France: Perez (2g); Couston, Palisses, Ratier, Pons; Espugna, Dumas; Storer, Mantese, Rabot, Verdes, Palanque, Bernabe. Subs: Rocci, Titeux
Referee: M. Stone (Australia)

GREAT BRITAIN 42
PAPUA NEW GUINEA 0
Wigan: 24 October 1987 9,121

Britain: Hampson (Wigan); Drummond (Warrington), Stephenson (Wigan, 7g), Lydon (Wigan, 1t), Ford (Bradford N., 1t); Edwards (Wigan, 2t); Gregory (Wigan, 1t); Ward (Castleford), Groves (St. Helens), Case (Wigan), Medley (Leeds, 1t), Goodway (Wigan), Hanley (Wigan, 1t). Subs: Woods (Warrington), Fairbank (Bradford N.)
Papua New Guinea: Kovae; Saea, Atoi, Numapo, Krewanty; Haili, Kila; Tep, Heni, Lomutopa, Kombra, Waketsi, Taumaku. Subs: Kitimun, Gaius
Referee: F. Desplas (France)

FRANCE 21 PAPUA NEW GUINEA 4
Carcassonne: 15 November 1987 5,000

France: Pougeau; Ratier (1t), Delaunay, Fraisse (2t), Pons (1t); Moliner, Bourrel (2g,1dg); Rabot, Khedimi, Ailleres, Montgaillard, Divet, G. Laforgue. Subs: Dumas, Verdes
Papua New Guinea: Kovae (1t); Krewanty, Saea, Atoi, Morea; Numapo, Kila; Lomutopa, Heni, Taumaku, Waketsi, Ako, Kouoru. Subs: Haili, Kombra
Referee: J. Holdsworth (England)

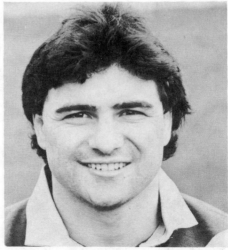
Australia hooker Ben Elias, scorer of a drop goal in the 1988 World Cup final.

Wayne Pearce, Australia's loose forward in their three 1988 World Cup fixtures, including the final.

PAPUA NEW GUINEA 22
GREAT BRITAIN 42
Port Moresby: 22 May 1988   12,077

Papua New Guinea: Kovae (2t); Saea, Morea, Numapo (3g), Krewanty (1t); Haili, Kila; Rop (1t), Matmillo, Bom, Kombra, Evei, Kouoru. Subs: Rombuk, Lapan
Britain: Loughlin (St. Helens, 7g); Ford (Bradford N.), Schofield (Leeds, 2t), Stephenson (Leeds, 1t), Gill (Wigan, 2t); Edwards (Wigan), A. Gregory (Wigan); Ward (Castleford), K. Beardmore (Castleford), Case (Wigan), Medley (Leeds, 1t), M. Gregory (Warrington, 1t), Hanley (Wigan). Subs: D. Hulme (Widnes), Dixon (Halifax)
Referee: G. McCallum (Australia)

AUSTRALIA 12   GREAT BRITAIN 26
Sydney: 9 July 1988   15,994

Australia: Jack; Ettingshausen, O'Connor (2g), Jackson, Currie; Lewis (1t), Sterling; Bella, Conescu, Backo (1t), Fullerton-Smith, Vautin, Pearce. Subs: Belcher, Lindner
Britain: P. Ford (Bradford N., 1t); Gill (Wigan, 2t), Stephenson (Leeds), Loughlin (St. Helens, 3g), Offiah (Widnes, 1t); D. Hulme (Widnes), A. Gregory (Wigan); Ward (Castleford), P. Hulme (Widnes), Waddell (Oldham), M. Gregory (Warrington, 1t), Powell (Leeds), Hanley (Wigan). Sub: Case (Wigan)
Referee: F. Desplas (France)

NEW ZEALAND 66
PAPUA NEW GUINEA 14
Auckland: 10 July 1988   8,392

New Zealand: Williams (1t); S. Horo (3t), Bell, K. Iro (3t), Mercer (2t); Cooper, Friend; Brown (9g), Wallace (1t), Shelford (1t), Graham (1t), Stewart, M. Horo. Subs: Freeman, Faimalo
Papua New Guinea: Kovae (1t); Krewanty, Numapo (3g), Atoi, Morea; Haili, Kila; Ben-Moide, Matmillo (1t), Bom, Evei, Kombra, Kouoru. Subs: Wanega, Kouru
Referee: G. McCallum (Australia)

NEW ZEALAND 12   GREAT BRITAIN 10
Christchurch: 17 July 1988   8,525

New Zealand: Williams; S. Horo, Bell, K. Iro, Mercer; Cooper, Friend; Brown (2g), Wallace, Shelford, Graham, Stewart, M. Horo. Sub: Freeman
Britain: P. Ford (Bradford N.); Gill (Wigan), Stephenson (Leeds), Loughlin (St. Helens, 1t,1g), Offiah (Widnes); D. Hulme (Widnes, 1t), A. Gregory (Wigan); K. Ward (Castleford), K. Beardmore (Castleford), Waddell (Oldham), M. Gregory (Warrington), Powell (Leeds), Hanley (Wigan). Sub: P. Hulme (Widnes)
Referee: M. Stone (Australia)

AUSTRALIA 70   PAPUA NEW GUINEA 8
Wagga Wagga: 20 July 1988   11,685

Australia: Jack (1t); O'Connor (4t,7g), Jackson, Meninga (2t), Currie (1t); Lewis (1t), Langer (2t); Daley, Conescu (1t), Dunn, Miller (1t), Fullerton-Smith (1t), Pearce. Subs: Hasler, Vautin
Papua New Guinea: Wanega; Krewanty, Kovae, Numapo (2g), Morea (1t); Atoi, Haili; Rombuk, Matmillo, Ben-Moide, Kombra, Evei, Gispe. Subs: Karara, Kuno
Referee: N. Kesha (New Zealand)

FINAL TABLE

	P	W	D	L	F	A	Pts
Australia	7	5	0	2	252	91	12*
New Zealand	7	4	1	2	158	86	11*
Great Britain	8	4	2	2	203	90	10
Papua New Guinea	7	1	0	6	84	325	4*
France	5	1	1	3	35	140	3

*Awarded two points in lieu of non-fulfilment of French fixtures Down Under.

Australia Test prop Sam Backo, an ever-present for Queensland in the 1988 State of Origin Series.

DOWN UNDER

THE SYDNEY PREMIERSHIP GRAND FINAL

1988 Final

Ellery Hanley joined the growing number of British players who have played in a Sydney Grand Final when he appeared for Balmain against Canterbury on 11 September 1988.

Although most of the others had also played at Wembley, the Wigan captain became the first to appear in the Challenge Cup final and the Grand Final in the same year.

But while he enjoyed a Wigan victory over Halifax at Wembley in April, Hanley was on the losing side in Sydney as Balmain went down 24-12. He also missed most of the match after being concussed in the 28th minute, returning 10 minutes later but being unable to play in the second half.

Balmain were leading 6-4 when Hanley first went off but conceded a try and goal six minutes after his departure. Although Balmain were only 10-8 behind at the interval they posed no real threat without Hanley in the second half and finished well beaten.

Hanley had been the major factor in Balmain making a late surge for honours, battling through to the final after qualifying for the semi-finals by beating Penrith in a play-off for fifth place.

Canterbury won the trophy from second place after beating leaders Cronulla in the major semi-final.

It was the first Grand Final to be played at the new Sydney Football Stadium with the capacity crowd of 40,000 falling well below the many vast attendances at the old and larger Sydney Cricket Ground.

SYDNEY GRAND FINAL

11 September 1988
CANTERBURY 24

Sydney Football Stadium
BALMAIN 12

British style numbering

Canterbury	No.	Balmain
Jason Alchin	1.	Garry Jack
Glenn Nissen	2.	Russell Gartner
Andrew Farrar	3.	Ellery Hanley
Tony Currie	4.	Michael Pobjie
Robin Thorne	5.	Ross Conlon
Terry Lamb	6.	Michael Neil
Michael Hagan	7.	Gary Freeman
Peter Tunks, Capt.	8.	Bruce McGuire
Joe Thomas	9.	Ben Elias
Paul Dunn	10.	Kerry Hemsley
David Gillespie	11.	Paul Sironen
Steve Folkes	12.	David Brooks
Paul Langmack	13.	Wayne Pearce, Capt.

T: Nissen, Gillespie, Lamb, Hagan
G: Lamb (4)
Substitutions:
Brandon Lee for Tunks (66 min.)
Steve Mortimer for Hagan (71 min.)
Darren McCarthy for Currie (75 min.)
Mark Bugden for Thomas (75 min.)
Sin bin: Tunks (6 min.)
Coach: Phil Gould
Half-time: 10-8
Referee: Michael Stone
Clive Churchill Medal for Man of the Match: Paul Dunn (Canterbury).

T: Elias, McGuire
G: Conlon (2)
Substitutions:
Steve Edmed for Hemsley (34 min.)
Scott Gale for Hanley (Half-time)
Kevin Hardwick for Brooks (75 min.)
*Head bin: Gale for Hanley (28 min.)
Coach: Warren Ryan
Scrums: 6-9
Penalties: 7-9
Attendance: 40,000
*Temporary (10 min.) substitution for a player with head injury.

1988 WINFIELD CUP

	P.	W.	D.	L.	F.	A.	Pts
Cronulla-Sutherland	22	16	2	4	507	330	34
Canterbury-Bankstown	22	16	0	6	412	268	32
Canberra	22	15	0	7	596	346	30
Manly-Warringah	22	15	0	7	538	347	30
Penrith	22	15	0	7	394	258	30
Balmain	22	15	0	7	402	341	30
Brisbane	22	14	0	8	474	368	28
South Sydney	22	12	2	8	425	383	24★
North Sydney	22	9	2	11	366	424	20
St. George	22	9	0	13	352	493	18
Parramatta	22	8	0	14	359	412	16
Eastern Suburbs	22	6	3	13	387	443	15
Illawarra	22	6	1	15	353	510	13
Newcastle	22	5	1	16	270	460	11
Gold Coast	22	4	2	16	238	484	10
Western Suburbs	22	4	1	17	287	493	9

★ 2 points deducted for fielding ineligible player against Manly.

WINFIELD CUP PLAY-OFF
Fifth place play off
Balmain 28 v. Penrith 8
Minor preliminary semi-final
Balmain 19 v. Manly 6
Major preliminary semi-final
Canterbury 19 v. Canberra 18
Minor semi-final
Balmain 14 v. Canberra 6
Major semi-final
Canterbury 26 v. Cronulla 8
Preliminary final
Balmain 9 v. Cronulla 2
Grand Final
Canterbury 24 v. Balmain 12

● All matches played at the
Sydney Football Stadium except for
the fifth place play-off at
Parramatta Stadium.

LEADING SCORERS
● Not including play-offs

Tries
John Ferguson (Canberra) 19
Goals
Gary Belcher (Canberra) 85
Points
Gary Belcher (Canberra) 210

Gary Belcher, 1988 Winfield Cup top goals and points scorer.

BRITISH PLAYERS IN GRAND FINALS

British players who have appeared in the Sydney Grand Final are:

Dick Huddart (St. George) 1966 winners, 1 try
Dave Bolton (Balmain) 1966 losers; 1969 winners, 2 drop goals
Mervyn Hicks (Canterbury) 1967 losers
Ken Batty (St. George) 1971 losers
Malcolm Reilly (Manly) 1972 winners, 1973 winners
Tommy Bishop (Cronulla) 1973 losers
Bob Wear (Cronulla) 1973 losers
Cliff Watson (Cronulla) 1973 losers
Brian Lockwood (Canterbury) 1974 losers
Gary Stephens (Manly) 1976 winners
Steve Norton (Manly) 1976 winners
Phil Lowe (Manly) 1976 winners, 1 try
Kevin Ward (Manly) 1987 winners
Ellery Hanley (Balmain) 1988 losers

Apart from Hicks and Wear, all the above also appeared in a Challenge Cup final at Wembley. In addition Len Killeen, the South African winger who began his league career with St. Helens, also played at Wembley and got a Grand Final winners' medal with Balmain in 1969 when he kicked two goals.

Ellery Hanley is the only player to appear in both major finals in the same year. In 1988 he led Wigan to success at Wembley and four months later was in Balmain's beaten Grand Final team.

Australians who have achieved the big double since the Grand Final became mandatory in 1954 are: Chris Anderson, Harry Bath, Graham Eadie, John Ferguson, Kerry Hemsley, Brett Kenny, John Muggleton, Peter Sterling, Michael O'Connor and Paul Vautin.

There were a record four British players in the 1973 Grand Final. Reilly got a winners' medal with Manly, while Bishop, Watson and Wear were in the beaten Cronulla side.

Three British players — Stephens, Norton and Lowe — were also in the Manly side which won the final in 1976.

BRITISH PLAYERS IN 1988 SYDNEY PREMIERSHIP

Only four British players appeared in the Sydney Premiership during the 1988 season.

The most notable was Ellery Hanley of Wigan who joined Balmain after captaining the Great Britain tourists Down Under. Hanley signed in time to play in the last three rounds of the Premiership and played a major role in getting Balmain into the play-offs and through to the final.

Hanley, reported to have been paid £1,500 per match, played eight matches and scored five tries.

Darryl Powell, the Sheffield Eagles utility player, also had a spell with Balmain, scoring two tries in four appearances.

Kevin Ward of Castleford joined Manly after the British Lions tour and the prop played in four matches, scoring one try.

Neil James, the Halifax forward, made two substitute appearances for Gold Coast.

Following an agreement between the two countries no British player who was in contention for a place in Great Britain's tour squad was allowed to join an Australian club until after the tour or before he was ruled out of the trip.

● British players granted clearance to play in the 1989 Sydney Premiership by 1 June were:

David Croft (Bradford N. to Western Suburbs)
Andy Currier (Widnes to Balmain)
Bernard Dwyer (St. Helens to Manly)
Shaun Edwards (Wigan to Balmain)
Des Foy (Oldham to Newcastle Knights)
Andy Gregory (Wigan to Illawara)
Graeme Hallas (Hull K.R. to Canterbury)
Steve Hampson (Wigan to Illawara)
Ellery Hanley (Wigan to Western Suburbs)
Tracy Lazenby (Wakefield T. to Penrith)
Joe Lydon (Wigan to Eastern Suburbs)
Craig O'Brien (Hull K.R. to Canterbury)
Martin Offiah (Widnes to Western Suburbs)
Garry Schofield (Leeds to Western Suburbs)
Kelvin Skerrett (Bradford N. to Western Suburbs)
Graham Steadman (Featherstone R. to Gold Coast Giants)
Paul Vannet (Workington T. to Cronulla)
Hugh Waddell (Leeds to Manly)

STATE OF ORIGIN

The State of Origin matches between New South Wales and Queensland began in 1980 and are now established as a major part of the Australian Rugby League scene.

Their introduction revived interest in the inter-state matches which had been dominated by New South Wales, who had won the last 15 matches by mainly wide margins.

Under the old system players appeared for the state in which they were playing club rugby at the time and this gave a big advantage to New South Wales because many of Queensland's best players were with Sydney clubs.

But in State of Origin matches players appear for the state in which they were born and this has resulted in the matches becoming more fiercely and evenly fought before increased attendances.

NEW SOUTH WALES v. QUEENSLAND RESULTS
State of Origin only.

Date	Winner	Score	Venue	Attendance
8 July 1980	Queensland	20 - 10	Brisbane	31,000
28 July 1981	Queensland	22 - 15	Brisbane	25,613
1 June 1982	New South Wales	20 - 16	Brisbane	27,326
8 June 1982	Queensland	11 - 7	Brisbane	19,435
22 June 1982	Queensland	10 - 5	Sydney	20,242
7 June 1983	Queensland	24 - 12	Brisbane	29,412
21 June 1983	New South Wales	10 - 6	Sydney	21,620
28 June 1983	Queensland	43 - 22	Brisbane	26,084
29 May 1984	Queensland	29 - 12	Brisbane	33,662
19 June 1984	Queensland	14 - 2	Sydney	29,088
17 July 1984	New South Wales	22 - 12	Brisbane	16,599
28 May 1985	New South Wales	18 - 2	Brisbane	33,011
11 June 1985	New South Wales	21 - 14	Sydney	39,068
23 July 1985	Queensland	20 - 6	Brisbane	18,825
27 May 1986	New South Wales	22 - 16	Brisbane	33,000
10 June 1986	New South Wales	24 - 20	Sydney	40,707
1 July 1986	New South Wales	18 - 16	Brisbane	21,097
2 June 1987	New South Wales	20 - 16	Brisbane	33,411
16 June 1987	Queensland	12 - 6	Sydney	42,048
15 July 1987	Queensland	10 - 8	Brisbane	33,000
6 Aug. 1987	New South Wales	30 - 18	California	12,349
17 May 1988	Queensland	26 - 18	Sydney	26,441
31 May 1988	Queensland	16 - 6	Brisbane	31,817
21 June 1988	Queensland	38 - 22	Sydney	16,910

SUMMARY
New South Wales won 10; Queensland won 14.
Since it became a three-match series in 1982 Queensland have won five series to New South Wales' two.

1988 STATE OF ORIGIN MATCHES

*Denotes captain

17 May
Sydney
New South Wales 18

Docking (Cronulla)
B. Johnston (St. George)
McGaw (Cronulla) 1t
O'Connor (Manly) 1t, 3g
Ettingshausen (Cronulla) 1t
Lyons (Manly)
Sterling (Parramatta)
Davidson (Souths)
Simmons (Penrith)
Roach (Balmain)
Folkes (Canterbury)
Cleal (Manly)
*Pearce (Balmain)

Subs: Lamb (Canterbury)
Trewhella (Easts)

Queensland 26

Belcher (Canberra) 1t, 3g
McIndoe (Illawarra) 1t
Currie (Canterbury)
Miles (Brisbane)
Kilroy (Brisbane)
Jackson (Canberra) 1t
Langer (Brisbane) 2t
Bella (Norths)
Conescu (Brisbane)
Backo (Canberra)
Fullerton-Smith (St. George)
Lindner (Parramatta)
*Vautin (Manly)

Subs: B. French (Norths)
Tronc (Wests)

Referee: Barry Gomersall
Man of the Match: Langer

31 May
Brisbane
New South Wales 6

Jack (Balmain)
Ferguson (Canberra)
McGaw (Cronulla)
O'Connor (Manly) 1t, 1g
Ettingshausen (Cronulla)
Lamb (Canterbury)
Sterling (Parramatta)
Daley (Manly)
Elias (Balmain)
Roach (Balmain)
*Pearce (Balmain)
Folkes (Canterbury)
Langmack (Canterbury)

Subs: Dunn (Canterbury)
Hasler (Manly)

Queensland 16

Belcher (Canberra) 4g
McIndoe (Illawarra)
Jackson (Canberra)
Miles (Brisbane)
Currie (Canterbury)
*Lewis (Brisbane)
Langer (Brisbane) 1t
Bella (Norths)
Conescu (Brisbane)
Backo (Canberra) 1t
Fullerton-Smith (St. George)
Lindner (Parramatta)
Vautin (Manly)

Subs: B. French (Norths)
Gillmeister (Easts)

Referee: Mick Stone
Man of the Match: Backo

21 June
Sydney
New South Wales 22

Jack (Balmain)
Ferguson (Canberra) 1t
McGaw (Cronulla)
O'Connor (Manly) 1t, 3g
Ettingshausen (Cronulla)
Lyons (Manly)
Hasler (Manly)
Hanson (Norths) 1t
Elias (Balmain)
Roach (Balmain)
Folkes (Canterbury)
*Pearce (Balmain) 1t
Langmack (Canterbury)

Subs: Florimo (Norths)
Cleal (Manly)

Queensland 38

Belcher (Canberra) 5g
McIndoe (Illawarra)
Jackson (Canberra) 1t
Currie (Canterbury)
Kilroy (Brisbane) 1t
*Lewis (Brisbane) 1t
Langer (Brisbane) 1t
Bella (Norths)
Conescu (Brisbane)
Backo (Canberra) 2t
Fullerton-Smith (St. George)
Lindner (Parramatta)
Vautin (Manly)

Subs: B. French (North) 1t
Gillmeister (Easts)

Referee: Greg McCallum
Man of the Match: Backo

NEW SOUTH WALES v. QUEENSLAND RECORDS
State of Origin only

NEW SOUTH WALES

Highest score:	30-18 at California, 6 August 1987
Widest margin:	18-2 at Brisbane, 28 May 1985
Most appearances:	16 + 1 sub. by Brett Kenny (Parramatta)
Most tries in a match:	3 by Chris Anderson (Canterbury), 28 June 1983
Most goals in a match:	No player has kicked more than five
Most points in a match:	18 (2t, 5g) Michael O'Connor (Manly), 28 May 1985
Biggest home attendance:	42,048, 16 June 1987

QUEENSLAND

Highest score:	43-22 at Brisbane, 28 June 1983 (Also widest margin)
Most appearances:	23 by Wally Lewis (Fortitude Valley, Wynum Manly, Brisbane)
Most tries:	3 by Kerry Boustead (Manly), 29 May 1984
Most goals:	7 by Mal Meninga (Souths, B), 8 July 1980
Most points:	14 (7g) Mal Meninga (Souths, B), 8 July 1980
Biggest home attendance:	33,662, 29 May 1984

Coaches:

New South Wales: Ted Glossop (1980, 1981, 1983); Frank Stanton (1982, 1984); Terry Fearnley (1985); Ron Willey (1986, 1987); John Peard (1988)

Queensland: John McDonald (1980); Arthur Beetson (1981, 1982, 1983, 1984); Des Morris (1985); Wayne Bennett (1986, 1987, 1988)

English referees

English referees who have taken charge of State of Origin matches are: Billy Thompson on 8 July 1980 and Robin Whitfield on 28 June 1983.

QUEENSLAND REGISTER

The following is a register of players who have appeared for Queensland in the State of Origin series plus the match against New South Wales in the United States of America, up to and including 1988. + indicates number of matches played as a substitute. B-Brisbane, S-Sydney.

BACKER, Brad (3) Easts, B
BACKO, Sam (3) Canberra
BEETSON, Arthur (1) Parramatta
BELCHER, Gary (9) Canberra
BELLA, Martin (5) North, S
BOUSTEAD, Kerry (6) Easts, S 3; Manly 3
BRENNAN, Mitch (4) Souths, S 3; Redcliffe 1
BROHMAN, Darryl (2) Penrith
BROWN, Dave (10) Manly 6; Easts, S 4
BUTLER, Terry (1) Wynnum Manly

CARR, Norm (2) Wests, B
CLOSE, Chris (9) Manly 7; Redcliffe 2
CONESCU, Greg (20) Norths, B 4; Redcliffe 10; Gladstone 3; Brisbane 3
CURRIE, Tony (5 + 3) Wests, B +1; Redcliffe +1; Canterbury 5 +1

DOWLING, Greg (11) Wynnum Manly 7; Norths, B 4
DOWLING, John (3) St. George

FRENCH, Brett (1 + 3) Wynnum Manly; Norths S +3
FRENCH, Ian (3 + 6) Wynnum Manly 2 + 3; Norths, S 1 + 3
FULLERTON-SMITH, Wally (10) Redcliffe 7; St. George 3

GILLMEISTER, Trevor (4 + 2) Easts, S

HANCOCK, Rohan (5) Souths, B 3; Easts, B 1; Toowoomba 1
HENRICK, Ross (2) Norths, B 1; Fortitude Valley 1
HEUGH, Cavill (2 + 1) Easts, B

JACKSON, Peter (7 + 1) Canberra 7; Souths, B +1
JONES, Gavin (3) Norths, S

KELLAWAY, Bob (+ 1) Souths, B
KHAN, Paul (4) Easts, B 3; Cronulla 1
KILROY, Joe (2) Brisbane
KISS, Les (2) Norths, S

LANG, John (1) Easts, S
LANGER, Allan (7) Ipswich 4, Brisbane 3
LEWIS, Wally (23) Wynnum Manly 13; Fortitude Valley 8; Brisbane 2
LINDNER, Bob (12) Souths, B 1; Wynnum Manly 5; Parramatta 6

McCABE, Paul (5) Easts, S 1; Manly 4
McINDOE, Alan (3) Illawarra
MENINGA, Mal (16) Souths, B 13; Canberra 3
MILES, Gene (16) Wynnum Manly 14; Brisbane 2
MORRIS, Rod (4) Balmain 2; Wynnum Manly 2
MURRAY, Mark (14) Fortitude Valley 3, Redcliffe 11

NIEBLING, Bryan (9) Fortitude Valley 3; Redcliffe 6

OLIPHANT, Greg (1) Balmain

PHELAN, Chris (2) Souths, B 1; Parramatta 1

QUINN, Greg (1) Ipswich

REDDY, Rod (1) St. George
RIBOT, John (8) Manly 5; Redcliffe 3

SCOTT, Colin (16 + 1) Wynnum Manly 15 + 1; Easts, B 1
SHEARER, Dale (10) Manly
SMITH, Alan (1) Norths, S
SMITH, Gary (+ 1) Brothers
STACEY, Steve (2) Easts, B

TESSMAN, Brad (4 + 1) Souths, B 3; Easts, S 1 + 1
TRONC, Scott (+ 1) Wests, S

VAUTIN, Paul (16 + 1) Manly

WALKER, Bruce (1) Manly

NEW SOUTH WALES REGISTER

The following is a register of players who have appeared for New South Wales in the State of Origin series plus the match against Queensland in the United States of America, up to and including 1988. + indicates number of matches played as a substitute. B-Brisbane, S-Sydney.

ANDERSON, Chris (4) Canterbury
AYLIFFE, Royce (1 + 2) Easts, S

BOWDEN, Steve (1) Newtown
BOYD, Les (3) Manly
BOYLE, David (2 + 2) Souths, S
BRENTNALL, Greg (4) Canterbury
BROOKS, David (1) Balmain
BROWN, Ray (1 + 2) Manly
BUGDEN, Geoff (2) Parramatta

CLEAL, Noel (11 + 1) Manly
CONLON, Ross (3) Canterbury
COOPER, Bob (1) Wests, S
COVENEY, John (2) Canterbury
CRONIN, Mick (6) Parramatta

DALEY, Phil (3) Manly
DAVIDSON, Les (5) Souths, S
DOCKING, Jonathan (2) Cronulla
DUKES, Phillip (1) Moree
DUNN, Paul (+1) Canterbury

EADIE, Graham (1) Manly
EDGE, Steve (1) Parramatta
ELIAS, Ben (5) Balmain
ELLA, Steve (3 + 4) Parramatta
ETTINGSHAUSEN, Andrew (6) Cronulla

FAHEY, Terry (2) Easts, S
FARRAR, Andrew (4) Canterbury
FERGUSON, John (5) Easts, S 3; Canberra 2
FIELD, Paul (2) Cootamundra
FLORIMO, Greg (+1) Norths, S
FOLKES, Steve (8 + 1) Canterbury

GERARD, Geoff (2) Manly
GILLESPIE, David (+3) Canterbury
GROTHE, Eric (9) Parramatta
GURR, Marty (2) Easts, S

HAMBLY, Gary (1) Souths, S
HANSON, Steve (1) Norths, S
HASLER, Des (2 + 3) Manly
HASTINGS, Kevin (+1) Easts, S
HETHERINGTON, Brian (1 + 1) Illawarra
HILDITCH, Ron (1) Parramatta
HUNT, Neil (2) Parramatta

IZZARD, Brad (2 + 1) Penrith

JACK, Garry (14) Balmain
JARVIS, Pat (6 + 2) St. George (4 + 2), Canterbury 2
JENSEN, Barry (1) Newtown
JOHNSTON, Brian (7) St. George
JOHNSTON, Lindsay (2) Norths, S
JURD, Stan (1 + 1) Parramatta

KENNY, Brett (16 + 1) Parramatta
KRILICH, Max (5) Manly

LAMB, Terry (3 + 3) Canterbury 2 + 3, Wests, S 1
LANGMACK, Paul (3 + 1) Canterbury
LEIS, Jim (1) Wests, S
LYONS, Cliff (4) Manly

McGAW, Mark (6 + 1) Cronulla
McKINNON, Don (1) Norths, S
MERLO, Paul (1) Wests, S
MELROSE, Tony (1) Souths, S
MILLER, Gavin (2) Cronulla
MORRIS, Steve (2) St. George
MORTIMER, Chris (7) Canterbury
MORTIMER, Steve (8) Canterbury
MUGGLETON, John (2) Parramatta

NISZCOTT, Ziggy (2) Souths, S

O'CONNOR, Michael (13) St. George 6, Manly 7

PEARCE, Wayne (15) Balmain
POTTER, Michael (+1) Canterbury
PRICE, Ray (8) Parramatta

RAMPLING, Tony (2 + 1) Souths, S
RAUDONIKIS, Tom (1) Newtown
ROACH, Steve (12) Balmain
ROGERS, Steve (4) Cronulla

SIGSWORTH, Phil (3) Newtown 2, Manly 1
SIMMONS, Royce (10) Penrith
STERLING, Peter (13) Parramatta
STONE, Robert (+1) St. George

THOMPSON, Alan (5 + 1) Manly
TREWHELLA, David (+1) Easts, S
TUNKS, Peter (7 + 1), Souths 1, Canterbury 6 + 1

WALSH, Chris (1) St. George
WRIGHT, Rex (1) N. Newcastle
WYNN, Graeme (1) St. George
WYNN, Peter (4) Parramatta

YOUNG, Craig (4 + 1) St. George

Terry Lamb, six appearances for New South Wales.

PAPUA NEW GUINEA TOUR OF NEW ZEALAND AND AUSTRALIA 1988
IN NEW ZEALAND

Date	Result	Score	Opposition	Venue	Attendance
3 July	W	58-0	Midlands Region T: Atoi (3), Numapo (3), Morea, Ben-Moide, Evei, Kombra G: Numapo (9)	Tokoroa	
5 July	W	38-12	Waikato T: Atoi (2), H. Kouoru (2) Gispe, Rombuk, Kuno G: Numapo (5)	Huntly	
10 July	L	14-66	NEW ZEALAND **New Zealand:** Williams (1t); S. Horo (3t), D. Bell (Capt.), K. Iro (3t), Mercer (2t); Cooper, Friend; Brown (9g) Wallace (1t), A. Shelford (1t), Graham (1t), Stewart, M. Horo. Subs: Freeman, Faimalo (both played) **Papua New Guinea:** Kovae (1t); Krewanty, Numapo (Capt. 3g), Atoi, Morea; Haili, Kila; Bom, Matmillo (1t), Ben-Moide, Evei, Kombra, G. Kouoru. Subs: Wanega, H. Kouoru (played) Referee: Greg McCallum (Australia)	Auckland	8,397
13 July	W	58-14	Northland T: Rop (2), Numapo (2), Kaeta (2), Evei, H. Kouoru, Rombuk, Lapan, Tivelit. G: Numapo (7)	Whangarei	

IN AUSTRALIA

Date	Result	Score	Opposition	Venue	Attendance
16 July	L	18-26	Southern Division (NSW) T: Evei, Krewanty, Numapo G: Numapo (3)	Nowra	800
20 July	L	8-70	AUSTRALIA **Australia:** Jack (1t); O'Connor (4t, 7g), Meninga (2t), Jackson, Currie (1t); Lewis (Capt. 1t), Langer (2t); Dunn, Conescu (1t), Daley, Fullerton-Smith (1t), Miller (1t), Pearce. Subs: Hasler, Vautin (both played) **Papua New Guinea:** Wanega; Krewanty, Kovae, Numapo (Capt. 2g), Morea (1t); Atoi, Haili; Rombuk, Matmillo, Ben-Moide, Kombra, Evei, Gispe. Subs: Karara, Kuno (both played) Referee: Neville Kesha (New Zealand)	Wagga Wagga	11,685
24 July	L	10-28	New South Wales Country T: Numapo, Haili G: Numapo	Bathurst	1,000
26 July	W	18-12	Central Coast Division (NSW) T: Morea: Karara, Evei, Matmillo, G: Lapan	Gosford	1,000

TOUR SUMMARY			F	A
P	W	L	Pts	Pts
8	4	4	222	228

TOUR REGISTER

Player	Club	App	Sub	T	G	Pts
ATOI, Louta	Dolphins, Bougainville	7	—	5	—	20
BEN-MOIDE, Daroa	Petone, Wellington, NZ	5	1	1	—	4
BOM, Yer	Brothers, Pt. Moresby	4	—	—	—	—
EVEI, Tuyo	Tarangau, Goroka	7	1	4	—	16
GISPE, Joe	Muruks, Rabaul	5	—	1	—	4
HAILI, Darius	Brothers, Kimbe	6	1	1	—	4
KAETA, Sawi	Air Niugini, Pt. Moresby	3	1	2	—	8
KARARA, Sam	Tigers, Gooroka	2	2	1	—	4
KILA, Tony	Air Niugini, Pt. Moresby	4	1	—	—	—
KOMBRA, Mathias	Bulldogs, Mendi	4	—	1	—	4
KOUORU, Gideon	Wests, Pt. Moresby	2	—	—	—	—
KOUORU, Haoda	Wests, Pt. Moresby	4	1	3	—	12
*KOVAE, Dairi	North Sydney	2	—	1	—	4
KREWANTY, Arnold	Defence, Pt. Moresby	7	—	1	—	4
KUNO, Andrew	Panthers, Lae	2	3	1	—	4
LAPAN, Ngala	Panthers, Lae	3	2	1	1	6
MATMILLO, Michael	Kone, Pt. Moresby	8	—	2	—	8
MOREA, Mea	DCA, Pt. Moresby	5	—	3	—	12
NUMAPO, Bal	Brothers, Kundiawa	7	1	7	30	88
ROMBUK, Thomas	United, Kimbe	5	—	2	—	8
ROP, Isaac	Magani, Pt. Moresby	2	1	2	—	8
TIVELIT, Arnold	Paga, Pt. Moresby	4	—	1	—	4
WANEGA, Ipisa	Brothers, Kundiawa	6	—	—	—	—

*available Tests only
Captain: Bal Numapo
Coach: Skerry Palanga
Team Manager: Stanley Pil
Tour Manager: Tau Peruka
Finance Manager: Rod Sweeney-Hunt

AUSTRALIA BICENTENNIAL CHALLENGE MATCH
Australia 22 Rest of the World 10

27 July: Sydney Football Stadium
Attendance: 15,301

Australia: Jack; Ettingshausen, Meninga, McGaw, McIndoe; Lewis (Capt.), Langer; Roach, Conescu, Backo, Miles, Miller, Pearce. Subs: Hasler, Fullerton-Smith (both played)
T: McGaw (2), Lewis, Ettingshausen
G: Meninga (3)

Rest of the World: Mercer (NZ); Kovae (PNG), Bell (NZ), K. Iro (NZ), Gill (GB); Cooper (NZ), A. Gregory (GB); Ward (GB), Wallace (NZ), A. Shelford (NZ), Graham (NZ, Capt.), M. Gregory (GB), Hanley (GB). Subs: Pougeau (F), Stewart (NZ) (both played)
T: Iro, M. Gregory G: Mercer.
Referee: Graham Ainui (PNG)

AUSTRALIA IN NEW ZEALAND
Australia played a Wellington Invitation side in a warm-up game for the World Cup final against New Zealand. Australia fielded their full World Cup line-up including the two substitutes who both played.

The scorers in Australia's 24-12 victory on 2 October were — Tries: McGaw, Lewis, Sironen, Elias. Goals: O'Connor 4.

● See WORLD CUP section for final between New Zealand and Australia.

Halifax full back Colin Whitfield outstrips the French defence in his Man of the Match performance.

FRENCH TOUR

FRENCH TOUR

France mounted a three-match official mini-tour of Britain as part of *French Enterprise,* a preparation programme in advance of their 1989 summer tour Down Under.

The October triple fixture was undertaken by a 22-man squad under the control of flamboyant coach Jacques Jorda, the opening victory at Warrington being followed by narrow defeats at the hands of Cumbria and Halifax.

A return to the traditional Gallic style of fast running and support play was particularly evident in the five-try romp at Warrington, although the customary lack of discipline — with two players sin-binned — crept in at Whitehaven and leaky defence allowed Halifax to build a 24-8 lead at Thrum Hall.

Fourteen of the tour squad went on to meet Great Britain in the Whitbread Trophy Tests three months later, top scorer being scrum half Gilles Dumas who tallied 11 points from a try, three goals and a drop goal in his two appearances.

Skipper Hugues Ratier was one of seven ever-presents, touching down twice in the opening encounter at Warrington, before staying for a further week to represent the Rest of the World, along with young hooker Thierry Valero, in the Whitbread Trophy Challenge against Great Britain.

Charismatic French coach Jacques Jorda.

TOUR RESULTS

Date		Result	Score	Opposition	Venue	Attendance
Oct.	16	W	29-6	Warrington	Warrington	3,200
	19	L	13-18	Cumbria	Whitehaven	4,000
	23	L	18-24	Halifax	Halifax	4,674

TOUR SUMMARY

					FOR				AGAINST			
P	W	D	L	T	G	Dr	Pts	T	G	Dr	Pts
3	1	0	2	11	7	2	60	8	8	0	48

296

TOUR PARTY
Coach: Jacques Jorda
Captain: Hugues Ratier

Player	Club	App	Sub	T	G	Dr	Pts
AILLIERES, Pierre	Toulouse	1	—	—	—	—	—
BOURREL, Freddy	Limoux	1	1	—	4	1	9
BUTTIGNOL, Thierry	Avignon	2	—	—	—	—	—
CRIOTIER, Marcel	Le Pontet	1	—	—	—	—	—
DELAUNAY, Guy	St. Esteve	3	—	—	—	—	—
DUMAS, Gilles	St. Gaudens	2	—	1	3	1	11
FRISON, Jean	Toulouse	2	1	1	—	—	4
GRANDJEAN, Georges	Lezignan	1	—	—	—	—	—
LIMONGI, Patrick	Carcassonne	1	—	—	—	—	—
MOLINER, Jacques	Pamiers	3	—	2	—	—	8
MONTGAILLARD, Pierre	Catalan XIII	2	1	—	—	—	—
PALISSES, Roger	St. Esteve	3	—	2	—	—	8
PECH, Jacques	Pamiers	1	—	—	—	—	—
PIREDDA, Christian	Carpentras	1	—	—	—	—	—
PONS, Cyril	St. Gaudens	2	—	2	—	—	8
RABOT, Jean-Luc	Villeneuve	1	1	—	—	—	—
RATIER, Hugues	St. Esteve	3	—	2	—	—	8
STORER, Yves	St. Gaudens	2	—	—	—	—	—
TISSEYRE, Marc	Pamiers	1	—	—	—	—	—
VALERO, Thierry	Pamiers	2	1	—	—	—	—
VERDES, Daniel	Villeneuve	2	—	1	—	—	4
VERGNIOL, Eric	Villeneuve	2	—	—	—	—	—

MATCH BY MATCH

16 October

WARRINGTON   **6**
FRANCE   **29**

1. Frison
2. Ratier
3. Delaunay
4. Vergniol
5. Pons
6. Palisses (Bourrel)
7. Dumas
8. Buttignol
9. Tisseyre (Valero)
10. Montgaillard
11. Storer
12. Verdes
13. Moliner

T: Ratier (2), Pons, Palisses, Moliner
G: Dumas (2, 1dg), Bourrel (2)

Warrington:
Turner; Drummond, Blake, Thorniley, Carbert; Woods, Bishop; Roach, Thursfield, Humphries, Sanderson, McGinty, Duane. Subs: Roberts, Tamati:
T: Blake
G: Woods
Half-time: 0-14
Referee: Ray Tennant (Castleford)
Attendance: 3,200

France marked the opening encounter of their three-match mini-tour with a display of running rugby in traditional Gallic style.

Led by two-try captain Ratier, the French ran in five touchdowns to a solitary effort from Australian Blake as the flamboyant Gauls dazzled the Wire with a series of high speed breaks, criss-crossing the field with improvised passing and exciting running.

Scrum half Dumas was outstanding, along with packmen Storer and Moliner as the revitalised visitors combined enterprise on attack with steel on defence.

Skipper Woods tried hard to inspire an injury-hit Warrington but France were very much on song with wingman Ratier opening and closing their try account in the second and 74th minutes.

19 October
Whitehaven

CUMBRIA	**18**
FRANCE	**13**

1. Limongi
2. Ratier
3. Piredda (Frison)
4. Delaunay
5. Criotier
6. Palisses
7. Bourrel
8. Aillieres
9. Valero
10. Rabot
11. Moliner
12. Grandjean (Montgaillard)
13. Pech

T: Moliner, Palisses
G: Bourrel (2, 1dg)

Cumbria:
Lowden (Workington T.); Solarie (Whitehaven), Pape (Carlisle), Fisher (Whitehaven), Quirk (St. Helens); Rea (Barrow), Murdock (Carlisle); Armstrong (Carlisle), Thomason (Carlisle), D. Kendall (Carlisle), Kirkby (Carlisle), Hetherington (Whitehaven), Huddart (Whitehaven). Sub: Walker (Barrow) for Armstrong. Non-playing sub: G. Smith (Workington T.).
T: Rea, Murdock
G: Lowden (5)
Half-time: 12-12
Referee: Colin Steele (Barrow)
Attendance: 4,000

After the cavalier performance at Warrington, France showed the less attractive side of their character by conceding a string of penalties for high tackles, with Moliner and Delaunay sent to the sin bin.

Workington Town full back Lowden punished the Gallic indiscipline, hitting three successful penalty goals in the last 24 minutes to seal Cumbria's hard-earned victory after scrum half Bourrel had given the visitors a 13-12 lead on the hour with a 35-yard drop goal.

France raced into a nine minute lead with a Moliner try and Bourrel goal before their Cumbrian hosts punished slack defence with tries for half backs Rea and home Man of the Match Murdock, Lowden adding the goals.

France produced a flash of their flair immediately before the interval when Delaunay and Pech combined to send in Palisses for a try, Bourrel again adding the goal for a 12-12 half-time scoreline.

23 October

HALIFAX	**24**
FRANCE	**18**

1. Frison
2. Ratier
3. Vergniol
4. Delaunay
5. Pons
6. Palisses
7. Dumas
8. Buttignol
9. Valero
10. Montgaillard (Rabot)
11. Storer
12. Verdes
13. Moliner

T: Pons, Frison, Verdes, Dumas
G: Dumas

Halifax:
Whitfield; Taylor, Grogan, Anderson, Wilson; Coyne, Holmes; Fairbank, McCallion, Kemp, Dixon, Stains (Bell), Ramshaw
T: Taylor, Coyne, Whitfield, Wilson, Dixon
G: Whitfield (2)
Half-time: 16-4
Referee: John Holdsworth (Kippax)
Attendance: 4,674

Man of the Match Whitfield orchestrated Halifax's 16-4 half-time lead, the Thrum Hall tries coming from Taylor, Coyne and the full back himself, also adding two goals.

The French replied on either side of the break with unconverted tries from Pons and Frison, the latter in free-flowing style. Halifax hit back with two further touchdowns, by Wilson and Dixon, but then sat back with the scoreline at 24-8.

The tourists wound up their encounter with a fiery 20 minutes of committed running and eagerness for the loose ball, their reward being tries for back row man Verdes and scrum half Dumas, who added the goal to round off an entertaining encounter.

Widnes full back Alan Tait on his 1989 Test debut against France at Wigan in January.

GREAT BRITAIN

GREAT BRITAIN

1988-89 TEST REVIEW

Great Britain experienced the highs and lows of international Rugby League in a packed round-the-world programme of seven Test matches — three World Cup-rated — and a challenge encounter with the Rest of the World.

The success-hungry Lions roared when:

* Great Britain maintained their unbeaten record against Papua New Guinea in the opening fixture of the 18th tour Down Under.

* Malcolm Reilly's injury-savaged line-up beat Australia 26-12 in the third Test in Sydney to end a run of 15 consecutive defeats by the Kangaroos.

* The British beat the Rest of the World 30-28 to celebrate the opening of the Whitbread Trophy Hall of Fame.

* The record books were rewritten as Britain achieved the double over France, the return encounter in Avignon being the 50th Anglo-French Test.

Down went morale when:

* Great Britain lost the Ashes for the seventh successive series.

* The Lions failed to secure at least a draw against New Zealand which would have set up a World Cup final date with Australia.

A chronicle of the 10-week trip Down Under is featured in the chapter 1988 LIONS TOUR.

The Whitbread Trophy Challenge between Great Britain and the select Rest of the World side at Headingley, Leeds, rounded off a week of celebrations surrounding the opening of the Hall of Fame at the Bentley Arms, Oulton, near Leeds. This was not a Test match and is not included in players' Great Britain appearances record. Seven world stars were flown in to complement a host of overseas imports in the World XIII, Australian World Cup-winning coach Don Furner being brought over to be at the helm. Unfortunately, Wally Lewis withdrew after Australia's captain broke an arm in the World Cup final.

He was replaced as the World captain by Mark Graham of New Zealand.

A crowd of nearly 12,500 saw Britain pull away to lead 30-18 with 17 minutes left, only for the visitors to score two tries in the last 10 minutes and leave the British hanging on by 30-28. British prop Kevin Ward produced a Herculean performance to earn the Man of the Match award, ahead of fellow front row man Hugh Waddell, giving the game a competitive edge without kindling the fire of a Test match. The World XIII strength was contained in their back row of Graham and Australians Noel Cleal and Gavin Miller.

Britain stayed loyal to those players on tour duty, the only non-tourist being Castleford winger David Plange. With the Rest of the World's star import, scrum half Allan Langer, failing to shine, their individual award went to Miller.

The 1989 Anglo-French home-and-away series was marked by a host of good football, top-class discipline in once torrid Test encounters, a bout of record-breaking and a world-class refereeing performance.

Great Britain achieved a record-equalling sixth successive Test victory over France in the opening match at Wigan, the French playing a major part in an entertaining game despite relentless rain.

France opened the tryscoring after 14 minutes from one of a series of fast attacks, loose forward Jacques Moliner rounding off a sweeping move. Five minutes later Britain replied in fortunate fashion as centre Paul Loughlin's bid for a second penalty goal struck the post for stand off Shaun Edwards to follow up and touch down, Loughlin this time adding the goal. Shortly before the break, scrum half Andy Gregory sent in skipper Ellery Hanley for a try which gave Britain a 12-4 half-time lead.

The French preparation of hosting a visit from Sydney club Penrith and staging a mini-tour to Britain showed dividends in a vastly improved display but Britain's pack laid the foundations for a satisfying second period considering the conditions. By the hour, Britain had extended their lead to 26-4 with tries from wingmen Phil Ford and Martin Offiah, plus one from centre Joe Lydon, celebrating his return to the international scene with an outstanding all-round display. Loughlin added a third goal, while France were rewarded for a never-say-die spirit when scrum half Gilles Dumas scooted through for a 79th minute touchdown, full back David Fraisse adding the goal.

The Whitbread Trophy Man of the Match award went to debutant full back Alan Tait, the ex-Scotland RU star being a midweek replacement for the injured Steve Hampson, while another former Rugby Union international, England's Peter Williams, made his first appearance as a 66th minute substitute.

A fortnight later, the 50th Test between the two countries was staged in Avignon, Great Britain celebrating in style with a 30-8 victory, their highest score and widest winning margin in France. The assured success extended the winning sequence against the Tricolours to a record seven matches.

While France did not maintain the improvement displayed at Wigan two weeks earlier, Britain controlled the game superbly, coach Reilly encouraging individual flair within a tight gameplan.

Hanley marked a record seventh captaincy against the French by opening the try account after only three minutes, stretching his consecutive tryscoring sequence against France to six matches. Two minutes later winger Ford rounded off a marvellous 45-yard move for Lydon to add the goal and open up a 10-0 lead.

Scrum half Andy Gregory shook off the effects of a cold to have a hand in both the opening tries before featuring in the first French try, his pass being intercepted by opposite number Dumas. Gregory was again the trymaker in the 23rd minute when his defence splitting pass sent Salford centre Williams

racing in for his first Test touchdown. Ford took advantage of slack French passing to kick ahead for his second try five minutes before the interval, Lydon's goal providing a 20-4 half-time scoreline.

Britain made another flying start after the break, the commanding figures of Hanley and Lee Crooks, returning to the Test scene after a two-year absence through lack of full fitness, sending Edwards through for a 44th minute try, Lydon adding the goal.

France rallied with skipper Hugues Ratier clinching a superb individual try after 55 minutes, swerving in and out of three defenders on a twisting 45-yard run. With five minutes left Britain rewrote the records when Tait, moved to the wing to make room at full back for substitute Hampson, raced 40 yards in a touchline dash for a sixth and final touchdown.

After a double success hallmarked by a top-class display of refereeing from Sydney whistler Greg McCallum, coach Reilly summed up Britain's progress: 'Many of the players have now established themselves as world-class performers in a squad which, benefiting from the tour Down Under, work together like a club side.'

Widnes packman, Richard Eyres, a Test debut as substitute at Wigan.

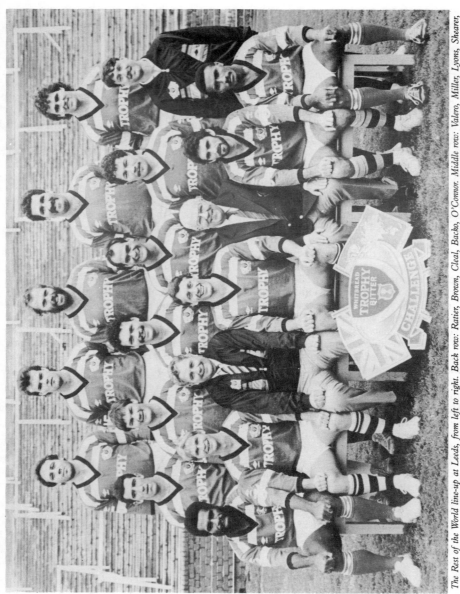

The Rest of the World line-up at Leeds, from left to right. Back row: Ratier, Brown, Cleal, Backo, O'Connor. Middle row: Valero, Miller, Lyons, Shearer, Sorensen, Tim Deykin (Physio). Front row: Numapo, Langer, Don Furner (Coach), Graham (Captain), Harry Jepson (Manager), Ella, Krewanty.

WHITBREAD TROPHY CHALLENGE

29 October   **Leeds**

GREAT BRITAIN 30

Paul Loughlin (St. Helens)	1.
David Plange (Castleford)	2.
Garry Schofield (Leeds)	3.
David Stephenson (Leeds)	4.
Martin Offiah (Widnes)	5.
Shaun Edwards (Wigan)	6.
Andy Gregory (Wigan)	7.
Kevin Ward (Castleford)	8.
Kevin Beardmore (Castleford)	9.
Hugh Waddell (Leeds)	10.
Mike Gregory (Warrington)	11.
Andy Platt (Wigan)	12.
Ellery Hanley (Wigan) Capt.	13.
David Hulme (Widnes)	14.
Roy Powell (Leeds)	15.

T: Edwards, Stephenson, Offiah, Hanley, Schofield
G: Stephenson (5)
Substitutions:
Powell for Platt (53 min.)
Hulme for Edwards (67 min.)
Referee: John Holdsworth (Kippax)
Attendance: 12,409

REST OF THE WORLD 28

Dale Shearer (Australia)
Arnold Krewanty (PNG)
Bal Numapo (PNG)
Michael O'Connor (Australia)
Hugues Ratier (France)
Steve Ella (Australia)
Allan Langer (Australia)
Kurt Sorensen (New Zealand)
Thierry Valero (France)
Sam Backo (Australia)
Mark Graham (New Z'd) Capt.
Noel Cleal (Australia)
Gavin Miller (Australia)
Cliff Lyons (Australia)
Peter Brown (New Zealand)

T: Graham, Cleal, Brown, Ratier, O'Connor
G: O'Connor (4)
Substitutions:
Brown for Backo (33 min.)
Lyons for Cleal (50 min.)
Half-time: 12-12

Scorechart

Minute	Score	GB	R of W
16:	Graham (T)		
	O'Connor (G)	0	6
19:	Edwards (T)		
	Stephenson G)	6	6
23:	Cleal (T)		
	O'Connor (G)	6	12
27:	Stephenson (P)	8	12
34:	Stephenson (T)	12	12
44:	Offiah (T)		
	Stephenson (G)	18	12

Minute	Score	GB	R of W
52:	Brown (T)		
	O'Connor (G)	18	18
55:	Hanley (T)		
	Stephenson (G)	24	18
63:	Schofield (T)		
	Stephenson (G)	30	18
70:	Ratier (T)	30	22
79:	O'Connor (T)		
	O'Connor (G)	30	28

	GB	R of W
Scrums	12	6
Penalties	6	7

FIRST WHITBREAD TROPHY TEST

21 January   **Wigan**

GREAT BRITAIN 26   **FRANCE 10**

Alan Tait (Widnes)	1.	David Fraisse (Le Pontet)
Phil Ford (Leeds)	2.	Hugues Ratier (St. Esteve) Capt.
Paul Loughlin (St. Helens)	3.	Eric Vergniol (Villeneuve)
Joe Lydon (Wigan)	4.	Guy Delaunay (St. Esteve)
Martin Offiah (Widnes)	5.	Marcel Criotier (Le Pontet)
Shaun Edwards (Wigan)	6.	Roger Palisses (St. Esteve)
Andy Gregory (Wigan)	7.	Gilles Dumas (St. Gaudens)
Kevin Ward (Castleford)	8.	Jean-Luc Rabot (Villeneuve)
Kevin Beardmore (Castleford)	9.	Thierry Valero (Pamiers)
Hugh Waddell (Leeds)	10.	Pierre Ailleres (Toulouse)
Mike Gregory (Warrington)	11.	Thierry Buttignol (Avignon)
Roy Powell (Leeds)	12.	Daniel Verdes (Villeneuve)
Ellery Hanley (Wigan) Capt.	13.	Jacques Moliner (Pamiers)
Peter Williams (Salford)	14.	Marc Tisseyre (Pamiers)
Richard Eyres (Widnes)	15.	Patrick Rocci (Le Pontet)

T: Edwards, Hanley, Ford, Lydon, Offiah

G: Loughlin (3)

Substitutions:

Eyres for Powell (62 min.)

Williams for Offiah (66 min.)

Referee: Greg McCallum (Sydney)

Attendance: 8,266

T: Moliner, Dumas

G: Fraisse

Substitutions:

Tisseyre for Rabot (62 min.)

Rocci for Palisses (69 min.)

Half-time: 12-4

Scorechart

Minute	Score	GB	France
10:	Loughlin (PG)	2	0
15:	Moliner (T)	2	4
20:	Edwards (T)		
	Loughlin (G)	8	4
34:	Hanley (T)	12	4
45:	Ford (T)	16	4
57:	Offiah (T)		
	Loughlin (G)	22	4
61:	Lydon (T)	26	4
79:	Dumas (T)		
	Fraisse (G)	26	10

	Scrums	10	13
	Penalties	5	4

Wigan's Joe Lydon, recalled for Test duty after a 15-month absence.

SECOND WHITBREAD TROPHY TEST

5 February   **Avignon**

GREAT BRITAIN 30		FRANCE 8
Alan Tait (Widnes)	1.	Jean Frison (Toulouse)
Phil Ford (Leeds)	2.	Hugues Ratier (St. Esteve) Capt.
Peter Williams (Salford)	3.	Eric Vergniol (Villeneuve)
Joe Lydon (Wigan)	4.	Guy Delaunay (St. Esteve)
Martin Offiah (Widnes)	5.	David Fraisse (Le Pontet)
Shaun Edwards (Wigan)	6.	Roger Palisses (St. Esteve)
Andy Gregory (Wigan)	7.	Gilles Dumas (St. Gaudens)
Kevin Ward (Castleford)	8.	Jean-Luc Rabot (Villeneuve)
Kevin Beardmore (Castleford)	9.	Thierry Valero (Pamiers)
Lee Crooks (Leeds)	10.	Pierre Ailleres (Toulouse)
Mike Gregory (Warrington)	11.	Thierry Buttignol (Avignon)
Roy Powell (Leeds)	12.	Daniel Verdes (Villeneuve)
Ellery Hanley (Wigan) Capt.	13.	Jacques Moliner (Pamiers)
Steve Hampson (Wigan)	14.	Marc Tisseyre (Pamiers)
Keith England (Castleford)	15.	Patrick Rocci (Le Pontet)

T: Ford (2), Hanley, Williams,
Edwards, Tait
G: Lydon (3)
Substitutions:
England for Powell (62 min.)
Hampson for Ford (69 min.)
Referee: Greg McCallum (Sydney)

T: Dumas, Ratier
Substitutions:
Rocci for Dumas (46 min.)
Tisseyre for Rabot (61 min.)
Half-time: 20-4
Attendance: 6,500

Scorechart

Minute	Score	GB	France
3:	Hanley (T)	4	0
5:	Ford (T)		
	Lydon (G)	10	0
10:	Dumas (T)	10	4
23:	Williams (T)	14	4
35:	Ford (T)		
	Lydon (G)	20	4
44:	Edwards (T)		
	Lydon (G)	26	4
55:	Ratier (T)	26	8
75:	Tait (T)	30	8

	Scrums	16	8
	Penalties	5	10

Roy Powell, who took his total of caps to nine in Avignon.

TESTS

● Although early Tests were played under the titles of Northern Union or England, it is acceptable to regard them as Great Britain.
W-Win, D-Drawn, L-Lost refer to Great Britain.

GREAT BRITAIN v. AUSTRALIA

Date	Result	Score	Venue	Attendance
12 Dec. 1908	D	22-22	QPR, London	2,000
23 Jan. 1909	W	15-5	Newcastle	22,000
15 Feb. 1909	W	6-5	Birmingham	9,000
18 Jun. 1910	W	27-20	Sydney	42,000
2 Jul. 1910	W	22-17	Brisbane	18,000
8 Nov. 1911	L	10-19	Newcastle	6,500
16 Dec. 1911	D	11-11	Edinburgh	6,000
1 Jan. 1912	L	8-33	Birmingham	4,000
27 Jun. 1914	W	23-5	Sydney	40,000
29 Jun. 1914	L	7-12	Sydney	55,000
4 Jul. 1914	W	14-6	Sydney	34,420
26 Jun. 1920	L	4-8	Brisbane	28,000
3 Jul. 1920	L	8-21	Sydney	40,000
10 Jul. 1920	W	23-13	Sydney	32,000
1 Oct. 1921	W	6-5	Leeds	32,000
5 Nov. 1921	L	2-16	Hull	21,504
14 Jan. 1922	W	6-0	Salford	21,000
23 Jun. 1924	W	22-3	Sydney	50,000
28 Jun. 1924	W	5-3	Sydney	33,842
12 Jul. 1924	L	11-21	Brisbane	36,000
23 Jun. 1928	W	15-12	Brisbane	39,200
14 Jul. 1928	W	8-0	Sydney	44,548
21 Jul. 1928	L	14-21	Sydney	37,000
5 Oct. 1929	L	8-31	Hull K.R.	20,000
9 Nov. 1929	W	9-3	Leeds	31,402
4 Jan. 1930	D	0-0	Swinton	34,709
15 Jan. 1930	W	3-0	Rochdale	16,743
6 Jun. 1932	W	8-6	Sydney	70,204
18 Jun. 1932	L	6-15	Brisbane	26,500
16 Jul. 1932	W	18-13	Sydney	50,053
7 Oct. 1933	W	4-0	Belle Vue, Manchester	34,000
11 Nov. 1933	W	7-5	Leeds	29,618
16 Dec. 1933	W	19-16	Swinton	10,990
29 Jun. 1936	L	8-24	Sydney	63,920
4 Jul. 1936	W	12-7	Brisbane	29,486
18 Jul. 1936	W	12-7	Sydney	53,546
16 Oct. 1937	W	5-4	Leeds	31,949
13 Nov. 1937	W	13-3	Swinton	31,724
18 Dec. 1937	L	3-13	Huddersfield	9,093
17 Jun. 1946	D	8-8	Sydney	64,527
6 Jul. 1946	W	14-5	Brisbane	40,500
20 Jul. 1946	W	20-7	Sydney	35,294
9 Oct. 1948	W	23-21	Leeds	36,529
6 Nov. 1948	W	16-7	Swinton	36,354
29 Jan. 1949	W	23-9	Bradford	42,000
12 Jun. 1950	W	6-4	Sydney	47,215
1 Jul. 1950	L	3-15	Brisbane	35,000
22 Jul. 1950	L	2-5	Sydney	47,178
4 Oct. 1952	W	19-6	Leeds	34,505
8 Nov. 1952	W	21-5	Swinton	32,421
13 Dec. 1952	L	7-27	Bradford	30,509
12 Jun. 1954	L	12-37	Sydney	65,884
3 Jul. 1954	W	38-21	Brisbane	46,355
17 Jul. 1954	L	16-20	Sydney	67,577
17 Nov. 1956	W	21-10	Wigan	22,473
1 Dec. 1956	L	9-22	Bradford	23,634
15 Dec. 1956	W	19-0	Swinton	17,542
14 Jun. 1958	L	8-25	Sydney	68,777
5 Jul. 1958	W	25-18	Brisbane	32,965
19 Jul. 1958	W	40-17	Sydney	68,720
17 Oct. 1959	L	14-22	Swinton	35,224
21 Nov. 1959	W	11-10	Leeds	30,184
12 Dec. 1959	W	18-12	Wigan	26,089
9 Jun. 1962	W	31-12	Sydney	70,174
30 Jun. 1962	W	17-10	Brisbane	34,766
14 Jul. 1962	L	17-18	Sydney	42,104
16 Oct. 1963	L	2-28	Wembley	13,946
9 Nov. 1963	L	12-50	Swinton	30,833
30 Nov. 1963	W	16-5	Leeds	20,497
25 Jun. 1966	W	17-13	Sydney	57,962
16 Jul. 1966	L	4-6	Brisbane	45,057
23 Jul. 1966	L	14-19	Sydney	63,503
21 Oct. 1967	W	16-11	Leeds	22,293
3 Nov. 1967	L	11-17	White City, London	17,445
9 Dec. 1967	L	3-11	Swinton	13,615
6 Jun. 1970	L	15-37	Brisbane	42,807
20 Jun. 1970	W	28-7	Sydney	60,962
4 Jul. 1970	W	21-17	Sydney	61,258
3 Nov. 1973	W	21-12	Wembley	9,874
24 Nov. 1973	L	6-14	Leeds	16,674
1 Dec. 1973	L	5-15	Warrington	10,019
15 Jun. 1974	L	6-12	Brisbane	30,280
6 Jul. 1974	W	16-11	Sydney	48,006
20 Jul. 1974	L	18-22	Sydney	55,505
21 Oct. 1978	L	9-15	Wigan	17,644
5 Nov. 1978	W	18-14	Bradford	26,447
18 Nov. 1978	L	6-23	Leeds	29,627
16 Jun. 1979	L	0-35	Brisbane	23,051
30 Jun. 1979	L	16-24	Sydney	26,837
14 Jul. 1979	L	2-28	Sydney	16,844
30 Oct. 1982	L	4-40	Hull C. AFC	26,771
20 Nov. 1982	L	6-27	Wigan	23,216
28 Nov. 1982	L	8-32	Leeds	17,318
9 Jun. 1984	L	8-25	Sydney	30,190
26 Jun. 1984	L	6-18	Brisbane	26,534
7 Jul. 1984	L	7-20	Sydney	18,756

25 Oct. 1986	L	16-38	Man U. AFC	50,583
8 Nov. 1986	L	4-34	Elland Rd,	
			Leeds	30,808
*22 Nov. 1986	L	15-24	Wigan	20,169

11 Jun. 1988	L	6-17	Sydney	24,202
28 Jun. 1988	L	14-34	Brisbane	27,103
*9 Jul. 1988	W	26-12	Sydney	15,994

* Also World Cup match.

	Played	Won	Drawn	Lost	Tries	Goals	Dr	Pts for
Great Britain	102	50	4	48	250	256	5	1284
Australia	102	48	4	50	293	321	6	1565

GREAT BRITAIN-AUSTRALIA TEST MATCH RECORDS

Britain

Highest score: 40-17 Third Test at Sydney 19 July 1958 (Also widest margin win)

Most tries in a match: 4 by J. Leytham (Wigan) Second Test at Brisbane 2 July 1910

Most goals in a match: 10 by B. L. Jones (Leeds) Second Test at Brisbane 3 July 1954

Most points in a match: 20 by B. L. Jones (as above)

20 (7g,2t) by R. Millward (Hull KR) Second Test at Sydney 20 June 1970.

Biggest attendance: 50,583 First Test at Old Trafford, Manchester, 25 Oct 1986

Australia

Highest score: 50-12 Second Test at Swinton, 9 Nov 1963 (Also widest margin win)

Most tries in a match: 3 by J. Devereux, First Test at QPR, London, 12 Dec 1908

3 by R. Gasnier, First Test at Swinton, 17 Oct 1959

3 by R. Gasnier, First Test at Wembley, 16 Oct 1963

3 by K. Irvine, Second Test at Swinton, 9 Nov 1963

3 by K. Irvine, Third Test at Sydney, 23 July 1966

3 by G. Miles, First Test at Old Trafford, Manchester, 25 Oct 1986

3 by M. O'Connor, First Test at Old Trafford, Manchester, 25 Oct 1986

Most goals in a match: 10 by M. Cronin, First Test at Brisbane, 16 June 1979

Most points in a match: 22 (5g,3t) by M. O'Connor First Test at Old Trafford, Manchester, 25 Oct 1986

Biggest attendance: 70,204 First Test at Sydney, 6 June 1932

● In a World Cup match at Perpignan, France, on 29 October 1972, R. Fulton scored 3 tries.

Great Britain winger Phil Ford dives in for a try in the Test against France at Wigan in January 1989.

307

GREAT BRITAIN v. NEW ZEALAND

Date	Result	Venue	Attendance
25 Jan. 1908	W 14-6	Leeds	8,182
8 Feb. 1908	L 6-18	Chelsea	14,000
15 Feb. 1908	L 5-8	Cheltenham	4,000
30 Jul. 1910	W 52-20	Auckland	16,000
1 Aug. 1914	W 16-13	Auckland	15,000
31 Jul. 1920	W 31-7	Auckland	34,000
7 Aug. 1920	W 19-3	Christchurch	10,000
14 Aug. 1920	W 11-10	Wellington	4,000
2 Aug. 1924	L 8-16	Auckland	22,000
6 Aug. 1924	L 11-13	Wellington	6,000
9 Aug. 1924	W 31-18	Dunedin	14,000
2 Oct. 1926	W 28-20	Wigan	14,500
13 Nov. 1926	W 21-11	Hull	7,000
15 Jan. 1927	W 32-17	Leeds	6,000
4 Aug. 1928	L 13-17	Auckland	28,000
18 Aug. 1928	W 13-5	Dunedin	12,000
25 Aug. 1928	W 6-5	Christchurch	21,000
30 Jul. 1932	W 24-9	Auckland	25,000
13 Aug. 1932	W 25-14	Christchurch	5,000
20 Aug. 1932	W 20-18	Auckland	6,500
8 Aug. 1936	W 10-8	Auckland	25,000
15 Aug. 1936	W 23-11	Auckland	17,000
10 Aug. 1946	L 8-13	Auckland	10,000
4 Oct. 1947	W 11-10	Leeds	28,445
8 Nov. 1947	L 7-10	Swinton	29,031
20 Dec. 1947	W 25-9	Bradford	42,680
29 Jul. 1950	L 10-16	Christchurch	10,000
12 Aug. 1950	L 13-20	Auckland	20,000
6 Oct. 1951	W 21-15	Bradford	37,475
10 Nov. 1951	W 20-19	Swinton	29,938
15 Dec. 1951	W 16-12	Leeds	18,649
24 Jul. 1954	W 27-7	Auckland	22,097
31 Jul. 1954	L 14-20	Greymouth	4,240
14 Aug. 1954	W 12-6	Auckland	6,186
8 Oct. 1955	W 25-6	Swinton	21,937
12 Nov. 1955	W 27-12	Bradford	24,443
17 Dec. 1955	L 13-28	Leeds	10,438
26 Jul. 1958	L 10-15	Auckland	25,000
9 Aug. 1958	W 32-15	Auckland	25,000
30 Sept. 1961	L 11-29	Leeds	16,540
21 Oct. 1961	W 23-10	Bradford	19,980
4 Nov. 1961	W 35-19	Swinton	22,536
28 Jul. 1962	L 0-19	Auckland	14,976
11 Aug. 1962	L 8-27	Auckland	16,411
25 Sept. 1965	W 7-2	Swinton	8,541
23 Oct. 1965	W 15-9	Bradford	15,740
6 Nov. 1965	D 9-9	Wigan	7,919
6 Aug. 1966	W 25-8	Auckland	14,494
20 Aug. 1966	W 22-14	Auckland	10,657
11 Jul. 1970	W 19-15	Auckland	15,948
19 Jul. 1970	W 23-9	Christchurch	8,600
25 Jul. 1970	W 33-16	Auckland	13,137
25 Sept. 1971	L 13-18	Salford	3,764
16 Oct. 1971	L 14-17	Castleford	4,108
6 Nov. 1971	W 12-3	Leeds	5,479
27 Jul. 1974	L 8-13	Auckland	10,466
4 Aug. 1974	W 17-8	Christchurch	6,316
10 Aug. 1974	W 20-0	Auckland	11,574
21 Jul. 1979	W 16-8	Auckland	9,000
5 Aug. 1979	W 22-7	Christchurch	8,500
11 Aug. 1979	L 11-18	Auckland	7,000
18 Oct. 1980	D 14-14	Wigan	7,031
2 Nov. 1980	L 8-12	Bradford	10,946
15 Nov. 1980	W 10-2	Leeds	8,210
14 Jul. 1984	L 0-12	Auckland	10,238
22 Jul. 1984	L 12-28	Christchurch	3,824
28 Jul. 1984	L 16-32	Auckland	7,967
19 Oct. 1985	L 22-24	Leeds	12,591
2 Nov. 1985	W 25-8	Wigan	15,506
*9 Nov. 1985	D 6-6	Elland Rd, Leeds	22,209
*17 Jul. 1988	L 10-12	Christchurch	8,525

* Also World Cup match

	Played	Won	Lost	Drawn	Tries	Goals	Dr	Pts for
Great Britain	71	43	25	3	256	206	3	1196
New Zealand	71	25	43	3	165	206	0	928

GREAT BRITAIN-NEW ZEALAND TEST MATCH RECORDS

Britain

Highest score:	52-20 First Test at Auckland, 30 July 1910 (Also widest margin win)
Most tries in a match:	4 by W. Boston (Wigan) First Test at Auckland, 24 July 1954
	4 by G. Schofield (Hull) Second Test at Wigan, 2 Nov 1985
Most goals in a match:	7 by N. Fox (Wakefield T.) Third Test at Swinton, 4 Nov 1961
	7 by E. Fraser (Warrington) Second Test at Auckland, 9 Aug 1958

Most points in a match: 16 (4t) by G. Schofield (Hull) Second Test at Wigan, 2 Nov 1985
Biggest attendance: 42,680 Third Test at Bradford, 20 Dec 1947
● In a World Cup match at Pau, France, on 4 November 1972, Britain won 53-19 with J. Holmes (Leeds) scoring 26 points from 10 goals and two tries.
In a World Cup match at Sydney on 8 June 1968, Bev Risman scored 7 goals.

New Zealand
Highest score: 32-16 Third Test at Auckland, 28 July 1984
Widest margin win: 19-0 First Test at Auckland, 28 July 1962
                      27-8 Second Test at Auckland, 11 Aug 1962
No player has scored three tries or more in a Test.
Most goals and points: 7g-14pts by D. White, Second Test at Greymouth, 31 July 1954
                       J. Fagan, First Test at Headingley, 30 Sep 1961
                       E. Wiggs, Second Test at Auckland, 20 Aug 1966
Biggest attendance: 34,000 First Test at Auckland, 31 July 1920
● In a World Cup match at Sydney, Australia, on 25 June 1957, W. Sorensen also scored 7 goals, 14 points.

GREAT BRITAIN v. FRANCE
● **Results since France were given Test match status.**

Date	Result	Venue	Attendance
26 Jan. 1957	W 45-12	Leeds	20,221
3 Mar. 1957	D 19-19	Toulouse	16,000
10 Apr. 1957	W 29-14	St. Helens	23,250
3 Nov. 1957	W 25-14	Toulouse	15,000
23 Nov. 1957	W 44-15	Wigan	19,152
2 Mar. 1958	W 23-9	Grenoble	20,000
14 Mar. 1959	W 50-15	Leeds	22,000
5 Apr. 1959	L 15-24	Grenoble	8,500
6 Mar. 1960	L 18-20	Toulouse	15,308
26 Mar. 1960	D 17-17	St. Helens	14,000
11 Dec. 1960	W 21-10	Bordeaux	8,000
28 Jan. 1961	W 27-8	St Helens	18,000
17 Feb. 1962	L 15-20	Wigan	17,277
11 Mar. 1962	L 13-23	Perpignan	14,000
2 Dec. 1962	L 12-17	Perpignan	5,000
3 Apr. 1963	W 42-4	Wigan	19,487
8 Mar. 1964	W 11-5	Perpignan	4,326
18 Mar. 1964	W 39-0	Leigh	4,750
6 Dec. 1964	L 8-18	Perpignan	15,000
23 Jan. 1965	W 17-7	Swinton	9,959
16 Jan. 1966	L 13-18	Perpignan	6,000
5 Mar. 1966	L 4-8	Wigan	14,004
22 Jan. 1967	W 16-13	Carcassonne	10,650
4 Mar. 1967	L 13-23	Wigan	7,448
11 Feb. 1968	W 22-13	Paris	8,000
2 Mar. 1968	W 19-8	Bradford	14,196
30 Nov. 1968	W 34-10	St. Helens	6,080
2 Feb. 1969	L 9-13	Toulouse	10,000
7 Feb. 1971	L 8-16	Toulouse	14,960
17 Mar. 1971	W 24-2	St. Helens	7,783
6 Feb. 1972	W 10-9	Toulouse	11,508
12 Mar. 1972	W 45-10	Bradford	7,313
20 Jan. 1974	W 24-5	Grenoble	5,500
17 Feb. 1974	W 29-0	Wigan	10,105
6 Dec. 1981	W 37-0	Hull	13,173
20 Dec. 1981	L 2-19	Marseilles	6,500
20 Feb. 1983	W 20-5	Carcassonne	3,826
6 Mar. 1983	W 17-5	Hull	6,055
29 Jan. 1984	W 12-0	Avignon	4,000
17 Feb. 1984	W 10-0	Leeds	7,646
1 Mar. 1985	W 50-4	Leeds	6,491
17 Mar. 1985	L 16-24	Perpignan	5,000
*16 Feb. 1986	D 10-10	Avignon	4,000
1 Mar. 1986	W 24-10	Wigan	8,112
*24 Jan. 1987	W 52-4	Leeds	6,567
8 Feb. 1987	W 20-10	Carcassonne	2,000
24 Jan. 1988	W 28-14	Avignon	6,500
6 Feb. 1988	W 30-12	Leeds	7,007
21 Jan. 1989	W 26-10	Wigan	8,266
5 Feb. 1989	W 30-8	Avignon	6,500

★ Also World Cup match.

	Played	Won	Drawn	Lost	Tries	Goals	Dr	Pts for
Great Britain	50	34	3	13	223	212	0	1144
France	50	13	3	34	94	126	3	554

GREAT BRITAIN-FRANCE TEST MATCH RECORDS

Britain

Highest score:	52-4 at Leeds, 24 January 1987
	(Also widest margin win)
Most tries in a match:	4 by A. Murphy (St. Helens) at Leeds, 14 March 1959
Most goals in a match:	10 by B. Ganley (Oldham) at Wigan, 23 November 1957
Most points in a match:	21 (9g, 1t) by B.L. Jones (Leeds) at Leeds, 26 January 1957
	21 (9g,1t) by N. Fox (Wakefield T.) at Wigan, 3 April 1963
	21 (9g,1t) by N. Fox (Wakefield T.) at Leigh, 18 March 1964
Biggest attendance:	23,250 at St. Helens, 10 April 1957

France

Highest score:	24-15 at Grenoble, 5 April 1959
	24-16 at Perpignan, 17 March 1985
Widest margin win:	19-2 at Marseilles, 20 December 1981
Most tries in a match:	3 by D. Couston at Perpignan, 17 March 1985
Most goals in a match:	7 by P. Lacaze at Wigan, 4 March 1967
Most points in a match:	14 by P. Lacaze (as above).
	14 (4g,2t) by G. Benausse at Wigan, 17 February 1962
Biggest attendance:	20,000 at Grenoble, 2 March 1958

●In a World Cup match at Toulouse on 7 November 1954, there were 37,471

Additional Great Britain v. France

Pre-Test status

22 May 1952	L	12-22	Paris	16,466
24 May 1953	L	17-28	Lyons	
27 Apr. 1954	W	17-8	Bradford	14,153
11 Dec. 1955	L	5-17	Paris	18,000
11 Apr. 1956	W	18-10	Bradford	10,453

Other match

31 July 1982	L	7-8	Venice	1,500

GREAT BRITAIN v PAPUA NEW GUINEA

5 Aug. 1984	W	38-20	Mt. Hagen	7,510
* 24 Oct. 1987	W	42-0	Wigan	9,121
* 22 May 1988	W	42-22	Port Moresby	12,107

* Also World Cup

Mike Gregory, who took his Test cap tally to nine in 1988-89.

GREAT BRITAIN REPRESENTATION
CLUB-BY-CLUB

Wigan beat their own record by fielding eight players in the Great Britain side which met Papua New Guinea at Wigan on 24 October 1987. The octet was backs Steve Hampson, David Stephenson, Joe Lydon, Shaun Edwards and Andy Gregory, plus forwards Brian Case, Andy Goodway and Ellery Hanley. The previous best of seven were backs Martin Ryan, Gordon Ratcliffe, Ernie Ashcroft, Jack Hilton and Tommy Bradshaw; plus forwards Ken Gee and Joe Egan in the 6-4 victory over Australia at Sydney on 12 June, 1950. Wigan also hold the record for the total of players selected with a remarkable 72.

Mick Sullivan gained Test honours with four clubs — Huddersfield (16), Wigan (19), St. Helens (10) and York (1). Billy Boston gained the most Test honours with a single club, making all 31 of his appearances for Britain while with Wigan.

Only six of last season's clubs have not had a player selected for Great Britain in Test or World Cup matches — Chorley Borough, Bramley, Doncaster, Carlisle, Mansfield Marksman and Sheffield Eagles. Of the extinct clubs only Broughton Rangers (later Belle Vue Rangers), Merthyr Tydfil, St. Helens Recs and the old Runcorn had players selected for Britain.

The following is a club-by-club register of Great Britain players. The figure in brackets after a player's name is the number of Great Britain appearances he made while serving the club under whose entry he is listed, and the number after the + sign indicates playing substitute. This is followed by the time span between his first and last British cap while at that club.

BARROW (19 players)
W. Burgess (16) 1924-29
W. Burgess (13) 1962-68
D. Cairns (2) 1984
C. Camilleri (2) 1980
C. Carr (7) 1924-26
F. Castle (4) 1952-54
R. Francis (1) 1947
H. Gifford (2) 1908
D. Goodwin (5) 1957-58
J. Grundy (12) 1955-57
P. Hogan (4 + 1) 1977-78
W. Horne (8) 1946-52
P. Jackson (27) 1954-58
J. Jones (1) 1946
B. Knowelden (1) 1946
E. Szymala (1 + 1) 1981
E. Toohey (3) 1952
L. A. Troup (2) 1936
J. Woods (1) 1933

BATLEY (4 players)
N. Field (1) 1963
F. Gallagher (8) 1924-26
C. Gibson (+ 1) 1985
J. Oliver (4) 1928

BRADFORD NORTHERN (28 players)
D. Barends (2) 1979
E. Batten (4) 1946-47
I. Brooke (5) 1966
L. Casey (5) 1979
W. T. H. Davies (3) 1946-47
K. Fairbank (+ 1) 1987
A. Fisher (8) 1970-78
P. Ford (7) 1987-88
T. Foster (3) 1946-48
J. Grayshon (11) 1979-82
E. Hanley (10 + 1) 1984-85
R. Jasiewicz (1) 1984
J. Kitching (1) 1946
A. Mann (2) 1908
K. Mumby (11) 1982-84
B. Noble (11) 1982-84
T. Price (1) 1970
J. Rae (1) 1965
W. Ramsey (+ 1) 1974
A. Rathbone (4 + 1) 1982-85
A. Redfearn (1) 1979
D. Redfearn (6 + 1) 1972-74
T. Smales (3) 1965
H. Smith (2) 1926
J. Thompson (1) 1978
K. Traill (8) 1950-54
E. Ward (20) 1946-52
F. Whitcombe (2) 1946

BROUGHTON/BELLE VUE RANGERS (8 players)
W. Bentham (2) 1924
L. Clampitt (3) 1907-14
E. Gwyther (6) 1947-51
A. Hogg (1) 1907
S. McCormick (2) 1948
D. Phillips (1) 1950
J. Price (2) 1921
J. Ruddick (3) 1907-10

CASTLEFORD (23 players)
A. Atkinson (11) 1929-36
K. Beardmore (10 + 1) 1984-89
W. Bryant (4 + 1) 1964-67
A. Croston (1) 1937
B. Cunniffe (1) 1937
W. J. Davies (1) 1933
D. Edwards (3 + 2) 1968-71
K. England (1 + 2) 1987-89
A. Hardisty (12) 1964-70
D. Hartley (9) 1968-70
K. Hepworth (11) 1967-70
J. Joyner (14 + 2) 1978-84
B. Lockwood (7) 1972-74
A. Marchant (3) 1986
R. Millward (1) 1966
S. Norton (2 + 1) 1974
D. Plange (1) 1988
M. Reilly (9) 1970
P. Small (1) 1962
G. Stephens (5) 1979

D. Walton (1) 1965
J. Ward (3) 1963-64
K. Ward (14) 1984-89

DEWSBURY (6 players)
A. Bates (2 + 2) 1974
F. Gallagher (4) 1920-21
J. Ledgard (2) 1947
R. Pollard (1) 1950
M. Stephenson (5 + 1) 1971-72
H. Street (4) 1950

FEATHERSTONE ROVERS (13 players)
T. Askin (6) 1928
K. Bridges (3) 1974
T. Clawson (2) 1962
M. Dixon (2) 1962-64
S. Evans (5 + 3) 1979-80
Deryck Fox (9) 1985-86
Don Fox (1) 1963
D. Hobbs (7 + 1) 1984
G. Jordan (2) 1964-67
A. Morgan (4) 1968
S. Nash (16) 1971-74
P. Smith (1 + 5) 1977-84
J. Thompson (19 + 1) 1970-77

FULHAM (1 player)
J. Dalgreen (1) 1982

HALIFAX (29 players)
A. Ackerley (2) 1952-58
A. Bassett (2) 1946
J. Beames (2) 1921
N. Bentham (2) 1929
H. Beverley (2) 1937
O. Burgham (1) 1911
A. Daniels (3) 1952-55
W. T. Davies (1) 1911
C. Dixon (1) 1968
P. Dixon (3 + 3) 1987-88
P. Eccles (1) 1907
T. Fogerty (+ 1) 1966
A. Halmshaw (1) 1971
N. James (1) 1986
R. Lloyd (1) 1920
A. Milnes (2) 1920
S. Prosser (1) 1914
D. Rees (1) 1926
C. Renilson (7 + 1) 1965-68
J. Riley (1) 1910
K. Roberts (10) 1963-66
A. Robinson (3) 1907-08
D. Schofield (1) 1955
J. Shaw (5) 1960-62
J. C. Stacey (1) 1920
J. Thorley (4) 1954
J. Wilkinson (6) 1954-55
F. Williams (2) 1914
D. Willicombe (1) 1974

HUDDERSFIELD (24 players)
J. Bowden (3) 1954
K. Bowman (3) 1962-63
B. Briggs (1) 1954
S. Brogden (9) 1929-33
J. Chilcott (3) 1914
D. Clark (11) 1911-20
D. Close (1) 1967
R. Cracknell (2) 1951
J. Davies (2) 1911
F. Dyson (1) 1959
B. Gronow (7) 1911-20
F. Longstaff (2) 1914
K. Loxton (1) 1971
S. Moorhouse (2) 1914
R. Nicholson (3) 1946-48
J. Rogers (7) 1914-21
K. Senior (2) 1965-67
T. Smales (5) 1962-64
M. Sullivan (16) 1954-57
G. Thomas (8) 1920-21
D. Valentine (15) 1948-54
R. Valentine (1) 1967
H. Wagstaff (12) 1911-21
H. Young (1) 1929

HULL (30 players)
W. Batten (1) 1921
H. Bowman (8) 1924-29
F. Boylen (1) 1908
R. Coverdale (4) 1954
M. Crane (1) 1982
L. Crooks (11 + 2) 1982-87
A. Dannatt (2) 1985
G. Divorty (2) 1985
J. Drake (1) 1960
W. Drake (1) 1962
S. Evans (2) 1982
V. Farrar (1) 1978
R. Gemmell (2) 1968-69
T. E. Gwynne (3) 1928-29
T. Harris (25) 1954-60
M. Harrison (7) 1967-73
W. Holder (1) 1907
A. Keegan (9) 1966-69
E. Morgan (2) 1921
S. Norton (9) 1978-82
W. Proctor (+ 1) 1984
P. Rose (1) 1982
G. Schofield (15) 1984-87
T. Skerrett (6) 1980-82
W. Stone (8) 1920-21
C. Sullivan (17) 1967-73
H. Taylor (3) 1907
R. Taylor (2) 1921-26
D. Topliss (1) 1982
J. Whiteley (15) 1957-62

HULL KINGSTON ROVERS (25 players)
C. Burton (8 + 1) 1982-87
A. Burwell (7 + 1) 1967-69
L. Casey (7 + 2) 1977-83
G. Clark (3) 1984-85
A. Dockar (1) 1947
G. Fairbairn (3) 1981-82
J. Feetham (1) 1929
P. Flanagan (14) 1962-70
F. Foster (1) 1967
D. Hall (2) 1984
P. Harkin (+ 1) 1985
S. Hartley (3) 1980-81
P. Hogan (2 + 2) 1979
R. Holdstock (2) 1980
W. Holliday (8 + 1) 1964-67
D. Laws (1) 1986
B. Lockwood (1 + 1) 1978-79
P. Lowe (12) 1970-78
R. Millward (27 + 1) 1967-78
H. Poole (1) 1964
P. Rose (1 + 3) 1974-78
M. Smith (10 + 1) 1979-84
B. Tyson (3) 1963-67
D. Watkinson (12 + 1) 1979-86
C. Young (5) 1967-68

HUNSLET (23 players)
W. Batten (9) 1907-11
H. Beverley (4) 1936-37
A. Burnell (3) 1951-54
H. Crowther (1) 1929
J. Evans (4) 1951-52
K. Eyre (1) 1965
B. Gabbitas (1) 1959
G. Gunney (11) 1954-65
D. Hartley (2) 1964
J. Higson (2) 1908
D. Jenkins (1) 1929
A. Jenkinson (2) 1911
W. Jukes (6) 1908-10
B. Prior (1) 1966
W. Ramsey (7) 1965-66
B. Shaw (5) 1956-60
G. Shelton (7) 1964-66
F. Smith (9) 1910-14
S. Smith (4) 1954
C. Thompson (2) 1951
L. White (7) 1932-33
R. Williams (3) 1954
H. Wilson (3) 1907

KEIGHLEY (1 player)
T. Hollindrake (1) 1955

LEEDS (66 players)
L. Adams (1) 1932
J. Atkinson (26) 1968-80
J. Bacon (11) 1920-26
R. Batten (3) 1969-73
J. Birch (1) 1907
S. Brogden (7) 1936-37
J. Brough (5) 1928-36
G. Brown (6) 1954-55
M. Clark (5) 1968
T. Clawson (3) 1972
D. Creasser (2 + 2) 1985-88
L. Crooks (1) 1989
W. A. Davies (2) 1914
K. Dick (2) 1980
R. Dickinson (2) 1985
L. Dyl (11) 1974-82
P. Ford (2) 1989
R. Gemmell (1) 1964
J. Grayshon (2) 1985
R. Haigh (3 + 1) 1970-71
D. Hallas (2) 1961
F. Harrison (3) 1911
D. Heron (1 + 1) 1982
J. Holmes (14 + 6) 1971-82
S. Hynes (12 + 1) 1970-73
J. W. Jarman (2) 1914
D. Jeanes (3) 1972

*Leeds utility back David Creasser,
capped four times between 1985
and 1988.*

D. Jenkins (1) 1947
B. L. Jones (15) 1954-57
K. Jubb (2) 1937
J. Lowe (1) 1932
P. Medley (3 + 1) 1987-88
I. Owens (4) 1946
S. Pitchford (4) 1977
H. Poole (2) 1966
R. Powell (7 + 2) 1985-89
D. Prosser (1) 1937
Keith Rayne (4) 1984
Kevin Rayne (1) 1986
B. Risman (5) 1968
D. Robinson (5) 1956-60
D. Rose (4) 1954
G. Schofield (4) 1988
B. Seabourne (1) 1970
B. Shaw (1) 1961
M. Shoebottom (10 + 2) 1968-71
B. Simms (1) 1962
A. Smith (10) 1970-73
S. Smith (10) 1929-33
D. Stephenson (4 + 1) 1988
J. Stevenson (15) 1955-58
S. Stockwell (3) 1920-21
A. Terry (1) 1962
A. Thomas (4) 1926-29
P. Thomas (1) 1907
J. Thompson (12) 1924-32
A. Turnbull (1) 1951
H. Waddell (1) 1989
D. Ward (12) 1977-82
W. Ward (1) 1910
F. Webster (3) 1910
R. Williams (9) 1948-51
H. Woods (1) 1937
G. Wriglesworth (5) 1965-66
F. Young (1) 1908

LEIGH (19 players)
K. Ashcroft (5) 1968-70
J. Cartwright (7) 1920-21
D. Chisnall (2) 1970
J. Darwell (5) 1924
S. Donlan (+ 2) 1984
D. Drummond (22) 1980-86
P. Foster (3) 1955
C. Johnson (1) 1985
F. Kitchen (2) 1954
J. Ledgard (9) 1948-54
G. Lewis (1) 1965
M. Martyn (2) 1958-59
W. Mooney (2) 1924
S. Owen (1) 1958
C. Pawsey (7) 1952-54
W. Robinson (2) 1963
Joe Walsh (1) 1971
W. Winstanley (2) 1910
J. Woods (7 + 3) 1979-83

MERTHYR TYDFIL (1 player)
D. Jones (2) 1907

OLDHAM (40 players)
A. Avery (4) 1910-11
C. Bott (1) 1966
A. Brough (2) 1924
T. Clawson (9) 1973-74
A. Davies (20) 1955-60
E. Davies (3) 1920
T. Flanagan (4) 1983-84
D. Foy (3) 1984-85
B. Ganley (3) 1957-58
A. Goodway (11) 1983-85
W. Hall (4) 1914
H. Hilton (7) 1920-21
D. Hobbs (2) 1987
D. Holland (4) 1914
R. Irving (8 + 3) 1967-72
K. Jackson (2) 1957
E. Knapman (1) 1924
S. Little (10) 1956-58
T. Llewellyn (2) 1907
J. Lomas (2) 1911
W. Longworth (3) 1908
L. McIntyre (1) 1963
T. O'Grady (5) 1954
J. Oster (1) 1929
D. Parker (2) 1964
D. Phillips (3) 1946
F. Pitchford (2) 1958-62
T. Rees (1) 1929
S. Rix (9) 1924-26
R. Sloman (5) 1928
A. Smith (6) 1907-08
I. Southward (7) 1959-62
L. Thomas (1) 1947
D. Turner (11) 1956-58
G. Tyson (4) 1907-08
H. Waddell (4) 1988
T. White (1) 1907
C. Winslade (1) 1959
A. Wood (4) 1911-14
M. Worrall (3) 1984

ROCHDALE HORNETS
(8 players)
J. Baxter (1) 1907
J. Bennett (6) 1924
J. Bowers (1) 1920
T. Fogerty (1) 1974
E. Jones (4) 1920
M. Price (2) 1967
J. Robinson (2) 1914
T. Woods (2) 1911

RUNCORN (2 players)
J. Jolley (3) 1907
R. Padbury (1) 1908

RUNCORN HIGHFIELD/ HUYTON/LIVERPOOL/WIGAN HIGHFIELD (4 players)
R. Ashby (1) 1964
W. Belshaw (6) 1936-37
N. Bentham (6) 1928
H. Woods (5) 1936

ST. HELENS (46 players)
C. Arkwright (+2) 1985
L. Aston (3) 1947
W. Benyon (5+1) 1971-72
T. Bishop (15) 1966-69
F. Carlton (1) 1958
E. Chisnall (4) 1974
E. Cunningham (1) 1978
R. Dagnall (4) 1961-65
D. Eckersley (2+2) 1973-74
A. Ellaby (13) 1928-33
L. Fairclough (6) 1926-29
J. Fieldhouse (1) 1986
A. Fildes (4) 1932
A. Frodsham (3) 1928-29
P. Gorley (2+1) 1980-81
D. Greenall (6) 1951-54
P. Groves (1) 1987
R. Haggerty (2) 1987
M. Hicks (1) 1965
N. Holding (4) 1984
R. Huddart (12) 1959-63
L. Jones (1) 1971
A. Karalius (4+1) 1971-72
V. Karalius (10) 1958-61
K. Kelly (2) 1972
B. Ledger (2) 1985-86
P. Loughlin (7) 1988-89
J. Mantle (13) 1966-73
S. McCormick (1) 1948
T. McKinney (1) 1957
R. Mathias (1) 1979
G. Moses (9) 1955-57
A. Murphy (26) 1958-66
F. Myler (9) 1970
G. Nicholls (22) 1973-79
H. Pinner (5+1) 1980-86
A. Platt (4+3) 1985-88
A. Prescott (28) 1951-58
A. Rhodes (4) 1957-61
J. Stott (1) 1947
M. Sullivan (10) 1961-62
J. Tembey (2) 1963-64
A. Terry (10) 1958-61
John Walsh (4+1) 1972
J. Warlow (3+1) 1964-68
C. Watson (29+1) 1963-71

ST. HELENS RECS (5 players)
F. Bowen (3) 1928
A. Fildes (11) 1926-29
J. Greenall (1) 1921
J. Owen (1) 1921
J. Wallace (1) 1926

SALFORD (28 players)
W. Burgess (1) 1969
P. Charlton (17+1) 1970-74
M. Coulman (2+1) 1971
G. Curran (6) 1946-48
E. Curzon (1) 1910
T. Danby (3) 1950
C. Dixon (11+2) 1969-74
A. Edwards (7) 1936-37
J. Feetham (7) 1932-33
K. Fielding (3) 1974-77
K. Gill (5+2) 1974-77
J. Gore (1) 1926
C. Hesketh (21+2) 1970-74
B. Hudson (8) 1932-37
E. Jenkins (9) 1933-37
J. Lomas (5) 1908-10
T. McKinney (7) 1951-54
A. Middleton (1) 1929
S. Nash (8) 1977-82
M. Richards (2) 1974
A. Risman (17) 1932-46
J. Spencer (1) 1907
J. Ward (1) 1970
S. Warwick (2) 1907
D. Watkins (2+4) 1971-74
W. Watkins (7) 1933-37
P. Williams (1+1) 1989
W. Williams (2) 1929-32

SWINTON (15 players)
T. Armitt (8) 1933-37
A. Buckley (7) 1963-66
F. Butters (2) 1929
W. Davies (1) 1968
B. Evans (10) 1926-33
F. Evans (4) 1924
J. Evans (3) 1926
K. Gowers (14) 1962-66
H. Halsall (1) 1929
M. Hodgson (16) 1929-37
R. Morgan (2) 1963
W. Rees (11) 1926-29
D. Robinson (12) 1965-67
J. Stopford (12) 1961-66
J. Wright (1) 1932

WAKEFIELD TRINITY (22 players)
I. Brooke (8) 1967-68
N. Fox (29) 1959-69
R. Haigh (2) 1968-70
W. Horton (14) 1928-33
D. Jeanes (5) 1971-72
B. Jones (3) 1964-66
H. Kershaw (2) 1910
F. Mortimer (2) 1956
H. Murphy (1) 1950
H. Newbould (1) 1910
J. Parkin (17) 1920-29
C. Pollard (1) 1924
E. Pollard (2) 1932

H. Poynton (3) 1962
D. Robinson (5) 1954-55
G. Round (8) 1959-62
T. Skerrett (4) 1979
S. Smith (1) 1929
D. Topliss (3) 1973-79
D. Turner (13) 1959-62
D. Vines (3) 1959
J. Wilkinson (7) 1959-62

WARRINGTON (43 players)
J. Arkwright (6) 1936-37
K. Ashcroft (+1) 1974
W. Aspinall (1) 1966
W. Belshaw (2) 1937
N. Bentham (2) 1929
J. Bevan (6) 1974-78
T. Blinkhorn (1) 1929
E. Brooks (3) 1908
J. Challinor (3) 1958-60
N. Courtney (+1) 1982
W. Cunliffe (11) 1920-26
G. Dickenson (1) 1908
W. Dingsdale (3) 1929-33
D. Drummond (2) 1987-88
R. Duane (3) 1983-84
R. Eccles (1) 1982
J. Featherstone (6) 1948-52
M. Forster (2) 1987
E. Fraser (16) 1958-61
L. Gilfedder (5) 1962-63
R. Greenough (1) 1960
A. Gregory (1) 1986
M. Gregory (9) 1987-89
G. Helme (12) 1948-54
K. Holden (1) 1963
A. Johnson (6) 1946-47
K. Kelly (2) 1980-82
T. McKinney (1) 1955
J. Miller (6) 1933-36
A. Murphy (1) 1971
A. Naughton (2) 1954
T. O'Grady (1) 1961
H. Palin (2) 1947
K. Parr (1) 1968
A. Pimblett (3) 1948
R. Price (9) 1954-57
R. Ryan (5) 1950-52
R. Ryder (1) 1952
F. Shugars (1) 1910
G. Skelhorne (7) 1920-21
G. Thomas (1) 1907
D. Whitehead (3) 1971
J. Woods (+1) 1987

WHITEHAVEN (5 players)
V. Gribbin (1) 1985
W. Holliday (1) 1964
R. Huddart (4) 1958
P. Kitchin (1) 1965
A. Walker (1) 1980

WIDNES (39 players)

M. Adams (11 + 2) 1979-84
J. Basnett (2) 1984-86
K. Bentley (1) 1980
M. Burke (14 + 1) 1980-86
F. Collier (1) 1964
R. Dutton (6) 1970
K. Elwell (3) 1977-80
R. Eyres (+ 1) 1989
J. Fieldhouse (6) 1985-86
R. French (4) 1968
L. Gorley (4 + 1) 1980-82
A. Gregory (8 + 1) 1981-84
I. Hare (1) 1967
F. Higgins (6) 1950-51
H. Higgins (2) 1937
E. Hughes (8) 1978-82
D. Hulme (4 + 1) 1988
P. Hulme (1 + 2) 1988
A. Johnson (4) 1914-20
V. Karalius (2) 1963
G. Kemel (2) 1965
D. Laughton (4) 1973-79
J. Lydon (9 + 1) 1983-85
T. McCue (6) 1936-46
J. Measures (2) 1963
J. Mills (6) 1974-79
A. Myler (14) 1983-86
F. Myler (14 + 1) 1960-67
G. Nicholls (7) 1971-72
M. Offiah (7) 1988-89
D. O'Neill (2 + 1) 1971-72
M. O'Neill (3) 1982-83
H. Pinner (1) 1986
G. Shaw (1) 1980
N. Silcock (12) 1932-37
A. Tait (2) 1989
J. Warlow (3) 1971
D. Wright (+ 1) 1988
S. Wright (7) 1977-78

*Widnes packman Glyn Shaw,
capped once against New Zealand
in 1980.*

WIGAN (72 players)

R. Ashby (1) 1965
E. Ashcroft (11) 1947-54
E. Ashton (26) 1957-63
W. Ashurst (3) 1971-72
F. Barton (1) 1951
J. Barton (2) 1960-61
J. Bennett (1) 1926
D. Bevan (1) 1952
W. Blan (3) 1951
D. Bolton (23) 1957-63
W. Boston (31) 1954-63
T. Bradshaw (6) 1947-50
F. Carlton (1) 1962
B. Case (6 + 1) 1984-88
N. Cherrington (1) 1960
C. Clarke (7) 1965-73
A. Coldrick (4) 1914
F. Collier (1) 1963
J. Cunliffe (4) 1950-54
S. Edwards (10 + 2) 1985-89
J. Egan (14) 1946-50
R. Evans (4) 1961-62
G. Fairbairn (14) 1977-80
T. Fogerty (1) 1967
P. Ford (1) 1985
W. Francis (4) 1967-77
D. Gardiner (1) 1965
K. Gee (17) 1946-51
H. Gill (14 + 1) 1981-88
A. Goodway (8) 1985-87
J. Gray (5 + 3) 1974
A. Gregory (10) 1987-89
S. Hampson (3 + 1) 1987-89
E. Hanley (17) 1985-89
C. Hill (1) 1966
D. Hill (1) 1971
J. Hilton (4) 1950
T. Howley (6) 1924
W. Hudson (1) 1948
D. Hurcombe (8) 1920-24
B. Jenkins (12) 1907-14
K. Jones (2) 1970
R. Kinnear (1) 1929
N. Kiss (1) 1985
D. Laughton (11) 1970-71
J. Lawrenson (3) 1948
J. Leytham (5) 1907-10
J. Lydon (9) 1986-89
B. McTigue (25) 1958-63
J. Miller (1) 1911
J. Morley (2) 1936-37
I. Potter (7 + 1) 1985-86
J. Price (4) 1924
R. Ramsdale (8) 1910-14
G. Ratcliffe (7) 1947-50
J. Ring (2) 1924-26
D. Robinson (1) 1970
M. Ryan (4) 1947-50
W. Sayer (7) 1961-63
J. Sharrock (4) 1910-11

N. Silcock (3) 1954
R. Silcock (1) 1908
D. Stephenson (5) 1982-87
J. Sullivan (25) 1924-33
M. Sullivan (19) 1957-60
G. Thomas (1) 1914
J. Thomas (8) 1907-11
S. Wane (2) 1985-86
E. Ward (3) 1946-47
L. White (2) 1947
D. Willicombe (2) 1974
W. Winstanley (3) 1911

WORKINGTON TOWN (9 players)

E. Bowman (4) 1977
P. Charlton (1) 1965
B. Edgar (11) 1958-66
N. Herbert (6) 1961-62
W. Martin (1) 1962
V. McKeating (2) 1951
A. Pepperell (2) 1950-51
I. Southward (4) 1958
G. Wilson (3) 1951

YORK (7 players)

E. Dawson (1) 1956
H. Field (3) 1936
G. Smith (3) 1963-64
J. Stevenson (4) 1959-60
M. Sullivan (1) 1963
B. Watts (5) 1954-55
L. White (4) 1946

*Workington Town second row man
Eddie Bowman. Four appearances
in the 1977 World Cup.*

315

GREAT BRITAIN TEAMS
...A 20-year review

The following is a compendium of Great Britain Test and World Cup teams since the end of the 1968-69 season.

Initials are included where more than one celebrated player shared a surname in the same era. Only playing substitutes are included on the teamsheet.

(WC): World Cup t: try g: goal dg: drop goal * captain

Hooker Tony Fisher, who appeared in five of the six Tests on the 1970 tour.

1970 Australia
Brisbane: 6 June
Lost 15-37
Price, T (Bradford) 3g
Sullivan, C (Hull)
*Myler (St. Helens)
Shoebottom (Leeds)
Atkinson, J (Leeds)
Hardisty (Castleford)
Hepworth (Castleford)
Chisnall, D (Leigh)
Flanagan (Hull KR) 1t
Watson (St. Helens) 1t
Laughton (Wigan) 1t
Robinson, D (Wigan)
Reilly (Castleford)
Sub: Irving (Oldham)

1970 Australia
Sydney: 20 June
Won 28-7
Edwards, D (Castleford)
Smith, A (Leeds)
Hynes (Leeds) 1g
*Myler (St. Helens)
Atkinson, J (Leeds) 1t
Millward (Hull KR) 7g,2t
Hepworth (Castleford)
Hartley, D (Castleford)
Fisher (Bradford) 1t
Watson (St. Helens)
Laughton (Wigan)
Thompson, J (Featherstone)
Reilly (Castleford)
Sub: Shoebottom (Leeds)

1970 Australia
Sydney: 4 July
Won 21-17
Shoebottom (Leeds)
Smith, A (Leeds)
Hynes (Leeds) 1t
*Myler (St. Helens)
Atkinson, J (Leeds) 2t
Millward (Hull KR) 3g,1t
Hepworth (Castleford)
Hartley, D (Castleford) 1t
Fisher (Bradford)
Watson (St. Helens)
Laughton (Wigan)
Thompson, J (Featherstone)
Reilly (Castleford)

1970 New Zealand
Auckland: 11 July
Won 19-15
Shoebottom (Leeds)
Smith, A (Leeds)
Hynes (Leeds) 2g,1t
*Myler (St. Helens)
Atkinson, J (Leeds) 1t
Millward (Hull KR) 1t
Seabourne (Leeds)
Hartley, D (Castleford)
Fisher (Bradford)
Watson (St. Helens)
Laughton (Wigan) 2t
Thompson, J (Featherstone)
Reilly (Castleford)

1970 New Zealand
Christchurch: 19 July
Won 23-9
Dutton (Widnes) 4g
Smith, A (Leeds)
Hynes (Leeds)
*Myler (St. Helens) 1t
Atkinson, J (Leeds)
Millward (Hull KR) 2t
Hepworth (Castleford)
Hartley, D (Castleford)
Fisher (Bradford)
Watson (St. Helens)
Laughton (Wigan) 1t
Thompson, J (Featherstone)
Reilly (Castleford) 1t

1970 New Zealand
Auckland: 25 July
Won 33-16
Dutton (Widnes) 5g
Smith, A (Leeds) 1t
Hesketh (Salford) 1t
*Myler (St. Helens)
Atkinson, J (Leeds)
Millward (Hull KR) 1g
Hepworth (Castleford) 1t
Watson (St. Helens) 1t
Fisher (Bradford)
Ward, J (Salford)
Irving (Oldham)
Lowe, P (Hull KR) 2t
Reilly (Castleford)
Sub: Hynes (Leeds) 1t

1970 Australia (WC)

Leeds: 24 Oct

Won 11-4

Dutton (Widnes) 3g
Smith, A (Leeds)
Hynes (Leeds) 1t,1g
*Myler (St. Helens)
Atkinson, J (Leeds)
Shoebottom (Leeds)
Hepworth (Castleford)
Hartley, D (Castleford)
Fisher (Bradford)
Watson (St. Helens)
Laughton (Wigan)
Thompson, J (Featherstone)
Reilly (Castleford)

1970 France (WC)

Castleford: 28 Oct

Won 6-0

Dutton (Widnes) 3g
Jones, K (Wigan)
Hynes (Leeds)
*Myler (St. Helens)
Atkinson, J (Leeds)
Shoebottom (Leeds)
Hepworth (Castleford)
Hartley, D (Castleford)
Ashcroft, K (Leigh)
Watson (St. Helens)
Laughton (Wigan)
Thompson, J (Featherstone)
Reilly (Castleford)

1970 New Zealand (WC)

Swinton: 31 Oct

Won 27-17

Dutton (Widnes) 6g
Jones, K (Wigan)
Hynes (Leeds) 1t
Hesketh (Salford) 1t
Atkinson, J (Leeds) 1t
Shoebottom (Leeds)
Hepworth (Castleford)
Chisnall, D (Leigh)
Ashcroft, K (Leigh)
Watson (St. Helens) 1t
Haigh (Leeds)
Thompson, J (Featherstone)
*Laughton (Wigan) 1t
Sub: Charlton (Salford)

1970 Australia (WC)

Leeds: 7 Nov

Lost 7-12

Dutton (Widnes) 1g
Smith, A (Leeds)
Hynes (Leeds) 1g
*Myler (St. Helens)
Atkinson, J (Leeds) 1t
Shoebottom (Leeds)
Hepworth (Castleford)
Hartley, D (Castleford)
Fisher (Leeds)
Watson (St. Helens)
Laughton (Wigan)
Thompson, J (Featherstone)
Reilly (Castleford)
Sub: Hesketh (Salford)
     Haigh (Leeds)

1971 France

Toulouse: 7 Feb

Lost 8-16

Whitehead (Warrington) 1g
Smith, A (Leeds) 1t
*Hynes (Leeds)
Benyon (St. Helens)
Atkinson, J (Leeds)
Hill, D (Wigan)
Shoebottom (Leeds)
Jeanes (Wakefield) 1t
Fisher (Leeds)
Warlow (Widnes)
Mantle (St. Helens)
Haigh (Leeds)
Laughton (Wigan)
Sub: Hesketh (Salford)
     Thompson, J (Featherstone)

1971 France

St. Helens: 17 March

Won 24-2

Whitehead (Warrington) 1t,3g
Smith, A (Leeds) 1t
Hesketh (Salford)
Benyon (St. Helens) 1t
Atkinson, J (Leeds)
Millward (Hull KR) 2t
Nash (Featherstone)
Warlow (Widnes)
Fisher (Leeds)
Watson (St. Helens)
Mantle (St. Helens)
Thompson, J (Featherstone) 1t
*Laughton (Wigan)
Sub: Watkins, D (Salford)
     Coulman (Salford)

1971 New Zealand

Salford: 25 Sep

Lost 13-18

Whitehead (Warrington) 2g
Jones, L (St. Helens)
Benyon (St. Helens) 1t
Hesketh (Salford) 1t
Sullivan, C (Hull)
*Millward (Hull KR)
Nash (Featherstone)
Warlow (Widnes)
Karalius, A (St. Helens)
Jeanes (Wakefield)
Ashurst (Wigan) 1t
Coulman (Salford)
Mantle (St. Helens)
Sub: Edwards, D (Castleford)

1971 New Zealand

Castleford: 16 Oct

Lost 14-17

Edwards, D (Castleford)
Sullivan, C (Hull) 1t
Watkins, D (Salford) 1g
Hesketh (Salford)
Walsh, Joe (Leigh) 1t
*Millward (Hull KR) 1t
Murphy, A (Warrington)
Harrison, M (Hull)
Karalius, A (St. Helens)
Coulman (Salford) 1t
Dixon, C (Salford)
Mantle (St. Helens)
Haigh (Leeds)
Sub: Benyon (St. Helens)
     Stephenson, M (Dewsbury)

1971 New Zealand

Leeds: 6 Nov

Won 12-3

Edwards, D (Castleford)
Sullivan, C (Hull)
Hesketh (Salford)
Holmes (Leeds) 2g,2dg
Atkinson, J (Leeds) 2t
*Millward (Hull KR)
Loxton (Huddersfield)
Harrison, M (Hull)
Karalius, A (St. Helens)
Jeanes (Wakefield)
Irving (Oldham)
Nicholls (Widnes)
Halmshaw (Halifax)
Sub: O'Neill, D (Widnes)

1972 France
Toulouse: 6 Feb
Won 10-9
Charlton (Salford)
*Sullivan, C (Hull) 1t
Holmes (Leeds) 2g
Benyon (St. Helens) 1t
Atkinson, J (Leeds)
Kelly (St. Helens)
Nash (Featherstone)
Harrison, M (Hull)
Karalius, A (St. Helens)
Jeanes (Wakefield)
Ashurst (Wigan)
Lowe, P (Hull KR)
Nicholls (Widnes)

1972 France
Bradford: 12 March
Won 45-10
Charlton (Salford) 1t
*Sullivan, C (Hull) 1t
Holmes (Leeds) 1t,6g
Benyon (St. Helens) 1t
Atkinson, J (Leeds) 1t
Kelly (St. Helens)
Nash (Featherstone)
Harrison, M (Hull)
Stephenson, M (Dewsbury) 1t
Jeanes (Wakefield) 1t
Ashurst (Wigan) 2t
Lowe, P (Hull KR) 1t
Nicholls (Widnes)
Sub: Walsh, John (St. Helens) 1t
    Irving (Oldham)

1972 Australia (WC)
Perpignan: 29 Oct
Won 27-21
Charlton (Salford)
*Sullivan, C (Hull) 1t
Hesketh (Salford)
Walsh, John (St. Helens)
Atkinson, J (Leeds) 1t
O'Neill, D (Widnes) 1t
Nash (Featherstone)
Clawson (Leeds) 6g
Stephenson, M (Dewsbury) 1t
Jeanes (Leeds)
Lockwood (Castleford)
Lowe, P (Hull KR) 1t
Nicholls (Widnes)
Sub: Holmes (Leeds)

1972 France (WC)
Grenoble: 1 Nov
Won 13-4
Charlton (Salford)
*Sullivan, C (Hull) 1t
Hesketh (Salford)
Walsh, John (St. Helens)
Atkinson, J (Leeds)
O'Neill, D (Widnes)
Nash (Featherstone)
Clawson (Leeds) 2g
Stephenson, M (Dewsbury)
Lockwood, B (Castleford)
Dixon, C (Salford)
Lowe, P (Hull KR) 2t
Nicholls (Widnes)

1972 New Zealand (WC)
Pau: 4 Nov
Won 53-19
Charlton (Salford) 1t
*Sullivan, C (Hull) 1t
Hesketh (Salford) 1t
Walsh, John (St. Helens)
Atkinson, J (Leeds) 2t
Holmes (Leeds) 10g,2t
Nash (Featherstone) 1t
Jeanes (Leeds) 1t
Stephenson, M (Dewsbury) 1t
Lockwood (Castleford)
Irving (Oldham)
Lowe, P (Hull KR)
Nicholls (Widnes) 1t
Sub: Redfearn, D (Bradford)
    Karalius, A (St. Helens)

1972 Australia (WC)
Lyon: 11 Nov
Drew 10-10
Charlton (Salford)
*Sullivan, C (Hull) 1t
Hesketh (Salford)
Walsh, John (St. Helens)
Atkinson, J (Leeds)
Holmes (Leeds)
Nash (Featherstone)
Clawson (Leeds) 2g
Stephenson, M (Dewsbury) 1t
Jeanes (Leeds)
Lockwood, B (Castleford)
Lowe, P (Hull KR)
Nicholls (Widnes)
Sub: Irving (Oldham)

1973 Australia
Wembley: 3 Nov
Won 21-12
Charlton (Salford)
*Sullivan (Hull)
Hynes (Leeds)
Hesketh (Salford)
Atkinson, J (Leeds)
Topliss (Wakefield)
Nash (Featherstone) 1dg
Clawson (Oldham) 4g
Clarke (Wigan) 1t
Lockwood (Castleford) 1t
Nicholls (St. Helens)
Lowe, P (Hull KR) 2t
Batten (Leeds)

1973 Australia
Leeds: 24 Nov
Lost 6-14
Charlton (Salford)
*Sullivan (Hull)
Hynes (Leeds)
Hesketh (Salford)
Atkinson, J (Leeds)
Topliss (Wakefield)
Nash (Featherstone)
Clawson (Oldham) 3g
Clarke (Wigan)
Lockwood (Castleford)
Mantle (St. Helens)
Lowe, P (Hull KR)
Batten, R (Leeds)
Sub: Eckersley (St. Helens)
    Dixon, C (Salford)

1973 Australia
Warrington: 1 Dec
Lost 5-15
Charlton (Salford)
Smith, A (Leeds)
Hynes (Leeds)
Hesketh (Salford)
*Sullivan, C (Hull)
Eckersley (St. Helens)
Millward (Hull KR) 1t,1g
Clawson (Oldham)
Clarke (Wigan)
Harrison, M (Hull)
Nicholls (St. Helens)
Lowe, P (Hull KR)
Laughton (Widnes)
Sub: Watkins, D (Salford)
    Dixon, C (Salford)

1974 France

Grenoble: 20 Jan

Won 24-5

Charlton (Salford)
Fielding (Salford) 3t
Willicombe (Halifax) 1t
Hesketh (Salford)
Redfearn, D (Bradford)
Gill, K (Salford) 1t
Bates, A (Dewsbury)
Clawson (Oldham) 3g
Bridges (Featherstone)
Lockwood (Castleford)
Dixon, C (Salford)
Nicholls (St. Helens)
*Laughton (Widnes) 1t
Sub: Watkins, D (Salford)
     Gray (Wigan)

1974 Australia

Sydney: 6 July

Won 16-11

Charlton (Salford)
Dyl (Leeds)
Eckersley (St. Helens)
*Hesketh (Salford)
Millward (Hull KR)
Gill, K (Salford) 1t
Nash (Featherstone)
Mills (Widnes)
Gray (Wigan) 3g,1dg
Thompson, J (Featherstone)
Dixon, C (Salford) 1t
Chisnall, E (St. Helens) 1t
Nicholls (St. Helens)
Sub: Norton (Castleford)

1974 New Zealand

Christchurch: 4 Aug

Won 17-8

Charlton (Salford)
Redfearn, D (Bradford) 1t
Dyl (Leeds) 1t
Dixon, C (Salford)
Richards (Salford)
*Hesketh (Salford) 1t
Nash (Featherstone)
Mills (Widnes)
Gray (Wigan) 4g
Thompson, J (Featherstone)
Chisnall, E (St. Helens)
Norton (Castleford)
Nicholls (St. Helens)
Sub: Bates, A (Dewsbury)

1974 France

Wigan: 17 Feb

Won 29-0

Charlton (Salford) 2t
Fielding (Salford)
Willicombe (Wigan) 1t
Hesketh (Salford)
Redfearn, D (Bradford) 2t
Gill, K (Salford)
Bates, A (Dewsbury)
Clawson (Oldham) 2g
Bridges (Featherstone)
Fogerty (Rochdale)
Dixon, C (Salford)
Nicholls (St. Helens)
*Laughton (Widnes) 1t
Sub: Watkins, D (Salford) 1g
     Gray (Wigan) 1t,1g

1974 Australia

Sydney: 20 July

Lost 18-22

Charlton (Salford)
Richards (Salford) 1t
Dyl (Leeds) 1t
*Hesketh (Salford)
Bevan, J (Warrington)
Gill, K (Salford)
Nash (Featherstone)
Clawson (Oldham)
Gray (Wigan) 6g
Thompson, J (Featherstone)
Dixon, C (Salford)
Chisnall, E (St. Helens)
Nicholls (St. Helens)
Sub: Millward (Hull KR)
     Rose, P (Hull KR)

1974 New Zealand

Auckland: 10 Aug

Won 20-0

Charlton (Salford)
Redfearn, D (Bradford)
Willicombe (Wigan)
Dyl (Leeds) 1t
Bevan, J (Warrington) 2t
*Hesketh (Salford) 1t
Nash (Featherstone)
Clawson (Oldham)
Gray (Wigan) 4g
Thompson, J (Featherstone)
Chisnall, E (St. Helens)
Dixon, C (Salford)
Nicholls (St. Helens)
Sub: Bates, A (Dewsbury)
     Ramsey (Bradford)

1974 Australia

Brisbane: 15 June

Lost 6-12

Charlton (Salford)
Redfearn, D (Bradford)
Watkins, D (Salford) 1g
*Hesketh (Salford)
Bevan, J (Warrington)
Millward (Hull KR)
Nash (Featherstone)
Clawson (Oldham) 2g
Bridges (Featherstone)
Mills (Widnes)
Dixon, C (Salford)
Thompson, J (Featherstone)
Nicholls (St. Helens)
Sub: Eckersley (St. Helens)
     Gray (Wigan)

1974 New Zealand

Auckland: 27 July

Lost 8-13

Charlton (Salford)
Redfearn, D (Bradford)
Dyl (Leeds)
*Hesketh (Salford)
Bevan, J (Warrington) 1t
Gill, K (Salford)
Nash (Featherstone) 1t
Clawson (Oldham) 1g
Gray (Wigan)
Thompson, J (Featherstone)
Dixon, C (Salford)
Norton (Castleford)
Nicholls (St. Helens)
Sub: Ashcroft (Warrington)

1977 France (WC)

Auckland: 5 June

Won 23-4

Fairbairn (Wigan) 7g
Fielding (Salford)
Holmes (Leeds)
Dyl (Leeds) 1t
Wright, S (Widnes) 1t
*Millward (Hull KR) 1t
Nash (Salford)
Thompson, J (Featherstone)
Ward, D (Leeds)
Pitchford, S (Leeds)
Bowman, E (Workington)
Nicholls (St. Helens)
Hogan (Barrow)
Sub: Gill, K (Salford)
     Casey (Hull KR)

1977 New Zealand (WC)
Christchurch: 12 June

Won 30-12

Fairbairn (Wigan) 6g
Wright, S (Widnes) 2t
Holmes (Leeds)
Dyl (Leeds)
Francis, W (Wigan)
*Millward (Hull KR) 1t
Nash (Salford)
Thompson, J (Featherstone)
Ward, D (Leeds)
Pitchford, S (Leeds)
Bowman, E (Workington) 1t
Nicholls (St. Helens) 1t
Hogan (Barrow) 1t
Sub: Casey (Hull KR)

1977 Australia (WC)
Brisbane: 18 June

Lost 5-19

Fairbairn (Wigan) 1g
Wright, S (Widnes)
Francis, W (Wigan)
Dyl (Leeds)
Fielding (Salford)
*Millward (Hull KR) 1t
Nash (Salford)
Thompson, J (Featherstone)
Ward, D (Leeds)
Pitchford, S (Leeds)
Bowman, E (Workington)
Nicholls (St. Helens)
Hogan (Barrow)
Sub: Holmes (Leeds)
     Smith, P (Featherstone)

1977 Australia (WC)
Sydney: 25 June

Lost 12-13

Fairbairn (Wigan) 3g
Wright, S (Widnes)
Holmes (Leeds)
Dyl (Leeds)
Francis, W (Wigan)
*Millward (Hull KR)
Nash (Salford)
Thompson, J (Featherstone)
Elwell (Widnes)
Pitchford, S (Leeds) 1t
Bowman, E (Workington)
Casey (Hull KR)
Hogan (Barrow)
Sub: Gill, K (Salford) 1t
     Smith, P (Featherstone)

1978 Australia
Wigan: 21 Oct

Lost 9-15

Fairbairn (Wigan) 3g
Wright, S (Widnes)
Hughes (Widnes)
Cunningham (St. Helens)
Bevan, J (Warrington) 1t
*Millward (Hull KR)
Nash (Salford)
Thompson, J (Bradford)
Ward, D (Leeds)
Rose, P (Hull KR)
Nicholls (St. Helens)
Casey (Hull KR)
Norton (Hull)
Sub: Holmes (Leeds)
     Hogan (Barrow)

1978 Australia
Bradford: 5 Nov

Won 18-14

Fairbairn (Wigan) 6g
Wright, S (Widnes) 2t
Joyner (Castleford)
Dyl (Leeds)
Atkinson, J (Leeds)
*Millward (Hull KR)
Nash (Salford)
Mills (Widnes)
Fisher (Bradford)
Lockwood (Hull KR)
Nicholls (St. Helens)
Lowe, P (Hull KR)
Norton (Hull)
Sub: Holmes (Leeds)
     Rose, P (Hull KR)

1978 Australia
Leeds: 18 Nov

Lost 6-23

Fairbairn (Wigan)
Wright, S (Widnes)
Joyner (Castleford)
Bevan, J (Warrington) 1t
Atkinson, J (Leeds)
*Millward (Hull KR) 1t
Nash (Salford)
Mills (Widnes)
Fisher (Bradford)
Farrar (Hull)
Nicholls (St. Helens)
Lowe, P (Hull KR)
Norton (Hull)
Sub: Holmes (Leeds)
     Rose, P (Hull KR)

1979 Australia
Brisbane: 16 June

Lost 0-35

Woods, J (Leigh)
Barends (Bradford)
Joyner (Castleford)
Hughes (Widnes)
Mathias (St. Helens)
Holmes (Leeds)
Stephens (Castleford)
Mills (Widnes)
Ward, D (Leeds)
Skerrett (Wakefield)
Nicholls (St. Helens)
*Laughton (Widnes)
Norton (Hull)
Sub: Evans, S (Featherstone)
     Hogan (Hull KR)

1979 Australia
Sydney: 30 June

Lost 16-24

Fairbairn (Wigan)
Barends (Bradford)
Joyner (Castleford) 1t
Woods, J (Leigh) 5g
Hughes (Widnes) 1t
Holmes (Leeds)
Stephens (Castleford)
*Nicholls (St. Helens)
Ward, D (Leeds)
Skerrett (Wakefield)
Casey (Bradford)
Grayshon (Bradford)
Adams, M (Widnes)
Sub: Evans, S (Featherstone)
     Watkinson (Hull KR)

1979 Australia
Sydney: 14 July

Lost 2-28

Fairbairn (Wigan) 1g
Evans, S (Featherstone)
Joyner (Castleford)
Woods, J (Leigh)
Hughes (Widnes)
Topliss (Wakefield)
Redfearn, A (Bradford)
*Nicholls (St. Helens)
Ward, D (Leeds)
Casey (Bradford)
Hogan (Hull KR)
Grayshon (Bradford)
Norton (Hull)
Sub: Holmes (Leeds)
     Adams, M (Widnes)

1979 New Zealand
Auckland: 21 July
Won 16-8
Fairbairn (Wigan) 1t,2g
Evans, S (Featherstone) 1t
Joyner (Castleford)
Smith, M (Hull KR) 1t
Hughes (Widnes) 1t
Holmes (Leeds)
Stephens (Castleford)
Casey (Bradford)
Ward, D (Leeds)
*Nicholls (St. Helens)
Hogan (Hull KR)
Grayshon (Bradford)
Adams, M (Widnes)
Sub: Lockwood (Hull KR)

1980 New Zealand
Wigan: 18 Oct
Drew 14-14
*Fairbairn (Wigan) 4g
Camilleri (Barrow) 1t
Joyner (Castleford)
Smith, M (Hull KR) 1t
Bentley (Widnes)
Hartley, S (Hull KR)
Dick (Leeds)
Holdstock (Hull KR)
Watkinson (Hull KR)
Skerrett (Hull)
Gorley, L (Widnes)
Grayshon (Bradford)
Casey (Hull KR)
Sub: Pinner (St. Helens)

1981 France
Hull: 6 Dec
Won 37-0
Fairbairn (Hull KR) 1g
Drummond (Leigh) 2t
Smith, M (Hull KR)
Woods, J (Leigh) 1t,7g
Gill (Wigan) 3t
Hartley (Hull KR) 1t
Gregory, A (Widnes)
Grayshon (Bradford)
*Ward, D (Leeds)
Skerrett (Hull)
Gorley, L (Widnes)
Gorley, P (St. Helens)
Norton (Hull)
Sub: Burke (Widnes)
     Szymala (Barrow)

1979 New Zealand
Christchurch: 5 Aug
Won 22-7
Fairbairn (Wigan) 5g
Evans, S (Featherstone) 1t
Joyner (Castleford)
Smith, M (Hull KR)
Hughes (Widnes) 1t
Holmes (Leeds)
Stephens (Castleford)
*Nicholls (St. Helens)
Ward, D (Leeds)
Skerrett (Wakefield)
Casey (Bradford) 1t
Grayshon (Bradford) 1t
Adams, M (Widnes)

1980 New Zealand
Bradford: 2 Nov
Lost 8-12
*Fairbairn (Wigan) 4g
Drummond (Leigh)
Joyner (Castleford)
Smith, M (Hull KR)
Camilleri (Barrow)
Kelly (Warrington)
Dick (Leeds)
Holdstock (Hull KR)
Elwell (Widnes)
Shaw, G (Widnes)
Casey (Hull KR)
Grayshon (Bradford)
Pinner (St. Helens)
Sub: Evans, S (Featherstone)
     Gorley, L (Widnes)

1981 France
Marseilles: 20 Dec
Lost 2-19
Burke (Widnes)
Drummond (Leigh)
Smith, M (Hull KR)
Woods, J (Leigh) 1g
Gill (Wigan)
Hartley (Hull KR)
Gregory, A (Widnes)
*Grayshon (Bradford)
Watkinson (Hull KR)
Skerrett (Hull)
Gorley, L (Widnes)
Szymala (Barrow)
Norton (Hull)
Sub: Gorley, P (St. Helens)

1979 New Zealand
Auckland: 11 Aug
Lost 11-18
Fairbairn (Wigan) 1g
Evans, S (Featherstone)
Joyner (Castleford)
Smith, M (Hull KR) 1t
Hughes (Widnes) 1t
Holmes (Leeds)
Stephens (Castleford) 1t
Skerrett (Wakefield)
Ward, D (Leeds)
*Nicholls (St. Helens)
Casey (Bradford)
Grayshon (Bradford)
Adams, M (Widnes)
Sub: Woods, J (Leigh)
     Hogan (Hull KR)

1980 New Zealand
Leeds: 15 Nov
Won 10-2
Burke (Widnes) 2g
Drummond (Leigh) 2t
Joyner (Castleford)
Evans, S (Featherstone)
Atkinson, J (Leeds)
Woods, J (Leigh)
Walker (Whitehaven)
Skerrett (Hull)
Elwell (Widnes)
*Casey (Hull KR)
Gorley, P (St. Helens)
Adams, M (Widnes)
Norton (Hull)

1982 Australia
Hull City FC: 30 Oct
Lost 4-40
Fairbairn (Hull KR)
Drummond (Leigh)
Hughes (Widnes)
Dyl (Leeds)
Evans, S (Hull)
Woods, J (Leigh)
*Nash (Salford)
Grayshon (Bradford)
Ward, D (Leeds)
Skerrett (Hull)
Gorley, L (Widnes)
Crooks, L (Hull) 2g
Norton (Hull)
Sub: D. Heron (Leeds)

1982 Australia

Wigan: 20 Nov

Lost 6-27

Mumby (Bradford) 3g
Drummond (Leigh)
Smith, M (Hull KR)
Stephenson, D (Wigan)
Gill (Wigan)
Holmes (Leeds)
Kelly, K (Warrington)
*Grayshon (Bradford)
Dalgreen (Fulham)
Skerrett (Hull)
Eccles (Warrington)
Burton (Hull KR)
Heron, D (Leeds)
Sub: Woods, J (Leigh)
　　　Rathbone (Bradford)

1983 France

Hull: 6 March

Won 17-5

Mumby (Bradford) 4g
Drummond (Leigh)
Joyner (Castleford)
Duane, R (Warrington) 1t
Lydon (Widnes)
Myler, A (Widnes)
Gregory, A (Widnes) 1t
O'Neill, M (Widnes)
Noble (Bradford)
Goodway (Oldham)
*Casey (Hull KR)
Rathbone (Bradford)
Flanagan (Oldham)
Sub: Smith, P (Featherstone) 1t

1984 Australia

Sydney: 9 June

Lost 8-25

Burke (Widnes) 2g
Drummond (Leigh)
Schofield (Hull) 1t
Mumby (Bradford)
Hanley (Bradford)
Foy, D (Oldham)
Holding (St. Helens)
Crooks, L (Hull)
*Noble (Bradford)
Goodway (Oldham)
Burton (Hull KR)
Worrall, M (Oldham)
Adams (Widnes)
Sub: Lydon (Widnes)
　　　Hobbs, D (Featherstone)

1982 Australia

Leeds: 28 Nov

Lost 8-32

Fairbairn (Hull KR)
Drummond (Leigh)
Stephenson, D. (Wigan)
Smith, M (Hull KR)
Evans (Hull) 1t
*Topliss (Hull)
Gregory, A (Widnes)
O'Neill, M (Widnes)
Noble (Bradford)
Rose (Hull)
Smith, P (Featherstone)
Crooks, L (Hull) 2g,1dg
Crane (Hull)
Sub: Courtney (Warrington)

1984 France

Avignon: 29 Jan

Won 12-0

*Mumby (Bradford)
Drummond (Leigh)
Duane, R (Warrington)
Foy, D (Oldham) 1t
Clark (Hull KR)
Lydon (Widnes)
Cairns (Barrow)
Rayne, Keith (Leeds)
Watkinson (Hull KR)
Goodway (Oldham) 1t
Worrall, M (Oldham)
Hobbs, D (Featherstone)
Hall (Hull KR)
Sub: Hanley (Bradford)
　　　Crooks, L (Hull) 2g

1984 Australia

Brisbane: 26 June

Lost 6-18

Burke (Widnes) 1g
Drummond (Leigh)
Schofield (Hull) 1t
Mumby (Bradford)
Hanley (Bradford)
Myler, A (Widnes)
Holding (St. Helens)
Rayne, Keith (Leeds)
*Noble (Bradford)
Crooks, L (Hull)
Burton (Hull KR)
Goodway (Oldham)
Worrall (Oldham)
Sub: Gregory, A (Widnes)
　　　Adams (Widnes)

1983 France

Carcassonne: 20 Feb

Won 20-5

Burke (Widnes) 1g
Drummond (Leigh)
Joyner (Castleford) 1t
Duane, R (Warrington)
Lydon (Widnes) 1t,3g
Myler, A (Widnes)
Gregory, A (Widnes)
O'Neill, M (Widnes)
Noble (Bradford) 1t
Goodway (Oldham) 1t
*Casey (Hull KR)
Rathbone (Bradford)
Flanagan (Oldham)
Sub: Woods, J (Leigh)
　　　Smith, P (Featherstone)

1984 France

Leeds: 17 Feb

Won 10-0

Mumby (Bradford)
Clark (Hull KR)
Joyner (Castleford)
Schofield (Hull)
Basnett (Widnes)
Hanley (Bradford)
Cairns (Barrow)
Rayne, Keith (Leeds)
*Noble (Bradford)
Ward, K (Castleford)
Jasiewicz (Bradford)
Hobbs, D (Featherstone) 5g
Hall (Hull KR)
Sub: Smith, M (Hull KR)
　　　Smith, P (Featherstone)

1984 Australia

Sydney: 7 July

Lost 7-20

Burke (Widnes) 1g
Drummond (Leigh)
Schofield (Hull)
Mumby (Bradford)
Hanley (Bradford) 1t
Myler, A (Widnes)
Holding (St. Helens) 1dg
Hobbs, D (Featherstone)
*Noble (Bradford)
Case (Wigan)
Burton (Hull KR)
Goodway (Oldham)
Adams (Widnes)

1984 New Zealand
Auckland: 14 July
Lost 0-12
Burke (Widnes)
Drummond (Leigh)
Schofield (Hull)
Mumby (Bradford)
Hanley (Bradford)
Smith, M (Hull KR)
Holding (St. Helens)
Hobbs, D (Featherstone)
*Noble (Bradford)
Case (Wigan)
Burton (Hull KR)
Goodway (Oldham)
Adams (Widnes)

1984 Papua New Guinea
Mount Hagen: 5 Aug
Won 38-20
Burke (Widnes) 1t,5g
Drummond (Leigh) 2t
Hanley (Bradford) 1t
Mumby (Bradford) 1t
Lydon (Widnes)
Myler, A (Widnes)
Gregory, A (Widnes)
Rayne, Keith (Leeds) 1t
*Noble (Bradford)
Goodway (Oldham)
Flanagan (Oldham)
Hobbs, D (Featherstone) 1t
Adams (Widnes)
Sub: Donlan (Leigh)
    Proctor (Hull)

1985 New Zealand
Leeds: 19 Oct
Lost 22-24
Burke (Widnes) 3g
Drummond (Leigh)
Schofield (Hull)
Hanley (Wigan) 1t
Lydon (Widnes) 1t,2g
Myler, A (Widnes)
Fox (Featherstone)
Crooks, L (Hull)
Watkinson (Hull KR)
Fieldhouse (Widnes)
Goodway (Wigan) 1t
*Pinner (St. Helens)
Sub: Arkwright (St. Helens)

1984 New Zealand
Christchurch: 22 July
Lost 12-28
Burke (Widnes) 2g
Drummond (Leigh)
Hanley (Bradford) 1t
Mumby (Bradford)
Lydon (Widnes)
Myler, A (Widnes) 1t
Gregory, A (Widnes)
Hobbs, D (Featherstone)
*Noble (Bradford)
Case (Wigan)
Burton (Hull KR)
Goodway (Oldham)
Adams (Widnes)
Sub: Joyner (Castleford)
    Beardmore, K (Castleford)

1985 France
Leeds: 1 March
Won 50-4
Edwards (Wigan)
Ledger (St. Helens)
Creasser (Leeds) 8g
Gribbin (Whitehaven) 1t
Gill (Wigan) 1t
Hanley (Bradford) 2t
Fox (Featherstone) 2t,1g
Dickinson (Leeds)
Watkinson (Hull KR) 1t
Dannatt (Hull)
*Goodway (Oldham)
Rathbone (Bradford)
Divorty (Hull) 1t
Sub: Gibson (Batley)
    Platt (St. Helens)

1985 New Zealand
Wigan: 2 Nov
Won 25-8
Burke (Widnes)
Drummond (Leigh)
Schofield (Hull) 4t
Hanley (Wigan)
Lydon (Widnes) 4g
Myler, A (Widnes)
Fox (Featherstone)
Grayshon (Leeds)
Watkinson (Hull KR)
Fieldhouse (Widnes)
Goodway (Wigan)
Potter (Wigan)
*Pinner (St. Helens) 1dg
Sub: Edwards (Wigan)
    Burton (Hull KR)

1984 New Zealand
Auckland: 28 July
Lost 16-32
Burke (Widnes) 4g
Drummond (Leigh)
Hanley (Bradford) 1t
Mumby (Bradford) 1t
Lydon (Widnes)
Myler, A (Widnes)
Gregory, A (Widnes)
Hobbs, D (Featherstone)
*Noble (Bradford)
Case (Wigan)
Adams (Widnes)
Goodway (Oldham)
Flanagan (Oldham)
Sub: Donlan (Leigh)
    Joyner (Castleford)

1985 France
Perpignan: 17 March
Lost 16-24
Johnson, C (Leigh)
Clark (Hull KR)
Creasser (Leeds) 1g
Foy, D (Oldham) 1t
Ford, P (Wigan) 2t
*Hanley (Bradford)
Fox (Featherstone)
Dickinson (Leeds)
Kiss (Wigan)
Wane (Wigan)
Dannatt (Hull)
Rathbone (Bradford)
Divorty (Hull) 1g
Sub: Harkin (Hull KR)
    Powell (Leeds)

1985 New Zealand (Also WC)
Elland Rd, Leeds: 9 Nov
Drew 6-6
Burke (Widnes)
Drummond (Leigh)
Schofield (Hull)
Edwards (Wigan)
Lydon (Widnes)
Hanley (Wigan)
Fox (Featherstone)
Grayshon (Leeds)
Watkinson (Hull KR)
Fieldhouse (Widnes)
Goodway (Wigan)
Potter (Wigan)
*Pinner (St. Helens)
Sub: Arkwright (St. Helens)
Sub: Crooks, L (Hull) 3g

1986 France (Also WC)
Avignon: 16 Feb
Drew 10-10
Burke (Widnes)
Drummond (Leigh)
Schofield (Hull)
Hanley (Wigan) 1t
Gill (Wigan)
Myler, A (Widnes)
Fox (Featherstone)
Crooks, L (Hull) 3g
Watkinson (Hull KR)
Wane (Wigan)
Potter (Wigan)
Fieldhouse (Widnes)
*Pinner (St. Helens)
Sub: Platt (St. Helens)

1986 France
Wigan: 1 March
Won 24-10
Lydon (Wigan)
Drummond (Leigh) 1t
Schofield (Hull) 1t,2g
Marchant (Castleford) 1t
Laws (Hull KR)
Myler, A (Widnes)
Fox (Featherstone)
Crooks, L (Hull) 2g
*Watkinson (Hull KR)
Fieldhouse (Widnes)
Rayne, Kevin (Leeds)
James (Halifax) 1t
Potter (Wigan)
Sub: Platt (St. Helens)

1986 Australia
Manch. U. FC: 25 Oct
Lost 16-38
Lydon (Wigan) 1t
Marchant (Castleford)
Schofield (Hull) 2t
Hanley (Wigan)
Gill (Wigan) 1g
Myler, A (Widnes)
Fox (Featherstone)
Ward (Castleford)
*Watkinson (Hull KR)
Fieldhouse (Widnes)
Crooks, L (Hull) 1g
Potter (Wigan)
Goodway (Wigan)

1986 Australia
Elland Rd, Leeds: 8 Nov
Lost 4-34
Lydon (Wigan)
Ledger (St. Helens)
Schofield (Hull) 1t
Marchant (Castleford)
Gill (Wigan)
Myler, A (Widnes)
Fox (Featherstone)
Ward (Castleford)
*Watkinson (Hull KR)
Fieldhouse (St. Helens)
Crooks, L (Hull)
Potter (Wigan)
Goodway (Wigan)
Sub: Edwards (Wigan)
     Platt (St. Helens)

1986 Australia (Also WC)
Wigan: 22 Nov
Lost 15-24
Lydon (Wigan) 2g
Gill (Wigan) 1g
Schofield (Hull) 2t,1dg
Stephenson (Wigan)
Basnett (Widnes)
Myler, A (Widnes)
Gregory, A (Warrington)
Ward (Castleford)
*Watkinson (Hull KR)
Crooks, L (Hull)
Burton (Hull KR)
Goodway (Wigan)
Pinner (Widnes)
Sub: Potter (Wigan)

1987 France (Also WC)
Leeds: 24 Jan
Won 52-4
Lydon (Wigan) 1t,8g
Forster (Warrington) 1t
Schofield (Hull)
Stephenson (Wigan)
Gill (Wigan)
*Hanley (Wigan) 2t
Edwards (Wigan) 2t
Hobbs (Oldham)
Beardmore, K (Castleford)
Crooks, L (Hull)
Goodway (Wigan) 1t
Haggerty (St. Helens)
Gregory, M (Warrington) 2t
Sub: Creasser (Leeds)
     England (Castleford)

1987 France
Carcassonne: 8 Feb
Won 20-10
Lydon (Wigan) 4g
Forster (Warrington)
Schofield (Hull)
*Hanley (Wigan) 1t
Gill (Wigan) 1t
Edwards (Wigan)
Gregory, A (Wigan)
Hobbs (Oldham)
Beardmore, K (Castleford) 1t
England (Castleford)
Burton (Hull KR)
Haggerty (St. Helens)
Gregory, M (Warrington)
Sub: Dixon (Halifax)

1987 Papua New Guinea (Also WC)
Wigan: 24 Oct
Won 42-0
Hampson (Wigan)
Drummond (Warrington)
Stephenson (Wigan) 7g
Lydon (Wigan) 1t
Ford (Bradford) 1t
Edwards (Wigan) 2t
Gregory, A (Wigan) 1t
Ward (Castleford)
Groves (St. Helens)
Case (Wigan)
Medley (Leeds) 1t
Goodway (Wigan)
*Hanley (Wigan) 1t
Sub: Woods (Warrington)
     Fairbank (Bradford)

1988 France
Avignon: 24 Jan
Won 28-14
Hampson (Wigan)
Drummond (Warrington) 1t
Schofield (Leeds) 2t
Loughlin (St. Helens) 3g
Offiah (Widnes) 1t
*Hanley (Wigan) 1t
Edwards (Wigan)
Ward (Castleford)
Beardmore, K (Castleford)
Waddell (Oldham)
Powell (Leeds)
Medley (Leeds)
Platt (St. Helens)
Sub: Creasser (Leeds) 1g
     Dixon (Halifax)

1988 France
Leeds: 6 Feb
Won 30-12

Hampson (Wigan)
Plange (Castleford) 1t
Schofield (Leeds) 1t,5g
*Hanley (Wigan) 2t
Ford (Bradford)
Edwards (Wigan)
Gregory, A (Wigan) 1t
Ward (Castleford)
Beardmore, K (Castleford)
Waddell (Oldham)
Powell (Leeds)
Dixon (Halifax)
Platt (St. Helens)
Sub: Stephenson (Leeds)
     Medley (Leeds)

1988 Australia
Brisbane: 28 June
Lost 14-34

Loughlin (St. Helens) 3g
Gill (Wigan)
Ford (Bradford) 1t
*Hanley (Wigan)
Offiah (Widnes) 1t
Hulme, D (Widnes)
Gregory, A (Wigan)
Ward (Castleford)
Beardmore, K (Castleford)
Powell (Leeds)
Dixon (Halifax)
Platt (St. Helens)
Gregory, M (Warrington)
Subs: Wright (Widnes)
      Hulme, P (Widnes)

1989 France
Wigan: 21 Jan
Won 26-10

Tait (Widnes)
Ford (Leeds) 1t
Loughlin (St. Helens) 3g
Lydon (Wigan) 1t
Offiah (Widnes) 1t
Edwards (Wigan) 1t
Gregory, A (Wigan)
Ward (Castleford)
Beardmore, K (Castleford)
Waddell (Leeds)
Gregory, M (Warrington)
Powell (Leeds)
*Hanley (Wigan) 1t
Sub: Williams (Salford)
     Eyres (Widnes)

1988 Papua New Guinea (Also WC)
Port Moresby: 22 May
Won 42-22

Loughlin (St. Helens) 7g
Ford (Bradford)
Schofield (Leeds) 2t
Stephenson (Leeds) 1t
Gill (Wigan) 2t
Edwards (Wigan)
Gregory, A (Wigan)
Ward (Castleford)
Beardmore, K (Castleford)
Case (Wigan)
Medley (Leeds) 1t
Gregory, M (Warrington) 1t
*Hanley (Wigan)
Subs: Hulme, D (Widnes)
      Dixon (Halifax)

1988 Australia (Also WC)
Sydney: 9 July
Won 26-12

Ford (Bradford) 1t
Gill (Wigan) 2t
Stephenson (Leeds)
Loughlin (St. Helens) 3g
Offiah (Widnes) 1t
Hulme, D (Widnes)
Gregory, A (Wigan)
Ward (Castleford)
Hulme, P (Widnes)
Waddell (Oldham)
Gregory, M (Warrington) 1t
Powell (Leeds)
*Hanley (Wigan)
Sub: Case (Wigan)

1989 France
Avignon: 5 Feb
Won 30-8

Tait (Widnes) 1t
Ford (Leeds) 2t
Williams (Salford) 1t
Lydon (Wigan) 3g
Offiah (Widnes)
Edwards (Wigan) 1t
Gregory, A (Wigan)
Ward (Castleford)
Beardmore, K (Castleford)
Crooks, L (Leeds)
Gregory, M (Warrington)
Powell (Leeds)
*Hanley (Wigan) 1t
Sub: Hampson (Wigan)
     England (Castleford)

1988 Australia
Sydney: 11 June
Lost 6-17

Loughlin (St. Helens) 1g
Ford (Bradford)
Schofield (Leeds)
Stephenson (Leeds)
Offiah (Widnes)
Hulme, D (Widnes)
Gregory, A (Wigan)
Ward (Castleford)
Beardmore, K (Castleford)
Dixon (Halifax)
Gregory, M (Warrington)
Platt (St. Helens)
*Hanley (Wigan) 1t
Subs: Gill (Wigan)
      Powell (Leeds)

1988 New Zealand (Also WC)
Christchurch: 17 July
Lost 10-12

Ford (Bradford)
Gill (Wigan)
Stephenson (Leeds)
Loughlin (St. Helens) 1t,1g
Offiah (Widnes)
Hulme, D (Widnes) 1t
Gregory, A (Wigan)
Ward (Castleford)
Beardmore, K (Castleford)
Waddell (Oldham)
Gregory, M (Warrington)
Powell (Leeds)
*Hanley (Wigan)
Sub: Hulme, P (Widnes)

*Shaun Edwards, who earned
his 12th cap in Avignon in
February 1989.*

GREAT BRITAIN RECORDS

Most appearances

46	Mick Sullivan★
31	Billy Boston
29 + 1	Cliff Watson
29	George Nicholls
29	Neil Fox
28 + 1	Roger Millward
28	Alan Prescott
27 + 1	Ellery Hanley
27	Phil Jackson
27	Alex Murphy
26	Eric Ashton
26	John Atkinson
25	Brian McTigue
25	Jim Sullivan
25	Tommy Harris

★Mick Sullivan's record number of appearances include a record run of 36 successive matches. In addition he played in two matches against France before they were given Test status.

Most tries

41, Mick Sullivan, also scoring two against France before they were given Test status.

Most goals and points

93 goals, (14 tries), 228 points, Neil Fox.

Longest Test careers

14 years — Gus Risman
1932 to 1946 (17 appearances)

13 years 9 months — Billy Batten
1908 to 1921 (10 appearances)

13 years 6 months — Alex Murphy
1958 to 1971 (27 appearances)

12 years 9 months — Roger Millward
1966 to 1978 (28 + 1 appearances)

12 years 6 months — John Atkinson
1968 to 1980 (26 appearances)

12 years 6 months — Terry Clawson
1962 to 1974 (14 appearances)

Youngest Test player

Shaun Edwards was 18 years 135 days old when he made his Great Britain Test debut against France at Leeds on 1 March 1985. Born on 17 October 1966, he beat the previous record held by Roger Millward (born 16 September 1947) who was not quite 18 years 6 months old when he made his debut for Britain against France at Wigan on 5 March 1966. Five months earlier Millward was a non-playing substitute for the second Test against New Zealand.

Oldest Test player

Jeff Grayshon (born 4 March 1949), was 36 years 8 months when he played in his last Test for Britain, against New Zealand at Elland Road, Leeds, on 9 November 1985.

Record team changes

The record number of team changes made by the Great Britain selectors is 10. This has happened on three occasions — all against Australia — and in the first two cases resulted in unexpected victories.

In 1929, Britain crashed 31-8 to Australia in the first Test at Hull KR and retained only three players for the second Test at Leeds where they won 9-3.

After their biggest ever defeat of 50-12 in the 1963 second Test at Swinton, Britain dropped nine players and were forced to make another change when Vince Karalius was injured and replaced by Don Fox. Britain stopped Australia making a clean sweep of the series by winning 16-5 at Leeds in the last Test.

Following the 40-4 first Test defeat at Hull City's soccer ground in 1982, the selectors again made 10 changes, not including substitutes. The changes made little difference this time as Britain went down 27-6 in the second Test at Wigan.

Britain have never fielded the same team for three or more successive Tests.

GREAT BRITAIN REGISTER

The following is a record of the 570 players who have appeared for Great Britain in 251 Test and World Cup matches.

It does not include matches against France before 1957, the year they were given official Test match status.

Figures in brackets are the total of appearances, with the plus sign indicating substitute appearances, e.g. (7 + 3).

For matches against touring teams, the year given is for the first half of the season.

World Cup matches are in bold letters except when also classified as Test matches. Substitute appearances are in lower case letters.

A - Australia, F - France, NZ - New Zealand, P - Papua New Guinea.

ACKERLEY, A (2) Halifax: 1952 A; 1958 NZ
ADAMS, L (1) Leeds: 1932 A
ADAMS, M (11 + 2) Widnes: 1979 Aa, NZ3; 1980 NZ; 1984 A2a, NZ3, P
ARKWRIGHT, C (+ 2) St. Helens: 1985 nz2
ARKWRIGHT, J (6) Warrington: 1936 A2, NZ; 1937 A3
ARMITT, T (8) Swinton: 1933 A; 1936 A2, NZ2; 1937 A3
ASHBY, R (2) Liverpool: 1964 F; Wigan: 1965 F
ASHCROFT, E (11) Wigan: 1947 NZ2; 1950 A3, NZ; 1954 A3, NZ2
ASHCROFT, K (5 + 1) Leigh: **1968 A**; 1968 F; 1969 F; **1970 F,NZ**; Warrington: 1974 nz
ASHTON, A (26) Wigan: **1957 A,NZ**; 1958 A2,NZ2; 1959 F, A3; 1960 F2; **1960 NZ,A**; 1961 NZ3; 1962 F3,A3; 1963 F,A2
ASHURST, W (3) Wigan: 1971 NZ; 1972 F2
ASKIN, T (6) Featherstone R: 1928 A3,NZ3
ASPINALL, W (1) Warrington: 1966 NZ
ASTON, L (3) St. Helens: 1947 NZ3
ATKINSON, A (11) Castleford: 1929 A3; 1932 A3,NZ3; 1933 A; 1936 A
ATKINSON, J (26) Leeds: **1968 F,NZ**; 1970 A3,NZ3; **1970 A2,F,NZ**; 1971 F2,NZ; 1972 F2; **1972 A2,F,NZ**; 1973 A2; 1978 A2; 1980 NZ
AVERY, A (4) Oldham: 1910 A,NZ; 1911 A2

BACON, J (11) Leeds: 1920 A3,NZ3; 1921 A3; 1924 A; 1926 NZ
BARENDS, D (2) Bradford N: 1979 A2
BARTON, F (1) Wigan: 1951 NZ
BARTON, J (2) Wigan: 1960 F; 1961 NZ
BASNETT, J (2) Widnes: 1984 F; 1986 A
BASSETT, A (2) Halifax: 1946 A2
BATES, A (2 + 2) Dewsbury: 1974 F2,nz2
BATTEN, E (4) Bradford N: 1946 A2,NZ; 1947 NZ
BATTEN, R (3) Leeds: 1969 F; 1973 A2
BATTEN, W (10) Hunslet: 1907 NZ; 1908 A3; 1910 A2,NZ; 1911 A2; Hull: 1921 A
BAXTER, J (1) Rochdale H: 1907 NZ

BEAMES, J (2) Halifax: 1921 A2
BEARDMORE, K (10 + 1) Castleford: 1984 nz; 1987 F2; 1988 F2, P, A2, NZ; 1989 F2
BELSHAW, W (8) Liverpool S: 1936 A3,NZ2; 1937 A; Warrington: A2
BENNETT, J (7) Rochdale H: 1924 A3,NZ3; Wigan: 1926 NZ
BENTHAM, N (10) Wigan H: 1928 A3,NZ3; Halifax: 1929 A2; Warrington: 1929(cont) A2
BENTHAM, W (2) Broughton R: 1924 NZ2
BENTLEY, K (1) Widnes: 1980 NZ
BENYON, W (5 + 1) St. Helens: 1971 F2,NZ,nz; 1972 F2
BEVAN, D (1) Wigan: 1952 A
BEVAN, J (6) Warrington: 1974 A2,NZ2; 1978 A2
BEVERLEY, H (6) Hunslet: 1936 A3; 1937 A; Halifax: A2
BIRCH, J (1) Leeds: 1907 NZ
BISHOP, T (15) St. Helens: 1966 A3,NZ2; 1967 A3; 1968 F3; **1968 A,F,NZ**; 1969 F
BLAN, W (3) Wigan: 1951 NZ3
BLINKHORN, T (1) Warrington: 1929 A
BOLTON, D (23) Wigan: 1957 F3; 1958 F,A2; 1959 F,A3; 1960 F2; 1961 NZ3; 1962 F2,A,NZ2; 1963 F,A2
BOSTON, W (31) Wigan: 1954 A2,NZ3; 1955 NZ; 1956 A3; 1957 F5; **1957 F,A**; 1958 F; 1959 A; 1960 F; **1960 A**; 1961 F,NZ3; 1962 F2,A3,NZ; 1963 F
BOTT, C (1) Oldham: 1966 F
BOWDEN, J (3) Huddersfield: 1954 A2,NZ
BOWEN, F (3) St. Helens Rec: 1928 NZ3
BOWERS, J (1) Rochdale H: 1920 NZ
BOWMAN, E (4) Workington T: **1977 F, NZ, A2**
BOWMAN, H (8) Hull: 1924 NZ2; 1926 NZ2; 1928 A2,NZ; 1929 A
BOWMAN, K (3) Huddersfield: 1962 F; 1963 F,A
BOYLEN, F (1) Hull: 1908 A
BRADSHAW, T (6) Wigan: 1947 NZ2; 1950 A3,NZ
BRIDGES, K (3) Featherstone R: 1974 F2,A
BRIGGS, B (1) Huddersfield: 1954 NZ

BROGDEN, S (16) Huddersfield: 1929 A; 1932 A3, NZ3; 1933 A2; Leeds: 1936 A3,NZ2; 1937 A2
BROOKE, I (13) Bradford N: 1966 A3,NZ2; Wakefield: 1967 A3; 1968 F2; **1968 A,F,NZ**
BROOKS, E (3) Warrington: 1908 A3
BROUGH, A (2) Oldham: 1924 A,NZ
BROUGH, J (5) Leeds: 1928 A2,NZ2; 1936 A
BROWN, G (6) Leeds: **1954 F2,NZ,A**; 1955 NZ2
BRYANT, W (4+1) Castleford: 1964 F2; 1966 Aa; 1967 F
BUCKLEY, A (7) Swinton: 1963 A; 1964 F; 1965 NZ; 1966 F,A2,NZ
BURGESS, W (16) Barrow: 1924 A3,NZ3; 1926 NZ3: 1928 A3,NZ2; 1929 A2
BURGESS, W (14) Barrow: 1962 F; 1963 A; 1965 NZ2; 1966 F,A3,NZ2; 1967 F,A; 1968 F; Salford: 1969 F
BURGHAM, O (1) Halifax: 1911 A
BURKE, M (14+1) Widnes: 1980 NZ; 1981 fF; 1983 F; 1984 A3, NZ3, P; 1985 NZ3; 1986 F
BURNELL, A (3) Hunslet: 1951 NZ2; 1954 NZ
BURTON, C (8+1) Hull KR: 1982 A; 1984 A3, NZ2; 1985 nz; 1986 A; 1987 F
BURWELL, A (7+1) Hull KR: 1967 a; 1968 F3; **1968 A,F,NZ**; 1969 F
BUTTERS, F (2) Swinton: 1929 A2

CAIRNS, D (2) Barrow: 1984 F2
CAMILLERI, C (2) Barrow: 1980 NZ2
CARLTON, F (2) St. Helens: 1958 NZ; Wigan: 1962 NZ
CARR, C (7) Barrow: 1924 A2,NZ2; 1926 NZ3
CARTWRIGHT, J (7) Leigh: 1920 A,NZ3; 1921 A3
CASE, B (6+1) Wigan: 1984 A, NZ3; 1987 P; 1988 P, a
CASEY, L (12+2) Hull KR: **1977 f,nz,A**; 1978 A; Bradford N: 1979 A2,NZ3; Hull KR: 1980 NZ3; 1983 F2
CASTLE, F (4) Barrow: 1952 A3; 1954 A
CHALLINOR, J (3) Warrington: 1958 A,NZ; **1960 F**
CHARLTON, P (18+1) Workington T: 1965 NZ; Salford: **1970 nz**; 1972 F2; **1972 A2,F,NZ**; 1973 A3; 1974 F2,A3,NZ3
CHERRINGTON, N (1) Wigan: 1960 F
CHILCOTT, J (3) Huddersfield: 1914 A3
CHISNALL, D (2) Leigh: 1970 A; **1970 NZ**
CHISNALL, E (4) St. Helens: 1974 A2,NZ2
CLAMPITT, L (3) Broughton R: 1907 NZ; 1911 A; 1914 NZ
CLARK, D (11) Huddersfield: 1911 A2; 1914 A3; 1920 A3,NZ3
CLARK, G (3) Hull KR: 1984 F2; 1985 F
CLARK, M (5) Leeds: 1968 F2; **1968 A,F,NZ**
CLARKE, C (7) Wigan: 1965 NZ; 1966 F,NZ; 1967 F; 1973 A3
CLAWSON, T (14) Featherstone R: 1962 F2; Leeds: **1972 A2,F**; Oldham: 1973 A3; 1974 F2,A2,NZ2
CLOSE, D (1) Huddersfield: 1967 F
COLDRICK, A (4) Wigan: 1914 A3,NZ

COLLIER, F (2) Wigan: 1963 A; Widnes: 1964 F
COULMAN, M (2+1) Salford: 1971 f,NZ2
COURTNEY, N (+1) Warrington: 1982 a
COVERDALE, R (4) Hull: **1954 F2,NZ,A**
CRACKNELL, R (2) Huddersfield: 1951 NZ2
CRANE, M (1) Hull: 1982 A
CREASSER, D (2+2) Leeds: 1985 F2; 1987 f; 1988 f
CROOKS, L (12+2) Hull: 1982 A2; 1984 f, A2; 1985 NZ, nz; 1986 F2, A3; 1987 F; Leeds: 1989 F
CROSTON, A (1) Castleford: 1937 A
CROWTHER, H (1) Hunslet: 1929 A
CUNLIFFE, J (4) Wigan: 1950 A,NZ; 1951 NZ; 1954 A
CUNLIFFE, W (11) Warrington: 1920 A,NZ2; 1921 A3; 1924 A3,NZ; 1926 NZ
CUNNIFFE, B (1) Castleford: 1937 A
CUNNINGHAM, E (1) St. Helens: 1978 NZ
CURRAN, G (6) Salford: 1946 A,NZ; 1947 NZ; 1948 A3
CURZON, E (1) Salford: 1910 A

DAGNALL, R (4) St.Helens: 1961 NZ2; 1964 F; 1965 F
DALGREEN, J (1) Fulham: 1982 A
DANBY, T (3) Salford: 1950 A2,NZ
DANIELS, A (3) Halifax: 1952 A2; 1955 NZ
DANNATT, A (2) Hull: 1985 F2
DARWELL, J (5) Leigh: 1924 A3,NZ2
DAVIES, A (20) Oldham: 1955 NZ; 1956 A3; **1957 F,A**; 1957 F2; 1958 F,A2,NZ2; 1959 F2,A; **1960 NZ,F,A**; 1960 F
DAVIES, E (3) Oldham: 1920 NZ3
DAVIES, J (2) Huddersfield: 1911 A2
DAVIES, W (1) Swinton: 1968 F
DAVIES, W.A (2) Leeds: 1914 A,NZ
DAVIES, W.J (1) Castleford: 1933 A
DAVIES, W.T (1) Halifax: 1911 A
DAVIES, W.T.H (3) Bradford N: 1946 NZ; 1947 NZ2
DAWSON, E (1) York: 1956 A
DICK, K (2) Leeds: 1980 NZ2
DICKENSON, G (1) Warrington: 1908 A
DICKINSON, R (2) Leeds: 1985 F2
DINGSDALE, W (3) Warrington: 1929 A2; 1933 A
DIVORTY, G (2) Hull: 1985 F2
DIXON, C (12+2) Halifax: 1968 F; Salford: 1969 F; 1971 NZ; **1972 F**; 1973 a2; 1974 F2,A3,NZ3
DIXON, M (2) Featherstone R: 1962 F; 1964 F
DIXON, P (3+3) Halifax: 1987 f; 1988 f, F, p, A2
DOCKAR, A (1) Hull KR: 1947 NZ
DONLAN, S (+2) Leigh: 1984 nz, p
DRAKE, J (1) Hull: 1960 F
DRAKE, W (1) Hull: 1962 F
DRUMMOND, D (24) Leigh: 1980 NZ2; 1981 F2; 1982 A3; 1983 F2; 1984 F, A3, NZ3, P; 1985 NZ3; 1986 F2; Warrington: 1987 P;1988 F
DUANE, R (3) Warrington: 1983 F2; 1984 F
DUTTON, R (6) Widnes: 1970 NZ2; **1970 A2,F,NZ**

DYL, L (11) Leeds: 1974 A2,NZ3; **1977 F,NZ,A2**; 1978 A; 1982 A
DYSON, F (1) Huddersfield: 1959 A

ECCLES, P (1) Halifax: 1907 NZ
ECCLES, R (1) Warrington: 1982 A
ECKERSLEY, D (2+2) St.Helens: 1973 Aa; 1974 Aa
EDGAR, B (11) Workington T: 1958 A,NZ; 1961 NZ; 1962 A3,NZ; 1965 NZ; 1966 A3
EDWARDS, A (7) Salford: 1936 A3,NZ2; 1937 A2
EDWARDS, D (3+2) Castleford: 1968 f; 1970 A; 1971 NZ2nz
EDWARDS, S (10+2) Wigan: 1985 F,nzNZ; 1986 a; 1987 F2, P; 1988 F2, P; 1989 F2
EGAN, J (14) Wigan: 1946 A3; 1947 NZ3; 1948 A3; 1950 A3,NZ2
ELLABY, A (13) St.Helens: 1928 A3,NZ2; 1929 A2; 1932 A3,NZ2; 1933 A
ELWELL, K (3) Widnes: **1977 A;** 1980 NZ2
ENGLAND, K (1+2) Castleford: 1987 fF; 1989 f
EVANS, B (10) Swinton: 1926 NZ; 1928 NZ; 1929 A; 1932 A2,NZ3; 1933 A2
EVANS, F (4) Swinton: 1924 A2,NZ2
EVANS, J (4) Hunslet: 1951 NZ; 1952 A3
EVANS, J (3) Swinton: 1926 NZ3
EVANS, R (4) Wigan: 1961 NZ2; 1962 F,NZ
EVANS, S (7+3) Featherstone R: 1979 Aa2,NZ3; 1980 NZnz; Hull: 1982 A2
EYRE, K (1) Hunslet: 1965 NZ
EYRES, R (+1) Widnes: 1989 f
FAIRBAIRN, G (17) Wigan: **1977 F,NZ,A2**; 1978 A3; 1979 A2,NZ3; 1980 NZ2; Hull KR: 1981 F; 1982 A2
FAIRBANK, K (+1) Bradford N: 1987 p
FAIRCLOUGH, L (6) St.Helens: 1926 NZ; 1928 A2,NZ2; 1929 A
FARRAR, V (1) Hull: 1978 A
FEATHERSTONE, J (6) Warrington: 1948 A; 1950 NZ2; 1952 A3
FEETHAM, J (8) Hull KR: 1929 A; Salford: 1932 A2,NZ2; 1933 A3
FIELD, H (3) York: 1936 A,NZ2
FIELD, N (1) Batley: 1963 A
FIELDHOUSE, J (7) Widnes: 1985 NZ3; 1986 F2, A; St.Helens: 1986 A
FIELDING, K (3) Salford: 1974 F2; **1977 F**
FILDES, A (15) St.Helens Recs: 1926 NZ2; 1928 A3,NZ3; 1929 A3; St.Helens 1932 A,NZ3
FISHER, A (11) Bradford N: 1970 A2,NZ3; **1970 A**; Leeds: **A;** 1971 F2; Bradford N: 1978 A2
FLANAGAN, P (14) Hull KR: 1962 F; 1963 F; 1966 A3,NZ; 1967 A3; 1968 F2; **1968 F,NZ**; 1970 A
FLANAGAN, T (4) Oldham: 1983 F2; 1984 NZ, P
FOGERTY, T (2+1) Halifax: 1966 nz; Wigan: 1967 F; Rochdale H: 1974 F
FORD, P (10) Wigan: 1985 F; Bradford N: 1987 P; 1988 F, P, A3, NZ; Leeds: 1989 F2

FORSTER, M (2) Warrington: 1987 F2
FOSTER, F (1) Hull KR: 1967 A
FOSTER, P (3) Leigh: 1955 NZ3
FOSTER, T (3) Bradford N: 1946 NZ; 1948 A2
FOX, Deryck (9) Featherstone R: 1985 F2, NZ3; 1986 F2, A2
FOX, Don (1) Featherstone R: 1963 A
FOX, N (29) Wakefield T: 1959 F,A2; 1960 F3; 1961 NZ2; 1962 F3,A3,NZ2; 1963 A2,F; 1964 F; 1965 F; 1966 F; 1967 F2,A; 1968 F3; 1969 F
FOY, D (3) Oldham: 1984 F, A; 1985 F
FRANCIS, R (1) Barrow: 1947 NZ
FRANCIS, W (4) Wigan: 1967 A; **1977 NZ,A2**
FRASER, E (16) Warrington: 1958 A3,NZ2; 1959 F2,A; 1960 F3; **1960 F,NZ**; 1961 F,NZ2
FRENCH, R (4) Widnes: 1968 F2; **1968 A,NZ**
FRODSHAM, A (3) St.Helens: 1928 NZ2; 1929 A

GABBITAS, B (1) Hunslet: 1959 F
GALLAGHER, F (12) Dewsbury: 1920 A3; 1921 A; Batley: 1924 A3,NZ3; 1926 NZ2
GANLEY, B (3) Oldham: 1957 F2; 1958 F
GARDINER, D (1) Wigan: 1965 NZ
GEE, K (17) Wigan: 1946 A3,NZ; 1947 NZ3; 1948 A3; 1950 A3,NZ2; 1951 NZ2
GEMMELL, R (3) Leeds: 1964 F; Hull: 1968 F; 1969 F
GIBSON, C (+1) Batley: 1985 f
GIFFORD, H (2) Barrow: 1908 A2
GILFEDDER, L (5) Warrington: 1962 A,NZ2,F; 1963 F
GILL, H (14+1) Wigan: 1981 F2; 1982 A; 1985 F; 1986 F, A3; 1987 F2; 1988 P, A2a, NZ
GILL, K (5+2) Salford: 1974 F2,A2,NZ; **1977 f,a**
GOODWAY, A (19) Oldham: 1983 F2; 1984 F, A3, NZ3, P; 1985 F; Wigan: 1985 NZ3; 1986 A3; 1987 F, P
GOODWIN, D (5) Barrow: 1957 F2; 1958 F,NZ2
GORE, J (1) Salford: 1926 NZ
GORLEY, L (4+1) Widnes: 1980 NZnz; 1981 F2; 1982 A
GORLEY, P (2+1) St.Helens: 1980 NZ; 1981 Ff
GOWERS, K (14) Swinton: 1962 F; 1963 F,A3; 1964 F2; 1965 NZ2; 1966 F2,A,NZ2
GRAY, S (5+3) Wigan: 1974 F2,A2a,NZ3
GRAYSHON, J (13) Bradford N: 1979 A2,NZ3; 1980 NZ2; 1981 F2; 1982 A2; Leeds: 1985 NZ2
GREENALL, D (6) St.Helens: 1951 NZ3; 1952 A2; 1954 NZ
GREENALL, J (1) St.Helens Rec: 1921 A
GREENOUGH, R (1) Warrington: **1960 NZ**
GREGORY, A (19+1) Widnes: 1981 F2; 1982 A; 1983 F2; 1984 a, NZ2, P; Warrington: 1986 A; Wigan: 1987 F, P; 1988 F, P, A3, NZ; 1989 F2
GREGORY, M (9) Warrington: 1987 F2; 1988 P, A3, NZ; 1989 F2
GRIBBIN, V (1) Whitehaven: 1985 F

GRONOW, B (7) Huddersfield: 1911 A2, 1920 A2, NZ3

GROVES, P (1) St. Helens: 1987 P

GRUNDY, J (12) Barrow: 1955 NZ3; 1956 A3; 1957 F3; **1957 F,A,NZ**

GUNNEY, G (11) Hunslet: 1954 NZ3; 1956 A; 1957 F3; **1957 F,NZ**; 1964 F; 1965 F

GWYNNE, T. E (3) Hull: 1928 A,NZ; 1929 A

GWYTHER, E (6) Belle Vue R: 1947 NZ2; 1950 A3; 1951 NZ

HAGGERTY, R (2) St. Helens: 1987 F2

HAIGH, R (5+1) Wakefield T: **1968 A,F**; Leeds: **1970 NZ,a**; 1971 F,NZ

HALL, D (2) Hull KR: 1984 F2

HALL, W (4) Oldham: 1914 A3,NZ

HALLAS, D (2) Leeds: 1961 F,NZ

HALMSHAW, A (1) Halifax: 1971 NZ

HALSALL, H (1) Swinton: 1929 A

HAMPSON, S (3+1) Wigan: 1987 P; 1988 F2; 1989 f

HANLEY, E (27+1) Bradford N: 1984 fF, A3, NZ3, P; 1985 F2; Wigan: 1985 NZ3; 1986 F, A; 1987 F2, P; 1988 F2, P, A3, NZ; 1989 F2

HARDISTY, A (12) Castleford: 1964 F3; 1965 F,NZ; 1966 A3,NZ; 1967 F2; 1970 A

HARE, I (1) Widnes: 1967 F

HARKIN, P (+1) Hull KR: 1985 f

HARRIS, T (25) Hull: 1954 NZ2; 1956 A3; 1957 F5; **1957 F,A**; 1958 A3,NZ,F; 1959 F2,A3; 1960 F2; **1960 NZ**

HARRISON, F (3) Leeds: 1911 A3

HARRISON, M (7) Hull: 1967 F2; 1971 NZ2; 1972 F2; 1973 A

HARTLEY, D (11) Hunslet: 1964 F2; Castleford: 1968 F; 1969 F; 1970 A2,NZ2; **1970 A2,F**

HARTLEY, S (3) Hull KR: 1980 NZ; 1981 F2

HELME, G (12) Warrington: 1948 A3; 1954 A3,NZ2; **1954 F2,A,NZ**

HEPWORTH, K (11) Castleford: 1967 F2; 1970 A3,NZ2; **1970 A2,F,NZ**

HERBERT, N (6) Workington T: 1961 NZ; 1962 F,A3,NZ

HERON, D (1+1) Leeds: 1982 aA

HESKETH, C (21+2) Salford: 1970 NZ; **1970 NZ,a**; 1971 Ff,NZ3; **1972 A2,F,NZ**; 1973 A3; 1974 F2,A3,NZ3

HICKS, M (1) St.Helens: 1965 NZ

HIGGINS, F (6) Widnes: 1950 A3,NZ2; 1951 NZ

HIGGINS, H (2) Widnes: 1937 A2

HIGSON, J (2) Hunslet: 1908 A2

HILL, C (1) Wigan: 1966 F

HILL, D (1) Wigan: 1971 F

HILTON, H (7) Oldham: 1920 A3,NZ3; 1921 A

HILTON, J (4) Wigan: 1950 A2,NZ2

HOBBS, D (9+1) Featherstone R: 1984 F2, Aa, NZ3, P; Oldham: 1987 F2

HODGSON, M (16) Swinton: 1929 A2; 1932 A3,NZ3; 1933 A3; 1936 A3,NZ; 1937 A

HOGAN, P (6+3) Barrow: **1977 F,NZ,A2**; 1978 a; Hull KR: 1979 Aa,NZ,nz

HOGG, A (1) Broughton R: 1907 NZ

HOLDEN, K (1) Warrington: 1963 A

HOLDER, W (1) Hull: 1907 NZ

HOLDING, N (4) St. Helens: 1984 A3, NZ

HOLDSTOCK, R (2) Hull KR: 1980 NZ2

HOLLAND, D (4) Oldham: 1914 A3,NZ

HOLLIDAY, W (9+1) Whitehaven: 1964 F; Hull KR: 1965 F,NZ3; 1966 Ff; 1967 A3

HOLLINDRAKE, T (1) Keighley: 1955 NZ

HOLMES, J (14+6) Leeds: 1971 NZ; 1972 F2; **1972 Aa,NZ**; **1977 F,NZ,Aa**; 1978 a3; 1979 A2a,NZ3; 1982 A

HORNE, W (8) Barrow: 1946 A3; 1947 NZ; 1948 A; 1952 A3

HORTON, W (14) Wakefield T: 1928 A3,NZ3; 1929 A; 1932 A3,NZ; 1933 A3

HOWLEY, T (6) Wigan: 1924 A3,NZ3

HUDDART, R (16) Whitehaven: 1958 A2,NZ2; St.Helens: 1959 A; 1961 NZ3; 1962 F2,A3,NZ2; 1963 A

HUDSON, B (8) Salford: 1932 NZ; 1933 A2; 1936 A,NZ2; 1937 A2

HUDSON, W (1) Wigan: 1948 A

HUGHES, E (8) Widnes: 1978 A; 1979 A3,NZ3; 1982 A

HULME, D (4+1) Widnes: 1988 p, A3, NZ

HULME, P (1+2) Widnes: 1988 Aa, nz

HURCOMBE, D (8) Wigan: 1920 A2,NZ; 1921 A; 1924 A2,NZ2

HYNES, S (12+1) Leeds: 1970 A2,NZ2nz; **1970 A2,F,NZ**; 1971 F; 1973 A3

IRVING, R (8+3) Oldham: 1967 F2,A3; 1970 a,NZ; 1971 NZ; 1972 f; **1972 NZ,a**

JACKSON, K (2) Oldham: 1957 F2

JACKSON, P (27) Barrow: 1954 A3,NZ3; **1954 F2,A,NZ**; 1955 NZ3; 1956 A3; **1957 F,NZ**; 1957 F5; 1958 F,A2,NZ

JAMES, N (1) Halifax: 1986 F

JARMAN, J W (2) Leeds: 1914 A2

JASIEWICZ, R (1) Bradford N: 1984 F

JEANES, D (8) Wakefield T: 1971 F,NZ2; 1972 F2; Leeds: **1972 A2,NZ**

JENKINS, B (12) Wigan: 1907 NZ3; 1908 A3; 1910 A,NZ; 1911 A2, 1914 A,NZ

JENKINS, D (1) Hunslet: 1929 A

JENKINS, D (1) Leeds: 1947 NZ

JENKINS, E (9) Salford: 1933 A; 1936 A3,NZ2; 1937 A3

JENKINSON, A (2) Hunslet: 1911 A2

JOHNSON, A (4) Widnes: 1914 A,NZ; 1920 A2

JOHNSON, A (6) Warrington: 1946 A2,NZ; 1947 NZ3

JOHNSON, C (1) Leigh: 1985 F

JOLLEY, J (3) Runcorn: 1907 NZ3

JONES, B (3) Wakefield T: 1964 F; 1965 F; 1966 F

JONES, B.L (15) Leeds: 1954 A3,NZ3; 1955 NZ3; 1957 F3; **1957 F,A,NZ**
JONES, D (2) Merthyr: 1907 NZ2
JONES, E (4) Rochdale H: 1920 A,NZ3
JONES, J (1) Barrow: 1946 NZ
JONES, K (2) Wigan: **1970 F,NZ**
JONES, L (1) St.Helens: 1971 NZ
JORDAN, G (2) Featherstone R: 1964 F; 1967 A
JOYNER, J (14+2) Castleford: 1978 A2; 1979 A3,NZ3; 1980 NZ3; 1983 F2; 1984 F, nz2
JUBB, K (2) Leeds: 1937 A2
JUKES, W (6) Hunslet: 1908 A3; 1910 A2,NZ

KARALIUS, A (4+1) St.Helens: 1971 NZ3; 1972 F; **1972 nz**
KARALIUS, V (12) St.Helens: 1958 A2,NZ2; 1959 F; **1960 NZ,F,A**; 1960 F; 1961 F; Widnes: 1963 A2
KEEGAN, A (9) Hull: 1966 A2; 1967 F2,A3; 1968 F; 1969 F
KELLY, K (4) St.Helens: 1972 F2; Warrington: 1980 NZ; 1982 A
KEMEL, G (2) Widnes: 1965 NZ2
KERSHAW, H (2) Wakefield T: 1910 A,NZ
KINNEAR, R (1) Wigan: 1929 A
KISS, N (1) Wigan: 1985 F
KITCHEN, F (2) Leigh: **1954 A,NZ**
KITCHIN, P (1) Whitehaven: 1965 NZ
KITCHING, J (1) Bradford N: 1946 A
KNAPMAN, E (1) Oldham: 1924 NZ
KNOWELDEN, B (1) Barrow: 1946 NZ

LAUGHTON, D (15) Wigan: 1970 A3,NZ2; **1970 A2,F,NZ**; 1971 F2; Widnes: 1973 A; 1974 F2; 1979 F
LAWRENSON, J (3) Wigan: 1948 A3
LAWS, D (1) Hull K.R: 1986 F
LEDGARD, J (11) Dewsbury: 1947 NZ2; Leigh: 1948 A; 1950 A2,NZ; 1951 NZ; **1954 F2,A,NZ**
LEDGER, B (2) St. Helens: 1985 F; 1986 A
LEWIS, G (1) Leigh: 1965 NZ
LEYTHAM, J (5) Wigan: 1907 NZ2; 1910 A2,NZ
LITTLE, S (10) Oldham: 1956 A; 1957 F5; **1957 F,A,NZ**; 1958 F
LLEWELLYN, T (2) Oldham: 1907 NZ2
LLOYD, R (1) Halifax: 1920 A
LOCKWOOD, B (8+1) Castleford: **1972 A2,F,NZ**; 1973 A2; 1974 F; Hull KR: 1978 A; 1979 nz
LOMAS, J (7) Salford: 1908 A2; 1910 A2,NZ; Oldham: 1911 A2
LONGSTAFF, F (2) Huddersfield: 1914 A,NZ
LONGWORTH, W (3) Oldham: 1908 A3
LOUGHLIN, P (7) St.Helens: 1988 F, P, A3, NZ; 1989 F
LOWE, J (1) Leeds: 1932 NZ
LOWE, P (12) Hull KR: 1970 NZ; 1972 F2; **1972 A2,F,NZ**; 1973 A3, 1978 A2

LOXTON, K (1) Huddersfield: 1971 NZ
LYDON, J (18+1) Widnes: 1983 F2; 1984 F, a, NZ2, P; 1985 NZ3; Wigan: 1986 F, A3; 1987 F2, P; 1989 F2

MANN, A (2) Bradford N: 1908 A2
MANTLE, J (13) St.Helens: 1966 F2,A3; 1967 A2; 1969 F; 1971 F2,NZ2; 1973 A
MARCHANT, A (3) Castleford: 1986 F, A2
MARTIN, W (1) Workington T: 1962 F
MARTYN, M (2) Leigh: 1958 A; 1959 A
McCORMICK, S (3) Belle Vue R: 1948 A2; St.Helens: A
McCUE, T (6) Widnes: 1936 A; 1937 A; 1946 A3,NZ
McINTYRE, L (1) Oldham: 1963 A
McKEATING, V (2) Workington T: 1951 NZ2
McKINNEY, T (11) Salford: 1951 NZ; 1952 A2; 1954 A3,NZ; Warrington: 1955 NZ3; St.Helens: **1957 NZ**
McTIGUE, B (25) Wigan: 1958 A2,NZ2; 1959 F2,A3; 1960 F2; **1960 NZ,F,A**; 1961 F,NZ3; 1962 F,A3,NZ2; 1963 F
MATHIAS, R (1) St.Helens: 1979 A
MEASURES, J (2) Widnes: 1963 A2
MEDLEY, P (3+1) Leeds: 1987 P; 1988 Ff, P
MIDDLETON, A (1) Salford: 1929 A
MILLER, J (1) Wigan: 1911 A
MILLER, J (6) Warrington: 1933 A3; 1936 A,NZ2
MILLS, J (6) Widnes: 1974 A2,NZ; 1978 A2; 1979 A
MILLWARD, R (28+1) Castleford: 1966 F; Hull KR: 1967 A3; 1968 F2; **1968 A,F,NZ**; 1970 A2,NZ3; 1971 F,NZ3; 1973 A; 1974 A2a; **1977 F,NZ,A2**; 1978 A3
MILNES, A (2) Halifax: 1920 A2
MOONEY, W (2) Leigh: 1924 NZ2
MOORHOUSE, S (2) Huddersfield: 1914 A,NZ
MORGAN, A (4) Featherstone R: 1968 F2; **1968 F,NZ**
MORGAN, E (2) Hull: 1921 A2
MORGAN, R (2) Swinton: 1963 F,A
MORLEY, J (2) Wigan: 1936 A; 1937 A
MORTIMER, F (2) Wakefield T: 1956 A2
MOSES, G (9) St.Helens: 1955 NZ2; 1956 A; 1957 F3; **1957 F,A,NZ**
MUMBY, K (11) Bradford N: 1982 A; 1983 F; 1984 F2, A3, NZ3, P
MURPHY, A (27) St.Helens: 1958 A3,NZ; 1959 F2,A; **1960 NZ,F,A**; 1960 F; 1961 F,NZ3; 1962 F,A3; 1963 A2; 1964 F; 1965 F,NZ; 1966 F2; Warrington: 1971 NZ
MURPHY, H (1) Wakefield T: 1950 A
MYLER, A (14) Widnes: 1983 F2; 1984 A2, NZ2, P; 1985 NZ2; 1986 F2, A3
MYLER, F (23+1) Widnes: **1960 NZ,F,A**; 1960 F; 1961 F; 1962 F; 1963 A; 1964 F; 1965 F,NZ; 1966 A,NZnz; 1967 F2; St.Helens: 1970 A3,NZ3; **1970 A2,F**

NASH, S (24) Featherstone R: 1971 F,NZ; 1972 F2;
1972 A2,F,NZ; 1973 A2; 1974 A3,NZ3; Salford:
1977 F,NZ,A2; 1978 A3; 1982 A
NAUGHTON, A (2) Warrington: **1954 F2**
NEWBOULD, H (1) Wakefield T: 1910 A
NICHOLLS, G (29) Widnes: 1971 NZ; 1972 F2;
1972 A2,F,NZ; St.Helens: 1973 A2; 1974
F2,A3,NZ3; **1977 F,NZ,A**; 1978 A3; 1979
A3,NZ3
NICHOLSON, R (3) Huddersfield: 1946 NZ;
1948 A2
NOBLE, B (11) Bradford N: 1982 A; 1983 F2; 1984
F, A3, NZ3, P
NORTON, S (11 + 1) Castleford: 1974 a,NZ2; Hull:
1978 A3; 1979 A2; 1980 NZ; 1981 F2; 1982 A

OFFIAH, M (7) Widnes: 1988 F, A3, NZ; 1989 F2
O'GRADY, T (6) Oldham: 1954 A2,NZ3;
Warrington: 1961 NZ
OLIVER, J (4) Batley: 1928 A3,NZ
O'NEILL, D (2 + 1) Widnes: 1971 nz; **1972 A,F**
O'NEILL, M (3) Widnes: 1982 A; 1983 F2
OSTER, J (1) Oldham: 1929 A
OWEN, J (1) St.Helens Recs: 1921 A
OWEN, S (1) Leigh: 1958 F
OWENS, I (4) Leeds: 1946 A3,NZ

PADBURY, R (1) Runcorn: 1908 A
PALIN, H (2) Warrington: 1947 NZ2
PARKER, D (2) Oldham: 1964 F2
PARKIN, J (17) Wakefield T: 1920 A2,NZ3; 1921
A2;1924 A3,NZ; 1926 NZ2; 1928 A,NZ; 1929 A2
PARR, K (1) Warrington: 1968 F
PAWSEY, C (7) Leigh: 1952 A3; 1954 A2,NZ2
PEPPERELL, A (2) Workington T: 1950 NZ; 1951
NZ
PHILLIPS, D (4) Oldham: 1946 A3, Belle Vue R:
1950 A
PIMBLETT, A (3) Warrington: 1948 A3
PINNER, H (6 + 1) St.Helens: 1980 nzNZ; 1985
NZ3; 1986 F; Widnes: 1986 A
PITCHFORD, F (2) Oldham: 1958 NZ; 1962 F
PITCHFORD, S (4) Leeds: **1977 F,NZ,A2**
PLANGE, D (1) Castleford: 1988 F
PLATT, A (4 + 3) St. Helens: 1985 f; 1986 fa;
1988 F2, A2
POLLARD, C (1) Wakefield T: 1924 NZ
POLLARD, E (2) Wakefield T: 1932 A2
POLLARD, R (1) Dewsbury: 1950 NZ
POOLE, H (3) Hull KR: 1964 F; Leeds: 1966 NZ2
POTTER, I (7 + 1) Wigan: 1985 NZ3; 1986 F2, A2a
POWELL, R (7 + 2) Leeds: 1985 f; 1988 F2, A2a,
NZ; 1989 F2
POYNTON, H (3) Wakefield T: 1962 A2,NZ
PRESCOTT, A (28) St.Helens: 1951 NZ2; 1952 A3;
1954 A3,NZ3; 1955 NZ3; 1956 A3; 1957 F5;
1957 F,A,NZ; 1958 F,A2

PRICE, J (6) Broughton R: 1921 A2; Wigan: 1924
A2,NZ2
PRICE, M (2) Rochdale H: 1967 A2
PRICE, R (9) Warrington: 1954 A,NZ2; 1955 NZ;
1956 A3; 1957 F2
PRICE, T (1) Bradford N: 1970 A
PRIOR, B (1) Hunslet: 1966 F
PROCTOR, W (+1) Hull: 1984 p
PROSSER, D (1) Leeds: 1937 A
PROSSER, S (1) Halifax: 1914 A

RAE, J (1) Bradford N: 1965 NZ
RAMSDALE, R (8) Wigan: 1910 A2; 1911 A2; 1914
A3,NZ
RAMSEY, W (7 + 1) Hunslet: 1965 NZ2; 1966
F,A2,NZ2; Bradford N; 1974 nz
RATCLIFFE, G (3) Wigan: 1947 NZ; 1950 A2
RATHBONE, A (4 + 1) Bradford N: 1982 a; 1983 F2;
1985 F2
RAYNE, KEITH (4) Leeds: 1984 F2, A, P
RAYNE, KEVIN (1) Leeds: 1986 F
REDFEARN, A (1) Bradford N: 1979 A
REDFEARN, D (6 + 1) Bradford N: **1972 nz**; 1974
F2,A,NZ3
REES, D (1) Halifax: 1926 NZ
REES, T (1) Oldham: 1929 A
REES, W (1) Swinton: 1926 NZ2; 1928 A3,NZ3;
1929 A3
REILLY, M (9) Castleford: 1970 A3,NZ3; **1970 A2,F**
RENILSON, C (7 + 1) Halifax: 1965 NZ; 1967 a;
1968 F3; **1968 A,F,NZ**
RHODES, A (4) St.Helens: **1957 NZ**; **1960 F,A**;
1961 NZ
RICHARDS, M (2) Salford: 1974 A,NZ
RILEY, J (1) Halifax: 1910 A
RING, J (2) Wigan: 1924 A; 1926 NZ
RISMAN, A (17) Salford: 1932 A,NZ3; 1933 A3;
1936 A2,NZ2; 1937 A3; 1946 A3
RISMAN, B (5) Leeds: 1968 F2; **1968 A,F,NZ**
RIX, S (9) Oldham: 1924 A3,NZ3; 1926 NZ3
ROBERTS, K (10) Halifax: 1963 A; 1964 F2; 1965
F,NZ3; 1966 F,NZ2
ROBINSON, A (3) Halifax: 1907 NZ; 1908 A2
ROBINSON, Dave (13) Swinton: 1965 NZ; 1966
F2,A3,NZ2; 1967 F2,A2; Wigan: 1970 A
ROBINSON, Don (10) Wakefield T: **1954 F2,NZ,A**;
1955 NZ; Leeds: 1956 A2; 1959 A2; 1960 F
ROBINSON, J (2) Rochdale H: 1914 A2
ROBINSON, W (2) Leigh: 1963 F,A
ROGERS, J (7) Huddersfield: 1914 A; 1920 A3;
1921 A3
ROSE, D (4) Leeds: **1954 F2,A,NZ**
ROSE, P (2 + 3) Hull KR: 1974 a; 1978 Aa2; Hull:
1982 A
ROUND, G (8) Wakefield T: 1959 A; 1962
F2,A3,NZ2
RUDDICK, J (3) Broughton R: 1907 NZ2; 1910 A

RYAN, M (4) Wigan: 1947 NZ; 1948 A2; 1950 A
RYAN, R (5) Warrington: 1950 A,NZ2; 1951 NZ;
1952 A
RYDER, R (1) Warrington: 1952 A

SAYER, W (7) Wigan: 1961 NZ; 1962 F,A3,NZ;
1963 A
SCHOFIELD, D (1) Halifax: 1955 NZ
SCHOFIELD, G (19) Hull: 1984 F, A3, NZ; 1985
NZ3; 1986 F2, A3; 1987 F2; Leeds: 1988 F2,P,A
SEABOURNE, B (1) Leeds: 1970 NZ
SENIOR, K (2) Huddersfield: 1965 NZ; 1967 F
SHARROCK, J (4) Wigan: 1910 A2,NZ; 1911 A
SHAW, B (6) Hunslet: 1956 A2; **1960 F,A**; 1960 F;
Leeds: 1961 F
SHAW, G (1) Widnes: 1980 NZ
SHAW, J (5) Halifax: **1960 F,A**; 1960 F; 1961 F;
1962 NZ
SHELTON, G (7) Hunslet: 1964 F2; 1965 NZ3;
1966 F2
SHOEBOTTOM, M (10 + 2) Leeds: **1968 A,nz**; 1969
F; 1970 A2a,NZ; **1970 A2,F,NZ**; 1971 F
SHUGARS, F (1) Warrington: 1910 NZ
SILCOCK, N (12) Widnes: 1932 A2,NZ2; 1933 A3;
1936 A3; 1937 A2
SILCOCK, N (3) Wigan: 1954 A3
SILCOCK, R (1) Wigan: 1908 A
SIMMS, B (1) Leeds: 1962 F
SKELHORNE, G (7) Warrington: 1920 A,NZ3;
1921 A3
SKERRETT, T (10) Wakefield T: 1979 A2,NZ2;
Hull: 1980 NZ2; 1981 F2; 1982 A2
SLOMAN, R (5) Oldham: 1928 A3,NZ2
SMALES, T (8) Huddersfield: 1962 F; 1963 F,A;
1964 F2; Bradford N: 1965 NZ3
SMALL, P (1) Castleford: 1962 NZ
SMITH, A (6) Oldham: 1907 NZ3; 1908 A3
SMITH, A (10) Leeds: 1970 A2,NZ3; **1970 A2**; 1971
F2; 1973 A
SMITH, F (9) Hunslet: 1910 A,NZ; 1911 A3; 1914
A3,NZ
SMITH, G (3) York: 1963 A; 1964 F2
SMITH, H (2) Bradford N: 1926 NZ2
SMITH, M (10 + 1) Hull KR: 1979 NZ3; 1980 NZ2;
1981 F2; 1982 A2; 1984 f,NZ
SMITH, P (1 + 5) Featherstone R: **1977 a2**; 1982 A;
1983 f2; 1984 f
SMITH, S (11) Wakefield T: 1929 A; Leeds: A2;
1932 A3,NZ3; 1933 A2
SMITH, S (4) Hunslet: **1954 A,NZ,F2**
SOUTHWARD, I (11) Workington T: 1958 A3,NZ;
Oldham: 1959 F2,A2; 1960 F2; 1962 NZ
SPENCER, J (1) Salford: 1907 NZ
STACEY, J.C (1) Halifax: 1920 NZ
STEPHENS, G (5) Castleford: 1979 A2,NZ3
STEPHENSON, D (9 + 1) Wigan: 1982 A2; 1986 A;
1987 F, P; Leeds: 1988 f, P, A2, NZ

STEPHENSON, M (5 + 1) Dewsbury: 1971 nz; 1972
F; **1972 A2,F,NZ**
STEVENSON, J (19) Leeds: 1955 NZ3; 1956 A3;
1957 F5; **1957 F,A,NZ**; 1958 F; York: 1959 A2;
1960 F2
STOCKWELL, S (3) Leeds: 1920 A; 1921 A2
STONE, W (8) Hull: 1920 A3,NZ3; 1921 A2
STOPFORD, J (12) Swinton: 1961 F; 1963 F,A2;
1964 F2; 1965 F,NZ2; 1966 F2,A
STOTT, J (1) St.Helens: 1947 NZ
STREET, H (4) Dewsbury: 1950 A3,NZ
SULLIVAN, C (17) Hull: 1967 F; **1968 A,F,NZ**;
1970 A; 1971 NZ3; 1972 F2; **1972 A2,F,NZ**;
1973 A3
SULLIVAN, J (25) Wigan: 1924 A3,NZ; 1926 NZ3;
1928 A3,NZ3; 1929 A3; 1932 A3,NZ3; 1933 A3
SULLIVAN, M (46) Huddersfield: **1954 F2,NZ,A**;
1955 NZ3; 1956 A3; 1957 F3; **1957 F,A,NZ**;
Wigan: 1957 F2; 1958 F,A3,NZ2; 1959 F2,A3;
1960 F3; **1960 F,NZ,A**; St.Helens: 1961 F,NZ2;
1962 F3,A3,NZ; York: 1963 A
SZYMALA, E (1 + 1) Barrow: 1981 fF

TAIT, A (2) Widnes: 1989 F2
TAYLOR, H (3) Hull: 1907 NZ3
TAYLOR, R (2) Hull: 1921 A; 1926 NZ
TEMBEY, J (2) St.Helens: 1963 A; 1964 F
TERRY, A (11) St.Helens: 1958 A2; 1959 F2,A3;
1960 F; 1961 F,NZ; Leeds: 1962 F
THOMAS, A (4) Leeds: 1926 NZ2; 1929 A2
THOMAS, G (1) Warrington: 1907 NZ
THOMAS, G (9) Wigan: 1914 A; Huddersfield: 1920
A3,NZ2; 1921 A3
THOMAS, J (8) Wigan: 1907 NZ; 1908 A3; 1910
A2,NZ; 1911 A
THOMAS, L (1) Oldham: 1947 NZ
THOMAS, P (1) Leeds: 1907 NZ
THOMPSON, C (2) Hunslet: 1951 NZ2
THOMPSON, J (12) Leeds: 1924 A,NZ2; 1928
A,NZ; 1929 A; 1932 A3,NZ3
THOMPSON, J (20 + 1) Featherstone R: 1970
A2,NZ2; **1970 A2,F,NZ**; 1971 Ff; 1974 A3,NZ3;
1977 F,NZ,A2; Bradford N: 1978 A
THORLEY, J (4) Halifax: **1954 F2,NZ,A**
TOOHEY, E (3) Barrow: 1952 A3
TOPLISS, D (4) Wakefield T: 1973 A2; 1979 A;
Hull: 1982 A
TRAILL, K (8) Bradford N: 1950 NZ2; 1951 NZ;
1952 A3; 1954 A,NZ
TROUP, L A (2) Barrow: 1936 NZ2
TURNBULL, A (1) Leeds: 1951 NZ
TURNER, D (24) Oldham: 1956 A2; 1957 F5; **1957
F,A,NZ**; 1958 F; Wakefield: 1959 A; 1960 F3;
1960 NZ,A; 1961 F,NZ; 1962 A2,NZ2,F
TYSON, B (3) Hull KR: 1963 A; 1965 F; 1967 F
TYSON, G (4) Oldham: 1907 NZ; 1908 A3

VALENTINE, D (15) Huddersfield: 1948 A3; 1951 NZ; 1952 A2; 1954 A3,NZ2; **1954 F2,NZ,A**
VALENTINE, R (1) Huddersfield: 1967 A
VINES, D (3) Wakefield T: 1959 F2,A

WADDELL, H (5) Oldham: 1988 F2, A, NZ; Leeds: 1989 F
WAGSTAFF, H (12) Huddersfield: 1911 A2; 1914 A3,NZ; 1920 A2,NZ2; 1921 A2
WALKER, A (1) Whitehaven: 1980 NZ
WALLACE, J (1) St.Helens Recs: 1926 NZ
WALSH, Joe (1) Leigh: 1971 NZ
WALSH, John (4+1) St.Helens: 1972 f; **1972 A2,F,NZ**
WALTON, D (1) Castleford: 1965 F
WANE, S (2) Wigan: 1985 F; 1986 F
WARD, D (12) Leeds: **1977 F,NZ,A**; 1978 A; 1979 A3,NZ3;1981 F; 1982 A
WARD, Edward (3) Wigan: 1946 A2; 1947 NZ
WARD, Ernest (20) Bradford N: 1946 A3,NZ; 1947 NZ2; 1948 A3; 1950 A3,NZ2; 1951 NZ3; 1952 A3
WARD, J (4) Castleford: 1963 A; 1964 F2; Salford: 1970 NZ
WARD, K (14) Castleford: 1984 F; 1986 A3; 1987 P; 1988 F2, P, A3, NZ; 1989 F2
WARD, W (1) Leeds: 1910 A
WARLOW, J (6+1) St.Helens: 1964 F; **1968 f,NZ**; 1968 F; Widnes: 1971 F2,NZ
WARWICK, S (2) Salford: 1907 NZ2
WATKINS, D (2+4) Salford: 1971 f,NZ; 1973 a; 1974 f2,A
WATKINS, W (7) Salford: 1933 A; 1936 A2,NZ2; 1937 A2
WATKINSON, D (12+1) Hull KR: 1979 a; 1980 NZ; 1981 F; 1984 F; 1985 F, NZ3; 1986 F2, A3
WATSON, C (29+1) St.Helens: 1963 A2; 1966 F2,A3,NZ2; 1967 F,A3; 1968 F2; **1968 A,F,nz**; 1969 F; 1970 A3,NZ3; **1970 A2,F,NZ**; 1971 F
WATTS, B (5) York: **1954 F2,NZ,A**; 1955 NZ
WEBSTER, F (3) Leeds: 1910 A2,NZ
WHITCOMBE, F (2) Bradford N: 1946 A2
WHITE, L (7) Hunslet: 1932 A3,NZ2; 1933 A2
WHITE, L (6) York: 1946 A3,NZ; Wigan: 1947 NZ2
WHITE, T (1) Oldham: 1907 NZ
WHITEHEAD, D (3) Warrington: 1971 F2,NZ
WHITELEY, J (15) Hull: **1957 A**; 1958 A3,NZ; 1959 F2,A2; 1960 F; **1960 NZ,F**; 1961 NZ2; 1962 F
WILKINSON, J (13) Halifax: 1954 A,NZ2; 1955 NZ3; Wakefield T: 1959 A; 1960 F2; **1960 NZ,F,A**; 1962 NZ
WILLIAMS, F (2) Halifax: 1914 A2
WILLIAMS, P (1+1) Salford: 1989 fF
WILLIAMS, R (12) Leeds: 1948 A2; 1950 A2,NZ2; 1951 NZ3; Hunslet: 1951 NZ3
WILLIAMS, W (2) Salford: 1929 A; 1932 A
WILLICOMBE, D (3) Halifax: 1974 F; Wigan: F,NZ
WILSON, G (3) Workington T: 1951 NZ3

WILSON, H (3) Hunslet: 1907 NZ3
WINSLADE, C (1) Oldham: 1959 F
WINSTANLEY, W (5) Leigh: 1910 A,NZ; Wigan: 1911 A3
WOOD, A (4) Oldham: 1911 A2; 1914 A,NZ
WOODS, H (6) Liverpool S: 1936 A3,NZ2; Leeds: 1937 A
WOODS, J (1) Barrow: 1933 A
WOODS, J (7+4) Leigh: 1979 A3,nz; 1980 NZ; 1981 F2; 1982 Aa; 1983 f; Warrington: 1987 p
WOODS, T (2) Rochdale H: 1911 A2
WORRALL, M (3) Oldham: 1984 F, A2
WRIGHT, D (+1) Widnes: 1988 a
WRIGHT, J (1) Swinton: 1932 NZ
WRIGHT, S (7) Widnes: **1977 F,NZ,A2**; 1978 A3
WRIGLESWORTH, G (5) Leeds: 1965 NZ; 1966 A2,NZ2

YOUNG, C (5) Hull KR: 1967 A3; 1968 F2
YOUNG, F (1) Leeds: 1908 A
YOUNG, H (1) Huddersfield: 1929 A

Peter Williams, two appearances against the French in 1989.

GREAT BRITAIN TOUR SQUADS
Captains in bold

1910 Tour

J. Lomas (Salford)
A. Avery (Oldham)
J. Bartholomew (Huddersfield)
W. Batten (Hunslet)
F. Boylen (Hull)
E. Curzon (Salford)
J. Davies (Huddersfield)
F. Farrar (Hunslet)
T. Helm (Oldham)
B. Jenkins (Wigan)
T. Jenkins (Ebbw Vale)
W. Jukes (Hunslet)
H. Kershaw (Wakefield T.)
J. Leytham (Wigan)
T. Newbould (Wakefield T.)
R. Ramsdale (Wigan)
J. Riley (Halifax)
G. Ruddick (Broughton R.)
J. Sharrock (Wigan)
F. Shugars (Warrington)
F. Smith (Hunslet)
J. Thomas (Wigan)
W. Ward (Leeds)
F. Webster (Leeds)
W. Winstanley (Leigh)
F. Young (Leeds)

Managers: J. Clifford
(Huddersfield) and J.
Houghton (St. Helens)

1924 Tour

J. Parkin (Wakefield T.)
J. Bacon (Leeds)
J. Bennett (Rochdale H.)
W. Bentham (Broughton R.)
H. Bowman (Hull)
A. Brough (Oldham)
W. Burgess (Barrow)
C. Carr (Barrow)
W. Cunliffe (Warrington)
J. Darwell (Leigh)
F. Evans (Swinton)
F. Gallagher (Batley)
B. Gronow (Huddersfield)
T. Howley (Wigan)

1914 Tour

H. Wagstaff (Huddersfield)
J. Chilcott (Huddersfield)
J. Clampitt (Broughton R.)
D. Clark (Huddersfield)
A. Coldrick (Wigan)
W. Davies (Leeds)
A. Francis (Hull)
J. Guerin (Hunslet)
W. Hall (Oldham)
D. Holland (Oldham)
J. Jarman (Leeds)
B. Jenkins (Wigan)
A. Johnson (Widnes)
F. Longstaff (Huddersfield)
S. Moorhouse (Huddersfield)
J. O'Garra (Widnes)
W. Prosser (Halifax)
R. Ramsdale (Wigan)
J. Robinson (Rochdale H.)
J. Rogers (Huddersfield)
W. Roman (Rochdale H.)
J. Smales (Hunslet)
F. Smith (Hunslet)
G. Thomas (Wigan)
F. Williams (Halifax)
A. Wood (Oldham)

Managers: J. Clifford
(Huddersfield) and J.
Houghton (St. Helens)

D. Hurcombe (Wigan)
E. Knapman (Oldham)
W. Mooney (Leigh)
C. Pollard (Wakefield T.)
J. Price (Wigan)
D. Rees (Halifax)
J. Ring (Wigan)
S. Rix (Oldham)
R. Sloman (Oldham)
J. Sullivan (Wigan)
J. Thompson (Leeds)
S. Whitty (Hull)

Managers: J.H. Dannatt
(Hull) and E. Osborne
(Warrington)

1920 Tour

H. Wagstaff (Huddersfield)
J. Bacon (Leeds)
J. Bowers (Rochdale H.)
J. Cartwright (Leigh)
D. Clark (Huddersfield)
W. Cunliffe (Warrington)
E. Davies (Oldham)
J. Doyle (Barrow)
F. Gallagher (Dewsbury)
B. Gronow (Huddersfield)
H. Hilton (Oldham)
D. Hurcombe (Wigan)
A. Johnson (Widnes)
E. Jones (Rochdale H.)
R. Lloyd (Halifax)
A. Milnes (Halifax)
J. Parkin (Wakefield T.)
G. Rees (Leeds)
W. Reid (Widnes)
J. Rogers (Huddersfield)
G. Skelhorne (Warrington)
J. Stacey (Halifax)
S. Stockwell (Leeds)
W. Stone (Hull)
G. Thomas (Huddersfield)
A. Wood (Oldham)

Managers: S. Foster (Halifax)
and J. Wilson (Hull K.R.)

1928 Tour

J. Parkin (Wakefield T.)
T. Askin (Featherstone R.)
N. Bentham (Wigan Highfield)
F. Bowen (St. Helens Recs)
H. Bowman (Hull)
J. Brough (Leeds)
W. Burgess (Barrow)
O. Dolan (St. Helens Recs)
A. Ellaby (St. Helens)
B. Evans (Swinton)
J. Evans (Swinton)
L. Fairclough (St. Helens)
A. Fildes (St. Helens Recs)
A. Frodsham (St. Helens)

W. Gowers (Rochdale H.)
T. Gwynne (Hull)
B. Halfpenny (St. Helens)
W. Horton (Wakefield T.)
J. Oliver (Batley)
W. Rees (Swinton)
M. Rosser (Leeds)
R. Sloman (Oldham)
J. Sullivan (Wigan)
J. Thompson (Leeds)
W. Williams (Salford)
H. Young (Bradford N.)

Managers: G. Hutchins
(Oldham) and E. Osborne
(Warrington)

1932 Tour

J. Sullivan (Wigan)
A. Atkinson (Castleford)
L. Adams (Leeds)
S. Brogden (Huddersfield)
F. Butters (Swinton)
I. Davies (Halifax)
W. Dingsdale (Warrington)
A. Ellaby (St. Helens)
B. Evans (Swinton)
J. Feetham (Salford)
N. Fender (York)
A. Fildes (St. Helens)
M. Hodgson (Swinton)
W. Horton (Wakefield T.)
B. Hudson (Salford)
J. Lowe (Leeds)
E. Pollard (Wakefield T.)
A. Risman (Salford)
G. Robinson (Wakefield T.)
N. Silcock (Widnes)
S. Smith (Leeds)
J. Thompson (Leeds)
L. White (Hunslet)
W. Williams (Salford)
J. Woods (Barrow)
J. Wright (Swinton)

Managers: R. Anderton
(Warrington) and G. Hutchins
(Oldham)

1936 Tour

J. Brough (Leeds)
J. Arkwright (Warrington)
T. Armitt (Swinton)
A. Atkinson (Castleford)
W. Belshaw (Liverpool S.)
H. Beverley (Hunslet)
S. Brogden (Leeds)
E. Davies (Wigan)
A. Edwards (Salford)
H. Ellerington (Hull)
G. Exley (Wakefield T.)
H. Field (York)
F. Harris (Leeds)
M. Hodgson (Swinton)
B. Hudson (Salford)
E. Jenkins (Salford)
H. Jones (Keighley)
T. McCue (Widnes)
J. Miller (Warrington)
J. Morley (Wigan)
A. Risman (Salford)
N. Silcock (Widnes)
S. Smith (Leeds)
L. Troup (Barrow)
W. Watkins (Salford)
H. Woods (Liverpool S.)

Managers: R. Anderton
(Warrington) and
W. Popplewell (Bramley)

1946 Tour

A. Risman (Salford)
A. Bassett (Halifax)
E. Batten (Bradford N.)
G. Curran (Salford)
W. Davies (Bradford N.)
J. Egan (Wigan)
T. Foster (Bradford N.)
K. Gee (Wigan)
W. Horne (Barrow)
F. Hughes (Workington T.)
D. Jenkins (Leeds)
A. Johnson (Warrington)
J. Jones (Barrow)
J. Kitching (Bradford N.)

B. Knowelden (Barrow)
J. Lewthwaite (Barrow)
T. McCue (Widnes)
H. Murphy (Wakefield T.)
R. Nicholson (Huddersfield)
I. Owens (Leeds)
D. Phillips (Oldham)
M. Ryan (Wigan)
Edward Ward (Wigan)
Ernest Ward (Bradford N.)
F. Whitcombe (Bradford N.)
L. White (York)

Managers: W. Popplewell
(Bramley) and W. Gabbatt
(Barrow)

1950 Tour

E. Ward (Bradford N.)
E. Ashcroft (Wigan)
T. Bradshaw (Wigan)
J. Cunliffe (Wigan)
T. Danby (Salford)
A. Daniels (Halifax)
J. Egan (Wigan)
J. Featherstone (Warrington)
K. Gee (Wigan)
E. Gwyther (Belle Vue R.)
F. Higgins (Widnes)
J. Hilton (Wigan)
W. Horne (Barrow)
J. Ledgard (Leigh)
H. Murphy (Wakefield T.)
D. Naughton (Widnes)
F. Osmond (Swinton)
A. Pepperell (Workington T.)
D. Phillips (Belle Vue R.)
R. Pollard (Dewsbury)
G. Ratcliffe (Wigan)
M. Ryan (Wigan)
R. Ryan (Warrington)
H. Street (Dewsbury)
K. Traill (Bradford N.)
R. Williams (Leeds)

Managers: G. Oldroyd
(Dewsbury) and T. Spedding
(Belle Vue R.)

1954 Tour

R. Williams (Hunslet)
E. Ashcroft (Wigan)
W. Boston (Wigan)
J. Bowden (Huddersfield)
B. Briggs (Huddersfield)
A. Burnell (Hunslet)
E. Cahill (Rochdale H.)
F. Castle (Barrow)
J. Cunliffe (Wigan)
D. Greenall (St. Helens)
G. Gunney (Hunslet)
T. Harris (Hull)
G. Helme (Warrington)
J. Henderson (Workington T.)
P. Jackson (Barrow)
B. L. Jones (Leeds)
T. McKinney (Salford)
T. O'Grady (Oldham)
C. Pawsey (Leigh)
A. Prescott (St. Helens)
R. Price (Warrington)
N. Silcock (Wigan)
K. Traill (Bradford N.)
A. Turnbull (Leeds)
D. Valentine (Huddersfield)
J. Wilkinson (Halifax)

Managers: T. Hesketh
(Wigan) and H. Rawson
(Hunslet)

1958 Tour

A. Prescott (St. Helens)
A. Ackerley (Halifax)
H. Archer (Workington T.)
E. Ashton (Wigan)
D. Bolton (Wigan)
F. Carlton (St. Helens)
J. Challinor (Warrington)
A. Davies (Oldham)
B. Edgar (Workington T.)
E. Fraser (Warrington)
D. Goodwin (Barrow)
T. Harris (Hull)
R. Huddart (Whitehaven)
K. Jackson (Oldham)
P. Jackson (Barrow)
V. Karalius (St. Helens)

M. Martyn (Leigh)
B. McTigue (Wigan)
G. Moses (St. Helens)
A. Murphy (St. Helens)
F. Pitchford (Oldham)
I. Southward (Workington T.)
M. Sullivan (Wigan)
A. Terry (St. Helens)
J. Whiteley (Hull)
W. Wookey (Workington T.)

Managers: B. Manson
(Swinton) and T. Mitchell
(Workington T.)
Coach: J. Brough
(Workington T.)

1962 Tour

E. Ashton (Wigan)
D. Bolton (Wigan)
W. Boston (Wigan)
F. Carlton (Wigan)
G. Cooper (Featherstone R.)
B. Edgar (Workington T.)
R. Evans (Wigan)
N. Fox (Wakefield T.)
D. Fox (Featherstone R.)
E. Fraser (Warrington)
L. Gilfedder (Warrington)
N. Herbert (Workington T.)
R. Huddart (St. Helens)
B. McTigue (Wigan)
A. Murphy (St. Helens)
K. Noble (Huddersfield)
H. Poynton (Wakefield T.)
G. Round (Wakefield T.)
W. Sayer (Wigan)
J. Shaw (Halifax)
P. Small (Castleford)
I. Southward (Workington T.)
M. Sullivan (St. Helens)
J. Taylor (Hull K.R.)
D. Turner (Wakefield T.)
J. Wilkinson (Wakefield T.)

Managers: S. Hadfield
(Wakefield T.) and A. Walker
(Rochdale H.)
Coach: C. Hutton (Hull K.R.)

1966 Tour

H. Poole (Leeds)
W. Aspinall (Warrington)
T. Bishop (St. Helens)
I. Brooke (Bradford N.)
W. Bryant (Castleford)
A. Buckley (Swinton)
W. Burgess (Barrow)
C. Clarke (Wigan)
G. Crewdson (Keighley)
C. Dooler (Featherstone R.)
B. Edgar (Workington T.)
P. Flanagan (Hull K.R.)
T. Fogerty (Halifax)
K. Gowers (Swinton)
A. Hardisty (Castleford)
B. Jones (Wakefield T.)
A. Keegan (Hull)
J. Mantle (St. Helens)
F. Myler (Widnes)
W. Ramsey (Hunslet)
K. Roberts (Halifax)
D. Robinson (Swinton)
G. Shelton (Hunslet)
J. Stopford (Swinton)
C. Watson (St. Helens)
G. Wriglesworth (Leeds)

Managers: W. Spaven (Hull
K.R.) and J. Errock (Oldham)

1970 Tour

F. Myler (St. Helens)
J. Atkinson (Leeds)
D. Chisnall (Leigh)
R. Dutton (Widnes)
D. Edwards (Castleford)
A. Fisher (Bradford N.)
P. Flanagan (Hull K.R.)
A. Hardisty (Castleford)
D. Hartley (Castleford)
K. Hepworth (Castleford)
C. Hesketh (Salford)
S. Hynes (Leeds)
R. Irving (Oldham)
D. Laughton (Wigan)
P. Lowe (Hull K.R.)
R. Millward (Hull K.R.)
T. Price (Bradford N.)

M. Reilly (Castleford)
D. Robinson (Wigan)
B. Seabourne (Leeds)
M. Shoebottom (Leeds)
A. Smith (Leeds)
C. Sullivan (Hull)
J. Thompson (Featherstone R.)
J. Ward (Salford)
C. Watson (St. Helens)

Manager: J. Harding (Leigh)
Coach: J. Whiteley (Hull)

1974 Tour

C. Hesketh (Salford)
K. Ashcroft (Warrington)
J. Atkinson (Leeds)
A. Bates (Dewsbury)
J. Bates (Dewsbury)
J. Bevan (Warrington)
J. Bridges (Featherstone R.)
J. Butler (Rochdale H.)
P. Charlton (Salford)
E. Chisnall (St. Helens)
T. Clawson (Oldham)
C. Dixon (Salford)
L. Dyl (Leeds)
D. Eckersley (St. Helens)
K. Gill (Salford)
J. Gray (Wigan)
J. Mills (Widnes)
R. Millward (Hull K.R.)
S. Nash (Featherstone R.)
G. Nicholls (St. Helens)
S. Norton (Castleford)
D. Redfearn (Bradford N.)
P. Rose (Hull K.R.)
J. Thompson (Featherstone R.)
D. Watkins (Salford)
D. Willicombe (Wigan)

Replacements during tour
W. Ramsey (Bradford N.) for
J. Bates; M. Richards
(Salford) for Atkinson

Manager: R. Parker
(Blackpool B.)
Coach: J. Challinor
(St. Helens)

1979 Tour

D. Laughton (Widnes)
M. Adams (Widnes)
D. Barends (Bradford N.)
L. Casey (Bradford N.)
S. Evans (Featherstone R.)
P. Glynn (St. Helens)
J. Grayshon (Bradford N.)
P. Hogan (Hull K.R.)
J. Holmes (Leeds)
E. Hughes (Widnes)
M. James (St. Helens)
J. Joyner (Castleford)
G. Liptrot (St. Helens)
B. Lockwood (Hull K.R.)
T. Martyn (Warrington)
R. Mathias (St. Helens)
J. Mills (Widnes)
R. Millward (Hull K.R.)
K. Mumby (Bradford N.)
S. Nash (Salford)
G. Nicholls (St. Helens)
S. Norton (Hull)
A. Redfearn (Bradford N.)
T. Skerrett (Wakefield T.)
M. Smith (Hull K.R.)
G. Stephens (Castleford)
C. Stone (Hull)
D. Ward (Leeds)
D. Watkinson (Hull K.R.)
J. Woods (Leigh)

Replacements during tour
J. Burke (Wakefield T.) for
Mills; G. Fairbairn (Wigan)
for Martyn; D. Topliss
(Wakefield T.) for Millward

Managers: H. Womersley
(Bradford N.) and
R. Gemmell (Hull)
Coach E. Ashton (St. Helens)

1984 Tour

B. Noble (Bradford N.)
M. Adams (Widnes)
R. Ashton (Oldham)
K. Beardmore (Castleford)
M. Burke (Widnes)

C. Burton (Hull K.R.)
B. Case (Wigan)
G. Clark (Hull K.R.)
L. Crooks (Hull)
S. Donlan (Leigh)
D. Drummond (Leigh)
R. Duane (Warrington)
T. Flanagan (Oldham)
D. Foy (Oldham)
A. Goodway (Oldham)
A. Gregory (Widnes)
E. Hanley (Bradford N.)
D. Hobbs (Featherstone R.)
N. Holding (St. Helens)
J. Joyner (Castleford)
J. Lydon (Widnes)
K. Mumby (Bradford N.)
A. Myler (Widnes)
M. O'Neill (Widnes)
H. Pinner (St. Helens)
W. Proctor (Hull)
Keith Rayne (Leeds)
G. Schofield (Hull)
M. Smith (Hull K.R.)
M. Worrall (Oldham)

Replacement during tour
J. Basnett (Widnes) for Duane

Managers: R. Gemmell (Hull)
and R. Davis (RLHQ)
Coach: Frank Myler (Oldham)

1988 Tour

E. Hanley (Wigan)
K. Beardmore (Castleford)
B. Case (Wigan)
L. Crooks (Leeds)
P. Dixon (Halifax)
S. Edwards (Wigan)
K. Fairbank (Bradford N.)
M. Ford (Oldham)
P. Ford (Bradford N.)
C. Gibson (Leeds)
H. Gill (Wigan)
A. Gregory (Wigan)
M. Gregory (Warrington)
P. Groves (St. Helens)
R. Haggerty (St. Helens)
D. Hulme (Widnes)

P. Loughlin (St. Helens)
P. Medley (Leeds)
M. Offiah (Widnes)
A. Platt (St. Helens)
R. Powell (Leeds)
G. Schofield (Leeds)
D. Stephenson (Leeds)
H. Waddell (Oldham)

K. Ward (Castleford)
I. Wilkinson (Halifax)

Replacements during tour
D. Wright (Widnes) for
Edwards; A. Currier (Widnes)
and P. Hulme (Widnes) for
Schofield and Medley; R.

Eyres (Widnes) and J. Joyner
(Castleford) for Crooks, Dixon
and Platt

Managers: L. Bettinson
(Salford) and D. Howes
(RLHQ)
Coach: M. Reilly

GREAT BRITAIN IN THE WORLD CUP

A — Australia, Fr — France, GB — Great Britain, NZ — New Zealand

1954 in France   *Winners:* Great Britain

30 Oct.	Fr	22	NZ	13	Paris	13,240
31 Oct.	GB	28	A	13	Lyons	10,250
7 Nov.	GB	13	Fr	13	Toulouse	37,471
7 Nov.	A	34	NZ	15	Marseilles	20,000
11 Nov.	GB	26	NZ	6	Bordeaux	14,000
11 Nov.	A	5	Fr	15	Nantes	13,000

Play off

| 13 Nov. | GB | 16 | Fr | 12 | Paris | 30,368 |

Final Table

	P.	W.	D.	L.	F.	A.	Pts.
Great Britain	3	2	1	0	67	32	5
France	3	2	1	0	50	31	5
Australia	3	1	0	2	52	58	2
New Zealand	3	0	0	3	34	82	0

1957 in Australia   *Winners:* Australia

15 June	GB	23	Fr	5	Sydney	50,007
15 June	A	25	NZ	5	Brisbane	29,636
17 June	GB	6	A	31	Sydney	57,955
17 June	NZ	10	Fr	14	Brisbane	28,000
22 June	A	26	Fr	9	Sydney	35,158
25 June	GB	21	NZ	29	Sydney	14,263

Final Table

	P.	W.	D.	L.	F.	A.	Pts.
Australia	3	3	0	0	82	20	6
Great Britain	3	1	0	2	50	65	2
New Zealand	3	1	0	2	44	60	2
France	3	1	0	2	28	59	2

1960 in England   *Winners:* Great Britain

24 Sept.	GB	23	NZ	8	Bradford	20,577
24 Sept.	A	13	Fr	12	Wigan	20,278
1 Oct.	A	21	NZ	15	Leeds	10,773
1 Oct.	GB	33	Fr	7	Swinton	22,923
8 Oct.	A	3	GB	10	Bradford	32,773
8 Oct.	NZ	9	Fr	0	Wigan	2,876

Final Table

	P.	W.	D.	L.	F.	A.	Pts.
Great Britain	3	3	0	0	66	18	6
Australia	3	2	0	1	37	37	4
New Zealand	3	1	0	2	32	44	2
France	3	0	0	3	19	55	0

1968 in Australia   *Winners:* Australia
and New Zealand

25 May	A	25	GB	10	Sydney	62,256
25 May	Fr	15	NZ	10	Auckland	18,000
1 June	A	31	NZ	12	Brisbane	23,608
2 June	Fr	7	GB	2	Auckland	15,760
8 June	A	37	Fr	4	Brisbane	32,600
8 June	GB	38	NZ	14	Sydney	14,105

Final Table

	P.	W.	D.	L.	F.	A.	Pts.
Australia	3	3	0	0	93	26	6
France	3	2	0	1	26	49	4
Great Britain	3	1	0	2	50	46	2
New Zealand	3	0	0	3	36	84	0

Play off final

| 10 June | A | 20 | Fr | 2 | Sydney | 54,290 |

1970 in England   *Winners:* Australia

21 Oct.	A	47	NZ	11	Wigan	9,586
24 Oct.	GB	11	A	4	Leeds	15,084
25 Oct.	NZ	16	Fr	15	Hull	3,824
28 Oct.	GB	6	Fr	0	Castleford	8,958
31 Oct.	GB	27	NZ	17	Swinton	5,609
1 Nov.	Fr	17	A	15	Bradford	6,215

Final Table

	P.	W.	D.	L.	F.	A.	Pts.
Great Britain	3	3	0	0	44	21	6
Australia	3	1	0	2	66	39	2
France	3	1	0	2	32	37	2
New Zealand	3	1	0	2	44	89	2

Play off final

| 7 Nov. | A | 12 | GB | 7 | Leeds | 18,776 |

1972 in France   *Winners:* Great Britain

28 Oct.	Fr	20	NZ	9	Marseilles	20,748
29 Oct.	GB	27	A	21	Perpignan	6,324
1 Nov.	A	9	NZ	5	Paris	8,000
1 Nov.	GB	13	Fr	4	Grenoble	5,321
4 Nov.	GB	53	NZ	19	Pau	7,500
5 Nov.	A	31	Fr	9	Toulouse	10,332

Final Table

	P.	W.	D.	L.	F.	A.	Pts.
Great Britain	3	3	0	0	93	44	6
Australia	3	2	0	1	61	41	4
France	3	1	0	2	33	53	2
New Zealand	3	0	0	3	33	82	0

Play off final

| 11 Nov. | GB | 10 | A | 10 | Lyon | 4,231 |

No further score after extra-time so Great Britain took the championship because they had scored the greatest number of points in the qualifying League table.

1977 in Australia and New Zealand   *Winners:* Australia

29 May	A	27	NZ	12	Auckland	18,000
5 June	GB	23	Fr	4	Auckland	10,000
11 June	A	21	Fr	9	Sydney	13,231
12 June	GB	30	NZ	12	C'church	7,000
18 June	A	19	GB	5	Brisbane	27,000
19 June	NZ	28	Fr	20	Auckland	8,000

Final Table

	P.	W.	D.	L.	F.	A.	Pts.
Australia	3	3	0	0	67	26	6
Great Britain	3	2	0	1	58	35	4
New Zealand	3	1	0	2	52	77	2
France	3	0	0	3	33	72	0

Play off final

| 25 June | A | 13 | GB | 12 | Sydney | 24,457 |

● Details of the World Cup series staged between 1985 and 1988 are chronicled in the chapter World Cup.

GREAT BRITAIN WORLD CUP SQUADS

Captains in bold

1954 IN FRANCE

D. Valentine (Huddersfield)
W. Banks (Huddersfield)
H. Bradshaw (Huddersfield)
G. Brown (Leeds)
R. Coverdale (Hull)

Manager: G. Shaw (Castleford)

G. Helme (Warrington)
P. Jackson (Barrow)
F. Kitchen (Leigh)
J. Ledgard (Leigh)
A. Naughton (Warrington)
D. Robinson (Wakefield T)
D. Rose (Leeds)

R. Rylance (Huddersfield)
S. Smith (Hunslet)
M. Sullivan (Huddersfield)
J. Thorley (Halifax)
B. Watts (York)
J. Whiteley (Hull)

1957 IN AUSTRALIA

A. Prescott (St. Helens)
E. Ashton (Wigan)
W. Boston (Wigan)
A. Davies (Oldham)
J. Grundy (Barrow)

G. Gunney (Hunslet)
T. Harris (Hull)
P. Jackson (Barrow)
L. Jones (Leeds)
S. Little (Oldham)
T. McKinney (St. Helens)
G. Moses (St. Helens)

R. Price (Warrington)
A. Rhodes (St. Helens)
J. Stevenson (Leeds)
M. Sullivan (Huddersfield)
D. Turner (Oldham)
J. Whiteley (Hull)

Managers: W. Fallowfield (RL Secretary) and H. Rawson (Hunslet)

1960 IN ENGLAND

E. Ashton (Wigan)
W. Boston (Wigan)
J. Challinor (Warrington)
A. Davies (Oldham)
E. Fraser (Warrington)

R. Greenough (Warrington)
T. Harris (Hull)
V. Karalius (St. Helens)
B. McTigue (Wigan)
A. Murphy (St. Helens)
F. Myler (Widnes)
A. Rhodes (St. Helens)

B. Shaw (Hunslet)
J. Shaw (Halifax)
M. Sullivan (Wigan)
D. Turner (Wakefield T)
J. Whiteley (Hull)
J. Wilkinson (Wakefield T)

Manager: W. Fallowfield (RL Secretary)

1968 IN AUSTRALIA AND NEW ZEALAND

B. Risman (Leeds)
K. Ashcroft (Leigh)
J. Atkinson (Leeds)
T. Bishop (St. Helens)
I. Brooke (Wakefield T)
A. Burwell (Hull KR)
M. Clark (Leeds)

D. Edwards (Castleford)
P. Flanagan (Hull KR)
R. French (Widnes)
R. Haigh (Wakefield T)
R. Millward (Hull KR)
A. Morgan (Featherstone R)
C. Renilson (Halifax)

M. Shoebottom (Leeds)
C. Sullivan (Hull)
J. Warlow (St. Helens)
C. Watson (St. Helens)
C. Young (Hull KR)

Manager: W. Fallowfield (RL Secretary)   Coach: C. Hutton (Hull KR)

1970 IN ENGLAND

F. Myler (St. Helens)
K. Ashcroft (Leigh)
J. Atkinson (Leeds)
P. Charlton (Salford)
D. Chisnall (Leigh)
R. Dutton (Widnes)
A. Fisher (Bradford N & Leeds)

R. Haigh (Leeds)
D. Hartley (Castleford)
K. Hepworth (Castleford)
C. Hesketh (Salford)
S. Hynes (Leeds)
K. Jones (Wigan)
D. Laughton (Wigan)

M. Reilly (Castleford)
M. Shoebottom (Leeds)
A. Smith (Leeds)
J. Thompson (Featherstone R)
C. Watson (St. Helens)

Manager: J. Harding (Leigh)   Coach: J. Whiteley (Hull KR)

1972 IN FRANCE

C. Sullivan (Hull)
J. Atkinson (Leeds)
P. Charlton (Salford)
T. Clawson (Leeds)
C. Dixon (Salford)
C. Hesketh (Salford)
J. Holmes (Leeds)

R. Irving (Oldham)
D. Jeanes (Leeds)
A. Karalius (St. Helens)
B. Lockwood (Castleford)
P. Lowe (Hull KR)
S. Nash (Featherstone R)
G. Nicholls (Widnes)

D. O'Neill (Widnes)
D. Redfearn (Bradford N)
M. Stephenson (Dewsbury)
D. Topliss (Wakefield T)
John Walsh (St. Helens)

Manager: W. Spaven (Hull KR)　　　　　　Coach: J. Challinor (St. Helens)

1977 IN AUSTRALIA AND NEW ZEALAND

R. Millward (Hull KR)
E. Bowman (Workington T)
L. Casey (Hull KR)
L. Dyl (Leeds)
K. Elwell (Widnes)
G. Fairbairn (Wigan)
K. Fielding (Salford)

W. Francis (Wigan)
K. Gill (Salford)
A. Hodkinson (Rochdale H)
P. Hogan (Barrow)
J. Holmes (Leeds)
S. Lloyd (Castleford)
S. Nash (Salford)

G. Nicholls (St. Helens)
S. Pitchford (Leeds)
P. Smith (Featherstone R)
J. Thompson (Featherstone R)
D. Ward (Leeds)
S. Wright (Widnes)

Manager: R. Parker (Blackpool B)　　　　Coach: D. Watkins (Salford)

ALL TIME TOUR RECORDS

IN AUSTRALIA
Highest score: 101-0 v. South Australia in 1914

Biggest defeat: 42-6 v. New South Wales in 1920
(Also *widest margin*)

Fewest defeats: 1 (and 1 draw) from 21 matches in
1958 and from 17 matches in 1970

Most defeats: 9 from 22 matches in 1966

Biggest attendances: 70,419 v. New South Wales
(Sydney) in 1950

IN NEW ZEALAND
Highest score: 81-14 v. Bay of Plenty in 1962

Widest margin win: 72-3 v. Buller in 1928
　　　　　　　　　　 72-3 v. North Island in 1958

Biggest defeat: 46-13 v. Auckland in 1962 (Also *widest
margin)*

Fewest defeats: The tourists have won all their matches
in the following years: 1910 (4 matches), 1914 (6),
1932 (8), 1936 (8), 1966 (8), 1970 (7).

Most defeats: 4 from 8 matches in 1984

Biggest attendance: 35,000 v. Auckland in 1920

PLAYERS' FULL TOUR RECORDS
Most full appearances: 24 by Dick Huddart in 1958

Most tries: 38 by Mick Sullivan in 1958

Most goals and points: 127g, 278 pts by Lewis Jones in
1954

Most tours: 3 by　Jonathan Parkin (1920, 1924, 1928)
　　　　　　　　　　Jim Sullivan (1924, 1928, 1932)
　　　　　　　　　　Joe Thompson (1924, 1928, 1932)
　　　　　　　　　　Augustus Risman (1932, 1936, 1946)
　　　　　　　　　　Brian Edgar (1958, 1962, 1966)
　　　　　　　　　　Roger Millward (1970, 1974, 1979)
　　　　　　　　　　John Joyner (1979, 1984, 1988 as
　　　　　　　　　　replacement)

Biggest club representation: 8 by Wigan in 1950 —
Ernie Ashcroft, Tommy Bradshaw, Jack Cunliffe, Joe
Egan, Ken Gee, Jack Hilton, Gordon Ratcliffe, Martin
Ryan

Brothers touring together: Bryn and Jack Evans (1928),
Don and Neil Fox (1962), Alan and John Bates
(1974), David and Paul Hulme (1988, Paul as
replacement)

Hull's Under-21 debutant Richard Price
in action in Carpentras.

UNDER-21s

UNDER-21s

Great Britain Under-21s, with Wakefield Trinity's David Topliss in charge for the first time, gave widely differing displays in the home-and-away junior contest. Scrum half Roy Southernwood earned the Man of the Match award in the opening 30-0 trouncing of the French at Leeds, while virtually this same line-up gave an undisciplined display in the return encounter in Carpentras.

At Headingley, the Friday night fixture was dominated by Castleford half back Southernwood who had a hand or a boot in five of Britain's seven tries, including his own touchdown in the 57th minute, a classic piece of scrum half play from a close range scrum.

France included three 17-year-olds, the lack of size and experience often being exploited by the British Under-21s, virtually all regular first team panel members.

Providing four of the back division, Castleford's influence was exerted as early as the 11th minute when Southernwood instigated a move for Grant Anderson to send in centre partner Shaun Irwin. Four minutes later, Southernwood's high kick was well retrieved by Anderson who fed clubmate Giles Boothroyd to send over Wakefield Trinity second row man Gary Price for the second touchdown. A total French collapse was on the cards but the visitors rallied to curtail Britain to only one further first half score, a Dennis Betts try after 22 minutes as the Wigan back row forward strode in from Southernwood's long pass.

Only spirited French defence and Britain's poor goalkicking — Paul Newlove taking over from Betts — kept the score down in the second half as Newlove, Richard Price and then Gary Price touched down. Britain's only successful kick at goal came two minutes from the end, Newlove adding the goal to Gary Price's second try. Newlove and Betts each missed four goal kicks.

Apart from two brief skirmishes the match was kept well under control by the impressive French referee Alain Sablayrolles, who sent opposing number eights Ian Lucas and Jean-Claude Rodriguez to the sin bin in the 54th minute.

The same could not be said for the return fixture two weeks later, the Carpentras encounter being marred by a 30-second brawl. The all-in melée flared up after a scrum in the 30th minute and broke into several kicking, punching gangs spread over a wide area. There was a further four-minute delay while Widnes referee Dave Carter lectured both sets of players, although no one was dismissed.

Leigh prop forward Tim Street angered the French players and supporters with his over-robust style as Britain were unable to find the fluent form of a fortnight earlier.

The French, however, benefited from six changes to the side which started at Leeds, although again restricting themselves to Under-21 players, unlike previous years when they exceeded the limit. The Tricolours' support play was top class, producing three tries to Britain's one. Stand off Jean-Marc Garcia was outstanding, touching down twice and putting in half back partner Frederic Mas for the other.

Britain opened the scoring with a 21st minute penalty goal from Newlove, who ran strongly after switching from the wing to the centre following Shaun Irwin's 34th minute withdrawal through injury. Garcia's first try, Daniel Vergniol adding the goal, gave the home side a 6-2 interval lead.

Great Britain coach Malcolm Reilly visited the juniors' dressing room at the interval asking for concentration on football and his plea was rewarded with a 53rd minute try from Castleford's Kenny Hill, Newlove's goal putting the visitors ahead 8-6. But France finished more strongly and two further tries and a Vergniol goal gave them their third victory in the last four meetings.

Referee Carter sent opposing props Ian Lucas and Joel Roux to the sin bin in the second half in separate incidents.

344

20 January   **Leeds**

GREAT BRITAIN 30   FRANCE 0

Chris Bibb (Featherstone R.)	1.	Pascal Fages (Pia)
Giles Boothroyd (Castleford)	2.	Philippe Chiron (Carpentras)
Shaun Irwin (Castleford)	3.	Mohamed Amar (Avignon)
Grant Anderson (Castleford)	4.	David Despin (Villeneuve)
Paul Newlove (Featherstone R.)	5.	Ahmed Djebarni (Villeneuve)
Richard Price (Hull)	6.	Jean-Marc Garcia (St. Esteve),
Roy Southernwood (Castleford)	7.	Christopher Delbert (Villeneuve)
Ian Lucas (Wigan)	8.	Jean-Claude Rodriguez (Carcassonne)
Martin Dermott (Wigan), Capt.	9	Charles Guidicelli (Albi)
Tim Street (Leigh)	10.	Djanel Louazani (Carpentras)
Dennis Betts (Wigan)	11.	Pierre Chamorin (St. Esteve)
Gary Price (Wakefield T.)	12.	Didier Cabestany (St. Esteve), Capt.
Ian Gildart (Wigan)	13.	Nicolas Iafratte (St. Gaudens)
Anthony Farrell (Huddersfield)	14.	Regis Ascencio (Carcassonne)
Neil Harmon (Warrington)	15.	Luc Durand (Avignon)

T: G. Price (2), Irwin, Betts,
Southernwood, Newlove
G: Newlove
Substitutions:
Harmon for Dermott (32 min.)
Farrell for Bibb (68 min.)
Manager: Harry Jepson
Coach: David Topliss

Substitutions:
Durand for Despin (Half-time)
Ascencio for Louazani (Half-time)
Half-time: 12-0

Referee: Alain Sablayrolles (France)
Attendance: 3,313

---

4 February   **Carpentras**

GREAT BRITAIN 8   FRANCE 16

Chris Bibb (Featherstone R.)	1.	Pascal Fages (Pia)
Anthony Farrell (Huddersfield)	2.	Philippe Chiron (Carpentras)
Shaun Irwin (Castleford)	3.	Daniel Vergniol (Villeneuve)
Grant Anderson (Castleford)	4.	David Despin (Villeneuve)
Paul Newlove (Featherstone R.)	5.	Nicolas Reyre (Avignon)
Richard Price (Hull)	6.	Jean-Marc Garcia (St. Esteve),
Roy Southernwood (Castleford), Capt.	7.	Frederic Mas (Avignon)
Ian Lucas (Wigan)	8.	Jean-Claude Rodriguez (Carcassonne)
Kenny Hill (Castleford)	9.	Charles Guidicelli (Carpentras)
Tim Street (Leigh)	10.	Joel Roux (Carpentras)
Dennis Betts (Wigan)	11.	Patrick Jammes (Limoux)
Gary Price (Wakefield T.)	12.	Didier Cabestany (St. Esteve), Capt.
Ian Gildart (Wigan)	13.	Michel Aubert (Le Pontet)
Steve Lay (Hunslet)	14.	Luc Durand (Avignon)
Neil Harmon (Warrington)	15.	Pierre Chamorin (St. Esteve)

T: Hill
G: Newlove (2)
Substitutions:
Lay for Irwin (34 min.)
Harmon for Street (71 min.)
Half-time: 2-6
Manager: H. Jepson; Coach: D. Topliss

T: Garcia (2), Mas
G: Vergniol (2)
Substitutions:
Chamorin for Rodriguez (12 min.)
Durand for Jammes (55 min.)
Referee: Dave Carter (Widnes)
Attendance: 1,500

GREAT BRITAIN
UNDER-21s RESULTS

25 Nov.	1984	W 24-8	v. F	Castleford
16 Dec.	1984	W 8-2	v. F	Albi
9 Oct.	1985	L 12-16	v. NZ	Bradford
19 Jan.	1986	L 6-19	v. F	St. Esteve
2 Feb.	1986	W 6-2	v. F	Whitehaven
8 Mar.	1987	W 40-7	v. F	St. Jean de Luz
21 Mar.	1987	W 54-6	v. F	St. Helens
6 Mar.	1988	L 13-14	v. F	Ausillon
19 Mar.	1988	L 4-8	v. F	St. Helens
20 Jan.	1989	W 30-0	v. F	Leeds
4 Feb.	1989	L 8-16	v. F	Carpentras

Key: F - France,
NZ - New Zealand

Huddersfield's Anthony Farrell dumps Frenchman Pascal Fages onto the Carpentras pitch.

GREAT BRITAIN UNDER-21s
REGISTER

The following is a register of appearances for Great Britain Under-21s since this classification of match was introduced in 1984.

Figures in brackets are the total appearances, with the plus sign indicating substitute appearances, e.g. (3 + 1).

Away matches are in bold letters. Substitute appearances are in lower case letters.

ALLEN, S. (1) St. Helens: 1984 F
ANDERSON, G. (2) Castleford: 1989 F, **F**

BECKWITH, M. (1 + 1) Whitehaven: 1986 f, **F**
BETTS, D. (2) Wigan: 1989 F, **F**
BIBB, C. (5) Featherstone R.: 1987 **F**, F; 1988 F; 1989 F, **F**
BISHOP, P. (1 + 1) Warrington: 1987 **F**, f
BOOTHROYD G. (1) Castleford: 1989 F

CARBERT, B. (3) Warrington: 1985 NZ; 1986 F, **F**
CASSIDY, F. (1 + 1) Swinton: 1988 f, **F**
CLARK, G. (2) Hull K.R.: 1984 F, **F**
CONWAY, M. (1) Leeds: 1984 F
CREASSER, D. (5) Leeds: 1984 F, **F**; 1985 NZ; 1986 **F**, F
CROOKS, L. (2) Hull: 1984 F, **F**
CURRIER, A. (2) Widnes: 1984 F, **F**

DALTON, J. (3) Whitehaven: 1985 NZ; 1986 **F**, F
DANNATT, A. (6) Hull: 1984 F, **F**; 1985 NZ; 1986 **F**; 1987 F, F
DERMOTT, M. (5) Wigan: 1987 **F**, F; 1988 **F**, **F**; 1989 F
DISLEY, G. (+ 1) Salford: 1987 f
DIVORTY, G. (6) Hull: 1984 F; 1985 NZ; 1986 **F**, F; 1987 **F**, F

EASTWOOD, P. (2) Hull: 1987 **F**, F
EDWARDS, S. (4) Wigan: 1984 F; 1985 NZ; 1987 **F**, F

FARRELL, A. (1 + 1) Huddersfield: 1989 f, **F**
FLETCHER, M. (2) Hull K.R.: 1988 **F**, F
FORD, M. (3 + 1) Wigan: 1985 NZ; 1986 **F**; Leigh: 1987 f, F
FORSTER, M. (3) Warrington: 1985 NZ; 1986 **F**, F
FOX, D. (1) Featherstone R.: 1984 **F**

GILDART, I. (4) Wigan: 1988 **F**, **F**; 1989 **F**, **F**
GREGORY, M. (1) Warrington: 1984 **F**
GRIBBIN, V. (1+1) Whitehaven: 1984 f, **F**
GROVES, P. (3) Salford: 1984 F, **F**; 1985 NZ

HARCOMBE, K. (1) Rochdale H.: 1986 F
HARMON, N. (1+3) Warrington: 1988 f, **F**; 1989 f, f
HILL, B. (+1) Leeds: 1986 f
HILL, K. (3) Castleford: 1988 **F**, **F**; 1989 **F**
HUGHES, G. (1) Leigh: 1986 F
HULME, D. (2+1) Widnes: 1985 nz; 1986 **F**, **F**

IRWIN, S. (3) Castleford: 1988 **F**; 1989 F, **F**

JOHNSON, E. (2) Leeds: 1988 **F**, **F**

LAY, S. (+1) Hunslet: 1989 **f**
LORD, G. (1) Castleford: 1988 **F**
LOUGHLIN, P. (2) St. Helens: 1987 **F**, **F**
LUCAS, I. (4) Wigan: 1988 **F**, **F**; 1989 F, **F**
LYMAN, P. (3) Featherstone R.: 1985 NZ; 1986 **F**, **F**
LYON, D. (2) Widnes: 1985 NZ; 1986 **F**

McCORMACK, K. (2) St. Helens: 1987 **F**, **F**
MEDLEY, P. (2) Leeds: 1987 **F**, **F**
MOUNTAIN, D. (+1) Castleford: 1987 **f**

NEWLOVE, P. (2) Featherstone R: 1989 F, **F**

PARKER, W. (2) Hull K.R.: 1988 **F**, **F**
POWELL, R. (5) Leeds: 1984 F, **F**; 1985 NZ;
    1986 **F**, **F**
PRATT, R. (2) Leeds: 1988 **F**, **F**
PRICE, G. (2+1) Wakefield T.: 1988 **f**; 1989 F, **F**
PRICE, R. (2) Hull: 1989 F, **F**
PROCTOR, W. (+1) Hull: 1984 **f**
PUCKERING, N. (4) Hull: 1986 **F**, **F**; 1987 **F**, **F**

RIPPON, A. (1) Swinton: 1984 **F**
ROBINSON, S. (1) Halifax: 1988 **F**
ROUND, P. (1+1) St. Helens: 1984 F, **f**
RUSSELL, R. (1+1) Wigan: 1987 **F**; 1988 **f**

SAMPSON, D. (1) Castleford: 1988 **F**
SANDERSON, G. (4) Warrington: 1987 F, **F**;
    1988 **F**, **F**
SCHOFIELD, G. (2) Hull: 1984 **F**, **F**
SOUTHERNWOOD, R. (2) Castleford: 1989 F, **F**
STREET, T. (2) Leigh: 1989 F, **F**

WANE, S. (3) Wigan: 1984 **F**; 1985 NZ; 1986 **F**
WESTHEAD, J. (1+2) Leigh: 1985 nz; 1986 f, **F**
WRIGHT, D. (2) Widnes: 1987 **F**; 1988 **F**

GREAT BRITAIN UNDER-24s RESULTS

3 Apr. 1965	W 17-9	v. F	Toulouse
20 Oct. 1965	W 12-5	v. F	Oldham
26 Nov. 1966	L 4-7	v. F	Bayonne
17 Apr. 1969	W 42-2	v. F	Castleford
14 Nov. 1976	W 19-2	v. F	Hull K.R.
5 Dec. 1976	W 11-9	v. F	Albi
12 Nov. 1977	W 27-9	v. F	Hull
18 Dec. 1977	W 8-4	v. F	Tonneins
4 Oct. 1978	L 8-30	v. A	Hull K.R.
14 Jan. 1979	W 15-3	v. F	Limoux
24 Nov. 1979	W 14-2	v. F	Leigh
13 Jan. 1980	W 11-7	v. F	Carcassonne
5 Nov. 1980	L 14-18	v. NZ	Fulham
10 Jan. 1981	W 9-2	v. F	Villeneuve
16 Jan. 1982	W 19-16	v. F	Leeds
21 Feb. 1982	W 24-12	v. F	Tonneins
16 Jan. 1983	W 19-5	v. F	Carpentras
11 Nov. 1983	W 28-23	v. F	Villeneuve
4 Dec. 1983	W 48-1	v. F	Oldham

GREAT BRITAIN UNDER-24s REGISTER
Since reintroduction in 1976 to 1984

The following is a register of appearances for Great Britain Under-24s since this classification of match was reintroduced in 1976, until it was replaced by the new Under-21 level in 1984.

Figures in brackets are the total appearances, with the plus sign indicating substitute appearances, e.g. (7+3).

Away matches are in bold letters. Substitute appearances are in lower case letters.

ARKWRIGHT, C. (1) St. Helens: 1982 F
ASHTON, R. (3) Oldham: 1983 **F**, **F**, F

BANKS, B. (1) York: 1979 **F**
BELL, K. (2) Featherstone R.: 1977 F, **F**
BENTLEY, K. (+1) Widnes: 1980 nz
BURKE, M. (5) Widnes: 1979 F; 1980 **F**, NZ;
    1982 F; 1983 **F**
BURTON, B. (2) Castleford: 1976 F, **F**

CAIRNS, D. (2) Barrow: 1979 F; 1982 **F**
CASE, B. (3+1) Warrington: 1979 **F**; 1980 NZ: 1981 **F**; 1982 f
CLARK, G. (3) Hull K.R.: 1983 **F, F,** F
CRAMPTON, J. (4) Hull: 1976 F, **F**; 1977 F, **F**
CROOKS, L. (1) Hull: 1983 F

DICKINSON, R. (5) Leeds: 1976 F, **F**; 1977 F, **F**; 1978 A
DRUMMOND, D. (5) Leigh: 1979 F; 1980 **F**; 1981 **F**; 1982 F, **F**
DUANE, R. (2) Warrington: 1983 **F, F**
DUNN, B. (2) Wigan: 1983 **F,** F

ECCLES, R. (2) Warrington: 1978 A; 1979 F
ENGLAND, K. (+1) Castleford: 1983 f
EVANS, S. (3) Featherstone R.: 1980 NZ; 1981 **F**; Hull: 1982 **F**

FENNELL, D. (1) Featherstone R.: 1978 A
FENTON, S. (6) Castleford: 1977 F, **F**; 1979 **F**; 1980 **F**, NZ; 1981 **F**
FIELDHOUSE, J. (1+1) Warrington: 1983 **F,** f
FLANAGAN, T. (5) Oldham: 1980 NZ; 1981 **F**; 1983 **F, F,** F
FORD, Phil (1) Warrington: 1982 **F**
FOX, V. (1) Whitehaven: 1980 NZ
FOY, D. (2) Oldham: 1983 **F,** F

GIBBINS, M. (2) Featherstone R.: 1977 F, **F**
GILBERT, J. (2+1) Featherstone R.: 1977 F; 1977 f; 1981 **F**
GILL, H. (1) Wigan: 1982 F
GOODWAY, A. (2) Oldham: 1983 **F,** F
GREGORY, A. (1) Widnes: 1982 F

HALL, D. (+1) Hull K.R.: 1976 f
HANLEY, E. (2) Bradford N.: 1982 F; 1983 F
HARKIN, P. (1) Hull K.R.: 1981 **F**
HARTLEY, I. (1) Workington T.: 1979 **F**
HOBBS, D. (2) Featherstone R.: 1982 F, **F**
HOGAN, P. (2) Barrow: 1978 A; Hull K.R.: 1979 **F**
HOLDING, N. (4) St. Helens: 1979 **F**; 1980 **F**, NZ; 1983 **F**
HOLDSTOCK, R. (3) Hull K.R.: 1978 A; 1979 F; 1980 **F**
HORNBY, J. (2) Wigan: 1978 A; 1979 **F**
HYDE, G. (1+1) Castleford: 1980 NZ; 1982 f

JAMES, K. (1) Bramley: 1980 **F**
JOHNSON, B. (2) Castleford: 1982 F, **F**
JOYNER, J. (4+1) Castleford: 1976 f; 1977 F, **F**; 1978 A; 1979 **F**

LEDGER, B. (2) St. Helens: 1983 **F,** F
LIPTROT, G. (4) St. Helens: 1977 F, **F**; 1978 A; 1979 **F**
LYDON, J. (3) Widnes: 1983 **F, F,** F

MASKILL, C. (1) Wakefield T.: 1983 **F**
MOLL, D. (1) Keighley: 1983 **F**
MUMBY, K. (6) Bradford N.: 1976 F, **F**; 1977 F, **F**; 1978 A; 1981 **F**
MUSCROFT, P. (3) New Hunslet: 1976 F, **F**; 1978 A
MYLER, A. (3) Widnes: 1982 **F**; 1983 **F,** F
MYLER, J. (1+1) Widnes: 1982 f; **F**

NOBLE, B. (4) Bradford N.: 1982 F, **F**; 1983 **F,** F
NULTY, J. (2) Wigan: 1976 F, **F**

O'NEILL, M. (3+2) Widnes: 1980 nz; 1982 F, f; 1983 **F,** F
O'NEILL, P. (3) Salford: 1980 **F**, NZ; 1981 **F**
O'NEILL, S. (2) Wigan: 1979 **F**; 1981 **F**

PINNER, H. (4+4) St. Helens: 1976 F, **F**; 1977 f, f; 1978 a; 1979 f, **F**; 1980 **F**
POTTER, I. (4) Warrington: 1979 **F**; 1981 **F**; Leigh: 1982 F, **F**
PROCTOR, W. (1) Hull: 1983 **F**

RATHBONE, A. (+1) Leigh: 1979 f
RAYNE, Keith (2) Wakefield T.: 1979 F; 1980 **F**
RICHARDSON, T. (1) Castleford: 1979 F
ROE, P. (4) Bradford N.: 1976 F, **F**; 1977 F, **F**
RUDD, I. (1+1) Workington T.: 1979 f; 1980 **F**

SCHOFIELD, G. (+2) Hull: 1983 f, f
SHEPHERD, M. (2) Huddersfield: 1977 F, **F**
SKERRETT, T. (1) Wakefield T.: 1977 F
SMITH, D. (2) Leeds: 1976 F, **F**
SMITH, Malcolm (1) Wigan: 1979 F
SMITH, Mike (7) Hull K.R.: 1976 F, **F**; 1977 **F**; 1978 A; 1979 **F**, F; 1980 **F**
SMITH, P. (1) Featherstone R.: 1978 A
SMITH, R. (+1) Salford: 1983 f
STEPHENSON, D. (5) Salford: 1979 F; 1980 **F**, NZ; 1982 F; Wigan: 1982 **F**
SWANN, M. (1) Leigh: 1979 F
SYZMALA, E. (2) Barrow: 1976 F, **F**

THACKRAY, R. (1) Warrington: 1980 NZ
TIMSON, A. (2) Castleford: 1982 F, **F**
TURNBULL, S. (2) Salford: 1976 F, **F**

VAN BELLEN, G. (2) Bradford N.: 1980 NZ; 1982 **F**

WARD, D. (+2) Leeds: 1976 f, f
WARD, K. (3) Castleford: 1980 **F**, NZ; 1981 **F**
WHITFIELD, C. (1) Salford: 1981 **F**
WILKINSON, A. (1) Leigh: 1977 F
WOOD, J. (2) Widnes: 1977 F, **F**
WOODS, J. (5) Leigh: 1977 F, **F**; 1978 A; 1979 **F,** F
WORRALL, M. (3) Oldham: 1983 **F, F,** F

England prop Jeff Grayshon off-loads despite the attentions of Wales debutant Paul Ringer in the Anglo-Welsh clash in Cardiff in 1981.

ENGLAND AND WALES

ENGLAND & WALES

The following is a register of England and Wales appearances since the reintroduction of European and World Championship matches in 1975, but does not include England's challenge match against Australia played after the 1975 World Championship.

Figures in brackets are the total appearances since 1975, with the plus sign indicating substitute appearances, e.g. (7 + 3).

A few players also played in the 1969-70 European Championship and this is shown as an additional total outside bracket, e.g. (11)2.

World Championship matches are in bold letters. Substitute appearances are in lower case letters.

A - Australia, E - England, F - France, NZ - New Zealand, W - Wales.

ENGLAND REGISTER
Since reintroduction in 1975

ADAMS, M. (3 + 2) Widnes: 1975 **NZ**, a; 1978 F; 1979 W; 1981 w
ARKWRIGHT, C. (+1) St. Helens: 1984 w
ATKINSON, J. (7) 4 Leeds: 1975 W, **F, W, NZ, W**; 1978 F, W

BANKS, B. (+1) York: 1979 f
BEARDMORE, K. (1) Castleford: 1984 W
BEVERLEY, H. (1) Workington T: 1979 W
BRIDGES, K. (7) Featherstone R: 1975 **NZ, A, W, F, NZ, A**; 1977 W
BURKE, M. (1) Widnes: 1984 W

CAIRNS, D. (1) Barrow: 1984 W
CASE, B. (1) Warrington: 1981 F
CASEY, L. (5) Hull K.R.: 1978 F, W; 1980 W; 1981 F, W
CHARLTON, P. (1) Salford: 1975 **F**
CHISNALL, D. (3 + 1) Warrington: 1975 w, **F, W, NZ**
CHISNALL, E. (3 + 1) St. Helens: 1975 F, **W, NZ**, a
CLARK, G. (1) Hull K.R.: 1984 W
COOKSON, P. (2) Leeds: 1975 **NZ, A**
COULMAN, M. (5) Salford: 1975 F, W, **W, A**; 1977 F
CUNNINGHAM, J. (2) Barrow: 1975 F, W

DONLAN, S. (1) Leigh: 1984 W
DRUMMOND, D. (5) Leigh: 1980 W, F; 1981 F, W; 1984 W
DUNN, G. (6) Hull K.R.: 1975 W, **A, F, NZ, A**; 1977 F
DYL, L. (12 + 1) Leeds: 1975 F, W, **F, W, NZ, A**, nz, A; 1977 W, F; 1978 F, W; 1981 W

ECKERSLEY, D. (+5) St. Helens: 1975 f, **w, f**; Widnes: 1977 w; 1978 w
ELWELL, K. (2) Widnes: 1978 F, W
EVANS, S. (3) Featherstone R: 1979 F; 1980 W, F

FAIRBAIRN, G. (15) Wigan: 1975 **W, NZ, A, W, F, NZ, A**; 1977 W, F; 1978 F; 1980 W, F; 1981 F, W; Hull K.R.: 1981 W

FARRAR, V. (1) Featherstone R: 1977 F
FENTON, S. (2) Castleford: 1981 F, W
FIELDING, K. (7) Salford: 1975 F, **F, W, NZ, A, W, F**
FORSYTH, C. (3) Bradford N: 1975 **W, F, NZ**

GILL, H. (1) Wigan: 1981 W
GILL, K. (9 + 2) Salford: 1975 W, **F, w, NZ**, a, **W, F, NZ, A**; 1977 W, F
GLYNN, P. (2) St. Helens: 1979 W, F
GOODWAY, A. (1) Oldham: 1984 W
GORLEY, L. (1 + 1) Workington T: 1977 W. Widnes: 1981 w
GORLEY, P. (2 + 1) St. Helens: 1980 W, f; 1981 W
GRAY, J. (3) Wigan: 1975 F, W, **F**
GRAYSHON, J. (9 + 1) Dewsbury: 1975 **W, F, NZ, A**; 1977 W. Bradford N: 1979 W, F; 1980 w, F; 1981 W

HANLEY, E. (1) Bradford N.: 1984 W
HARRISON, M. (2) Leeds: 1978 F, W
HOBBS, D. (1) Featherstone R.: 1984 W
HOGAN, B. (5) Wigan: 1975 **W, F, NZ, A**; 1977 W
HOGAN, P. (1) Hull K.R.: 1979 F
HOLDING, N. (1) St. Helens: 1980 W
HOLDSTOCK, R. (3) Hull K.R.: 1980 W, F; 1981 W
HOLMES, J. (5 + 2) Leeds: 1975 **W, F, NZ, A**; 1977 W, f; 1978 f
HUDDART, M. (1) Whitehaven: 1984 W
HUGHES, E. (8 + 1) Widnes: 1975 **W, F, NZ, a**; 1977 F; 1978 F, W; 1979 W, F
IRVING, R. (3) Wigan: 1975 **W, F, A**

JACKSON, P. (2) Bradford N.: 1975 W, **F**
JONES, L. (1) St. Helens: 1977 W
JOYNER, J. (4) Castleford: 1980 W, F; 1981 F, W
KELLY, A. (1) Hull K.R.: 1984 W
KELLY, K. (3) Warrington: 1979 W; 1981 F, W
LAUGHTON, D. (1) Widnes: 1977 W
LEDGER, B. (+1) St. Helens: 1984 w

LIPTROT, G. (2) St. Helens: 1979 W, F
LOCKWOOD, B. (2)+1 Hull K.R.: 1979 W, F
LOWE, P. (3)2 Hull K.R.: 1977 F; 1978 F; 1981 W

MARTYN, T. (4+1) Warrington: 1975 W, **F, w**; 1979 W, F
MILLINGTON, J. (2) Hull K.R.: 1975 F; 1981 W
MILLWARD, R. (13)3+1 Hull K.R.: 1975 F, W, **F, W, A, W, F, NZ, A**; 1977 W, F; 1978 F, W
MORGAN, M. (3+3) Wakefield T: 1975 f, W, f, **W, nz, A**
MUMBY, K. (2) Bradford N: 1979 W, F
MURPHY, M. (1) Oldham: 1975 F

NASH, S. (7) Featherstone R: 1975 **W, NZ, A.** Salford: 1978 F, W; 1981 W, W
NICHOLLS, G. (7+4) St. Helens: 1975 F, **F, W, NZ, A, w, nz, f**; 1977 f; 1978 F, W
NOONAN, D. (3) Warrington: 1975 W, **F, W**
NORTON, J. (11) Castleford: 1975 **W, NZ, A, W, F, NZ, A**; 1977 F. Hull: 1978 W; 1981 W, W

O'NEILL, S. (1) Wigan: 1981 F

PATTINSON, W. (1+1) Workington T: 1981 f, W
PHILBIN, B. (1) Warrington: 1975 **F**
PIMBLETT, G. (1) St. Helens: 1978 W
PINNER, H. (3) St. Helens: 1980 W, F; 1981 F
POTTER, I. (2) Warrington: 1981 F, W

RAYNE, Keith (2) Wakefield T: 1980 W, F

REDFEARN, A. (2) Bradford N: 1979 F; 1980 F
REDFEARN, D. (2) Bradford N: 1975 F, **A**
REILLY, M. (+1)2 Castleford: 1977 w
RICHARDSON, T. (1) Castleford: 1981 W
ROSE, P. (2) Hull K.R.: 1977 F; 1978 W

SCHOFIELD, G. (1) Hull: 1984 W
SHEARD, L. (1) Wakefield T: 1975 W
SMITH, D. (1) Leeds: 1977 F
SMITH, K. (1) Wakefield T: 1979 W
SMITH, M. (5) Hull K.R.: 1980 W, F; 1981 F, W, W
SMITH, P. (1) Featherstone R: 1980 F
STEPHENS, G. (1) Castleford: 1979 W
SZYMALA, E. (+1) Barrow: 1979 f

THOMPSON, J. (2+1)1 Featherstone R: 1975 **A**; 1977 W. Bradford N: 1978 w
TINDALL, K. (1) Hull: 1979 F
TOPLISS, D. (1) Wakefield T: 1975 F

WADDELL, H. (1) Blackpool B.: 1984 W
WALKER, A. (1) Whitehaven: 1981 F
WALSH, J. (3) St. Helens: 1975 F, **NZ, A**
WARD, D. (6) Leeds: 1977 F; 1980 W, F; 1981 F, W, W
WATKINSON, D. (+1) Hull K.R.: 1977 w
WOODS, J. (3+4) Leigh: 1979 w, F; 1980 w, F; 1981 f, w, **W**
WRIGHT, S. (7) Wigan: 1975 **NZ**. Widnes: 1977 W; 1978 F, W; 1979 W, F; 1980 W

WALES REGISTER
Since reintroduction in 1975

BANNER, P. (9) Salford: 1975 F, E, **F, E, NZ.** Featherstone R: 1975 (cont.) **E, A, NZ, F**
BAYLISS, S. (1) St. Helens: 1981 E
BEVAN, J. (17) Warrington: 1975 F, E, **E, A, NZ, F**; 1977 E; 1978 A; 1979 F, E; 1980 F, E; 1981 F, E, E; 1982 A
BOX, H. (5) Featherstone R: 1979 F, E; 1980 F, E. Wakefield T: 1981 F
BUTLER, B. (2+2) Swinton: 1975 **F, nz**. Warrington: 1975 (cont.) f; 1977 F

CAMBRIANI, A. (3) Fulham: 1981 F, E, E
CAMILLERI, C. (3) Barrow: 1980 F. Widnes: 1982 A. Bridgend: 1984 E
COSLETT, K. (8)2 St. Helens: 1975 F, E, **F, E, A, NZ, E, A**
CUNNINGHAM, E (8) St. Helens: 1975 **E, A, E, A**; 1977 E; 1978 F, E, A
CUNNINGHAM, T. (2) Warrington: 1979 F, E
CURLING, D. (+1) Warrington: 1977 f

DAVID, T. (2) Cardiff C: 1981 E; 1982 A
DAVIES, F. (1) New Hunslet: 1978 E
DAVIES, M. (1) Bridgend: 1984 E
DIAMOND, S. (2+1) Wakefield T: 1980 F, e; 1981 F
DIXON, C. (10)3 Salford: 1975 F, E, **F, E, NZ, A**; 1977 E, F; 1978 F. Hull K.R.: 1981 E

EVANS, R. (5) Swinton: 1975 E, **F, F**; 1978 F; Salford: 1978 E

FENWICK, S. (2) Cardiff C: 1981 E; 1982 A
FISHER, A. (10)4 Leeds: 1975 F, **E, A, NZ.** Castleford: 1975 (cont.) **E, A, NZ**; 1977 E, F. Bradford N: 1978 A
FLOWERS, N. (4) Wigan: 1980 F, E; 1981 E. Bridgend: 1984 E
FORD, Phil (1) Warrington: 1984 E
FRANCIS, W. (19) Wigan: 1975 F, E, **F, E, A, NZ, E, A, NZ, F**; 1977 E, F. St. Helens: 1978 F, E, A; 1979 F, E. Oldham: 1980 F, E

GALLACHER, S. (3+1) Keighley: 1975 f, E, **NZ, F**
GREGORY, B. (3) Wigan: 1975 **E, NZ, F**
GRIFFITHS, C. (+2) St. Helens: 1980 f; 1981 f

HALLETT, L. (2) Cardiff C: 1982 A. Bridgend:
 1984 E
HERDMAN, M. (2+1) Fulham: 1981 e, E; 1982 A
HOPKINS, L. (1) Workington T: 1982 A

JAMES, M. (11) St. Helens: 1975 **E**; 1978 F, E, A;
 1979 F, E; 1980 F, E; 1981 F, E, E
JOHNS, G. (+2) Salford: 1979 f. Blackpool B: 1984 e
JONES, C. (1+3) Leigh: 1975 **nz, F**; 1978 f, e
JULIFF, B. (8) Wakefield T: 1979 F, E; 1980 F, E;
 1981 F, E: Wigan: 1982 A; 1984 E

McJENNETT, M. (2+1) Barrow: 1980 F; 1982 a;
 1984 E
MANTLE, J. (11+1)3 St. Helens: 1975 F, E, **F, e,
 A, NZ, E, A, NZ, F**; 1977 E; 1978 E
MATHIAS, R. (20) St. Helens: 1975 F, E, **F, E, A,
 NZ, A, NZ, F**; 1977 E, F; 1978 F, E, A;
 1979 F, E; 1980 F, E; 1981 F, E
MILLS, J. (13)4 Widnes: 1975 F, E, **E, A, NZ, A,
 NZ**; 1977 E, F; 1978 F, E, A; 1979 F
MURPHY, M. (4+1) Bradford N: 1975 **F, NZ, F**;
 1977 f. St. Jacques, France: 1979 F

NICHOLAS, M. (4+2) Warrington: 1975 F, e;
 1977 E, F; 1978 F; 1979 e

O'BRIEN, C. (1) Bridgend: 1984 E
OWEN, G. (2) Oldham: 1981 E, F
OWEN, R. (+2) St. Helens: 1981 f, e

PARRY, D. (6) Blackpool B: 1980 F, E; 1981 F, E, E:
 1982 A
PREECE, C. (1) Bradford N: 1984 E
PRENDIVILLE, P. (4+2) Hull: 1979 e; 1980 E;
 1981 F, e; 1982 A; 1984 E
PRITCHARD, G. (1+2) Barrow: 1978 f, e;
 Cardiff C.: 1981 E

RICHARDS, M. (2)1 Salford: 1975 **F**; 1977 E
RINGER, P. (2) Cardiff C: 1981 E; 1982 A
RISMAN, J. (2+1) Workington T: 1978 F; 1979 f, E
ROWE, P. (4+3)2 Blackpool B: 1975 **a, e, a**.
 Huddersfield: 1977 E, F; 1979 F, E
RULE, S. (1) Salford: 1981 E

SELDON, C. (1+1) St. Helens: 1980 f, E
SHAW, G. (7) Widnes: 1978 F, A; 1980 F, E; 1981 E.
 Wigan: 1982 A; 1984 E
SKERRETT, T. (7) Wakefield T: 1978 A; 1979 F, E;
 1980 F. Hull: 1981 F, E; 1984 E
SULLIVAN, C. (10)4 Hull K.R.: 1975 **E, A, NZ, E**;
 1977 F; 1978 F, E, A; 1979 F, E

TREASURE, D. (5) Oldham: 1975 **E, A, NZ, E**;
 1977 F
TURNER, G. (3+3) Hull K.R.: 1975 e, **A, e, A, f**.
 Hull: 1978 E

WALLACE, R. (+1) York: 1975 f
WALTERS, G. (2+1) Hull: 1980 E. 1981 E.
 Bridgend 1984 e
WANBON, R. (3)3+1 Warrington: 1975 **E, A, NZ**
WATKINS, D. (14) Salford: 1975 F, E, **F, E, A, NZ,
 E, A, NZ, F**; 1977 E; 1978 E, A; 1979 F
WILKINS, R. (1+1) Workington T: 1977 e, F
WILLIAMS, B. (1) Cardiff C: 1982 A
WILLICOMBE, D. (11)+2 Wigan: 1975 F, E, **F, E,
 A, NZ, NZ, F**; 1978 F, E, A
WILSON, D. (4) Swinton: 1981 F, E, E; 1984 E
WILSON, F. (7+2)4 St. Helens: 1975 F, E, **F, e, a,
 E, A, NZ, F**
WOODS, P. (10) Widnes: 1977 E, F; 1978 F, E, A.
 Rochdale H: 1979 F, E. Hull: 1980 E; 1981 F, E

*Rodstock War of the Roses debutants Kelvin Skerrett
(left) and Paul Hulme in the 1988 Headingley clash.*

WAR OF THE ROSES

WAR OF THE ROSES

1988 RODSTOCK WAR OF THE ROSES
Ace interception merchant Garry Schofield struck again seven minutes from time to ward off a Lancashire revival and maintain Yorkshire's 100 per cent stranglehold on the Rodstock Trophy while levelling the all-time tally at 41 wins apiece.

Having trailed 18-4 after 53 minutes, the Red Rose outfit, fielding six debutants, pulled back to 18-14 with 11 minutes left and Man of the Match, skipper Andy Gregory, in inspirational form.

Leeds centre Schofield delivered the killer blow by intercepting a lightning pass from Widnes prop forward Derek Pyke to race near enough to the posts to make David Hobbs' kick at goal a formality and take the final scoreline to 24-14. It was Schofield's fourth interception try in the last four matches and extended Yorkshire's unbeaten record to four matches in the new-style county-of-origin annual series.

Coach Peter Fox's loyalty in selection provided basic teamwork, coupled with intense passion and commitment, which Lancashire — despite fielding 13 Widnes and Wigan players — were unable to match.

White Rose skipper Ellery Hanley, playing his first game since a return from Sydney Premiership club football with Grand Finalists Balmain, opened the scoring after only three minutes, powering over for a try, Hobbs adding the goal.

It was that man Schofield, in only his second county match, who displayed world-class centre skills to set up Yorkshire's second touchdown in the 23rd minute. Andy Goodway provided the ball 75 yards out, Schofield breaking away in great style to turn the Red Rose defence inside out with a variety of dummies and swerves to serve winger Henderson Gill with a clear run to the line for a classic try. A Hobbs' penalty goal four minutes later gave the home side a 12-0 interval lead.

Captaining Lancashire for the fourth successive War of the Roses battle, scrum half Gregory refused to wilt and his non-stop efforts, albeit littered with a handful of errors through trying too hard, were finally rewarded 10 minutes after the break when he sent in Widnes winger Rick Thackray at the corner for a debutant try.

Within two minutes of going on as substitute for Bradford Northern's Kelvin Skerrett, Leeds loose forward David Heron fed a long, long pass to first-cap full back David Roockley who sent clubmate Tony Marchant dummying his way over for a 53rd minute touchdown, Hobbs again adding the goal.

Showing increased drive, Lancashire bounced straight back and within five minutes Widnes centre Andy Currier, returning after half an hour on the bench, burst onto a pass from club colleague Mike O'Neill to narrow the gap to 18-8. With 11 minutes to go, Currier's pass was deflected off Yorkshire substitute Graham Steadman to allow Widnes utility back Barry Dowd to touch down, Currier adding the goal to close the margin to only four points.

Then Schofield stepped in with his trade-mark interception try to keep the Rodstock Trophy in Yorkshire to the delight of a Headingley crowd of 8,244, the best attendance for a county game East of the Pennines for 22 years.

Yorkshire coach Fox took his winning run to six matches, including tour fixtures against New Zealand and Papua New Guinea, while new Lancashire coach Doug Laughton was left to reflect, as Alex Murphy had done in the previous three Rodstock encounters, how to overcome Yorkshire's intense county pride and passion.

RODSTOCK WAR OF THE ROSES

21 September   **Leeds**

YORKSHIRE 24		**LANCASHIRE 14**
David Roockley (Castleford)	1.	Joe Lydon (Wigan)
Henderson Gill (Wigan)	2.	Rick Thackray (Widnes)
Garry Schofield (Leeds)	3.	Andy Currier (Widnes)
Tony Marchant (Castleford)	4.	Paul Loughlin (St. Helens)
Carl Gibson (Leeds)	5.	Mark Preston (Wigan)
Ellery Hanley (Wigan) Capt.	6.	David Hulme (Widnes)
Deryck Fox (Featherstone R.)	7.	Andy Gregory (Wigan) Capt.
David Hobbs (Bradford N.)	8.	Derek Pyke (Widnes)
Kevin Beardmore (Castleford)	9.	Nicky Kiss (Wigan)
Kelvin Skerrett (Bradford N.)	10.	Shaun Wane (Wigan)
Paul Dixon (Halifax)	11.	Mike O'Neill (Widnes)
Roy Powell (Leeds)	12.	Mark Roberts (Warrington)
Andy Goodway (Wigan)	13.	Paul Hulme (Widnes)
Graham Steadman (Featherstone R.)	14.	Barry Dowd (Widnes)
David Heron (Leeds)	15.	Richard Eyres (Widnes)

T: Hanley, Gill, Marchant, Schofield
G: Hobbs (4)
Substitutions:
Heron for Skerrett (51 min.)
Steadman for Gill (59 min.)
Half-time: 12-0
Attendance: 8,244

T: Thackray, Currier, Dowd
G: Loughlin
Substitutions:
Dowd for Currier (19 min.)
Eyres for Roberts (59 min.)
Referee: Robin Whitfield (Widnes)

Yorkshire captain Ellery Hanley with the Rodstock Trophy, a fourth successive White Rose triumph.

LANCASHIRE v. YORKSHIRE RESULTS

All county championship matches except where stated.

Date	Result		Score	Venue	Attendance
7 Dec. 1895	Yorkshire	won	8 - 0	Oldham	9,059
29 Feb. 1896	Lancashire	won	8 - 3	Huddersfield	5,300
21 Nov. 1896	Lancashire	won	7 - 3	Oldham	15,000
20 Nov. 1897	Yorkshire	won	7 - 6	Bradford P.A.	11,000
5 Nov. 1898	Yorkshire	won	20 - 9	Salford	8,000
4 Nov. 1899	Lancashire	won	16 - 13	Halifax	9,000
3 Nov. 1900	Lancashire	won	24 - 5	Rochdale	18,000
15 Feb. 1902	Yorkshire	won	13 - 8	Hull	15,000
15 Nov. 1902	Lancashire	won	13 - 0	Salford	14,000
14 Nov. 1903	Lancashire	won	8 - 0	Leeds	11,000
12 Nov. 1904	Yorkshire	won	14 - 5	Oldham	8,500
4 Nov. 1905	Lancashire	won	8 - 0	Hull	8,000
3 Nov. 1906	Lancashire	won	19 - 0	Salford	5,000
2 Nov. 1907	Yorkshire	won	15 - 11	Halifax	7,000
31 Oct. 1908	Lancashire	won	13 - 0	Salford	5,000
4 Nov. 1909	Yorkshire	won	27 - 14	Hull	6,000
7 Nov. 1910	Lancashire	won	17 - 3	Wigan	2,000
25 Jan. 1912	Lancashire	won	13 - 12	Halifax	3,199
16 Dec. 1912	Yorkshire	won	20 - 8	Oldham	4,000
10 Dec. 1913	Yorkshire	won	19 - 11	Huddersfield	3,500
24 Sept. 1919	Lancashire	won	15 - 5	Broughton	5,000
21 Oct. 1920	Yorkshire	won	18 - 3	Hull	7,000
4 Oct. 1921	Yorkshire	won	5 - 2	Rochdale	4,000
7 Dec. 1922	Match drawn	—	11 - 11	Hull K.R.	8,000
8 Dec. 1923	Lancashire	won	6 - 5	Oldham	8,000
29 Nov. 1924	Lancashire	won	28 - 9	Halifax	6,000
12 Dec. 1925	Lancashire	won	26 - 10	St. Helens	13,000
30 Oct. 1926	Lancashire	won	18 - 13	Wakefield	9,000
29 Oct. 1927	Lancashire	won	35 - 19	Warrington	12,000
3 Nov. 1928	Lancashire	won	33 - 10	Halifax	6,520
22 Mar. 1930	Lancashire	won	18 - 3	Rochdale	4,000
18 Oct. 1930	Yorkshire	won	25 - 15	Wakefield	9,000
17 Oct. 1931	Lancashire	won	11 - 8	Warrington	10,049
*29 Oct. 1932	Yorkshire	won	30 - 3	Wakefield	4,000
25 Sept. 1933	Yorkshire	won	15 - 12	Oldham	2,000
*9 Jan. 1935	Match drawn	—	5 - 5	Leeds	1,500
12 Oct. 1935	Lancashire	won	16 - 5	Widnes	6,700
21 Oct. 1936	Lancashire	won	28 - 6	Castleford	7,648
12 Feb. 1938	Lancashire	won	10 - 9	Rochdale	3,653
*26 Oct. 1938	Match drawn	—	10 - 10	Leeds	3,000
10 Nov. 1945	Lancashire	won	17 - 16	Swinton	11,059
9 Nov. 1946	Yorkshire	won	13 - 10	Hunslet	5,000
12 Nov. 1947	Lancashire	won	22 - 10	Wigan	6,270
3 May 1949	Lancashire	won	12 - 3	Halifax	7,000
5 Oct. 1949	Lancashire	won	22 - 13	Warrington	15,000

Date	Result		Score	Venue	Attendance
18 Oct. 1950	Yorkshire	won	23 - 15	Huddersfield	6,547
10 Oct. 1951	Yorkshire	won	15 - 5	Leigh	11,573
28 Apr. 1953	Yorkshire	won	16 - 8	Hull	8,400
14 Oct. 1953	Lancashire	won	18 - 10	Leigh	12,870
6 Oct. 1954	Yorkshire	won	20 - 10	Bradford	8,500
26 Sept. 1955	Lancashire	won	26 - 10	Oldham	8,000
26 Sept. 1956	Lancashire	won	35 - 21	Hull	8,500
23 Sept. 1957	Yorkshire	won	25 - 11	Widnes	6,200
24 Sept. 1958	Yorkshire	won	35 - 19	Hull K.R.	5,000
29 Oct. 1958	Yorkshire	won	16 - 15	Leigh	8,500
11 Nov. 1959	Yorkshire	won	38 - 28	Leigh	6,417
31 Aug. 1960	Lancashire	won	21 - 20	Wakefield	15,045
9 Oct. 1961	Lancashire	won	14 - 12	Leigh	4,970
26 Sept. 1962	Yorkshire	won	22 - 8	Wakefield	7,956
11 Sept. 1963	Lancashire	won	45 - 20	St. Helens	11,200
23 Sept. 1964	Yorkshire	won	33 - 10	Hull	7,100
10 Nov. 1965	Yorkshire	won	16 - 13	Swinton	5,847
21 Sept. 1966	Lancashire	won	22 - 17	Leeds	10,528
24 Jan. 1968	Lancashire	won	23 - 17	Widnes	8,322
25 Sept. 1968	Yorkshire	won	10 - 5	Hull K.R.	6,656
3 Sept. 1969	Lancashire	won	14 - 12	Salford	4,652
13 Jan. 1971	Yorkshire	won	32 - 12	Castleford	2,000
24 Feb. 1971	Yorkshire	won	34 - 8	Castleford	4,400
29 Sept. 1971	Yorkshire	won	42 - 22	Leigh	4,987
11 Oct. 1972	Yorkshire	won	32 - 18	Castleford	2,474
19 Sept. 1973	Lancashire	won	17 - 15	Widnes	3,357
25 Sept. 1974	Yorkshire	won	20 - 14	Keighley	1,219
16 Oct. 1974	Lancashire	won	29 - 11	Widnes	3,114
20 Dec. 1975	Yorkshire	won	17 - 7	Wigan	700
1 Mar. 1977	Yorkshire	won	18 - 13	Castleford	2,730
††19 Oct. 1977	Lancashire	won	33 - 8	Widnes	5,056
27 Sept. 1978	Lancashire	won	23 - 7	Widnes	4,283
12 Sept. 1979	Yorkshire	won	19 - 16	Castleford	2,738
24 Sept. 1980	Lancashire	won	17 - 9	Widnes	1,593
9 Sept. 1981	Yorkshire	won	21 - 15	Castleford	1,222
26 May 1982	Yorkshire	won	22 - 21	Leigh	1,738
WR11 Sept. 1985	Yorkshire	won	26 - 10	Wigan	6,743
WR17 Sept. 1986	Yorkshire	won	26 - 14	Leeds	5,983
WR16 Sept. 1987	Yorkshire	won	16 - 10	Wigan	9,748
WR21 Sept. 1988	Yorkshire	won	24 - 14	Leeds	8,244

* Match abandoned but result stands   †† Queen's Jubilee match   WR War of the Roses
● There were also a few Lancashire-Yorkshire matches played during the war years but not of a competitive nature.

SUMMARY
Lancashire won 41   Yorkshire won 41   Drawn 3

LANCASHIRE v. YORKSHIRE RECORDS

LANCASHIRE

Highest score:	45-20 at St. Helens, 11 Sept. 1963
Widest margin win:	As above and 33-8 at Widnes, 19 Oct. 1977
Most tries in a match:	No player has scored more than 3
Most goals in a match:	9 by L. Gilfedder (Wigan) at St. Helens, 11 Sept. 1963
Most points in a match:	18 by L. Gilfedder (Wigan) as above
Biggest home attendance:	18,000 at Rochdale, 3 Nov. 1900

OTHER RECORDS (not involving Yorkshire)

Highest score:	60-12 v. Cumberland at Wigan, 10 Sept. 1958
Most tries in a match:	4 by T. O'Grady (Oldham) v. Cumberland at Wigan, 6 Sept. 1956
	4 by W. Burgess (Barrow) v. Cumberland at Widnes, 12 Sept. 1962
Most goals in a match:	12 by E. Fraser (Warrington) v. Cumberland at Wigan, 10 Sept. 1958
Most points in a match:	24 by E. Fraser (Warrington) as above
Biggest home attendance:	24,000 v. Australia at Warrington, 26 Sept. 1929

YORKSHIRE

Highest score:	42-22 at Leigh, 29 Sept. 1971
Widest margin win:	30-3 at Wakefield, 29 Oct. 1932
Most tries in a match:	No player has scored more than 3
Most goals in a match:	10 by V. Yorke (York) at Hull K.R., 24 Sept. 1958
Most points in a match:	20 by V. Yorke (York) as above
Biggest home attendance:	15,045 at Wakefield, 31 Aug. 1960

OTHER RECORDS (not involving Lancashire)

Highest score:	51-12 v. Cumberland at Hunslet, 17 Oct. 1923
Highest against:	55-11 v. Australia at Huddersfield, 26 Nov. 1952
Most tries in a match:	5 by J. Parkin (Wakefield T.) v. Cumberland at Halifax, 14 Nov. 1921
Most goals in a match:	10 also by N. Fox (Wakefield T.) v. Australia at York, 28 Sept. 1959
Most points in a match:	23 by N. Fox (Wakefield T.) as above
Biggest home attendance:	19,376 v. Australia at Wakefield, 4 Oct. 1967

Hull's Andy Dannatt, a substitute for Yorkshire in 1985.

One Yorkshire 1982 substitute role for Kevin Rayne.

Keighley's Trevor Skerrett, capped three times for Yorkshire while with Hull.

Yorkshire hooker Kevin Beardmore hands on to David Hobbs, Lancashire skipper Andy Gregory forming the rearguard.

Lancashire centre Paul Loughlin outstrips the Yorkshire cover of Ellery Hanley and Andy Goodway (right).

LANCASHIRE TEAMS

. . . **A 20-year review.** Initials are included where more than one celebrated player shared a surname in the same era. Only playing substitutes are listed.

1969 Yorkshire

Salford: 3 Sept.

Won 14-12

Dutton (Widnes) 4g
Jones (St. Helens)
Hesketh (Salford)
Benyon (St. Helens)
Murray (Barrow) 1t
W. Davies (Swinton)
Gordon (Warrington)
J. Stephens (Wigan)
Taylor (Oldham)
Fletcher (Wigan)
Nicholls (Widnes)
Welding (Leigh)
Laughton (Wigan) 1t
Subs: Tees (Rochdale)
      B. Hogan (Wigan)

1971 Yorkshire

Castleford: 13 Jan.

Lost 12-32

Dutton (Widnes) 3g
S. Wright (Wigan)
Benyon (St. Helens)
D. O'Neill (Widnes)
Joe Walsh (Leigh)
W. Davies (Swinton) 1t
A. Murphy (Leigh)
Mick Murphy (Barrow)
Clarke (Wigan)
Brown (Rochdale)
E. Chisnall (St. Helens)
E. Prescott (St. Helens)
Laughton (Wigan) 1t
Subs: Boylan (Widnes)
      Nicholls (Widnes)

1971 Yorkshire

Leigh: 29 Sept.

Lost 22-42

Dutton (Widnes) 5g
Jones (St. Helens)
Benyon (St. Helens)
Hesketh (Salford)
Joe Walsh (Leigh)
D. O'Neill (Widnes)
Kenny (Swinton) 1t
J. Stephens (St. Helens) 1t
A. Karalius (St. Helens)
Mick Murphy (Barrow)
Lester (Leigh)
Ashurst (Wigan)
Clark (Oldham) 1t
Subs: Eckersley (Leigh)
      Welding (Rochdale) 1t

1969 Cumberland

Workington: 24 Sept.

Won 30-10

Dutton (Widnes) 6g
Burgess (Salford)
Hesketh (Salford)
F. Myler (St. Helens)
Murray (Barrow)
A. Murphy (Leigh) 3t
Gordon (Warrington) 1t
J. Stephens (Wigan)
Ashcroft (Leigh)
Sanderson (Barrow)
Robinson (Swinton) 1t
Welding (Leigh)
Laughton (Wigan) 1t
Sub: D. Hill (Wigan)

1971 Yorkshire (Play-off)

Castleford: 24 Feb.

Lost 8-34

Tyrer (Wigan) 1g
Joe Walsh (Leigh)
Buckley (Swinton)
Hesketh (Salford)
Jones (St. Helens) 1t
D. O'Neill (Widnes)
Boylan (Widnes)
J. Stephens (St. Helens)
Ashcroft (Leigh)
B. Hogan (Wigan)
Nicholls (Widnes) 1t
Cramant (Swinton)
Robinson (Wigan)
Subs: Eckersley (Leigh)
      Clarke (Wigan)

1972 Cumberland

Warrington: 27 Sept.

Won: 26-16

Martin Murphy (Oldham)
Hodgkinson (Oldham)
Benyon (St. Helens)
John Walsh (St. Helens) 1t, 4g
E. Hughes (Widnes)
K. Kelly (St. Helens) 1t
Banner (Salford)
Halsall (Swinton)
A. Karalius (St. Helens) 2t
J. Stephens (St. Helens)
E. Prescott (Salford)
B. Gregory (Warrington) 1t
Nicholls (Widnes) 1t
Subs: Hesketh (Salford)
      Birchall (Rochdale)

1970 Cumberland

Barrow: 11 Nov.

Won 28-5

John Walsh (St. Helens) 5g
S. Wright (Wigan) 1t
Benyon (St. Helens)
Hesketh (Salford) 1t
Joe Walsh (Leigh)
F. Myler (St. Helens) 2t
Boylan (Widnes)
D. Chisnall (Leigh)
Ashcroft (Leigh) 1t
Brown (Rochdale)
E. Prescott (St. Helens) 1t
E. Chisnall (St. Helens)
Laughton (Wigan)
Subs: Martin Murphy (Oldham)
      Nicholls (Widnes)

1971 Cumberland

Workington: 15 Sept.

Lost 7-17

Dutton (Widnes) 2g
Keiron O'Loughlin (Wigan)
Benyon (St. Helens) 1t
Eckersley (Leigh)
Fuller (Wigan)
D. O'Neill (Widnes)
Boylan (Leigh)
D. Chisnall (Warrington)
A. Karalius (St. Helens)
Brown (Rochdale)
Cunningham (Wigan)
Wills (Huyton)
Nicholls (Widnes)
Subs: Whittle (St. Helens)
      Welding (Rochdale)

1972 Yorkshire

Castleford: 11 Oct.

Lost 18-32

Dutton (Widnes) 2g
Hodgkinson (Oldham) 1t
Benyon (St. Helens)
John Walsh (St. Helens) 1g
E. Hughes (Widnes) 1t
D. O'Neill (Widnes) 1t
Banner (Salford)
Halsall (Swinton)
A. Karalius (St. Helens)
J. Stephens (St. Helens) 1t
E. Chisnall (St. Helens)
B. Gregory (Warrington)
Ashurst (Wigan)

1973 Cumbria
Barrow: 5 Sept.
Won 18-6
D. Whitehead (Warrington) 3g
Brelsford (Rochdale)
Benyon (St. Helens) 1t
Hesketh (Salford)
E. Hughes (Widnes) 1t
Eckersley (St. Helens)
Gordon (Warrington)
Fiddler (Leigh) 1t
Evans (Swinton)
Brady (Warrington)
Nicholls (St. Helens)
Welding (Rochdale)
Laughton (Widnes)
Sub: Noonan (Warrington) 1t

1974 Cumbria
Warrington: 18 Sept.
Won 29-4
D. Whitehead (Warrington) 4g, 1t
S. Wright (Wigan) 1t
Noonan (Warrington) 2t
Hesketh (Salford)
E. Hughes (Widnes) 1t
Whittle (Warrington)
Nulty (Wigan)
D. Chisnall (Warrington) 1t
Evans (Swinton)
Fiddler (Leigh)
Robinson (Wigan)
B. Gregory (Oldham)
T. Martyn (Leigh) 1t

1975 Other Nationalities
St. Helens: 25 Nov.
Won 36-7
Dutton (Widnes) 6g
J. Davies (Leigh)
Pimblett (St. Helens)
Butler (Salford)
George (Widnes)
Gill (Salford) 1t
Bowden (Widnes) 1t
B. Hogan (Wigan)
Elwell (Widnes) 1t
Nelson (Widnes)
Nicholls (St. Helens) 1t
T. Martyn (Warrington) 2t
Adams (Widnes) 1t
Subs: Eckersley (St. Helens)
Hodkinson (Rochdale) 1t

1973 Yorkshire
Widnes: 19 Sept.
Won 17-15
D. Whitehead (Warrington) 3g
Brelsford (Rochdale)
Benyon (St. Helens) 1t
Hesketh (Salford)
E. Hughes (Widnes)
Eckersley (St. Helens)
Gordon (Warrington)
Fiddler (Leigh) 1g
Evans (Swinton)
Brady (Warrington)
Nicholls (St. Helens) 1t
Welding (Rochdale)
E. Prescott (Salford) 1t
Subs: Noonan (Warrington)
Briggs (Warrington)

1974 Yorkshire
Keighley: 25 Sept.
Lost 14-20
D. Whitehead (Warrington) 4g
S. Wright (Wigan)
John Walsh (St. Helens)
Hesketh (Salford) 1t
E. Hughes (Widnes)
Whittle (Warrington)
Gordon (Warrington)
D. Chisnall (Warrington)
Evans (Swinton)
Fiddler (Leigh)
T. Martyn (Leigh) 1t
B. Gregory (Oldham)
B. Philbin (Warrington)
Sub: Robinson (Wigan)

1975 Cumbria
Workington: 6 Dec.
Won 22-17
Dutton (Widnes) 5g
Davies (Leigh) 1t
Butler (Salford) 1t
George (Widnes)
Jones (St. Helens)
Gill (Salford)
Bowden (Widnes) 2t
B. Hogan (Wigan)
Elwell (Widnes)
Hodkinson (Rochdale)
Nicholls (St. Helens)
T. Martyn (Warrington)
Adams (Widnes)
Subs: Eckersley (St. Helens)
Turnbull (Salford)

1974 Other Nationalities
Salford: 11 Sept.
Won 14-13
D. Whitehead (Warrington) 1g
S. Wright (Wigan)
John Walsh (St. Helens)
Noonan (Warrington)
Jones (St. Helens)
Whittle (Warrington) 1t
Gordon (Warrington)
D. Chisnall (Warrington)
Evans (Swinton)
Fiddler (Leigh) 3g
Nicholls (St. Helens)
E. Prescott (Salford)
B. Philbin (Warrington)
Sub: B. Gregory (Oldham) 1t

1974 Yorkshire (Play-off)
Widnes: 16 Oct.
Won 29-11
Dutton (Widnes) 7g
S. Wright (Wigan) 1t
Hesketh (Salford) 1t
Noonan (Warrington) 2t
E. Hughes (Widnes)
Gill (Salford) 1t
Gordon (Warrington)
D. Chisnall (Warrington)
Ashcroft (Warrington)
Brady (Warrington)
Nicholls (St. Helens)
E. Prescott (Salford)
B. Philbin (Warrington)
Subs: Aspey (Widnes)
T. Martyn (Leigh)

1975 Yorkshire
Wigan: 20 Dec.
Lost 7-17
Dutton (Widnes) 2g
Jones (St. Helens)
Butler (Salford)
George (Widnes)
E. Hughes (Widnes)
Gill (Salford)
Bowden (Widnes)
B. Hogan (Wigan)
Evans (Swinton)
Hodkinson (Rochdale)
Turnbull (Salford) 1t
T. Martyn (Warrington)
Adams (Widnes)
Subs: Benyon (St. Helens)
Nelson (Widnes)

1977 Cumbria

Leigh: 2 Feb.

Won 18,14

M. Hogan (Leigh)
Fielding (Salford) 1t
Stacey (Leigh)
Butler (Salford)
S. Wright (Widnes) 1t
Gill (Salford)
Bowden (Widnes)
Coulman (Salford) 1t
Elwell (Widnes)
Wilkinson (Leigh)
T. Martyn (Warrington)
Adams (Widnes)
Boyd (Leigh)
Sub: Hesford (Warrington) 1t, 3g

1977 Yorkshire

Widnes: 1 Mar.

Lost 13-18

Fairbairn (Wigan) 3g
Fielding (Salford)
Hughes (Widnes) 1t
Hesford (Warrington)
S. Wright (Widnes)
Gill (Salford)
Bowden (Widnes)
Hodkinson (Rochdale)
Elwell (Widnes) 1dg
J. Wood (Widnes)
T. Martyn (Warrington) 1t
Adams (Widnes)
Boyd (Leigh)
Subs: Aspey (Widnes)
      Pinner (St. Helens)

1977 Yorkshire (Jubilee)

Widnes: 19 Oct.

Won 33-8

Pimblett (St. Helens) 5g
Jones (St. Helens)
Aspey (Widnes) 1t
Woods (Leigh) 2t, 2g
S. Wright (Widnes) 1t
Gill (Salford)
Bowden (Widnes)
Wilkinson (Leigh) 1t
Elwell (Widnes) 1t
Gourley (Rochdale)
Adams (Widnes) 1dg
Nicholls (St. Helens)
E. Prescott (Salford)
Sub: Macko (Leigh)

1978 Yorkshire

Widnes: 27 Sept.

Won 23-7

Fairbairn (Wigan) 4g
Fielding (Salford) 2t
Aspey (Widnes)
Cunningham (St. Helens) 1t
Bevan (Warrington) 1t
K. Kelly (Warrington) 1t
Bowden (Widnes)
D. Chisnall (St. Helens)
Elwell (Widnes)
Hodkinson (Rochdale)
Adams (Widnes)
Nicholls (St. Helens)
E. Prescott (Salford)
Subs: Glynn (St. Helens)
      Pinner (St. Helens)

1978 Cumbria

Whitehaven: 11 Oct.

Lost 15-16

Glynn (St. Helens) 3g
S. Wright (Widnes) 2t
Aspey (Widnes)
E. Hughes (Widnes)
Jones (St. Helens)
K. Kelly (Warrington)
Bowden (Widnes)
D. Chisnall (St. Helens)
Liptrot (St. Helens)
Hodkinson (Rochdale)
Adams (Widnes)
Nicholls (St. Helens)
E. Prescott (Salford)
Subs: Keiron O'Loughlin (Wigan) 1t
      Pinner (St. Helens)

1979 Cumbria

St. Helens: 5 Sept.

Won 23-15

Eckersley (Widnes) 2g
Arkwright (St. Helens) 1t
Woods (Leigh) 1t, 3g
E. Hughes (Widnes) 2t
Hornby (Wigan)
K. Kelly (Warrington)
Bowden (Widnes)
B. Hogan (Widnes)
Elwell (Widnes)
S. O'Neill (Wigan)
W. Melling (Wigan)
Nicholls (St. Helens)
Pinner (St. Helens) 1dg
Subs: Glynn (St. Helens)
      E. Prescott (Salford)

1979 Yorkshire

Castleford: 12 Sept.

Lost 16-19

Eckersley (Widnes) 1t
Arkwright (St. Helens)
Keiron O'Loughlin (Wigan)
E. Hughes (Widnes)
Glynn (St. Helens)
Burke (Widnes) 3g
Bowden (Widnes)
S. O'Neill (Wigan)
Elwell (Widnes)
Gourley (Salford)
Adams (Widnes)
W. Melling (Wigan)
Pinner (St. Helens) 2t, 1dg
Subs: Hull (Widnes)
      E. Prescott (Salford)

1980 Cumbria

Barrow: 3 Sept.

Lost 16-19

Burke (Widnes) 2g
Bilsbury (Leigh) 1t
Stephenson (Salford)
Glynn (St. Helens)
Bentley (Widnes)
Woods (Leigh) 2t
Holding (St. Helens)
M. O'Neill (Widnes)
Elwell (Widnes)
Eccles (Warrington) 1t
Dearden (Widnes)
Gittins (Leigh)
Adams (Widnes)
Sub: Flanagan (Oldham)

1980 Yorkshire

Widnes: 24 Sept.

Won 17-9

C. Whitfield (Salford) 4g
Bentley (Widnes)
Bilsbury (Leigh) 1t
M. Foy (Wigan)
Hornby (Wigan) 1t
Woods (Leigh)
Holding (St. Helens) 1t
M. O'Neill (Widnes)
Liptrot (St. Helens)
Eccles (Warrington)
S. O'Neill (Wigan)
Dearden (Widnes)
Adams (Widnes)
Subs: A. Fairhurst (Leigh)
      Gittins (Leigh)

1981 Yorkshire
Castleford: 9 Sept.
Lost 15-21
C. Whitfield (Salford) 3g
Drummond (Leigh) 2t
Stephenson (Salford)
M. Foy (Wigan)
Bentley (Widnes) 1t
K. Kelly (Warrington)
A. Gregory (Widnes)
M. O'Neill (Widnes)
Kiss (Wigan)
Case (Warrington)
Potter (Warrington)
Adams (Widnes)
Pinner (St. Helens)
Sub: Donlan (Leigh)

1982 Cumbria
Workington: 30 May
Won 46-8
Burke (Widnes) 8g
Meadows (St. Helens) 3t
Stephenson (Wigan) 2t
Donlan (Leigh) 3t
Basnett (Widnes)
Keiron O'Loughlin (Widnes)
A. Gregory (Widnes)
M. O'Neill (Widnes) 1t
Kiss (Wigan)
Wilkinson (Leigh)
Potter (Leigh)
Tabern (Leigh) 1t
Flanagan (Oldham)
Subs: C. Whitfield (Wigan)
Fieldhouse (Warrington)

1987 Yorkshire
Wigan: 16 Sept.
Lost 10-16
Hampson (Wigan) 1t
McCormack (St. Helens)
Cullen (Warrington)
Whitfield (Halifax) 1g
D. Wright (Widnes)
Woods (Warrington)
A. Gregory (Wigan)
Case (Wigan)
Dermott (Wigan)
Humphries (Warrington)
Round (Oldham) 1t
Potter (Wigan)
M. Gregory (Warrington)
Subs: McCulloch (Leigh)
McGinty (Warrington)

1981 Cumbria
Wigan: 16 Sept.
Lost 15-27
C. Whitfield (Salford) 3g
Drummond (Leigh) 1t
George (Widnes)
Glynn (St. Helens) 1t
Bentley (Widnes)
K. Kelly (Warrington) 1t
Peters (St. Helens)
Hodkinson (Wigan)
Kiss (Wigan)
M. O'Neill (Widnes)
Potter (Warrington)
Case (Warrington)
Pinner (St. Helens)
Subs: Kirwan (Oldham)
Yates (Salford)

1985 Yorkshire
Wigan: 11 Sept.
Lost 10-26
Burke (Widnes) 1g
Ledger (St. Helens)
Stephenson (Wigan)
Keiron O'Loughlin (Salford)
Lydon (Widnes)
A. Myler (Widnes)
A. Gregory (Warrington) 1t
M. O'Neill (Widnes)
Webb (Warrington)
Forber (St. Helens)
Eccles (Warrington) 1t
Fieldhouse (Widnes)
Pendlebury (Salford)
Subs: Edwards (Wigan)
Wane (Widnes)

1987 Papua New Guinea
St. Helens: 14 Oct.
Drew: 22-22
Hampson (Wigan)
Drummond (Warrington)
Lydon (Wigan) 1t, 1g
Henderson (Leigh) 1t
Offiah (Widnes)
Edwards (Wigan) 2t
A. Gregory (Wigan)
Pyke (Leigh)
Groves (St. Helens)
Round (Oldham)
M. Gregory (Warrington)
Roberts (Warrington) 1t
Arkwright (St. Helens)
Subs: D. Hulme (Widnes)
Cottrell (Leigh)

1982 Yorkshire
Leigh: 26 May
Lost 21-22
Burke (Widnes) 1t, 6g
Drummond (Leigh)
Stephenson (Wigan) 1t
Woods (Leigh)
Basnett (Widnes)
A. Myler (Widnes) 1t
A. Gregory (Widnes)
M. O'Neill (Widnes)
Kiss (Wigan)
Wilkinson (Leigh)
Potter (Leigh)
F. Whitfield (Widnes)
Flanagan (Oldham)
Sub: Fieldhouse (Warrington)

1986 Yorkshire
Leeds: 17 Sept.
Lost 14-26
Lydon (Wigan)
Forster (Warrington)
R. Duane (Warrington)
Stephenson (Wigan) 1t, 3g
Basnett (Widnes) 1t
Edwards (Wigan)
A. Gregory (Warrington)
Pyke (Leigh)
Liptrot (St. Helens)
Fieldhouse (Widnes)
Arkwright (St. Helens)
Platt (St. Helens)
M. Gregory (Warrington)
Subs: Henderson (Leigh)
Haggerty (St. Helens)

1988 Yorkshire
Leeds: 21 Sept
Lost 14-24
Lydon (Wigan)
Thackray (Widnes) 1t
Currier (Widnes) 1t
Loughlin (St. Helens) 1g
Preston (Wigan)
D. Hulme (Widnes)
A. Gregory (Wigan)
Pyke (Widnes)
Kiss (Wigan)
Wane (Wigan)
M. O'Neill (Widnes)
P. Hulme (Widnes)
Roberts (Warrington)
Subs: Dowd (Widnes) 1t
R. Eyres (Widnes)

LANCASHIRE REGISTER

The following is a register of current players who have appeared for Lancashire. Each played at least one first team game last season.

ARKWRIGHT, C. (4) St. Helens
ASHURST, W. (2) Wigan

BASNETT, J. (3) Widnes
BENTLEY, K. (4) Widnes
BURKE, M. (5) Widnes

CASE, B. (3) Warrington 2, Wigan
COTTRELL, A. (+1) Leigh
CULLEN, P. (1) Warrington
CURRIER, A. (1) Widnes

DERMOTT, M. (1) Wigan
DONLAN, S. (1+1) Leigh
DOWD, B. (+1) Widnes
DRUMMOND, D. (4) Leigh 3, Warrington
DUANE, R. (1) Warrington

ECCLES, R. (3) Warrington
EDWARDS, S. (2+1) Wigan
EYRES, R. (+1) Widnes

FAIRBAIRN, G. (2) Wigan
FAIRHURST, A. (+1) Leigh
FIELDHOUSE, J. (2+2) Warrington +2, Widnes 2
FLANAGAN, T. (2+1) Oldham
FORBER, P. (1) St. Helens
FORSTER, M. (1) Warrington

GLYNN, P. (4+2) St. Helens
GREGORY, A. (8) Widnes 3, Warrington 2, Wigan 3
GREGORY, M. (3) Warrington
GROVES, P. (1) St. Helens

HAGGERTY, R. (+1) St. Helens
HAMPSON, S. (2) Wigan
HENDERSON, J. (1+1) Leigh
HOLDING, N. (2) St. Helens
HULME, D. (1+1) Widnes
HULME, P. (1) Widnes
HUMPHRIES, A. (1) Warrington

KISS, N. (5) Wigan

LEDGER, B. (1) St. Helens
LOUGHLIN, P. (1) St. Helens
LYDON, J. (4) Widnes, Wigan 3

McCORMACK, K. (1) St. Helens
McCULLOCH, N. (+1) Leigh
McGINTY, W. (+1) Warrington
MEADOWS, K. (1) St. Helens
MYLER, A. (2) Widnes

OFFIAH, M. (1) Widnes
O'LOUGHLIN, Keiron (4+1) Wigan 2+1, Widnes, Salford
O'NEILL, M. (8) Widnes
O'NEILL, S. (3) Wigan

PENDLEBURY, J. (1) Salford
PETERS, S. (1) St. Helens
PINNER, H. (4+3) St. Helens
PLATT, A. (1) St. Helens
POTTER, I. (5) Warrington 2, Leigh 2, Wigan
PRESCOTT, E. (9+2) Salford 7+2, St. Helens 2
PRESTON, M. (1) Wigan
PYKE, D. (3) Leigh 2, Widnes

ROBERTS, M. (2) Warrington
ROUND, P. (2) Oldham

STEPHENSON, D. (6) Salford 2, Wigan 4

TABERN, R. (1) Leigh
THACKRAY, R. (1) Widnes

WANE, S. (1+1) Wigan
WEBB, C. (1) Warrington
WHITFIELD, C. (4+1) Salford 3, Wigan +1, Halifax
WOODS, J. (6) Leigh 5, Warrington
WRIGHT, D. (1) Widnes

Warrington winger Des Drummond, capped four times for Lancashire.

Swinton packman Steve O'Neil, three appearances for the Red Rose county while with Wigan.

Five Lancashire caps for Colin Whitfield.

YORKSHIRE TEAMS

. . . **A 20-year review.** Initials are included where more than one celebrated player shared a surname in the same era. Only playing substitutes are listed.

1969 Lancashire

Salford: 3 Sept.

Lost 12-14

Keegan (Hull)
A. Smith (Leeds)
Hynes (Leeds)
A. Burwell (Hull KR)
Francis (Wigan)
Millward (Hull KR) 2g
K. Hepworth (Castleford) 1t
Denis Hartley (Castleford)
C. Dickinson (Castleford)
Macklin (Hull) 1g
P. Lowe (Hull KR) 1t
Lockwood (Castleford)
Batten (Leeds)
Subs: Edwards (Castleford)
    A. Morgan (Featherstone)

1971 Lancashire

Castleford: 13 Jan.

Won 32-12

Jefferson (Keighley) 6g
A. Smith (Leeds) 2t
Hynes (Leeds) 1t
N. Stephenson (Dewsbury) 2t
Atkinson (Leeds)
Topliss (Wakefield)
Shoebottom (Leeds) 1g
Clawson (Hull KR)
C. Dickinson (Castleford)
Jeanes (Wakefield)
Haigh (Leeds)
J. Thompson (Featherstone)
Batten (Leeds) 1t

1971 Cumberland

Wakefield: 20 Oct.

Won 17-12

Edwards (Castleford)
Slater (Wakefield)
Watson (Bradford) 2t
N. Stephenson (Dewsbury) 2t
Lamb (Bradford)
Millward (Hull KR) 1g
A. Bates (Dewsbury)·
Harrison (Hull)
M. Stephenson (Dewsbury)
Farrar (Featherstone)
Boxall (Hull) 1t
Irving (Oldham)
Halmshaw (Halifax)

1969 Cumberland

Hull KR: 1 Oct.

Won 42-3

Keegan (Hull) 1t
Lowndes (Castleford) 1t
Moore (Hull KR) 3t
A. Burwell (Hull KR)
T. Thompson (Hunslet) 1t
Millward (Hull KR) 6g, 2t
Davidson (Hull) 1t
Harrison (Hull)
M. Stephenson (Dewsbury)
J. Ward (Castleford)
Haigh (Wakefield) 1t
J. Thompson (Featherstone)
Doyle (Batley)

1971 Lancashire (Play-off)

Castleford: 24 Feb.

Won 34-8

Jefferson (Keighley) 1t,1g
Slater (Wakefield) 2t
Stenton (Castleford)
N. Stephenson (Dewsbury) 3g, 2t
Young (York)
Hardisty (Castleford) 1g
K. Hepworth (Castleford)
Clawson (Hull KR)
C. Dickinson (Castleford)
Jeanes (Wakefield) 1t
Lockwood (Castleford)
Irving (Oldham) 1t
Halmshaw (Halifax)
Subs: Topliss (Wakefield) 1t
    M. Stephenson (Dewsbury)

1972 Cumberland

Whitehaven: 13 Sept.

Lost: 14-23

Rushton (Dewsbury)
A. Smith (Leeds)
Dyl (Leeds)
N. Stephenson (Dewsbury) 4g
D. Redfearn (Bradford)
Millward (Hull KR)
Nash (Featherstone) 2t
Clawson (Leeds)
M. Stephenson (Dewsbury)
Jeanes (Wakefield)
Cookson (Leeds)
J. Bates (Dewsbury)
Halmshaw (Halifax)
Subs: Wraith (Wakefield)
    Irving (Oldham)

1970 Cumberland

Whitehaven: 14 Sept.

Lost 15-21

Edwards (Castleford)
Slater (Wakefield)
Shoebottom (Leeds)
Watson (Leeds)
Lamb (Bradford) 1t
Wolford (Bramley)
Davidson (Hull)
Denis Hartley (Castleford)
M. Stephenson (Dewsbury) 1t
Clawson (Hull KR) 3g
Lockwood (Castleford)
J. Thompson (Featherstone) 1t
Batten (Leeds)
Sub: Firth (Hull)

1971 Lancashire

Leigh: 29 Sept.

Won 42-22

Edwards (Castleford)
Slater (Wakefield)
Watson (Bradford) 1t
N. Stephenson (Dewsbury) 5g,1t
Lamb (Bradford) 1t
Millward (Hull KR) 4g,1t
Nash (Featherstone) 1t
Harrison (Hull)
M. Stephenson (Dewsbury)
Jeanes (Wakefield)
Boxall (Hull)
Irving (Oldham)
Halmshaw (Halifax) 1t
Subs: Topliss (Wakefield) 1t
    Farrar (Featherstone) 1t

1972 Lancashire

Castleford: 11 Oct.

Won 32-18

Jefferson (Keighley) 7g
Lamb (Bradford) 2t
Worsley (Castleford) 1t
Pickup (Huddersfield) 1t
D. Redfearn (Bradford) 1t
Blacker (Bradford)
A. Bates (Dewsbury)
Naylor (Batley)
M. Stephenson (Dewsbury)
T. Lowe (Dewsbury)
Irving (Oldham) 1t
Lockwood (Castleford)
Norton (Castleford)
Subs: Wraith (Wakefield)
    C. Dickinson (Castleford)

1973 Cumberland (Play-off)

Leeds: 17 Jan.

Won 20-7

Jefferson (Keighley) 4g
Lamb (Bradford)
Worsley (Castleford)
Dyl (Leeds)
D. Redfearn (Bradford) 1t
Topliss (Wakefield) 1t
Hudson (Hull KR)
Dixon (York) 1t
M. Stephenson (Dewsbury)
Lyons (Wakefield) 1t
Irving (Oldham)
Lockwood (Castleford)
Batten (Leeds)
Subs: N. Stephenson (Dewsbury)
      B. Kear (Featherstone)

1974 Cumbria

Workington: 11 Sept.

Lost 7-10

Jefferson (Keighley) 2g
Lamb (Bradford)
Dave Hartley (Featherstone) 1t
M. Smith (Featherstone)
D. Redfearn (Bradford)
Topliss (Wakefield)
Nash (Featherstone)
Harrison (Leeds)
Spurr (Castleford)
Farrar (Featherstone)
Grayshon (Dewsbury)
J. Bates (Dewsbury)
Norton (Castleford)
Subs: Burton (Halifax)
      Ramsey (Bradford)

1974 Lancashire (Play-off)

Widnes: 16 Oct.

Lost 11-29

Sheard (Wakefield)
Lamb (Bradford)
Roe (Keighley) 1t
Burton (Halifax) 1g
Atkinson (Leeds) 1t
Topliss (Wakefield)
A. Bates (Dewsbury)
Dixon (York)
Raistrick (Keighley)
Millington (Hull KR)
Grayshon (Dewsbury)
Irving (Wigan)
Norton (Castleford) 1t

1973 Cumbria

Bramley: 12 Sept.

Won 37-12

Jefferson (Keighley) 7g, 1t
A. Smith (Leeds) 3t
Newlove (Featherstone)
Dyl (Leeds)
Atkinson (Leeds)
Topliss (Wakefield) 1t
Nash (Featherstone) 1g
Ballantyne (Wakefield)
M. Morgan (Wakefield) 1t
Davies (Huddersfield)
Irving (Wigan)
J. Thompson (Featherstone) 1t
Stone (Featherstone)
Sub: Idle (Bramley)

1974 Other Nationalities

Hull KR: 18 Sept.

Won 22-15

Marshall (Leeds) 5g
D. Redfearn (Bradford)
Hughes (Bramley)
M. Smith (Featherstone) 1t
Atkinson (Leeds) 1t
Burton (Halifax) 1t
A. Bates (Dewsbury)
Harrison (Leeds)
Farrar (Featherstone)
Ramsey (Bradford) 1t
Grayshon (Dewsbury)
J. Thompson (Featherstone)
Norton (Castleford)
Subs: Langley (Leeds)
      J. Bates (Dewsbury)

1975 Cumbria

Dewsbury: 19 Nov.

Won 10-7

Wraith (Castleford)
D. Smith (Wakefield) 1t
Holmes (Leeds) 1t, 2g
Dyl (Leeds)
Dunn (Hull KR)
Newlove (Featherstone)
Millward (Hull KR)
Beverley (Dewsbury)
Bridges (Featherstone)
J. Thompson (Featherstone)
Grayshon (Dewsbury) .
Irving (Wigan)
Norton (Castleford)
Subs: N. Stephenson (Dewsbury)
      M. Morgan (Wakefield)

1973 Lancashire

Widnes: 19 Sept.

Lost 15-17

Jefferson (Keighley) 3g
A. Smith (Leeds) 1t
Hynes (Leeds)
Holmes (Leeds)
Atkinson (Leeds) 1t
Topliss (Wakefield)
Nash (Featherstone)
Harrison (Hull)
M. Morgan (Wakefield)
Davies (Huddersfield) 1t
Grayshon (Dewsbury)
J. Thompson (Featherstone)
Stone (Featherstone)
Sub: J. Bates (Dewsbury)

1974 Lancashire

Keighley: 25 Sept.

Won 20-14

Marshall (Leeds) 4g
D. Redfearn (Bradford)
Hughes (Bramley)
Roe (Keighley)
Atkinson (Leeds) 1t
Millward (Hull KR) 1t
A. Bates (Dewsbury) 1t
Dixon (York)
Raistrick (Keighley)
Irving (Wigan) 1t
Grayshon (Dewsbury)
Idle (Bramley)
Norton (Castleford)
Subs: Clark (N. Hunslet)
      J. Bates (Dewsbury)

1975 Other Nationalities

Bradford: 6 Dec.

Drew 16-16

Wraith (Castleford)
D. Smith (Wakefield) 1t
Holmes (Leeds) 2g
N. Stephenson (Dewsbury)
Dunn (Hull KR)
Newlove (Featherstone)
Nash (Salford)
Beverley (Dewsbury)
Bridges (Featherstone) 1t
J. Thompson (Featherstone) 2t
Grayshon (Dewsbury)
Irving (Wigan)
Norton (Castleford)
Subs: Topliss (Wakefield)
      M. Morgan (Wakefield)

1975 Lancashire
Wigan: 20 Dec.
Won 17-7
Langley (Dewsbury)
D. Smith (Wakefield)
Holmes (Leeds) 4g
Dyl (Leeds)
Atkinson (Leeds) 1t
Topliss (Wakefield)
Stephens (Castleford)
Millington (Hull KR)
Bridges (Featherstone)
Farrar (Featherstone)
Grayshon (Dewsbury)
M. Morgan (Wakefield) 2t
Norton (Castleford)
Subs: Hancock (Hull)
     J. Thompson (Featherstone)

1977 Cumbria (Jubilee)
York: 5 Oct.
Won 28-10
Banks (York)
D. Smith (Leeds) 2t
Marston (York) 1t
Quinn (Featherstone) 5g
Atkinson (Leeds) 2t
Hancock (Hull)
Shepherd (Huddersfield)
Beverley (Dewsbury)
Bridges (Featherstone)
Farrar (Featherstone)
M. Morgan (York)
Boxall (Hull) 1t
Bell (Featherstone)
Subs: Hague (Leeds)
     Branch (Huddersfield)

1978 Lancashire
Widnes: 27 Sept.
Lost 7-23
Mumby (Bradford)
Muscroft (N. Hunslet)
Joyner (Castleford)
M. Smith (Hull KR) 1t
D. Redfearn (Bradford)
Francis (St. Helens)
Stephens (Castleford)
Ballantyne (Castleford)
Wileman (York)
Pitchford (Leeds)
Lloyd (Hull) 2g
P. Smith (Featherstone)
Branch (Huddersfield)
Subs: Topliss (Wakefield)
     Farrar (Hull)

1977 Cumbria
Whitehaven: 15 Feb.
Drew 12-12
Wraith (Castleford)
Muscroft (N. Hunslet)
Joyner (Castleford) 1t
Roe (Bradford)
Atkinson (Leeds)
Topliss (Wakefield) 1t
Stephens (Castleford)
J. Thompson (Featherstone)
D. Ward (Leeds)
A. Dickinson (Castleford)
Grayshon (Dewsbury)
Lloyd (Castleford) 3g
M. Morgan (Wakefield)

1977 Lancashire (Jubilee)
Widnes: 19 Oct.
Lost 8-33
Mumby (Bradford)
D. Smith (Leeds)
Hague (Leeds)
Quinn (Featherstone) 1g
Atkinson (Leeds) 1t
Francis (Wigan)
Nash (Salford)
J. Thompson (Bradford)
Bridges (Featherstone)
Farrar (Featherstone)
M. Morgan (York) 1t
Branch (Huddersfield)
Bell (Featherstone)
Subs: Hancock (Hull)
     Griffiths (N. Hunslet)

1979 Cumbria
Workington: 29 Aug.
Lost 13-17
Box (Featherstone)
Fletcher (Wakefield) 1t
M. Parrish (Hunslet) 3g
Banks (York) 1t
Fenton (Castleford)
Evans (Featherstone)
Dean (Hunslet) 1dg
Tindall (Hull)
Wileman (Hull)
Gibbins (Featherstone)
Grayshon (Bradford)
Hankins (Dewsbury)
Bell (Featherstone)
Sub: G. Smith (York)

1977 Lancashire
Castleford: 1 Mar.
Won 18-13
Mumby (Bradford) 1g
Muscroft (N. Hunslet) 1t
Crook (Wakefield)
Francis (Wigan)
Atkinson (Leeds)
Topliss (Wakefield)
Stephens (Castleford)
J. Thompson (Featherstone)
D. Ward (Leeds) 1t
Farrar (Featherstone)
Rose (Hull KR)
P. Lowe (Hull KR)
Norton (Castleford)
Subs: N. Stephenson (Dewsbury) 1t
     Lloyd (Castleford) 2g

1978 Cumbria
Hull: 20 Sept.
Won 37-9
Mumby (Bradford) 4g
T. Morgan (York)
Joyner (Castleford) 1t
N. Stephenson (Dewsbury) 1t, 1g
Atkinson (Leeds)
Francis (St. Helens) 2t
Nash (Salford)
Harrison (Leeds)
Dalgreen (Warrington) 1t
Pitchford (Leeds) 1t
Casey (Hull KR) 1t
P. Lowe (Hull KR) 1t
Crane (Leeds) 1t
Subs: Topliss (Wakefield)
     Farrar (Hull)

1979 Lancashire
Castleford: 12 Sept.
Won 19-16
Box (Featherstone) 3g
Fletcher (Wakefield)
Joyner (Castleford)
Evans (Featherstone)
Fenton (Castleford)
Burton (Castleford) 1t
Stephens (Castleford)
Beverley (Workington)
Raistrick (Halifax) 1t, 1dg
Gibbins (Featherstone)
Branch (Huddersfield) 1t
Hankins (Dewsbury)
Adams (Leeds) 1t
Subs: P. Johnson (Castleford)
     R. Dickinson (Leeds)

1980 Cumbria
Hull KR: 17 Sept.

Lost 16-17

Wraith (Castleford)
Fletcher (Wakefield) 1t
Joyner (Castleford)
Quinn (Featherstone) 4g
Fenton (Castleford)
Hague (Leeds)
Dick (Leeds) 1t, 2dg
Holdstock (Hull KR)
Spurr (Castleford)
Skerrett (Hull)
Grayshon (Bradford)
Kevin Rayne (Wakefield)
Norton (Hull)
Sub: D. Heron (Leeds)

1980 Lancashire
Widnes: 24 Sept.

Lost 9-17

Wraith (Castleford)
Fletcher (Wakefield) 1t
Joyner (Castleford)
Quinn (Featherstone) 3g
Fenton (Castleford)
Topliss (Wakefield)
Stephens (Castleford)
Holdstock (Hull KR)
Watkinson (Hull KR)
Skerrett (Hull)
Grayshon (Bradford)
Kevin Rayne (Wakefield)
Norton (Hull)
Subs: Wilby (Hull)
      D. Heron (Leeds)

1981 Lancashire
Castleford: 9 Sept.

Won 21-15

Mumby (Bradford) 1t
Richardson (Castleford)
Joyner (Castleford) 2t
Dyl (Leeds) 1t
Fenton (Castleford)
Holmes (Leeds)
Nash (Salford)
Grayshon (Bradford)
D. Ward (Leeds) 1t
Millington (Hull KR)
Finch (Castleford) 3g
P. Smith (Featherstone)
Norton (Hull)

1981 Cumbria
Whitehaven: 23 Sept.

Lost 10-20

Box (Wakefield)
Richardson (Castleford)
Hague (Leeds)
Quinn (Featherstone) 1g
A. Parker (Bradford) 1t
Holmes (Leeds)
Nash (Salford)
R. Dickinson (Leeds)
D. Ward (Leeds)
Standidge (Halifax)
Finch (Castleford) 1t, 1g
Idle (Bradford)
Bell (Featherstone)
Subs: Evans (Featherstone)
      White (York)

1982 Cumbria
Castleford: 23 May

Won 22-7

Mumby (Bradford)
Richardson (Castleford) 3t
Joyner (Castleford) 2t
Day (Hull)
Gant (Bradford)
Holmes (Leeds)
Dick (Leeds) 1t, 2g
Tindall (Hull)
D. Ward (Leeds)
R. Dickinson (Leeds)
G. Van Bellen (Bradford)
Casey (Hull KR)
Norton (Hull)
Subs: Dyl (Leeds)
      D. Hobbs (Featherstone)

1982 Lancashire
Leigh: 26 May

Won 22-21

Mumby (Bradford)
Pryce (York) 3t
Joyner (Castleford)
Day (Hull)
Gant (Bradford)
Holmes (Leeds)
Dick (Leeds) 1t, 3g, 1dg
Tindall (Hull)
D. Ward (Leeds)
R. Dickinson (Leeds)
G. Van Bellen (Bradford)
P. Smith (Featherstone)
K. Ward (Castleford) 1t
Subs: Dyl (Leeds)
      Keith Rayne (Leeds)

1985 Lancashire
Wigan: 11 Sept.

Won 26-10

Kay (Hunslet)
Gibson (Batley)
Hyde (Castleford) 1t
Mason (Bramley) 2t
Laws (Hull KR)
Joyner (Castleford)
Fox (Featherstone) 3g
Hill (Leeds)
Watkinson (Hull KR)
M. Morgan (Oldham)
D. Hobbs (Oldham) 1t
Burton (Hull KR)
D. Heron (Leeds) 1t
Subs: Lyman (Featherstone)
      Dannatt (Hull)

1985 New Zealand
Bradford: 23 Oct.

Won 18-8

Mumby (Bradford)
Gibson (Batley) 1t
Creasser (Leeds)
Schofield (Hull) 1dg
Mason (Bramley)
Hanley (Wigan) 1t, 1dg
Fox (Featherstone) 2g
Grayshon (Bradford)
Noble (Bradford)
Skerrett (Hull)
Crooks (Hull)
Goodway (Wigan) 1t
D. Heron (Leeds)
Subs: Steadman (York)
      Lyman (Featherstone)

1986 Lancashire
Leeds: 17 Sept.

Won 26-14

Wilkinson (Leeds)
Gibson (Leeds)
Marchant (Castleford) 1t
Hanley (Wigan) 1t
Gill (Wigan) 1t
Joyner (Castleford)
Fox (Featherstone)
Kelly (Hull KR)
Noble (Bradford)
Hobbs (Oldham) 5g
P. Smith (Featherstone)
Price (York)
Lyman (Featherstone) 1t
Subs: Mason (Bramley)
      Medley (Leeds)

1987 Lancashire
Wigan: 16 Sept.
Won 16-10
Wilkinson (Halifax)
Gibson (Leeds)
Marchant (Castleford) 1t
Mason (Wakefield)
Gill (Wigan) 1t
Hanley (Wigan) 1t
Fox (Featherstone) 1g
Ward (Castleford)
K. Beardmore (Castleford)
Hobbs (Bradford) 1g
Crooks (Leeds)
Burton (Hull K.R.)
Goodway (Wigan)
Sub: Dixon (Halifax)

1987 Papua New Guinea
Leeds: 27 Oct.
Won 28-4
Mumby (Bradford)
Eastwood (Hull)
Marchant (Castleford) 1t
Gibson (Leeds) 3t
Mason (Wakefield)
Joyner (Castleford)
Fox (Featherstone)
Hobbs (Bradford) 2g
McCallion (Halifax)
Powell (Leeds)
Burton (Hull K.R.)
K. Fairbank (Bradford) 1t
Dixon (Halifax)
Subs: Creasser (Leeds) 1t
D. Heron (Leeds)

1988 Lancashire
Leeds: 21 Sept.
Won 24-14
Roockley (Castleford)
Gill (Wigan) 1t
Schofield (Leeds) 1t
Marchant (Castleford) 1t
Gibson (Leeds)
Hanley (Wigan) 1t
Fox (Featherstone)
Hobbs (Bradford) 4g
K. Beardmore (Castleford)
K. Skerrett (Bradford)
Dixon (Halifax)
Powell (Leeds)
Goodway (Wigan)
Subs: Steadman (Featherstone)
D. Heron (Leeds)

YORKSHIRE REGISTER
The following is a register of current players who have appeared for Yorkshire. Each played at least one first team game last season.

BEARDMORE, K. (2) Castleford
BELL, K. (4) Featherstone R.
BURTON, C. (3) Hull K.R.

CREASSER, D. (1+1) Leeds
CROOKS, L. (2) Hull, Leeds

DANNATT, A (+1) Hull
DICK, K. (3) Leeds
DICKINSON, R. (3+1) Leeds
DIXON, P. (2+1) Halifax
DYL, L. (6+2) Leeds

EASTWOOD, P. (1) Hull
EVANS, S. (2+1) Featherstone R.

FAIRBANK, K. (1) Bradford N.
FLETCHER, A. (4) Wakefield T.
FOX, D. (6) Featherstone R.

GIBSON, C. (6) Batley 2, Leeds 4
GILL, H. (3) Wigan
GOODWAY, A. (3) Wigan
GRAYSHON, J. (14) Dewsbury 9, Bradford N. 5

HAGUE, N. (3+1) Leeds
HANLEY, E. (4) Wigan
HERON, D. (2+4) Leeds
HILL, B. (1) Leeds
HOBBS, D. (5+1) Featherstone R. +1, Oldham 2, Bradford N. 3
HYDE, G. (1) Castleford

IDLE, G. (1+1) Bramley +1, Bradford N.

JOHNSON, Phil. (+1) Castleford
JOYNER, J. (12) Castleford

KAY, A. (1) Hunslet
KELLY, A. (1) Hull K.R.

LAWS, D. (1) Hull K.R.
LYMAN, P. (1+2) Featherstone R.

McCALLION, S. (1) Halifax
MARCHANT, A. (4) Castleford
MASON, A. (4+1) Bramley (2+1), Wakefield T. 2
MEDLEY, P. (+1) Leeds
MUMBY, K. (9) Bradford N.

NASH, S. (10) Featherstone R. 5, Salford 5
NOBLE, B. (2) Bradford N.
NORTON, S. (13) Castleford 9, Hull 4

POWELL, R. (2) Leeds
PRICE, G. (1) York
PRYCE, G. (1) York

QUINN, S. (5) Featherstone R.

RAYNE, Keith (+1) Leeds
RAYNE, Kevin (2) Wakefield T.
ROOCKLEY, D. (1) Castleford

SCHOFIELD, G. (2) Hull, Leeds
SKERRETT, K. (1) Bradford N.
SKERRETT, T. (3) Hull
SMITH, G. (+1) York
SMITH, M. (1) Hull K.R.
SMITH, P. (4) Featherstone R.
STEADMAN, G. (+2) York, Featherstone R.
STEPHENS, G. (6) Castleford
STEPHENSON, N. (7+3) Dewsbury

VAN BELLEN, G. (2) Bradford N.

WARD, D. (6) Leeds
WARD, K. (2) Castleford
WATKINSON, D. (2) Hull K.R.
WHITE, B. (+1) York
WILKINSON, I. (2) Leeds, Halifax

COUNTY CHAMPIONSHIP TITLES
(including joint titles)

Lancashire 34
Yorkshire 24
Cumbria 16
Cheshire 1

1895-96	Lancashire	1937-38	Lancashire
1896-97	Lancashire	1938-39	Lancashire
1897-98	Yorkshire	1945-46	Lancashire
1898-99	Yorkshire	1946-47	Yorkshire
1899-1900	Lancashire	1947-48	Lancashire
1900-01	Lancashire	1948-49	Cumberland
1901-02	Cheshire	1949-50	Undecided
1902-03	Lancashire	1950-51	Undecided
1903-04	Lancashire	1951-52	Yorkshire
1904-05	Yorkshire	1952-53	Lancashire
1905-06	Lancashire / Cumberland	1953-54	Yorkshire
		1954-55	Yorkshire
1906-07	Lancashire	1955-56	Lancashire
1907-08	Cumberland	1956-57	Lancashire
1908-09	Lancashire	1957-58	Yorkshire
1909-10	Cumberland / Yorkshire	1958-59	Yorkshire
		1959-60	Cumberland
1910-11	Lancashire	1960-61	Lancashire
1911-12	Cumberland	1961-62	Cumberland
1912-13	Yorkshire	1962-63	Yorkshire
1913-14	Undecided	1963-64	Cumberland
1919-20	Undecided	1964-65	Yorkshire
1920-21	Yorkshire	1965-66	Cumberland
1921-22	Yorkshire	1966-67	Cumberland
1922-23	Lancashire / Yorkshire	1967-68	Lancashire
		1968-69	Yorkshire
1923-24	Lancashire	1969-70	Lancashire
1924-25	Lancashire	1970-71	Yorkshire
1925-26	Lancashire	1971-72	Yorkshire
1926-27	Lancashire	1972-73	Yorkshire
1927-28	Cumberland	1973-74	Lancashire
1928-29	Lancashire	1974-75	Lancashire
1929-30	Lancashire	1975-76	Yorkshire
1930-31	Yorkshire	1976-77	Yorkshire
1931-32	Lancashire	1977-78	Not Held
1932-33	Cumberland	1978-79	Lancashire
1933-34	Cumberland	1979-80	Lancashire
1934-35	Cumberland	1980-81	Cumbria
1935-36	Lancashire	1981-82	Cumbria
1936-37	Lancashire	1982-83	Yorkshire

Record Rugby Union recruit, former Wales skipper Jonathan Davies, a January 1989 signing by Widnes.

TRANSFERS

TRANSFERS

TRANSFER REVIEW
1 June 1988 to 31 May 1989

The top cash transfer deal during the period was set early on when Great Britain Test back row forward Andy Platt moved from St. Helens to Wigan for £140,000 on 5 September, having been on the transfer list at £175,000 for five months.

Forwards continued to demand the biggest fees with Bradford Northern's Brendan Hill going to Halifax for £90,000 — easily a record for a specialist prop, although utility pack man Lee Crooks remains the costliest forward following his £150,000 transfer from Hull to Leeds the previous season.

Hill's move to Halifax concluded an extraordinary affair after St. Helens claimed he had signed for them two days before in a deal which would have taken prop Tony Burke to Bradford. The confusion meant Hill was signed shortly after the Cup transfer deadline and Burke stayed at St. Helens long enough to go to Wembley before being transferred to Warrington for £50,000. Halifax and Hill were later reprimanded by the Rugby League for contravening transfer practices.

Other £50,000 or more straight cash transfers were:

£65,000 Darren Bloor, Salford to St. Helens.
£50,000 John Henderson, Leigh to Oldham.

Players-plus-cash exchanges became increasingly popular with some major and rather complicated deals taking place. The biggest was reckoned to be worth £140,000 for an exchange of Test second row forwards with Paul Medley going from Leeds to Halifax and Paul Dixon moving in the opposite direction. Halifax had valued Dixon around £140,000, which Wigan had bid for him, while Leeds rated Medley at £100,000 and let half back John Lyons go to Halifax as part of the deal.

Leeds were also involved in another major transfer when they signed Test winger Phil Ford from Bradford in a deal reckoned to be worth £95,000, including utility back Mark Wilson joining Northern. Although Leeds would not put a price on Wilson they agreed the cash paid for Ford beat the record for a winger of £55,000 which St. Helens paid for Barrow's Les Quirk in October 1987. Ford had originally been listed at £200,000 after returning from Britain's tour of Australia and refusing to play for Bradford because of a contract dispute. Northern later reduced his list price to £140,000.

Leeds were involved in yet another big exchange deal when they obtained Oldham Test prop Hugh Waddell for £50,000 plus former amateur international prop John Fairbank. Waddell had been put on offer at £90,000 during the summer tour Down Under, but had agreed to stay at Watersheddings when Leeds moved in.

Hull Kingston Rovers signed loose forward Paul Lyman from Featherstone Rovers for £55,000 plus veteran forward Chris Burton in a deal worth £90,000, although Burton had been listed several months earlier at £80,000.

There was a total of 212 transfers between clubs plus 33 players going on loan, including those who returned to their original club. The previous year there were 168 transfers plus 20 players on loan.

Fees were determined by the Tribunal in 10 transfers during 1988-89, compared with seven in the previous 12 months.

RUGBY UNION SIGNINGS

Widnes' capture of Jonathan Davies, the Wales Rugby Union captain and stand off, made a bigger impact on the national media than any other event in the game's history. The Llanelli half back was one of six Rugby Union internationals to switch codes during the period but his signing received more coverage than all the others put together.

Davies, aged 26, signed for Widnes on 5

January in a world record deal variously reported as being up to £400,000 on a four-year contract. Widnes later said the official figure was £150,000.

The previous record for a Rugby Union player is equally difficult to establish since new tax regulations meant fees were spread over longer periods. It is generally accepted that the record single cash fee was the £80,000 Terry Holmes, the Wales international scrum half, received from Bradford Northern in 1985.

A crowd of 11,871 — almost double their average at that time — and more than 100 media men turned up for Davies' debut at home to Salford in a Stones Bitter Championship match on 15 January but he did little of note after going on as a 53rd minute substitute centre with Widnes already well on the way to a 50-8 victory.

Davies made another substitute appearance before making his first full appearance at stand off when he scored a try and five goals in a 38-14 home league defeat of Oldham on 5 February.

The total of six international Rugby Union signings during the 12-month period was the greatest number of top players to switch codes for many years. The others were:

● David Bishop (Pontypool) to Hull Kingston Rovers. Scrum half, played once for Wales.

● John Bentley (Sale) to Leeds. Wing or centre, played once for England.

● Adrian Hadley (Cardiff) to Salford. Wing, played 27 times for Wales.

● Paul Moriarty (Swansea) to Widnes. Forward, played 22 times for Wales.

● Jonathan Griffiths (Llanelli) to St. Helens. Scrum half, played twice for Wales.

In addition to the full international recruits there were other notable Rugby Union signings. St. Helens paid a substantial fee for Neath and Wales B winger Mark Carrington and Halifax captured Sheffield

Widnes-bound ex-Swansea RU international forward Paul Moriarty.

and England B scrum half David Holmes.

Perhaps the biggest impact was made by Emosi Koloto, the big Tongan forward signed by Widnes from the Wellington RU club in New Zealand. Another signing from New Zealand was Basil Ake, a centre from Ponsonby RU who joined Bradford after gaining junior All Black honours.

Altogether a total of 24 Rugby Union players joined professional Rugby League clubs compared with 18 the previous year.

AMATEUR SIGNINGS

A total of 211 amateur Rugby League players turned professional compared with 227 in the previous year.

Alan Hunte, the Great Britain youth captain and centre, was reported to have received a record contract for an amateur of more than £50,000 when he signed for St. Helens on 1 March. The Eastmoor (Wakefield) junior had already made two appearances, including one as substitute, for Wakefield Trinity, scoring a try, when he decided to join St. Helens.

Hunte's fee was held in trust so that he could remain an amateur until after he had toured Australia with the Great Britain youth squad in the summer.

OVERSEAS SIGNINGS

Despite further restrictions on the signing of overseas players a total of 125 made first team appearances during the season, only nine fewer than the record 134 in 1986-87 when clubs were limited to four plus any with British passports or who did not need work permits.

The following season there were 128 overseas players when the quota was cut to three plus passport and non-work permit players.

Last season clubs were allowed three imports plus only one other and this season there will be a strict quota of three with no extras other than the exempt overseas players who have resided in Britain for five consecutive years.

Fulham were allowed the normal quota allocation with an unlimited number of lower grade overseas players temporarily resident in the capital. The Londoners took full advantage with 14 Australians and three New Zealanders making first team appearances.

A total of 73 Australians played first team rugby last season compared with 79 the year before, but they included a record 12 Test players. Seven of the Test men were playing English club rugby for the first time — Sam Backo (Leeds), Gary Belcher (Castleford), Chris Close (Hull K.R.), Les Davidson and Steve Roach (Warrington), Michael O'Connor and Paul Vautin (St. Helens).

A record 48 New Zealanders played first team rugby, one more than the previous season. Of the 15 Test players last season the only newcomers were: Mark Graham and Brent Todd (Wakefield Trinity), and Mark Horo (Salford).

The following is a list of all overseas players who made at least one first team appearance during the season.

Salford signing, New Zealand Test prop Peter Brown.

OVERSEAS REGISTER 1988-89

*Test players as at 1 June 1989

AUSTRALIA (73)

Tony Anderson	(Halifax)
*Sam Backo	(Leeds)
David Baker	(Fulham)
*Gary Belcher	(Castleford)
Phil Blake	(Warrington)
Steve Bleakley	(York)
Bob Boyce	(Fulham)
*Les Boyd	(Warrington)
David Boyle	(Hull)
Brian Brown	(Fulham)
Jeff Burns	(Barrow)
Phil Carey	(Featherstone R.)
Tony Catton	(Carlisle)
Paul Cheetham	(Fulham)
*Chris Close	(Hull K.R.)
John Cogger	(Oldham, Runcorn H.)
Craig Coleman	(Hull)
Jeffrey Coutts	(Fulham)
Peter Coyne	(Halifax)
*Les Davidson	(Warrington)
Joe Dutton	(Fulham)
Tim Dwyer	(Barrow)
*Graham Eadie	(Halifax)
*Steve Ella	(Wakefield T.)
*Andrew Ettingshausen	(Leeds)
Earnie Garland	(Fulham)
Graham Gerrard	(Bramley)
Mark Geyer	(Sheffield E.)
Ron Gibbs	(Castleford)
Steve Gibson	(Salford)
Ashley Gilbert	(Oldham)
Bob Grogan	(Halifax)
Neil Henry	(Hull)
Cavill Heugh	(Barrow)
Terry Hooklyn	(Dewsbury)
Scott Jennings	(Fulham)
Mark Jones	(Hull K.R.)
Gary Lane	(Fulham)
Cliff Lyons	(Leeds)
Brett McEvoy	(Bramley)
Phil McKenzie	(Widnes)
Chris Macklin-Shaw	(York)
David Maguire	(Mansfield M.)
Kevin Manning	(Fulham)
Glenn Mansfield	(Fulham)
*Gavin Miller	(Hull K.R.)
David Moon	(Hull)

Paul Mulherin	(York)
Vincent O'Brien	(Keighley)
*Michael O'Connor	(St. Helens)
Chris O'Sullivan	(Oldham)
David Perry	(Batley)
Darryl Pitt	(Carlisle)
Michael Porter	(Hull K.R.)
*Steve Roach	(Warrington)
Wayne Sanchez	(Mansfield M.)
Aaron Sawyer	(Rochdale H.)
Paul Shaw	(Salford)
Greg Shuttleworth	(Huddersfield, Workington T.)
Warren Smiles	(Bramley, Sheffield E.)
Dan Stains	(Halifax)
Craig Taylor	(Fulham)
Paul Taylor	(Oldham)
Peter Thornton	(Workington T.)
Greg Totten	(Barrow, Doncaster)
*Paul Vautin	(St. Helens)
Phil Veivers	(St. Helens)
Nick Webster	(Huddersfield)
Ian Wightman	(Fulman)
Mark Wilkes	(Carlisle)
Sean Willey	(York)
Brian Winkell	(Doncaster)
Andrew Zillman	(Fulham, Mansfield M.)

Australian Test packman Les Davidson on duty for Warrington.

NEW ZEALAND (48)

Basil Ake	(Bradford N.)
*Dean Bell	(Wigan)
Glenn Bell	(Featherstone R.)
Mark Brooke-Cowden	(Leeds)
*Peter Brown	(Salford)
Danny Campbell	(Runcorn H.)
Trevor Clark	(Featherstone R.)
*Shane Cooper	(St. Helens)
Shane Cummins	(Oldham)
Chris Curtis	(Keighley)
Logan Edwards	(Rochdale H.)
Morvin Edwards	(Swinton)
David Gillan	(Fulham)
*Mark Graham	(Wakefield T.)
Joe Grima	(Widnes)
Albert Helg	(Fulham)
*Mark Horo	(Salford)
*Shane Horo	(Castleford)
*Kevin Iro	(Wigan)
*Tony Iro	(Wigan)
Michael Kuiti	(Swinton)
*James Leuluai	(Wakefield T.)
Charlie McAlister	(Oldham)
George Mann	(Leigh)
*Gary Mercer	(Bradford N.)
Robert Moimoi	(Leigh)
Herbert Moore	(Hunslet)
Roby Muller	(Runcorn H., Warrington)
*Dane O'Hara	(Hull)
Paul Okesene	(Sheffield E.)
Graeme Reynolds	(Whitehaven)
Peter Ropati	(Leigh)
*Adrian Shelford	(Wigan)
Stuart Simcott	(Rochdale H.)
Masauwee Solomona	(Sheffield E.)
*Kurt Sorensen	(Widnes)
Dennis Smith	(Swinton)
Russell Stewart	(Bradford N.)
Peter Subritzky	(Huddersfield)
*Kevin Tamati	(Warrington)
Willie Tangira	(Swinton)
*Brent Todd	(Wakefield T.)
Dennis Trembath	(Fulham)
Shane Tupeae	(Rochdale H.)
Dave Watson	(Whitehaven)
Nigel White	(Whitehaven)
Tom White	(Chorley B.)
Walter Wilson	(Rochdale H.)

MOROCCO (1)

Hussein M. Barki	(Fulham)

TONGA (2)

Lawrence Johansson	(Fulham)
Emosi Koloto	(Widnes)

SOUTH AFRICA (1)

Nick Du Toit	(Barrow)

Kiwi centre Kevin Iro touches down for Wigan in the 1989 Silk Cut Challenge Cup Final, brother Tony (right) in support.

RECORD TRANSFERS

The first £1,000 transfer came in 1921 when Harold Buck joined Leeds from Hunslet, although there were reports at the time that another player was involved in the deal to make up the four-figure transfer. Other claims for the first £1,000 transfer are attached to Stan Brogden's move from Bradford Northern to Huddersfield in 1929.

The following list gives an indication of how transfer fees have grown this century in straight cash deals only:

Season	Player	Position	From	To	Fee
1901-02	Jim Lomas	Centre	Bramley	Salford	£100
1910-11	Jim Lomas	Centre	Salford	Oldham	£300
1912-13	Billy Batten	Centre	Hunslet	Hull	£600
1921-22	Harold Buck	Wing	Hunslet	Leeds	£1,000
1929-30	Stanley Smith	Wing	Wakefield T.	Leeds	£1,075
1933-34	Stanley Brogden	Wing/centre	Huddersfield	Leeds	£1,200
1937-38	Billy Belshaw	Full back	Liverpool S.	Warrington	£1,450
1946-47	Bill Davies	Full back/centre	Huddersfield	Dewsbury	£1,650
1947-48	Bill Hudson	Forward	Batley	Wigan	£2,000
1947-48	Jim Ledgard	Full back	Dewsbury	Leigh	£2,650
1948-49	Ike Owens	Forward	Leeds	Castleford	£2,750
1948-49	Ike Owens	Forward	Castleford	Huddersfield	£2,750
1948-49	Stan McCormick	Wing	Belle Vue R.	St. Helens	£4,000
1949-50	Albert Naughton	Centre	Widnes	Warrington	£4,600
1950-51	Bruce Ryan	Wing	Hull	Leeds	£4,750
1950-51	Joe Egan	Hooker	Wigan	Leigh	£5,000
1950-51	Harry Street	Forward	Dewsbury	Wigan	£5,000
1957-58	Mick Sullivan	Wing	Huddersfield	Wigan	£9,500
1958-59	Ike Southward	Wing	Workington T.	Oldham	£10,650
1960-61	Mick Sullivan	Wing	Wigan	St. Helens	£11,000
1960-61	Ike Southward	Wing	Oldham	Workington T.	£11,002 10s
1968-69	Colin Dixon	Forward	Halifax	Salford	£12,000
1969-70	Paul Charlton	Full back	Workington T.	Salford	£12,500
1972-73	Eric Prescott	Forward	St. Helens	Salford	£13,500
1975-76	Steve Nash	Scrum half	Featherstone R.	Salford	£15,000
1977-78	Bill Ashurst	Forward	Wigan	Wakefield T.	£18,000
1978-79	Clive Pickerill	Scrum half	Castleford	Hull	£20,000
1978-79	Phil Hogan	Forward	Barrow	Hull K.R.	£35,000
1979-80	Len Casey	Forward	Bradford N.	Hull K.R.	£38,000
1980-81	Trevor Skerrett	Forward	Wakefield T.	Hull	£40,000
1980-81	George Fairbairn	Full back	Wigan	Hull K.R.	£72,500
1985-86	Ellery Hanley	Centre/stand off	Bradford N.	Wigan	£85,000
1985-86	Joe Lydon	Centre	Widnes	Wigan	£100,000
1986-87	Andy Gregory	Scrum half	Warrington	Wigan	£130,000
1987-88	Lee Crooks	Forward	Hull	Leeds	£150,000
1987-88	Garry Schofield	Centre	Hull	Leeds	£155,000

MOST MOVES

Geoff Clarkson extended his record number of transfers to 12 when he left Leigh for Featherstone Rovers on 27 October 1983. He played for 10 different English clubs and had a brief spell in Australia.

Clarkson, born on 12 August 1943 was 40 years old when he finished playing regular first team rugby in 1983-84. He turned professional with Wakefield Trinity in 1966 after gaining Yorkshire County forward honours with Wakefield Rugby Union Club.

Clarkson's club career in England is as follows:

1966 — Wakefield T.
1968 — Bradford N.
1970 — Leigh
1971 — Warrington
1972 — Leeds
1975 — York
1976 — Bramley
1978 — Wakefield T. and Hull K.R.
1980 — Bradford N. and Oldham
1981 — Leigh
1983 — Featherstone R.

1988-89 SIGNINGS

The following is a register of signings by clubs from 1 June 1988 to 31 May 1989. The right-hand column lists the club from which the player was recruited (ARL Amateur Rugby League, RU — Rugby Union).

In some instances a player who wishes to retain his amateur status is not registered although he may be named in the club's list of appearances.

Although this is a register of signings, it is possible to trace a club's transfers by scrutinising the right hand column.

Indicates where clubs have agreed to a player being signed 'on loan', a temporary transfer, the Rugby Football League prohibiting a subsequent transfer within 28 days. Where a player on loan has not been retained his return to his original club is also marked.

BARROW

Signed	Player	Club From
27.5.88	Pemberton, Keith	Millom ARL
17.8.88	Clayton, Stephen	Walney Central ARL
26.8.88	Middleton, Glen	Barrow Island, ARL
26.8.88	Hadley, Derek	Ulverston ARL
26.8.88	Heugh, Cavill	Illawara, Aus
30.9.88	Burns, Jeffrey	Past Brothers, Aus
6.10.88	Dwyer, Tim	Manly Warringah, Aus
4.11.88	Payne, Darren	Railway ARL
2.1.89	Tees, Gary	Holker Pioneers ARL
9.1.89	Richardson, John	Carlisle
3.2.89	James, Mike	Whitehaven
10.2.89	O'Neill, Ian	Millom ARL
21.2.89	Rowan, Stephen	Walney Central ARL
7.3.89	Beckwith, Mark	Whitehaven
23.3.89	Thompson, Phil	Holker Pioneers ARL
28.3.89	Totten, Greg	Doncaster

BATLEY

Signed	Player	Club From
6.9.88	*Thornton, Gary	Wakefield T.
7.10.88	Hinchcliffe, Mark	Featherstone R.
1.11.88	Wragg, Nicholas	Lock Lane ARL
16.11.88	Smith, Garry	Sheffield E.
26.12.88	*Carroll, Dean	Carlisle
4.1.89	Waites, Brian	Featherstone R.
6.1.89	*McCleary, Jack	Doncaster
26.1.89	Kaye, Andrew	Hunslet
18.2.89	*Kellett, Neil	Sheffield E.
13.3.89	Marshall, Paul	Shaw Cross ARL

BRADFORD NORTHERN

Signed	Player	Club From
26.6.88	Pinner, Harry	Leigh
1.7.88	Albone, Mark	Bradford Colts
1.7.88	Moxon, Darren	Bradford Colts
2.9.88	Ake, Basil	Ponsonby RU, NZ
20.9.88	Johnson, Errol	Leeds
30.12.88	Wilson, Mark	Leeds
30.12.88	*Robinson, Andy	Bramley
31.12.88	Wilkinson, Ian	Halifax
17.1.89	Langton, Steve	Carlisle
24.1.89	Pendlebury, John	Halifax
2.2.89	Cornforth, Phil	West Bowling ARL
14.3.89	Snee, Gavin	Stanningley ARL
14.3.89	Cooper, David	Bramley RU

BRAMLEY

Signed	Player	Club From
19.7.88	Dyl, Les	Leeds
19.7.88	Langley, Paul	—
2.8.88	Idle, Graham	Rochdale H.
12.8.88	Jackson, Robert	Bradford N.
18.8.88	*Sygrove, Andy	Wakefield T.
25.8.88	Durham, Steve	Batley
28.8.88	Holden, Barry	Dewsbury
28.8.88	Agar, Malcolm	Halifax

29.8.88	Armitage, Des	Leeds
1.9.88	Birch, Richard	Kippax ARL
13.10.88	Smiles, Warren	Applecross, Aus
22.10.88	McEvoy, Brett	Mt Pritchard, Aus
22.10.88	Gerrard, Graham	Mt Pritchard, Aus
26.10.88	*Bridgeman, Derek	Sheffield E.
27.10.88	Holmes, John	East Leeds ARL
1.11.88	Illingworth, Neil	Batley
18.11.88	*Robinson, Andy	Bradford N.
17.12.88	Johnson, Barry	Castleford
27.1.89	*Thornton, Gary	Wakefield T.
14.2.89	Gibson, Andy	Redhill ARL
7.4.89	Ellis, Andy	Stanningley ARL
12.4.89	*Kilner, Shaun	Mansfield M.
19.5.89	Fraser, Paul	Wheldale ARL

CARLISLE

Signed	Player	Club From
14.7.88	Wilkes, Mark	Eastern Suburbs, Aus
10.10.88	Pitt, Darryl	Valleys Diehards, Aus
10.10.88	Catton, Tony	Valleys Diehards, Aus
15.11.88	Richardson, John	Barrow
5.1.89	Thomason, Bryan	Broughton Red Rose ARL
31.1.89	White, Nigel	Whitehaven
28.2.89	Pollard, Damian	Holker Pioneers ARL
1.3.89	*Carroll, Dean	Batley
2.3.89	Rea, Steve	Barrow
7.3.89	Ferguson, Garry	Flimby ARL

CASTLEFORD

Signed	Player	Club From
19.8.88	Gibbs, Ron	Gold Coast Giants, Aus
10.9.88	Belcher, Gary	Canberra Raiders, Aus
11.10.88	Yemm, Clive	Wakefield RU
11.10.88	Clarke, Andrew	Wakefield RU
10.11.88	Southernwood, Graham	Redhill ARL
9.1.89	Gibson, Mark	Bramley
14.2.89	McAllister, Terry	Redhill ARL
9.3.89	Whitehead, Paul	Redhill ARL

CHORLEY BOROUGH

Signed	Player	Club From
28.7.88	Meadows, Mark	Swinton
28.7.88	Sheals, Mark	Swinton
24.8.88	Abram, Darren	Warrington
2.9.88	*Wilkinson, Chris	Fulham
6.9.88	Stansfield, Phil	—
6.9.88	Wiltshire, Roy	Salford
22.9.88	Glynn, Peter	Salford
12.10.88	Smith, Graham	Woolston R. ARL
5.11.88	Phythian, David	Blackbrook ARL
5.11.88	McCarthy, Kevin	Woolston ARL
5.11.88	Hindley, Alan	Culcheth ARL
23.12.88	Reynolds, Paul	Crosfields ARL
30.12.88	Tong, Michael	Dewsbury Colts
30.12.88	Mayo, John	Fulham
4.1.89	Middlehurst, Chris	Runcorn H.
4.1.89	Shaw, Mark	Runcorn H.
6.1.89	Whittle, Stephen	Swinton

10.2.89	Brown, David	Rochdale H.
18.2.89	Clayton, Richard	St. Judes ARL
18.2.89	Iddon, Tim	Crosfields ARL
18.2.89	Jones, David	Rose Bridge ARL
18.2.89	O'Rourke, Michael	Crosfields ARL

DEWSBURY

Signed	Player	Club From
1.6.88	Gill, Richard	Gate Inn ARL
27.6.88	Hopkinson, Ian	Wakefield T.
25.8.88	Rose, Tony	Whitehaven
10.9.88	Simpson, Karl	Dewsbury Albion ARL
19.9.88	Diskin, Richard	Dewsbury Colts
5.10.88	Spooner, Chris	Hanging Heaton ARL
11.10.88	Fairhurst, Ian	Keighley
20.10.88	Northcott, Lee	Normanton ARL
20.10.88	Firth, Stephen	Oulton ARL
27.10.88	Kelly, Neil	Wakefield T.
3.11.88	Hooklyn, Terry	South Grafton, Aus
18.11.88	McCraw, Tom	Wakefield T.
1.12.88	McCabe, Martin	Wibsey RU
6.12.88	Potts, Martin	Bradford N.
16.12.88	Jones, Keith	Castleford
30.12.88	Graham, Nathan	Dewsbury Colts
5.1.89	Johnson, Willie	Mansfield M.
6.1.89	Carroll, John	Hull
6.1.89	Pickerill, Neil	Featherstone R.
6.1.89	Bell, David	Doncaster
6.1.89	Ellis, Kevin	Doncaster
14.1.89	Abraham, Steven	Wakefield T.
24.1.89	Wilkinson, Chris	Fulham
6.3.89	Moore, Gary	Doncaster

DONCASTER

Signed	Player	Club From
2.8.88	Sigfugson, Karl	Doncaster ARL
2.8.88	Aldridge, David	Doncaster ARL
2.8.88	Aveling, Martin	Rotherham Rangers ARL
2.8.88	Heptinstall, Jason	Doncaster ARL
2.8.88	O'Reilly, Chris	Hillsboro Hawks ARL
2.8.88	Bobb, Lee	Doncaster ARL
2.8.88	Bailey, Stuart	Sharlston ARL
19.8.88	*McLeary, Jack	Batley
23.8.88	Carter, Darrel	Normanton ARL
23.8.88	Hudson, Shaun	Streethouse ARL
23.8.88	Rafferty, Roy	Sheffield E.
23.8.88	Tonks, Les	Normanton ARL
24.8.88	Hartley, Iain	Dewsbury
13.9.88	Winkel, Brian	Life Savers, Aus
22.9.88	*Timson, Andy	York
14.10.88	Roberts, Howard	Moorends ARL
14.10.88	Chappell, Anthony	Moorends ARL
20.10.88	Totten, Gregory	Eastern Suburbs, Aus
2.11.88	Rayne, Kevin	Leeds
2.2.89	Smeeton, Tony	Skellow Grange ARL
2.2.89	Truelove, Mark	Pudsey ARL
14.3.89	Sims, Mark	Nottingham RU
28.3.89	Jones, Keith	Castleford
28.3.89	Shillito, Alan	York
28.3.89	Fletcher, Ian	York
28.3.89	Abraham, Steven	Wakefield T.

FEATHERSTONE ROVERS

Signed	Player	Club From
13.6.88	Palmer, Craig	Featherstone M.W. ARL
25.6.88	Whiteley, Lee	Featherstone M.W. ARL
5.7.88	Pearse, Wayne	Redhill ARL
10.8.88	Newlove, Paul	Featherstone M.W. ARL
18.8.88	Grayshon, Jeff	Bradford N.
18.8.88	Fennell, Dale	Bradford N.
8.9.88	Clark, Trevor	Leeds
17.9.88	Carey, Phil	Canberra, Aus
20.9.88	Knapper, Mark	Jubilee ARL
18.10.88	Benson, Paul	Featherstone M.W. ARL
3.11.88	Pearson, Martin	Travellers ARL
17.11.88	Booth, Glenn	Jubilee ARL
17.11.88	Pickerill, Neil	Hunslet
8.12.88	Hall, Richard	Sharlston ARL
7.1.89	Bell, Glen	Mannakew, NZ
8.1.89	Burton, Chris	Hull K.R.
17.1.89	Fisher, Andrew	Eastmoor ARL
8.3.89	Campbell, Mark	Mansfield M.
8.3.89	Slatter, Tim	Mansfield M.
8.3.89	*Hopkins, Calvin	Mansfield M.
3.4.89	*Pearson, Martin	Travellers ARL
11.4.89	*Forsyth, Craig	Heworth ARL

FULHAM

Signed	Player	Club From
20.8.88	Brown, Robert	—
20.8.88	Leslie, Roy	South London ARL
20.8.88	Callow, Steve	West London Inst. ARL
20.8.88	Helg, Albert	—
20.8.88	Harris, Paul	Glenora, NZ
20.8.88	Gemmell, Brent	South London ARL
20.8.88	Boyce, Bob	London Colonials ARL
20.8.88	Brown, Brian	Western Suburbs, Aus
20.8.88	Garland, Earnie	Western Suburbs, Aus
25.8.88	Mighty, Andy	South London ARL
25.8.88	Coutts, Jeff	Seagulls Diehards, Aus
17.9.88	Mansfield, Glenn	Parramatta, Aus
24.9.88	Keeting, Noel	Fulham Colts
24.9.88	Johansson, Lawrence	—
24.9.88	Jennings, Scott	South Suburbs, Aus
24.9.88	Dutton, Joe	South Suburbs, Aus
24.9.88	Wright, Robert	Fulham Colts
4.10.88	M'Barki, Hussein	Hull
31.12.88	Mayo, John	Warrington
7.1.89	Walker, Paul	West London Inst. ARL
15.1.89	Render, Andrew	St. Mary's College RU
19.2.89	Rotherham, David	West London Institute
26.2.89	Zillman, Andrew	Mansfield M.
5.3.89	Pearce, Greg	Hemel Hempstead ARL
5.3.89	Baker, David	Hemel Hempstead ARL
24.3.89	Braniff, Gary	Workington T.
26.3.89	Trembath, Dennis	—

HALIFAX

Signed	Player	Club From
20.6.88	Holmes, David	Sheffield RU
5.7.88	Hutchinson, Robert	Norland ARL
15.8.88	Finn, Brendan	Halifax Colts

16.9.88	Stains, Danny	Cronulla, Aus
26.9.88	Coyne, Peter	Brisbane Valleys, Aus
4.1.89	Medley, Paul	Leeds
4.1.89	Lyons, John	Leeds
5.1.89	Milner, Richard	Milford ARL
9.1.89	Hill, Brendan	Bradford N.
20.1.89	*Fleming, Mark	Sheffield E.
26.1.89	Mellors, Ian	Sunnybank RU, Aus
26.1.89	Hutchinson, Darren	Norland ARL
19.2.89	Atkinson, Colin	Keighley
10.3.89	Kevin, Dick	Hull

HUDDERSFIELD

Signed	Player	Club From
7.9.88	Ventola, Roy	Paddock ARL
11.11.88	Stephenson, Nigel	Hunslet
13.11.88	*Senior, Gary	Hunslet
3.1.89	Bailey, Stuart	Shortston ARL
3.1.89	MacDonald, Gordon	—
3.1.89	Simpson, Andy	Earlsheaton ARL
3.1.89	Southern, Nigel	Featherstone R. Colts
3.1.89	Brook, Tim	Moldgreen ARL
3.1.89	Wells, Trevor	David Brown ARL
3.1.89	Mackintosh, Andy	Featherstone R.
3.1.89	Massa, Mark	Leeds
5.1.89	Johnson, Phil	Bramley
5.1.89	Wilson, Michael	Batley
9.1.89	Heselwood, David	Featherstone R.
27.2.89	*Naidole, Tom	Oldham
11.3.89	Subritzky, Peter	Carlisle
27.3.89	St. Hilaire, Darren	York
6.4.89	Shuttleworth, Greg	Workington T.

HULL

Signed	Player	Club From
21.6.88	Brown, David	Greatfield ARL
22.6.88	Jackson, Tony	Greatfield ARL
22.6.88	Harold, Karl	Eureka ARL
1.8.88	Boyle, David	South Sydney, Aus
5.8.88	Moon, David	South Sydney, Aus
18.8.88	Sutton, Mick	Carlisle
26.8.88	Marsden, Lee	NDLB ARL
30.8.88	Hunter, Paul	Eureka ARL
22.9.88	Harrison, Paul	Featherstone M.W. ARL
24.9.88	Smart, David	—
28.9.88	Henry, Neil	Cooma, Aus
21.12.88	Blacker, Brian	Barrow
5.1.89	Bullock, Adrian	Villa ARL
5.1.89	Eastwood, Jason	Hull White Star
5.1.89	Catar, Lance	Hull White Star
5.1.89	McCure, Steve	Hullensians RU
5.1.89	Branton, Richard	Hull White Star
5.1.89	Kingdom, Matthew	Isberg Easts ARL
5.1.89	Barrett, Robert	Hull White Star
8.1.89	Doherty, Paul	St. Helens
19.1.89	Busby, David	Featherstone R.
7.2.89	Bullock, Adrian	Villa ARL
21.3.89	More, Peter	Hull Boys Club ARL
22.3.89	Rowles, David	Balmain, Aus
27.3.89	Mighty, Andy	Fulham

HULL KINGSTON ROVERS

Signed	Player	Club From
25.7.88	Bishop, David	Pontypool RU
25.7.88	Schultz, Stuart	NDLB ARL
3.8.88	Fletcher, Paul	Eureka ARL
23.8.88	Porter, Michael	Cronulla, Aus
1.9.88	Close, Chris	Gold Coast Giants, Aus
24.9.88	O'Brien, Craig	West Hull ARL
30.9.88	Charlton, Gary	Sheffield E.
5.10.88	Jones, Mark	Woy Woy, Aus
26.10.88	Pratt, Richard	Leeds
19.11.88	Hallas, Graeme	Dudley Hill ARL
29.12.88	Armstrong, Colin	Carlisle
30.12.88	Irvine, Jimmy	Hunslet
7.1.89	Lyman, Paul	Featherstone R.
14.1.89	Robinson, Steve	Halifax
22.5.89	*Smith,Steve	York

HUNSLET

Signed	Player	Club From
30.8.88	Whittington, Mark	Dewsbury Moor ARL
31.8.88	Stephenson, Nigel	York
15.9.88	Hague, Neil	York
22.9.88	Moore, Herbert	Mangere East, NZ
13.12.88	Rollinson, James	Pointer Panthers ARL
24.1.89	Oldroyd, Thomas	Dewsbury Moor ARL
24.1.89	Wilby, Simon	Dewsbury Moor ARL
1.2.89	*Senior, Gary	Huddersfield
3.2.89	Brook, Richard	Dewsbury Moor ARL
9.4.89	Burrow, Paul	—
27.4.89	Evans, Garry	Batley Victoria ARL

Manly-Warringah half back Cliff Lyons, a second spell at Leeds.

KEIGHLEY

Signed	Player	Club From
20.10.88	O'Brien, Vince	Past Brothers, Aus
24.11.88	Curtis, Chris	Ngotaha, NZ
1.12.88	Mason, Max	Worth Village ARL
29.12.88	Rose, Kevin	Yew Tree ARL

LEEDS

Signed	Player	Club From
25.5.88	Ettingshausen, Andrew	Cronulla, Aus
11.7.88	Lyons, Cliff	Manly-Warringah, Aus
29.7.88	Backo, Sam	Canberra, Aus
1.9.88	Lord, Gary	Castleford
9.9.88	Waddell, Hugh	Oldham
21.11.88	Bentley, John	Sale RU
15.12.88	Vasey, Chris	Dewsbury
30.12.88	Ford, Phil	Bradford N.
5.1.89	Dixon, Paul	Halifax
9.2.89	*Lord, Mark	Oldham

LEIGH

Signed	Player	Club From
28.7.88	Ledger, Barry	St. Helens
4.8.88	Herbert, Graham	Leigh East ARL
16.8.88	Platt, Alan	Hunslet
22.9.88	Street, Tim	Wigan
4.10.88	Hill, David	Blackbrook ARL
4.10.88	Moimoi, Robert	Northcote, NZ
18.10.88	Ropati, Peter	Te Atatu, NZ
19.10.88	Ogden, Michael	Golborne ARL
3.11.88	Evans, Andrew	Leigh Miners ARL
8.12.88	Mann, George	Mangere East, NZ
29.12.88	Knight, Mark	Warrington
6.1.89	*Atherton, Wayne	Workington T.
8.1.89	McGrory, Paul	Widnes Albert ARL
17.1.89	Gaskell, Paul	Portside ARL
19.1.89	Hudspith, Mark	Golborne ARL

MANSFIELD MARKSMAN

Signed	Player	Club From
5.8.88	Sheldon, Michael	Jubilee ARL
5.8.88	Andrews, Brent	Mayfield ARL
5.8.88	Gillespie, Michael	Huddersfield
6.8.88	Stapleton, John	Rochdale H.
6.8.88	Ashcroft, John	Blackbrook ARL
5.9.88	Yarrow, Julian	Dewsbury Moor ARL
16.9.88	Moulder, Darren	Bradford N.
16.9.88	Sanchez, Wayne	Cronulla, Aus
25.9.88	Fox, Joseph	Lock Lane ARL
25.9.88	Zillman, Andrew	Brisbane Valleys, Aus
2.10.88	Powell, Paul	Batley Boys ARL
2.10.88	Maguire, David	Illawara, Aus
30.10.88	Burgess, Andrew	Culcheth ARL
16.11.88	Sanderson, Mark	Milford ARL
18.12.88	Cockayne, Phil	Spotland Rangers ARL
30.12.88	Oates, David	Park Amateurs ARL
1.1.89	Woolford, Neil	Travellers ARL
2.1.89	Hitchins, Gary	Seddon Atkinson ARL

4.1.89	Wilson, Nick	St. Josephs ARL
6.1.89	Nash, Steve	Rochdale H.
6.1.89	McLeary, Jack	Batley
6.1.89	Tuffs, Simon	Bradford N.
7.1.89	Madden, Shaun	Batley
12.1.89	*Hopkins, Colin	Featherstone R.
12.1.89	*Slatter, Tim	Featherstone R.
3.2.89	Wardle, Chris	Ovenden ARL
3.2.89	*Campbell, Mark	Featherstone R.
24.2.89	Jascwiez, Paul	Dewsbury
26.2.89	Roberts, Carl	George ARL
1.3.89	*Kilner, Shaun	Bramley
18.3.89	Taylor, Adrian	Clowne Angels ARL
5.4.89	Langton, Terry	Featherstone R.
6.4.89	Maher, Harry	Waterhead ARL

OLDHAM

Signed	Player	Club From
1.8.88	Ruane, Andy	Rochdale H.
17.8.88	Miller, Tony	Cutsyke ARL
28.8.88	*Parrish, Mick	Batley
6.9.88	Taylor, Paul	Parramatta, Aus
10.9.88	Fairbank, John	Leeds
15.9.88	Gilbert, Ashley	Canberra, Aus
15.9.88	O'Sullivan, Chris	Canberra, Aus
22.9.88	Henderson, John	Leigh
29.9.88	*Willis, Chris	Mansfield M.
2.12.88	Platt, Duncan	Widnes
8.12.88	Hyde, Gary	Castleford
4.1.89	Newton, Keith	Widnes
5.1.89	*Lord, Mark	Leeds
3.2.89	Martyn, Thomas	Leigh M.W. ARL
6.2.89	Blackman, Richard	Dewsbury Moor ARL
6.2.89	Cogger, John	Runcorn H.
19.2.89	Flanagan, Neil	St. Annes ARL
3.3.89	Allen, Shaun	St. Helens
16.3.89	Leech, Tony	Blackbrook ARL
19.3.89	Barrow, Tony	Thatto Heath ARL
1.4.89	Entwhistle, Steve	Waterhead ARL
27.4.89	Joynt, Chris	Wigan St. Patricks ARL

ROCHDALE HORNETS

Signed	Player	Club From
5.7.88	Brown, Jeff	Swinton
26.7.88	Turner, Steve	Mayfield ARL
1.8.88	Myler, Chris	Oldham
9.8.88	Derbyshire, Alan	Swinton
27.8.88	Brown, David	Chorley B.
2.9.88	Edwards, Jeff	Oldham
8.9.88	Higgins, Brian	Swinton
11.9.88	Edwards, Tony	Huddersfield
17.9.88	Sawyer, Aaron	Manly Warringah, Aus
1.10.88	Charnock, Les	Rylands ARL
8.10.88	Sealey, Camrel	Mansfield M.
14.10.88	Gamble, Paul	Chorley B.
2.2.89	Chadwick, Les	Mansfield M.

RUNCORN HIGHFIELD

Signed	Player	Club From
29.7.88	Caunce, Tommy	Spring View ARL
29.7.88	Gunning, Phil	Leigh East ARL
29.7.88	Dwyer, Mark	Rose Bridge ARL
29.7.88	Walls, David	St. Judes
26.8.88	Milner, John	Wigan
26.8.88	Jones, Charlie	Fulham
25.9.88	Muller, Roby	Swinton
13.11.88	Fildes, Tony	Clockface ARL
13.11.88	Greenall, Billy	Clockface ARL

ST. HELENS

Signed	Player	Club From
2.8.88	Vautin, Paul	Manly-Warringah, Aus
5.8.88	O'Connor, Michael	Manly-Warringah, Aus
5.8.88	Webster, Mark	Normanton ARL
17.8.88	Green, Iyan	Golborne ARL
15.9.88	Cosgrove, David	Farnworth ARL
18.9.88	Fairclough, Andrew	Wigan St. Patricks ARL
30.9.88	Bloor, Darren	Salford
6.10.88	Carrington, Mike	Neath RU
28.10.88	Cooper, Carl	Blackbrook ARL
1.12.88	Clare, Jeff	Wigan
12.12.88	Connolly, Gary	Blackbrook ARL
27.1.89	Hodgkinson, Thomas	Blackbrook ARL
1.3.89	Hunte, Alan	Wakefield T.
11.5.89	Roach, Jason	St. Helens U-19s ARL
13.5.89	Griffiths, Jonathan	Llanelli RU

SALFORD

Signed	Player	Club From
9.8.88	Evans, Tex	Swinton
5.9.88	Hadley, Adrian	Cardiff RU
14.9.88	Shaw, Paul	Manly-Warringah, Aus
12.10.88	Brown, Peter	Te Atatu, NZ
12.10.88	Horo, Mark	Te Atatu, NZ
17.11.88	Bragger, Ian	Keighley
6.12.88	Kerry, Steve	Preston Grasshoppers RU
9.12.88	Dobson, Mark	Rochdale H.
5.1.89	Rodden, Michael	Rose Bridge ARL

SHEFFIELD EAGLES

Signed	Player	Club From
3.8.88	Cartwright, Phil	Rochdale H.
4.8.88	Okesene, Paul	Richmond Rovers, NZ
9.8.88	Salomona, Masauwee	Richmond Rovers, NZ
23.8.88	Charlton, Gary	Egremont ARL
24.8.88	Halafihi, Nick	Bridlington RU
8.9.88	Evans, Steve	Bradford N.
9.9.88	Idle, Graham	Bramley
22.9.88	Geyer, Mark	Penrith, Aus
30.11.88	*Bridgeman, Derek	Bramley
31.12.88	Grimoldby, Nick	Fulham
6.1.89	Smiles, Warren	Bramley
6.1.89	Van Bellen, Gary	Wakefield T.
24.2.89	*Fleming, Mark	Halifax
23.3.89	Nickle, Sonny	Hunslet

SWINTON

Signed	Player	Club From
24.7.88	Wood, John	Widnes
26.7.88	Bond, Gary	Carlisle
31.7.88	Connor, Ian	West Park RU
11.8.88	Kinsey, Tony	Huddersfield
14.8.88	Wakefield, Stuart	Thatto Heath ARL
12.9.88	Kuiti, Michael	Upper Hutt, NZ
12.9.88	Tangira, Willie	Pentone, NZ
22.10.88	O'Neill, Steve	Widnes
22.10.88	Myler, John	Widnes
24.11.88	Smith, Dennis	Blackpool Stanley ARL
6.12.88	Edwards, Morvin	Upper Hutt, NZ
19.2.89	Ashell, John	Thatto Heath ARL
28.2.89	Pickavance, Ian	St. Helens Colts
16.3.89	Jackson, Steve	Lowerhouse ARL

WAKEFIELD TRINITY

Signed	Player	Club From
1.7.88	Timmins, Jason	Normanton ARL
1.7.88	Slater, Richard	Normanton ARL
8.8.88	Glancy, John	Sheffield E.
23.8.88	Kelly, Neil	Hunslet
26.8.88	Ella, Steve	Parramatta, Aus
26.8.88	Graham, Mark	North Sydney, Aus
8.9.88	Todd, Brent	Canberra, Aus
9.10.88	*Thornton, Gary	Batley
10.10.88	*Sygrove, Andy	Bramley
13.10.88	Norton, Steve	Hull
13.10.88	Leuluai, James	Hull
4.11.88	Wilson, Andy	Queens ARL
13.12.88	Hirst, John	Stanley Rangers ARL
7.1.89	McElhetton, Craig	Normanton ARL
9.1.89	*Hughes, Ian	York
9.1.89	Hunte, Alan	Eastmoor ARL
9.1.89	McCrew, Tom	Dewsbury
10.2.89	Slater, Martin	Featherstone R.
10.3.89	*Thornton, Gary	Bramley

WARRINGTON

Signed	Player	Club From
1.6.88	Rudd, Chris	Kells ARL
14.6.88	Sumner, Phil	Wigan St. Patricks ARL
15.6.88	Roach, Steve	Balmain, Aus
4.7.88	Chambers, Gary	Kells ARL
5.7.88	Richards, Basil	Queensbury ARL
8.7.88	Geary, Nigel	Wigan St. Judes ARL
11.7.88	Blake, Phil	South Sydney, Aus
11.7.88	Davidson, Les	South Sydney, Aus
11.7.88	Bishop, Paul	Cronulla, Aus
2.8.88	Abram, Darren	Swinton
8.9.88	Mayo, John	Fulham
24.11.88	Rea, Kevin	Millom ARL
5.12.88	Kenyon, Neil	Bold ARL
5.12.88	Massey, Neil	Woolston Rovers ARL
8.12.88	Darbyshire, Paul	Wigan St. Patricks ARL
29.12.88	Thomas, Mark	Leigh
5.1.89	Malloy, Frank	Simms Cross ARL
10.2.89	Muller, Roby	Runcorn H.
4.3.89	*Carroll, Dean	Carlisle
25.5.89	Burke, Tony	St. Helens

WHITEHAVEN

Signed	Player	Club From
28.6.88	Davidson, Alan	Kells ARL
27.7.88	Fryer, Steve	Flimby ARL
4.8.88	Geffney, Francis	Whitehaven RU
12.8.88	Huddart, Milton	Leigh
8.9.88	Sanders, Kevin	Distington ARL
10.9.88	White, Nigel	Manakare, NZ
10.9.88	Watson, David	Mangere, NZ
6.10.88	James, Michael	Barrow
6.1.89	Reynolds, Graeme	Mangere East, NZ
4.2.89	Williams, Barry	Broughton Red Rose RU
2.3.89	Burns, Bill	Kells ARL
9.3.89	Hewer, Gary	Barrow
21.3.89	McGlennan, Garry	St. Bees ARL

Australian Test prop forward Steve Roach, a short term recruit by Warrington from Balmain and flown back for the Silk Cut Challenge Cup semi-final at Manchester City.

383

WIDNES

Signed	Player	Club From
1.8.88	Myers, David	Blackbrook ARL
21.10.88	Koloto, Emosi	Wellington RU, NZ
6.1.89	Davies, Jonathan	Llanelli RU
25.3.89	Moriarty, Paul	Swansea RU

WIGAN

Signed	Player	Club From
1.9.88	Goulding, Robert	Widnes St. Maries ARL
5.9.88	Platt, Andy	St. Helens
27.9.88	Barr, Brendan	St. Judes ARL
4.10.88	Atta, Hamza	Hull University ARL
6.1.89	Welsby, Mark	Blackbrook ARL
9.2.89	Gilfillan, John	Orrell RU

WORKINGTON TOWN

Signed	Player	Club From
19.7.88	Ward, David	Leeds
11.8.88	Wilson, Robert	Great Clifton ARL
12.8.88	Torley, Iain	Glasson Rangers ARL
14.8.88	Lamb, Keith	Ellenborough ARL
6.9.88	Shuttleworth, Greg	Canterbury B., Aus
18.9.88	Johnson, Robert	Flimby ARL
24.9.88	Thornton, Peter	Tugun ARL
22.10.88	Vannet, Paul	Great Clifton ARL
8.11.88	Barker, Brian	Ellenborough ARL
8.12.88	Platt, Billy	Mansfield M.
19.1.89	McMullen, Alan	Carlisle
14.2.89	Walker, William	Broughton Red Rose ARL

YORK

Signed	Player	Club From
5.7.88	Macklin-Shaw, Chris	Illawara, Aus
14.7.88	Stephens, Gary	Halifax
14.7.88	St. Hilaire, Darren	Halifax
20.8.88	Pool, Philip	York All Blacks ARL
20.8.88	Warters, Nick	York Colts
9.9.88	Skelly, Michael	Queanbeyan, Aus
15.9.88	Bleakley, Steve	Redcliffe, Aus
4.10.88	Mulherin, Paul	Parramatta, Aus
10.11.88	Walker, Stuart	INL ARL
17.11.88	Payne, Phil	Doncaster
25.11.88	Crossley, John	Featherstone R.
8.12.88	*Hughes, Ian	Wakefield T.
15.12.88	Atkins, Paul	York All Blacks ARL
12.1.89	Hayes, Richard	York All Blacks ARL
12.1.89	Scott, Mick	Halifax
20.1.89	Hughes, Ian	Wakefield T.
1.2.89	Willey, Sean	North Sydney, Aus
17.2.89	Williams, Dean	Rochdale H.
10.3.89	*Smith, Steve	Hull K.R.
12.4.89	Morris, Stuart	Dewsbury
8.5.89	Hutchinson, Paul	Redhill ARL

Greenalls Man of Steel 1989, Great Britain and Wigan skipper Ellery Hanley.

AWARDS

THE 1989 MAN OF STEEL AWARDS

Launched in the 1976-77 season, the Rugby Football League's official awards are presented to the Man of Steel, the personality judged to have made the most impact on the season; the First and Second Division Players of the Year, decided by a ballot of the players; the Young Player of the Year, under 21 at the start of the season; the Coach of the Year and Referee of the Year all chosen by a panel of judges.

Having been sponsored by Trumanns Steel for the first seven years, the awards were taken over by Greenall Whitley in 1983-84. Last season they presented a record £7,000 in prizes at the Variety Centre, Salford.

Greenalls Man of Steel

Great Britain and Wigan skipper Ellery Hanley took his record haul of Man of Steel titles to three, earning £2,000 and an inscribed £300 silver champagne goblet. Hanley was voted Man of the Series in the Australian Tests Down Under; Man of the Match in both the Silk Cut Challenge Cup and John Player Special Trophy finals; captained his country, county and club to glory; plus inspiring Balmain to the Sydney Grand Final during a two-month stay. He also finished fourth in the try chart with 29 touchdowns and broke the First Division career total of tries, becoming the seventh most capped British Test player.

Greenalls First Division Player of the Year

Widnes stand off and vice-captain David Hulme topped the poll of fellow Stones Bitter Championship players, votes being cast in January and April. A 1988 Lion, he appeared in all five Tests Down Under and missed only a couple of games as Widnes lifted the Championship, the Premiership and the Charity Shield, plus being runners-up in the John Player Special Trophy. Nominees for the title were Andy Gregory (Wigan) and Kelvin Skerrett (Bradford Northern).

Greenalls Second Division Player of the Year

His fellow players' choice in the twin ballot was Sheffield Eagles skipper Darryl Powell who led the side to promotion and Second Division Premiership success in only their fifth season. The centre or loose forward established new club records with 28 tries in the season and five tries in a match, against Mansfield Marksman. Nominees were Cavill Heugh, of Barrow, and Leigh's Chris Johnson.

Greenalls Young Player of the Year

Featherstone Rovers centre Paul Newlove became the youngest-ever winner of the title — three months short of his 18th birthday — in his first season as a professional. Son of former Featherstone and Hull back, John, he was the Colliers' top try scorer with 18, plus nine goals, and scored a try and three goals on his debut appearances for Great Britain Under-21s at Leeds and Carpentras. Nominees were Grant Anderson (Castleford) and Wigan's Denis Betts.

Greenalls Referee of the Year

Kippax-based whistler John Holdsworth lifted the title for the third time having topped the assessment chart and taken charge of the Great Britain versus Rest of the World encounter, the John Player Special Trophy and the Premiership final. Nominees were Ray Tennant, of Castleford, and Widnes-based Robin Whitfield.

Greenalls Coach of the Year

Two days after announcing his departure from Wigan, New Zealander Graham Lowe took the annual award for the second time in three years. He had masterminded the capture of the Silk Cut Challenge Cup, the John Player Special Trophy, the Grunhalle Lager Lancashire Cup, plus runners-up spot in the Stones Bitter Championship after a last match title decider at Widnes. Nominees were Peter Fox (Featherstone Rovers) and Hull's Brian Smith.

THE MAN OF STEEL AWARDS ROLL OF HONOUR

	Man of Steel	1st Division Player	2nd Division Player	Young Player	Coach	Referee
1977	David Ward (Leeds)	Malcolm Reilly (Castleford)	Ged Marsh (Blackpool B.)	David Ward (Leeds)	Eric Ashton MBE (St. Helens)	Billy Thompson (Huddersfield)
1978	George Nicholls (St. Helens)	George Nicholls (St. Helens)	John Woods (Leigh)	John Woods (Leigh)	Frank Myler (Widnes)	Billy Thompson (Huddersfield)
1979	Doug Laughton (Widnes)	Mick Adams (Widnes)	Steve Norton (Hull)	Steve Evans (Featherstone R.)	Doug Laughton (Widnes)	Mick Naughton (Widnes)
1980	George Fairbairn (Wigan)	Mick Adams (Widnes)	Steve Quinn (Featherstone R.)	Roy Holdstock (Hull K.R.)	Peter Fox (Bradford N.)	Fred Lindop (Wakefield)
1981	Ken Kelly (Warrington)	Ken Kelly (Warrington)	John Crossley (York)	Des Drummond (Leigh)	Billy Benyon (Warrington)	John Holdsworth (Kippax)
1982	Mick Morgan (Carlisle)	Steve Norton (Hull)	Mick Morgan (Carlisle)	Des Drummond (Leigh)	Arthur Bunting (Hull)	Fred Lindop (Wakefield)
1983	Allan Agar (Featherstone R.)	Keith Mumby (Bradford N.)	Steve Nash (Salford)	Brian Noble (Bradford N.)	Arthur Bunting (Hull)	Robin Whitfield (Widnes)
1984	Joe Lydon (Widnes)	Joe Lydon (Widnes)	David Cairns (Barrow)	Joe Lydon (Widnes)	Tommy Dawes (Barrow)	Billy Thompson (Huddersfield)
1985	Ellery Hanley (Bradford N.)	Ellery Hanley (Bradford N.)	Graham Steadman (York)	Lee Crooks (Hull)	Roger Millward MBE (Hull K.R.)	Ron Campbell (Widnes)
1986	Gavin Miller (Hull K.R.)	Gavin Miller (Hull K.R.)	Derek Pyke (Leigh)	Shaun Edwards (Wigan)	Chris Anderson (Halifax)	Fred Lindop (Wakefield)
1987	Ellery Hanley (Wigan)	Andy Gregory (Wigan)	John Cogger (Runcorn H.)	Shaun Edwards (Wigan)	Graham Lowe (Wigan)	John Holdsworth (Kippax)
1988	Martin Offiah (Widnes)	Steve Hampson (Wigan)	Peter Smith (Featherstone R.)	Shaun Edwards (Wigan)	Doug Laughton (Widnes)	Fred Lindop (Wakefield)
1989	Ellery Hanley (Wigan)	David Hulme (Widnes)	Darryl Powell (Sheffield E.)	Paul Newlove (Featherstone R.)	Graham Lowe (Wigan)	John Holdsworth (Kippax)

DAILY MIRROR-STONES BITTER TEAM AWARDS 1988-89

Introduced in the 1979-80 season, the scheme acknowledges the adjudged Team of the Month in both Division One and Two.

A panel of judges representing the *Daily Mirror*, Stones Bitter and the Rugby League selected the two monthly winners, the First Division winners receiving £400, the Second Division £300, plus a framed citation.

Promoted by the *Daily Mirror*, the awards were sponsored for the first four seasons by Shopacheck before Lada Cars took over in the 1983-84 season and introduced the first-ever Team of the Year title. Stones Bitter took over the sponsorship in 1987-88, the 1989 Team of the Year receiving £1,500.

	First Division	Second Division
Aug./Sept.	Castleford	Keighley
Oct.	Leeds	Doncaster
Nov.	Widnes	Leigh
Dec.	Hull	Huddersfield
Jan.	Wigan	Sheffield E.
Feb.	Widnes	Leigh
Mar.	Wigan	Batley
Apr./May	Hull	Sheffield E.

Team of the Year
1983-84: Widnes
1984-85: Hull K.R.
1985-86: Halifax
1986-87: Wigan
1987-88: Widnes
1988-89: Wigan

STONES BITTER – DAILY STAR STARMEN AWARDS

Introduced in 1982-83, the scheme was sponsored by Stones Bitter and promoted by the *Daily Star*. For 1987-88 the top three players for each side in every Stones Bitter Championship and Second Division game were awarded a rating out of 10. The top pollster in the Championship — Featherstone Rovers skipper Deryck Fox — received £1,000 and a trophy, with £500 and a trophy being presented to the top Second Division player, Sheffield Eagles captain Darryl Powell.

The roll of honour is:

Championship

1982-83	Harry Pinner (St. Helens)
1983-84	John Woods (Leigh)
1984-85	Ellery Hanley (Bradford N.)
1985-86	Deryck Fox (Featherstone R.)
1986-87	Deryck Fox (Featherstone R.)
1987-88	Kurt Sorensen (Widnes)
1988-89	Deryck Fox (Featherstone R.)

Second Division

1982-83	Graham Beale (Keighley)
1983-84	John Wolford (Hunslet)
1984-85	Graham Steadman (York)
1985-86	Dean Carroll (Carlisle)
1986-87	Billy Platt (Mansfield M.)
1987-88	Chris Vasey (Dewsbury)
1988-89	Darryl Powell (Sheffield E.)

TRAVELEADS TOP FAN AWARD 1989

Huddersfield handyman Keith Burhouse (44) was declared official Supporter of the Year in recognition of his voluntary groundsman duties at Fartown. He won a £4,000 holiday for two featuring a trip to Milwaukee for the Warrington-Wigan promotional encounter.

GREENALL WHITLEY TOP SCORERS AWARDS 1988-89

Launched in the 1976-77 season, the scheme was designed to reward the top try and goal scorers in the League. Sponsored by brewers Greenall Whitley, the 1989 awards were worth £25 a try and £5 a goal.

For the second successive season, the top try merchant was Widnes winger Martin Offiah. The ex-Rosslyn Park RU flier touched down 60 times to earn a cheque for £1,500, beating his own Widnes club record with 58 tries for the Chemics, plus two for Great Britain.

Sheffield Eagles stand off Mark Aston topped the goal chart with 148, a new club record. He received a cheque for £740.

Top goal scorer Mark Aston, of Sheffield Eagles.

WALLACE ARNOLD – SUNDAY MIRROR ENTERTAINER AWARDS 1988-89

Introduced in 1986-87, the scheme was sponsored by Wallace Arnold and promoted by the *Sunday Mirror*.

Each month an adjudged player was chosen as Entertainer of the Month to receive a Wallace Arnold holiday voucher for £300. The Entertainer of the Year was awarded a £1,000 holiday voucher, the 1989 winner being Widnes winger Martin Offiah, the league's top try scorer, with 60, and top try scorer on the 1988 Lions tour Down Under with 19.

Entertainer of the Month 1988-89

Sept.	Graham Steadman (Featherstone R.)
Oct.	Kevin Ward (Castleford)
Nov.	Gavin Miller (Hull K.R.)
Dec.	Joe Lydon (Wigan)
Jan.	Darryl Powell (Sheffield E.)
Feb.	Mike O'Neill (Widnes)
Mar.	Gary Pearce (Hull)
Apr./May	Martin Offiah (Widnes)

Entertainer of the Year

1987:	Ellery Hanley (Wigan)
1988:	Martin Offiah (Widnes)
1989:	Martin Offiah (Widnes)

Hull stand off Gary Pearce, Entertainer of the Month for March 1989.

REFEREES

Silk Cut Challenge Cup final:
Ray Tennant

John Player Special Trophy final:
John Holdsworth

Stones Bitter Premiership final:
John Holdsworth

Second Division Premiership final:
Robin Whitfield

Grunhalle Lager Lancashire Cup final:
Kevin Allatt

John Smiths Yorkshire Cup final:
Robin Whitfield

Great Britain v Rest of World:
John Holdsworth

Under-21. France v Great Britain:
Dave Carter

European Club Championship:
Ray Tennant

Cumbria v France:
Colin Steele

Rodstock War of the Roses:
Robin Whitfield

Okells Charity Shield:
Ray Tennant

SENIOR REFEREES 1989-90

KEVIN ALLATT (Southport)
Date of birth: 29.12.42
Grade Two: 1970-71
Grade One: 1972-73
Premiership Trophy 1986-87
Lancashire Cup 1983-84, 1988-89
Yorkshire Cup 1987-88 (+replay)
Lancashire v Yorkshire 1975-76

DAVID ASQUITH (York)
Date of birth: 20.6.53
Grade One: 1989-90

GEOFF BERRY (Batley)
Date of birth: 26.4.54
Grade Two: 1981-82
Grade One: 1983-84

ALEX BOWMAN (Whitehaven)
Date of birth: 20.9.56
Grade One: 1986-87

ALAN BURKE (Oldham)
Date of birth: 21.1.57
Grade One: 1987-88

DAVID CAMPBELL (St. Helens)
Date of birth: 9.10.54
Grade One: 1989-90

DAVE CARTER (Widnes)
Date of birth: 29.11.55
Grade One: 1984-85
France v Great Britain Under-21s 1988-89

PAUL CRASHLEY (Wakefield)
Date of birth: 1.8.50
Grade One: 1989-90

STEVE CROSS (Hull)
Date of birth: 23.3.50
Grade One: 1986-87

BRIAN GALTRESS (Bradford)
Date of birth: 9.8.60
Grade One: 1988-89

STEPHEN HAIGH (Ossett)
Date of birth: 5.4.45
Grade Two: 1980-81
Grade One: 1983-84

JOHN HOLDSWORTH (Kippax)
Date of birth: 25.1.47
Grade Two: 1979-80
Grade One: 1980-81
Challenge Cup 1986-87
John Player Trophy 1985-86, 1986-87, 1988-89
Premiership Trophy 1980-81, 1987-88, 1988-89
Lancashire Cup 1982-83, 1985-86
World Club Challenge 1987-88
Wales v England 1980-81
Great Britain v Rest of World 1988-89
RL Chairman's XIII v Papua New Guinea 1987-88
Cumbria v Yorkshire 1981-82
France v Great Britain Under-24s 1982-83
War of the Roses 1987-88
Charity Shield 1987-88

GARY HOLGATE (Barrow)
Date of birth: 26.4.48
Grade One: 1987-88

JOHN KENDREW (Castleford)
Date of birth: 22.4.50
Grade Two: 1982-83
Grade One: 1983-84
Lancashire v Papua New Guinea 1987-88

GERRY KERSHAW (Easingwold)
Date of birth: 24.10.43
Grade Two: 1969-70
Grade One: 1970-71
Challenge Cup 1980-81
Lancashire Cup 1980-81
Floodlit Trophy 1973-74
John Player Trophy 1973-74
Wales v England 1981-82
Wales v Australia 1982-83
France v Great Britain Under-24s 1981-82
Lancashire v Yorkshire 1971-72
Lancashire v Cumbria 1972-73
Cumbria v Other Nationalities 1974-75
Cumbria v Lancashire 1978-79, 1980-81

COLIN MORRIS (Huddersfield)
Date of birth: 14.3.57
Grade One: 1989-90

KEIRON MORRIS (Widnes)
Date of birth: 29.9.48
Grade One: 1988-89

BRIAN SIMPSON (Manchester)
Date of birth: 23.6.44
Grade One: 1985-86

JIM SMITH (Halifax)
Date of birth: 2.3.44
Grade Two: 1977-78
Grade One: 1983-84
Lancashire Cup 1986-87

COLIN STEELE (Dalton-in-Furness)
Date of birth: 11.9.60
Grade One: 1987-88
Cumbria v France 1988-89

RAY TENNANT (Castleford)
Date of birth: 7.4.49
Grade One: 1985-86
Challenge Cup 1988-89
European Club Championship 1988-89
Charity Shield 1988-89
Cumbria v Papua New Guinea 1987-88

FRANK TICKLE (St. Helens)
Date of birth: 26.10.45
Grade One: 1984-85

CHARLIE TIDBALL (Wakefield)
Date of birth: 25.12.48
Grade One: 1987-88

JOHN WHITELAM (Hull)
Date of birth: 11.5.53
Grade One: 1988-89

ROBIN WHITFIELD (Widnes)
Date of birth: 26.11.43
Grade Two: 1979-80
Grade One: 1980-81
Challenge Cup 1982-83, 1985-86
Yorkshire Cup 1981-82, 1988-89
Second Division Premiership 1987-88, 1988-89
France v Australia (2) 1982-83
New Zealand v Australia 1983
Australia v New Zealand (3) 1986
Yorkshire v Lancashire 1981-82
War of the Roses 1988-89

Ray Tennant, in charge of the 1989 Silk Cut Challenge Cup final.

THE ALLIANCE

SLALOM LAGER ALLIANCE

FINAL TABLES 1988-89

FIRST DIVISION

	P.	W.	D.	L.	Dr.	Gls.	Trs.	Pts.	Dr.	Gls.	Trs.	Pts.	Pts.
						FOR				**AGAINST**			
Wigan	26	18	1	7	14	95	126	708	5	53	62	359	37
Castleford	26	17	2	7	7	102	112	659	5	60	74	421	36
St. Helens	26	16	1	9	6	94	108	626	4	77	89	514	33
Leeds	26	16	0	10	5	85	119	651	5	72	76	453	32
Hull K.R.	26	15	1	10	5	92	91	553	5	68	84	477	31
Widnes	26	13	1	12	2	90	102	590	1	89	88	531	27
Salford	26	13	1	12	3	76	96	539	9	75	79	475	27
Hull	26	12	3	11	5	79	80	483	3	63	79	445	27
Halifax	26	11	1	14	0	51	79	418	5	80	83	497	23
Warrington W.	26	11	0	15	2	85	92	540	8	93	94	570	22
Swinton C.	26	9	2	15	2	59	76	424	4	94	111	636	20
Hunslet	26	9	0	17	9	72	71	437	4	84	115	632	18
Carlisle	26	8	1	17	2	61	69	400	2	77	95	536	17
Whitehaven	26	6	2	18	0	48	55	316	2	104	147	798	14

● Bottom two clubs relegated

SECOND DIVISION

	P.	W.	D.	L.	Dr.	Gls.	Trs.	Pts.	Dr.	Gls.	Trs.	Pts.	Pts
						FOR				**AGAINST**			
Featherstone R.	24	22	0	2	5	99	114	659	5	54	51	317	44
Oldham	24	20	1	3	0	103	124	702	3	54	51	315	41
Bradford N.	24	14	2	8	4	79	106	586	5	64	65	393	30
Barrow	24	14	1	9	3	63	80	449	1	50	68	373	29
Bramley	24	11	3	10	1	57	68	387	5	70	84	481	25
Wakefield T.	24	12	0	12	3	64	84	467	7	56	68	391	24
York	24	11	0	13	9	74	86	501	3	62	77	435	22
Workington T.	24	11	0	13	13	53	62	367	6	58	57	350	22
Huddersfield	24	9	2	13	6	44	57	322	4	63	91	494	20
Doncaster	24	9	0	15	5	53	63	363	6	75	107	584	18
Dewsbury	24	7	3	14	3	51	61	349	5	75	101	559	17
Leigh	24	8	0	16	4	43	58	322	2	75	86	496	16
Trafford B.	24	2	0	22	3	59	55	341	7	86	112	627	4

● Top two clubs promoted

1988-89 RESULTS

FIRST DIVISION

Home: \ Away:	Carlisle	Castleford	Halifax	Hull	Hull K.R.	Hunslet	Leeds	St. Helens	Salford	Swinton C.	Warrington W.	Whitehaven	Widnes	Wigan
Carlisle	—	26-24	28-0	12-17	10-25	14-0	16-28	14-18	9-8	33-6	24-48	22-4	24-12	14-32
Castleford	28-22	—	40-18	26-4	30-12	40-14	24-18	66-12	17-22	29-4	34-0	34-16	12-28	24-23
Halifax	12-8	14-9	—	10-10	30-4	50-8	12-20	14-10	36-26	36-2	20-16	40-6	16-4	10-2
Hull	18-16	13-24	31-6	—	20-2	26-10	16-7	32-8	16-16	18-12	22-10	40-6	20-30	12-12
Hull K.R.	38-4	4-4	20-8	18-22	—	44-14	24-10	22-12	26-7	40-10	21-14	46-6	24-15	23-26
Hunslet	32-10	14-30	25-8	20-16	8-13	—	18-28	20-12	26-20	14-22	16-28	20-12	24-26	14-26
Leeds	32-16	12-20	24-10	19-16	22-12	18-30	—	50-14	42-6	34-14	38-22	38-12	52-2	4-54
St. Helens	22-10	22-21	46-16	44-12	28-18	22-19	18-16	—	18-8	41-15	27-18	50-22	20-4	37-6
Salford	34-8	12-20	38-4	22-16	14-39	10-11	6-21	16-14	—	14-10	8-0	60-8	26-12	30-14
Swinton C.	20-16	24-24	14-10	21-12	16-20	34-16	4-28	12-38	18-26	—	20-32	30-28	32-6	18-40
Warrington W.	10-18	21-26	42-6	30-12	24-32	19-20	28-26	24-21	36-25	10-14	—	50-6	14-20	16-15
Whitehaven	8-8	22-16	28-10	10-23	16-10	14-10	12-50	6-36	20-18	20-20	4-12	—	18-6	0-19
Widnes	28-12	14-26	20-12	32-20	42-12	66-22	26-2	24-24	20-44	14-22	34-8	80-8	—	13-5
Wigan	32-6	30-12	17-10	22-19	65-4	24-12	21-12	29-12	14-23	37-10	61-8	50-4	32-12	—

SECOND DIVISION

Home: \ Away:	Barrow	Bradford N.	Bramley	Dewsbury	Doncaster	Featherstone R.	Huddersfield	Leigh	Oldham	Trafford B.	Wakefield	Workington T.	York
Barrow	—	12-42	19-10	26-0	54-4	12-26	22-0	26-4	14-30	18-12	22-2	9-0	30-0
Bradford N.	28-18	—	12-12	33-0	40-0	16-18	20-31	34-6	26-26	29-19	12-20	28-2	26-19
Bramley	32-6	18-17	—	14-14	24-12	0-38	10-22	32-6	6-18	24-16	18-12	6-3	18-11
Dewsbury	10-24	24-48	14-14	—	28-12	10-18	14-14	12-17	24-22	22-18	18-12	26-6	14-25
Doncaster	12-28	28-36	11-22	24-12	—	6-34	10-26	22-8	16-24	22-19	11-25	10-7	30-16
Featherstone R.	23-14	32-23	28-26	44-14	38-22	—	38-2	38-9	24-16	40-8	4-26	32-15	26-18
Huddersfield	24-24	19-12	22-2	11-6	18-40	0-26	—	17-4	8-34	25-10	6-20	2-14	14-34
Leigh	10-17	20-30	49-12	29-8	18-0	12-26	11-0	—	10-32	26-10	10-24	22-10	11-24
Oldham	18-6	20-6	28-30	40-6	38-17	12-18	44-7	22-8	—	30-10	44-20	36-10	38-2
Trafford B.	16-28	12-16	44-8	18-19	8-16	14-28	10-40	10-14	14-36	—	8-30	6-1	36-12
Wakefield	8-12	2-22	24-5	24-38	15-20	10-18	26-6	22-10	16-26	46-18	—	12-9	6-22
Workington T.	38-0	17-10		20-16	13-14	14-30	36-4	38-18	12-24	21-9	23-11	—	23-13
York	24-8	18-20	20-30	46-0	33-4	19-12	27-4	28-4	23-24	54-12	6-34	7-11	—

Captain Paul Gill shows off the Slalom Lager Alliance Challenge Cup after their 1989 final success over St. Helens.

Slalom Lager Alliance final Man of the Match and Leeds skipper Paul Gill drives into the St. Helens defence.

SLALOM LAGER ALLIANCE CHALLENGE CUP 1989

First Round

Barrow	4	Hull	24
Bradford N.	38	Carlisle	12
Doncaster	15	Hull K.R.	30
Featherstone R.	30	Castleford	20
Hunslet	12	Bramley	4
Leigh	33	Trafford B.	10
Oldham	26	Dewsbury	15
Warrington W.	10	Wigan	32
Whitehaven	6	Leeds	16
Workington T.	18	Huddersfield	6
York	33	Salford	30

Byes: Halifax, St. Helens, Swinton, Wakefield T., Widnes

Second Round

Bradford N.	8	St. Helens	11
Hull	12	Halifax	25
Hull K.R.	19	York	12
Leigh	10	Leeds	37
Wakefield T.	17	Swinton C.	22
Widnes	4	Featherstone R.	8
Wigan	20	Oldham	12
Workington T.	7	Hunslet	10

Third Round

Leeds	10	Hull K.R.	2
St. Helens	56	Featherstone R.	6
Swinton C.	8	Hunslet	17
Wigan	4	Halifax	14

Semi-Finals

Leeds	30	Hunslet	18
St. Helens	24	Halifax	4

Final

Leeds	24	St. Helens	12

SLALOM LAGER ALLIANCE PLAYER OF THE YEAR

1986: Steve Gill (Castleford)
1987: Shaun Fairhurst (Leigh)
1988: Mike O'Hara (Blackpool S.)
1989: Alan Moses (Barrow)

LANCASHIRE COUNTY CHALLENGE SHIELD 1988-89

First Round

Barrow	8	Thatto Heath	18
Leigh	12	Oldham	13
St. Helens	32	Runcorn H.	0
Trafford B.	10	Carlisle	21
Warrington	36	Workington T.	18
Whitehaven	18	Salford	16
Widnes	26	Swinton	16
Wigan	28	Crossfields	8

Second Round

Oldham	9	Wigan	10
St. Helens	0	Widnes	34
Warrington	22	Carlisle	20
Whitehaven	28	Thatto Heath	16

Semi-Finals

Warrington	15	Widnes	16
Wigan	34	Whitehaven	6

Final

Wigan	22	Widnes	16

YORKSHIRE SENIOR COMPETITION CHALLENGE CUP 1988-89

First Round

Bradford N.	16	Hull K.R.	12
Bramley	14	Hull	26
Castleford	68	Streethouse	0
Dewsbury	28	Jubilee	18
Halifax	32	Hunslet	24
Leeds	124	Huddersfield	0
Wakefield T.	10	Doncaster	28
York	14	Featherstone R.	12

Second Round

Bradford N.	24	York	2
Castleford	30	Halifax	26
Doncaster	20	Hull	22
Leeds	30	Dewsbury	12

Semi-Finals

Hull	18	Castleford	29
Leeds	32	Bradford N.	13

Final

Leeds	22	Castleford	20

POT POURRI

HALL OF FAME

The Whitbread Trophy Hall of Fame opened on 24 October 1988 with nine selected all-time greats featured on sepia prints in an oak-panelled gallery in the Bentley Arms at Oulton, near Leeds.

Record points scorer Neil Fox became the 10th entry, joining the 13-a-side code's elite in August 1989.

Fox made a delayed entry into the line up of legends because of one of the two major ground rules, that a player had to have been retired for at least 10 years, the other guideline being that a player had to grace the British scene for the majority of his career.

His inclusion in the Hall of Fame came exactly a decade after his retirement to end a 23-year playing career.

Officially opened by the chairman of Whitbreads, Sam Whitbread, the Hall of Fame fulfilled its original concept of providing a Rugby League shrine featuring memorabilia of the League scenario, including photographs of great players, trophies, caps, medals and jerseys.

The opening ceremony was graced by the four living entrants into the Hall of Fame — Brian Bevan, Billy Boston, Alex Murphy and Gus Risman. Family dependants represented the five deceased Hall of Famers — Billy Batten, Jonty Parkin, Albert Rosenfeld, Jim Sullivan and Harold Wagstaff. Specially designed commemorative medals, struck by the Queen's jewellers, were presented by the League.

Rugby League's first-ever Hall of Fame — a £250,000 project — was celebrated by the staging of a Great Britain versus the Rest of the World encounter at Leeds on 29 October, a crowd of more than 12,000 watching the home side record a 30-28 victory.

NEIL FOX
1956-1979

The most prolific points scorer of all time, amassing 6,220 points from 358 tries and 2,574 goals, including four one-point drop goals, in 828 club and representative matches.

He broke many other records but was much more than a points machine. His big, powerful physique allied to an abundance of skills made him one of Great Britain's greatest-ever centres. He reigned supreme at international level for 10 years, his 29 Test appearances still being a record for a British centre.

After 14 years as an outstanding centre with Wakefield Trinity and briefly Bradford Northern, Fox moved into the pack and had another nine years as a shrewd, ball distributing back-row forward with Trinity, Hull K.R., York, Bramley, Huddersfield and Bradford.

Fox made his senior debut for Wakefield a month short of his 17th birthday and played his last match at 40 when he was injured playing for Bradford in the opening match of the 1979-80 season.

Among his many records is most points in a Challenge Cup final with 20 for Wakefield in the 38-5 defeat of Hull at Wembley in 1960.

Fox had a brief spell with Wellington in New Zealand during 1975 scoring 102 points, but they are not included in his records.

DIARY OF LANDMARKS

1895 August 29... the beginning. The Northern Rugby Football Union formed at The George Hotel, Huddersfield, following the breakaway from the English RU by 21 clubs who wanted to pay players for taking time off work to play.

September 7... season opens with 22 clubs.

Joseph Platt appointed Rugby League Secretary.

1897 April 24... Batley won the first Northern Union — later Rugby League — Challenge Cup final.

Line-out abolished and replaced by punt from touch.

All goals to be worth two points.

1898 Professionalism allowed but players must be in full-time employment.

1899 Scrum if player cannot release the ball after a tackle.

1901 Punt from touch replaced by 10-yard scrum when ball is carried into touch.

1902 Two divisions introduced.

Punt from touch abolished completely. Touch-finding rule introduced with the ball having to bounce before entering touch.

1905 Two divisions scrapped.

Lancashire and Yorkshire County Cup competitions inaugurated.

1906 Thirteen-a-side introduced, from traditional 15.

Play-the-ball introduced.

1907 First tour — New Zealand to England. The tour party were RU 'rebels'.

First Top Four play-off for championship.

1908 Australia and New Zealand launch Rugby League.

First Australian tour of England.

1910 First British tour of Australia and New Zealand.

1915 Competitive rugby suspended for duration of First World War.

1919 Competitive rugby resumed in January.

1920 John Wilson appointed Rugby League Secretary.

1922 Title of Northern Rugby Football Union changed to Rugby Football League.

Goal from a mark abolished.

1927 First radio broadcast of Challenge Cup Final — Oldham v. Swinton at Wigan.

1929 Wembley staged its first RL Challenge Cup final — Wigan v. Dewsbury.

1932 London exhibition match under floodlights at White City — Leeds v. Wigan.

1933 France staged its first Rugby League match — an exhibition between England and Australia in Paris.

London Highfield, formerly Wigan Highfield, became capital's first Rugby League team, also first to play regularly under floodlights.

1934 A French squad made a short tour of England before Rugby League was officially launched in France.

1935 European Championship introduced, contested by England, France and Wales.

1939 Second World War. Emergency war-time competitions introduced.

1945 War-time emergencies over.

Bill Fallowfield appointed Rugby League Secretary.

1946 First all-ticket match — Hull v. Hull K.R.

1948 King George VI became first reigning monarch to attend Rugby League match — Wigan v. Bradford Northern Cup final at Wembley.

First televised match — at Wembley — but shown only in London area.

Wembley's first all-ticket final.

International Board formed.

1949 Welsh League formed.

1950 Italian squad made brief tour of England.

1951 First televised match in the North — Britain v. New Zealand at Swinton.

First floodlights installation by Northern club, Bradford Northern.

1952 First nationally televised Challenge Cup final — Workington Town v. Featherstone Rovers.

1954 First World Cup, staged in France.

1955	London staged series of televised floodlit matches for the Independent Television Association Trophy. Welsh League disbanded.
1956	Sunday rugby for amateurs permitted by the Rugby Football League.
1962	Two divisions reintroduced, with Eastern and Western Divisions also formed.
1964	Substitutes allowed for injuries, but only up to half-time. Two division and regional leagues scrapped. One league system with Top-16 play-off for championship.
1965	BBC-2 Floodlit Trophy competition began with regular Tuesday night series. Substitutes allowed for any reason up to and including half-time. English Schools Rugby League formed.
1966	Four-tackle rule introduced for Floodlit Trophy competition in October, then for all games from December.
1967	First Sunday fixtures played, two matches on December 17th.
1969	Substitutes allowed at any time. University Rugby League Association formed.
1971	John Player Trophy competition launched.
1972	Six-tackle rule introduced. Timekeepers with hooter system to signal end of match introduced. Colts League formed.
1973	Two divisions re-introduced. March 4... British Amateur Rugby League Association formed.
1974	Drop goal value halved to one point. Had been reduced earlier in international matches. David Oxley appointed Rugby League Secretary. David Howes appointed first full-time Public Relations Officer to the Rugby Football League. National Coaching Scheme launched.
1975	Premiership Trophy competition launched.
1976	Differential penalty introduced for technical scrum offences.
1977	County Championship not held for first time since 1895, excluding war years. Anglo-Australian transfer ban agreed.
1978	Papua New Guinea admitted as full members of International Board.
1981	Rugby League Professional Players' Association formed.
1982	County Championship scrapped.
1983	January 1... Sin bin introduced. Try value increased to four points. Handover after sixth tackle introduced, among several other new or amended laws following meeting of International Board. Anglo-Australia transfer ban lifted.
1984	Alliance League introduced in reserve grade reorganisation.
1985	First Charity Shield match played in Isle of Man. War of the Roses launched on Lancashire v. Yorkshire county of origin basis. Relegation-promotion reduced to three down, three up.
1986	Relegation-promotion altered for one year only to four down, two up to provide a 14-strong First Division for the 1987-88 season.
1987	Division Two Premiership Trophy competition launched. New players' contracts system introduced.
1988	Colts scrapped for new youth scheme. Six-man League Board of Directors appointed, plus first-ever Controller of Referees, ex-match official Fred Lindop.
1989	First-ever Sales Marketing Executive, Mike Turner, appointed by the League.

DISCIPLINARY RECORDS

This sub-section is a compilation of sendings off and disciplinary verdicts for first team players.

The following information is based on the workings of the League's Disciplinary Committee which meets weekly during a season.

DISMISSALS .... A review

The following is a review of the number of first team players sent off in each season since 1982-83.
— indicates where a club was not in existence.

	1988-89	1987-88	1986-87	1985-86	1984-85	1983-84	1982-83
Sheffield E.	4	0	3	6	4	—	—
Southend I.	—	—	—	—	3	3	—
Swinton	2	3	3	2	2	0	4
Wakefield T.	1	5	5	6	7	5	2
Warrington	2	3	6	6	1	6	5
Whitehaven	3	3	2	3	3	6	2
Widnes	2	2	4	5	6	7	4
Wigan	3	5	3	3	2	2	3
Workington T.	3	5	5	9	5	4	3
York	3	4	3	2	1	4	2
Totals	**91**	**101**	**116**	**139**	**124**	**137**	**104**

	1988-89	1987-88	1986-87	1985-86	1984-85	1983-84	1982-83
Barrow	4	4	4	3	6	2	2
Batley	2	1	7	3	3	3	4
Bradford N.	2	2	2	4	0	3	3
Bramley	2	4	3	3	2	3	2
Bridgend	—	—	—	—	4	6	2
Carlisle	4	9	3	2	3	8	4
Castleford	4	3	1	3	1	5	4
Chorley B.	2	2	4	5	4	3	3
Dewsbury	3	5	3	4	4	2	5
Doncaster	1	3	2	4	1	10	2
Featherstone R.	1	2	0	0	3	1	1
Fulham	0	0	6	5	4	6	8
Halifax	1	1	2	1	5	3	4
Huddersfield	3	0	4	4	4	4	2
Hull	1	2	5	5	2	3	4
Hull K.R.	3	1	4	8	2	5	4
Hunslet	5	2	1	2	4	3	1
Keighley	3	5	7	8	7	0	3
Leeds	0	2	1	2	4	0	3
Leigh	3	6	2	1	1	3	2
Mansfield M.	7	2	6	3	3	—	—
Oldham	3	4	3	6	5	5	3
Rochdale H.	3	5	1	3	4	9	1
Runcorn H.	6	3	3	12	5	5	3
St. Helens	3	1	3	0	4	3	3
Salford	2	2	5	6	5	5	6

DISCIPLINARY ANALYSIS 1988-89

The following is a club-by-club disciplinary record for last season, showing the players sent off in first team matches and the findings of the League's Disciplinary Committee.

The committee's verdict is featured in the brackets after the player's name, each number indicating the match ban imposed. SOS stands for sending off sufficient and NG for not guilty. A suspension reduced or increased on appeal is shown as follows, 6 to 4.

During 1988-89 the totting-up system for sin-bin suspensions was abandoned. Previously two points were issued for a 10-minute temporary dismissal, a one-match ban being imposed when the total reached six. Instead, the sin bins were recorded and taken into account when considering a full dismissal.

* indicates where video evidence was submitted. The 1984-85 season was the first time video action other than official BBC or ITV tapes could be offered in evidence. In 1987-88 the committee considered video evidence in 37 individual cases, six more than during 1987-88. Five cases were considered by the committee after viewing a video, the player not having been dismissed.

Club	Total sent off	Dismissed Player	Number of Sin Bins
Barrow	4	M. James (2), G. Kendall (2), S. McGuire (*2), K. Pemberton (*2)	10
Batley	2	M. Scott (2), P. Geary (SOS)	10
Bradford N.	2	D. Hobbs (2), B. Hill (*3)	21
Bramley	2	S. Bond (*1), A. Gascoigne (*2)	5
Carlisle	4	M. Doyle (2), S. Kirkby (SOS), T. Catton (*1), B. Vickers (1)	7
Castleford	4	R. Gibbs (3, *NG), R. Southernwood (*2), M. Gibson (*NG)	7
Chorley B.	2	C. Brisco (2), J. Mayo (3)	7
Dewsbury	3	A. Shaw (*2), J. Moore (4), C. Wilkinson (2)	10
Doncaster	1	A. Timson (2)	10
Featherstone R.	1	C. Burton (3)	5
Fulham	0		7
Halifax	1	J. Pendlebury (*SOS)	13
Huddersfield	3	J. Johnson (4), D. Nelson (*2), F. Simpson (*1)	13
Hull	1	A. Dannatt (*2)	3
Hull K.R.	3	J. Irvine (*SOS), G. Miller (*SOS), M. Beall (*NG)	15
Hunslet	5	A. Marson (NG), G. Coates (2), K. Mason (*2, 3), C. Bowden (2)	13
Keighley	3	M. Fairbank (4), K. Rose (2), J. Bardgett (*SOS)	18
Leeds	0		11
Leigh	3	J. Kerr (*3 to 1), T. Street (3, *6 to 8)	18
Mansfield M.	7	B. Kellett (*SOS), N. Rudd (*3), C. Whitehead (4), L. Chadwick (*2), M. Howarth (*2), B. Andrews (*2), D. Moulden (*3)	7
Oldham	3	J. Fairbank (1), K. Newton (NG), P. Round (*3)	11
Rochdale H.	3	S. Hoare (2), L. Charnock (3), P. Gamble (SOS)	14
Runcorn H.	6	J. Brown (2), W. Ashurst (4), T. Jackson (6), P. Fraser (3), D. Walsh (2), H. Henney (4)	14
St. Helens	3	B. Dwyer (1), S. Evans (3), D. Tanner (2)	13
Salford	2	S. Gibson (*2), P. Brown (*3)	9
Sheffield E.	4	C. McDermott (3), P. Broadbent (2), A. Dickinson (SOS), S. Evans (2)	7
Swinton	2	J. Horrocks (*4), S. O'Neill (2)	13
Wakefield T.	1	A. Mason (*1)	10
Warrington	2	S. Roach (3 to *2), J. Woods (*SOS)	14
Whitehaven	3	S. Howse (2), D. McCartney (4), N. Lofthouse (3)	8

Widnes	2	R. Eyres (*1), E. Koloto (*2)	13
Wigan	3	D. Betts (NG), D. Bell (6), G. Byrne (3)	12
Workington T.	3	G. Phillips (4), A. McMullen (4), G. Burgess (2)	7
York	3	M. Scott (SOS), P. Payne (*1), S. Willey (4)	12

• In addition, the Disciplinary Committee carried out five *trials by video*, calling up, after viewing video tapes, players who had not been dismissed. Neil Clawson of Oldham was given a four match ban; Paul Delaney of Leeds three matches; Des Harrison of Hull K.R. two matches; and Brent Todd of Wakefield T. one match. Ron Gibbs of Castleford was reprimanded.

SPONSORSHIP
This updated sub-section is a record of the sponsorship programme under the control of the Rugby Football League.

1988-89 COMPETITIONS:

Silk Cut Challenge Cup	£170,000
John Player Special Trophy	£170,000
Stones Bitter Championship and Premiership	£150,000
Whitbread Trophy Bitter Tests	£ 80,000
British Coal Nines	£ 25,000
Okells Charity Shield	£ 7,000
Rodstock War of the Roses	£ 4,000
	£606,000
Awards:	£ 28,000
Miscellaneous:	£ 45,000
GRAND TOTAL	£679,000

COMPETITION SPONSORSHIP
The following is a review of sponsorship of the game's major competitions.

SILK CUT CHALLENGE CUP

	Prel.	1st	2nd	3rd	S.F.	R.U.	Winners	Development Fund	Total
	£	£	£	£	£	£	£	£	£
1979	—	750	1,160	2,000	3,555	6,555	12,555	4,500	60,000
1980	—	750	1,160	2,000	3,555	6,555	12,555	19,500	75,000
1981	—	750	1,160	2,000	3,555	6,555	12,555	29,500	85,000
1982	1,000	1,000	1,400	2,400	4,325	8,000	14,555	30,000	100,000
1983	1,000	1,000	1,400	2,400	4,325	8,000	14,555	40,000	110,000
1984	1,000	1,000	1,400	2,400	4,325	8,000	14,555	48,000	120,000
1985	1,100	1,100	1,500	2,500	4,500	9,000	16,000	47,600	130,000
1986	1,100	1,100	1,500	2,500	4,500	9,000	16,000	57,600	140,000
1987	1,200	1,200	1,650	2,750	4,500	9,000	16,000	58,200	150,000
1988	1,200	1,200	1,800	3,000	5,000	10,000	18,000	62,000	160,000
1989	1,300	1,300	2,000	3,250	5,500	11,000	20,000	62,600	170,000

• Sponsored by State Express 1979-84.

JOHN PLAYER SPECIAL TROPHY

	Prel.	1st	2nd	3rd	S.F.	R.U.	Winners	Development Fund	Total
	£	£	£	£	£	£	£	£	£
1971-72	—	—	—	—	1,000	2,500	5,000	—	9,500
1972-73	—	150	300	450	1,000	2,500	5,000	—	16,100
1973-74	—	150	300	450	1,000	2,500	5,000	—	16,100
1974-75	—	150	300	450	1,000	2,500	5,000	—	16,100
1975-76	—	300	450	600	1,500	3,000	6,000	—	22,800
1976-77	—	400	550	700	1,500	3,000	6,000	—	25,600
1977-78	—	450	600	750	1,750	3,500	8,000	—	30,000
1978-79	—	550	700	900	1,750	3,500	8,000	—	33,000
1979-80	—	600	800	1,000	2,000	4,000	8,500	—	36,500
1980-81	—	600	800	1,000	2,000	4,000	8,500	3,500	40,000
1981-82	700	700	900	1,175	2,500	4,500	9,000	7,000	50,000
1982-83	700	700	900	1,175	2,500	5,000	10,000	10,500	55,000
1983-84	700	700	900	1,175	2,500	5,000	10,000	15,500	60,000
1984-85	750	750	1,000	1,500	2,500	5,000	10,000	20,000	75,000
1985-86	750	750	1,000	1,500	2,750	5,500	11,000	26,000	80,000
1986-87	800	800	1,100	1,700	3,000	6,000	12,000	26,200	85,000
1987-88	1,100	1,100	1,600	2,825	4,750	9,000	16,000	65,000	150,000
1988-89	1,250	1,250	1,850	3,175	5,250	10,000	18,000	74,000	170,000

STONES BITTER

	Championship winners	R.U.	2nd Division winners	R.U.	Premiership winners	R.U.	2nd Division Premiership winners	R.U.	Development Fund	Total
	£	£	£	£	£	£	£	£	£	£
1980-81	6,000	—	3,000	—	4,000	—	—	—	42,000	55,000
1981-82	10,000	—	6,000	—	6,000	—	—	—	48,000	70,000
1982-83	12,000	—	7,000	—	7,000	—	—	—	54,000	80,000
1983-84	12,000	—	7,000	—	7,000	—	—	—	59,000	85,000
1984-85	13,000	—	9,000	—	8,000	—	—	—	60,000	90,000
1985-86	13,000	—	9,000	—	8,000	—	—	—	65,000	95,000
1986-87	20,000	8,000	10,000	4,000	9,000	3,500	4,000	1,500	60,000	120,000
1987-88	20,000	8,000	10,000	4,000	9,000	3,500	4,000	1,500	70,000	123,000
1988-89	25,000	10,000	12,000	5,000	10,000	4,000	5,000	2,000	77,000	150,000

● Sponsored by Slalom Lager from 1980-86

GRUNHALLE LAGER LANCASHIRE CUP

	Winners	Total
	£	£
1976	1,000	4,000
1977	1,500	5,000
1978	1,800	5,500
1979	1,900	6,000
1980	2,530	10,000
1981	2,700	11,000
1982	3,000	11,500
1983	3,200	12,500
1984	3,400	13,250
1985	3,400	13,250
1986	4,300	17,000
1987	4,600	18,600
1988	5,000	19,000

● Sponsored by Burtonwood Brewery 1976-85

YORKSHIRE CUP

	Sponsor	Winners	Total
		£	£
1972	Esso	800	4,000
1973	Esso	1,500	6,000
1974	Esso	1,400	6,000
1975	Esso	1,200	6,000
1976	Esso	1,200	6,000
1977	Esso	1,600	8,000
1978	Esso	2,000	9,000
1979	Esso	2,000	9,500
1980	Websters Brewery	2,750	13,000
1981	Websters Brewery	3,000	14,000
1982	Websters Brewery	2,500	15,000
1983	Philips Video	2,500	15,000
1984	Philips Video	2,500	15,000
1985	John Smiths	2,500	5,000
1986	John Smiths	2,500	12,500
1987	John Smiths	3,000	12,500
1988	John Smiths	3,500	27,500

INTERNATIONAL

Great Britain v Australia Tests 1978
Forward Chemicals: £17,500

Great Britain v Australia Tests 1982
Dominion Insurance: £40,000

Great Britain v France Tests 1983
Dominion Insurance: £5,000

Great Britain v France Tests 1984
Dominion Insurance: £5,000

Great Britain Tour 1984
Modern Maintenance Products: £100,000

Great Britain 1985-86
Whitbread Trophy Bitter: £85,000

Great Britain 1986-87
Whitbread Trophy Bitter: £85,000

Great Britain 1987-88
Whitbread Trophy Bitter: £80,000

Great Britain 1988-89
Whitbread Trophy Bitter: £80,000

NINE-A-SIDES

The second British Coal Nines tournament was again staged at Central Park, Wigan. Featured on BBC TV's Sportsnight, the 2½-hour tourney was won by Warrington who defeated the Rest of the World outfit in the final. The £25,000 sponsored event was entered by the top six clubs in the 1987-88 Stones Bitter Championship table, plus invitation sides, the Rest of the World and a President's IX selected by Les Bettinson. All matches were played seven minutes each way, except the final which was extended to nine minutes each half. First round losers received £2,000 each, semi-finalists £3,000 each, the runners-up £4,000 and the winners £6,000, the remaining £1,000 being allocated to travel expenses. The 1988 results were:

First Round

Leeds	6	President's IX	4
St. Helens	14	Widnes	12
Bradford N.	0	Rest of the World	4
Warrington	12	Wigan	6

Semi-Finals

Rest of the World	16	Leeds	12
Warrington	6	St. Helens	0

Final

Warrington	24	Rest of the World	0

Attendance: 7,141
Man of the Tournament: John Woods (Warrington)

ATTENDANCES

CLUB ATTENDANCE REVIEW

The following is a review of clubs' home attendances for league matches from 1980-81.

The main figure is the individual club's average gate for league games during that season. The figure in brackets indicates an upward or downward trend compared with the previous season.

Also indicated is the division the club competed in that season, i.e.

1 — First Division, 2 — Second Division.

Club	80-81	81-82	82-83	83-84	84-85	85-86	86-87	87-88	88-89
Barrow	1 4065 (+922)	1 4162 (+97)	1 3852 (−310)	2 3218 (−450)	1 2728 (−490)	2 1926 (−802)	1 2664 (+738)	2 1624 (−1040)	2 1594 (−30)
Batley	2 1329 (−1)	2 1052 (−277)	2 916 (−136)	2 864 (−52)	2 1015 (+151)	2 930 (−85)	2 744 (−186)	2 859 (+115)	2 924 (+65)
Bradford N.	1 6105 (−131)	1 5816 (−289)	1 4920 (−896)	1 5316 (+386)	1 4251 (−1065)	1 3975 (−276)	1 4312 (+377)	1 4723 (+411)	1 4969 (+246)
Bramley	2 1050 (−154)	2 928 (−122)	2 809 (−119)	2 759 (−50)	2 858 (+99)	2 831 (−27)	2 737 (−94)	2 858 (+121)	2 1004 (+146)
Bridgend	—	2 2008 —	2 854 (−1154)	2 581 (−273)	2 510 (−70)	—	—	—	—
Carlisle	—	2 2950 (−1026)	1 1924 (−1172)	2 752 (+244)	2 986 (−368)	2 618 (+171)	2 789 (+171)	2 763 (−26)	2 678 (−85)
Castleford	1 4612 (+898)	1 3791 (−821)	1 3548 (−243)	1 4288 (+740)	1 3217 (−1071)	1 3701 (+430)	1 4758 (+1057)	1 4520 (−238)	1 6580 (+2060)
Chorley B.	2 684 (−892)	2 768 (+84)	2 679 (−89)	2 625 (−54)	2 555 (−70)	2 534 (−21)	2 475 (−59)	2 922 (+447)	2 512 (−410)
Dewsbury	2 1377 (−175)	2 1048 (−329)	2 779 (−269)	2 706 (−73)	2 995 (+189)	1 1819 (+824)	2 669 (−1150)	2 658 (−41)	2 772 (+114)
Doncaster	2 628 (+200)	2 556 (−72)	2 441 (−115)	2 255 (−186)	2 266 (+11)	2 689 (+423)	2 1543 (+854)	2 1450 (−93)	2 1906 (+456)
Featherstone R.	1 3007 (+706)	1 2806 (−201)	1 2647 (−159)	1 3032 (+385)	1 2541 (−491)	1 2320 (−221)	1 2606 (+286)	2 1879 (−727)	1 4379 (+2500)
Fulham	2 6096 —	1 4321 (−1775)	2 2688 (−1633)	1 2238 (−450)	2 949 (−1289)	2 817 (−132)	2 684 (−133)	2 615 (−69)	2 588 (−27)
Halifax	1 4090 (+1121)	2 2818 (−1272)	1 2270 (−548)	2 1254 (−1016)	1 3497 (+2243)	1 4944 (+1447)	1 4891 (−53)	1 6521 (+1630)	1 8022 (+1501)
Huddersfield	2 1769 (+115)	2 1185 (−584)	2 776 (−409)	2 699 (−77)	2 905 (+206)	2 678 (−227)	2 524 (−154)	2 601 (+77)	2 1114 (+513)
Hull	1 11711 (+1690)	1 13190 (+1479)	1 11525 (−1665)	1 10679 (−846)	1 8525 (−2154)	1 6245 (−1280)	1 5538 (−707)	1 5111 (−427)	1 6804 (+1693)
Hull K. R.	1 8904 (+1951)	1 8723 (−181)	1 7379 (−1344)	1 6966 (−413)	1 6715 (−215)	1 4855 (−1860)	1 4651 (−204)	1 4186 (−465)	1 5298 (+1111)
Hunslet	2 921 (−797)	2 744 (−177)	2 1195 (+451)	2 1338 (+143)	1 2246 (+908)	2 722 (−1524)	1 1050 (+338)	1 2678 (+1050)	2 947 (−1731)

Club	80-81	81-82	82-83	83-84	84-85	85-86	86-87	87-88	88-89
Keighley	2 1612 (+19)	2 1576 (−36)	2 1085 (−491)	2 734 (−351)	2 822 (+88)	2 685 (−137)	2 445 (−240)	2 958 (+503)	2 961 (+3)
Leeds	1 5934 (−747)	1 5599 (−335)	1 5893 (+294)	1 6542 (+649)	1 7330 (+788)	1 6928 (−402)	1 6393 (−535)	1 9911 (+3518)	1 12060 (+2149)
Leigh	1 4498 (+80)	1 5939 (+1441)	1 4617 (−1322)	1 4434 (−183)	1 3822 (−612)	2 2710 (−1112)	1 4232 (+1522)	1 4516 (+284)	2 2346 (−2170)
Mansfield M.	—	—	—	—	2 1020 —	2 487 (−553)	2 368 (−119)	2 368 —	2 560 (+192)
Oldham	1 3220 (+853)	1 2395 (−825)	1 3721 (+1326)	1 4138 (+417)	1 4562 (+424)	1 4333 (−229)	1 3915 (−418)	2 3790 (−125)	1 5759 (+1696)
Rochdale H.	2 1149 (−61)	2 888 (−261)	2 619 (−269)	2 538 (−81)	2 542 (+4)	2 1267 (+725)	2 877 (−390)	2 1106 (+229)	2 1027 (−79)
Runcorn H.	2 270 (+32)	2 385 (+115)	2 224 (−161)	2 172 (−52)	2 509 (+337)	2 363 (−146)	2 331 (−35)	2 515 (+184)	2 298 (−217)
St. Helens	1 4934 (−643)	1 4862 (−72)	1 4543 (−319)	1 4656 (+113)	1 7336 (+2680)	1 6022 (−1314)	1 7341 (+1391)	1 8417 (+1076)	1 9514 (+1097)
Salford	1 3458 (−1388)	2 2404 (−1054)	2 1928 (−476)	1 2399 (+471)	2 1795 (−604)	1 2520 (+725)	1 2826 (+306)	1 3747 (+921)	1 5470 (+1723)
Sheffield E.	—	—	—	—	2 885 —	2 698 (−187)	2 708 (+10)	2 847 (+139)	2 838 (−9)
Southend Invicta	—	—	—	2 731	2 216 (−515)	—	—	—	—
Swinton	2 1935 (+426)	2 1567 (−368)	2 1314 (−253)	2 1077 (−237)	2 1590 (+513)	1 2706 (+1116)	2 1622 (−1084)	1 2987 (+1365)	2 1435 (−1543)
Wakefield T.	1 4814 (+255)	1 3716 (−1098)	2 2344 (−1372)	1 3483 (+1139)	2 1568 (−1915)	2 1714 (+146)	1 2637 (+923)	2 2416 (−221)	1 5151 (+2735)
Warrington	1 4917 (−205)	1 3838 (−1079)	1 3824 (−14)	1 4059 (+235)	1 3801 (−258)	1 3618 (−183)	1 4172 (+554)	1 4974 (+820)	1 4893 (−81)
Whitehaven	2 2733 (+972)	1 2710 (−23)	2 1742 (−968)	1 1639 (−103)	2 1540 (−99)	2 1878 (+333)	2 1800 (−78)	2 1772 (−28)	2 1310 (−462)
Widnes	1 5306 (−837)	1 5485 (+179)	1 4703 (−782)	1 4687 (−16)	1 4266 (−421)	1 4019 (−247)	1 3840 (−179)	1 6262 (+2422)	1 8648 (+2386)
Wigan	2 4693 (+28)	1 5497 (+804)	1 7426 (+1929)	1 7479 (+53)	1 10056 (+2577)	1 12515 (+2459)	1 12732 (+217)	1 13021 (+289)	1 14543 (+1519)
Workington T.	1 2188 (+354)	2 1969 (−219)	1 1470 (−499)	2 934 (−536)	1 920 (−14)	2 702 (−218)	2 653 (−49)	2 737 (+84)	2 774 (+37)
York	2 3827 (−107)	1 3677 (−150)	2 1685 (−1992)	2 1215 (−470)	2 1528 (+313)	1 2828 (+1300)	2 1520 (−1380)	2 1406 (−114)	2 2021 (+615)

COMPETITION ATTENDANCE REVIEW

		80-81	81-82	82-83	83-84	84-85	85-86	86-87	87-88	88-89
FIRST	Total	1,226,428	1,264,520	1,113,915	1,140,548	1,137,195	1,100,329	1,162,666	1,060,296	1,327,192
DIVISION	Av.	5,110	5,268	4,641	4,752	4,738	4,585	4,844	5,826	7,292
SECOND	Total	420,994	403,652	321,226	279,673	266,730	310,311	217,552	381,825	298,776
DIVISION	Av.	2,005	1,484	1,181	914	953	1,014	863	1,364	1,067
LEAGUE TOTALS (1st & 2nd)	Total	1,647,422	1,668,172	1,435,141	1,420,221	1,403,925	1,410,640	1,380,218	1,442,121	1,625,968
	Av.	3,661	3,258	2,803	2,601	2,700	2,584	2,805	3,121	3,519
R.L. CUP	Av.	9,993	11,388	8,355	8,399	8,497	8,280	6,965	8,764	8,666
JOHN PLAYER	Av.	5,362	5,590	4,219	3,893	4,881	4,232	4,122	3,570	4,987
PREMIER	Av.	11,689	9,454	10,099	8,136	10,115	9,273	15,154	13,462	15,856
10,000 + (No. of)		36	36	37	26	27	36	43	46	59

20,000-plus crowds . . . . A 10-year review

All matches except the Rugby League Challenge Cup final at Wembley

20,775	Bradford N. v. Hull	RL Cup round 3	Bradford	9 Mar. 1980
29,448	Hull v. Hull K.R.	Premiership final	Leeds	16 May 1981
25,245	Hull v. Hull K.R.	John Player final	Leeds	23 Jan. 1982
21,207	Hull v. Castleford	RL Cup semi-final	Leeds	27 Mar. 1982
41,171	Hull v. Widnes	RL Cup final replay	Elland Rd, Leeds	19 May 1982
26,771	Britain v. Australia	First Test	Hull C. FC	30 Oct. 1982
23,216	Britain v. Australia	Second Test	Wigan	20 Nov. 1982
26,031	Hull v. Castleford	RL Cup semi-final	Elland Rd, Leeds	2 Apr. 1983
20,569	Hull v. Hull K.R.	Division One	Hull	8 Apr. 1983
20,077	St. Helens v. Wigan	RL Cup round 3	St. Helens	11 Mar. 1984
25,237	Hull v. Hull K.R.	Yorks Cup final	Hull C. FC	27 Oct. 1984
26,074	St. Helens v. Wigan	Lancs Cup final	Wigan	28 Oct. 1984
25,326	Hull v. Hull K.R.	John Player final	Hull C. FC	26 Jan. 1985
20,982	Hull v. Castleford	RL Cup semi-final	Leeds	6 Apr. 1985
20,968	Hull v. Castleford	RL Cup semi-final replay	Leeds	10 Apr. 1985
22,209	Britain v. New Zealand	Third Test	Elland Rd, Leeds	9 Nov. 1985
21,813	Wigan v. St. Helens	Division One	Wigan	26 Dec. 1985
23,866	Hull K.R. v. Leeds	RL Cup semi-final	Elland Rd, Leeds	29 Mar. 1986
32,485	Hull K.R. v. Leeds	RL Cup semi-final replay	Elland Rd, Leeds	3 Apr. 1986
28,252	Wigan v. St. Helens	Lancs Cup semi-final	Wigan	1 Oct. 1986
30,622	Wigan v. Australia	Tour	Wigan	12 Oct. 1986
20,180	Oldham v. Wigan	Lancs Cup final	St. Helens	19 Oct. 1986
50,583	Britain v. Australia	First Test	Manchester U. FC	25 Oct. 1986
30,808	Britain v. Australia	Second Test	Elland Rd, Leeds	8 Nov. 1986

(continued)

20,169	Britain v. Australia	Third Test	Wigan	22 Nov. 1986
21,214	St. Helens v. Wigan	Division One	St. Helens	26 Dec. 1986
21,144	Warrington v. Wigan	John Player final	Bolton W. FC	10 Jan. 1987
20,355	Wigan v. St. Helens	Division One	Wigan	17 Apr. 1987
22,457	Wigan v. Halifax	Premiership semi-final	Wigan	10 May 1987
38,756	Warrington v. Wigan	Premiership final	Manchester U. FC	17 May 1987
36,895	Wigan v. Manly	World Club Challenge	Wigan	7 Oct. 1987
20,234	Wigan v. Warrington	Lancs Cup final	St. Helens	11 Oct. 1987
23,809	Wigan v. St. Helens	Division One	Wigan	27 Dec. 1987
25,110	Wigan v. Leeds	RL Cup round 2	Wigan	14 Feb. 1988
20,783	Salford v. Wigan	RL Cup semi-final	Bolton W. FC	12 Mar. 1988
20,534	Halifax v. Hull	RL Cup semi-final	Leeds	26 Mar. 1988
25,117	Hull v. Halifax	RL Cup semi-final replay	Elland Rd, Leeds	30 Mar. 1988
21,812	St. Helens v. Wigan	Division One	St. Helens	1 Apr. 1988
35,252	St. Helens v. Widnes	Premiership final	Manchester U. FC	15 May 1988
22,968	Castleford v. Leeds	Yorks Cup final	Elland Rd, Leeds	16 Oct. 1988
20,709	Widnes v. Wigan	John Player final	Bolton W. FC	7 Jan. 1989
26,080	Leeds v. Widnes	RL Cup round 2	Leeds	26 Feb. 1989
26,529	Warrington v. Wigan	RL Cup semi-final	Manchester C. FC	25 Mar. 1989
21,076	Wigan v. St. Helens	Division One	Wigan	12 Apr. 1989
40,194	Hull v. Widnes	Premiership Final	Manchester U. FC	14 May 1989

1988-89 ATTENDANCE ANALYSIS

FIRST DIVISION

Total 1,327,192
Average 7,292

Gates rose by 25 per cent compared with the 1987-88 figures of 1,060,296 and 5,826. Since the streamlining of the division from 16 to 14 clubs two years earlier, the average gate has gone up by 50 per cent. Only one club, Warrington, did not record an annual increase, Wigan topping the chart for the fifth consecutive season, up to 14,543, the highest average in two-division history. There were a host of massive increases in average gates, particularly the promoted trio of Featherstone Rovers (133 per cent), Wakefield Trinity (113 per cent) and Oldham (52 per cent), plus Salford (46 per cent), Castleford (45 per cent) and Widnes (38 per cent).

SECOND DIVISION

Total 298,776
Average 1,067

After a massive 40 per cent increase, Second Division gates fell by 11 per cent compared with the 1987-88 figures of 381,825 and 1,364. Nine of the 20 clubs recorded a rise in gates, notably York with a 44 per cent increase to finish second in the gates chart behind champions Leigh; Doncaster going up a further 31 per cent to third spot; and revitalised Huddersfield who registered an 85 per cent increase to move into seventh position.

LEAGUE CHAMPIONSHIP

Aggregate 1,625,968
Average 3,519

The average attendance for the 34 clubs in both divisions, staging a total of 462 matches, was up 13 per cent compared with the previous figures of 1,442,121 and 3,121.

SILK CUT CHALLENGE CUP

The 1989 Cup trail attracted a total of 320,642 to the 37 ties, including a new lower capacity of 78,000 at the Wembley final. The average of 8,666 was a one per cent decrease on the 1988 figure of 8,764.

JOHN PLAYER SPECIAL TROPHY

There was a 40 per cent upward trend for the 1988-89 tournament, which attracted a total of 179,532 fans to the 36 ties, including a replay, providing an average of 4,987 compared with the previous 3,570.

STONES BITTER PREMIERSHIP

The end of season top-eight competition was attended by a total of 110,992 fans, the average gate for the seven ties being 15,856. This was an 18 per cent increase on the 1988 figures of 94,235 and 13,462. The tournament featured a new record attendance for a Premiership final of 40,194 at Manchester United's Old Trafford ground.

SECOND DIVISION PREMIERSHIP

The six ties, including a replay, staged outside of the doubleheader at Old Trafford attracted a total of 13,845. The average of 2,307 was down 23 per cent compared with the 1988 figure of 2,845. The staging of the Second Division Premiership final as part of a double bill helped boost the Old Trafford gate to a tournament record 40,194.

GRUNHALLE LAGER LANCASHIRE CUP

Gates for the 15-tie competition went up by 16 per cent, the 1988-89 total being 94,107 and the average gate being 6,274 compared with the previous figures of 81,151 and 5,410.

JOHN SMITHS YORKSHIRE CUP

The White Rose county tournament attracted a 42 per cent rise in attendances. The 1988-89 returns were a total of 104,473 for an average of 6,145, compared with the previous average of 4,327.

FIVE-FIGURE CROWDS

There were 59 five-figure gates, a new record since the reintroduction of two-divisions in 1973 and beating the previous best of 47 set 12 months earlier. The traditional top gate was at Wembley for the 1989 Silk Cut Challenge Cup final, the new lower capacity of 78,000 being the seventh full house. The 40,000 barrier was broken for the Stones Bitter Premiership double-header at Manchester United, which attracted a tournament record of 40,194. The 10,000-plus gates were divided into the following categories.

League 33
Challenge Cup 9
Premiership Trophy 5
John Player Special Trophy 4
Yorkshire Cup 4
Lancashire Cup 3
GB v. Rest of World 1

STONES BITTER CHAMPIONSHIP

	1988-89 Average	Annual Difference
Wigan	14543	(+1519)
Leeds	12060	(+2149)
St. Helens	9514	(+1097)
Widnes	8648	(+2386)
Halifax	8022	(+1501)
Hull	6804	(+1693)
Castleford	6580	(+2060)
*Oldham	5759	(+1969)
Salford	5470	(+1723)
Hull Kingston Rovers	5298	(+1111)
*Wakefield Trinity	5151	(+2735)
Bradford Northern	4969	(+246)
Warrington	4893	(−81)
*Featherstone Rovers	4379	(+2500)

Promoted 1987-88

SECOND DIVISION

	1988-89 Average	Annual Difference
*Leigh	2346	(−2170)
York	2021	(+615)
Doncaster	1906	(+456)
Barrow	1594	(−30)
*Swinton	1435	(−1543)
Whitehaven	1310	(−462)
Huddersfield	1114	(+513)
Rochdale Hornets	1027	(−79)
Bramley	1004	(+146)
Keighley	961	(+3)
*Hunslet	947	(−1731)
Batley	924	(+65)
Sheffield Eagles	838	(−9)
Workington Town	774	(+37)
Dewsbury	772	(+114)
Carlisle	678	(−85)
Fulham	588	(−27)
Mansfield Marksman	560	(+192)
Chorley Borough	512	(−410)
Runcorn Highfield	298	(−217)

Relegated 1987-88

FIXTURES

PRINCIPAL DATES 1989-90

1989

27 August	CIS Insurance Charity Shield: Widnes v. Wigan (Anfield, Liverpool)
3 September	Stones Bitter Championship season commences
17 September	County Cup Competitions (1)
20 September	Rodstock War of the Roses
27 September	County Cup Competitions (2)
4 October	Foster's World Club Challenge (Old Trafford, Manchester)
5 October	Grunhalle Lager Lancashire Cup (SF)
11 October	John Smiths Yorkshire Cup (SF)
15 October	Grunhalle Lager Lancashire Cup (F)
21 October	British Coal Test: Great Britain v. New Zealand (1) (Old Trafford, Manchester)
28 October	British Coal Test: Great Britain v. New Zealand (2) (Elland Road, Leeds)
5 November	John Smiths Yorkshire Cup (F)
11 November	British Coal Test: Great Britain v. New Zealand (3) (Central Park, Wigan)
3 December	Regal Trophy (1)
10 December	Regal Trophy (2)
17 December	Regal Trophy (3)
23 December	Regal Trophy (SF1)
30 December	Regal Trophy (SF2)

1990

13 January	Regal Trophy (F)
21 January	British Coal Under-21 International: France v. Great Britain (Villeneuve)
28 January	Silk Cut Challenge Cup (1)
11 February	Silk Cut Challenge Cup (2)
16 February	British Coal Under-21 International: Great Britain v. France
25 February	Silk Cut Challenge Cup (3)
10 March	Silk Cut Challenge Cup (SF1)
18 March	British Coal Test: France v. Great Britain (Carcassonne)
31 March	Silk Cut Challenge Cup (SF2)
7 April	British Coal Test: Great Britain v. France
28 April	Silk Cut Challenge Cup (F) (Wembley)
13 May	Stones Bitter Premiership (F) (Old Trafford, Manchester)

STONES BITTER CHAMPIONSHIP 1989-90

SUNDAY, 27th AUGUST, 1989
CIS CHARITY SHIELD
Widnes   v.   Wigan at Anfield,
                            Liverpool

SUNDAY, 3rd SEPTEMBER, 1989
Bradford N.	v.	Hull
Castleford	v.	Featherstone R.
Leeds	v.	Wakefield T.
Leigh	v.	Barrow
Sheffield E.	v.	St. Helens
Widnes	v.	Salford
Wigan	v.	Warrington

WEDNESDAY, 6th SEPTEMBER, 1989
Leigh	v.	Wigan

SUNDAY, 10th SEPTEMBER, 1989
Barrow	v.	Leeds
Featherstone R.	v.	Sheffield E.
Hull	v.	Widnes
St. Helens	v.	Castleford
Salford	v.	Wigan
Wakefield T.	v.	Leigh
Warrington	v.	Bradford N.

SUNDAY, 17th SEPTEMBER, 1989
County Cup Competitions FIRST ROUND

WEDNESDAY, 20th SEPTEMBER, 1989
RODSTOCK WAR OF THE ROSES
Lancashire   v.   Yorkshire at Central Park,
                            Wigan

SUNDAY, 24th SEPTEMBER, 1989
Bradford N.	v.	St. Helens
Castleford	v.	Hull
Leeds	v.	Salford
Leigh	v.	Warrington
Sheffield E.	v.	Barrow
Widnes	v.	Featherstone R.
Wigan	v.	Wakefield T.

WEDNESDAY, 27th SEPTEMBER, 1989
County Cup Competitions SECOND ROUND

SUNDAY, 1st OCTOBER, 1989
Barrow	v.	Wigan
Featherstone R.	v.	Leigh
Hull	v.	Leeds
Salford	v.	Bradford N.
Wakefield T.	v.	Sheffield
Warrington	v.	Castleford
St. Helens	v.	NEW ZEALAND

TUESDAY, 3rd OCTOBER, 1989
Castleford	v.	NEW ZEALAND

WEDNESDAY, 4th OCTOBER, 1989
FOSTER'S WORLD CLUB CHALLENGE
Widnes   v.   Australia Premiers
(at Old Trafford)

THURSDAY, 5th OCTOBER, 1989
GRUNHALLE LAGER LANCASHIRE CUP
SEMI-FINALS

SUNDAY 8th OCTOBER, 1989
Bradford N.	v.	Barrow
Featherstone R.	v.	Leeds
Salford	v.	Leigh
Sheffield E.	v.	Widnes
Wakefield T.	v.	St. Helens
Warrington	v.	Hull
Wigan	v.	NEW ZEALAND

WEDNESDAY, 11th OCTOBER, 1989
Bradford N.   v.   NEW ZEALAND
JOHN SMITHS YORKSHIRE CUP SEMI-FINALS

SUNDAY, 15th OCTOBER, 1989
Barrow	v.	Warrington
Castleford	v.	Sheffield E.
Hull	v.	Salford
St. Helens	v.	Featherstone R.
Widnes	v.	Wakefield T.
Leeds	v.	NEW ZEALAND

GRUNHALLE LAGER LANCASHIRE CUP FINAL

TUESDAY, 17th OCTOBER, 1989
Cumbria	v.	NEW ZEALAND

SATURDAY, 21st OCTOBER, 1989
BRITISH COAL FIRST TEST
(at Old Trafford, Manchester)
GREAT BRITAIN v. NEW ZEALAND

SATURDAY, 28th OCTOBER, 1989
BRITISH COAL SECOND TEST
(at Elland Road, Leeds)
GREAT BRITAIN v. NEW ZEALAND

SUNDAY, 29th OCTOBER, 1989
Bradford N.	v.	Leigh
Featherstone R.	v.	Barrow
Salford	v.	Widnes
Sheffield E.	v.	Leeds
Wakefield T.	v.	Hull
Warrington	v.	St. Helens
Wigan	v.	Castleford

WEDNESDAY, 1st NOVEMBER, 1989
Featherstone R.   v.   NEW ZEALAND

SUNDAY, 5th NOVEMBER, 1989
Barrow	v.	Wakefield T.
Castleford	v.	Bradford N.
Leeds	v.	Warrington
Leigh	v.	Featherstone R.
St. Helens	v.	Salford
Sheffield E.	v.	Wigan
Widnes	v.	NEW ZEALAND

SUNDAY, 5th NOVEMBER, 1989
JOHN SMITHS YORKSHIRE CUP FINAL

TUESDAY, 7th NOVEMBER, 1989
Hull	v.	NEW ZEALAND

SATURDAY, 11th NOVEMBER, 1989
BRITISH COAL THIRD TEST
(at Central Park, Wigan)
GREAT BRITAIN v. NEW ZEALAND

SUNDAY, 12th NOVEMBER, 1989
Bradford N.	v.	Wigan
Featherstone R.	v.	Hull
St. Helens	v.	Barrow
Salford	v.	Leeds
Wakefield T.	v.	Castleford
Warrington	v.	Sheffield E.
Widnes	v.	Leigh

SUNDAY, 19th NOVEMBER, 1989
Barrow	v.	Salford
Castleford	v.	Warrington
Hull	v.	St. Helens
Leeds	v.	Widnes
Leigh	v.	Wakefield T.
Sheffield E.	v.	Bradford N.
Wigan	v.	Featherstone R.

SUNDAY, 26th NOVEMBER, 1989

Bradford N.	v.	Leeds
Featherstone R.	v.	St. Helens
Salford	v.	Sheffield E.
Wakefield T.	v.	Barrow
Warrington	v.	Leigh
Widnes	v.	Castleford
Wigan	v.	Hull

SUNDAY, 3rd DECEMBER, 1989
REGAL TROPHY FIRST ROUND

SUNDAY, 10th DECEMBER, 1989
REGAL TROPHY SECOND ROUND

SUNDAY, 17th DECEMBER, 1989
REGAL TROPHY THIRD ROUND

SUNDAY, 17th DECEMBER, 1989

Barrow	v.	Widnes
Castleford	v.	Wigan
Hull	v.	Leigh
St. Helens	v.	Bradford N.
Sheffield E.	v.	Featherstone R.
Warrington	v.	Salford

SATURDAY, 23rd DECEMBER, 1989
REGAL TROPHY SEMI-FINAL 1

TUESDAY, 26th DECEMBER, 1989

Featherstone R.	v.	Wakefield T.
Hull	v.	Sheffield E.
Leeds	v.	Castleford
Leigh	v.	Salford
Widnes	v.	Warrington
Wigan	v.	St. Helens

SATURDAY, 30th DECEMBER, 1989
REGAL TROPHY SEMI-FINAL 2

SUNDAY, 31st DECEMBER, 1989

Barrow	v.	Sheffield E.

1990

MONDAY, 1st JANUARY, 1990

Bradford N.	v.	Castleford
Leeds	v.	Hull
St. Helens	v.	Widnes
Wakefield T.	v.	Featherstone R.
Warrington	v.	Wigan

SUNDAY, 7th JANUARY, 1990

Castleford	v.	Wakefield T.
Hull	v.	Barrow
Leigh	v.	St. Helens
Salford	v.	Featherstone R.
Sheffield E.	v.	Warrington
Widnes	v.	Leeds
Wigan	v.	Bradford N.

SATURDAY, 13th JANUARY, 1990
REGAL TROPHY FINAL

SUNDAY, 14th JANUARY, 1989

Bradford N.	v.	Widnes
Featherstone R.	v.	Castleford
Leeds	v.	Leigh
St. Helens	v.	Hull
Wakefield T.	v.	Salford
Warrington	v.	Barrow
Wigan	v.	Sheffield E.

SUNDAY, 21st JANUARY, 1990

Barrow	v.	Featherstone R.
Castleford	v.	Widnes
Hull	v.	Wigan
Leeds	v.	Bradford N.
Leigh	v.	Sheffield E.
Salford	v.	St. Helens
Wakefield T.	v.	Warrington

SUNDAY, 21st JANUARY, 1990
BRITISH COAL UNDER-21 INTERNATIONAL
France v Great Britain at Villeneuve

SUNDAY, 28th JANUARY, 1990
SILK CUT CHALLENGE CUP FIRST ROUND

SUNDAY, 4th FEBRUARY, 1990

Featherstone R.	v.	Warrington
Hull	v.	Castleford
Leigh	v.	Bradford N.
Salford	v.	Barrow
Sheffield E.	v.	Wakefield T.
St. Helens	v.	Leeds
Widnes	v.	Wigan

SUNDAY, 11th FEBRUARY, 1990
SILK CUT CHALLENGE SECOND ROUND

FRIDAY, 16th FEBRUARY, 1990
BRITISH COAL UNDER-21 INTERNATIONAL

Great Britain	v.	France

SUNDAY, 18th FEBRUARY, 1990

Barrow	v.	St. Helens
Bradford N.	v.	Featherstone R.
Castleford	v.	Leigh
Leeds	v.	Sheffield E.
Warrington	v.	Wakefield T.
Widnes	v.	Hull
Wigan	v.	Salford

SUNDAY, 25th FEBRUARY, 1990
SILK CUT CHALLENGE CUP THIRD ROUND

SUNDAY, 25th FEBRUARY, 1990

Featherstone R.	v.	Widnes
Hull	v.	Bradford N.
Leigh	v.	Leeds
St. Helens	v.	Warrington
Salford	v.	Castleford
Wigan	v.	Barrow

SUNDAY, 4th MARCH, 1990

Barrow	v.	Hull
Bradford N.	v.	Salford
Castleford	v.	St. Helens
Leeds	v.	Wigan
Sheffield E.	v.	Leigh
Wakefield T.	v.	Widnes
Warrington	v.	Featherstone R.

SATURDAY, 10th MARCH, 1990
SILK CUT CHALLENGE CUP SEMI-FINAL 1

SUNDAY, 11th MARCH, 1990

Barrow	v.	Leigh
Featherstone R.	v.	Salford
Hull	v.	Wakefield T.
Sheffield E.	v.	Castleford
Warrington	v.	Leeds
Widnes	v.	Bradford N.

SUNDAY, 18th MARCH, 1990

Bradford N.	v.	Sheffield E.
Featherstone R.	v.	Wigan
Leeds	v.	Barrow
Leigh	v.	Widnes
St. Helens	v.	Wakefield T.
Salford	v.	Hull

BRITISH COAL TEST
France v. Great Britain at Carcassonne

SUNDAY, 25th MARCH, 1990

Bradford N.	v.	Warrington
Castleford	v.	Barrow
Hull	v.	Featherstone R.
St. Helens	v.	Leigh
Sheffield E.	v.	Salford
Wakefield T.	v.	Leeds
Wigan	v.	Widnes

SATURDAY, 31st MARCH, 1990
SILK CUT CHALLENGE CUP SEMI-FINAL 2

SUNDAY, 1st APRIL 1990

Barrow	v.	Bradford N.
Castleford	v.	Salford
Leeds	v.	St. Helens
Leigh	v.	Hull
Wakefield T.	v.	Wigan
Widnes	v.	Sheffield E.

SATURDAY, 7th APRIL, 1990
BRITISH COAL TEST

Great Britain	v.	France

SUNDAY, 8th APRIL, 1990

Featherstone R.	v.	Bradford N.
Hull	v.	Warrington
Leigh	v.	Castleford
St. Helens	v.	Sheffield E.
Salford	v.	Wakefield T.
Widnes	v.	Barrow
Wigan	v.	Leeds

GOOD FRIDAY, 13th APRIL, 1990

Barrow	v.	Castleford
Bradford N.	v.	Wakefield T.
Leeds	v.	Featherstone R.
St. Helens	v.	Wigan
Warrington	v.	Widnes

SUNDAY, 15th APRIL, 1990

Sheffield E.	v.	Hull

EASTER MONDAY, 16th APRIL, 1990

Castleford	v.	Leeds
Salford	v.	Warrington
Wakefield T.	v.	Bradford N.
Widnes	v.	St. Helens
Wigan	v.	Leigh

SATURDAY, 28th APRIL, 1990
SILK CUT CHALLENGE CUP FINAL AT WEMBLEY

SUNDAY, 13th MAY, 1990
STONES BITTER PREMIERSHIP FINAL AT
OLD TRAFFORD, MANCHESTER

SECOND DIVISION FIXTURES
Preliminary draft subject to Club amendments

SUNDAY, 3rd SEPTEMBER, 1989

Batley	v.	Nottingham City
Carlisle	v.	Runcorn H.
Doncaster	v.	Dewsbury
Fulham	v.	Ryedale York
Halifax	v.	Rochdale H.
Hunslet	v.	Bramley
Keighley	v.	Hull K.R.
Oldham	v.	Workington T.
Swinton	v.	Chorley
Whitehaven	v.	Huddersfield

WEDNESDAY, 6th SEPTEMBER, 1989

Carlisle	v.	Keighley
Chorley	v.	Bramley
Dewsbury	v.	Hull K.R.
Halifax	v.	Nottingham City
Hunslet	v.	Ryedale York
Runcorn H.	v.	Batley
Trafford B.	v.	Swinton
Whitehaven	v.	Rochdale H.

SUNDAY, 10th SEPTEMBER, 1989

Batley	v.	Ryedale York
Bramley	v.	Doncaster
Chorley	v.	Whitehaven
Dewsbury	v.	Keighley
Halifax	v.	Oldham
Huddersfield	v.	Fulham
Nottingham City	v.	Hunslet
Rochdale H.	v.	Swinton
Trafford B.	v.	Runcorn H.
Workington T.	v.	Carlisle

WEDNESDAY, 13th SEPTEMBER, 1989

Huddersfield	v.	Hunslet
Hull K.R.	v.	Trafford B.

Keighley	v.	Whitehaven
Swinton	v.	Doncaster

SUNDAY, 24th SEPTEMBER, 1989

Batley	v.	Bramley
Carlisle	v.	Trafford B.
Chorley	v.	Fulham
Doncaster	v.	Runcorn H.
Huddersfield	v.	Workington T.
Hull K.R.	v.	Halifax
Keighley	v.	Nottingham City
Rochdale H.	v.	Dewsbury
Swinton	v.	Ryedale York
Whitehaven	v.	Hunslet

SUNDAY, 1st October, 1989

Bramley	v.	Rochdale H.
Chorley	v.	Keighley
Dewsbury	v.	Swinton
Doncaster	v.	Whitehaven
Fulham	v.	Carlisle
Hunslet	v.	Batley
Nottingham City	v.	Halifax
Oldham	v.	Hull K.R.
Runcorn H.	v.	Huddersfield
Workington T.	v.	Ryedale York

WEDNESDAY, 4th OCTOBER, 1989
FOSTER'S WORLD CLUB CHALLENGE

Widnes	v.	Australia Premiers
(at Old Trafford).		

SUNDAY, 8th OCTOBER, 1989

Batley	v.	Swinton
Bramley	v.	Chorley
Carlisle	v.	Workington T.
Halifax	v.	Doncaster
Hull K.R.	v.	Nottingham City

Hunslet v. Dewsbury
Runcorn H. v. Oldham
Ryedale York v. Keighley
Trafford B. v. Huddersfield
Whitehaven v. Fulham

SUNDAY, 15th OCTOBER, 1989
Chorley v. Hunslet
Dewsbury v. Runcorn H.
Doncaster v. Ryedale York
Fulham v. Rochdale H.
Huddersfield v. Whitehaven
Keighley v. Trafford B.
Nottingham City v. Batley
Oldham v. Halifax
Swinton v. Carlisle
Workington T. v. Bramley

SATURDAY, 21st OCTOBER, 1989
FIRST TEST (at Old Trafford, Manchester)
GREAT BRITAIN v. NEW ZEALAND

SUNDAY, 22nd OCTOBER, 1989
Batley v. Whitehaven
Carlisle v. Oldham
Fulham v. Bramley
Halifax v. Dewsbury
Hull K.R. v. Swinton
Keighley v. Doncaster
Rochdale H. v. Workington T.
Runcorn H. v. Nottingham City
Trafford B. v. Hunslet

SATURDAY, 28th OCTOBER, 1989
SECOND TEST (at Elland Road, Leeds)
GREAT BRITAIN v. NEW ZEALAND

SUNDAY, 29th OCTOBER, 1989
Bramley v. Halifax
Dewsbury v. Chorley
Doncaster v. Workington T.
Hull K.R. v. Fulham
Hunslet v. Carlisle
Nottingham City v. Rochdale H.
Oldham v. Batley
Ryedale York v. Huddersfield
Trafford B. v. Keighley
Whitehaven v. Swinton

SUNDAY, 5th NOVEMBER, 1989
Chorley v. Nottingham City
Dewsbury v. Carlisle
Doncaster v. Oldham
Fulham v. Whitehaven
Halifax v. Hull K.R.
Keighley v. Batley
Rochdale H. v. Runcorn H.
Ryedale York v. Hunslet
Swinton v. Bramley
Workington T. v. Trafford B.

SATURDAY, 11TH NOVEMBER, 1989
THIRD TEST (at Central Park, Wigan)
GREAT BRITAIN v. NEW ZEALAND

SUNDAY, 12th NOVEMBER, 1989
Batley v. Runcorn H.
Bramley v. Fulham
Carlisle v. Ryedale York
Chorley v. Dewsbury
Hull K.R. v. Workington T.
Hunslet v. Huddersfield
Nottingham City v. Swinton
Oldham v. Keighley
Trafford B. v. Halifax
Whitehaven v. Doncaster

SUNDAY, 19th NOVEMBER, 1989
Doncaster v. Trafford B.

Fulham v. Oldham
Halifax v. Chorley
Huddersfield v. Nottingham City
Keighley v. Carlisle
Rochdale H. v. Ryedale York
Runcorn H. v. Bramley
Swinton v. Hull K.R.
Workington T. v. Batley

SUNDAY, 26th NOVEMBER, 1989
Batley v. Fulham
Bramley v. Huddersfield
Carlisle v. Halifax
Hull K.R. v. Dewsbury
Hunslet v. Rochdale H.
Nottingham City v. Runcorn H.
Oldham v. Doncaster
Ryedale York v. Chorley
Trafford B. v. Workington T.
Whitehaven v. Keighley

SUNDAY, 17th DECEMBER, 1989
Carlisle v. Nottingham City
Chorley v. Swinton
Dewsbury v. Halifax
Doncaster v. Hunslet
Fulham v. Hull K.R.
Huddersfield v. Ryedale York
Rochdale H. v. Bramley
Runcorn H. v. Whitehaven
Trafford B. v. Batley
Workington T. v. Oldham

TUESDAY, 26th DECEMBER, 1989
Batley v. Dewsbury
Bramley v. Keighley
Halifax v. Huddersfield
Hull K.R. v. Ryedale York
Hunslet v. Chorley
Nottingham City v. Doncaster
Rochdale H. v. Oldham
Runcorn H. v. Carlisle
Swinton v. Trafford B.
Workington T. v. Whitehaven

SUNDAY, 31st DECEMBER, 1989
Dewsbury v. Batley
Doncaster v. Fulham
Huddersfield v. Keighley
Hunslet v. Hull K.R.

MONDAY, 1st JANUARY, 1990
Chorley v. Runcorn H.
Halifax v. Bramley
Oldham v. Swinton
Ryedale York v. Workington T.
Trafford B. v. Rochdale H.
Whitehaven v. Carlisle

SUNDAY, 7th JANUARY, 1990
Bramley v. Batley
Carlisle v. Swinton
Dewsbury v. Doncaster
Fulham v. Trafford B.
Halifax v. Ryedale York
Huddersfield v. Runcorn H.
Keighley v. Rochdale H.
Nottingham City v. Hull K.R.
Oldham v. Hunslet
Workington T. v. Chorley

SUNDAY, 14th JANUARY, 1990
Batley v. Keighley
Bramley v. Workington T.
Hull K.R. v. Oldham
Hunslet v. Nottingham City
Rochdale H. v. Fulham
Runcorn H. v. Dewsbury
Ryedale York v. Carlisle

Swinton	v.	Huddersfield
Trafford B.	v.	Chorley
Whitehaven	v.	Halifax

SUNDAY, 21st JANUARY, 1990
Carlisle	v.	Bramley
Chorley	v.	Oldham
Dewsbury	v.	Hunslet
Doncaster	v.	Keighley
Fulham	v.	Batley
Huddersfield	v.	Trafford B.
Rochdale H.	v.	Whitehaven
Runcorn H.	v.	Ryedale York
Swinton	v.	Nottingham City
Workington T.	v.	Hull K.R.

SUNDAY, 4th FEBRUARY, 1990
Batley	v.	Trafford B.
Bramley	v.	Hull K.R.
Chorley	v.	Workington T.
Hunslet	v.	Doncaster
Keighley	v.	Dewsbury
Nottingham City	v.	Huddersfield
Oldham	v.	Fulham
Ryedale York	v.	Rochdale H.
Whitehaven	v.	Runcorn H.

SUNDAY, 18th FEBRUARY, 1990
Dewsbury	v.	Rochdale H.
Doncaster	v.	Bramley
Hull K.R.	v.	Runcorn H.
Nottingham City	v.	Fulham
Oldham	v.	Chorley
Swinton	v.	Whitehaven
Trafford B.	v.	Carlisle
Workington T.	v.	Huddersfield

SUNDAY, 25th FEBRUARY, 1990
Batley	v.	Workington T.
Bramley	v.	Hunslet
Chorley	v.	Ryedale York
Fulham	v.	Doncaster
Halifax	v.	Carlisle
Huddersfield	v.	Dewsbury
Keighley	v.	Oldham
Rochdale H.	v.	Nottingham City
Runcorn H.	v.	Trafford B.
Whitehaven	v.	Hull K.R.

SUNDAY, 4th MARCH, 1990
Carlisle	v.	Dewsbury
Chorley	v.	Halifax
Hull K.R.	v.	Keighley
Hunslet	v.	Whitehaven
Oldham	v.	Huddersfield
Runcorn H.	v.	Rochdale H.
Ryedale York	v.	Fulham
Swinton	v.	Batley
Trafford B.	v.	Doncaster
Workington T.	v.	Nottingham City

SUNDAY, 11th MARCH, 1990
Batley	v.	Oldham
Bramley	v.	Runcorn H.
Dewsbury	v.	Workington T.
Doncaster	v.	Swinton
Fulham	v.	Huddersfield
Keighley	v.	Ryedale York
Nottingham City	v.	Carlisle
Rochdale H.	v.	Halifax
Whitehaven	v.	Chorley

SUNDAY, 18th MARCH, 1990
Carlisle	v.	Hunslet
Halifax	v.	Batley
Huddersfield	v.	Bramley
Hull K.R.	v.	Whitehaven
Nottingham City	v.	Keighley
Oldham	v.	Runcorn H.

Swinton	v.	Dewsbury
Ryedale York	v.	Doncaster
Trafford B.	v.	Fulham
Workington T.	v.	Rochdale H.

SUNDAY, 25th MARCH, 1990
Batley	v.	Halifax
Bramley	v.	Carlisle
Fulham	v.	Nottingham City
Huddersfield	v.	Oldham
Keighley	v.	Chorley
Rochdale H.	v.	Hunslet
Runcorn H.	v.	Doncaster
Ryedale York	v.	Swinton
Trafford B.	v.	Hull K.R.
Workington T.	v.	Dewsbury

SUNDAY, 1st APRIL, 1990
Carlisle	v.	Fulham
Chorley	v.	Trafford B.
Dewsbury	v.	Huddersfield
Doncaster	v.	Halifax
Hull K.R.	v.	Bramley
Hunslet	v.	Oldham
Nottingham City	v.	Workington T.
Ryedale York	v.	Runcorn H.
Swinton	v.	Rochdale H.
Whitehaven	v.	Batley

SUNDAY, 8th APRIL, 1990
Batley	v.	Hunslet
Fulham	v.	Dewsbury
Halifax	v.	Whitehaven
Huddersfield	v.	Swinton
Nottingham City	v.	Chorley
Oldham	v.	Carlisle
Rochdale H.	v.	Keighley
Runcorn H.	v.	Hull K.R.
Workington T.	v.	Doncaster

GOOD FRIDAY, 13th APRIL, 1990
Fulham	v.	Chorley
Huddersfield	v.	Halifax
Keighley	v.	Bramley
Rochdale H.	v.	Trafford B.
Ryedale York	v.	Hull K.R.
Swinton	v.	Oldham
Whitehaven	v.	Workington T.

EASTER MONDAY, 16th APRIL, 1990
Bramley	v.	Swinton
Carlisle	v.	Whitehaven
Dewsbury	v.	Fulham
Doncaster	v.	Nottingham City
Halifax	v.	Trafford B.
Hull K.R.	v.	Hunslet
Keighley	v.	Huddersfield
Oldham	v.	Rochdale H.
Runcorn H.	v.	Chorley
Ryedale York	v.	Batley